Advance Praise for *Handbook of Evidence-Based Mental Health Practice with Sexual and Gender Minorities*

"Pachankis and Safren have done the field a great service with the publication of this important and timely handbook. This volume is a must-read for researchers and practitioners who seek to develop and disseminate affirmative, evidence-based mental health treatments for sexual and gender minority populations."
—**Mark L. Hatzenbuehler, PhD**, Associate Professor of Sociomedical Sciences and Sociology, Columbia University

"This up-to-date, comprehensive volume integrates findings from cutting edge empirical research with affirming and nuanced case examples and practical suggestions for culturally responsive clinical work, making it a must-read for all practitioners and educators in the mental health professions. The chapters in this important and timely volume include both population- specific and problem-specific approaches for the diverse and dynamic treatment needs of sexual and gender minority clients in the 21st century."
—**Kimberly Balsam, PhD**, Clinical Psychology Professor at Palo Alto University and Past President of the American Psychological Association's Society for the Psychology of Sexual Orientation and Gender Diversity

Handbook of Evidence-Based Mental Health Practice with Sexual and Gender Minorities

Handbook of Evidence-Based Mental Health Practice with Sexual and Gender Minorities

EDITED BY

JOHN E. PACHANKIS, PHD

AND

STEVEN A. SAFREN, PHD

OXFORD
UNIVERSITY PRESS

Oxford University Press is a department of the University of Oxford. It furthers
the University's objective of excellence in research, scholarship, and education
by publishing worldwide. Oxford is a registered trade mark of Oxford University
Press in the UK and certain other countries.

Published in the United States of America by Oxford University Press
198 Madison Avenue, New York, NY 10016, United States of America.

Library of Congress Cataloging-in-Publication Data
Names: Pachankis, John E., editor. | Safren, Steven A., editor.
Title: Handbook of evidence-based mental health practice with sexual
and gender minorities / edited by John E. Pachankis, Steven A. Safren.
Description: New York : Oxford University Press, 2019. |
Includes bibliographical references and index.
Identifiers: LCCN 2019008911 (print) | LCCN 2019011120 (ebook) |
ISBN 9780190669317 (UPDF) | ISBN 9780190669324 (EPUB) |
ISBN 9780190669300 (paperback)
Subjects: LCSH: Gays—Mental health services. | Lesbians—Mental health services. |
Sexual minorities—Mental health services. | BISAC: PSYCHOLOGY / Clinical Psychology. |
SOCIAL SCIENCE / Gender Studies.
Classification: LCC RC451.4.G39 (ebook) | LCC RC451.4.G39 H35 2019 (print) |
DDC 362.196/89008664—dc23
LC record available at https://lccn.loc.gov/2019008911

CONTENTS

SECTION III Evidence-Based Treatments for Specific Mental Health
Problems Among Sexual and Gender Minority Clients

SECTION IV Evidence-Based Treatments for Sexual and Gender Minorities
Using Novel Modalities

Within the past three decades, there has been a major change in societal acceptance of lesbian, gay, bisexual, and transgender (LGBT) individuals, and although there clearly continues to exist discrimination and aggression against sexual and gender minorities, the shift has been dramatic. Although a bit late in coming, the shift also exists within the mental health profession. Once labeled as a mental disorder, identifying as LGBT is no longer considered to be pathological. Furthermore, the stress and discrimination that LGBT individuals experience in their lives are now recognized as a key source of the mental health disparities that exist. Research clearly demonstrates that compared to their heterosexual counterparts, LGBT individuals show higher rates of psychopathology, greater impairment due to psychological problems, and, as a result, utilize services at a higher rate.

In the past, mental health professionals contributing to the literature on LGBT issues needed to do so at their own professional risk. Indeed, we know of one such researcher who was closeted in his personal and professional life and kept a separate curriculum vitae that included his research on gay issues. This clearly no longer needs to be the case, and we indeed now have a new generation of researchers—not all of whom identify as LGBT—who are openly dedicated to our improved understanding of sexual and gender minorities and the development of more effective therapy interventions.

Another change within the profession is the fact that past writings on LGBT issues were typically written for other professionals who had an interest in learning more about what it is to be a sexual or gender minority. Consequently, the literature on LGBT issues typically appeared in specific journals dedicated to that topic and was ignored within mainstream psychology. For example, textbooks on human development typically said nothing about the identity issues that sexual minorities had to deal with while growing up. Thus, although LGBT professionals were telling, mainstream psychology was not listening.

A vivid example of this is an experience we had some years ago when conducting a panel on LGBT issues, in which four participants gave presentations. What was striking about this presentation was that there were fewer members in the audience than there were panelists. This has clearly changed over the years. Panels on LGBT issues are common and well-attended at mainstream conferences. Mainstream journals, including the premier journals in clinical psychology, regularly publish work of relevance to sexual and gender minority issues, and mental health professionals have recognized that there is much to be learned from studying sexual and gender minorities. For example, one prominent researcher studying partner abuse changed her feminist conceptualization of abuse after reading the literature on partner abuse in same-sex couples.

Given the long-standing history of paying little attention to LGBT issues, therapists have typically not received the kind of clinical training that prepared them for working with LGBT individuals. Fortunately, there is now a new generation of researchers and clinicians dedicated to learning more about how to work with sexual and gender minority clients. This is critically important. Despite the progress that has been made in the United States in terms of acceptance of LGBT individuals and their rights, LGBT individuals remain at high risk for discrimination, violence, and resulting mental health problems, and they are greatly in need of culturally sensitive and affirming interventions. This book was designed to serve as a guide for such intervention.

This volume contains the work of a new generation of clinical scientists who are dedicated to developing and providing the most effective treatments designed to address the unique needs of sexual and gender minority individuals. Importantly, it focuses on evidence-based practice, making use of all available research evidence and clinical observations to guide effective clinical intervention. Furthermore, the contributions do not assume that all LGBT individuals or issues should be treated the same. The term "LGBT" implies the commonalities that everyone included under that umbrella shares, but it would be a grave mistake, particularly from a clinical perspective, to not recognize within-group differences. As such, the chapters reflect the specific issues facing, for example, transgender individuals, LGBT youth, LGBT older adults, couples, parents, HIV-negative men, and HIV-positive men. Although the chapters deal with the most common clinical problems experienced by sexual and gender minority individuals, they also move the field well past the stage of how to work with LGBT clients in general to how to work with LGBT clients on the specific issues they have and symptoms they are experiencing. In addition, the book provides not just one option for clinicians with regard to type of treatment but, rather, a range of options that can allow providers to select what might be most appropriate for their specific client and for their own strengths in how they work clinically.

With the publication of this volume, gone are the days when therapists could say that they do not know how to work with sexual and gender minority issues or clients. This book can and should serve as a key resource in training the next generation of diversity-competent professionals who can effectively work with LGBT clients.

Joanne Davila, PhD
Marvin R. Goldfried, PhD
Stony Brook University

John E. Pachankis, PhD, is Associate Professor at the Yale School of Public Health and the Director of the Esteem Research Group in New York City. He received his PhD in clinical psychology in 2008 from the State University of New York at Stony Brook and completed his clinical psychology internship at Harvard Medical School/McLean Hospital. His research seeks to bring evidence-based mental health interventions to LGBTQ people in the United States and throughout the world. With National Institutes of Health funding, he examines the efficacy of LGBTQ-affirmative interventions delivered via novel technologies (e.g., smartphones), in diverse settings (e.g., Eastern Europe and Appalachia), and with diverse segments of the LGBTQ community (e.g., rural youth, queer women). He has published widely (more than 90 publications) in the areas of stigma, LGBTQ mental health, and psychosocial mechanisms linking stigma to mental health. This work appears in journals such as *Psychological Bulletin, Developmental Psychology, Journal of Consulting and Clinical Psychology*, and *Health Psychology*. His research has had national and international scholarly, legal, and popular impact, having been referenced in national professional guidelines for LGBTQ mental health practice; cited in numerous amici curiae briefs before US state and federal courts, including the US Supreme Court; and featured in national and international media outlets.

Steven A. Safren, PhD, is Professor of Psychology at the University of Miami; Co-Director of the Miami Center for AIDS Research (CFAR) at the University of Miami, Behavioral/Social Sciences and Community Outreach Core; and an expert on working with sexual and gender minorities, as well as on health-related behavior change. He earned his PhD from the State University of New York at Albany and did his internship and postdoctoral fellowship at Massachusetts General Hospital (MGH)/Harvard Medical School. Before moving to the University of Miami in August 2015, he was the founding director of the current MGH Behavioral Medicine Service at Massachusetts General Hospital and of the Harvard University Behavioral and Social Science Core for the Harvard University CFAR. In addition, for more than 15 years, he led behavioral science research projects at the Fenway Institute at Fenway Health in Boston, one of the nation's largest health centers for sexual and gender minorities. He has been principal investigator (PI) or protocol chair of 15 National Institutes of Health-funded grants and has authored more than 300 peer-reviewed publications in his professional areas of interest. In addition to studies in which he has served as PI, he has regularly served as co-PI or mentor on studies related to sexual and gender minority health, HIV prevention and treatment, work with other medical illnesses, and on cognitive–behavioral approaches to managing adult and adolescent attention-deficit/hyperactivity disorder (ADHD). He has co-authored books on cognitive–behavioral therapy (CBT) with LGBT individuals and integrating CBT with motivational interviewing, and he is editor of a book on behavioral medicine interventions across various illnesses. He has co-authored two sets of published treatment manuals on CBT for treating depression and adherence in chronic illness and on treating adult ADHD, respectively. He is currently the Publications Coordinator for ABCT and Associate Editor for the *Journal of Consulting and Clinical Psychology*. He has also served as Editor and Associate Editor for ABCT's clinical journal, *Cognitive and Behavioral Practice*.

CONTRIBUTORS

Edward J. Alessi
Associate Professor
School of Social Work
Rutgers University
New Brunswick, New Jersey

Ashley Austin
Associate Professor
School of Social Work
Barry University
Miami Shores, Florida

Aaron J. Blashill
Assistant Professor
Department of Psychology
San Diego State University
San Diego, California

Rotem Boruchovitz-Zamir
PhD Candidate
Department of Psychology
Ben-Gurion University
Be'er-Sheva, Israel

Tiffany A. Brown
Postdoctoral Fellow
Department of Psychiatry
University of California, San Diego
San Diego, California

Charles L. Burton
Associate Research Scientiest
Department of Social and Behavioral
    Sciences
School of Public Health
Yale University
New Haven, Connecticut

Adam Carmel
Clinical Assistant Professor
Department of Psychology
University of Washington
Seattle, Washington

Adam W. Carrico
Associate Professor
Department of Public Health Sciences
University of Miami
Miami, Florida

Andrew Young Choi
Doctoral Candidate
Department of Counseling, Clinical,
    and School Psychology
Gevirtz Graduate School of Education
University of California, Santa Barbara
Santa Barbara, California

Jeffrey M. Cohen
Clinical Instructor of Psychology
    (in Psychiatry)
Department of Psychiatry
Columbia University Medical Center
New York, New York

Shelley L. Craig
Associate Professor
Factor-Inwentash Faculty of
   Social Work
University of Toronto
Toronto, Ontario, Canada

Joanne Davila
Professor of Clinical Psychology
Department of Psychology
Stony Brook University
Stony Brook, New York

Gary M. Diamond
Professor
Department of Psychology
Ben-Gurion University
Be'er-Sheva, Israel

Emily R. Dworkin
Postdoctoral Fellow
Department of Psychiatry and
   Behavioral Sciences
University of Washington
Seattle, Washington

Brian A. Feinstein
Research Assistant Professor
Institute for Sexual and Gender
   Minority Health and Wellbeing
Northwestern University
Chicago, Illinois

Reihonna L. Frost
Doctoral Student
Department of Psychology
Clark University
Worcester, Massachusetts

Inbal Gat
PhD Candidate
Department of Psychology
Ben-Gurion University
Be'er-Sheva, Israel

Abbie E. Goldberg
Associate Professor
Department of Psychology
Clark University
Worcester, Massachusetts

Marvin R. Goldfried
Professor of Clinical Psychology
Department of Psychology
Stony Brook University
Stony Brook, New York

Walter Gómez
Doctoral Student
School of Social Welfare
University of California, Berkeley
Berkeley, California

W. Kim Halford
Professor of Clinical Psychology
School of Psychology
University of Queensland
Brisbane, Australia

Audrey Harkness
Postdoctoral Fellow
Department of Psychology
University of Miami
Miami, Florida

Trevor A. Hart
Professor
Department of Psychology
Ryerson University
Toronto, Ontario, Canada

Brandon Hoeflein
PhD Candidate
Department of Psychology
Pacific Graduate School of Psychology
Palo Alto University
Palo Alto, California

Natalie R. Holt
Doctoral Student
Department of Psychology
University of Nebraska–Lincoln
Lincoln, Nebraska

Debra A. Hope
Professor
Department of Psychology
University of Nebraska–Lincoln
Lincoln, Nebraska

Tania Israel
Professor
Department of Counseling, Clinical,
  and School Psychology
Gevirtz Graduate School of Education
University of California, Santa Barbara
Santa Barbara, California

Debra Kaysen
Professor
Department of Psychiatry &
  Behavioral Sciences
School of Medicine
University of Washington
Seattle, Washington

Patrycja Klimek
Doctoral Student
Department of Psychology
San Diego State University/University
  of California, San Diego Joint
  Doctoral Program in Clinical
  Psychology
San Diego, California

Keren Lehavot
Investigator
Denver–Seattle Center of Innovation
  for Veteran-Centered and
  Value-Driven Care
Health Services Research &
  Development
VA Puget Sound Health Care System
Seattle, Washington

Anthony Lyons
Associate Professor
Australian Research Centre in Sex,
  Health, and Society
La Trobe University
Melbourne, Australia

Christopher R. Martell
Director and Lecturer
Psychological Services Center
Department of Psychological and
  Brain Sciences
University of Massachusetts
Amherst, Massachusetts

Michael E. Newcomb
Assistant Professor
Institute for Sexual and Gender
  Minority Health and Wellbeing
Northwestern University
Chicago, Illinois

Michelle G. Newman
Professor of Psychology and Psychiatry
Department of Psychology
The Pennsylvania State University
University Park, Pennsylvania

Ofir Nir-Gottlieb
PhD Candidate
Department of Psychology
Ben-Gurion University
Be'er-Sheva, Israel

Néstor Noyola
Doctoral Student
Department of Psychology
Clark University
Worcester, Massachusetts

David W. Pantalone
Associate Professor
Department of Psychology
University of Massachusetts
Boston, Massachusetts

Christopher A. Pepping
Lecturer in Clinical Psychology
Department of Psychology &
  Counselling
School of Psychology & Public Health
La Trobe University
Melbourne, Australia

Allura L. Ralston
Doctoral Student
Department of Psychology
University of Nebraska–Lincoln
Lincoln, Nebraska

Cathy J. Reback
Core Director
Center for HIV Identification,
  Prevention and Treatment Services
University of California, Los Angeles
Los Angeles, California

Craig Rodriguez-Seijas
Doctoral Candidate
Department of Psychology
Stony Brook University
Stony Brook, New York

Daniel Ryu
PsyD Candidate
Department of Psychiatry
PGSP-Stanford Psy.D. Consortium
Palo Alto University
Palo Alto, California

Jillian C. Shipherd
Director
Lesbian, Gay, Bisexual, and
    Transgender (LGBT) Health
    Program
Veterans Health Administration
Washington, DC
Clinical Research Psychologist
National Center for PTSD
VA Boston Healthcare System
Boston, Massachusetts

Matthew D. Skinta
Clinical Faculty
Department of Psychology
Pacific Graduate School of
    Psychology
Palo Alto University
Palo Alto, California

Colleen A. Sloan
Assistant Professor
Department of Psychiatry
Boston University School of Medicine
Boston, Massachusetts

Nathan Grant Smith
Associate Professor
Department of Psychological, Health,
    and Learning Sciences
College of Education
University of Houston
Houston, Texas

Sarah E. Valentine
Assistant Professor of Psychiatry
Department of Psychiatry
Boston University School of Medicine
Boston, Massachusetts

Julia R. G. Vernon
Graduate Student
Department of Psychology
Ryerson University
Toronto, Ontario, Canada

Julie Woulfe
Attending Psychologist
Department of Psychiatry and
    Behavioral Sciences
Montefiore Medical Center
The University Hospital for Albert
    Einstein College of Medicine
Bronx, New York

Background

Adapting Evidence-Based Practice for Sexual and Gender Minorities

The Current State and Future Promise of Scientific and Affirmative Treatment Approaches

JOHN E. PACHANKIS AND STEVEN A. SAFREN ■

Today represents the first time in history that a critical mass of empirical evidence exists regarding suitable treatment goals and delivery methods for sexual and gender minority (SGM)-affirmative mental health practice. Taking advantage of this unprecedented situation, this handbook compiles the strongest examples of evidence-based SGM-affirmative practice to guide clinicians and researchers in considering ways in which SGM individuals' unique presenting concerns might be affirmatively addressed using evidence-based techniques. As an introduction to this handbook, this chapter first reviews the historical application of science to SGM mental health, current barriers toward evidence-based mental health treatments for SGM, and the recent progress to overcome these barriers as showcased throughout this handbook. The chapter reviews pressing questions and potential solutions regarding evidence-based SGM-affirmative practice, including why existing evidence-based treatments need to be adapted to address SGM-specific concerns, how existing evidence-based treatments can be adapted to address these concerns, and how clinical wisdom of expert mental health providers can serve to guide the adaptation of existing evidence-based treatments to facilitate their ability to affirm SGM as they improve SGM mental health.

HISTORICAL BACKGROUND

Across its history, the mental health profession has used science to both harm and help the mental health of SGM (Drescher, Shidlo, & Schroeder, 2002; Haldeman, 1994). Throughout the first half of the 20th century, the mental health profession used its scientific authority to perpetuate societal stigma toward SGM individuals. Specifically, during this time, the profession peddled oppressive diagnoses and psychologically and physically harmful treatments to ensure that homosexuality remained the illness that society assumed it was. Science, in this case, was used to subjugate an already vulnerable population. Following years of advocacy, in 1973, the profession made the landmark decision that homosexuality was no longer a mental illness and gradually shifted toward a more affirmative treatment approach that empowered, rather than further imprisoned, this vulnerable population (Krajeski, 1996). Although today's affirmative treatments no doubt represent a surer route to mental health than the unethical and harmful conversion therapies of the past (and today), scientific guidance for how such treatments should be developed and delivered has lagged. As described in the following section, several barriers have historically impeded scientific progress toward SGM-affirmative practice, which are currently being challenged to pave a more promising path forward.

BARRIERS AND PROGRESS TOWARD EVIDENCE-BASED SGM-AFFIRMATIVE PRACTICE

Despite clear professional, ethical, and scientific justifications for bringing a greater evidence base to SGM-affirmative practice, several barriers have impeded this goal (Pachankis, in press). Here, four such barriers are reviewed: (1) a lack of clear treatment targets; (2) a lack of treatment studies specific to SGM mental health; (3) failure to report SGM status in existing treatment studies; and (4) stigma itself, which perpetuates the lack of necessary resources to ultimately overcome the aforementioned barriers.

Lack of Clear Treatment Mechanisms

Only in the past two decades has the mental health field possessed accurate knowledge regarding the disparity in the prevalence of mental health problems that exists between sexual minority and heterosexual populations (Cochran & Mays, 2000a, 2000b; Gilman et al., 2001; King et al., 2008; Sandfort, de Graaf, Bijl, & Schnabel, 2001). Population-based data regarding gender minorities have only recently begun to emerge (Bränström & Pachankis, 2018). As this knowledge has emerged, researchers have used methodologically rigorous approaches to show that the root of this substantial disparity lies in SGM disproportionate exposure to stigma-related stress. Specifically, using population-based studies (Mays

& Cochran, 2001), interviewer-based assessments (Meyer, Schwartz, & Frost, 2008), experimental designs (Bosson, Haymovitz, & Pinel, 2004), and measures of exposure to structural stigma (e.g., discriminatory policy environments; Hatzenbuehler, Keyes, & Hasin, 2009), accumulating research has shown that stigma exposure explains SGM individuals' consistently elevated prevalence of stress-sensitive mental health problems (e.g., depression, anxiety, and substance use disorder).

Although this research points to the elimination of stigma as the surest route to reducing mental health disparities affecting SGM, stigma, through its persistent mechanisms and lasting effects, is not easy to change (Hatzenbuehler, Phelan, & Link, 2013). Furthermore, although the advocacy of mental health professionals can certainly play an important role in reducing stigma (Drescher, 2012, 2015), such advocacy does not always represent the most immediately relevant goal in clinical contexts. Without knowing the modifiable psychosocial mechanisms through which stigma compromises SGM mental health, until recently the field has been without clear, evidence-based treatment mechanisms for SGM clients who present for mental health services. Therefore, identifying the psychological mechanisms through which stigma operates to impair mental health has become a paramount goal for clinical researchers attempting to bring a greater evidence base to SGM mental health treatment.

Consistent with clinical recommendations spanning several decades (Hetrick & Martin, 1987; Malyon, 1982; Perez, DeBord, & Bieschke, 2000; Savin-Williams & Rodriguez, 1993), an emerging body of research has sought to determine the psychological pathways that are driven by stigma; that cause mental health problems; and that, because they are psychological in nature, can be modified with psychological treatments (Hatzenbuehler, 2009; Meyer, 2003). These pathways include psychological processes that are both specific to SGM, such as internalized homophobia (Newcomb & Mustanski, 2010), rejection sensitivity (Pachankis, Goldfried, & Ramrattan, 2008), and sexual identity concealment (Pachankis, 2007), and also universal risk factors for psychopathology that are elevated among SGM compared to heterosexuals, including social isolation (Safren & Heimberg, 1999), emotion dysregulation (Hatzenbuehler, McLaughlin, & Nolen-Hoeksema, 2008), and behavioral unassertiveness (Pachankis et al., 2008). Because these pathways are cognitive, affective, and behavioral, they lend themselves to being addressed through existing cognitive–behavioral (Fairburn et al., 2009; Farchione et al., 2012), emotion-focused (Elliott, Watson, Goldman, & Greenberg, 2004), and other evidence-based approaches (Diamond et al., 2010). Many chapters contained in this handbook illustrate the adaptation of these existing treatment approaches to address the minority stress treatment mechanisms reviewed here.

Lack of Treatment Studies Specific to SGM Mental Health

One paradoxical outcome of the HIV/AIDS crisis of the 1980s and 1990s was greater research attention to the health of SGM communities. This research illustrated not only that sexual minority men and transgender women are at vastly disproportionate risk of HIV infection compared to heterosexual and cisgender individuals but also that their greater risk for HIV co-occurs with other health disparities to synergistically exacerbate this risk (Stall et al., 2003). In particular, this research showed that mental health problems represent a prominent concern in the lives of many, if not most, SGM populations, that both co-occur with HIV risk, and also stand on their own to compromise SGM health (D'Augelli, 1989; Garnets, Herek, & Levy, 1990; McKirnan & Peterson, 1988; Meyer, 1995).

This era of research also ushered in the first randomized controlled trials of psychosocial treatments applied to SGM. This first set of treatment studies focused on stress coping and HIV risk reduction among gay and bisexual men (Antoni et al., 2000; Lutgendorf et al., 1998). Still to this day, nearly every randomized controlled trial conducted with SGM has been limited to the context of HIV prevention and care among sexual minority men (Mustanski et al., 2017; Parsons, Lelutiu-Weinberger, Botsko, & Golub, 2014; Safren et al., 2009). Although such studies provide invaluable evidence-based guidance to practicing clinicians regarding the sexual health needs of SGM populations, they typically address mental health only as one of several determinants of HIV-related behavioral health (e.g., medication adherence, condom usage) and have been limited to sexual minority men.

Despite the historic lack of randomized controlled trial data for SGM, several notable attempts have nonetheless been made to incorporate professional recommendations for SGM-affirmative practice into evidence-based practice (American Psychological Association, 2017). In general, these attempts have been in the form of either (1) clinical suggestions for applying observational research regarding SGM mental health in practice (Brown, 1988; Davies, 1996; Martell, Safren, & Prince, 2003; Ritter & Terndrup, 2002) or (2) clinical case studies incorporating SGM-affirmative principles into existing evidence-based approaches (Glassgold, 2009; Kaysen, Lostutter, & Goines, 2005; Safren & Rogers, 2001; Walsh & Hope, 2010). This first source of SGM-affirmative treatment guidance draws upon research regarding common developmental experiences of SGM individuals to increase therapists' awareness of these experiences and help SGM clients adapt to the stressors typical of each stage. This guidance also draws upon consumer report studies of treatment-seeking SGM to guide therapists toward gaining SGM-specific knowledge and avoiding heterocentric assumptions about their SGM clients, which SGM clients consistently specify as critical therapeutic requirements (Burckell & Goldfried, 2006).

Several existing SGM-specific case studies have described the application of cognitive–behavioral treatments to SGM clients. That so many case studies of SGM-affirmative evidence-based practice describe the application of cognitive–behavioral therapy is not surprising given the natural fit between minority stress conceptualizations of SGM mental health and the stress-coping orientation of cognitive–behavioral interventions (Balsam, Martell, & Safren, 2006). These case studies report helping SGM clients challenge negative attitudes about themselves and SGM peers, weigh the objective risks and benefits of sexual orientation disclosure, identify a supportive niche within the SGM community, and understand current symptomatology against a backdrop of societal homophobia. The chapters in this handbook draw upon, and extend, the best of both of these traditions to suggest strategies for merging this clinical wisdom into current evidence-based mental health practice.

Failure to Report SGM Status in Existing Treatment Studies

Although nearly every randomized controlled trial conducted with the general population includes SGM individuals by virtue of the random and diffuse distribution of SGM individuals in the general population, hardly any randomized controlled trials report the SGM status of their samples and none has stratified results by SGM status (Heck, Mirabito, LeMaire, Livingston, & Flentje, 2017). Thus, despite having the potential to relatively easily provide much-needed information regarding the efficacy of existing evidence-based practices for SGM individuals, this opportunity is currently lost. This pervasive tendency has left unanswered the question of whether SGM individuals experience comparable benefit to heterosexuals from existing evidence-based practice.

Nonetheless, a few recent studies, mostly conducted in naturalistic treatment settings, have examined whether SGM respond similarly or differently to treatment, with mixed results. For instance, in a hospital-based sample, SGM patients were found to experience equal treatment outcomes compared to heterosexual patients after participating in a general cognitive and dialectical behavioral treatment program, although subgroup analyses found that bisexual patients reported more thoughts related to self-injury and suicide and worse perceptions of care compared to other patients (Beard et al., 2017). In a large sample of students who sought therapy at college counseling centers throughout the United States, sexual minorities presented with greater depressive and anxious symptoms compared to heterosexuals but did not exhibit different treatment outcomes (Lefevor, Janis, & Park, 2017). In one of the few randomized controlled trials to examine treatment efficacy according to sexual orientation, homeless sexual minority adolescents experienced greater reductions in internalizing symptoms and drug use compared to homeless heterosexual adolescents after receiving a cognitive–behavioral substance use treatment (Grafsky, Letcher, Slesnick, & Serovich, 2011). Overall, these studies do not paint a definitive picture regarding the efficacy of existing treatments for SGM or answer the question of whether SGM-specific adaptations to existing evidence-based practice might be required. Notably, no studies have examined diverse gender identities as moderators or treatment efficacy.

Stigma as a Barrier to Evidence-Based Mental Health Practice with SGM

No doubt, stigma itself represents a fundamental obstacle to building a greater evidence base for SGM-affirmative mental health treatment (Pachankis, in press). Because stigma keeps marginalized groups away from the necessary power, resources, and social conditions necessary for creating more equitable social conditions (Bränström, Hatzenbuehler, Pachankis, & Link, 2016), it is not surprising that stigma would also interfere with the necessary conditions for generating accurate knowledge about mental health treatments for SGM. For instance, although SGM have been a visible and vibrant segment of the US population for decades and although a critical body of research has suggested that SGM experience substantial mental health disparities, among the largest in all of psychiatric epidemiology, and that these disparities are due to stigma-related stress, hardly any SGM-affirmative mental health treatment approaches have ever been tested for efficacy with SGM individuals (Chaudoir, Wang, & Pachankis, 2017).

Outside of HIV/AIDS-related research, which itself initially required dramatic acts of protest to receive adequate attention and funding resources (Epstein, 1996), SGM health has simply not received resources commensurate with the size of the problem. In fact, three-fourths of the National Institutes of Health's portfolio for SGM health research is allocated to HIV/AIDS research, typically among gay and bisexual men, despite the fact that mental health problems, especially suicide, have likely surpassed HIV/AIDS as the leading cause of premature mortality among SGM (Hottes, Ferlatte, & Gesink, 2015). Although HIV/AIDS research pertaining to SGM certainly merits funding resources given the disproportionate impact of HIV/AIDS on gay and bisexual men and transgender women in the United States and in many world regions, to rely on this research for knowledge about SGM *mental* health likely overestimates risk and overlooks the distinct concerns of sexual minority women and gender diverse individuals.

Another way that stigma interferes with accurate evidence regarding SGM mental health is through diminished academic power. Until recently, with a few courageous exceptions, it was nearly impossible to stake an academic career on studying SGM mental health given the reality of professional homophobia. Therefore, despite the fact that SGM seek mental health services at significantly higher rates than the general population (Cochran, Björkenstam, & Mays, 2017), mental health training programs often lacked sufficient coverage of SGM-relevant topics, thereby perpetuating a lack of SGM-specific treatment knowledge across successive generations of mental health trainees. Today represents the first time in history that mental health trainees can seek training in SGM-specific training with the goal of making SGM mental health a core focus of their careers. The following chapters of this handbook, in fact, suggest ambitious programs of SGM treatment research that could easily require many entire careers to pursue. Fortunately, the field now possesses a critical mass of scholars with just such goals.

DO EXISTING EVIDENCE-BASED TREATMENTS NEED TO BE ADAPTED TO ADDRESS SGM-SPECIFIC CONCERNS?

The mental health professions aspire to deliver both SGM-affirmative treatments and evidence-based treatments as a matter of ethical and professional practice (American Psychological Association, 2012; APA Presidential Task Force on Evidence-Based Practice, 2006). These aspirations suggest that evidence-based practice should be delivered to SGM in a way that is SGM affirmative and that SGM-affirmative practice should be tested for empirical support. In terms of progress toward these goals, although existing research and clinical recommendations strongly encourage clinicians to employ an SGM-affirmative stance when delivering all treatments, including evidence-based treatments, only one SGM-affirmative mental health treatment has been tested for efficacy in a randomized controlled trial (Pachankis, Hatzenbuehler, Rendina, Safren, & Parsons, 2015).

A distinct but equally pressing question is whether existing evidence-based mental health treatments need to be *adapted*—that is, changed from their current form—to address the specific concerns that SGM might bring to treatment (Johnson, 2012). Here, we review evidence for and against this possible need. On the one hand, emerging empirical findings and practical considerations suggest that SGM-specific adaptations to existing practice might not be required. First, SGM mental health disparities have been found to be driven by universal psychosocial risk factors (Hatzenbuehler, 2009), suggesting that existing evidence-based treatments that address these risk factors should be helpful for SGM clients without adaptation. In fact, as reviewed previously, the few studies that have examined differential efficacy of existing mental health treatments according to sexual orientation have found that, with the exception of hospital-based treatment for bisexuals, sexual minorities seem to benefit just as much, if not more than, heterosexuals from existing practice (Beard et al., 2017; Grafsky et al., 2011; Lefevor et al., 2017). Furthermore, rather than SGM experiencing barriers to engagement in existing treatments, population-based research suggests that sexual minorities are actually more likely to engage in existing treatments, even after accounting for their greater burden of mental health problems (Cochran et al., 2017). One might additionally argue that whether novel SGM-specific adaptations of evidence-based treatments are needed should be weighed against the prodigious outlay of resources required to develop and test new interventions. Indeed, if every population subgroup were to require its own treatment approach, the field would be in the untenable position of having to create thousands of distinct treatments (Kazdin, 2000). Therefore, novel adaptations to evidence-based practice might only be required when a given population experiences unique mechanisms underlying their mental health disparities or when that population does not benefit from existing practice (National Institute of Mental Health, 2010). Whether SGM mental health needs rise to this threshold remains to be determined.

On the other hand, the case for creating novel, SGM-specific adaptations of evidence-based treatments can be considered on ethical grounds (Pachankis, in press). SGM individuals seek mental health services at higher rates than do heterosexuals, in some cases even after accounting for their greater burden of mental health problems (Cochran et al., 2017). Creating novel adaptations of evidence-based treatments for such frequent consumers of mental health services would be an important reparation for the field's historic perpetuation of psychologically, and sometimes physically, harmful treatments. Indeed, for much of its early history in the United States, the mental health profession, rather than seeking a scientific base for empowering SGM, proffered unscientific, homophobic treatments that further harmed this already vulnerable population (Pachankis, in press). Indeed, only 10 US states and the District of Columbia currently ban sexual orientation conversion therapy, and Vice President Mike Pence is an avowed supporter of the practice (Stack, 2016). Throughout the world, only two countries have legal sanctions against conversion therapy, and outright abuse abounds at the hands of the mental health profession (International Lesbian, Gay, Bisexual, Trans, and Intersex Association, 2017). In China, for instance, which has one of the world's largest populations of SGM given its overall population size, one study found that 36% of mental health professionals support conversion therapy and 14% report practicing it (Beijing LGBT Center, 2014). Therefore, ethical reasons might compel the field to create novel adaptations of evidence-based treatments for SGM. It is simply morally inexcusable that Western societies have been more successful at disseminating abusive conversion therapies than evidence-based alternatives for SGM people.

The case for creating novel SGM-specific evidence-based treatments can also be considered on professional grounds. Several professional mental health associations throughout the world have adopted SGM-affirmative practice guidelines to promote appropriate treatment of SGM populations (American Psychological Association, 2017). According to these guidelines, SGM-affirmative treatment requires that therapists treating SGM possess awareness of the unique stressors facing this population; avoid homophobia and heterocentric assumptions; and become familiar with SGM developmental experiences, families, communities, and relationship norms (American Psychological Association, 2012). Yet, the field currently lacks an evidence base for translating these principles into evidence-based practice. To the extent that novel adaptations of existing evidence-based practice could incorporate concrete clinical strategies for implementing these SGM-affirmative clinical recommendations, the field will facilitate the implementation of its professional mandate. Another professional reason for creating treatments that address SGM-specific concerns is that treatment studies are themselves experiments and can provide needed knowledge regarding the impact of stigma and its alleviation on SGM mental health.

Overall, although empirical findings and practical realities suggest that the field must carefully justify the creation of novel SGM-specific adaptations to existing evidence-based practice, for ethical and professional reasons, such adaptations should at least be explored more than they have been to date. Importantly, this consideration does not speak to the need to deliver SGM-affirmative evidence-based care; as noted previously, such care represents an obvious practice requirement, as specified in professional guidelines. Instead, this discussion is intended to outline reasons that SGM might benefit from existing, non-adapted practice even as they might additionally benefit from SGM-specific adaptations to current practice. Regardless of whether or not the field decides that SGM-specific adaptations are justified, there is reason for optimism that the field's trajectory away from unscientific, harmful approaches toward SGM-affirmative evidence-based practice will continue.

HOW SHOULD EXISTING EVIDENCE-BASED TREATMENTS BE ADAPTED TO ADDRESS SGM-SPECIFIC CONCERNS?

Assuming that future research and ethical and professional considerations determine that existing evidence-based practice as applied to SGM clients can be made more effective by addressing SGM-specific presenting concerns, a key question becomes *how* SGM-specific adaptations to these treatments should best be made. Two potential options for addressing SGM-specific concerns in evidence-based practice are creating altogether novel approaches for SGM individuals and adapting existing evidence-based practice to address SMG-specific presenting concerns. Notably, all of the approaches described in this handbook represent adaptations of existing evidence-based approaches that make them responsive to SGM-specific presenting concerns. That no treatments described herein represent brand new treatment approaches created specifically for SGM likely reflects the fact that existing evidence-based approaches are relatively seamlessly consistent with minority stress conceptualizations of SGM mental health, given that both minority stress theory and evidence-based practice focus on modifiable cognitive, affective, and behavioral stress pathways, as noted previously. Thus, assuming that brand new treatments are not required for SGM, the question becomes how to best adapt existing treatments for this population.

The cultural adaptation literature, which typically addresses how to adapt mental health treatments for racial and ethnic minorities (Bernal, Jiménez-Chafey, & Domenech Rodríguez, 2009; Hall, 2001; Lau, 2006), has been relatively silent on how to adapt mental health treatments for SGM. Nonetheless, this literature suggests that cultural adaptations of evidence-based practice must strike a balance between preserving fidelity to the original intervention given that its efficacy rests in science and sensitively attending to unique presenting features of culturally diverse clients. This literature also suggests that adaptation attempts consider whether adaptations should focus on addressing barriers to engagement in existing evidence-based treatments or on how existing treatments can accommodate the unique context surrounding the presenting concerns of diverse populations (Lau, 2006). Given that no evidence suggests the existence of barriers to sexual minorities' engagement in treatment and, in fact, that sexual minority individuals are disproportionately likely to *seek* care, it seems most reasonable that adaptation for SGM should primarily focus on addressing the unique context surrounding SGM's presenting concerns. Of course, research is needed to determine whether the same applies to transgender individuals, for whom substantial barriers to mental health care might exist alongside unique clinically relevant contextual challenges (White Hughto, Reisner, & Pachankis, in press).

The adaptations specified in this handbook address how this unique context—namely stigma, discrimination, and related minority stressors—serves as a key determinant of mental health problems for many SGM individuals. Notably, these approaches are careful to avoid suggesting that although SGM-specific contextual adaptations might be required, all SGM experience their stigmatizing contexts similarly and that a one-size-fits-all approach to adaptation is warranted. These chapters are also careful to suggest ways that treatment adaptations can focus on SGM's unique community and individual strengths, also following recommendations for cultural adaptation of evidence-based practice (Lau, 2006).

Borrowing from the cultural adaptation literature, the psychotherapy adaptation process for SGM can be conceptualized along a continuum. On one end of the continuum lies no adaptation. As applied to SGM, this would simply involve delivering existing evidence-based practice using a general SGM-affirmative therapeutic stance. On the other end of the continuum lies the creation of brand new treatment approaches that address processes that are uniformly shared by the specific cultural group that fundamentally alters their presenting concerns and experience of mental health. Perhaps one way in which the experience of SGM might demand a novel treatment approach is through universally challenging the pervasive, often subtle, way in which homophobic worldviews become internalized and get under the skin to harm SGM mental health. Notably, this approach would stand in stark contrast to cultural development approaches, which typically seek to radically accept culturally diverse clients' worldviews and align those with therapeutic goals. One role of the therapist working with SGM clients, however, might be to challenge clients' deeply held worldviews (e.g., regarding the inferiority of homosexuality) that stem from pervasive structural homophobia and interfere with mental health.

For the most part, the approaches suggested in this handbook lie somewhere in between these two ends of the continuum. Although all of the chapters encourage the application of an SGM-affirmative stance in treating SGM, none of them describe a radically distinct approach. However, all of the approaches suggested in this handbook deeply consider how the tenets of existing approaches can be made to align with common experiences, minority stress processes, and worldviews of SGM clients. First, several chapters describe how evidence-based practice can be adapted for subpopulations of SGM. For instance, Pepping, Halford, and Lyons (Chapter 5) suggest ways to address the distinct features of many same-sex relationships, including non-monogamy agreements and challenges of relationship disclosure, using SGM-affirmative adaptations of relationship education programs originally created for heterosexuals (Halford, Markman, Kling, & Stanley, 2003). Similarly, Goldberg, Frost, and Noyola (Chapter 6) describe how existing parenting interventions can address the unique experience of same-sex parents. Other chapters suggest SGM-affirmative adaptations for SGM youth (Chapters 2 and 3), transgender individuals (Chapter 4), and bisexual individuals (Chapter 7).

Several chapters review how specific mental health problems might result from SGM-specific determinants and manifest with distinct functions (e.g., as coping strategies for minority stress). These chapters suggest how to address the determinants and functions of these problems in an SGM-affirmative manner. Mental health problems addressed include anxiety disorders (Chapter 8), depression (Chapter 9), substance use disorders (Chapter 10), trauma-related stress (Chapters 11 and 12), eating and body image disorders (Chapter 13), and sexual health problems (Chapters 14 and 15). Furthermore, recognizing that several features of minority stress align seamlessly with existing evidence-based approaches, chapters in the final section discuss how to adapt these approaches to address SGM-specific presenting concerns. These chapters discuss, for instance, how principles of group-based cognitive–behavioral therapy (Chapter 16), mindfulness- and acceptance-based approaches (Chapter 17), dialectical behavior therapy (Chapter 18), attachment-based family therapy (Chapter 19), and transdiagnostic approaches (Chapter 20) can address the distinct stressors that often bring SGM to mental health treatment. All chapters in this handbook present vivid examples of how these adaptations might play out in practice. Overall, every chapter suggests ways to incorporate SGM-affirmative adaptations into existing evidence-based practice, thereby suggesting intervention approaches to be tested in future randomized controlled trials. The approaches described herein strike a reasonable balance between the need for SGM-affirmative evidence-based practice and the challenges and potential lack of necessity for creating treatments anew.

FUTURE RESEARCH DIRECTIONS IN EVIDENCE-BASED PRACTICE FOR SGM

As the chapters in this handbook illustrate, the field has made significant progress in laying the foundation for evidence-based practice for SGM clients. At the same time, several existing knowledge gaps suggest exciting avenues for future study. As reviewed here, these future research directions include randomized controlled trials of SGM-specific treatment approaches, methods for greater understanding of the moderators of SGM-specific treatment efficacy, and tests of psychotherapy process factors with this population. From spanning the largest contexts to the finest in-session processes, this future research can inform where, why, how, and for whom SGM-specific psychotherapies work best.

Randomized Controlled Trials

Randomized controlled trials represent the gold-standard test of psychotherapy efficacy (Leichsenring & Steinert, 2017). As mentioned previously, to date, only one randomized controlled trial has been conducted for mental health concerns among SGM, and no known randomized controlled trials in the general population have stratified analyses by sexual orientation or diverse gender identities (Heck et al., 2017; Pachankis et al., 2015). For the ethical and professional reasons discussed previously, randomized controlled trials of SGM-specific treatments represent a needed remedy to the historic lack of evidence-based practice with this population and the potential for harmful treatments to proliferate without a stronger evidence base for SGM-affirmative alternatives. The chapters contained in this handbook propose specific treatments that could be examined in such trials. At the same time, for the reasons outlined previously, future research is also needed to examine differential benefit from existing evidence-based treatments according to SGM status.

Clinically Useful, Empirically Derived Treatment Principles

As important as randomized controlled trials are for establishing the superiority of a given treatment over others, more clinically useful data are needed to maximally inform practice (Westen, Novotny, & Thompson-Brenner, 2004). Convincing arguments have been made elsewhere that the primary product of randomized controlled trials—a manualized protocol—often does not provide the most useable guidance in actual practice (Goldfried & Eubanks-Carter, 2004; Pachankis & Goldfried, 2007; Westen et al., 2004). Given that clinicians often do not find manualized treatment protocols applicable to the complexity of their actual cases, research that identifies treatment *principles* that can be flexibly applied across SGM presenting concerns represents a necessary adjunct to traditional randomized controlled trial data (Goldfried, 1980; Pachankis, 2015). Indeed, research that distills core principles has the additional benefit of preventing a situation in which dozens of, if not more, distinct treatments are tested and created for numerous distinct presenting concerns among distinct subpopulations of SGM. Such a research climate would no doubt place an undue demand on already constrained treatment resources without appreciably increasing clinically useful knowledge or advancing science.

Tests of Treatment Moderators

As important as knowing whether various treatments are efficacious for SGM individuals in general is knowing under what circumstances and for whom such treatments are efficacious and also under what circumstances and for which subpopulations such treatments are not. Emerging research in related areas suggests that several potential moderators, such as the structural environment, race/ethnicity, and minority stress processes, represent important future areas for exploration. With respect to the structural environment, one analysis found that across 99 randomized controlled trials of HIV-prevention interventions for African Americans, the race-related conditions of the location in which the treatment was delivered were associated with treatment efficacy (Reid, Dovidio, Ballester, & Johnson, 2014). Applying this to SGM clients, these results suggest the possibility that the structural climate (i.e., how oppressive or homophobic it is) in which SGM-affirmative treatments are delivered might similarly influence the efficacy of such treatments on SGM individuals' mental health. With respect to race and ethnicity, with few notable exceptions (e.g., Cochran, Mays, Alegria, Ortega, & Takeuchi, 2007; Rodriguez-Seijas, Eaton, & Pachankis, in press), very few population-based studies have examined the basic question of whether racial and ethnic minority SGM are disproportionately affected by mental health problems compared to White SGM. Furthermore, no mental health treatment studies with SGM have stratified efficacy results by race or ethnicity. Existing data, from both population-based data sets and randomized controlled trials, offer future researchers a relatively straightforward means for addressing these particular gaps. Such research might consider the utility of adopting an intersectional lens to capture the multiple sources of stigma-related disadvantage that can affect vulnerable subpopulations of SGM communities.

Minority stress processes themselves represent another potential treatment outcome moderator that has only recently received empirical attention. These recent data suggest an important role of minority stress processes, such as internalized homophobia, in determining who might benefit most (and least) from SGM-affirmative treatments. For instance, in a reanalysis of a randomized controlled trial of SGM-affirmative therapy, Millar, Wang, and Pachankis (2016) found that gay and bisexual men who endorsed higher levels of implicit anti-gay bias at the start of treatment experienced more improvement from the treatment than did men with lower levels of implicit anti-gay bias. However, these results contradict those of two other recent studies indicating that sexual minority men who endorse more self-reported internalized homophobia experience less benefit from both a group-delivered HIV-prevention intervention (Huebner, Davis, Nemeroff, & Aiken, 2002) and a relationship education intervention (Newcomb et al., 2017). Future research might investigate other personal moderators of treatment efficacy, such as identity concealment, making sure to also explore the role of such factors beyond samples of sexual minority men. This research might help pinpoint those subpopulations of SGM for whom specifically adapted treatments might be required, thereby bypassing the flawed approach of assuming that all SGM warrant SGM-adapted treatments.

Psychotherapy Process Research

Finally, given the dearth of psychotherapy process-outcome research among SGM clients and the clinically useful information that can emerge from such work, future research should explore facets of the psychotherapeutic process that can facilitate or hinder positive treatment outcomes for SGM clients. This research might explore, for instance, how minority stress narratives unfold over the course of treatment and which therapist responses are most conducive to using those narratives constructively. Therapists who focus on stigma-related stress despite an SGM client's beliefs that stigma is irrelevant to their presenting concerns may influence poorer outcomes among their clients. Process-outcome research can also link in-session events, such as alliance ruptures caused by therapists' misunderstanding of SGM-specific concerns, to ultimate treatment outcome (Sullivan & Pachankis, 2018). Whether, how, and when therapists disclose their own sexual orientation or gender identities in treatment can also be linked to treatment outcomes, thereby providing clinicians with highly concrete guidance for how to handle this particular situation especially relevant to working with SGM clients. How therapists react to clients' own SGM identity disclosures represents a similarly important future direction. Drawing upon the clinical wisdom currently being applied to SGM-affirmative practice in naturalistic community settings represents a highly promising approach for determining future adaptations to existing evidence-based practice.

CONCLUSION

The field of SGM-affirmative mental health care has arrived at an exciting juncture. A burgeoning literature is awakening to suggest how existing evidence-based treatments can be adapted to best address SGM clients' presenting concerns in a manner consistent with professional guidelines for both SGM-affirmative practice and evidence-based treatment adaptation. The chapters featured in this handbook represent the best available guidance for how to deliver SGM-affirmative evidence-based practice to overcome the historic barriers that have hindered this possibility to date. Unfortunately, SGM-affirmative evidence-based practice has not been the historic norm, but the wisdom contained in the following chapters suggests that future optimism is warranted.

REFERENCES

American Psychological Association. (2012). Guidelines for psychological practice with lesbian, gay, and bisexual clients. *American Psychologist, 67*, 10–42.

American Psychological Association. (2017). *Guidelines and practice position statements.* Washington, DC: IPsyNet.

Antoni, M. H., Cruess, D. G., Cruess, S., Lutgendorf, S., Kumar, M., Ironson, G., . . . Schneiderman, N. (2000). Cognitive–behavioral stress management intervention effects on anxiety, 24-hr urinary norepinephrine output, and T-cytotoxic/suppressor cells over time among symptomatic HIV-infected gay men. *Journal of Consulting and Clinical Psychology, 68*, 31–45.

APA Presidential Task Force on Evidence-Based Practice. (2006). Evidence-based practice in psychology. *The American Psychologist, 61*(4), 271–285.

Balsam, K. F., Martell, C. R., & Safren, S. A. (2006). Affirmative cognitive–behavior therapy with lesbian, gay, and bisexual people. In P. A. Hays & G. Y. Iwamasa (Eds.), *Culturally responsive cognitive–behavioral therapy: Assessment, supervision, and practice* (pp. 223–244). Washington, DC: American Psychological Association.

Beard, C., Kirakosian, N., Silverman, A. L., Winer, J. P., Wadsworth, L. P., & Björgvinsson, T. (2017). Comparing treatment response between LGBQ and heterosexual individuals attending a CBT- and DBT-skills-based partial hospital. *Journal of Consulting and Clinical Psychology, 85*(12), 1171–1181.

Beijing LGBT Center. (2014). *Chinese LGBT Mental Health Survey Report*. Beijing, China: Author.

Bernal, G., Jiménez-Chafey, M. I., & Domenech Rodríguez, M. M. (2009). Cultural adaptation of treatments: A resource for considering culture in evidence-based practice. *Professional Psychology: Research and Practice, 40*(4), 361–368.

Bosson, J. K., Haymovitz, E. L., & Pinel, E. C. (2004). When saying and doing diverge: The effects of stereotype threat on self-reported versus non-verbal anxiety. *Journal of Experimental Social Psychology, 40*(2), 247–255.

Bränström, R., Hatzenbuehler, M. L., Pachankis, J. E., & Link, B. G. (2016). Sexual orientation disparities in preventable disease: A fundamental cause perspective. *American Journal of Public Health, 106*(6), 1109–1115.

Bränström, R., & Pachankis, J. E. (2018). Mental health and gender dysphoria: A total population study in Sweden. Manuscript in preparation.

Brown, L. S. (1988). Lesbians, gay men and their families: Common clinical issues. *Journal of Gay & Lesbian Psychotherapy, 1*(1), 65–78.

Burckell, L. A., & Goldfried, M. R. (2006). Therapist qualities preferred by sexual-minority individuals. *Psychotherapy: Theory, Research, Practice, Training, 43*(1), 32.

Chaudoir, S. R., Wang, K., & Pachankis, J. E. (2017). What reduces sexual minority stress? A review of the intervention "toolkit." *Journal of Social Issues, 73*, 586–617.

Cochran, S. D., Björkenstam, C., & Mays, V. M. (2017). Sexual orientation differences in functional limitations, disability, and mental health services use: Results from the 2013–2014 National Health Interview Survey. *Journal of Consulting and Clinical Psychology, 85*(12), 1111–1121.

Cochran, S. D., & Mays, V. M. (2000a). Lifetime prevalence of suicide symptoms and affective disorders among men reporting same-sex sexual partners: Results from NHANES III. *American Journal of Public Health, 90*, 573–578.

Cochran, S. D., & Mays, V. M. (2000b). Relation between psychiatric syndromes and behaviorally defined sexual orientation in a sample of the US population. *American Journal of Epidemiology, 151*, 516–523.

Cochran, S. D., Mays, V. M., Alegria, M., Ortega, A. N., & Takeuchi, D. (2007). Mental health and substance use disorders among Latino and Asian American lesbian, gay, and bisexual adults. *Journal of Consulting and Clinical Psychology, 75*, 785–794.

D'Augelli, A. R. (1989). Lesbians' and gay men's experiences of discrimination and harassment in a university community. *American Journal of Community Psychology, 17*, 317–321.

Davies, D. (1996). Towards a model of gay affirmative therapy. In D. Davies & C. Neal (Eds.), *Pink therapy: A guide for counsellors and therapists working with lesbian, gay and bisexual clients* (pp. 24–40). Maidenhead, UK: Open University Press.

Diamond, G. S., Wintersteen, M. B., Brown, G. K., Diamond, G. M., Gallop, R., Shelef, K., & Levy, S. (2010). Attachment-based family therapy for adolescents with suicidal ideation: A randomized controlled trial. *Journal of the American Academy of Child & Adolescent Psychiatry, 49*(2), 122–131.

Drescher, J. (2012). The removal of homosexuality from the DSM: Its impact on today's marriage equality debate. *Journal of Gay & Lesbian Mental Health, 16*, 124–135.

Drescher, J. (2015). Queer diagnoses revisited: The past and future of homosexuality and gender diagnoses in DSM and ICD. *International Review of Psychiatry, 27*, 386–395.

Drescher, J., Shidlo, A., & Schroeder, M. (2002). *Sexual conversion therapy: Ethical, clinical and research perspectives.* Boca Raton, FL: CRC Press.

Elliott, R., Watson, J., Goldman, R. N., & Greenberg, L. S. (2004). *Learning emotion-focused therapy: The process-experiential approach to change.* Washington, DC: American Psychological Association.

Epstein, S. (1996). *Impure science: AIDS, activism, and the politics of knowledge.* Berkeley, CA: University of California Press.

Fairburn, C. G., Cooper, Z., Doll, H. A., O'Connor, M. E., Bohn, K., Hawker, D. M., . . . Palmer, R. L. (2009). Transdiagnostic cognitive–behavioral therapy for patients with eating disorders: A two-site trial with 60-week follow-up. *American Journal of Psychiatry, 166*(3), 311–319.

Farchione, T. J., Fairholme, C. P., Ellard, K. K., Boisseau, C. L., Thompson-Hollands, J., Carl, J. R., & Barlow, D. H. (2012). Unified protocol for transdiagnostic treatment of emotional disorders: A randomized controlled trial. *Behavior Therapy, 43*, 666–678.

Garnets, L., Herek, G. M., & Levy, B. (1990). Violence and victimization of lesbians and gay men: Mental health consequences. *Journal of Interpersonal Violence, 5*, 366–383.

Gilman, S. E., Cochran, S. D., Mays, V. M., Hughes, M., Ostrow, D., & Kessler, R. C. (2001). Risk of psychiatric disorders among individuals reporting same-sex sexual partners in the National Comorbidity Survey. *American Journal of Public Health, 91*, 933–939.

Glassgold, J. M. (2009). Key facets in Felix's case: The therapist's cultural competency, masculine socialization, and sexual orientation stigma. *Pragmatic Case Studies in Psychotherapy, 5*(4), 39–43.

Goldfried, M. R. (1980). Toward the delineation of therapeutic change principles. *American Psychologist, 35*, 991–999.

Goldfried, M. R., & Eubanks-Carter, C. (2004). On the need for a new psychotherapy research paradigm: Comment on Westen, Novotny, and Thompson-Brenner (2004). *Psychological Bulletin, 130*, 669–673.

Grafsky, E. L., Letcher, A., Slesnick, N., & Serovich, J. M. (2011). Comparison of treatment response among GLB and non-GLB street living youth. *Children and Youth Services Review, 33*, 569–574.

Haldeman, D. C. (1994). The practice and ethics of sexual orientation conversion therapy. *Journal of Consulting and Clinical Psychology, 62*(2), 221.

Halford, W. K., Markman, H. J., Kling, G. H., & Stanley, S. M. (2003). Best practice in couple relationship education. *Journal of Marital and Family Therapy, 29*(3), 385–406.

Hall, G. C. N. (2001). Psychotherapy research with ethnic minorities: Empirical, ethical, and conceptual issues. *Journal of Consulting and Clinical Psychology, 69*(3), 502.

Hatzenbuehler, M. L. (2009). How does sexual minority stigma "get under the skin"? A psychological mediation framework. *Psychological Bulletin, 135*, 707–730.

Hatzenbuehler, M. L., Keyes, K. M., & Hasin, D. S. (2009). State-level policies and psychiatric morbidity in lesbian, gay, and bisexual populations. *American Journal of Public Health*, 99, 2275–2281.

Hatzenbuehler, M. L., McLaughlin, K. A., & Nolen-Hoeksema, S. (2008). Emotion regulation and internalizing symptoms in a longitudinal study of sexual minority and heterosexual adolescents. *Journal of Child Psychology and Psychiatry*, 49, 1270–1278.

Hatzenbuehler, M. L., Phelan, J. C., & Link, B. G. (2013). Stigma as a fundamental cause of population health inequalities. *American Journal of Public Health*, 103(5), 813–821.

Heck, N. C., Mirabito, L. A., LeMaire, K., Livingston, N. A., & Flentje, A. (2017). Omitted data in randomized controlled trials for anxiety and depression: A systematic review of the inclusion of sexual orientation and gender identity. *Journal of Consulting and Clinical Psychology*, 85, 72–76.

Hetrick, E. S., & Martin, A. D. (1987). Developmental issues and their resolution for gay and lesbian adolescents. *Journal of Homosexuality*, 14(1–2), 25–43.

Hottes, T. S., Ferlatte, O., & Gesink, D. (2015). Suicide and HIV as leading causes of death among gay and bisexual men: A comparison of estimated mortality and published research. *Critical Public Health*, 25, 513–526.

Huebner, D. M., Davis, M. C., Nemeroff, C. J., & Aiken, L. S. (2002). The impact of internalized homophobia on HIV preventive interventions. *American Journal of Community Psychology*, 30, 327–348.

International Lesbian, Gay, Bisexual, Trans and Intersex Association. (2017). *State-sponsored homophobia 2017: A world survey of sexual orientation laws: Criminalisation, protection and recognition*. Geneva, Switzerland: Author.

Johnson, S. D. (2012). Gay affirmative psychotherapy with lesbian, gay, and bisexual individuals: Implications for contemporary psychotherapy research. *American Journal of Orthopsychiatry*, 82(4), 516–522.

Kaysen, D., Lostutter, T. W., & Goines, M. A. (2005). Cognitive processing therapy for acute stress disorder resulting from an anti-gay assault. *Cognitive and Behavioral Practice*, 12, 278–289.

Kazdin, A. E. (2000). Developing a research agenda for child and adolescent psychotherapy. *Archives of General Psychiatry*, 57, 829–835.

King, M., Semlyen, J., Tai, S. S., Killaspy, H., Osborn, D., Popelyuk, D., & Nazareth, I. (2008). A systematic review of mental disorder, suicide, and deliberate self harm in lesbian, gay and bisexual people. *BMC Psychiatry*, 8(1), 70.

Krajeski, J. (1996). Homosexuality and the mental health professions: A contemporary history. In R. P. Cabaj & T. S. Stein (Eds.), *Textbook of homosexuality and mental health* (pp. 17–31). Washington, DC: American Psychiatric Press.

Lau, A. S. (2006). Making the case for selective and directed cultural adaptations of evidence-based treatments: Examples from parent training. *Clinical Psychology: Science and Practice*, 13(4), 295–310.

Lefevor, G. T., Janis, R. A., & Park, S. Y. (2017). Religious and sexual identities: An intersectional, longitudinal examination of change in therapy. *The Counseling Psychologist*, 45, 387–413.

Leichsenring, F., & Steinert, C. (2017). Is cognitive behavioral therapy the gold standard for psychotherapy? The need for plurality in treatment and research. *JAMA*, 318, 1323–1324.

Lutgendorf, S. K., Antoni, M. H., Ironson, G., Starr, K., Costello, N., Zuckerman, M., . . . Schneiderman, N. (1998). Changes in cognitive coping skills and social support during cognitive behavioral stress management intervention and distress outcomes in symptomatic human immunodeficiency virus (HIV)-seropositive gay men. *Psychosomatic Medicine, 60,* 204–214.

Malyon, A. K. (1982). Psychotherapeutic implications of internalized homophobia in gay men. *Journal of Homosexuality, 7*(2–3), 59–69.

Martell, C. R., Safren, S. A., & Prince, S. (2003). *Cognitive behavioral therapy with gay, lesbian, and bisexual clients.* New York, NY: Guilford.

Mays, V. M., & Cochran, S. D. (2001). Mental health correlates of perceived discrimination among lesbian, gay, and bisexual adults in the United States. *American Journal of Public Health, 91,* 1869–1876.

McKirnan, D. J., & Peterson, P. L. (1988). Stress, expectancies, and vulnerability to substance abuse: A test of a model among homosexual men. *Journal of Abnormal Psychology, 97,* 461–466.

Meyer, I. H. (1995). Minority stress and mental health in gay men. *Journal of Health and Social Behavior, 36,* 38–56.

Meyer, I. H. (2003). Prejudice, social stress, and mental health in lesbian, gay, and bisexual populations: Conceptual issues and research evidence. *Psychological Bulletin, 129,* 674–697.

Meyer, I. H., Schwartz, S., & Frost, D. M. (2008). Social patterning of stress and coping: Does disadvantaged social status confer more stress and fewer coping resources? *Social Science & Medicine, 67,* 368–379.

Millar, B. M., Wang, K., & Pachankis, J. E. (2016). The moderating role of internalized homonegativity on the efficacy of LGB-affirmative psychotherapy: Results from a randomized controlled trial with young adult gay and bisexual men. *Journal of Consulting and Clinical Psychology, 84,* 565–570.

Mustanski, B., Madkins, K., Greene, G. J., Parsons, J. T., Johnson, B. A., Sullivan, P., . . . Abel, R. (2017). Internet-based HIV prevention with at-home sexually transmitted infection testing for young men having sex with men: Study protocol of a randomized controlled trial of Keep It Up! 2.0. *JMIR Research Protocols, 6*(1), e1.

National Institute of Mental Health. (2010). *From discovery to cure: Accelerating the development of new and personalized interventions for mental illnesses: Report of the National Advisory Mental Health Council's Workshop.* Bethesda, MD: Author.

Newcomb, M. E., Macapagal, K. R., Feinstein, B. A., Bettin, E., Swann, G., & Whitton, S. W. (2017). Integrating HIV prevention and relationship education for young same-sex male couples: A pilot trial of the 2GETHER intervention. *AIDS and Behavior, 21*(8), 2464–2478.

Newcomb, M. E., & Mustanski, B. (2010). Internalized homophobia and internalizing mental health problems: A meta-analytic review. *Clinical Psychology Review, 30*(8), 1019–1029.

Pachankis, J. E. (2007). The psychological implications of concealing a stigma: A cognitive–affective–behavioral model. *Psychological Bulletin, 133,* 328–345.

Pachankis, J. E. (2015). A transdiagnostic minority stress treatment approach for gay and bisexual men's syndemic health conditions. *Archives of Sexual Behavior, 44,* 1843–1860.

Pachankis, J. E. (in press). The scientific pursuit of sexual and gender minority mental health treatments: Toward evidence-based affirmative practice. *American Psychologist.*

Pachankis, J. E., & Goldfried, M. R. (2007). *An integrative, principle-based approach to psychotherapy.* In S. G. Hofmann & J. Weinberger (Eds.), *The art and science of psychotherapy* (pp. 49–68). New York, NY: Routledge.

Pachankis, J. E., Goldfried, M. R., & Ramrattan, M. E. (2008). Extension of the rejection sensitivity construct to the interpersonal functioning of gay men. *Journal of Consulting and Clinical Psychology, 76*(2), 306.

Pachankis, J. E., Hatzenbuehler, M. L., Rendina, H. J., Safren, S. A., & Parsons, J. T. (2015). LGB-affirmative cognitive–behavioral therapy for young adult gay and bisexual men: A randomized controlled trial of a transdiagnostic minority stress approach. *Journal of Consulting and Clinical Psychology, 83*, 875.

Parsons, J. T., Lelutiu-Weinberger, C., Botsko, M., & Golub, S. A. (2014). A randomized controlled trial utilizing motivational interviewing to reduce HIV risk and drug use in young gay and bisexual men. *Journal of Consulting and Clinical Psychology, 82*(1), 9.

Perez, R. M., DeBord, K. A., & Bieschke, K. J. (2000). *Handbook of counseling and psychotherapy with lesbian, gay, and bisexual clients.* Washington, DC: American Psychological Association.

Reid, A. E., Dovidio, J. F., Ballester, E., & Johnson, B. T. (2014). HIV prevention interventions to reduce sexual risk for African Americans: The influence of community-level stigma and psychological processes. *Social Science & Medicine, 103*, 118–125.

Ritter, K., & Terndrup, A. I. (2002). *Handbook of affirmative psychotherapy with lesbians and gay men.* New York, NY: Guilford.

Rodriguez-Seijas, C., Eaton, N., & Pachankis, J. E. (in press). Prevalence of psychiatric disorders at the intersection of race and sexual orientation: Results from the National Epidemiologic Survey of Alcohol and Related Conditions-III. *Journal of Consulting and Clinical Psychology.*

Safren, S. A., & Heimberg, R. G. (1999). Depression, hopelessness, suicidality, and related factors in sexual minority and heterosexual adolescents. *Journal of Consulting and Clinical Psychology, 67*(6), 859–866.

Safren, S. A., O'Cleirigh, C., Tan, J. Y., Raminani, S. R., Reilly, L. C., Otto, M. W., & Mayer, K. H. (2009). A randomized controlled trial of cognitive behavioral therapy for adherence and depression (CBT-AD) in HIV-infected individuals. *Health Psychology, 28*(1), 1.

Safren, S. A., & Rogers, T. (2001). Cognitive–behavioral therapy with gay, lesbian, and bisexual clients. *Journal of Clinical Psychology, 57*, 629 643.

Sandfort, T. G., de Graaf, R., Bijl, R. V., & Schnabel, P. (2001). Same-sex sexual behavior and psychiatric disorders: Findings from the Netherlands Mental Health Survey and Incidence Study (NEMESIS). *Archives of General Psychiatry, 58*, 85–91.

Savin-Williams, R. C., & Rodriguez, R. G. (1993). A developmental, clinical perspective on lesbian, gay male, and bisexual youths. In T. P. Gullotta, G. R. Adams, & R. Montemayor (Eds.), *Advances in adolescent development: Vol. 5. Adolescent sexuality* (pp. 77–101). Thousand Oaks, CA: Sage .

Stack, L. (2016). Mike Pence and "conversion therapy": A history. *New York Times*, p. 30.

Stall, R., Mills, T. C., Williamson, J., Hart, T., Greenwood, G., Paul, J., & Catania, J. A. (2003). Association of co-occurring psychosocial health problems and increased vulnerability to HIV/AIDS among urban men who have sex with men. *American Journal of Public Health, 93*, 939–942.

Sullivan, T. J., & Pachankis, J. E. (2018, June). *Therapeutic alliance and the efficacy of LGBQ-affirmative cognitive–behavioral therapy: The role of client minority stress.* Paper presented at the annual convention for the Society of Psychotherapy Research, Amsterdam, the Netherlands.

Walsh, K., & Hope, D. A. (2010). LGB-affirmative cognitive–behavioral treatment for social anxiety: A case study applying evidence-based practice principles. *Cognitive and Behavioral Practice, 17*, 56–65.

Westen, D., Novotny, C. M., & Thompson-Brenner, H. (2004). The empirical status of empirically supported psychotherapies: Assumptions, findings, and reporting in controlled clinical trials. *Psychological Bulletin, 130*(4), 631–663.

White Hughto, J. M., Pachankis, J. E., & Reisner, S. L. (in press). Healthcare mistreatment and avoidance in trans masculine adults: The mediating role of rejection sensitivity. *Psychology of Sexual Orientation and Gender Diversity.*

Evidence-Based Treatments for Specific Sexual and Gender Minority Populations

Cognitive–Behavioral Therapy for Sexual and Gender Minority Youth Mental Health

SHELLEY L. CRAIG, ASHLEY AUSTIN, AND EDWARD J. ALESSI ■

LESBIAN, GAY, BISEXUAL, AND TRANS* YOUTH MENTAL HEALTH

Diverse Sexual Orientations and Gender Identities in Adolescence

Lesbian, gay, bisexual, and transgender (LGBT) youth exist in a developmental context of emerging and shifting identities. Whereas awareness of gender identity (i.e., one's internal sense of being male, female, or something else) emerges in early childhood, adolescence is the developmental stage during which sexual orientation (i.e., romantic and/or sexual attraction to others) often plays an increasingly important role (Kitts, 2010). Awareness of a non-heterosexual identity has been shown to occur as early as age 12 years for some youth (Pew Research Center, 2013). Definitions of sexual orientation typically encompass attraction, behavior, and identity (e.g., heterosexual, bisexual, lesbian, and gay) (Institute of Medicine [IOM], 2011), which can evolve or change across the lifespan (Austin, Conron, Patel, & Freedner, 2007). The terms used to describe sexual identities are continuously changing, ranging from more traditional labels (e.g., heterosexual, gay, lesbian, and bisexual) to more contemporary ones (e.g., pansexual, greysexual, and queer) (McInroy & Craig, 2012). For varying reasons, some adolescents prefer not to adopt particular labels yet still engage in same-sex sexual behavior, experience same-sex attraction, and/or identify with a variety of non-heterosexual communities (Levine, 2013). Such identity development is considered normative

(Reitman et al., 2013). A recent study of sexual and gender minority youth (SGMY; $N = 6,309$) found that pansexual (30%), bisexual (26%), and queer (21%) labels were used most frequently, compared to gay (16%), lesbian (16%), or others (e.g., homoflexible) (Craig et al., 2017). Such terms reflect the diversity of sexual identities among adolescents and the influence of history on the identity context (Russell & Fish, 2016).

Gender identity may also vary considerably among adolescents. Although the term *transgender* (often abbreviated as trans*) is frequently used as an umbrella term to encompass the full range of gender identities, other terms indicating a gender identity and/or expression that do not align with biological sex or societal expectations are also used (e.g., gender variant and gender nonconforming). It is becoming increasingly clear that gender identity comprises a multidimensional spectrum of experiences (Gray, Carter, & Levitt, 2012). Contemporary gender identities beyond the male/female binary include, but are certainly not limited to, transgender, gender creative, gender diverse, gender neutral, genderqueer, and agender. Craig et al. (2017) examined gender identity among LGBT youth using non-mutually exclusive terms, and they found that many used non-binary/gender nonconforming (24%) and genderqueer/genderfluid terms (20%). The youth also identified other gender identity labels, including female (41%), male (17%), and trans* (18%), as well as a range of emerging terms (e.g., demigender, bigender, and genderfluid). Such terms convey a broad, flexible range of gender expressions with interests and behaviors that are not limited by restrictive boundaries of what it purportedly means to be "girl" or "boy." Genderfluidity may suggest that adolescents experience themselves as both a boy and a girl at the same time, that their gender identity varies from day to day or across circumstances, or that neither the term boy nor the term girl describes them accurately (IOM, 2011). However, the presentation and expression of gender associated with one's gender identity may continue to develop over time. This is further discussed in Chapter 4.

Mental Health Disparities

LGBT adolescents experience significant mental health disparities that may have severe and enduring consequences. One community-based study found that 30% of LGBT adolescents ($N = 246$) reported clinical levels of mental distress during the past week (Mustanski, Garafalo, & Emerson, 2010). The high prevalence of depression among LGBT adolescents is particularly troubling (Marshal et al., 2011), and it is also concerning that these mental health problems have been shown to persist into adulthood (Russell & Fish, 2016). For example, LGBT adults have a high prevalence of anxiety disorders (Tjepkema, 2008), and bisexual women are more than twice as likely as heterosexual women to have severe anxiety and anger (Macleod, Bauer, Robinson, MacKay, & Ross, 2015). In a study of young women ($N = 6,689$), Kerr, Santurri, and Peters (2013) found that bisexual and lesbian undergraduates were 4.7 times more likely than heterosexuals to report intentional self-injury (e.g., cutting, burning, and bruising).

Many LGBT adolescents are also at high risk of suicide. According to a meta-analysis, the risk for suicidal thoughts and behaviors among LGB adolescents was three times greater than that for heterosexual adolescents, with the greatest risk among bisexuals (Marshal et al., 2013). LGB youth are also more likely to engage in suicidal behaviors, suicide attempts, and suicide completion (22.8% compared to 6.6% for non-LGB adolescents) (Mustanski & Liu, 2013). General risk factors such as depression, impulsivity, and hopelessness, as well as identity-based risks such as homophobic discrimination and victimization, are associated with high prevalence of suicidal behavior (IOM, 2011). Risks may be particularly exacerbated among certain subgroups. For example, White, Latino, and American Native/Pacific Islander LGBT adolescents have been shown to have a higher prevalence of suicide attempts compared to Black and Asian LGBT adolescents in some studies (Bostwick et al., 2014). The lower prevalence of suicide among Black and Asian LGBT adolescents is often attributed to negative cultural views of suicide (Bostwick et al., 2014). Transgender adolescents have an exceptionally high risk of elevated suicidality (Nuttbrock et al., 2010). According to the National Transgender Discrimination Survey ($N = 6,400$), 45% of young adult respondents (aged 18–24 years) reported having attempted suicide (Grant et al., 2011). However, Newcomb, Heinz, and Mustanski (2012) found that gender nonconformity was not associated with a suicide attempt history.

Suicide is just one of many behavioral risks facing LGBT adolescents. The Centers for Disease Control and Prevention reports that compared to students who are not LGBT, "a disproportionate number of . . . [LGBT] students engage in a wide range of health risk behaviors" (Kann et al., 2011, p. 49). In their meta-analysis, Marshal and colleagues (2008) found that LGBT adolescents report earlier onset and heightened rates of substance use (nearly twice those of their non-LGBT peers), and they determined that certain subgroups experience even greater disparities. For example, bisexual adolescents demonstrate rates of substance use three times higher than those of heterosexual adolescents. Given these significant challenges, it is critical for clinicians to effectively address the mental health of LGBT adolescents.

Stigma, Discrimination, and Victimization

LGBT adolescents are disproportionately exposed to stigma and discrimination, as well as verbal, physical, and sexual victimization (Birkett, Newcomb, & Mustanski, 2015; Goldblum et al., 2012). The victimization of LGBT children and adolescents "pervades their school, family, religious, and community environments" (Dragowski, Halkitis, Grossman, & D'Augelli, 2011, p. 228). In a sample of LGBT adolescents (aged 14–21 years; $N = 350$), Dragowski et al. found that nearly three-fourths were verbally abused (72%), had objects thrown at them (13%), and/or were physically attacked (11%) because of their LGBT identities. Moreover, many young adults who identify with a nondominant sexuality face harassment and bullying for not conforming to normative expectations for sexual identity expression (Alessi, Kahn, & Chatterji, 2016).

Mounting research demonstrates pervasive experiences of bullying by LGBT adolescents in schools. The 2015 GLSEN National School Climate Survey (Kosciw, Greytak, Giga, Villenas, & Danischewski, 2015) explored feelings of safety and experiences of school-based victimization among 10,528 LGBT students (aged 13–21 years). An overwhelming majority experienced verbal harassment as a result of being LGBT (85%) and/or gender nonconforming (54%), with almost half (49%) being victimized through online formats (e.g., text messages and postings on social media), indicating that cyberbullying has become a major concern. Blumenfeld and Cooper (2010) found that 54% of LGBT youth ($N = 3,502$) reported being victims of cyberbullying in the 30 days prior to the survey and reported feeling depressed (45%) and suicidal (25%) because of these experiences.

In addition to school-based discrimination, research suggests that LGBT adolescents experience disparate rates of physical and sexual victimization by parents or caretakers. A meta-analysis of 37 studies conducted by Friedman and colleagues (2011) determined that LGBT adolescents were 3.8 times more likely to experience childhood sexual abuse and 1.2 times more likely to be physically abused by a parent or caretaker compared to non-LGBT peers. Trans* adolescents are at particular risk, encountering higher prevalence of all types of victimization (i.e., physical, sexual, verbal, and psychological abuse) by family members compared to adolescents whose presentation and behavior are gender-normative (D'Augelli, Grossman, & Starks, 2006). Family support is particularly critical to the mental health of LGBT youth. Needham and Austin (2010) found that (1) LGBT young adults experienced lower levels of parental support than their non-LGBT counterparts; (2) parental support was inversely related to health outcomes, including depression, substance use, and suicidal thoughts; and (3) parental support partially mediated associations between sexual orientation and marijuana and hard drug use among young lesbian women. Parental support can also be helpful for trans* adolescents. One study showed that for transgender adolescents (aged 12–24 years), the presence of parental support was correlated with greater life satisfaction and less depression (Simons, Schrager, Clark, Belzer, & Olson, 2013).

Conflict with parents is an important factor to consider with LGBT adolescents because it has been found to contribute to the increased likelihood of homelessness (Walls, Hancock, & Wisneski, 2007). In fact, LGBT adolescents comprise a disproportionate number of the adolescent homeless population (approximately 40%), with transgender and racial and ethnic minorities particularly overrepresented (Cray, Miller, & Durso, 2013). LGBT adolescents are also overrepresented in the child welfare and foster care systems due to higher rates of family victimization (Gallegos et al., 2011).

Victimization and discrimination may have devastating and lingering consequences for LGBT youth. Goldblum et al. (2012) found that transgender adults who experienced identity-based discrimination in school were four times more likely to have a history of suicide attempts compared to those who did not experience this type of discrimination. In addition to overt victimization, LGBT adolescents and emerging adults are also exposed to incessant LGBT-phobic stigma and microaggressions (i.e., frequent and brief verbal insults) across multiple life domains (Alessi, Sapiro, Kahn, & Craig, 2017; Nadal, Whitman, Davis, Erazo, & Davidoff, 2016). Such identity-based discrimination may manifest as family rejection (Alessi, Martin, Gyamerah, & Meyer, 2013); lack of inclusive legal protections (Grant et al., 2011); the absence of safe and inclusive school and community spaces (Birkett, Espelage, & Koenig, 2009); and discrimination by school personnel, religious institutions, and health care providers (Nadal et al., 2016). Studies indicate that experiences of discrimination, victimization, and rejection from others result in the internalization of homophobic and transphobic stigma (i.e., negative views of one's LGBT identity) (Mizock & Mueser, 2014; Vogel, Bitman, Hammer, & Wade, 2013). LGBT adolescents are at risk of internalizing implicit and explicit messages of homophobic and transphobic hate experienced on a daily basis (Kosciw et al., 2015). This is of notable concern because internalized stigma has been linked with poor mental health outcomes (Newcomb & Mustanski, 2010).

LGBT Youth and Minority Stress

Given the severity and enduring nature of victimization and stigmatization experienced by LGBT adolescents, health disparities among this population must be understood through a minority stress lens (Alessi, 2014; Meyer, 2003; Meyer, Dietrich, & Schwartz, 2008). Minority stress theory provides a framework for understanding the impact of stress associated with the persistent and pervasive devaluation and marginalization of an individual's minority identity (Meyer, 2003). An elaboration of stress and coping theory (Lazarus & Folkman, 1984), minority stress theory proposes that individuals from marginalized populations experience a unique form of stress due to conflict between their internal sense of self and their experiences of majority social norms and expectations (DiPlacido, 1998). Because LGBT children and adolescents do not usually share their LGBT identity with family members, they may not learn identity-specific coping strategies as many adolescents in other minority communities do (Craig, Austin, & Alessi, 2013). This leaves LGBT adolescents more vulnerable to health and mental health threats (Kelleher, 2009) as well as at increased likelihood of engaging in risky behaviors (Birkett et al., 2009). Minority stress stems from objective experiences of discrimination; internal processes, including internalized homophobia; expectations of rejection based on sexual orientation (i.e., perceived stigma); and feeling the need to conceal sexual orientation (Meyer, 2003). For LGBT adolescents, minority stress contributes to the development of mental and behavioral health issues during adolescence and adulthood. Hatzenbuehler and Pachankis (2016) identified that the stigma experienced by LGBT individuals can "disrupt cognitive, affective, interpersonal and physiologic processes" (p. 986) that may negatively impact health. For example, Newcomb et al. (2012) suggest that LGBT adolescents may struggle with emotion regulation because consistent exposure to discrimination can lead to more negative emotions, which in turn may contribute to maladaptive coping behaviors such as alcohol consumption. Minority stress can also negatively modify cognitive functioning (Hatzenbuehler, 2009). Specifically, the impact of discrimination can be seen in the cognitive appraisal of potential threats, and this in turn can be associated with depression for LGBT populations (Alessi, 2014; Hatzenbuehler & Pachankis, 2016). Cognitive appraisals assign meaning to stressful events (e.g., viewing stress as a challenge or a threat) and explain why the same experience contributes to differing levels of distress across individuals (Hojat, Gonnella, Erdmann, & Vogel, 2003). Such appraisals are important to coping with stressful events because they enable emotional regulation of responses (Steptoe & Voegele, 1986). These general psychological processes (e.g., cognitive appraisals, coping, and emotional regulation) may mediate the LGBT experiences of minority stress and mental health problems (Hatzenbuehler, 2009). Thus, because patterns of adolescent cognitive appraisal ultimately contribute to long-term mental health (Rowley, Roesch, Jurica, & Vaughn, 2005), attending to the psychological processes such as cognitive appraisals that are associated with minority stress may have a notable lifelong impact on emotions and behaviors (Safren, Hollander, Hart, & Heimberg, 2001). To counter negative appraisals, clinicians must incorporate affirmative approaches when using cognitive–behavioral therapy (CBT) with LGBT adolescents (Craig & Austin, 2016). An affirmative clinical approach recognizes that LGBT adolescents disproportionately experience identity-based stressors and that these stressors negatively impact the mental health of LGBT adolescents. Next, we review the relevance of CBT for LGBT youth.

COGNITIVE–BEHAVIORAL THERAPY FOR LGBT YOUTH

Introduction to Affirmative Cognitive–Behavioral Therapy for Youth and Relevant Empirical Support

Cognitive–behavioral therapy is considered an effective treatment for adolescents with mental health problems such as social anxiety (Baer & Garland, 2005), depression (Richardson, Stallard, & Velleman, 2010; Treatment for Adolescents with Depression Study, 2004), and suicidal ideation (Stanley et al., 2009). Evidence indicates that CBT can also facilitate resilience (or constructive adaptation; Pachankis, 2014) and improve self-esteem (Hyun, Chung, & Lee, 2005). Although practice literature suggests that CBT is an effective method for treating depression among lesbian and gay adults (Martell, Safren, & Prince, 2004)—and can enable clients to manage their own mental health, cope with identity disclosure, and establish social support (Safren & Rogers, 2001)—only recently have researchers applied CBT to LGBT adolescent populations (Duarté-Vélez, Bernal, & Bonilla, 2010).

Affirmative CBT (A-CBT) explores and validates the positive expression of LGBT identities and recognizes the impact of discrimination on mental health using the empirical framework of CBT (Craig et al., 2013). A-CBT holds particular promise for treating mental health problems among LGBT adolescents. For one, CBT focuses on changing maladaptive behaviors by changing problematic ways of thinking. Identifying as an LGBT person can negatively impact one's thoughts and beliefs, which in turn may cause feelings of low self-worth, anxiety, and depression. According to Pachankis, Goldfried, and Ramrattan (2008), the internalization of homophobia may negatively impact LGBT adolescents' self-perceptions and interactions with others, such as the ability to be assertive interpersonally. Challenging one's negative thoughts about their LGBT identity in a safe and supportive environment may help decrease internalized homophobia and transphobia. For example, a pansexual adolescent who believes she can never feel "happy or normal" because of her sexual orientation can learn to challenge these thoughts and replace them with more positive and realistic ones (e.g., "LGBT people create happy and satisfying lives"). CBT also helps clients recognize how their thoughts impact their behaviors. LGBT adolescents are taught to replace maladaptive coping skills (e.g., isolating from friends and family) with more effective ones (e.g., talking to an ally about family problems). These new skills are modeled and reinforced throughout the intervention process. Integrating new coping strategies is particularly important for LGBT adolescents who—as a result of fear, shame, and guilt associated with experiences of discrimination—may have learned to rely on unhealthy coping mechanisms, including substance abuse, disordered eating, or skipping school. By addressing maladaptive thoughts and beliefs regarding one's LGBT identity and subsequently teaching proactive coping skills to deal with stressors, CBT facilitates the use of adaptive, flexible thinking that can foster healthy emotional and behavioral functioning among LGBT adolescents (Craig et al., 2013).

Finally, A-CBT can promote cognitive reappraisal for LGBT adolescents. In their study of adolescent appraisal, Rowley et al. (2005) found that efficacious coping such as "active coping, positive reinterpretation, and growth were positively related to appraising stress as a challenge and maladaptive coping such as substance use, denial and emotional venting was associated with assessing stress as a threat" (p. 554). CBT can effectively address the complex stressors that exacerbate depression and psychological distress for LGBT adolescents by helping them evaluate the sources of, perceptions of, and reactions to stress, as well as mitigate feelings of self-blame and shame associated with discrimination (Craig et al., 2013; Lucassen, Merry, Hatcher, & Frampton, 2015). Table 2.1 highlights the A-CBT therapeutic framework. Three studies of small-scale, brief CBT interventions created and tested with LGBT adolescents can be used to highlight CBT's utility with LGBT youth: (1) a computerized intervention for LGBQ adolescents (Rainbow SPARX), (2) a community-based intervention for a range of LGBT adolescent identities (AFFIRM), and (3) a transdiagnostic intervention for gay and bisexual young adults (Effective Skills to Empower Effective Men [ESTEEM]).

Rainbow SPARX is a brief computerized CBT (seven sessions) designed specifically for LGBQ adolescents aged 13–19 years ($N = 21$; 11 male-identified: 15 New Zealand European, 4 Asian, and 2 Maori) (Lucassen et al., 2015). Rainbow

Table 2.1. AFFIRMATIVE COGNITIVE–BEHAVIORAL THERAPY (CBT) WITH LGBT ADOLESCENTS: THERAPEUTIC FRAMEWORK

Key Therapeutic Task	Clinical Concern/Description (Rationale)	Clinical Strategies
Establish affirmative therapeutic context.	By the time they enter therapy, most LGBT adolescents have been exposed to a host of homo/bi/transphobic beliefs, attitudes, and behaviors from peers, adults, and relevant institutions in their lives. A key to affirmative CBT is the immediate establishment of an LGBT affirming therapeutic stance and clinical context for intervention. An affirmative approach is particularly important because harmful and unethical reparative and conversion efforts aimed at LGBT youth continue to permeate religious and cultural communities in the United States and abroad.	Create visibly affirming spaces (e.g., rainbow stickers or posters, books, brochures, and magazines highlighting the lives of diverse LGBT people). Use intake forms with inclusive options for sexual orientation and gender identity and that allow for the use of a chosen/preferred name. Include statements on websites and/or other marketing material that affirm LGBT adolescents. When making initial introductions, include a statement that explicitly affirms LGBT adolescents (e.g., "I want to let you know that I embrace and value all sexual orientations and gender identities; this is a space where you are free to be who you really are and express yourself authentically.").
Emphasize collaboration.	Contemporary CBT approaches emphasize collaboration (rather than confrontation), and therapeutic collaboration may be even more important for LGBT adolescents who often have trouble finding supportive adults. The structure of CBT allows the therapist to provide a clear description of the rationale and process of the sessions, which can empower LGBT youth and foster collaboration. While explaining the process of CBT, clinicians should utilize terms familiar to LGBT adolescents so that they can make informed choices about their treatment.	Explain each step while encouraging collaboration and feedback. For example, "These counseling meetings are like a team project. I will explain the plan and then you can let me know if we need to change or add anything. For this session we will talk more about how discrimination makes you think and feel because our thoughts and feelings often influence what we do."

Affirm LGBT identities during assessment.	Assessment clarifies the client's needs, informs the direction of treatment, and provides a starting point for initiating behavioral change. With LGBT adolescents, it is critical to affirm their identities during assessment. Actively reflect with youth during the initial assessment and examine the extent to which they have experienced affirmation of their LGBT sexual and/or gender identities and how this impacted the engagement process.	"How would you describe your sexual and gender identity? Just a reminder that all identities are welcome and supported here." At the end of each session, the clinician could give the LGBT adolescent a feedback sheet in which statements such as "Please describe the ways in which you felt particularly affirmed in today's session," "The areas of today's session that didn't feel as good to me were," and "These are ideas for what to do next time" are presented with the ability for short qualitative responses.
Identify adolescent's comfort with their LGBT identity.	To appropriately tailor the treatment to the developmental stage of the LGBT adolescent, it is important to assess the affirmative stance of LGBT youth as well as those in their spheres.	Have the LGBT adolescent list positive feelings about identifying as xxx (e.g., pansexual). If this is challenging, have the youth identify positive traits related to other LGBT individuals (e.g., celebrities, icons, teachers, and friends). To fully understand their comfort with their identity, have the adolescent also list any negative feelings or about identifying as xxx (e.g., lesbian)

(continued)

Table 2.1. Continued

Key Therapeutic Task	Clinical Concern/Description (Rationale)	Clinical Strategies
Identify minority stressors.	Clinicians should acknowledge the impact of discrimination and address the impact of homo/bi/transphobia on their lived experiences. A functional assessment of the antecedents and consequences of the client's stress can encourage the youth to share their perspective about how environmental conditions contributed to their mental health concerns. Clinicians should openly communicate that they want to understand the impact of oppression on the client's lived experience.	"Given that you have stated that your identity is xxx, can you share some of the ways in which you have experienced discrimination?" or "In what ways has anyone made you feel bad about your identity/who you are/being xxx." "Can you describe some of the ways that these experiences have impacted you and your life?" For example, clinicians can ask clients to list their minority stressors on an erasable board. Then the practitioner and client can talk about each stressor together. Using this method conveys that the practitioner is different from other adults who have minimized the client's problem or even rejected the client for being LGBT.
Validate experiences of discrimination.	Although CBT encourages the exploration of other hypotheses to determine the "cause" of a problem, this may be perceived as doubting or minimizing the youth's experience. LGBT youth may also experience this response as a subtle form of homo/bi/transphobia, which could undermine the therapeutic relationship. Acknowledging the presence and impact of discrimination may increase youth engagement and further understanding of clinical concerns.	When an LGBT adolescent reports an incident of discrimination, the therapist should not automatically universalize it (e.g., "All youth are teased") or search for alternative reasons for the bully's behavior (e.g., "Doesn't he make fun of everyone?"). Instead, it is important that the therapist provide a validating response (e.g., "It must be really painful to be teased in front of everyone").

SPARX is an adaptation of SPARX, a computerized intervention shown to be efficacious for general populations of adolescents ($N = 187$; aged 12–19 years) with mild to moderate depression in a multicenter randomized controlled trial (RCT; Merry et al., 2012). With a focus on building and practicing core CBT skills (i.e., relaxation training, behavioral activation, social skills training, naming cognitive distortions, problem-solving, cognitive restructuring, and hope), SPARX has users identify the components of a "shield against depression" (Lucassen et al., 2015, p. 205). Rainbow SPARX closely follows the same format as SPARX with a seven-module interactive fantasy game using avatars that strive to destroy negative emotions but with specific content for LGBQ adolescents. Modules highlight strengths of being a sexual minority, social skills, and problem-solving around fears of disclosure. They also reflect upon the impact of homophobia, help clients reframe cognitive distortions, and offer them options for gender and sexual identities. Grounded in the results of the SPARX RCT, Rainbow SPARX was designed as an open pilot trial and collected data at three time points (pre-test, post-test, and 3-month follow-up). Lucassen et al. found that participants' depressive symptoms significantly decreased following the intervention ($p < .0001$), and these results persisted after 3 months. Rainbow SPARX had high acceptability with 80% of participants stating they would "recommend [it] to a friend" and that they learned about "depression" and "relaxing–slow breathing" (Lucassen et al., 2015, p. 212).

AFFIRM is a brief affirmative cognitive–behavioral coping skills group intervention (eight modules) with LGBT adolescents, adapted from a manualized depression intervention for culturally diverse youth (Rosselló & Bernal, 2007) and carefully developed through ongoing community partnerships (Craig & Austin, 2016). A diverse sample of LGBT participants aged 15–18 years ($N = 30$) in the pilot feasibility trial identified with the non-mutually exclusive gender identity categories of female (57%), trans*/gender nonconforming (31%), and/or male (18%), as well as the sexual orientation categories of pansexual (29%), lesbian (25%), queer (21%), bisexual (18%), and/or gay (11%). Measures of depression and stress appraisal were completed at three time points. Significant reductions were found in depression ($\eta^2 = .23$, $p < .05$) and appraising stress as a threat ($\eta^2 = .17$, $p < .05$) following the intervention. A significant increase was found in perceiving stress as a challenge ($\eta^2 = .52$, $p < .001$). Depression was positively correlated with threat appraisals and negatively correlated with challenge appraisals. The relationship between depression and cognitive appraisal indicates the potential importance of targeting perceptions of minority stressors within interventions designed to reduce psychological distress among LGBT adolescents. Consistent with the CBT model, findings suggest that LGBT adolescents developed a more adaptive way of appraising stressful situations as a result of participating in AFFIRM. Adolescents intended to "apply what they learned" (97%) and gleaned skills to "connect thoughts, feelings and behaviors" (90%) (Craig & Austin, 2016, p. 140).

Cognitive–behavioral therapy was also shown to effectively address the multiple health risks of young adult gay and bisexual males in the ESTEEM RCT. Participants were aged 18–35 years (58 identifying as gay and 5 as bisexual).

Compared to the waitlist (n = 31), participants in the intervention group (n = 32) experienced significant reductions in depressive symptoms, alcohol use problems, as well as risky sexual behaviors (Pachankis, Hatzenbuehler, Rendina, Safren, & Parsons, 2015). These findings indicate the promise of CBT using a transdiagnostic (i.e., unified) approach to positively impact intersecting risks for multiple and concurrent mental health problems linked by minority stress processes (Pachankis et al., 2015).

AFFIRMATIVE COGNITIVE–BEHAVIORAL THERAPY FOR LGBT ADOLESCENTS: CLINICAL APPROACHES

This section identifies critical components of A-CBT for LGBT adolescents and examines clinically relevant strategies, followed by a case example. The results of the studies described in the previous section underscore the promise of using a CBT-based approach that affirms LGBT identities, attends to minority stressors, actively targets maladaptive responses to stressors, and builds effective coping skills (Craig & Austin, 2016). As noted in Beck's (1993) approach to CBT, emotions and behaviors are influenced by how we perceive events. A-CBT encourages individuals to formulate alternative ways of thinking about situations and problems, which in turn prompts emotional and behavioral changes. However, prior to helping clients change their ways of thinking and engaging in cognitive or behavioral change strategies, A-CBT requires clinicians to validate the reality of stigma. In addition, clinicians must affirm the identities of LGBT adolescents. Doing so is more than just about being politically correct (Alessi, 2013); it is about celebrating LGBT identities. An affirmative approach, coupled with specific strategies to address the impact of discrimination, is critical for LGBT adolescents (Craig & Austin, 2016). The effectiveness of A-CBT is based on the competent delivery of CBT that attends to both process and content elements (Thordarson, Keller, Sullivan, Trafalis, & Friedberg, 2016). Thus, A-CBT should be a collaborative and individualized process (Craig et al., 2013).

A-CBT is relevant to clinical practice with LGBT adolescents in three primary ways. First, A-CBT targets behaviors for change with adolescents through a respectful, culturally responsive assessment that explores strengths, social supports, and goals. Clinicians working with LGBT adolescents must initially develop a comprehensive case conceptualization that incorporates the complex intersections often present in the lived experiences of these adolescents (e.g., being an African American lesbian female youth with a trauma history). Based on that formulation, clinicians should design CBT interventions that identify and subsequently address their maladaptive reactions to their social and psychological stressors while understanding that for some LGBT youth, the root cause of their psychosocial distress may persist (Thordarson et al., 2016).

Second, following an exploration of environmental factors, which includes a comprehensive examination of particular stressors related to prejudice and discrimination, CBT practitioners utilize cognitive restructuring interventions (e.g., evidence testing and decatastrophizing) to address obstacles (e.g., cognitive distortions and automatic thoughts) to clients' long-term goals (Hays, 2009). For example, an LGBT adolescent who dreams of becoming a computer animator but consistently has been skipping school because of bullying due to her sexual orientation and is at risk of failing 12th grade may benefit from A-CBT. Because A-CBT promotes personal agency (Pachankis, 2014), the initial step is to explore the adolescent's environmental obstacles, including safety within the school and the need for possible environmental changes (e.g., intervention with school staff and changing schools). Subsequently, through the identification of proactive coping skills to deal with stressors, CBT facilitates the use of flexible or adaptive thinking, which can foster healthy emotional and behavioral functioning among LGBT adolescents.

Third, A-CBT encourages alternative ways of thinking. For example, because A-CBT may positively impact stress appraisals and emotion regulation related to minority stress (Craig & Austin, 2016; Pachankis, 2014), clinicians can incorporate interventions to help LGBT adolescents manage perceived discrimination. For example, in the case of an LGBT adolescent who is reporting increased anxiety due to verbal harassment, the clinician should first validate the discrimination ("It sounds like it must be really painful to be bullied for just being yourself. This should not be happening to you."). After exploring the client's feelings and thoughts associated with this discrimination, the clinician might consider having the youth discuss their current coping strategies. If they are maladaptive, the clinician might state, "What might be one other way that you can deal with this bullying?" The clinician can then ask the client to try this strategy out at least twice this week and then in the next session discuss what it was like to try this strategy. Table 2.2 further illustrates these key clinical strategies and tasks for A-CBT with LGBT adolescents, and the following section explores the application of A-CBT through a detailed case study.

CLINICAL APPLICATION

The following case example of Bianca provides a description of minority stressors experienced by an LGBT adolescent (pansexual and genderqueer) and offers some approaches based on A-CBT that can be used by clinicians to help reduce symptomology and encourage alternate coping strategies.

CASE EXAMPLE

Bianca is a 15-year-old female adolescent who identifies as pansexual, genderqueer, and Latinx. During the assessment, Bianca presents with symptoms of anxiety. She discloses that she worries about what her family and people at her school think about her sexuality. She worries about attracting attention to herself and also worries about her grades and appearance. She has thoughts such as "They

Table 2.2. AFFIRMATIVE COGNITIVE–BEHAVIORAL THERAPY (CBT) WITH LGBT ADOLESCENTS: SESSION TASKS

Key Therapeutic Task	Clinical Rationale	Clinical Strategies
Help youth distinguish issues based on structural causes and those rooted in dysfunctional thoughts.	This is particularly important for CBT with LGBT adolescents who may struggle with situations outside of their control (e.g., biphobic bullying). LGBT adolescents may encounter events (e.g., rejection by family member) that cannot be easily changed by modifying dysfunctional thoughts or changing behavior. Failing to acknowledge that certain stressful circumstances stem from homo/bi/transphobic social conditions may be dangerous to the well-being of LGBT adolescents. Clinicians should validate their concerns and frustrations as well as teach them skills for coping with situations that are beyond their control (e.g., living with a rejecting parent until they start college).	For example, clinicians working with homeless LGBT adolescents should initially focus on the external factors (e.g., lack of safe, permanent housing) contributing to the client's feelings of hopelessness and subsequently address the dysfunctional thought patterns (e.g., things will never get better).
Question the helpfulness of the thought or belief.	An affirmative approach to cognitive restructuring includes evaluating the utility of the belief. This technique helps LGBT adolescents recognize dysfunctional thoughts that work against their long-term goals and also helps decrease feelings of hopelessness.	The therapist might ask, "Is it helpful for you to say that if you come out you will be homeless, or to hold onto this belief, or to repeat this thought or image to yourself?" Encourage youth to consider the advantages or disadvantages of each belief to assess whether it is currently helping them. For example, make a pro and con list for coming out to your grandmother, and then use the "helpful thoughts vs. not helpful thoughts" framework to assess the current utility of these thoughts.

Help youth develop their cognitive appraisal skill.	Specific negative experiences may contribute to LGBT adolescents' assumptions that they will always face similar results. LGBT adolescents may also perceive that their previous experiences of discrimination mean that all similar situations will result in their experiencing discrimination. As such, it is important that therapists provide opportunities for youth to reconsider their limiting ideas.	Questioning whether a thought is irrational or invalid may be interpreted by some LGBT adolescents as not affirmative or naive. For example, in an effort to demonstrate the irrational fear of coming out to one's family, a less-skilled practitioner might ask, "So what's the worst that could happen?" However, this question could intensify the client's realistic fears and may even backfire because some youth experience serious consequences after coming out to family members (e.g., violence, homelessness, or being disowned). "When I came to this school, I was bullied all the time for being gay. If I have to go to a new school because of my mom's new job, I am sure it will happen again." Clinicians can help youth search for evidence to support a reappraisal of the damaging experience and cultivate an alternative belief. For example, "When you were bullied, you say it happened all the time. Can you think of just one time when it didn't happen? Can you think of a time when someone was kind to you at your school? So can you say that bullying happened all the time?" *Or* "I went to that one support group in Toronto and that didn't help. Therefore I won't go to any other groups because they won't help either." Clinician: "Help me understand that experience. When you went to that support group and you say it didn't help, what were you looking for help with? Can you think of one small thing that was good or helpful about the group? So perhaps there may be some ways in which support groups could be helpful to you?"

(continued)

Table 2.2. CONTINUED

Key Therapeutic Task	Clinical Rationale	Clinical Strategies
Help youth build their skills for interacting with the social environment.	Affirmative CBT can help LGBT adolescents cope with stressful situations, even if they are unable to change their environment. Because they will undoubtedly encounter homophobia and heterosexism at different times in their lives, learning to effectively cope with such situations (e.g., challenging negative thoughts and replacing harmful behaviors with healthier ones) is essential.	For example, an LGBT adolescent that is experiencing bullying in the neighborhood can role play telling a parent or speaking up to the bully. When a youth is feeling angry about how they are being treated, they can practice some deep breathing and relaxation techniques that they have learned in session. To counter immobilization or rumination related to discriminatory experiences, therapists can suggest behavioral activation techniques such as trying out different activities, volunteering, or joining an online community.
Help youth increase supports.	Specific support for LGBT identity is critical to adolescent well-being. Clinicians should probe for affirmative sources of supports and identify areas in which supports could be strengthened.	Identify affirmative supports by asking who and how LGBT adolescents are supported by family of origin and family of choice (e.g., boyfriend's/girlfriend's family or best friend's family), informal supports (e.g., friends and partners), formal peer supports (e.g., Gay–Straight Alliances), and community groups (e.g., SMY support group). To help develop support, suggest LGBT adolescents' (1) participate in Gay–Straight Alliances or school-based support groups, (2) advocate for other vulnerable groups, and (3) attend Parents, Families and Friends of Lesbians and Gays (PFLAG) groups to connect with positive parental role models.

| Help youth identify strengths. | Acknowledging strengths is an important component of resilience. When LGBT adolescents try to create new thoughts to replace less helpful ones, the list of specific strengths generated during the initial assessment can be a concrete reminder of past successes. New "minority strengths" related to the increasing acceptance of their LGBT identities can also be identified and expressed. | Past successes can be formulated into positive self-statements, such as the following: "All the barriers I have coped with in the past has made me strong"; "If I got through last year, I can get through anything"; and "My differences are what make me unique and special." Youth can add these new thoughts and beliefs to their notes section of their phone or on a piece of paper to take with them. Have youth count the number of positive thoughts (generally and about being LGBT) and then try to increase them by 10% each week.

Have youth write down one negative thought, but write down two positive thoughts to counteract it. |
| Assign affirmative homework that is congruent with stage of identity development. | Clinicians should be aware that some LGBT adolescents experience unique barriers with regard to engaging in activities of their choice. For example, spending time with a romantic partner may be something that the adolescent identifies as both enjoyable and useful for "combating" negative thoughts and feelings. However, parents who reject a youth's LGBT identity may not permit such activities. Clinicians should attend to this reality when "assigning" homework to LGBT adolescents. | Consider renaming homework with the client (e.g., wellness plan). Review with the youth the short amount of time it will take to complete. Identify how likely they are to complete it (look for a high likelihood).

Ensure assignments are tailored to the client's stage of the coming out process. For example, while helping youth identify an "affirmative activity list," youth who are not yet out may not want to attend a Pride parade or join the Gay–Straight Alliance. However, they might feel comfortable watching an LGBT-affirmative movie, spending time with a straight ally, or watching gay affirmative videos on YouTube. In these instances, it may be helpful to ask the youth, "What is one small step that you can take to help you feel like you are making a difference with your problem?" In this case, the youth might attempt to socialize through Instagram or email rather than attend a support group. |

think I am stupid," "I am embarrassing my parents," and "I am the only pan girl in California":

> THERAPIST: Thank you for sharing these experiences and feelings with me. They sound like they are causing some painful feelings.
>
> BIANCA: I do find it very stressful.
>
> THERAPIST: I bet it is. It is especially hard when you have to constantly worry about what people are thinking of you.
>
> BIANCA: Exactly. It feels like a lot sometimes.
>
> THERAPIST: What happens when you start to have thoughts that you are embarrassing your parents or that you are the only pan girl in California?
>
> BIANCA: I feel anxious and nervous.
>
> THERAPIST: What do you do when that happens?
>
> BIANCA: I go online to look at Tumbler or Facebook to not have to think about my situation.
>
> THERAPIST: Does that help?
>
> BIANCA: Yes, I feel better.
>
> THERAPIST: Figuring out ways to soothe yourself is really important when you are feeling anxious. Can we talk some more about why do you think your thoughts cause you to feel stressed?
>
> BIANCA: Maybe because I feel bad about being pan.
>
> THERAPIST: I want you to know that this is a place where all identities are respected and I believe you deserve a lot of respect for being open and honest with me. Being pan is the way that many young people identify and many are happy and healthy but it is important that we are able to talk through your feelings together.

After the therapist validates Bianca's pansexual identity and her experiences, Bianca and the therapist discuss how, after taking time away from her troubled thoughts and putting space between her and her daily life, she sometimes feels a bit better. The therapist explains how thoughts impact feelings and behavior and has Bianca sketch out the cognitive triad. The therapist explores with Bianca the idea of thinking about her anxiety as a "person" who makes statements, similar to her online friends. With this frame, Bianca can then "talk back" in comments to her anxiety. To facilitate this approach, the therapist draws a box on a paper (to illustrate Facebook) and writes a statement from Bianca's anxiety like it is a Facebook post. Then Bianca can talk back to the Facebook post with a comment. In addition, Bianca can go online to gather evidence about her beliefs and slow down her thoughts as she finds evidence that refutes those beliefs. For example, instead of thinking she is "weird" because she is pansexual, Bianca can identify online examples of adolescents who have come out as pansexual.

As can be seen in the example, the goal of A-CBT is to help Bianca change some of her negative thoughts. However, the therapist does not question the validity of these thoughts. The therapist acknowledges that Bianca lives in a society that marginalizes LGBT identities and that LGBT people have to manage interactions during which they may experience discrimination. The therapist explains that Bianca is not the problem but that homophobia, biphobia, and transphobia contribute to her feeling bad about herself. The therapist talks about the importance of managing her thoughts and engaging in activities that not only distract her from her negative thoughts but also affirm her identity, such as reading Ellen's DeGeneres biography (a person she respects). Thus, A-CBT has an important psychoeducational component that provides a rationale for the affirmative interventions. Clients are instructed not only to manage their negative thoughts but also to transform this negativity into something constructive. For example, the therapist might suggest Bianca join an online group or Gay–Straight Alliance (Alessi, 2014).

EMERGING TRENDS IN COGNITIVE–BEHAVIORAL THERAPY FOR LGBT ADOLESCENTS AND PROMISING PRACTICES

Several emerging trends may impact A-CBT for LGBT adolescents. This section addresses the increased focus on resilience and the role of information and communication technologies (ICTs).

Promoting Resilience

The adversity encountered by LGBT adolescents necessitates a focus on the factors that support the development of resilience (Craig, McInroy, McCready, & Alaggia, 2015). Resilience includes minimization of perceived threats to well-being as well as creating meaning out of challenges (Craig et al., 2015; Goldstein & Brooks, 2005). For LGBT youth, threats to their well-being are real, and therapists should explore the existence of those challenges and provide concrete support as needed (e.g., calling child protective services for a child experiencing abuse or asking the adolescent's permission to speak to a principal or a parent if an LGBT youth is currently being bullied). Resilience and healthy coping skills are associated with better overall health, healthier decision-making, and lower likelihood of risky behaviors in adolescence (Levine, 2013). Social support, connectedness, and feelings of belonging have been found to positively influence self-esteem and contribute to reduced mental health challenges for adolescents (Snapp, Watson, Russell, Diaz, & Ryan, 2015). High self-esteem and social support may be negatively correlated with suicidality for some LGBT adolescents (Grossman & Kerner, 1998). However, Mustanksi, Newcomb, and Garofalo (2011) determined that social support contributes to better mental health but does not moderate the negative impact of victimization on psychological distress. Thus, LGBT adolescents need to learn skills to combat the effects of victimization on their own mental health. CBT can enhance resilience in vulnerable populations by providing opportunities to develop social support and skills to combat stigma and manage mental health

(Eamon, 2008). To enhance resilience for LGBT adolescents, clinicians should promote critical individual, interpersonal, and environmental factors (e.g., caring adults, role models, and positive school environments) (Hatzenbuehler, 2011; Higa et al., 2014). Group-based CBT may offer particular advantages for LGBT adolescents because group contexts offer opportunities for learning, observing, and practicing skills (Rosselló et al., 2008) and can support the development of the social supports necessary to combat minority stressors. Although this evidence suggests that A-CBT may contribute to the resilience of LGBT adolescents, future applications should consider utilizing empirical measures of resilience, such as the Brief Resilience Scale (Smith et al., 2008) or the Child Youth Resilience Measure (Ungar et al., 2008), in clinical and research activities.

Information and Communication Technologies

Due to their rapid uptake and broad accessibility, ICTs (e.g., internet, social media, smartphones, and mobile applications) have the potential to promote resilience among LGBT children and adolescents (Craig & McInroy, 2014). ICTs may be utilized to gain education, explore identity, and locate affirmative providers with expertise in adolescent-specific issues (Ybarra, Mitchell, Palmer, & Reisner, 2015). ICTs represent particularly critical avenues for enhancing LGBT adolescent well-being due to minority stressors that are exacerbated by geographic or social exclusion (Austin, 2016; Craig et al., 2015). ICTs have potential to facilitate the uptake of evidence-based interventions (Berry & Lai, 2014; Mustanski, Greene, Ryan, & Whitton, 2015). Because the majority of LGBT adolescents cannot or do not access professional support, and even fewer are likely to see a CBT-trained therapist (Richardson et al., 2010), computerized CBT (CCBT) is an important emerging area (Berry & Lai, 2014). As noted previously (Lucassen et al., 2015), CCBT is an effective way to engage adolescents and offers positive effects comparable to those of traditional CBT (Richardson et al., 2010). Furthermore, the structured format of CBT and online presentation allow for a certain anonymity, which may thus allow LGBT adolescents to more easily share personal information with a therapist (MacGregor, Hayward Peck, & Wilkes, 2009). Although there are challenges to widespread implementation, such as high attrition or programs that target inappropriate developmental stages (Stallard, 2004), CCBT could significantly increase access for underserved populations. Given the potential of A-CBT to promote well-being among LGBT adolescents, the possibility of further impacting youth mental health through integration into ICT platforms represents an exciting opportunity.

Based on the significant empirical foundation of CBT and emerging research on its utility for LGBT populations, A-CBT represents an important intervention approach for clinical practice with LGBT adolescents. Despite the vast array of minority stressors encountered by LGBT adolescents, A-CBT can disrupt the psychosocial stress trajectories that can lead to poor mental health. Future manifestations of A-CBT may include a focus on resilience and ICTs.

REFERENCES

Alessi, E. J. (2014). A framework for incorporating minority stress theory into treatment with sexual minority clients. *Journal of Gay & Lesbian Mental Health, 18*(1), 47–66.

Alessi, E. J., Kahn, S., & Chatterji, S. (2016). "The darkest times of my life": Recollections of child abuse among forced migrants persecuted because of their sexual orientation and gender identity. *Child Abuse & Neglect, 51*, 93–105.

Alessi, E. J., Martin, J. I., Gyamerah, A., & Meyer, I. H. (2013). Prejudice events and traumatic stress among heterosexuals and lesbians, gay men, and bisexuals. *Journal of Aggression, Maltreatment & Trauma, 22*(5), 510–526.

Alessi, E. J., Sapiro, B., Kahn, S., & Craig, S. L. (2017). The first-year university experience for sexual minority students: A grounded theory exploration. *Journal of LGBT Youth, 14*(1), 71–92.

Austin, A. (2016). "There I am": A grounded theory study of young adults navigating a transgender or gender nonconforming identity within a context of oppression and invisibility. *Sex Roles, 75*(5–6), 215–230.

Austin, S. B., Conron, K. J., Patel, A., & Freedner, N. (2007). Making sense of sexual orientation measures: Findings from a cognitive processing study with adolescents on health survey questions. *Journal of LBGT Health Research, 3*(1), 55–65.

Baer, S., & Garland, E. (2005). Pilot study of community-based cognitive behavioral group therapy for adolescents with social phobia. *Journal of the American Academy of Child and Adolescent Psychiatry, 44*, 258–264.

Beck, A. T. (1993). Cognitive therapy: Past, present, and future. *Journal of Consulting and Clinical Psychology, 61*, 194–198.

Berry, R., & Lai, B. (2014). The emerging role of technology in cognitive–behavioral therapy for anxious youth: A review. *Journal of Rational–Emotive & Cognitive–Behavior Therapy, 32*(1), 57–66.

Birkett, M., Espelage, D. L., & Koenig, B. (2009). LGB and questioning students in schools: The moderating effects of homophobic bullying and school climate on negative outcomes. *Journal of Youth and Adolescence, 38*(7), 989–1000.

Birkett, M., Newcomb, M. E., & Mustanski, B. (2015). Does it get better? A longitudinal analysis of psychological distress and victimization in lesbian, gay, bisexual, transgender, and questioning youth. *Journal of Adolescent Health, 56*(3), 280–285.

Blumenfeld, W., & Cooper, R. (2010). LGBT and allied youth responses to cyberbullying: policy implications. *International Journal of Critical Pedagogy, 3*(1), 114–133.

Bostwick, W. B., Meyer, I., Aranda, F., Russell, S., Hughes, T., Birkett, M., & Mustanski, B. (2014). Mental health and suicidality among racially/ethnically diverse sexual minority youths. *American Journal of Public Health, 104*(6), 1129–1136.

Craig, S. L., & Austin, A. (2016). The AFFIRM open pilot feasibility study: A brief affirmative cognitive behavioral coping skills group intervention for sexual and gender minority youth. *Children and Youth Services Review, 64*, 136–144.

Craig, S. L., Austin, A., & Alessi, E. (2013). Gay affirmative cognitive behavioral therapy for sexual minority youth: A clinical adaptation. *Clinical Social Work Journal, 41*(3), 258–266.

Craig, S. L., & McInroy, L. (2014). You can form a part of yourself online: The influence of new media on identity development and coming out for LGBTQ youth. *Journal of Gay & Lesbian Mental Health, 18*(1), 95–109.

Craig, S. L., McInroy, L., D'Souza, S., Austin, A., Eaton, A., McCready, L., & Shade, L. (2017). The influence of information and communication technologies on the resilience and coping of sexual and gender minority youth in the United States and Canada (Project #Queery): Mixed methods *JMIR Research Protocols, 6*(9), e189.

Craig, S. L., McInroy, L., McCready, L. T., & Alaggia, R. (2015). Media: A catalyst for resilience in lesbian, gay, bisexual, transgender, and queer youth. *Journal of LGBT Youth, 12*(3), 254–275.

Cray, A., Miller, K., & Durso, L. E. (2013). *Seeking shelter: The experiences and unmet needs of LGBT homeless youth*. Washington, DC: Center for American Progress.

D'Augelli, A. R., Grossman, A. H., & Starks, M. T. (2006). Childhood gender atypicality, victimization, and PTSD among lesbian, gay, and bisexual youth. *Journal of Interpersonal Violence, 21*(11), 1462–1482.

DiPlacido, J. (1998). *Minority stress among lesbians, gay men, and bisexuals: A consequence of heterosexism, homophobia, and stigmatization*. Thousand Oaks, CA: Sage.

Dragowski, E. A., Halkitis, P. N., Grossman, A. H., & D'Augelli, A. R. (2011). Sexual orientation victimization and posttraumatic stress symptoms among lesbian, gay, and bisexual youth. *Journal of Gay & Lesbian Social Services, 23*(2), 226–249.

Duarté-Vélez, Y., Bernal, G., & Bonilla, K. (2010). Culturally adapted cognitive–behavioral therapy: Integrating sexual, spiritual, and family identities in an evidence-based treatment of a depressed Latino. *Adolescent Journal of Clinical Psychology, 66*, 895–906.

Eamon, M. K. (2008). *Empowering vulnerable populations: Cognitive–behavioral interventions*. Chicago, IL: Lyceum.

Friedman, M. S., Marshal, M. P., Guadamuz, T. E., Wei, C., Wong, C. F., Saewyc, E. M., & Stall, R. (2011). A meta-analysis of disparities in childhood sexual abuse, parental physical abuse, and peer victimization among sexual minority and sexual nonminority individuals. *American Journal of Public Health, 101*(8), 1481–1494.

Gallegos, A., Roller White, C., Ryan, C., O'Brien, K., Pecora, P. J., & Thomas, P. (2011). Exploring the experiences of lesbian, gay, bisexual, and questioning adolescents in foster care. *Journal of Family Social Work, 14*(3), 226–236.

Goldblum, P., Testa, R., Pflum, S., Hendricks, M., Bradford, J., & Bongar, B. (2012). Gender-based victimization and suicide attempts among transgender people. *Professional Psychology Research and Practice, 43*(5), 465–475.

Goldstein, S., & Brooks, R. B. (2005). *Resilience in children*. New York, NY: Springer.

Grant, J. M., Mottet, L., Tanis, J. E., Harrison, J., Herman, J., & Keisling, M. (2011). *Injustice at every turn: A report of the National Transgender Discrimination Survey*. Washington, DC: National Center for Transgender Equality.

Gray, S. A., Carter, A. S., & Levitt, H. (2012). A critical review of assumptions about gender variant children in psychological research. *Journal of Gay & Lesbian Mental Health, 16*(1), 4–30.

Grossman, A. H., & Kerner, M. S. (1998). Support networks of gay male and lesbian youth. *International Journal of Sexuality and Gender Studies, 3*(1), 27–46.

Hatzenbuehler, M. L. (2009). How does sexual minority stigma "get under the skin"? A psychological mediation framework. *Psychological Bulletin, 135*(5), 707–730.

Hatzenbuehler, M. L. (2011). The social environment and suicide attempts in lesbian, gay, and bisexual youth. *Pediatrics, 127*(5), 896–903.

Hatzenbuehler, M. L., & Pachankis, J. E. (2016). Stigma and minority stress as social determinants of health among lesbian, gay, bisexual, and transgender youth: Research evidence and clinical implications. *Pediatrics Clinic of North America, 63*(6), 985–997.

Hays, P. (2009). Integrating evidence-based practice, cognitive–behavior therapy, and multicultural therapy: Ten steps for culturally competent practice. *Professional Psychology: Research and Practice, 40*(4), 354–360.

Higa, D., Hoppe, M. J., Lindhorst, T., Mincer, S., Beadnell, B., Morrison, D. M., . . . Mountz, S. (2014). Negative and positive factors associated with the well-being of lesbian, gay, bisexual, transgender, queer, and questioning (LGBTQ) youth. *Youth & Society, 46*(5), 663–687.

Hojat, M., Gonnella, J. S., Erdmann, J. B., & Vogel, W.H. (2003). Medical students' cognitive appraisal of stressful life events as related to personality, physical well-being, and academic performance: A longitudinal study. *Personality & Individual Differences, 35,* 219–235.

Hyun, M. S., Chung, H. I. C., & Lee, Y. J. (2005). The effect of cognitive–behavioral group therapy on the self-esteem, depression, and self-efficacy of runaway adolescents in a shelter in South Korea. *Applied Nursing Research, 18,* 160–166.

Institute of Medicine. (2011). *The health of lesbian, gay, bisexual, and transgender people: Building a foundation for better understanding.* Washington, DC: National Academies Press.

Kann, L., Olsen, E. O., McManus, T., Kinchen, S., Chyen, D., Harris, W. A., & Wechsler, H. (2011). Sexual identity, sex of sexual contacts, and health-risk behaviors among students in grades 9–12: Youth risk behavior surveillance, selected sites, United States, 2001–2009. *Morbidity and Mortality Weekly Report, 60*(SS07), 1–133.

Kelleher, C. (2009). Minority stress and health: Implications for lesbian, gay, bisexual, transgender, and questioning (LGBTQ) young people. *Counselling Psychology Quarterly, 22*(4), 373–379.

Kerr, D. L., Santurri, L., & Peters, P. (2013). A comparison of lesbian, bisexual, and heterosexual college undergraduate women on selected mental health issues. *Journal of American College Health, 61*(4), 185–194.

Kitts, R. L. (2010). Barriers to optimal care between physicians and lesbian, gay, bisexual, transgender, and questioning adolescent patients. *Journal of Homosexuality, 57*(6), 730–747.

Kosciw, J., Greytak, E., Giga, N., Villenas, C., & Danischewski, D. (2015). The 2015 National School Climate Survey. Retrieved March 16, 2017, from http://www.glsen.org.

Lazarus, R. S., & Folkman, S. (1984). *Stress, appraisal, and coping.* New York, NY: Springer.

Levine, D. A. (2013). Office-based care for lesbian, gay, bisexual, transgender, and questioning youth. *Pediatrics, 132*(1), e297–e313.

Lucassen, M. F., Merry, S. N., Hatcher, S., & Frampton, C. M. (2015). Rainbow SPARX: A novel approach to addressing depression in sexual minority youth. *Cognitive and Behavioral Practice, 22*(2), 203–216.

MacGregor, A. D., Hayward, L., Peck, D. F., & Wilkes, P. (2009). Empirically grounded clinical interventions clients' and referrers' perceptions of computer-guided CBT (FearFighter). *Behavioral and Cognitive Psychotherapy, 37*(1), 1–9.

MacLeod, M. A., Bauer, G. R., Robinson, M., MacKay, J., & Ross, L. E. (2015). Biphobia and anxiety among bisexuals in Ontario, Canada. *Journal of Gay & Lesbian Mental Health, 19*(3), 217–243.

Marshal, M. P., Dermody, S. S., Cheong, J., Burton, C. M., Friedman, M. S., Aranda, F., & Hughes, T. L. (2013). Trajectories of depressive symptoms and suicidality among heterosexual and sexual minority youth. *Journal of Youth and Adolescence, 42*(8), 1243–1256.

Marshal, M. P., Dietz, L. J., Friedman, M. S., Stall, R., Smith, H. A., McGinley, J., . . . Brent, D. A. (2011). Suicidality and depression disparities between sexual minority and heterosexual youth: A meta-analytic review. *Journal of Adolescent Health*, *49*(2), 115–123.

Marshal, M. P., Friedman, M. S., Stall, R., King, K. M., Miles, J., Gold, M. A., . . . Morse, J. Q. (2008). Sexual orientation and adolescent substance use: A meta-analysis and methodological review. *Addiction*, *103*(4), 546–556.

Martell, C. R., Safren, S. A., & Prince, S. E. (2004). *Cognitive-behavioral therapies with lesbian, gay, and bisexual clients*. New York, NY: Guilford.

McInroy, L., & Craig, S. L. (2012). Articulating identities: Language and practice with multiethnic sexual minority youth. *Counselling Psychology Quarterly*, *25*(2), 137–149.

Merry, S. N., Stasiak, K., Shepherd, M., Frampton, C., Fleming, T., & Lucassen, M. F. (2012). The effectiveness of SPARX, a computerised self help intervention for adolescents seeking help for depression: Randomised controlled non-inferiority trial. *British Medical Journal*, *344*, e2598.

Meyer, I. (2003). *Minority stress and mental health in gay men*. New York, NY: Columbia University Press.

Meyer, I. H., Dietrich, J., & Schwartz, S. (2008). Lifetime prevalence of mental disorders and suicide attempts in diverse lesbian, gay, and bisexual populations. *American Journal of Public Health*, *98*(6), 1004–1006.

Mizock, L., & Mueser, K. T. (2014). Employment, mental health, internalized stigma, and coping with transphobia among transgender individuals. *Psychology of Sexual Orientation and Gender Diversity*, *1*(2), 146–158.

Mustanski, B., Greene, G. J., Ryan, D., & Whitton, S. W. (2015). Feasibility, acceptability, and initial efficacy of an online sexual health promotion program for LGBT youth: The queer sex ed intervention. *Journal of Sex Research*, *52*(2), 220–230.

Mustanski, B., & Liu, R. T. (2013). A longitudinal study of predictors of suicide attempts among lesbian, gay, bisexual, and transgender youth. *Archives of Sexual Behavior*, *42*(3), 427–448.

Mustanski, B., Newcomb, M., & Garofalo, R. (2011). Mental health of lesbian, gay, and bisexual youth: A developmental resiliency perspective. *Journal of Gay & Lesbian Social Services*, *23*(2), 204–225.

Mustanski, B. S., Garofalo, R., & Emerson, E. M. (2010). Mental health disorders, psychological distress, and suicidality in a diverse sample of lesbian, gay, bisexual, and transgender youths. *American Journal of Public Health*, *100*(12), 2426–2432.

Nadal, K., Whitman, C., Davis, L., Erazo, T., & Davidoff, K. (2016). Microaggressions toward lesbian, gay, bisexual, transgender, queer, and genderqueer people: A review of the literature. *Journal of Sex Research*, *53*(4–5), 488–508.

Needham, B. L., & Austin, E. L. (2010). Sexual orientation, parental support, and health during the transition to young adulthood. *Journal of Youth and Adolescence*, *39*(10), 1189–1198.

Newcomb, M. E., Heinz, A. J., & Mustanski, B. (2012). Examining risk and protective factors for alcohol use in lesbian, gay, bisexual, and transgender youth: a longitudinal multilevel analysis. *Journal of Studies on Alchohol and Drugs*, *73*(5), 783–793.

Newcomb, M. E., & Mustanski, B. (2010). Internalized homophobia and internalizing mental health problems: A meta-analytic review. *Clinical Psychology Review*, *30*(8), 1019–1029.

Nuttbrock, L., Hwahng, S., Bockting, W., Rosenblum, A., Mason, M., Macri, M., & Becker, J. (2010). Psychiatric impact of gender-related abuse across the life course of male-to-female transgender persons. *Journal of Sex Research*, *47*(1), 12–23.

Pachankis, J. E. (2014). Uncovering clinical principles and techniques to address minority stress, mental health, and related health risks among gay and bisexual men. *Clinical Psychology: Science and Practice*, *21*, 313–330.

Pachankis, J. E., Goldfried, M. R., & Ramrattan, M. E. (2008). Extension of the rejection sensitivity construct to the interpersonal functioning of gay men. *Journal of Consulting and Clinical Psychology*, *76*(2), 306–317.

Pachankis, J. E., Hatzenbuehler, M., Rendina, H., Safren, S., & Parsons, J. (2015). LGB-affirmative cognitive–behavioral therapy for young adult gay and bisexual men: A randomized controlled trial of a transdiagnostic minority stress approach. *Journal of Consulting and Clinical Psychology*, *83*(5), 875–889.

Pew Research Center. (2013). A survey of LGBT Americans: Attitudes, experiences and values in changing times. Accessed from http://assets.pewresearch.org/wp-content/uploads/sites/3/2013/06/SDT_LGBT-Americans_06-2013.pdf

Reitman, D. S., Austin, B., Belkind, U., Chaffee, T., Hoffman, N. D., Moore, E., . . . Ryan, C. (2013). Recommendations for promoting the health and well-being of lesbian, gay, bisexual, and transgender adolescents. *Journal of Adolescent Health*, *52*(4), 506–510.

Richardson, R., Stallard, P., & Velleman, S. (2010). Computerized cognitive behavioral therapy for the prevention and treatment of depression and anxiety in children and adolescents: A systematic review. *Clinical Child and Family Psychological Review*, 13, 275–290.

Rosselló, J., Bernal, G., & Rivera-Medina, C. (2008). Individual and group CBT and IPT for Puerto Rican adolescents with depressive symptoms. *Cultural Diversity and Ethnic Minority Psychology*, *14*(3), 234–245.

Rosselló, J., & Bernal, G. (2007). Treatment manual for cognitive behavioural therapy for depression: Individual Format (Therapist's Manual). Adaptation for Puerto Rican adolescents. Center for Psychological Services and Research University of Puerto Rico, Río Piedras.

Rowley, R. A., Roesch, S. C., Jurica, B. J., & Vaughn, A. A. (2005). Developing and validating a stress appraisal measure for minority adolescents. *Journal of Adolescence*, 28, 547–557.

Russell, S., & Fish, J. (2016). Mental health in lesbian, gay, bisexual, and transgender (LGBT) youth. *Annual Review Clinical Psychology*, *12*, 465–487.

Safren, S. A., & Rogers, T. (2001). Cognitive behavioral therapy with gay, lesbian and bisexual clients. *Psychotherapy in Practice*, *57*, 629–643.

Safren, S., Hollander, G., Hart, T., & Heimberg, R. (2001). Cognitive-behavioral therapy with lesbian, gay, and bisexual youth. *Cognitive and Behavioral Practice*, *8*, 215–223.

Simons, L., Schrager, S. M., Clark, L. F., Belzer, M., & Olson, J. (2013). Parental support and mental health among transgender adolescents. *Journal of Adolescent Health*, *53*(6), 791–793.

Smith, B. W., Dalen, J., Wiggins, K., Tooley, E., Christopher, P., & Bernard, J. (2008). The Brief Resilience Scale: Assessing the ability to bounce back. *International Journal of Behavioral Medicine*, *15*(3), 194–200.

Snapp, S. D., Watson, R. J., Russell, S. T., Diaz, R. M., & Ryan, C. (2015). Social support networks for LGBT young adults: Low cost strategies for positive adjustment. *Family Relations, 64*(3), 420–430.

Stallard, P. (2004). Cognitive behaviour therapy with prepubertal children. In P. Graham (Ed.), *Cognitive behaviour therapy for children and families* (2nd ed., pp. 121–135). Cambridge, MA: Cambridge University Press.

Stanley, B., Brown, G., Brent, D., Wells, K., Poling, K., Curry, J., . . . Hughes, J. (2009). Cognitive behavior therapy for suicide prevention (CBT-SP): Treatment model, feasibility and acceptability. *Journal of the American Academy of Child and Adolescent Psychiatry, 48*, 1005–1013.

Steptoe, A., & Voegele, C. (1986). Are stress responses influenced by cognitive appraisal? An experimental comparison of coping strategies. *British Journal of Psychology, 77*, 243–255.

Thordarson, M. A., Keller, M., Sullivan, P. J., Trafalis, S., & Friedberg, R. D. (2016). Cognitive–behavioral therapy for immigrant youth: The essentials. In S. Patel & D. Reicherter (Eds.), *Psychotherapy for immigrant youth* (pp. 27–47). New York, NY: Springer.

Tjepkema, M. (2008). Health care use among gay, lesbian and bisexual Canadians. *Health Reports, 19*(1), 53–64.

Treatment for Adolescents with Depression Study. (2004). Fluoxetine, cognitive-behavioral therapy, and the combination for adolescents with depression. *JAMA, 292*, 807–821.

Ungar, M., Liebenberg, L., Boothroyd, R., Kwong, W. M., Lee, T. Y., Leblanc, J., . . . Maknach, A. (2008). The study of youth resilience across cultures: Lessons from a pilot study of measurement development. *Research in Human Development, 5*(3), 166–180.

Vogel, D. L., Bitman, R. L., Hammer, J. H., & Wade, N. G. (2013). Is stigma internalized? The longitudinal impact of public stigma on self-stigma. *Journal of Counseling Psychology, 60*(2), 311–316.

Walls, N. E., Hancock, P., & Wisneski, H. (2007). Differentiating the social service needs of homeless sexual minority youths from those of non-homeless sexual minority youths. *Journal of Children and Poverty, 13*(2), 177–205.

Ybarra, M. L., Mitchell, K. J., Palmer, N. A., & Reisner, S. L. (2015). Online social support as a buffer against online and offline peer and sexual victimization among US LGBT and non-LGBT youth. *Child Abuse & Neglect, 39*, 123–136.

3

Evidence-Based Approaches for Sexual Health and Substance Use Problems in Sexual and Gender Minority Youth

MICHAEL E. NEWCOMB AND BRIAN A. FEINSTEIN ■

Lesbian, gay, bisexual, transgender, and other sexual and gender minority (LGBTQ) youth are at higher risk for a host of negative mental and physical health outcomes relative to their heterosexual counterparts (Mustanski et al., 2014). Two behavioral health domains that disproportionately impact LGBTQ youth most are sexual health outcomes (i.e., HIV and sexually transmitted infections [STIs]) and substance use. Despite these well-documented disparities, very little attention has been paid to mitigating these health issues, and few evidence-based interventions that are tailored to the unique needs of LGBTQ youth have been developed to address these problems. Unfortunately, our understanding of the best evidence-based practices for addressing sexual health and substance use disparities among LGBTQ youth is truly in its nascence, and a great deal of research is needed in order to develop the prevention and treatment strategies that are necessary for improving the health and well-being of these young people.

With regard to sexual health, young gay, bisexual, and other men who have sex with men (YMSM) are at high and increasing risk for HIV infection (Centers for Disease Control and Prevention [CDC], 2016), particularly YMSM of color. Indeed, YMSM aged 13–24 and 25–34 years are the groups that are currently experiencing the highest incidence of new HIV infections in the United States (CDC, 2015). Although less research has been conducted on HIV risk among young transgender women and men, existing evidence suggests that these groups are also at disproportionate risk for HIV acquisition (Clark, Babu, Wiewel,

Opoku, & Crepaz, 2017; Poteat, Scheim, Xavier, Reisner, & Baral, 2016). Finally, less knowledge exists about the sexual health of young sexual minority women (Mustanski et al., 2014), but evidence suggests that these young people have lower rates of pregnancy prevention use and higher rates of unintended pregnancy compared to heterosexual women (Kann et al., 2016; Saewyc, Bearinger, Blum, & Resnick, 1999; Saewyc, Poon, Homma, & Skay, 2008). Together, these findings point to vast disparities in sexual health outcomes among LGBTQ youth relative to their heterosexual and cisgender peers.

LGBTQ youth are also at higher risk for alcohol and illicit drug use, as well as for onset of substance use disorders, than are heterosexual youth (Corliss et al., 2010; Garofalo, Wolf, Kessel, Palfrey, & DuRant, 1998; Kelly, Parsons, & Wells, 2006; Marshal et al., 2008; Marshal, Friedman, Stall, & Thompson, 2009; Phillips et al., 2017; Tucker, Ellickson, & Klein, 2008). Because LGBTQ youth experience numerous chronic, socially based stressors resulting from having a minority sexual orientation or gender identity (Hendricks & Testa, 2012; Meyer, 2003), they may develop deficits in healthy emotion regulation, which promotes negative affect. These youth may turn to maladaptive coping behaviors to manage this stress, including alcohol and drug use (Hatzenbuehler, 2009). LGBTQ youth experience rapid growth in alcohol, marijuana, and illicit drug use from adolescence into emerging adulthood (Marshal et al., 2009; Newcomb, Heinz, & Mustanski, 2012; Swann, Bettin, Clifford, Newcomb, & Mustanski, 2017), and these growth trajectories have been found to be steeper than those of heterosexual youth (Marshal et al., 2009). Indeed, high and increasing alcohol and marijuana use have been found to be associated with higher rates of substance use problems and a higher likelihood of substance use disorder in a 10-year longitudinal study of YMSM (Swann et al., 2017). Very little is known about alcohol and drug use specifically among transgender and other gender minority youth, largely because the vast majority of population-based surveys do not assess gender identity separate from sex assigned at birth.

This chapter summarizes the current state of the science in behavioral interventions for addressing sexual health and substance use among LGBTQ youth. As noted previously, relatively few evidence-based interventions have been developed for addressing these issues among LGBTQ youth. Where interventions are available, they tend to focus on HIV prevention for YMSM, in part due to the disproportionate burden of the domestic HIV epidemic that is shouldered by YMSM. With regard to substance use, this issue has most often been addressed in the context of reducing sexually risky behaviors (e.g., substance use before condomless sex). Furthermore, few interventions have reached the stage in their evaluation at which they have established strong evidence of efficacy via well-controlled randomized trials. As such, this chapter has three aims. First, we review the few interventions that have received strong support of efficacy, as well as highlight new and innovative intervention strategies that have shown preliminary evidence of efficacy and hold strong promise. Second, we provide two case examples, illustrating the use of evidence-based approaches to assist young people who entered treatment to address issues related to sexual health or substance use. Finally, we identify gaps in our scientific knowledge and discuss various opportunities for innovation in the development of evidence-based approaches for addressing the behavioral health needs of LGBTQ youth.

BEHAVIORAL INTERVENTIONS FOR SEXUAL HEALTH AND SUBSTANCE USE AMONG LGBTQ YOUTH

The past several decades have seen a great deal of behavioral intervention development efforts for various groups at increased risk for HIV and other sexual health outcomes, but these efforts have largely been directed toward HIV prevention among heterosexuals and adult gay and bisexual men (CDC, 2017; Mustanski, Newcomb, Du Bois, Garcia, & Grov, 2011). Far less attention has been paid to HIV prevention efforts among YMSM and transgender youth, although recent years have seen increases in behavioral intervention development efforts among YMSM in particular. Regrettably, very few (if any) evidence-based behavioral interventions for addressing the sexual health needs of young sexual minority women exist. As a result, there is a dearth of sexual health promotion programs for LGBTQ youth that have established efficacy via large randomized controlled trials (RCTs). However, a number of recently developed HIV prevention programs for YMSM and transgender youth have demonstrated promise and preliminary evidence of efficacy through pilot and other nonrandomized trials.

Even less work has been done to develop prevention and treatment strategies for reducing alcohol and drug use among LGBTQ youth, despite well-documented disparities in substance use among sexual minority youth (Marshal et al., 2008). The vast majority of programs that do address substance use do so as a precursor to sexual risk behavior. However, there are several exceptions that point to promising avenues for reducing substance use among LGBTQ youth. Given the current state of the literature, our review of sexual health and substance use programs for LGBTQ youth focuses primarily on HIV prevention programming for YMSM. We highlight the few approaches that do address substance use specifically, as well as the few programs that are available for young sexual minority women and transgender youth. We organized our review of the literature based on intervention delivery modality. We begin by reviewing more traditional face-to-face programs delivered to individuals and groups, followed by community-level and popular opinion leader programs and, finally, eHealth and other technology-based approaches to prevention and treatment.

Individual- and Group-Based Interventions

There are a handful of traditional individual- and group-based sexual health programs for YMSM and transgender youth that have shown promise, and several of these programs also address substance use as a primary outcome. In one of the earliest HIV prevention programs for YMSM, Remafedi (1994) developed a cognitive–behavioral HIV risk reduction program that sought to change HIV knowledge, beliefs, and risk behaviors. The program delivered individualized risk reduction, peer education, and referrals to needed services. This was a single-session program with one booster that was designed to be administered by a peer educator. Results showed a significant increase in condom use during anal intercourse at 3-month post-test, but this trial did not randomize participants to a control condition, which limits knowledge of its efficacy.

More recently, Parsons, Lelutiu-Weinberger, Botsko, and Golub (2014) developed the Young Men's Health Project (YMHP). YMHP is one of the few HIV prevention programs designed for YMSM that is a CDC-endorsed "best evidence" intervention, a designation that allows local health departments and community-based organizations to receive funding for implementing the program. YMHP utilizes motivational interviewing techniques and aims to reduce sexual risk behaviors and substance use across four one-on-one sessions. YMHP provides participants with information about the risks associated with condomless anal sex and substance use, and it enhances motivation and personal responsibility for behavior change. Sessions 1 and 2 focus on guiding the client toward change for each of the target behaviors (i.e., sexual risk and substance use) by collaboratively creating a plan for change, including detailing behavior change goals and identifying potential barriers. Upon completion of these exercises, the client also completes a decisional balance exercise in Session 2 that elicits the client's perceived benefits and risks for changing both behaviors. In Session 3, the therapist reviews the client's progress, including assessing readiness for change, motivation, and progress toward goals. Finally, the therapist focuses on termination in Session 4 by reviewing and revising the client's behavior change goals.

In an attention-matched RCT, YMHP resulted in significantly larger decreases in condomless anal sex and substance use at 12-month follow-up relative to a content-matched educational program. YMHP is advantageous in that it is brief compared to most other individual- or group-based interventions. Furthermore, although motivational interviewing requires some training, it does not necessitate an advanced degree, which allows for flexibility and cost-effectiveness when implementing the program in community settings. It is also noteworthy that YMHP is one of the few sexual health programs that also addresses substance use as a primary outcome of the intervention; most programs that integrate HIV prevention and substance use simply aim to reduce substance use before sex in order to reduce its impact on condomless sex. YMHP, in contrast, addresses both sexual health and substance use behaviors as primary outcomes, and the program significantly decreases both behaviors.

Another individually administered program that targets multiple health outcomes, Effective Skills to Empower Effective Men (ESTEEM), is a transdiagnostic, cognitive–behavioral prevention and treatment approach for young gay and bisexual men (Pachankis, 2014). The 10-session program was adapted from the Unified Protocol for the Transdiagnostic Treatment of Emotional Disorders (Barlow et al., 2010) in order to address sexual orientation-related stress (i.e., minority stress). The broad goal of ESTEEM is to reduce mental and behavioral health problems by targeting minority stress and universal risk factors. For instance, modules were adapted to teach participants how to recognize minority stress, to monitor their reactions, and to facilitate effective coping. In an RCT with young gay and bisexual men aged 18–35 years, ESTEEM resulted in significant reductions in alcohol use problems, sexual compulsivity, past-90-day condomless anal sex with casual partners, and depressive symptoms, as well as increases in condom use self-efficacy, compared to a waitlist (Pachankis, Hatzenbuehler, Rendina, Safren, & Parsons, 2015). Ongoing evaluation of ESTEEM in a large-scale RCT will provide more firm evidence of program efficacy, but this preliminary evidence that a single protocol can result in improvements across multiple health domains is certainly promising.

There are also several group-based programs that have been shown to reduce HIV risk, and in some cases substance use, among YMSM and transgender youth. In the early 1990s, Rotheram-Borus, Reid, and Rosario (1994) developed a 20-session group-based program to address HIV risk in young gay and bisexual men. One of the first programs to address HIV risk specifically among YMSM, this program used an open group format in which participants could join at any time, and session topics covered HIV prevention information, barriers to HIV risk reduction, access to health care and related resources, and coping with stress and stigma. Given the large number of sessions, the program experienced high attrition, but participants who attended more sessions experienced larger reductions in condomless anal sex that were maintained at 12-month follow-up. Nevertheless, this program represents an important step forward in early HIV prevention efforts for YMSM given that it was among the first to developmentally tailor content to the needs of the target population.

Many Men, Many Voices (3MV) is a CDC-endorsed group-based program that was originally designed to reduce HIV risk among adult Black MSM (Wilton et al., 2009). Black MSM peers facilitate the 3MV sessions, and the program consists of six 2- or 3-hour group sessions. 3MV focuses on behavioral and social determinants relevant to HIV risk among Black MSM, including cultural, religious, and community norms; connectedness to the Black and gay communities; relationship dynamics; and racism and homophobia. A unique component of 3MV is the development of a "menu of behavior change options" for reducing risk of HIV instead of focusing solely on condoms, as well as a focus on teaching skills for communicating effectively with partners about sexual risk behavior and prevention options. Furthermore, discussions about sexual behavior and relationships emphasize how culture and community norms influence these dynamics. In an RCT, 3MV participants reported significantly less condomless anal sex and more HIV testing relative to a waitlist control, which was a major factor in establishing 3MV as a CDC "best evidence" intervention. 3MV was more recently adapted for administration to YMSM of color (primarily Black and Latino YMSM) across several CDC-funded community sites (Stein et al., 2015). In this community demonstration project in New York City, Tampa, Florida, and New Orleans, Louisiana, the pace of delivery of group sessions varied (e.g., three sessions per week or one long retreat-style session), and analyses of aggregate data from the 3MV sites found significant reductions in HIV risk behaviors among YMSM of color at both 3 and 6 months post-intervention. As is evident from these data, it may not always be necessary to build new programs from the ground up, but adapting existing efficacious interventions to the developmental needs of YMSM and other LGBTQ youth may enhance the relevance of the prevention information to young people.

Although most newly developed individual and group-based programs are now online, there are also a handful of novel group-based interventions that involve in-person administration. These programs typically were designed for populations that are marginalized within the LGBTQ community or otherwise would benefit from programs that build community in vivo (e.g., transgender youth, LGBTQ youth of color, and young couples). For example, Life Skills is an HIV risk reduction program for young transgender women (aged 16–24 years) that consists of six group sessions focused on skills building and up to five individual sessions for skills implementation (Garofalo et al., 2012). Life Skills uses trained facilitators who are members of the community themselves, and the program aims to build community among transgender women. Based on Bronfenbrenner's (1979) social ecological theory, the program includes modules on transgender pride, communication skills, general life skills (e.g., employment and housing), HIV and safer sex, and partner negotiation. A pilot trial of the program measured outcomes at 3 months post-intervention and found trends of decreasing sexual risk behaviors. Life Skills was also adapted for transgender men who have sex with men, and evaluation of the adapted program found similar trends in decreasing sexual risk behaviors at 4 months post-intervention (Reisner et al., 2016). Although these programs show promise for improving the sexual health of transgender youth, more evaluation is necessary in order to establish their efficacy.

Another recently developed group-based program is 2GETHER, an integrated relationship education and HIV prevention program for young male couples (Newcomb et al., 2017). 2GETHER is a four-session program that consists of two group sessions and two individualized couples' sessions, facilitated by bachelor's-level trainees. In response to data showing that most new HIV infections among YMSM occur in the context of primary partnerships (Sullivan, Salazar, Buchbinder, & Sanchez, 2009), the creators of 2GETHER drew from the information, motivation, and behavioral skills (IMB) model of HIV prevention (Fisher, Fisher, Williams, & Malloy, 1994) and the vulnerability–stress–adaptation model of relationship functioning (Karney & Bradbury, 1995) to build the program. 2GETHER focuses on building communication and coping skills in order to help young male couples improve their relationship functioning and have more nuanced conversations about sexual health, including making decisions about HIV prevention in the context of both monogamous and nonmonogamous relationship agreements. The traditional group-based format of the program resulted from formative data suggesting that young male couples feel isolated and want to meet other young couples while learning skills to build and maintain their relationships (Greene, Fisher, Kuper, Andrews, & Mustanski, 2015). The program is also unique in that it enrolls both HIV-negative and HIV-positive individuals and integrates information on behavioral and biomedical HIV prevention to address the needs of all male couples, regardless of HIV status. In an uncontrolled pilot trial, 2GETHER showed significant improvements in relationship functioning and reductions in HIV risk behaviors at 2-week follow-up. More data are needed to firmly establish efficacy of this new program.

Finally, Smith and colleagues (2016) developed Project PRIDE (Promoting Resilience in Discriminatory Environments), an eight-session, cognitive–behavioral group program to reduce substance use and HIV risk behavior among HIV-negative young gay and bisexual men. The program draws from minority stress theory (Meyer, 2003) and stress and coping theory (Lazarus & Folkman, 1984), and it aims to help young gay and bisexual men cope with minority stress in order to promote sexual health and reduce substance use and negative mental health outcomes. Furthermore, the program provides participants with knowledge and skills related to stress and coping, safer sex strategies, and sexual communication (e.g., asking about HIV/STI status and condom negotiation). In an uncontrolled pilot trial with 33 young gay and bisexual men aged 18–25 years, the program led to reductions in frequency of alcohol use, number of sex partners, loneliness, and minority stress, as well as increases in self-esteem, at the 3-month follow-up assessment. In summary, findings suggest that Project PRIDE is a promising program to reduce substance use and sexual risk among young gay and bisexual men, but further evaluation is needed.

Community-Level and Popular Opinion Leader Interventions

Perhaps the most well-studied and widely disseminated HIV prevention program for YMSM is the Mpowerment Project, originally developed for 18- to 29-year-old YMSM and adapted for various populations and administration modalities (Kegeles, Hays, & Coates, 1996; Kegeles, Hays, Pollack, & Coates, 1999). This CDC-endorsed intervention was developed based on the theory that safer sex behaviors are learned via modeling and peer influence and that these learned behaviors can be diffused throughout communities by peer leaders. Mpowerment begins by developing a group of 12–15 core group members and volunteers who organize various social, outreach, and small group activities. Specifically, they work with their local community to develop and distribute safer sex materials and information tailored to the needs of their community (Hays, Rebchook, & Kegeles, 2003; Kegeles et al., 1996). In the 1990s, the Mpowerment creators evaluated the program in several controlled trials in urban communities throughout the United States and found it to be efficacious at decreasing various sexual risk behaviors, including condomless sex (Kegeles et al., 1996, 1999). Since that time, Mpowerment has been adopted by many community-based organizations (Hays et al., 2003; Rebchook, Kegeles, Huebner, & Team, 2006), and recent data from the Monitoring and Evaluation of Mpowerment Project suggest that it remains effective when implemented in populations at high risk for HIV acquisition (Shelley et al., 2017).

In Russia and Bulgaria, Amirkhanian, Kelly, Kabakchieva, McAuliffe, and Vassileva (2003) developed an innovative social network intervention specifically for reducing HIV risk among YMSM. In this program, peer leaders are trained through five 3- or 4-hour group sessions to provide information on HIV transmission and risk reduction to members in their social network. Evaluations of this program found significant reductions in condomless anal sex and other sexual risk behaviors among social network members at 3-month follow-up (Amirkhanian et al., 2003) and marginal decreases in these risk behaviors at 12-month follow-up (Amirkhanian, Kelly, & McAuliffe, 2005). More recently, Amirkhanian and colleagues (2015) evaluated this program in an RCT in Russia and Hungary in which social networks were randomly assigned to have peer leaders receive the training for the experimental intervention or to receive HIV/STI testing and counseling (control). This RCT found significant reductions in condomless anal sex at both 3- and 12-month follow-up among social network members in the experimental condition relative to control.

Hosek and colleagues (2015) used a similar popular opinion leader approach to develop an HIV prevention program for Black YMSM in the House Ball Community, called Promoting Ovahness through Safer Sex Education (POSSE). POSSE is an adaptation of an existing HIV prevention program for adult Black MSM (Jones et al., 2008); popular opinion leaders from the House Ball Community were trained to deliver HIV risk reduction messages to their peers through four group-based training sessions. Community-level surveys of the local House Ball Community assessed diffusion of messages and outcomes, and the researchers observed significant reductions in number of sexual encounters and condomless anal sex encounters at post-test. Although POSSE has not been evaluated in a more rigorous controlled trial, the use of existing tight-knit social networks to disseminate prevention messages via peer influence is a potentially powerful approach for preventing HIV in high-risk communities, particularly given that evidence suggests that HIV travels more rapidly through these insular social networks (Berry, Raymond, & McFarland, 2007; Mustanski, Birkett, Kuhns, Latkin, & Muth, 2015; Newcomb & Mustanski, 2013; Raymond & McFarland, 2009).

eHealth and Other Technology-Based Programs

As Internet access and mobile technology have become more universally accessible during the past decade, behavioral interventions have begun to utilize these technologies in order to enhance the reach of sexual health promotion programs. eHealth programs vary widely in their degree of automation and tailoring, as well as in the amount of personalized contact participants have with program facilitators. Our review of eHealth programs that address sexual health in LGBTQ youth highlights this diversity in content and format.

Given that these technologies are still relatively new, very few eHealth sexual health programs have reached the point in their development and evaluation at which they have established efficacy with a large-scale RCT. In one exception, the

Keep It Up! (KIU) program (Mustanski, Garofalo, Monahan, Gratzer, & Andrews, 2013) is an online HIV prevention program for YMSM up to age 29 years who have recently tested HIV-negative that utilized the IMB model of HIV prevention (Fisher, Fisher, Misovich, Kimble, & Malloy, 1996) in its development. Recognizing that HIV testing is an important window of opportunity for engaging YMSM in prevention messaging, KIU aims to provide YMSM with the information they need to "keep it up" and stay HIV-negative. KIU is a fully automated eHealth program with minimal tailoring that aims to address HIV-related information, motivation, and behavioral skills by using online media to immerse YMSM into the various contexts they may face when making safer sex decisions (meeting partners online, sex while under the influence, etc.). Several trials provide evidence that KIU reduces various HIV risk behaviors among YMSM, including a pilot RCT with 12-week follow-up (Mustanski et al., 2013) and a community implementation project (Greene, Madkins, Andrews, Dispenza, & Mustanski, 2016). A multisite RCT evaluated KIU compared to an attention-matched HIV information program, and participants in the experimental condition showed significant decreases in both condomless anal sex and rectal STI infections at 12-month follow-up (Mustanski, Parsons, et al., 2017). These data led KIU to be designated as a CDC-endorsed "best evidence" intervention.

In another fully automated eHealth program, Mustanski, Greene, Ryan, and Whitton (2015) developed Queer Sex Ed (QSE) to improve sexual health-related outcomes among LGBTQ youth in romantic relationships (aged 16–20 years). To our knowledge, this is the only evidence-based sexual health program designed to address the needs of young sexual minority women and transgender individuals, in addition to those of YMSM. Also based in large part on the IMB model (Fisher et al., 1996), QSE is a five-module multimedia program designed to provide LGBTQ-inclusive sex and relationship education. In a nonrandomized trial, participants showed improvements in several sexual health (e.g., HIV information and motivation), relationship (e.g., communication), and sexual orientation-related outcomes (e.g., internalized stigma). Although more rigorous evaluation of this program is needed via a large-scale randomized trial, this automated approach to providing universal sex education to LGBTQ youth has the potential to be a cost-effective and efficacious strategy for improving sexual health.

To our knowledge, Schwinn, Thom, Schinke, and Hopkins (2015) developed and evaluated the only program that specifically addresses substance use as the primary outcome. This web-based drug abuse prevention program for LGBTQ youth aged 15 or 16 years is a three-session program that was informed by minority stress theory (Meyer, 2003) and a social competency skill-building strategy (Bandura, Adams, & Beyer, 1977). The eHealth program also utilizes a high degree of automation, and it focuses on teaching skills related to stress management, decision-making, and drug use refusal. In a randomized trial, 236 LGBTQ youth were randomized to either complete the intervention or a no-intervention control condition. At 3-month follow-up, compared to youth who did not complete the intervention, youth who completed the intervention reported lower stress, peer drug use, and past 30-day other drug use (i.e., inhalant, club drug, steroid, cocaine, methamphetamine, prescription drug, and heroin use), as well as higher coping, problem-solving, and drug use refusal skills. In contrast, past 30-day alcohol, cigarette, and marijuana use did not differ between youth who completed the intervention and those who did not. These data provide preliminary support for the efficacy of a web-based drug abuse prevention program for sexual minority youth. In summary, the benefits of these types of highly automated eHealth programs are that they can be consistently administered in the exact same manner to all individuals (i.e., fidelity monitoring is unnecessary) and online media can simulate situations that may otherwise be difficult for more isolated youth to come across in their daily lives. On the other hand, technology changes rapidly, and a fair amount of technological support is needed to update and host online content, which may increase the cost of implementation.

With regard to more tailored eHealth strategies, Get Connected is a program that aims to increase HIV/STI testing among YMSM by tailoring content to participant's demographics and testing history (Bauermeister et al., 2015). The program consists of four webpages that can be viewed in a single sitting, and broadly speaking, the website provides HIV/STI information, seeks to improve testing motivation, and addresses barriers to accessing testing. In an RCT of Get Connected compared to an HIV/STI testing locator control condition, YMSM in the experimental condition were more likely to have received HIV/STI testing at 30-day follow-up (although this effect was not statistically significant). Another program that involves a fair amount of tailoring is HealthMpowerment.org (HMP), which is an online mobile-optimized HIV prevention program for Black YMSM and transgender women that utilizes behavior change and gaming theories to reduce sexual risk behaviors (Muessig, Baltierra, Pike, LeGrand, & Hightow-Weidman, 2014). The user-driven nature of the program allows participants to tailor the program content to their needs and experiences, and the website content includes information about sexual health, quizzes and games that allow participants to earn points and win prizes, and a choose-your-own-adventure narrative to enhance risk reduction motivation. Participants in HMP also interact with other participants in forums in order to build community, and the program is open to HIV-negative and HIV-positive youth. In a 4-week nonrandomized pilot trial, participants showed an increase in HIV-related information and motivation, although more data are needed in order to assess sexual behavior change and efficacy.

One underutilized technology-based approach to increasing the reach of traditional behavioral interventions is using online technology to deliver interventions live that were originally developed for face-to-face administration. This approach allows for a high degree of personalization in that the interventions are still administered by a live facilitator, but the use of technology to administer the intervention reduces barriers to accessing face-to-face programs because participants do not need to live near an organization that has LGBTQ-inclusive programming. In one example, YMHP (Parsons et al., 2014), which was described previously, was adapted for administration over social media platforms. MiCHAT (Motivational Interviewing Communication About Health, Attitudes and

Thoughts) is an eight-session program delivered over the Facebook live chat feature, and it integrates motivational interviewing and cognitive–behavioral skills training approaches to reduce sexual risk behavior, substance use, and mental health-related outcomes (Lelutiu-Weinberger et al., 2015). In a nonrandomized pilot trial, MiCHAT participants reported significant reductions in condomless anal sex and alcohol and drug use at 3-month follow-up. Although MiCHAT has not been evaluated in a large-scale RCT, the strong evidence supporting the efficacy of its parent intervention, YMHP, suggests that MiCHAT is a promising approach to reducing HIV risk and substance online.

CASE EXAMPLES FOR APPLICATION OF EVIDENCED-BASED PRINCIPLES FOR LGBTQ YOUTH

In this section, we provide two case examples that draw from our clinical experience. The overarching goal of this section is to highlight evidence-based strategies for reducing sexual risk behaviors and substance use in LGBTQ youth, drawing from the various interventions we reviewed in the prior section. We recognize that the case examples describe YMSM and therefore do not represent the diversity of identities within the LGBTQ youth community. Because the vast majority of evidence-based interventions in the scientific literature address risk behaviors in YMSM, we chose to focus our case examples on YMSM as well; without further evaluation, it is not appropriate to assume that the evidence-based principles reviewed in this chapter would be similarly efficacious for young sexual minority women and transgender youth. However, we did purposefully choose these examples to represent diversity of experiences within the YMSM population. As such, one of the examples focuses primarily on substance use, whereas the other focuses primarily on sexual behavior. Moreover, one case example represents an individual seeking treatment, and the other is a couple seeking counseling for relationship discord.

INDIVIDUAL CASE EXAMPLE

Thomas was an 18-year-old, Latino, gay man who presented for treatment because his friends had expressed concern about his drinking. Although he did not perceive his drinking to be a problem, he acknowledged that he typically drank more than he intended to and there were negative consequences to his drinking (e.g., hangovers and doing things he later regretted). During the initial assessment, Thomas reported drinking three or four times per week and consuming at least five drinks per occasion. He reported occasional marijuana use, but he denied other illicit drug use. Thomas typically drank at bars, and he often ended up in risky situations (e.g., having sex and not using a condom). Despite the negative consequences of his drinking, Thomas was ambivalent about changing his behavior because he was concerned about his social life changing as a result.

Given that Thomas did not perceive his drinking as a problem and that he was ambivalent about changing his behavior, the clinician began with a motivational approach. Similar to the YMHP intervention (Parsons et al., 2014), the clinician explored Thomas' ambivalence by asking him to describe the advantages and disadvantages of continuing to engage in his current behavior (i.e., binge drinking three or four times per week) versus changing his behavior. During this exercise, Thomas noted several negative consequences of his behavior (e.g., hangovers, blackouts, and engaging in risky sexual behavior), but he also noted benefits (e.g., it felt good in the moment). He was able to see potential benefits to changing his behavior (e.g., improved health and not putting himself at risk), but he was concerned that changing his behavior would also have negative consequences (e.g., fewer social opportunities). Throughout the exercise, the clinician remained non-judgmental and non-confrontational, using reflection to reinforce Thomas' commitment to change (e.g., the clinician made comments such as "It sounds like you're worried that your friends won't want to hang out with you if you don't drink as much, but you're tired of being hung over and doing things that you later regret" and "I'm hearing you say that if you had fewer drinks when you went out, then you would be more likely to use a condom if you had sex"). This approach increased Thomas' awareness of the negative consequences of his drinking, and he gradually became more open to making changes to his behavior.

Given that Thomas' drinking typically occurred in social contexts, the clinician hypothesized that social and interpersonal factors may be contributing to his problematic alcohol use. The clinician explored Thomas' motivation for drinking in different contexts and learned that Thomas felt uncomfortable and self-conscious in social situations. For example, he worried about being judged for acting effeminate, even among other gay men, and found that drinking calmed his nerves. To address Thomas' anxiety, the clinician used a cognitive–behavioral approach informed by minority stress theory, similar to the ESTEEM intervention (Pachankis, 2014). The clinician helped Thomas understand the connection between his anxious thoughts and his drinking by exploring the antecedents to his alcohol use and by educating him about the reinforcing nature of avoidant behavior (e.g., drinking can reduce anxiety in the moment but reinforce it over time). Thomas began to realize that he drank the most in situations that triggered anxious thoughts related to his sexual orientation (e.g., "No one is going to want to talk to me because I'm too effeminate"). The clinician helped Thomas become more aware of the extent to which his anxious thoughts were impacting his behavior and taught him how to challenge his anxious thoughts. For example, rather than accepting his thoughts as facts, Thomas learned how to evaluate the evidence for and against his thoughts. Over time, he was able to challenge his anxious thoughts with statements such as "I don't know whether or not anyone will want to talk to me, because I haven't tried. Some men may not want to talk to me, but I don't know if it's because I'm too effeminate or for a different reason." Thomas used this new self-talk while he gradually exposed himself to situations that he had previously avoided (e.g., talking to men at bars). Over the course of treatment, he was able to reduce his problematic drinking by learning adaptive coping skills (e.g., challenging anxious thoughts) and by no longer avoiding anxiety-provoking situations. In summary, the clinician integrated motivational and cognitive–behavioral techniques to help Thomas reduce his problematic drinking and subsequent sexual risk behavior and also to help him cope with minority stress using strategies other than drinking.

COUPLE CASE EXAMPLE

Tyler (26 years old, White) and Jesse (28 years old, Black) were a couple who had been together for 2 years and presented to treatment due to relationship discord. The couple stated that they argued frequently and that their arguments often became very emotional and escalated into yelling matches. They denied instances of intimate partner violence. The couple noted that their arguments typically arose from what they called jealousy and trust issues. Both partners were HIV-negative at the time of treatment, and the couple described having an open relationship agreement in which they were allowed to have sex with partners outside of the relationship. Tyler described becoming angry with Jesse because he believed that Jesse sometimes got "too close" to his outside sex partners (e.g., socializing with them in non-sexual settings). Jesse was upset with Tyler because on several occasions Tyler had sex with an outside partner without a condom, and Jesse worried that it could expose the couple to HIV.

Similar to the 2GETHER couples intervention (Newcomb et al., 2017), treatment initially focused on enhancing effective communication skills between Tyler and Jesse because it was clear that the couple were unable to discuss their concerns without quickly escalating to anger. The clinician first taught Tyler and Jesse distress tolerance skills in order to reduce the intensity of their emotions prior to entering into a discussion about a relationship issue. For example, Tyler noted that he calmed himself down by listening to music, whereas Jesse preferred to go for a walk. Next, the therapist observed the couple talking to one another about their concerns. It became clear that Tyler had a tendency to frame his concerns with "you" statements (e.g., "You don't care as much about our relationship as I do"), which was often followed by Jesse making insulting comments to Tyler and withdrawing from the conversation. By using "I" statements (e.g., "I feel hurt when you spend a lot of time with other guys"), Tyler's communication became less accusatory. In addition, Jesse was able to engage more in conversation by learning to be an active listener and paraphrasing Tyler's thoughts (e.g., "What I hear you saying is that you worry that I don't care about our relationship"). By addressing communication, the clinician was able to set the stage for helping the couple address their concerns about their relationship agreement and sexual behavior.

Because the couple noted that they periodically engaged in behaviors that put them at risk for HIV, the clinician utilized a framework that was adapted from the IMB model (Fisher et al., 1996) to help the couple reduce their risk of HIV acquisition. As described previously, this framework has been used as the basis for multiple HIV prevention interventions for YMSM (Mustanski et al., 2013;

Newcomb et al., 2017). First, the clinician provided the couple with HIV prevention information specific to YMSM couples; in particular, Tyler and Jesse knew very little about the effectiveness of pre-exposure prophylaxis (PrEP) as a prevention strategy. Given that the couple was not using condoms with one another and Tyler periodically had sex with outside partners without a condom, PrEP could be a highly effective prevention strategy for the couple. As such, the clinician used motivational interviewing techniques to assess and increase the couple's motivation to initiate PrEP. In a decisional balance exercise similar to that used in YMHP (Parsons et al., 2014), the couple identified the advantages and disadvantages of behavior change (i.e., initiating PrEP) and continuing with their current behavior. The therapist reflected the couple's ambivalence using non-judgmental language in order to enhance motivation (e.g., "It sounds like you guys don't like the idea of taking a pill every day, and taking PrEP would help ease your worry about getting HIV from an outside partner").

Finally, building a formal, mutually agreed upon relationship agreement is one of the primary HIV prevention behavioral skills for couples. While reviewing the rules of their agreement, it became clear that the couple had not thoroughly discussed the rules of their open relationship, including whether or not sex without a condom was permissible. Thus, it was not the open agreement itself that caused relationship conflict but, rather, the lack of clarity about the agreement rules led to different interpretations of the limitations of the agreement. The clinician encouraged Tyler and Jesse to use effective communication skills to discuss their concerns, and both members of the couple were able to make compromises when establishing their agreement. Based on Jesse's feedback, the couple set the rule that they had to use condoms for anal sex when they had sex with outside partners. With regard to Tyler's concerns, they agreed that outside partners had to be anonymous partners, and they were not allowed to spend time with these partners aside from the sexual encounter. In summary, the therapist integrated communication skills training, motivational interviewing, and HIV risk reduction in order to help improve their relationship functioning and optimize their sexual health.

FUTURE DIRECTIONS IN BEHAVIORAL INTERVENTIONS FOR LGBTQ YOUTH

In addition to continuing to evaluate the various promising programs reviewed in this chapter through more rigorous randomized trials, there are several other innovative and promising intervention approaches that deserve attention in future research. First, schools are a highly underutilized venue for delivering sexual health programming to LGBTQ youth. Although the feasibility of delivering LGBTQ-inclusive sex education varies by jurisdiction within the United States, delivering such education to middle school and high school students has the potential to not only improve sexual health outcomes but also improve acceptance of and the overall climate for LGBTQ students. In one early example, Blake et al. (2001) evaluated a program in Massachusetts in which teachers in some districts received LGBTQ inclusivity training, including LGBTQ health and LGBTQ-sensitive HIV instruction. Using data from the 1995 Youth Risk Behavior Surveillance (YRBS) in Massachusetts, the research found that sexual minority youth in schools that received LGBTQ inclusivity training reported fewer sexual risk behaviors than did youth in schools that did not receive such training. Despite the barriers inherent in delivering comprehensive sex education in many schools (let alone LGBTQ-inclusive sex education), more research and advocacy are needed to understand how to optimize school-based sex education. Similarly, Konishi, Saewyc, Homma, and Poon (2013) analyzed data from the 2008 British Columbia Adolescent Health Survey and found that students who attended schools with gay–straight alliances and anti-homophobia bullying policies reported significantly lower odds of problem substance use compared to students who did not attend such schools. This indicates that LGBTQ-inclusive substance use prevention programming in schools may also effectively reduce substance use problems among LGBTQ youth.

Parents and families of LGBTQ youth are also an underutilized resource for delivering sexual health promotion and substance use prevention programming. Family- or parent-based programs are commonly used strategies for addressing HIV risk and substance use among presumably heterosexual adolescents (Brown et al., 2014; Prado et al., 2012), and research indicates that parental support, communication, and monitoring are associated with fewer sexual risk and substance use behaviors among YMSM (Mustanski, Swann, Newcomb, & Prachand, 2017). Furthermore, qualitative evidence suggests that both parents and LGBTQ adolescents do indeed want to improve their relationships with one another (Bouris, Hill, Fisher, Erickson, & Schneider, 2015; Feinstein et al., 2018; Garofalo, Mustanski, & Donenberg, 2008; Newcomb, Feinstein, Matson, Macapagal, & Mustanski, 2018), pointing to a need for programming that builds supportive parent–adolescent relationships in order to enhance the health and well-being of LGBTQ youth. In the context of increasing societal acceptance of LGBTQ persons, the time is right for the development of family- and parent-based health promotion strategies for LGBTQ youth.

Newer technologies also provide innovative opportunities for sexual health promotion and substance use prevention. For example, programs that deliver behavior change strategies via text messaging may be effective at engaging young people in health-related interventions given the ubiquity of text message use by youth populations. Indeed, researchers have begun to develop text message-based HIV prevention programs for adolescent gay and bisexual boys (Ybarra et al., 2016), and a pilot RCT of this program found that participants in the experimental condition were more likely to receive HIV testing at 12-month follow-up relative to controls (Ybarra et al., 2017). However, the researchers observed no differences between conditions in sexual risk behavior, which indicates that this behavior change strategy may require more refinement. The same research team also recently identified online focus groups as a potential avenue for intervention (Ybarra, DuBois, Parsons, Prescott, & Mustanski, 2014). In the process of developing content for the previously described text message program, the team conducted online focus groups with adolescent gay and bisexual boys. Participants in these focus groups had a high level of engagement, and qualitative analysis found that most participants reported that upon completion of the focus group, they felt more comfortable talking about sex and more confident in making safer choices, such as negotiating condom use. The researchers note that online focus groups and facilitated discussion boards are low-cost and easy to manage, which enhances their appeal as a health promotion strategy.

In addition to the previously mentioned novel intervention modalities, there are several specific health topics that deserve more attention. For example, LGBTQ youth are increasingly expressing an interest in programs that address their health more broadly rather than focusing exclusively on HIV and sexual health (Greene et al., 2015). As such, it will be important for future program development efforts to address the broader health needs of LGBTQ youth—not just because that is what is most appealing to LGBTQ youth but also because sexual health disparities do not occur in a vacuum and are linked to their other health needs. In fact, certain programs reviewed in this chapter have begun to do so. For example, YMPH addresses both sexual risk and substance use behaviors in YMSM (Parsons et al., 2014), and the 2GETHER intervention provides both relationship education and HIV prevention skills for couples (Newcomb et al., 2017).

Related, existing sexual health promotion programs clearly do not fully address the needs of many youth within the LGBTQ community. The vast majority of sexual health programs for LGBTQ youth have been developed to address HIV risk among YMSM, and program development and evaluation efforts have largely ignored the specific needs of young sexual minority women, bisexual individuals, and transgender and gender expansive youth. For example, evidence from YRBS suggests that young bisexual women experience some of the largest disparities in alcohol and drug use (Newcomb et al., 2014; Talley, Hughes, Aranda, Birkett, & Marshal, 2014), yet little to no prevention or treatment programming is available that addresses the unique needs of bisexual individuals. At best, young bisexual men have been included in HIV prevention programming insofar as they are considered to be YMSM, but this approach may be ignoring the unique experiences of bisexuals that may increase or reduce risk for negative health outcomes. In summary, very little is currently known about the health needs of most groups within the LGBTQ youth population, despite the fact that they are disproportionately affected by negative sexual health outcomes, including HIV/STI risk and intimate partner violence.

Finally, LGBTQ youth are undoubtedly engaged in sexual health promotion and substance use prevention programming that was designed for presumably heterosexual youth, including sex education in schools and programs that were designed and evaluated for the broader population of adolescents and young adults. For example, analysis of data from five randomized trials of the Familias Unidas family-based sexual health and substance use prevention program for Hispanic adolescents found that 11.9% of adolescents enrolled in these trial were sexual minorities (Ocasio, Feaster, & Prado, 2016). This is important because it is unclear whether LGBTQ youth who receive these broader services benefit to the same degree as their heterosexual counterparts. It may be that broader programs do not sufficiently address the unique contexts in which LGBTQ youth live, which might render these programs less effective. Understanding which LGBTQ youth under which conditions benefit from universal interventions or need more tailored and LGBTQ-specific programs will help conserve much-needed prevention resources while maximizing their benefits.

CONCLUSION

Ample research has documented the various health inequities experienced by LGBTQ youth (Mustanski et al., 2014), but there has not been a commensurate prevention or treatment research response in the scientific literature. Even among the few evidence-based behavioral interventions that have been designed to address sexual health and substance use among LGBTQ youth, the vast majority are HIV prevention programs for young gay, bisexual, and other YMSM. Although a number of recent efforts have been made to address these inequities, a great deal of work is needed in order to address the diverse health needs of this population.

With regard to clinical practice, the existing literature on addressing sexual health and substance use in LGBTQ youth points to several promising strategies. Motivational interviewing techniques are advantageous for working with young people who may or may not be ready to change their behaviors because these techniques use the client's own intrinsic motivations to move the client toward behavior change and also because they encourage the client to develop their own behavior change plans that match their own goals and values. Pairing motivational interviewing techniques with known efficacious cognitive–behavioral principles may be an especially effective way to enact behavior change in LGBTQ youth. It is also clear that sexual health and substance use behaviors do not exist in a vacuum, and other psychosocial issues must also be addressed in order to effectively change behaviors. For example, successful approaches may need to treat HIV risk behaviors and substance use behaviors concurrently (e.g., YMHP); HIV risk in the context of relationship education (e.g., 2GETHER); or sexual health and substance use in the context of other mental health problems, such as depression and anxiety (e.g., ESTEEM). Finally, although clinicians who work with LGBTQ youth should continuously strive to educate themselves about LGBTQ issues, it is unreasonable to expect that clinicians will have knowledge of every aspect of LGBTQ life and culture. Fortunately, there are ample online resources for both therapists and clients, and eHealth programs are excellent supplements to in-person treatment approaches.

REFERENCES

Amirkhanian, Y. A., Kelly, J. A., Kabakchieva, E., McAuliffe, T. L., & Vassileva, S. (2003). Evaluation of a social network HIV prevention intervention program for young men who have sex with men in Russia and Bulgaria. *AIDS Education and Prevention, 15*(3), 205–220.

Amirkhanian, Y. A., Kelly, J. A., & McAuliffe, T. L. (2005). Identifying, recruiting, and assessing social networks at high risk for HIV/AIDS: Methodology, practice, and a case study in St. Petersburg, Russia. *AIDS Care, 17*(1), 58–75. doi:10.1080/ 09540120412331305133

Amirkhanian, Y. A., Kelly, J. A., Takacs, J., McAuliffe, T. L., Kuznetsova, A. V., Toth, T. P., . . . Meylakhs, A. (2015). Effects of a social network HIV/STD prevention intervention for MSM in Russia and Hungary: A randomized controlled trial. *AIDS, 29*(5), 583–593. doi:10.1097/QAD.0000000000000558

Bandura, A., Adams, N. E., & Beyer, J. (1977). Cognitive processes mediating behavioral change. *Journal of Personality and Social Psychology, 35*(3), 125–139.

Barlow, D. H., Farchione, T. J., Fairholme, C. P., Ellard, K. K., Boisseau, C. L., Allen, L. B., & May, J. T. E. (2010). *Unified protocol for transdiagnostic treatment of emotional disorders: Therapist guide*. New York, NY: Oxford University Press.

Bauermeister, J. A., Pingel, E. S., Jadwin-Cakmak, L., Harper, G. W., Horvath, K., Weiss, G., & Dittus, P. (2015). Acceptability and preliminary efficacy of a tailored online HIV/ STI testing intervention for young men who have sex with men: The Get Connected! program. *AIDS and Behavior, 19*(10), 1860–1874. doi:10.1007/s10461-015-1009-y

Berry, M., Raymond, H. F., & McFarland, W. (2007). Same race and older partner selection may explain higher HIV prevalence among Black men who have sex with men. *AIDS, 21*(17), 2349–2350. doi:10.1097/QAD.0b013e3282f12f41

Blake, S. M., Ledsky, R., Lehman, T., Goodenow, C., Sawyer, R., & Hack, T. (2001). Preventing sexual risk behaviors among gay, lesbian, and bisexual adolescents: The benefits of gay-sensitive HIV instruction in schools. *American Journal of Public Health, 91*(6), 940–946.

Bouris, A., Hill, B. J., Fisher, K., Erickson, G., & Schneider, J. A. (2015). Mother–son communication about sex and routine human immunodeficiency virus testing among younger men of color who have sex with men. *Journal of Adolescent Health, 57*(5), 515–522. doi:10.1016/j.jadohealth.2015.07.007

Bronfenbrenner, U. (1979). *The ecology of human development: Experiments by nature and design*. Cambridge, MA: Harvard University Press.

Brown, L. K., Hadley, W., Donenberg, G. R., DiClemente, R. J., Lescano, C., Lang, D. M., . . . Oster, D. (2014). Project STYLE: A multisite RCT for HIV prevention among youths in mental health treatment. *Psychiatric Services, 65*(3), 338–344. doi:10.1176/ appi.ps.201300095

Centers for Disease Control and Prevention. (2015). *HIV among gay and bisexual men*. Retrieved from https://www.cdc.gov/hiv/group/msm/index.html

Centers for Disease Control and Prevention. (2016). *HIV surveillance report, 2015*. Retrieved from https://www.cdc.gov/hiv/library/reports/surveillance

Centers for Disease Control and Prevention. (2017). *Compendium of evidence-based interventions and best practices for HIV prevention*. Retrieved from https://www.cdc. gov/hiv/research/interventionresearch/compendium/index.html

Clark, H., Babu, A. S., Wiewel, E. W., Opoku, J., & Crepaz, N. (2017). Diagnosed HIV infection in transgender adults and adolescents: Results from the National HIV Surveillance System, 2009–2014. *AIDS and Behavior, 21*(9), 2774–2783. doi:10.1007/ s10461-016-1656-7

Corliss, H. L., Rosario, M., Wypij, D., Wylie, S. A., Frazier, A. L., & Austin, S. B. (2010). Sexual orientation and drug use in a longitudinal cohort study of U.S. adolescents. *Addictive Behaviors*, 35(5), 517–521.

Feinstein, B. A., Thomann, M., Coventry, R., Macapagal, K., Mustanski, B., & Newcomb, M. E. (2018). Gay and bisexual males' perspectives on parent–adolescent relationships and parenting practices related to teen sex and dating. *Archives of Sexual Behavior*, 47(6), 1825–1837.

Fisher, J. D., Fisher, W. A., Misovich, S. J., Kimble, D. L., & Malloy, T. E. (1996). Changing AIDS risk behavior: Effects of an intervention emphasizing AIDS risk reduction information, motivation, and behavioral skills in a college student population. *Health Psychology*, 15(2), 114–123.

Fisher, J. D., Fisher, W. A., Williams, S. S., & Malloy, T. E. (1994). Empirical tests of an information–motivation–behavioral skills model of AIDS-preventive behavior with gay men and heterosexual university students. *Health Psychology*, 13(3), 238–250.

Garofalo, R., Johnson, A. K., Kuhns, L. M., Cotten, C., Joseph, H., & Margolis, A. (2012). Life skills: Evaluation of a theory-driven behavioral HIV prevention intervention for young transgender women. *Journal of Urban Health*, 89(3), 419–431. doi:10.1007/s11524-011-9638-6

Garofalo, R., Mustanski, B., & Donenberg, G. (2008). Parents know and parents matter; Is it time to develop family-based HIV prevention programs for young men who have sex with men? *Journal of Adolescent Health*, 43(2), 201–204. doi:10.1016/j.jadohealth.2008.01.017

Garofalo, R., Wolf, C. R., Kessel, S., Palfrey, J., & DuRant, R. H. (1998). The association between health risk behaviors and sexual orientation among a school-based sample of adolescents. *Pediatrics*, 101, 895–902.

Greene, G. J., Fisher, K. A., Kuper, L., Andrews, R., & Mustanski, B. (2015). "Is this normal? Is this not normal? There's no set example": Sexual health intervention preferences of LGBT youth in romantic relationships. *Sexuality Research & Social Policy*, 12(1), 1–14. doi:10.1007/s13178-014-0169-2

Greene, G. J., Madkins, K., Andrews, K., Dispenza, J., & Mustanski, B. (2016). Implementation and evaluation of the Keep It Up! online HIV prevention intervention in a community-based setting. *AIDS Education and Prevention*, 28(3), 231–245. doi:10.1521/aeap.2016.28.3.231

Hatzenbuehler, M. L. (2009). How does sexual minority stigma "get under the skin"? A psychological mediation framework. *Psychological Bulletin*, 135(5), 707–730.

Hays, R. B., Rebchook, G. M., & Kegeles, S. M. (2003). The Mpowerment Project: Community-building with young gay and bisexual men to prevent HIV1. *American Journal of Community Psychology*, 31(3–4), 301–312.

Hendricks, M. L., & Testa, R. J. (2012). A conceptual framework for clinical work with transgender and gender nonconforming clients: An adaptation of the minority stress model. *Professional Psychology: Research and Practice*, 43(5), 460–467. doi:10.1037/A0029597

Hosek, S. G., Lemos, D., Hotton, A. L., Fernandez, M. I., Telander, K., Footer, D., & Bell, M. (2015). An HIV intervention tailored for Black young men who have sex with men in the House Ball Community. *Aids Care*, 27(3), 355–362. doi:10.1080/09540121.2014.963016

Jones, K. T., Gray, P., Whiteside, Y. O., Wang, T., Bost, D., Dunbar, E., . . . Johnson, W. D. (2008). Evaluation of an HIV prevention intervention adapted for Black men who have sex with men. *American Journal of Public Health, 98*(6), 1043–1050. doi:10.2105/AJPH.2007.120337

Kann, L., Olsen, E. O., McManus, T., Harris, W. A., Shanklin, S. L., Flint, K. H., . . . Zaza, S. (2016). Sexual identity, sex of sexual contacts, and health-related behaviors among students in grades 9–12—United States and selected sites, 2015. *MMWR Surveillance Summaries, 65*(9), 1–202. doi:10.15585/mmwr.ss6509a1

Karney, B. R., & Bradbury, T. N. (1995). The longitudinal course of marital quality and stability: A review of theory, methods, and research. *Psychological Bulletin, 118*(1), 3–34. doi:10.1037/0033-2909.118.1.3

Kegeles, S. M., Hays, R. B., & Coates, T. J. (1996). The Mpowerment Project: A community-level HIV prevention intervention for young gay men. *American Journal of Public Health, 86*(8), 1129–1136.

Kegeles, S. M., Hays, R. B., Pollack, L. M., & Coates, T. J. (1999). Mobilizing young gay and bisexual men for HIV prevention: A two-community study. *AIDS, 13*(13), 1753–1762.

Kelly, B. C., Parsons, J. T., & Wells, B. E. (2006). Prevalence and predictors of club drug use among club-going young adults in New York City. *Journal of Urban Health, 83*(5), 884–895. doi:10.1007/s11524-006-9057-2

Konishi, C., Saewyc, E., Homma, Y., & Poon, C. (2013). Population-level evaluation of school-based interventions to prevent problem substance use among gay, lesbian and bisexual adolescents in Canada. *Preventive Medicine, 57*(6), 929–933. doi:10.1016/j.ypmed.2013.06.031

Lazarus, R. S., & Folkman, S. (1984). *Stress, appraisal, and coping.* New York, NY: Springer.

Lelutiu-Weinberger, C., Pachankis, J. E., Gamarel, K. E., Surace, A., Golub, S. A., & Parsons, J. T. (2015). Feasibility, acceptability, and preliminary efficacy of a live-chat social media intervention to reduce HIV risk among young men who have sex with men. *AIDS and Behavior, 19*(7), 1214–1227. doi:10.1007/s10461-014-0911-z

Marshal, M. P., Friedman, M. S., Stall, R., King, K. M., Miles, J., Gold, M. A., . . . Morse, J. Q. (2008). Sexual orientation and adolescent substance use: A meta-analysis and methodological review. *Addiction, 103*(4), 546–556.

Marshal, M. P., Friedman, M. S., Stall, R., & Thompson, A. L. (2009). Individual trajectories of substance use in lesbian, gay and bisexual youth and heterosexual youth. *Addiction, 104*(6), 974–981.

Meyer, I. H. (2003). Prejudice, social stress, and mental health in lesbian, gay, and bisexual populations: Conceptual issues and research evidence. *Psychological Bulletin, 129*(5), 674–697. doi:10.1037/0033-2909.129.5.674

Muessig, K. E., Baltierra, N. B., Pike, E. C., LeGrand, S., & Hightow-Weidman, L. B. (2014). Achieving HIV risk reduction through HealthMpowerment.org, a user-driven eHealth intervention for young Black men who have sex with men and transgender women who have sex with men. *Digital Culture & Education, 6*(3), 164.

Mustanski, B., Birkett, M., Greene, G. J., Hatzenbuehler, M. L., & Newcomb, M. E. (2014). Envisioning an America without sexual orientation inequities in adolescent health. *American Journal of Public Health, 104*(2), 218–225. doi:10.2105/AJPH.2013.301625

Mustanski, B., Birkett, M., Kuhns, L. M., Latkin, C. A., & Muth, S. Q. (2015). The role of geographic and network factors in racial disparities in HIV among young men who have sex with men: An egocentric network study. *AIDS and Behavior*, *19*(6), 1037–1047. doi:10.1007/s10461-014-0955-0

Mustanski, B., Garofalo, R., Monahan, C., Gratzer, B., & Andrews, R. (2013). Feasibility, acceptability, and preliminary efficacy of an online HIV prevention program for diverse young men who have sex with men: The Keep It Up! intervention. *AIDS and Behavior*, *17*(9), 2999–3012. doi:10.1007/s10461-013-0507-z

Mustanski, B., Greene, G. J., Ryan, D., & Whitton, S. W. (2015). Feasibility, acceptability, and initial efficacy of an online sexual health promotion program for LGBT youth: The Queer Sex Ed intervention. *Journal of Sex Research*, *52*(2), 220–230. doi:10.1080/00224499.2013.867924

Mustanski, B., Newcomb, M., Du Bois, S. N., Garcia, S. C., & Grov, C. (2011). HIV in young men who have sex with men: A review of epidemiology, risk and protective factors, and interventions. *Journal of Sex Research*, *48*(2–3), 218–253. doi:10.1080/00224499.2011.558645

Mustanski, B., Parsons, J. T., Sullivan, P., Madkins, K., Rosenberg, E., & Swann, G. (2017). eHealth intervention effects on sexually transmitted infection and condomless anal sex in young men who have sex with men: A randomized controlled trial. Manuscript under review.

Mustanski, B., Swann, G., Newcomb, M. E., & Prachand, N. (2017). Effects of parental monitoring and knowledge on substance use and HIV risk behaviors among young men who have sex with men: Results from three studies. *AIDS and Behavior*, *21*(7), 2046–2058. doi:10.1007/s10461-017-1761-2

Newcomb, M. E., Birkett, M., Corliss, H. L., & Mustanski, B. (2014). Sexual orientation, gender, and racial differences in illicit drug use in a sample of US high school students. *American Journal of Public Health*, *104*(2), 304–310. doi:10.2105/AJPH.2013.301702

Newcomb, M. E., Feinstein, B. A., Matson, M., Macapagal, K., & Mustanski, B. (2018). "I have no idea what's going on out there": Parents' perspectives on promoting sexual health in lesbian, gay, bisexual and transgender adolescents. *Sexuality Research and Social Policy*, *15*(2), 111–122.

Newcomb, M. E., Heinz, A. J., & Mustanski, B. (2012). Examining risk and protective factors for alcohol use in lesbian, gay, bisexual, and transgender youth: A longitudinal multilevel analysis. *Journal of Studies on Alcohol and Drugs*, *73*(5), 783–793.

Newcomb, M. E., Macapagal, K. R., Feinstein, B. A., Bettin, E., Swann, G., & Whitton, S. W. (2017). Integrating HIV prevention and relationship education for young same-sex male couples: A pilot trial of the 2GETHER intervention. *AIDS and Behavior*, *21*(8), 2464–2478. doi:10.1007/s10461-017-1674-0

Newcomb, M. E., & Mustanski, B. (2013). Racial differences in same-race partnering and the effects of sexual partnership characteristics on HIV risk in MSM: A prospective sexual diary study. *Journal of Acquired Immune Deficiency Syndromes*, *62*(3), 329–333. doi:10.1097/QAI.0b013e31827e5f8c

Ocasio, M. A., Feaster, D. J., & Prado, G. (2016). Substance use and sexual risk behavior in sexual minority Hispanic adolescents. *Journal of Adolescent Health*, *59*(5), 599–601. doi:10.1016/j.jadohealth.2016.07.008

Pachankis, J. E. (2014). Uncovering clinical principles and techniques to address minority stress, mental health, and related health risks among gay and bisexual men. *Clinical Psychology*, *21*(4), 313–330. doi:10.1111/cpsp.12078

Pachankis, J. E., Hatzenbuehler, M. L., Rendina, H. J., Safren, S. A., & Parsons, J. T. (2015). LGB-affirmative cognitive–behavioral therapy for young adult gay and bisexual men: A randomized controlled trial of a transdiagnostic minority stress approach. *Journal of Consulting and Clinical Psychology*, *83*(5), 875–889. doi:10.1037/ccp0000037

Parsons, J. T., Lelutiu-Weinberger, C., Botsko, M., & Golub, S. A. (2014). A randomized controlled trial utilizing motivational interviewing to reduce HIV risk and drug use in young gay and bisexual men. *Journal of Consulting and Clinical Psychology*, *82*(1), 9–18. doi:10.1037/a0035311

Phillips, G., 2nd, Turner, B., Salamanca, P., Birkett, M., Hatzenbuehler, M. L., Newcomb, M. E., . . . Mustanski, B. (2017). Victimization as a mediator of alcohol use disparities between sexual minority subgroups and sexual majority youth using the 2015 National Youth Risk Behavior Survey. *Drug and Alcohol Dependence*, *178*, 355–362. doi:10.1016/j.drugalcdep.2017.05.040

Poteat, T., Scheim, A., Xavier, J., Reisner, S., & Baral, S. (2016). Global epidemiology of HIV infection and related syndemics affecting transgender people. *Journal of Acquired Immune Deficiency Syndromes*, *72*(Suppl. 3), S210–S219. doi:10.1097/QAI.0000000000001087

Prado, G., Pantin, H., Huang, S., Cordova, D., Tapia, M. I., Velazquez, M. R., . . . Estrada, Y. (2012). Effects of a family intervention in reducing HIV risk behaviors among high-risk Hispanic adolescents: A randomized controlled trial. *Archives of Pediatrics & Adolescent Medicine*, *166*(2), 127–133. doi:10.1001/archpediatrics.2011.189

Raymond, H. F., & McFarland, W. (2009). Racial mixing and HIV risk among men who have sex with men. *AIDS and Behavior*, *13*(4), 630–637. doi:10.1007/s10461-009-9574-6

Rebchook, G. M., Kegeles, S. M., Huebner, D., & Team, T. R. (2006). Translating research into practice: The dissemination and initial implementation of an evidence-based HIV prevention program. *AIDS Education and Prevention*, *18*(4 Suppl. A), 119–136. doi:10.1521/aeap.2006.18.supp.119

Reisner, S. L., Hughto, J. M., Pardee, D. J., Kuhns, L., Garofalo, R., & Mimiaga, M. J. (2016). LifeSkills for Men (LS4M): Pilot evaluation of a gender-affirmative HIV and STI prevention intervention for young adult transgender men who have sex with men. *Journal of Urban Health*, *93*(1), 189–205. doi:10.1007/s11524-015-0011-z

Rotheram-Borus, M. J., Reid, H., & Rosario, M. (1994). Factors mediating changes in sexual HIV risk behaviors among gay and bisexual male adolescents. *American Journal of Public Health*, *84*(12), 1938–1946.

Saewyc, E. M., Bearinger, L. H., Blum, R. W., & Resnick, M. D. (1999). Sexual intercourse, abuse and pregnancy among adolescent women: Does sexual orientation make a difference? *Family Planning Perspectives*, *31*, 127–132.

Saewyc, E. M., Poon, C. S., Homma, Y., & Skay, C. L. . (2008). Stigma management? The links between enacted stigma and teen pregnancy trends among gay, lesbian, and bisexual students in British Columbia. *Canada Journal of Human Sexuality*, *17*(3), 123–139.

Schwinn, T. M., Thom, B., Schinke, S. P., & Hopkins, J. (2015). Preventing drug use among sexual-minority youths: Findings from a tailored, web-based intervention. *Journal of Adolescent Health*, *56*(5), 571–573. doi:10.1016/j.jadohealth.2014.12.015

Shelley, G., Williams, W., Uhl, G., Hoyte, T., Eke, A., Wright, C., . . . Kegeles, S. M. (2017). An evaluation of Mpowerment on individual-level HIV risk behavior, testing, and psychosocial factors among young MSM of color: The monitoring and evaluation of MP (MEM) Project. *AIDS Education and Prevention*, *29*(1), 24–37. doi:10.1521/aeap.2017.29.1.24

Smith, N. G., Hart, T. A., Moody, C., Willis, A. C., Andersen, M. F., Blais, M., & Adam, B. (2016). Project PRIDE: A cognitive–behavioral group intervention to reduce HIV risk behaviors among HIV-negative young gay and bisexual men. *Cognitive and Behavioral Practice*, *23*, 398–411.

Stein, R., Shapatava, E., Williams, W., Griffin, T., Bell, K., Lyons, B., & Uhl, G. (2015). Reduced sexual risk behaviors among young men of color who have sex with men: Findings from the Community-Based Organization Behavioral Outcomes of Many Men, Many Voices (CBOP-3MV) project. *Prevention Science*, *16*(8), 1147–1158. doi:10.1007/s11121-015-0565-8

Sullivan, P. S., Salazar, L., Buchbinder, S., & Sanchez, T. H. (2009). Estimating the proportion of HIV transmissions from main sex partners among men who have sex with men in five US cities. *AIDS*, *23*(9), 1153–1162. doi:10.1097/QAD.0b013e32832baa34

Swann, G., Bettin, E., Clifford, A., Newcomb, M. E., & Mustanski, B. (2017). Trajectories of alcohol, marijuana, and illicit drug use in a diverse sample of young men who have sex with men. *Drug and Alcohol Dependence*, *178*, 231–242. doi:10.1016/j.drugalcdep.2017.05.015

Talley, A. E., Hughes, T. L., Aranda, F., Birkett, M., & Marshal, M. P. (2014). Exploring alcohol-use behaviors among heterosexual and sexual minority adolescents: Intersections with sex, age, and race/ethnicity. *American Journal of Public Health*, *104*(2), 295–303. doi:10.2105/AJPH.2013.301627

Tucker, J. S., Ellickson, P. L., & Klein, D. J. (2008). Understanding differences in substance use among bisexual and heterosexual young women. *Women's Health Issues*, *18*(5), 387–398. doi:10.1016/j.whi.2008.04.004

Wilton, L., Herbst, J. H., Coury-Doniger, P., Painter, T. M., English, G., Alvarez, M. E., . . . Carey, J. W. (2009). Efficacy of an HIV/STI prevention intervention for Black men who have sex with men: Findings from the Many Men, Many Voices (3MV) project. *AIDS and Behavior*, *13*(3), 532–544. doi:10.1007/s10461-009-9529-y

Ybarra, M. L., DuBois, L. Z., Parsons, J. T., Prescott, T. L., & Mustanski, B. (2014). Online focus groups as an HIV prevention program for gay, bisexual, and queer adolescent males. *AIDS Education and Prevention*, *26*(6), 554–564. doi:10.1521/aeap.2014.26.6.554

Ybarra, M. L., Prescott, T. L., Philips, G. L., 2nd, Bull, S. S., Parsons, J. T., & Mustanski, B. (2016). Iteratively developing an mHealth HIV prevention program for sexual minority adolescent men. *AIDS and Behavior*, *20*(6), 1157–1172. doi:10.1007/s10461-015-1146-3

Ybarra, M. L., Prescott, T. L., Phillips, G. L., 2nd, Bull, S. S., Parsons, J. T., & Mustanski, B. (2017). Pilot RCT results of an mHealth HIV prevention program for sexual minority male adolescents. *Pediatrics*, *140*, pii: e20162999 *In Press*(1). doi:10.1542/peds.2016-2999

4

Transgender Affirmative Cognitive–Behavioral Therapy

ASHLEY AUSTIN AND SHELLEY L. CRAIG ■

OVERVIEW OF EXPERIENCES AMONG TRANSGENDER INDIVIDUALS

Although a growing body of literature illustrates high rates of discrimination and victimization as well as corresponding mental and behavioral health disparities among transgender and gender diverse individuals (Budge, Adelson, & Howard, 2013; Clements-Nolle, Marx, & Katz, 2006; James et al., 2016; Reisner et al., 2016; White Hughto, Reisner, & Pachankis, 2015), there remains a paucity of transgender affirming mental health interventions (Gridley et al., 2016; Kosenko, Rintamaki, Raney, & Maness, 2013; Shipherd, Green, & Abromovitz, 2014). The advent of several popular television programs focused on transgender issues and featuring famous transgender people has contributed to burgeoning awareness about transgender identities and experiences. However, understanding of contemporary transgender experiences is neither nuanced nor comprehensive. Rather, there remains a lack of awareness about transgender-specific experiences and needs among the general public and specifically among mental health care providers (Gridley et al., 2016; Shipherd et al., 2014). The limitations to transgender-specific knowledge among care providers likely result from many factors. One is a transgender research base lacking both breadth and depth. The limited scope of research may be related to several factors, including a history of pathologizing transgender identities within medical and mental health professions (Ansara, 2010, 2012; Ansara & Hegarty, 2012), the conceptualization of gender as a binary rather than a spectrum (Riley, Wong, & Sitharthan, 2011), and a deeply rooted cisgender bias in Western society (Ansara, 2010, 2012). Public discourse as well as a majority of research have focused narrowly on the dominant narrative of transgender experience, one that centers around a binary conceptualization of gender (i.e., the existence of only two genders, male and female) and a transition from living as one gender to "the other." However, emerging evidence indicates that for many transgender people, a binary (male or female) gender identity does not fit (James et al., 2016; Saltzburg & Davis, 2010). Recent data suggest that nearly one-third of transgender individuals do not identify exclusively as male or female (James et al., 2016), instead connecting with a variety of non-binary gender identities (i.e., agender, bigender, genderqueer, genderfluid, gender neutral, and gender expansive) (Riley et al., 2011). As such, the terms *transgender* and *trans* are used to represent the multidimensional spectrum of binary and non-binary gender identities embraced by individuals in the transgender community.

Transgender-Specific Stressors and Sources of Well-Being

The best available evidence in the absence of representative population-based surveys suggests that transgender individuals experience disproportionate rates of psychological distress (Budge et al., 2013; Clements-Nolle et al., 2006) and particularly high rates of suicidality (Haas, Rodgers, & Herman, 2014; James et al., 2016; Nuttbrock et al., 2010). It is well recognized that high rates of mental health problems among members of the transgender community are related to identity-based stigma, discrimination, and trauma (Bockting, Miner, Swinburne Romine, Hamilton, & Coleman, 2013; Hendricks & Testa, 2012). Pervasive verbal, physical, and sexual abuse, as well as stigma and discrimination, are common experiences for many transgender individuals (Goldblum et al., 2012; James et al., 2016; Kosciw, Greytak, Palmer, & Boesen, 2014). In fact, discrimination rooted in transphobia and cisgender privilege begins early, with transgender individuals reporting alarming rates of verbal abuse and physical and sexual victimization in childhood (Dragowski, Halkitis, Grossman, & D'Augelli, 2011). Although schools provide the context for a staggering amount of bullying and exclusion of transgender youth (Kosciw et al., 2014), trans-specific victimization is not limited to "any particular social context as it pervades school, family, religious, and community environments" (Dragowski et al., 2011, p. 227). Many of these events are experienced as traumatic for transgender youth and adults and are associated with symptoms consistent with post-traumatic stress disorder (Burnes, Dexter, Richmond, Singh, & Cherrington, 2016; Reisner et al., 2016; Richmond, Burnes, & Carroll, 2012).

Minority stress theory, based on the notion that sexual and gender minorities encounter high levels of stress due to homophobic and transphobic social conditions, is used to explain the deleterious impact of identity-based stressors among sexual and gender minority populations (Hendricks & Testa, 2012; Meyer, 2003, 2015). The consequences of pervasive minority stress associated with stigmatization of transgender identities appear to complicate pathways to well-being and self-acceptance for transgender individuals (Bockting et al., 2013; Hendricks & Testa, 2012). In addition to contributing to elevated rates of anxiety and depression, minority stress experiences such as discrimination, victimization, and rejection from others appear to result in self-stigma, or the internalization of stigma (Mizock & Mueser, 2014; Vogel, Bitman, Hammer, & Wade, 2013). In order to fully support transgender clients in mental health settings, clinicians must have a well-developed understanding of trans-specific sources of stress and their impact on mental health outcomes.

The Impact of Living Authentically on Well-Being

Because many transgender individuals identify as non-binary (James et al., 2016; Saltzburg & Davis, 2010), there needs to be broadened understanding of what it means for a transgender person to live authentically. Transitioning in the traditional sense (e.g., medical and/or legal transitions) may not be a primary need or goal of many non-binary transgender individuals (Riley et al., 2011). Moreover, for some clients, terms such as "living authentically" or "living my true gender" may be preferable to the term "transition." A growing number of transgender individuals achieve authenticity without any medical interventions, conveying a more flexible and expansive range of gender expressions. The opportunity to live one's authentic gender (male, female, or other) has long been recognized as a critical, often life or death, need of many transgender individuals. In fact, mounting empirical research demonstrates the positive impact of social, medical, and legal aspects of transitioning on mental health and overall well-being among transgender children (Ehrensaft, 2016; Olson, Durwood, DeMeules, & McLaughlin, 2016), teens (Simons, Schrager, Clark, Belzer, & Olson, 2013; Tishelman et al., 2015), and adults (Bauer, Scheim, Pyne, Travers, & Hammond; 2015; Davis & Colton Meier, 2014; Heylens, Verroken, De Cock, T'Sjoen, & De Cuypere, 2014; Keo-Meier et al., 2015; Riggs, Ansara, & Treharne, 2015).

Emerging research suggests that transgender children and teens who experienced familial support and acceptance associated with living authentically (e.g., socially and/or medically transitioning) are more likely to experience positive mental health outcomes (Olson et al., 2016; Ryan, Russell, Huebner, Diaz, & Sanchez, 2010; Simons et al., 2013). Research with transgender adults also indicates better outcomes among those who had supportive family and/or partners (Grant et al., 2010). Connection with other members of the transgender community may contribute to transgender individuals' well-being as they strive to live authentically (Testa, Jimenez, & Rankin, 2014). Testa and colleagues found that connection with other transgender people during early stages of identity development predicted decreased psychological distress and increased comfort with one's trans identity. Social connection to the transgender community has also been associated with elevated self-esteem (Austin & Goodman, 2017) and positive mental health (Frost & Meyer, 2012; Sánchez & Vilain, 2009).

Barriers to Living Authentically

Despite burgeoning research illustrating the benefits of transitioning/living authentically (findings that come as no surprise to members of the trans community and their allies), there remain many interpersonal, social, cultural, and economic barriers to identifying openly as transgender and to accessing transition-related care (Gridley et al., 2016; James et al., 2016; Shipherd et al., 2014). As a result of persistent stigma (external and internalized), the absence of family or social support, fears for safety, and/or economic security, many transgender clients (both youth and adults) continue to experience a multitude of challenges to living authentically. These challenges often contribute to the development or exacerbation of mental health conditions (James et al., 2016; Shipherd et al., 2014). As such, it is important that clinicians providing intervention and support to transgender clients possess a comprehensive understanding of trans-specific issues and embrace a transgender affirmative approach (Austin & Craig, 2015a).

OVERVIEW OF TRANSGENDER AFFIRMATIVE COGNITIVE–BEHAVIORAL THERAPY

Transgender affirmative cognitive–behavioral therapy (TA-CBT) is an evidence-informed intervention developed to address the specific mental health needs of transgender clients. This section provides an overview of TA-CBT's tenets, the process associated with developing TA-CBT, and a brief discussion of emerging evidence supporting its efficacy with trans populations.

Affirmative approaches to clinical practice for transgender individuals have emerged in response to unethical clinical practices that aim to change, pathologize, or invalidate transgender identities and experiences (Austin & Craig, 2015a; Craig, Austin, Alessi, 2013). The potential harm associated with "reparative" or "conversion" therapy is well documented, and clearly this therapy should be rejected as a clinical option (Substance Abuse and Mental Health Services Administration, 2015). In contrast, affirmative interventions, which support and validate the identities, strengths, and experiences of transgender individuals, can promote health and well-being (Austin, Craig, & D'Souza, 2018; Craig & Austin, 2016). It is critical that clinicians adopt, and make known, an affirming clinical position, which recognizes all experiences of gender as equally healthy and valuable. Affirmative practice must acknowledge and counter the oppressive contexts of the lives of transgender individuals (Austin & Craig, 2015a; Craig et al., 2013). Unconditional positive regard for the diversity of transgender identities and expressions that is integrated throughout all interactions with the transgender individual is perhaps the most fundamental component of a transgender affirmative clinical practice. As such, clinicians must diligently engage in self-exploration regarding their own gender-related attitudes, beliefs, and biases (American Psychological Association [APA], 2015; Burnes et al., 2010). Finally, interventions attending to the specific needs of transgender individuals should be practiced with trans-specific competency and rooted in empirical evidence.

TA-CBT is a version of CBT that has been adapted to meet the unique needs of transgender clients. CBTs have demonstrated empirical support for the treatment of a variety of mental health issues, including depression, anxiety, substance abuse, trauma, and suicidality, among both adolescents and adults across multiple settings (Hofmann, Asnaani, Vonk, Sawyer, & Fang, 2012; Morley, Sitharthan, Haber, Tucker, & Sitharthan, 2014; Pachankis, Hatzenbuehler, Rendina, Safren, & Parsons, 2015); these issues disproportionately impact the transgender community. Moreover, because CBT focuses on changing maladaptive behaviors by modifying unhelpful ways of thinking, it is a particularly relevant intervention for transgender clients who may have internalized the negative attitudes, thoughts, and beliefs about transgender individuals and trans lives in contemporary society. Challenging negative thoughts about trans identities in a safe and supportive environment may help modify transphobic beliefs and resultant painful emotions (e.g., shame, fear, and despair). In addition, through its emphasis on modifying unhelpful behaviors, transgender clients who may have learned to rely on less helpful coping mechanisms, such as substance use, isolation, or self-harm, can develop more effective and healthy coping strategies to deal with stress.

Through an in-depth, ongoing intervention development process (Austin & Craig, 2015b; Austin et al., 2018; Craig & Austin, 2016), TA-CBT was adapted from a manualized depression intervention for culturally diverse young people (Rosselló & Bernal, 2007) to ensure (1) an affirming stance toward gender diversity; (2) recognition and awareness of transgender-specific sources of stress (e.g., transphobia, gender dysphoria, and systematic oppression); and (3) the delivery of CBT content within an affirming, developmentally relevant, and trauma-informed framework. Given the potentially traumatic impact of stigma and discrimination (Resiner et al., 2016), a critical component of TA-CBT is that it is grounded in an understanding of transgender-specific sources of stress. In the face of notable structural oppression and obstacles to living authentically, TA-CBT aims to create a safe, affirming, and collaborative therapeutic relationship to facilitate positive change and healthy coping. TA-CBT recognizes that as a result of pervasive exposure to transphobic attitudes and beliefs (Bockting et al., 2013; Mizock & Mueser, 2014), clients may internalize negative or stigmatizing thoughts about themselves that affect emotional and behavioral responses. Clinicians who foster a trans-affirming view of transgender identities and experiences can help their clients overcome negative self-perceptions and views of the future. From a CBT perspective, embracing a trans-affirming worldview can decrease troubling thoughts and behaviors. Moreover, transgender clients are often faced with persistent barriers to transition-related care and other options for living whole and authentic lives, leading to a host of negative emotional responses (e.g., hopelessness and despair) and subsequent maladaptive behavioral responses. One of the many benefits of TA-CBT is its flexibility, allowing for an assessment of individual trans-specific risks, needs, and sources of resilience (Austin & Craig, 2015a; Austin, Craig, & Alessi, 2017; Austin et al., 2018).

Given the exacerbated mental health risks among transgender clients, it is critical that they have access to interventions representative of best practices in the field. TA-CBT was intentionally developed to meet the specific needs of the transgender community while retaining the key components of CBT, an intervention with extant evidence supporting its transdiagnostic efficacy (Pachankis et al., 2015; Weiss, 2014). Research on TA-CBT is in its infancy; however, preliminary findings from AFFIRM, an open pilot feasibility and efficacy study of TA-CBT, point to its utility for improving coping and reducing depression and sexual health risk (Austin et al., 2018; Craig & Austin, 2016) among sexual and gender minority young people. Findings from this project indicate high acceptability and satisfaction ratings among participants (Austin et al., 2018; Craig & Austin, 2016). Currently, a study is underway that is examining the feasibility and preliminary efficacy of TA-CBT for addressing mental and behavioral health risk and coping skills among a sample of transgender sex workers. Results from this research are anticipated to contribute to emerging support for TA-CBT as an evidence-based intervention addressing the specific needs of transgender clients.

CLINICAL APPLICATION OF TRANSGENDER AFFIRMATIVE COGNITIVE–BEHAVIORAL THERAPY

The following discussion focuses on considerations associated with applications of the TA-CBT model. Clinical examples are utilized to elucidate affirmative delivery of several important components of TA-CBT: transgender affirmative case conceptualization, psychoeducation, and the development of coping skills to promote identity-affirming changes.

Transgender Affirmative Case Formulation

Case formulation refers to collecting client data and developing working hypotheses to comprehensively explain presenting issues and underlying mechanisms contributing to the development and maintenance of presenting issues within relevant sociocultural contexts (Lee & Toth, 2016; Persons & Lisa, 2015). Affirmative case formulation is a collaborative, client-centered, iterative process aimed at developing an integrated assessment to guide treatment. The case formulation is meant to be responsive, flexible, and tailor-made to the evolving goals and unique needs of each transgender client (Henderson & Martin, 2014; Lee & Toth, 2016). TA-CBT explores and attempts to understand the development and maintenance of maladaptive thoughts, behaviors, and emotional reactions through the lenses of minority stress theory and transgender affirmative clinical practice. As clinicians utilize case formulations to describe and propose relationships among the psychological mechanisms and contextual factors that are causing and maintaining a client's presenting problems (Persons & Lisa, 2015), it is critical that they also affirmatively explore client experiences with attention to the transphobia and cisgender privilege that pervades social, cultural, political, and interpersonal contexts in contemporary society. Importantly, based on burgeoning research supporting the relevance of transdiagnostic approaches to intervention, particularly for sexual and gender minority clients (Pachankis, 2015; Pachankis et al., 2015; Weiss, 2014), affirmative case formulation avoids a diagnosis-driven approach, instead engaging in an exploration of transdiagnostic factors common among transgender clients with shared stress-related psychosocial and contextual risks (e.g., history of victimization and identity-based stressors resulting in anxiety, depression, and/or suicidality). The 4P model for case formulation, centered around an exploration of preconditions, precipitating factors, perpetuating factors, and protective factors, represents a particularly good fit with an affirmative approach to case formulation. A primary focus on exploring factors associated with the client's internal state (e.g., persistent negative thinking) and the client's environment (e.g., hostile work environment and non-affirming family) that perpetuate the client's presenting issues is fundamental to developing an affirmative case formulation. Like in many biopsychosocial models of case formulation, an in-depth exploration of client strengths and sources of resilience is an explicit component of the 4P model. Critical to TA-CBT is an emphasis on mobilizing client resilience, which begins during the initial phase of case conceptualization and extends throughout the course of treatment. Table 4.1 provides an example of employing the 4P model in TA-CBT.

Integrated Approach to Psychoeducation

Psychoeducation is an integral component of TA-CBT. In addition to helping clients understand the underlying tenets of CBT (e.g., interconnection among thoughts, emotions, and behaviors), TA psychoeducation may be necessary to help clients identify trans-specific minority stressors, recognize the link between external stigma (structural and interpersonal transphobia) and self-stigma (internalized transphobia), understand the potentially traumatic impact of trans-specific stressors, and acknowledge trans-specific sources of resilience and their positive impact on well-being (e.g., connectedness to trans community, achieving mind–body congruence, and living authentically). Although many transgender clients enter therapy with a deep understanding of their own identities, their goals and opportunities for living authentically, and the existing resources in the community to facilitate this process, some transgender clients know very little about the range of transgender identities (e.g., non-binary and binary) or the various options and processes associated with living authentically/transitioning. These clients may benefit from psychoeducation devoted to these issues; only then are they equipped with the requisite knowledge to fully engage with the clinician in the collaborative process of therapeutic goal setting and intervention planning. The following clinical example illustrates how TA psychoeducation helps a 43-year-old gay transman, "Dylan," recognize the role of minority stress in his life and normalizes the effects of this stress on psychosocial functioning:

Table 4.1. TRANS AFFIRMATIVE CASE FORMULATION USING THE 4P MODEL

4P Model Components	General Areas of Exploration	Examples of Trans Affirmative-Specific Areas of Exploration
Preconditions	Why is this person vulnerable to presenting problems/issues?	The role of early transphobic messages on current life stressors Experiences of discrimination, victimization, and violence
Precipitating factors	Why now? Why is this client having symptoms now? *and/or* Why is this client presenting to the clinician for treatment now?	Current trans-specific needs related to understanding gender identity, coming out, and/or transitioning/living authentically Explore current life stressors with attention to the potential role of transphobia (e.g., homelessness, job loss, and isolation) Mental health issues associated with identity-based stressors
Perpetuating factors	What factors continue to contribute to the existence and maintenance of the client's struggles?	Potential barriers to living authentically/transitioning Internalized transphobia
Protective factors	What factors support client well-being?	Gender identity pride Transgender affirming social support systems Hopes and dreams for the future

DYLAN: I guess I am more sensitive to criticism than most people. I don't understand why, but it really affects me—causes me a lot of anxiety and kind of hurls me into a spiral of self-doubt and self-hate—I feel totally rejected, even when I don't actually care about the person criticizing me—it's honestly horrible.

CLINICIAN: So this is a perfect time to consider how early transphobic messages may continue to have an impact. You shared experiences of being harassed and called names by bullies in middle school, as well as being relentlessly lectured by your grandparents about the sins and perils of acting like a boy. What we know is that often these early messages are internalized and manifest in negative self-perceptions and feelings, such as shame or worthlessness. As a result, when you experience criticism, it likely triggers negative automatic thoughts connected to feelings of shame. Does this make sense to you at all?

DYLAN: It actually does, because I remember coming home from my grandparents' house and feeling like a complete failure, just wanting to hide in my room listening to music and talking to no one. When I have an issue at work with my manager or a customer, I feel the same way. Last month after I had an issue at work, I called in sick and just laid in bed and watched TV for two days.

CLINICIAN: So, when you consider your current reactions to criticism within the context of your early life, perhaps you can recognize that you are having really normal emotional reactions to a lifetime of challenging and often non-affirming circumstances. What we can work on together are developing strategies to modify some of these negative internalizations and to cope more effectively with criticism.

Developing Coping Skills to Promote Transgender Affirming Change

As cognitive theory holds that problems develop and are maintained because of maladaptive or unhelpful cognitions that subsequently impact emotions and behaviors, a core feature of CBT approaches is an emphasis on exploring and modifying negative patterns of thinking (Beck, 2011). Transphobia pervades many interpersonal, social, political, cultural, and religious contexts (White Hughto et al., 2015). As such, children and adults are often shamed for being transgender or gender nonconforming and quickly learn to suppress, reject, or feel great ambivalence about their transgender identity (Austin, 2016; Wallace & Russell, 2013). These early experiences can be traumatic and contribute to core beliefs that one is unlovable or worthless. Core beliefs are conceptualized as a set of deeply embedded ideas about oneself, others, the world, and the future that are regarded as absolute truths (Beck, 2011). The following sections review two primary targets of the TA-CBT intervention: modifying core beliefs that may be rooted in transphobia and promoting resilience.

IDENTIFYING AND MODIFYING NEGATIVE CORE BELIEFS
Important foci of TA-CBT include exploring the existence of self-stigmatizing thoughts and core beliefs that may be rooted in transphobia, as well as examining the impact of these self-stigmatizing thoughts and beliefs on feelings, behaviors, and relationships. Although core beliefs drive feelings and behaviors, they are often hidden from view and difficult to recognize. Exercises that elucidate these beliefs are often important. By exploring situations or thoughts using specific probative questions such as "What does that mean about you?" "If that were true, what is so bad about it?" "What is the worst part about . . . ?" or "How is that a problem for you?" clients can develop insight and awareness about the deeply held beliefs guiding their feelings and behaviors. This technique is referred to as the downward arrow method (Burns, 1989) and is illustrated in the following exchange between "Chloe," a 27-year-old transfeminine client, and her clinician:

CLINICIAN: When Oscar [cisgender man she is dating] didn't call yesterday what went through your mind?

CHLOE: That he is over me.

CLINICIAN: Ok, and what does that mean?

CHLOE: That he found someone else and is done with me.

CLINICIAN: And if that were true, what is so bad about it?

CHLOE: Well, that I was really starting to like him, but no big surprise, I should've seen it coming.

CLINICIAN: What does it mean that you "should've seen it coming"?

CHLOE: Well, like why would he pick me when he can have a cis girl?

CLINICIAN: Ok, if that were so, what's the worst part about it?

CHLOE: That everyone would rather have a cis girl than a trans girl.

CLINICIAN: And if that were true, what does that mean for you?

CHLOE: That no one will actually ever love me, I will always be alone.

This example illustrates the way in which the downward arrow can uncover existing core beliefs that may have their roots in transphobic messages. In this case, the client had internalized the message that "because I am trans, I am less worthy than cisgender people, and therefore less lovable and desirable." Identifying this underlying belief provides a target of intervention in TA-CBT. The client and clinician can work together to challenge these erroneous beliefs and to replace them with more accurate and affirming perceptions about self, others, and the future. Useful activities for doing so revolve around cognitive restructuring, a strategy aimed at identifying inaccurate and unhelpful thoughts and replacing them with alternative thoughts that are more realistic, affirming, and helpful (Beck, 2011). For instance, in TA-CBT, the A-B-C-D method can be particularly useful for recognizing the negative emotional consequences of negative thoughts, as well as for developing realistic counterpoints to pessimistic and/or pathologizing thoughts (Table 4.2).

PROMOTING RESILIENCE

That transgender individuals continue to face countless barriers to well-being is undisputed (James et al., 2016; White Hughto et al., 2015). Aside from disparate risks for marginalization, victimization, and violence across the lifespan, transgender clients are four times as likely to live in poverty and twice as likely to be unemployed compared to their cisgender counterparts (Center for American Progress & Movement Advancement Project, 2015). In addition, for transgender clients seeking medical transitions, gaps in transgender-specific knowledge and competence among mental health and health care providers represent significant obstacles to well-being (Gridley et al., 2016; Shipherd et al., 2014) and often cause great distress. Consequently, a particularly important feature of TA-CBT is its emphasis on fostering internal and external sources of resilience among clients. Areas of focus include (1) developing active coping skills, (2) enhancing agency and self-efficacy, (3) strengthening community connection, and (4) fostering

Table 4.2. EXAMPLE OF THE A-B-C-D METHOD: "ALEX," A 19-YEAR-OLD CLIENT WHO
IDENTIFIES AS GENDERQUEER

A. *Activating event* (What happened?) "I was recently mistreated (gawked at, whispered about, and snickered at) while trying to order and eat lunch on campus."	B. *Belief* (Your thoughts and beliefs about what happened and what you told yourself about what happened that affected your reaction) "No one can be happy if they are genderqueer." "I will never fit in anywhere." "I won't be able to handle the discrimination and stigma associated with being genderqueer."
C. *Consequence* (How do you feel and/or how did you react?) "I feel hopeless and worried." "I become self-disparaging." "I isolate myself from friends and avoid going out of my dorm."	D. *Debate or dispute the belief* (Alternate thoughts that could help you react in a healthier way) "There are people who are genderqueer who are as happy as people who are cisgender." "Discrimination against genderqueer people happens, but it won't ruin each minute of my life." "I am a determined person, with many strengths who does not have to conform to the gender binary to be successful, happy, or accepted." "Instead of wasting energy doubting myself and feeling anxiety, I can use my energy to figure out the best way to live an authentic life."

self-compassion and hope. The following case narrative illustrates the application of specific evidence-based strategies, including developing coping and action plans, fostering social connection, and cultivating self-compassion (Austin & Goodman, 2017; Barr, Budge, & Adelson, 2016; Gutnick et al., 2014; Hoffman, Grossman, & Hinton, 2011; Neff & Germer, 2013; Testa et al., 2014).

CASE EXAMPLE

Jaqui, a 24-year-old transgender woman of Hispanic descent, entered therapy because she was experiencing symptoms of anxiety and depression in response to multiple life stressors. Jaqui currently lives in Miami, Florida, but was born and raised in a lower middle-class home in New Jersey. Jaqui moved to Miami at the age of 22 years after being kicked out of her family home and financially cut off by her father when she disclosed to the family that she was transgender. Jaqui is currently working as a line cook in a restaurant. She left her position as a server because she had a traumatic experience with a customer who was harassing and ridiculing her. Jaqui makes much less money now but feels incredibly fearful and anxious about the possibility of being stared at and ridiculed by transphobic customers. For Jaqui, living authentically as a woman includes changing her name legally on all of her documentation, accessing hormones legitimately through her doctor, having laser hair removal for the hair on her face and body, and having bottom surgery (gender confirming surgery). At this point, Jaqui is comfortable with the breasts she grew as a result of her hormone therapy and is not interested in top surgery (breast augmentation). Jaqui shares her frustration and despair related to the many transition-related barriers she is experiencing. After a difficult experience with an endocrinologist when she first moved to Miami that included "being taken" for $600 and never receiving her prescription for hormones, Jaqui has been buying her hormones on the street. Because they are expensive, she has not been able to take them consistently, particularly when she was unemployed. She will be eligible for health insurance at her current job after 3 months, but the health plan will not cover bottom surgery. Moreover, Jaqui is very distraught by the fact that her name has not been legally changed, and she has not yet saved the money for this process. The absence of correct and affirming legal documents is frightening, frustrating, and demeaning for her. Finally, Jaqui has identified laser hair removal as one of her primary goals, yet it is incredibly expensive, not covered by insurance, and a very lengthy process. Her facial hair is a significant source of stress and social anxiety for Jaqui, often contributing to feelings that she is unattractive and leading her to avoid, or drink heavily in, social situations. Because many of Jaqui's difficult circumstances will not change immediately, Jaqui has identified several needs, including "learning how to deal with all this" and "feeling better about myself."

TRANSGENDER AFFIRMING COPING AND ACTION PLANS

Several TA-CBT strategies can be used to support clients and help them cope with challenging situations. For instance, evidence indicates that helping clients create a clear, specific, time-limited, and feasible action plan associated with a personal goal promotes active coping and self-efficacy (Gutnick et al., 2014; Kwasnicka, Presseau, White, & Sniehotta, 2013). To develop an effective coping and action plan, the clinician should support the client's efforts to identify and prioritize an immediate goal, identify the significance of the goal, identify resources and next steps, and rate their current level of confidence (i.e., self-efficacy) associated with achieving the goal. The plan includes proactive coping components aimed at anticipating and troubleshooting barriers to achieving the client's goal (i.e., "What strategies can I use to address barriers I encounter?"). Setting and achieving small, self-determined goals helps clients regain a sense of ownership and authorship of their own lives. Enhanced self-efficacy and personal agency are particularly important for trans clients who may feel, generally for good reason, that many aspects of their lives are not in their immediate control. Table 4.3 provides an example of Jaqui's coping and action plan for finding a transgender affirming health care provider, an important step in her larger transition plan.

FOSTERING PERSONAL AGENCY AND TRANSGENDER-SPECIFIC SUPPORT

Because connections with other transgender people can foster well-being (Austin & Goodman, 2017; Barr et al., 2016; Testa et al., 2014), an integral component of

Table 4.3. EXAMPLE OF AN AFFIRMING COPING AND ACTION PLAN

What is my goal?	Find a transgender affirmative health care provider to prescribe and monitor my hormone therapy.
Why is this important to me?	My health is important to me, I want to be consistent with my hormones, and I want a doctor who values trans people.
When do I want to achieve this?	By next month.
Who can help me achieve this?	People who go to the trans support group, and my therapist.
What resources do I need?	My insurance information, my gender letter, and the internet.
How will I know if it has been achieved?	I will be taking hormones and I will feel comfortable being honest with my doctor.
What barriers might interfere with my goal?	If I lose my job and my insurance and money. If the doctor does not value me and my identity.
What strategies can I use to address these barriers?	I will look for local, regional, or national agencies that support trans health. I will use my contacts and the internet to find a new doctor. I will see my therapist to process these setbacks.
What are my best first steps?	Look online to see if I can find any potential providers, and send an email to my trans support group asking for names of trans affirming providers.
How confident am I that I can achieve this goal? (Scale of 1–10)	My confidence related to this goal is an 8. I think I have the internal and external resources to make it happen.

cultivating resilience in TA-CBT revolves around building or strengthening links with the transgender community. In TA-CBT, the focus is on identifying specific transgender affirming activities and sources of support that can be integrated into clients' lives. Specifically, TA-CBT clinicians help their clients generate realistic and meaningful lists of trans-affirming people, places, and activities. An enhanced sense of connection to the transgender community may also foster a greater connection to and appreciation of one's own trans identity (Raj, 2007; Testa et al., 2014). For some, an increased sense of belonging to the transgender community may be particularly important to positive mental health (Bariola et al., 2015; Barr et al., 2016). Table 4.4 provides an example of Jaqui's "affirming activities list," which identifies a range of support-building opportunities.

There are several considerations for clinicians helping clients enhance their connection to the transgender community. Because knowledge of transgender-specific

Table 4.4. Example of Affirming Activities List

Transgender Affirming Activity	Examples
Schedule time with affirming people.	• Go out at least once a week after work, with best friend (a gay, cis-male who has always been very supportive of her identity and her transition).
Schedule identity-affirming activities.	• Attend the local transgender support group at least once a month and try to build relationships that persist outside of the group. • Spend time reading trans-specific blogs that focus on successful transition stories. • Plan ahead to attend the local transgender conference in March.
Engage in trans-specific community-building activities.	• Volunteer to be on the planning committee of one of the local trans or LGBT events for the coming year.

resources and sources of support will vary widely across clients, it is important that TA-CBT clinicians have the requisite knowledge of local, regional, national, and online resources and sources of support. Clinicians must be attentive to potential barriers to accessing transgender-specific support. In addition to exploring emotional barriers (e.g., anxiety about meeting new people), it is important to explore economic and logistical barriers such as lack of consistent transportation to attend events or groups. Troubleshooting these challenges, and helping the client develop a feasible plan for gradually increasing transgender-specific involvement at a pace that feels safe and comfortable, is often an important component of fostering affirmative connections.

Cultivating Self-Compassion

In addition to goal-directed strategies, TA-CBT aims to cultivate self-compassion. Self-compassion has been defined by Neff (2003) as consisting of the following dimensions: (1) self-kindness, which entails being warm toward oneself when encountering pain and personal shortcomings rather than ignoring them or hurting oneself with self-criticism; (2) common humanity, which involves recognizing that suffering and personal failure are part of the shared human experience; and (3) taking a mindful, balanced approach to negative emotions so that feelings are neither exaggerated nor denied. Because transgender individuals continue to experience a general lack of compassion from society at large and may have internalized many transphobic messages, the ability to learn and practice self-compassion in conjunction with other CBT strategies may be particularly important. Cultivating self-compassion within the context of TA-CBT can be accomplished using a variety of strategies. For instance, the clinician may work with the client to identify meaningful and relevant self-affirming statements (e.g.,

"My life has meaning and purpose, even if I struggle to realize it at times," "I accept myself for who I am," and "I am a special person with a unique perspective") that can be practiced on a daily basis or in response to emotionally distressing situations. In addition, the integration of mindfulness strategies such as loving-kindness and compassion meditation may be useful (Hoffman et al., 2011). Emerging research with cisgender samples suggests that these strategies can enhance positive affect, support efforts to reduce stress and anxiety, and improve interpersonal processes and social connectedness (Hoffman et al., 2011). Interested clients can be introduced to specific self-compassion scripts (Neff, 2003) within the clinical sessions and then practice them for homework. Pilot data suggest that self-compassion interventions are associated with increases in well-being, including greater life satisfaction and decreased anxiety, depression, and stress (Neff & Germer, 2013), among cisgender adults. Self-compassion strategies may hold particular promise for transgender clients who experience deep feelings of shame and worthlessness associated with the internalization of transphobic stigma. Table 4.5 provides an example of self-compassion exercises based on the work of Neff (2003), Germer (2009), and Germer and Neff (2013) that are used with transgender clients in TA-CBT.

EMERGING TRENDS AND FUTURE DIRECTIONS

Two trends are particularly significant for clinicians: increasing recognition of the diversity within the trans community (James et al., 2016) and the burgeoning recognition of and responsiveness to gender diverse experiences in early and middle childhood (Ehrensaft, 2016). The increased visibility and attention given to transgender individuals and experiences in the media, popular culture, and politics, coupled with the role of the information and communication technologies in facilitating connection to trans-specific knowledge, resources, and support, have greatly contributed to the evolving landscape of transgender experiences in contemporary society. Results from the 2015 United States Transgender Survey, the largest study of transgender participants in the United States ($N = 27,715$), indicated that more than one-third (36%) of participants identified as non-binary (James et al., 2016). Of these participants, 35% were unsure whether they would ever want to live full-time in a gender that is different from the one assigned to them at birth, and 7% were clear that they did not. These findings, along with the broadening range of trans perspectives and experiences being shared in the media, literature, and research, contribute to an expanding conceptualization of gender identity inclusive of the full spectrum of non-binary and/or fluid experiences of gender. Living authentically and transitioning may look very different for non-binary individuals (Riley et al., 2011) than it does for binary transgender individuals; consequently, clinicians need to be prepared to practice competently and affirmatively with a broad spectrum of transgender clients. In order to engage in affirming and relevant clinical case conceptualization and intervention, clinicians must recognize the heterogeneity within the trans community,

Table 4.5. Self-Compassion Exercise

Self-Compassion Tenet	Self-Compassion Behavior	Self-Compassion Statements
Practicing kindness to self	When feeling emotional distress, clients can ask, "What do I need to hear right now to express kindness to myself?" Clients can be taught to offer words of kindness and compassion to themselves— slowly and affectionately.	May I be safe. May I accept myself. May I give myself the compassion that I need. May I forgive myself. May I be strong. May I be patient. May I be peaceful. May I maintain hope.
Connecting to common humanity	Clients can be taught to engage in a soothing touch. For some, placing their hands over their heart to feel the warmth on their chests will be comfortable. For others, this may lead to feelings of dysphoria. Clients should be encouraged to find a place on the body that feels comfortable to them.	Suffering is a part of life. Other people feel this way. I'm not alone. We all struggle in our lives.
Practicing mindfulness	Clients can be taught to observe negative thoughts and emotions with openness and clarity. Clients can learn to observe thoughts and feelings as they are, without trying to suppress them or being overtaken by negative reactivity.	This is a moment of suffering. This hurts. Ouch! This is stress. I am in pain.

be attuned to the relevance of dimensions of diversity for clinical practice needs among specific clients, and be prepared to meet their clinical needs with compassion and the requisite clinical knowledge (Austin & Goodman, 2018; Burnes et al., 2010).

The second societal trend that has implications for trans affirmative practice is the growing awareness of trans experiences and gender diversity among young children. Clinicians whose emphasis has been on supporting transgender teens and adults may need to broaden their focus to include transgender children and their caregivers. Children and families appear to be seeking transgender-specific consultation and intervention from qualified mental health care providers in historically high numbers (Wells, 2016), and it is widely anticipated that these numbers will continue to grow. To date, an overwhelming majority of the re-search and clinical practice for transgender clients has focused on trans adults, with some attention devoted to transgender adolescents. Because awareness of gender identity (e.g., male, female, and other) occurs relatively young, with children typically identifying themselves as boys or girls or other by age 3 years (American Pediatric Association, 2015), transgender children are increasingly being granted the opportunity to live authentically at increasingly younger ages (Olson et al., 2016). In some cases, this includes social transitions (Olson et al., 2016) for children of binary trans experience, whereas for other children this consists of a range of gender-creative expressions of self (Ehrensaft, 2016). As transgender children have gender experiences that may evolve over time, cor-responding needs for clinical support will also vary (Ehrensaft, 2016; Steensma, McGuire, Kreukels, Beekman, & Cohen-Kettenis, 2013). Clinical approaches that affirm the spectrum of gender diversity during childhood, create safe and supportive settings, and offer evidence-based interventions aimed at addressing mental health needs are critical. As such, TA-CBT represents a promising ap-proach for work with transgender and gender diverse children. The overarching framework of TA-CBT is both relevant and important to affirming clinical practice with transgender children and their families, and CBT is an efficacious approach for reducing mental health concerns among children (Hoffman et al., 2012). The specific CBT strategies, exercises, and protocols may require developmentally specific modification. Moreover, affirmative clinicians whose experience has pre-dominantly centered around the clinical needs of teens and adults may need to enhance knowledge related to the developmental components of navigating a trans identity during childhood. Likewise, clinicians with demonstrated exper-tise in working predominantly with cisgender children will likely need to de-velop their transgender affirmative expertise to meet the needs of the youngest generation of transgender individuals (Austin, 2017).

CONCLUSION

To a greater extent than ever before, transgender individuals across the lifespan are taking steps to live authentically (Lyons, 2016; Mosher & Gould, 2017; Wells, 2016). The affirmation of their authentic identities is recognized as paramount to well-being among trans individuals (APA, 2015; Bauer et al., 2015). Clinicians must be prepared to help transgender individuals manage minority stress and cope with the challenges of living in a society dominated by transphobic views and cisgender bias (Austin & Craig, 2015a; Bockting et al., 2013; White Hughto et al., 2015). Based on emerging research (Austin et al., 2018; Craig & Austin, 2016), TA-CBT represents a valuable clinical approach for working effectively with transgender clients. To meet the unique needs of diverse clients, TA-CBT offers individualized and flexible application of cognitive–behavioral strategies. Through the combination of empirically supported intervention strategies and an affirmative understanding of transgender experiences, TA-CBT facilitates the development of adaptive coping skills and the reduction of distress within a transgender affirming clinical context. TA-CBT validates the adversities experienced by transgender populations in contemporary society while enhancing the support, resources, and skills necessary to foster resilience and overall well-being.

REFERENCES

American Pediatric Association. (2015). Gender identity development in children. Section on Lesbian, Gay, Bisexual, Transgender, Health and Wellness. Retrieved from https://www.healthychildren.org/English/ages-stages/gradeschool/Pages/Gender-Identity-and-Gender-Confusion-In-Children.aspx

American Psychological Association. (2015). Guidelines for psychological practice with transgender and gender nonconforming people. *American Psychologist, 70* (9), 832–864. doi:10.1037/a0039906

Ansara, Y. G. (2010). Beyond cisgenderism: Counselling people with non-assigned gender identities. In L. Moon (Ed.), *Counselling ideologies: Queer challenges to heteronormativity* (pp. 167–200). Aldershot, UK: Ashgate.

Ansara, Y. G. (2012). Cisgenderism in medical settings: How collaborative partnerships can challenge structural violence. In I. Rivers & R. Ward (Eds.), *Out of the ordinary: LGBT lives* (pp. 102–122). Cambridge, UK: Cambridge Scholars Publishing.

Ansara, Y. G., & Hegarty, P. (2012). Cisgenderism in psychology: Pathologizing and misgendering children from 1999 to 2008. *Psychology & Sexuality, 3*, 137–160. doi:10.1080/19419899.2011.576696

Austin, A. (2016). "There I am": A grounded theory study of young adults navigating a transgender or gender nonconforming identity within a context of oppression and invisibility. *Sex Roles, 75*(5–6), 215–230.

Austin, A. (2018). Transgender and gender diverse children: Considerations for affirmative social work practice. *Child & Adolescent Social Work Journal, 35*(1), 73–84. doi:10.1007/s10560-017-0507-3

Austin, A., & Craig, S. L. (2015a). Transgender affirmative cognitive behavioral therapy: Clinical considerations and applications. *Professional Psychology: Research and Practice, 46*(1), 21–29.

Austin, A., & Craig, S. L. (2015b). Adapting empirically supported interventions for sexual and gender minority youth: A stakeholder driven model. *Journal of Evidence Informed Social Work, 12*(6), 567–578.

Austin, A., Craig, S. L., & Alessi, E. J. (2017). Affirmative cognitive behavioral therapy with transgender and gender nonconforming adults. Special Issue: Clinical Issues and Affirmative Treatment with Transgender Clients, *Psychiatric Clinics of North America, 40*, 141–156.

Austin, A., Craig, S. L., & D'Souza, S. A. (2018). An AFFIRMative cognitive behavioral intervention for transgender youth: Preliminary effectiveness. *Professional Psychology: Research and Practice, 49*(1), 1–8.

Austin, A., & Goodman, R. (2017). The impact of social connectedness and internalized transphobic stigma on self-esteem among transgender and gender non-conforming adults. *Journal of Homosexuality, 64*(6), 825–841. doi:10.1080/00918369.2016.1236587

Austin, A., & Goodman, R. (2018). Perceptions of transition-related health and mental health services among transgender adults. *Journal of Gay & Lesbian Social Services, 30*(1), 17–32.

Bariola, E., Lyons, A., Leonard, W., Pitts, M., Badcock, P., & Couch, M. (2015). Demographic and psychosocial factors associated with psychological distress and resilience among transgender individuals. *American Journal of Public Health, 105*(10), 2108–2116.

Barr, S. M., Budge, S. L., & Adelson, J. L. (2016). Transgender community belongingness as a mediator between strength of transgender identity and well-being. *Journal of Counseling Psychology, 63*(1), 87.

Bauer, G. R., Scheim, A. I., Pyne, J., Travers, R., & Hammond, R. (2015). Intervenable factors associated with suicide risk in transgender persons: A respondent driven sampling study in Ontario, Canada. *BMC Public Health, 15*(1), 509–519.

Beck, J. S. (2011). *Cognitive behavior therapy: Basics and beyond.* New York, NY: Guilford.

Bockting, W. O., Miner, M. H., Swinburne Romine, R. E., Hamilton, A., & Coleman, E. (2013). Stigma, mental health, and resilience in an online sample of the US transgender population. *American Journal of Public Health, 103*(5), 943–951.

Budge, S. L., Adelson, J. L., & Howard, K. A. (2013). Anxiety and depression in transgender individuals: The roles of transition status, loss, social support, and coping. *Journal of Consulting and Clinical Psychology, 81*, 545–557.

Burnes, T. R., Dexter, M. M., Richmond, K., Singh, A. A., & Cherrington, A. (2016). The experiences of transgender survivors of trauma who undergo social and medical transition. *Traumatology, 22*(1), 75–84.

Burnes, T. R., Singh, A. A., Harper, A. J., Harper, B., Maxon-Kann, W., Pickering, D. L., & Hosea, J. (2010). American Counseling Association: Competencies for counseling with transgender clients. *Journal of LGBT Issues in Counseling, 4*(3–4), 135–159.

Burns, D. D. (1989). *The feeling good handbook.* New York, NY: Morrow.

Center for American Progress & Movement Advancement Project. (2015). *Paying an unfair price: The financial penalty for being transgender in America.* Retrieved from http://www.lgbtmap.org/file/paying-an-unfair-price-transgender.pdf

Clements-Nolle, K., Marx, R., & Katz, M. (2006). Attempted suicide among transgender persons: The influence of gender-based discrimination and victimization. *Journal of Homosexuality, 51*, 53–69.

Craig, S. L., & Austin, A. (2016). The AFFIRM Open Pilot Feasibility Study: A brief affirmative cognitive behavioral coping skills group intervention for sexual and gender minority youth. *Child and Youth Services Review, 64*, 136–144. doi:10.1016/j.childyouth.2016.02.022

Craig, S. L., Austin, A., & Alessi, E. (2013). Gay affirmative cognitive behavioral therapy for sexual minority youth: A clinical adaptation. *Clinical Social Work Journal, 41*(3), 258–266.

Davis, S. A., & Colton Meier, S. (2014). Effects of testosterone treatment and chest reconstruction surgery on mental health and sexuality in female-to-male transgender people. *International Journal of Sexual Health, 26*(2), 113–128.

Dragowski, E. A., Halkitis, P. N., Grossman, A. H., & D'Augelli, A. R. (2011). Sexual orientation victimization and posttraumatic stress symptoms among lesbian, gay, and bisexual youth. *Journal of Gay & Lesbian Social Services, 23*(2), 226–249.

Ehrensaft, D. (2016). *The gender creative child: Pathways for nurturing and supporting children who live outside gender boxes.* New York, NY: The Experiment.

Frost, D. M., & Meyer, I. H. (2012). Measuring community connectedness among diverse sexual minority populations. *Journal of Sex Research, 49*(1), 36–49.

Germer, C. K. (2009). *The mindful path to self-compassion: Freeing yourself from destructive thoughts and emotions.* New York, NY: Guilford.

Germer, C. K., & Neff, K. D. (2013). Self-compassion in clinical practice. *Journal of Clinical Psychology, 69*(8), 856–867.

Goldblum, P., Testa, R. J., Pflum, S., Hendricks, M. L., Bradford, J., & Bongar, B. (2012). The relationship between gender-based victimization and suicide attempts in transgender people. *Professional Psychology: Research and Practice, 43*(5), 468–475.

Grant, J. M., Mattet, L. A., Tanis, J., Harrison, J., Herman, J. L., & Keisling, M. (2010). Injustice at every turn: A report of the National Transgender Discrimination Survey. Retrieved from http://endtransdiscrimination.org/report.html

Gridley, S. J., Crouch, J. M., Evans, Y., Eng, W., Antoon, E., Lyapustina, M., . . . Breland, D. J. (2016). Youth and caregiver perspectives on barriers to gender-affirming health care for transgender youth. *Journal of Adolescent Health, 59*(3), 254–261.

Gutnick, D., Reims, K., Davis, C., Gainforth, H., Jay, M., & Cole, S. (2014). Brief action planning to facilitate behavior change and support patient self-management. *Journal of Clinical Outcomes Management, 21*(1), 18–29.

Haas, A. P., Rodgers, P. L., & Herman, J. L. (2014). *Suicide attempts among transgender and gender non-conforming adults: Finding of the National Transgender Discrimination Survey.* Los Angeles, CA: American Foundation for Suicide Prevention and the Williams Institute. Retrieved from http://williamsinstitute.law.ucla.edu/wp-content/uploads/AFSP-Williams-Suicide-Report-Final.pdf

Henderson, S. W., & Martin, A. (2014). *Case formulation and integration of information in child and adolescent mental health* (IACAPAP e-Textbook of Child and Adolescent Mental Health). Geneva, Switzerland: International Association for Child and Adolescent Psychiatry and Allied Professions.

Hendricks, M. L. & Testa, R. J. (2012). A conceptual framework for clinical work with transgender and gender nonconforming clients: An adaptation of the minority stress model. *Professional Psychology: Research and Practice, 43*(5), 460–467.

Heylens, G., Verroken, C., De Cock, S., T'Sjoen, G., & De Cuypere, G. (2014). Effects of different steps in gender reassignment therapy on psychopathology: A prospective study of persons with a gender identity disorder. *Journal of Sexual Medicine, 11*(1), 119–126.

Hofmann, S. G., Grossman, P., & Hinton, D. E. (2011). Loving-kindness and compassion meditation: Potential for psychological interventions. *Clinical Psychology Review, 31*, 1126–1132.

Hofmann, S. G., Asnaani, A., Vonk, I. J., Sawyer, A. T., & Fang, A. (2012). The efficacy of cognitive behavioral therapy: A review of meta-analyses. *Cognitive Therapy and Research, 36*(5), 427–440.

James, S. E., Herman, J. L., Rankin, S., Keisling, M., Mottet, L., & Anafi, M. (2016). *The report of the 2015 U.S. Transgender Survey.* Washington, DC: National Center for Transgender Equality.

Keo-Meier, C. L., Herman, L. I., Reisner, S. L., Pardo, S. T., Sharp, C., & Babcock, J. C. (2015). Testosterone treatment and MMPI-2 improvement in transgender men: A prospective controlled study. *Journal of Consulting and Clinical Psychology, 83*(1), 143–156.

Kosciw, J., Greytak, E., Palmer, N., & Boesen, M. (2014). *GLESN National School Climate Survey*. Accessed January 24, 2016, from http://www.glsen.org/sites/default/files/2013%20National%20School%20Climate%20Survey%20Full%20Report_0.pdf

Kosenko, K., Rintamaki, L., Raney, S., & Maness, K. (2013). Transgender patient perceptions of stigma in health care contexts. *Medical Care, 51*(9), 819–822.

Kwasnicka, D., Presseau, J., White, M., & Sniehotta, F. F. (2013). Does planning how to cope with anticipated barriers facilitate health-related behaviour change? A systematic review. *Health Psychology Review, 7*(2), 129–145.

Lee, E., & Toth, H. (2016). An integrated case formulation in social work: Toward developing a theory of a client. *Smith College Studies in Social Work, 86*(3), 184–203.

Lyons, K. (2016, July 10). Gender identity clinic services under strain as referral rates soar. *The Guardian*. Retrieved from https://www.theguardian.com/society/2016/jul/10/transgender-clinic-waiting-times-patient-numbers-soar-gender-identity-services

Meyer, I. H. (2003). Prejudice, social stress, and mental health in lesbian, gay, and bisexual populations: Conceptual issues and research evidence. *Psychological Bulletin, 129*(5), 674–697.

Meyer, I. H. (2015). Resilience in the study of minority stress and health of sexual and gender minorities. *Psychology of Sexual Orientation and Gender Diversity, 2*(3), 209.

Mizock, L., & Mueser, K. T. (2014). Employment, mental health, internalized stigma, and coping with transphobia among transgender individuals. *Psychology of Sexual Orientation and Gender Diversity, 1*(2), 146.

Morley, K. C., Sitharthan, G., Haber, P. S., Tucker, P., & Sitharthan, T. (2014). The efficacy of an opportunistic cognitive behavioral intervention package (OCB) on substance use and comorbid suicide risk: A multisite randomized controlled trial. *Journal of Consulting and Clinical Psychology, 82*(1), 130.

Mosher, D., & Gould, S. (2017, May 22). Gender transition surgeries jumped nearly 20% in a year—But the new data highlight a worrisome problem. *Business Insider*. Retrieved from http://www.businessinsider.com/sex-transition-plastic-surgery-statistics-2017-5

Neff, K. (2003). Self-compassion: An alternative conceptualization of a healthy attitude toward oneself. *Self and Identity, 2*(2), 85–101.

Neff, K. D., & Germer, C. K. (2013). A pilot study and randomized controlled trial of the mindful self-compassion program. *Journal of Clinical Psychology, 69*(1), 28–44.

Nuttbrock, L., Hwahng, S., Bockting, W., Rosenblum, A., Mason, M., Macri, M., & Becker, J. (2010). Psychiatric impact of gender-related abuse across the life course of male-to-female transgender persons. *Journal of Sex Research, 47*(1), 12–23.

Olson, K., Durwood, L., DeMeules, M., & McLaughlin, K. A. (2016). Mental health of transgender children who are supported in their identities. *Pediatrics, 137*(3). doi:10.1542/peds.2015-3223.

Pachankis, J. E. (2015). A transdiagnostic minority stress treatment approach for gay and bisexual men's syndemic health conditions. *Archives of Sexual Behavior, 44*(7), 1843–1860.

Pachankis, J. E., Hatzenbuehler, M. L., Rendina, H. J., Safren, S. A., & Parsons, J. T. (2015). LGB-affirmative cognitive–behavioral therapy for young adult gay and bisexual men: A randomized controlled trial of a transdiagnostic minority stress approach. *Journal of Consulting and Clinical Psychology, 83*(5), 875–889.

Persons, B. J., & Lisa, S. T. (2015). Developing and using a case formulation to guide cognitive–behavior therapy. *Journal of Psychology & Psychotherapy, 5,*179. doi:10.4172/2161-0487.1000179

Raj, R. (2007). Transactivism as therapy: A client self-empowerment model linking personal and social agency. *Journal of Gay & Lesbian Psychotherapy, 11*(3–4), 77–98.

Reisner, S. L., White Hughto, J. M., Gamarel, K. E., Keuroghlian, A. S., Mizock, L., & Pachankis, J. E. (2016). Discriminatory experiences associated with posttraumatic stress disorder symptoms among transgender adults. *Journal of Counseling Psychology, 63*(5), 509–519.

Richmond, K. A., Burnes, T., & Carroll, K. (2012). Lost in trans-lation: Interpreting systems of trauma for transgender clients. *Traumatology, 18*, 45–57.

Riggs, D. W., Ansara, G. Y., & Treharne, G. J. (2015). An evidence based model for understanding the mental health experiences of transgender Australians. *Australian Psychologist, 50*(1), 32–39.

Riley, E. A., Wong, W. T., & Sitharthan, G. (2011). Counseling support for the forgotten transgender community. *Journal of Gay & Lesbian Social Services, 23*(3), 395–410.

Rosselló, J., & Bernal, G. (2007). *Treatment manual for cognitive behavioral therapy for depression: Adaptation for Puerto Rican adolescents.* Retrieved from http://ipsi.uprrp. edu/pdf/manuales_tara/group_manual_eng.pdf

Ryan, C., Russell, S., Huebner, D., Diaz, R., & Sanchez, J. (2010). Family acceptance in adolescents and the health of SGDCA young adults. *Journal Child Adolescent Psychiatric Nursing, 23*, 205–213.

Saltzburg, S., & Davis, T. S. (2010). Co-authoring gender-queer youth identities: Discursive tellings and retellings. *Journal of Ethnic & Cultural Diversity in Social Work, 19*(2), 87–108.

Sánchez, F. J., & Vilain, E. (2009). Collective self-esteem as a coping resource for male-to-female transsexuals. *Journal of Counseling Psychology, 56*(1), 202–209.

Shipherd, J. C., Green, K. E., & Abromovitz, S. (2014). Transgender clients: Identifying and minimizing barriers to mental health treatment. *Journal of Gay & Lesbian Mental Health, 14*(2), 94–108.

Simons, L., Schrager, S. M., Clark, L. F., Belzer, M., & Olson, J. (2013). Parental support and mental health among transgender adolescents. *Journal of Adolescent Health, 53*, 791–793.

Steensma, T. D., McGuire, J. K., Kreukels, B. P., Beekman, A. J., & Cohen-Kettenis, P. T. (2013). Factors associated with desistence and persistence of childhood gender dysphoria: A quantitative follow-up study. *Journal of American Academy of Child Adolescent Psychiatry, 52*(6), 582–590.

Substance Abuse and Mental Health Services Administration. (2015). *Ending conversion therapy: Supporting and affirming LGBTQ youth* (HHS Publication No. SMA 15-4928). Rockville, MD: Substance Abuse and Mental Health Services Administration. Retrieved January 20, 2016, from http://store.samhsa.gov/shin/content/SMA15-4928/SMA15-4928.pdf

Testa, R. J., Jimenez, C. L., & Rankin, S. (2014). Risk and resilience during transgender identity development: The effects of awareness and engagement with other transgender people on affect. *Journal of Gay & Lesbian Mental Health, 18*, 31–46.

Tishelman, A. C., Kaufman, R., Edwards-Leeper, L., Mandel, F. H., Shumer, D. E., & Spack, N. P. (2015). Serving transgender youth: Challenges, dilemmas, and clinical examples. *Professional Psychology: Research and Practice, 46*(1), 37.

Vogel, D. L., Bitman, R. L., Hammer, J. H., & Wade, N. G. (2013). Is stigma internalized? The longitudinal impact of public stigma on self-stigma. *Journal of Counseling Psychology, 60*(2), 311.

Wallace, R., & Russell, H. (2013). Attachment and shame in gender-nonconforming children and their families: Toward a theoretical framework for evaluating clinical interventions. *International Journal of Transgenderism, 14*(3), 113–126.

Weiss, J. A. (2014). Transdiagnostic case conceptualization of emotional problems in youth with ASD: An emotion regulation approach. *Clinical Psychology: Science and Practice, 21*(4), 331–350.

Wells, R. (2016, June 14). *Free to be he, she, they: Helping young people navigate gender identity.* University of San Francisco News Center. Retrieved from https://www.ucsf. edu/news/2016/06/403226/free-to-be-he-she-they

White Hughto, J. M., Reisner, S. L., & Pachankis, J. E. (2015). Transgender stigma and health: A critical review of stigma determinants, mechanisms, and interventions. *Social Science & Medicine, 147,* 222–231.

5

Couple Interventions for Same-Sex Couples

CHRISTOPHER A. PEPPING, W. KIM HALFORD,
AND ANTHONY LYONS ■

Most lesbian, gay, and bisexual (LGB) individuals desire a stable, satisfying romantic relationship (D'Augelli, Rendina, Sinclair, & Grossman, 2007; Frost, 2011), yet very little research has focused on the development and evaluation of couple interventions for same-sex couples. Existing evidence-based couple interventions are likely to benefit same-sex couples given that many predictors of relationship outcomes are similar across both same-sex and heterosexual couple relationships (Kurdek, 2004; Peplau & Fingerhut, 2007). Nonetheless, same-sex couples face some distinctive challenges (Andersson, Noack, Seierstad, & Weedon-Fekjaer, 2006; Kurdek, 2004; Pepping & Halford, 2014), and couple interventions likely need to be tailored to meet the specific needs of same-sex couples. This chapter describes the two major forms of couple intervention and their evidence base; reviews research pertaining to relationship stability and relationship satisfaction of same-sex couples, including similarities and differences in predictors of stability and satisfaction between heterosexual and same-sex couples; and outlines adaptations that may be required in couple interventions to meet the needs of same-sex couples.

COUPLE INTERVENTIONS

There are two broad forms of couple intervention: couple therapy and couple relationship education (RE). Couple therapy typically assists distressed couples to resolve ambivalence about the relationship and reduce their distress. Both cognitive–behavioral couple therapy and emotion-focused therapy for couples have been replicated as efficacious in reducing relationship distress in heterosexual couples (Lebow, Chambers, Christensen, & Johnson, 2012; Snyder, Castellani, & Whisman, 2006). Specifically, a review of meta-analyses found a large mean effect size for couple therapy relative to controls ($d = .84$; Shadish & Baldwin, 2003). Although there is much evidence that couple therapy is efficacious with heterosexual couples, evidence for its efficacy with same-sex couples remains limited. In one notable exception, Fals-Stewart, O'Farrell, and Lam (2009) found that behavioral couple therapy was efficacious for treatment of alcohol use disorders in same-sex couples in which one partner displayed problematic alcohol use, and it also led to improvements in relationship satisfaction. However, to date there has been no randomized controlled trial of couple therapy to treat relationship distress specifically tailored to meet the needs of same-sex couples.

Evidence-based RE teaches couples relationship knowledge and skills (Halford, Markman, & Stanley, 2008). RE is often provided to relatively satisfied couples, with the goal of helping them maintain satisfying romantic relationships and prevent future distress (Halford & Bodenmann, 2013). However, it can be a useful intervention for moderately distressed couples (Halford et al., 2015). Three RE programs have demonstrated efficacy from randomized controlled trials with heterosexual couples: the Prevention and Relationship Enhancement Program (PREP; Markman, Stanley, & Blumberg, 2010), Couples Coping Enhancement Training (CCET; Bodenmann & Shantinath, 2004), and Couple Commitment and Relationship Enhancement (Couple CARE; Halford et al., 2006). These programs have much in common: They all promote shared and realistic relationship expectations and aim to enhance couple commitment. However, there are some distinctive features between programs: PREP teaches specific relationship skills such as communication (Markman et al., 2010), whereas CCET aims to enhance dyadic coping, whereby partners manage life stress as a couple (Bodenmann & Shantinath, 2004). Finally, Couple CARE focuses on relationship self-regulation, whereby partners reflect on their relationship and implement self-change goals to enhance the relationship (Halford et al., 2006).

The evidence on the effects of RE is somewhat mixed. On the one hand, a meta-analysis of 117 studies found moderate effect size improvements in couple communication ($d = .44$) and small increases in satisfaction ($d = .36$) following RE (Hawkins, Blanchard, Baldwin, & Fawcett, 2008). However, a more recent meta-analysis of 38 studies of RE with low-income couples found only very small effects on satisfaction ($d = .067$) and no effect on relationship stability ($d = -.002$) (Hawkins & Erickson, 2015). It may be that RE is not sufficient in some stressful circumstances, such as financial stress, to help couples maintain satisfying relationships. However, there is also evidence that couples at high risk for future relationship problems and for whom RE can modify the risk factors that they experience also tend to benefit more from RE (Halford & Bodenmann, 2013). Thus, overall, it appears that RE may benefit some groups of couples more than others.

As the field of RE is maturing, adaptations of evidence-based RE programs have been developed and evaluated for specific populations that may be at risk for future relationship problems. Specifically, RE programs have been tailored and found to enhance relationships of military couples (Allen, Stanley, Rhoades, Markman, &

Loew, 2011; Bakhurst, McGuire, & Halford, 2017), couples making the transition to parenthood (Petch, Halford, Creedy, & Gamble, 2012), cultural minority groups (Beach et al., 2011), and stepfamilies (Lucier-Greer & Adler-Baeder, 2012). With regard to adaptations for same-sex couples, there have been two published trials, both for male same-sex couples (Buzzella, Whitton, & Tompson, 2012; Whitton, Weitbrecht, Kuryluk, & Hutsell, 2016). In both studies, there was an increase in relationship functioning and improved communication following RE, and effects were generally maintained at 3-month follow-up. Nonetheless, the samples were small, with only 7 (Buzzella et al., 2012) and 11 (Whitton et al., 2016) gay male couples receiving RE immediately; thus, further research examining RE for same-sex couples is clearly needed.

SAME-SEX COUPLE RELATIONSHIPS

Couple interventions typically target modifiable processes that predict relationship outcomes, and the predictors of relationship satisfaction and stability are quite similar in heterosexual and same-sex couples. For instance, well-established predictors of relationship outcomes such as psychological adjustment of each partner, communication, conflict styles, and social support predict relationship satisfaction and stability in both heterosexual and same-sex couples (Gottman et al., 2003; Khaddouma, Norona, & Whitton, 2015; Kurdek, 2004). This suggests that existing approaches to couple therapy and RE are likely to be beneficial for same-sex couples. Nonetheless, there are relationship differences between same-sex and heterosexual couples, including some distinctive challenges faced by same-sex couples that interventions may need to address. Here, we provide a brief overview of some of the key similarities and differences, and we outline some distinctive challenges faced by same-sex couples.

Most studies find no differences between same-sex couples and married heterosexual couples with regard to levels of relationship satisfaction (Patterson, 2000; Peplau & Cochran, 1990; Peplau & Fingerhut, 2007). However, several studies find that same-sex couples may be at greater risk of relationship break-up than their heterosexual counterparts (Andersson et al., 2006; Kurdek, 2004). These disparities are at least partially accounted for by differences in relationship formalization between couple types. Specifically, during a 3-year period, disparities in break-up rates largely disappeared in samples of same-sex and heterosexual couples when controlling for marriage and marriage-like commitments (Rosenfeld, 2014). However, in studies with larger sample sizes and longer follow-up periods (8–10 years) conducted in Europe, same-sex couples were at somewhat greater risk of break-up compared to heterosexual couples (Andersson et al., 2006; Kalmijn, Loeve, & Manting, 2007). Furthermore, these findings remain even when comparing only cohabiting heterosexual relationships with cohabiting same-sex relationships, or heterosexual and same-sex couples who are either married or legally registered (Andersson et al., 2006; Kalmijn et al., 2007).

The available evidence therefore suggests that same-sex relationships may be at higher risk of break-up compared to those of heterosexual couples (Andersson et al., 2006; Kalmijn et al., 2007; Kurdek, 2004). This is likely to be attributable to external challenges such as discrimination and stigmatization (Otis, Rostosky, Riggle, & Hamrin, 2006) and, for some couples, a lack of social support for the relationship from friends and family (Khaddouma et al., 2015). Much evidence reveals that minority stress, referring to the chronic stress associated with living in a heteronormative environment (Meyer, 2003), is associated with poorer life outcomes, including relationship functioning (Otis et al., 2006). Thus, it seems likely that the effects of minority stress may account for at least some of the higher rates of break-up in same-sex relationships.

A range of relationship differences have been identified across heterosexual, lesbian, and gay male couples. For instance, in heterosexual couples, partners often express rejection of traditional gender roles, yet the distribution of household chores often follows traditional gender role divisions (Aassve, Fuochi, & Mencarini, 2014; Kjeldstad & Lappegard, 2014), whereas in same-sex couples, the distribution of household labor tends to be more egalitarian (Kurdek, 1993; Peplau & Fingerhut, 2007). Specifically, lesbian couples tend to share completion of household tasks, whereas gay male couples often have one partner perform specific tasks (Kurdek, 1993; Peplau & Fingerhut, 2007). Overall, same-sex couples generally split household tasks more equally between partners than do heterosexual married couples.

As noted previously, couple conflict predicts relationship dissatisfaction in heterosexual and same-sex couple relationships, and there appears to be a similar frequency of conflict in same-sex and heterosexual couples (Kurdek, 1994, 2004). However, there are some distinctive challenges faced by same-sex couples that can feature in the content of the conflict. For instance, managing disclosure to friends, family members, and colleagues regarding their sexual orientation and relationship status is a distinctive challenge experienced by same-sex couples (Rostosky, Riggle, Gray, & Hatton, 2007), and low levels of "outness" are associated with relationship strain (Frost & Meyer, 2009). Similarly, managing reactions from family, friends, and colleagues regarding being in a same-sex relationship is often reported as a significant concern for many same-sex couples (Lewis, Derlega, Berndt, Morris, & Rose, 2001; Todosijevic, Rothblum, & Solomon, 2005).

Internalized homonegativity refers to the internalization of society's negative attitudes toward sexual minorities as a result of living in a heteronormative social environment (Meyer & Dean, 1998). Internalized homonegativity is associated with low self-esteem and increased shame, depression, and anxiety (Meyer & Dean, 1998; Newcomb & Mustanski, 2010), and it has important implications for couple relationships (Otis et al., 2006). Experiencing negative feelings about one's own sexual orientation is likely to lead to shame and dissatisfaction with one's romantic relationship, particularly given that being in a same-sex relationship is perhaps one of the most salient reminders of one's sexual orientation for sexual minorities in a relationship (Frost & Meyer, 2009; Rostosky et al., 2007). Consistent with this proposition, internalized homonegativity is associated with relationship distress in same-sex couples, and this association is mediated by depressive symptomatology (Frost & Meyer, 2009).

Gay male, lesbian, and heterosexual couples differ with regard to sexual behavior in a number of important ways. Although the frequency of sexual behavior declines with the duration of the relationship in each of these three groups (Kurdek, 1995), the type of relationship differentially predicts the magnitude of the decline. Specifically, the rate of decline in sexual behavior is lowest in gay male couples, then heterosexual couples, and highest in lesbian couples (Kurdek, 1995). Although female same-sex couples report the lowest frequency of sexual behavior, they report longer duration of sexual acts (Blair & Pukall, 2014) and more frequent occurrence of orgasm (Garcia, Lloyd, Wallen, & Fisher, 2014) compared to heterosexual women. Finally, nonmonogamous relationships are more common and more widely accepted in gay male relationships compared to lesbian or heterosexual relationships (Bailey, Gaulin, Agyei, & Gladue, 1994; Lyons & Hosking, 2014). Several studies show no differences in sexual satisfaction or relationship satisfaction between monogamous and nonmonogamous gay male couples (Bricker & Horne, 2007; Parsons, Starks, Gamarel, & Grov, 2012), although the extent to which partners agree on rules and expectations in nonmonogamous relationships is an important determinant of relationship functioning (Hosking, 2013a).

In summary, although many of the predictors of relationship outcomes are the same in heterosexual and same-sex couples, there are some important differences. The similarities suggest that couple interventions developed and evaluated with heterosexual couples are likely to be effective, at least to some degree, with same-sex couples. However, the unique challenges facing same-sex couples suggest that couple interventions need modification in order to be appropriate and effective for same-sex couples.

ADAPTATIONS OF COUPLE INTERVENTIONS FOR SAME-SEX COUPLES

Case Example

Jane (age 32 years) and Susan (age 35 years) have been together for 3 years and have experienced substantial stress in these early years as a couple. Jane has been out to her family, friends, and work colleagues since her early 20s, whereas Susan has felt unable to disclose her sexual orientation to anyone but a few close friends. Jane and Susan share many common interests, enjoy spending time together, and both have a desire to move in together. However, they have so far been unable to do this because Susan is concerned this will reveal her sexual orientation to friends and family. Although Jane is understanding of Susan's dilemma, she often feels hurt when Susan refers to her as a friend, and she is afraid that Susan is ashamed of her when they cannot hold hands in public. Susan feels guilty that Jane is affected by this, reports often feeling ashamed that she is in a same-sex relationship, and is fearful of judgments and reactions from others. She has never known other same-sex couples and feels somewhat alone in coping with these challenges because she does not wish to place further strain on Jane or the relationship. These challenges have made it very difficult for both Jane and Susan to feel secure in their relationship. They both report wanting to make their relationship work, but they are feeling increasingly unsure of how to improve it.

This case illustrates some of the distinctive challenges that can face same-sex couples, particularly surrounding internalized shame, concealment, and navigating a stable and satisfying relationship in the absence of role models of same-sex couples. Here, we review some of the adaptations to couple therapy and RE that may be beneficial for same-sex couples, and we use the case of Jane and Susan to illustrate these points.

Appropriate Materials

Existing couple interventions were designed for, and evaluated with, heterosexual couples. For instance, RE programs typically include workbooks and audiovisual material that may contain heterosexist bias to a greater or lesser extent. Same-sex couples may feel excluded by workbooks, vignettes, and audiovisual material that depict only heterosexual couples. This is consistent with previous research highlighting the importance of tailoring interventions and program material to make them inclusive and relevant to sexual minorities, which is likely to reduce access barriers, increase uptake, and be perceived as more effective (Lyons, Rozbroj, Pitts, Mitchell, & Christensen, 2015; Rozbroj, Lyons, Pitts, Mitchell, & Christensen, 2014). It is therefore important that program materials are free from heterosexist bias and use same-sex couple vignettes and images (Pepping & Halford, 2014; Whitton & Buzzella, 2012). Jane and Susan, for instance, may have difficulty relating to program material featuring only heterosexual couples. In addition, they may find that some of their more significant challenges, such as navigating Susan's fear of coming out, are not adequately addressed in programs designed for different-sex couples who do not experience that challenge.

Assessing Relationship Expectations

Most LGB individuals have been raised by heterosexual parents and often have not had exposure to positive role models of same-sex relationships. This may provide greater freedom for same-sex couples to create their own vision for their relationship rather than adopting socially defined, traditional norms. However, it is plausible that discrepancies in relationship expectations might also be one source of relationship distress in same-sex couples. Relationship education programs for same-sex couples (Halford & Pepping, 2015; Whitton et al., 2016) emphasize the importance of clarifying relationship expectations for both partners in the context of the benefits and challenges associated with having greater freedom to adopt their own beliefs and expectations about what makes for a good relationship. For instance, a recently developed RE program included material on topics that are relevant, and sometimes challenging, for gay male couples, including if and how to become parents and negotiated nonmonogamy (Whitton et al., 2016). The content pertaining to relationship expectations was designed to assist partners to identify and negotiate relationship expectations using effective communication skills. Participants who received RE did indeed display more effective observed communication following the intervention, and they reported increased relationship satisfaction at 3-month follow-up (Whitton et al., 2016).

As highlighted in the case of Jane and Susan, it may also be useful to explore relationship expectations pertaining to the level of outness and disclosure of the relationship, as well as the level of comfort with public displays of affection. For instance, asking both Jane and Susan about their relationship expectations with regard to openness as a couple, and highlighting points of agreement as well as differences in expectations, may be particularly useful. Some couples may also find it useful to discuss the potential impact of same-sex relationship role models growing up, including the lack of such role models where relevant. A discussion surrounding the potential impact of discrepancies in relationship expectations on the relationship is likely to be beneficial. It may then be useful to highlight the particular skills that may help Jane and Susan resolve some of these discrepancies, such as dyadic coping, effective communication, and conflict resolution skills. Therapists and relationship educators should clarify the relationship expectations of both partners, including general relationship expectations and those specific to same-sex couples; identify potential discrepancies; and help couples use effective skills to manage these challenges.

Managing the Effects of Minority Stress

As highlighted previously, same-sex couples often experience challenges associated with minority stress, including discrimination and stigmatization (Otis et al., 2006) and, for some couples, a lack of social support for the relationship from friends and family (Khaddouma et al., 2015). Gay and lesbian users of therapeutic programs have previously emphasized the importance of addressing minority stress-related issues in their lives (Lyons et al., 2015). In this work, a range of minority stress-related issues were identified as potentially important foci in therapeutic interventions, including difficulties with family disapproval of one's same-sex partner and challenges pertaining to the disclosure of one's relationship to others and displaying affection in public (Lyons et al., 2015).

Assisting couples to understand the external influences of minority stress-related difficulties, namely societal heterosexism, may be beneficial. This may be particularly useful when there is a discrepancy between partners' familial acceptance or comfort with outness and disclosure. For instance, in the case of Jane and Susan, highlighting the external influence of minority stress on their relationship may shift negative attributions about the self or partner toward accurately attributing these difficulties to living in a heteronormative society. It may be useful for therapists to ask same-sex couples about their experience of acceptance and support for their relationship from family and friends, as well as their broader experiences of potential discrimination and prejudice. Reflection and discussion of the impact of such issues may also facilitate effective negotiation and communication. For instance, a therapist might ask Jane and Susan about their individual experiences of disclosing or concealing their sexual orientation to family and friends, validate and normalize Susan's difficulties coming out to family and friends, and assist both Jane and Susan to view these challenges as the results of external minority stress. A therapist might then assist Jane and Susan to communicate about these challenges effectively by helping them each express their experiences and feelings surrounding these issues in a non-blaming way and teaching adaptive communication skills such as active listening and paraphrasing to effectively discuss these challenges.

Enhancing Dyadic Coping

A related point is helping couples cope with the negative effects of minority stress. Experiences of discrimination negatively impact on relationship quality. This has been documented in ethnic minorities (Trail, Goff, Bradbury, & Karney, 2012) and in same-sex couples (Otis et al., 2006). The RE programs developed for same-sex couples (Halford & Pepping, 2015; Whitton et al., 2016) both focus on enhancing couples' dyadic coping skills given much evidence that dyadic coping helps heterosexual couples dealing with stressful life circumstances (Badr, Carmack, Kashy, Cristofanilli, & Revenson, 2010). It seems likely that enhancing dyadic coping might buffer some effects of discrimination on same-sex couples as it has done for other minority groups. For instance, in an RE intervention for African American couples, Beach and colleagues (2011) provided an example of an African American couple supporting each other to deal with racism. The inclusion of a discussion and demonstration of these skills in the context of discrimination could assist couples to cope with implicit or explicit forms of discrimination and moderate some of the negative effects of discrimination on relationship quality. In the case of Jane and Susan, assisting them to cope with these challenges together as a couple would likely be useful, including potentially evaluating the risks and benefits of Susan coming out to others and widening their social environment as a couple to establish a more supportive network of friends.

Managing Internalized Homonegativity

As highlighted previously, internalized homonegativity can impact both the relationship functioning (Mohr & Fassinger, 2006; Otis et al., 2006) and the mental health (Newcomb & Mustanski, 2010) of sexual minority individuals. Internalized homonegativity within couple relationships may appear in numerous forms. For example, same-sex attracted individuals may hold beliefs that LGB individuals cannot maintain satisfying romantic relationships or are incapable of intimacy or feel substantial shame for being in a same-sex relationship (Frost & Meyer, 2009). Internalized homonegativity may also lead to relational ambivalence because people high in internalized homonegativity desire to be in a same-sex relationship while at the same time experiencing shame regarding their sexual orientation (Frost & Meyer, 2009; Mohr & Fassinger, 2006). For instance, internalized homonegativity is associated not only with poor relationship quality but also with increased sensitivity to stigma, confusion surrounding sexual identity, and less perceived similarity to one's partner (Mohr & Fassinger, 2006). Furthermore, those with high internalized homonegativity are less likely to be out to friends and family, report greater social anxiety, and less connected to the gay community (Lingiardi, Baiocco, & Nardelli, 2012).

Examples of internalized homonegativity include partners avoiding disclosing their relationship to others, even when it is safe to do so; a partner criticizing the other for being too feminine or masculine; and fears of public displays of affection. Although internalized homonegativity is associated with reduced relationship satisfaction broadly (Mohr & Fassinger, 2006; Otis et al., 2006), it is possible that discrepancies between partners in internalized homonegativity may be particularly problematic. The case of Jane and Susan is one such example. Susan feels shame surrounding her sexuality and relationship, is not out to significant others, and is uncomfortable with public displays of affection. Jane, on the other hand, is comfortable with these factors and feels hurt when Susan hides their relationship from others. Exploring the potential impact of internalized homonegativity on relationship processes and outcomes, as well as highlighting the external origins of internalized homonegativity, may be a useful focus for some same-sex couples in RE and couple therapy.

It is unlikely that couples will present to therapy stating they require assistance with internalized homonegativity, and it is therefore important that therapists be attentive to potential signs of internalized homonegativity. For instance, therapists might observe subtle behavioral cues, such as partners experiencing discomfort with intimacy in a same-sex relationship. Self-reported feelings of shame may also be related to internalized homonegativity, as well as behavioral indicators of shame such as withdrawal and, in some cases, identity concealment. Finally, explicit or implicit negative beliefs and assumptions about same-sex relationships and one's own sexuality are likely to also signal that internalized homonegativity may be problematic.

Inclusivity of Nonmonogamous Relationships

Nonmonogamous relationships are more common and more accepted in gay male relationships compared to lesbian or heterosexual couples (Bailey et al., 1994; Lyons & Hosking, 2014). There do not appear to be differences between monogamous and nonmonogamous male couples in relation to frequency of sex with primary partners, relationship satisfaction, and sexual satisfaction (Bricker & Horne, 2007). Nonetheless, effective negotiation surrounding boundaries, rules, and expectations about sexual exclusivity, including safe sex practices, is likely to be particularly important for relationship satisfaction (Hosking, 2013a). Specifically, recent research highlights the importance of partners perceiving relatively equal benefit to the nonmonogamous relationship (Hosking, 2013a) and that the agreements surrounding extra-dyadic sex are upheld (Hosking, 2013b).

It is therefore important that during assessment, therapists enquire about the exclusivity of the relationship, including rules, expectations, and boundaries for nonmonogamous relationships. In our own RE program currently being evaluated, Rainbow Couple CARE (Halford & Pepping, 2015), couples in a nonmonogamous relationship are encouraged to discuss potential rules and expectations, including the types of sexual activities partners wish to pursue outside of the primary relationship and any activities that are off-limits, as well as the frequency and nature of the contact with sexual partners. Discussion and negotiation of the rules and arrangements for nonmonogamous relationships are likely to be an important area of focus for couples involved in extra-dyadic sex.

EMERGING ISSUES AND FUTURE DIRECTIONS

Access to Couple Interventions and Flexible Delivery

Data pertaining to the uptake of evidence-based couple services, and barriers to accessing such services, among same-sex couples are limited. Research from heterosexual couples finds that couple services are often not accessed, with more than half of divorcing heterosexual couples never accessing services prior to the divorce (Johnson et al., 2002; Relationships Australia, 2011). Furthermore, heterosexual couples report facing substantial barriers to accessing evidence-based couple services, including the costs associated with accessing these services and the inconvenience of attending face-to-face sessions (Halford & Simons, 2005).

With regard to couple services for same-sex couples, we recently surveyed 363 Australian adults in same-sex relationships about their use of couple services and barriers to accessing these services (Pepping, Lyons, Halford, Cronin, & Pachankis, 2017). Most individuals reported never having accessed couple services, with only 4% of participants having accessed couple therapy. With regard to access to couple services, concerns such as financial constraints and time limitations were identified as barriers to accessing services, which is consistent with research pertaining to heterosexual couples. However, there were also some additional barriers related to minority stress, such as fear of discrimination from professionals and a lack of appropriately trained practitioners to work with same-sex couples.

To address the commonly reported practical barriers to accessing couple services, researchers have developed flexible delivery RE (Halford et al., 2010) and couple therapy (Doss et al., 2016) for heterosexual couples. These programs typically include access to online resources, self-directed activities, guidebooks, DVDs, and generally some contact with a relationship educator or therapist on-line or via telephone (Busby, Larson, Holman, & Halford, 2015). Flexible delivery of couple interventions can address many of the barriers to attending couple services, such as the inconvenience of attendance face-to-face. Flexible delivery also has the potential to increase the reach of couple services because research demonstrates that, at least among heterosexual couples, people are more more likely to read books (Doss, Rhoades, Stanley, & Markman, 2009) or access websites (Casey & Halford, 2010) to obtain relationship information than attend face-to-face interventions. To our knowledge, no similar flexible delivery programs exist for same-sex couples. Given the practical and minority stress-related barriers to accessing couple services (Pepping et al., 2017) and the importance of tailoring couple interventions for same-sex couples (Pepping & Halford, 2014), there is a great need for future research to develop tailored couple interventions for same-sex couples via flexible delivery.

Halford and Bodenmann (2013) recently argued that a stepped approach to couple interventions might enhance their uptake: Couples would have access to a number of interventions, ranging from brief, low-intensity programs to more intensive programs delivered by professionals. Couples at lower risk for relation-ship distress may only require low-intensity RE, such as books, video materials, or assessment with feedback. High-risk couples may benefit from the more intensive curriculum-based RE programs or couple therapy. Such stepped approaches have demonstrated efficacy in parenting interventions (Sanders, 2008) and may well enhance the reach and uptake of couple services.

Therapist Training in Same-Sex Couple Interventions

Training therapists and relationship educators to provide culturally sensitive services to same-sex couples is particularly important. Just as the importance of considering cross-cultural issues in psychotherapy has been widely recognized, researchers have highlighted the importance of service providers possessing the necessary attitudes, knowledge, and skills to work with same-sex couples (Pepping & Halford, 2014). For instance, it may well be important for both het-erosexual and same-sex attracted therapists to consider their own heterosexist biases resulting from living in a heteronormative society. Examples of such im-plicit biases or assumptions about same-sex relationships include the belief that gay male relationships are unstable, that relationship dissolution is less distressing in same-sex relationships, and that bisexual individuals cannot commit to one partner.

It is important that service providers possess the necessary knowledge to work effectively with same-sex couples. For instance, therapists need to educate them-selves about same-sex relationships and LGBT culture more broadly so as to avoid the client needing to educate the therapist (Moradi, Mohr, Worthington, & Fassinger, 2009). Similarly, it will be important that adequate training and supervision are provided to all educators and therapists, regardless of their own sexual orientation, to ensure they have the necessary attitudes, knowledge, and skills required to work effectively with same-sex couples. Future research on therapist training for working with same-sex couples and sexual minorities is greatly needed to investigate methods by which we can enhance therapists' knowledge about LGBT culture and the unique issues affecting same-sex couples, as well as methods to increase practitioners' skills pertaining to working with same-sex couples.

CONCLUSION

Much evidence reveals that RE and couple therapy are efficacious at enhancing couple relationship functioning and reducing distress (Halford & Bodenmann, 2013; Lebow et al., 2012), yet very little research has examined couple interventions for same-sex couples. Existing evidence-based couple interventions are likely to benefit same-sex couples to some degree given the similarities in predictors of relationship outcomes across same-sex and heterosexual couples. However, same-sex couples face some distinctive challenges (Kurdek, 2004; Pepping & Halford, 2014), and couple interventions may require some modification to successfully address the needs of same-sex couples. Couple therapists might incorporate some discussion of minority stress where relevant, including potential effects of internalized homonegativity and discrimination, and focus on enhancing dyadic coping to buffer the negative effects of minority stress. Therapists might also assess the potential relevance of unique areas of content with same-sex couples, such as comfort with disclosure of the relationship, level of outness to friends and family, and potentially rules and expectations regarding nonmonogamous or open relationships.

The challenge for researchers and clinicians is to develop and refine couple therapy and RE protocols that build on existing evidence-based approaches to couple intervention but make adaptations to address the specific issues faced by same-sex couples. Innovation is also needed to enhance the reach of couple services for same-sex couples, potentially making a range of couple interventions available, from brief, low-intensity programs to more intensive intervention delivered by professionals. Finally, rigorous outcome studies on the efficacy of couple services with same-sex couples are greatly needed, and the findings must be disseminated to consumers and clinicians.

CONFLICT OF INTEREST STATEMENT

Dr. W. Kim Halford is the author of the relationship education program Couple CARE published by Australian Academic Press and receives royalties from its sales. He also runs professional training workshops in how to conduct Couple

CARE, for which he has received fees. Dr. Christopher Pepping runs professional training workshops in how to conduct Couple CARE, for which he has received fees. Dr. Pepping and Dr. Halford are co-authors of Rainbow Couple CARE, a relationship education program for same-sex couples, which might be published commercially at some point in the future. Dr. Anthony Lyons declares no conflict of interest.

REFERENCES

Aassve, A., Fuochi, G., & Mencarini, L. (2014). Desperate housework: Relative resources, time availability, economic dependency, and gender ideology across Europe. *Journal of Family Issues, 35*, 1000–1002. doi:10.1177/0192513X14522248

Allen, E., Stanley, S. M., Rhoades, G. K., Markman, H. J., & Loew, B. A. (2011). Marriage education in the Army: Results of a randomized clinical trial. *Journal of Couple & Relationship Therapy, 10*(4), 309–326. doi:10.1080/15332691.2011.613309

Andersson, G., Noack, T., Seierstad, A., & Weedon-Fekjar, H. (2006). The demographics of same-sex marriages in Norway and Sweden. *Demography, 43*(1), 79–98. doi:10.1353/dem.2006.0001

Badr, H., Carmack, C. L., Kashy, D. A., Cristofanilli, M., & Revenson, T. A. (2010). Dyadic coping in metastatic breast cancer. *Health Psychology, 29*, 169–180. doi:10.1177/0011000091192003

Bailey, J. M., Gaulin, S., Agyei, Y., & Gladue, B. A. (1994). Effects of gender and sexual orientation on evolutionarily relevant aspects of human mating psychology. *Journal of Personality and Social Psychology, 66*, 1081–1093. doi:10.1037/0022-3514.66.6.1081

Bakhurst, M. G., McGuire, A. C., & Halford, W. K. (2017). Relationship education for military couples: A pilot randomized controlled trial of the effects of Couple CARE in Uniform. *Journal of Couple & Relationship Therapy, 16*(3), 167–187. doi:10.1080/15332691.2016.1238797

Beach, S. R. H., Hurt, T. R., Franklin, K. J., Fincham, F. D., McNair, L. M., & Stanley, S. M. (2011). Enhancing marital enrichment through spirituality: Efficacy data for prayer focused relationship enhancement. *Psychology of Religion & Spirituality, 3*, 201–216.

Blair, K. L., & Pukall, C. F. (2014). Can less be more? Comparing duration vs. frequency of sexual encounters in same-sex and mixed-sex relationships. *Canadian Journal of Human Sexuality, 23*(2), 123–136. doi:10.3138/cjhs.2393

Bodenmann, G., & Shantinath, S. D. (2004). The Couples Coping Enhancement Training (CCET): A new approach to prevention of marital distress based upon stress and coping. *Family Relations, 53*, 477–484. doi:10.1111/j.0197-6664.2004.00056.x

Bricker, M. E., & Horne, S. G. (2007). Gay men in long-term relationships. *Journal of Couple & Relationship Therapy, 6*(4), 27–47. doi:10.1300/J398v06n04_02

Busby, D. M., Larson, J. H., Holman, T. B., & Halford, W. K. (2015). Flexible delivery approaches to couple relationship education: Predictors of initial engagement and retention of couples. *Journal of Child and Family Studies, 24*(10), 3018–3029. doi:10.1007/s10826-014-0105-3

Buzzella, B. A., Whitton, S. W., & Tompson, M. C. (2012). A preliminary evaluation of a relationship education program for male same-sex couples. *Couple and Family Psychology: Research and Practice, 1*(4), 306–322. doi:10.1037/a0030380

Casey, L. M., & Halford, W. K. (2010). Couples and the Silicon chip: Applying information technology to couple relationship services. In K. Hahlweg, M. Grawe-Gerber, & D. H. Baucom (Eds.), *Enhancing couples: The shape of couple therapy to come* (pp. 216–230). Cambridge, MA: Hogrefe.

D'Augelli, A. R., Rendina, J., Sinclair, K. O., & Grossman, A. H. (2007). Lesbian and gay youth's aspirations for marriage and raising children. *Journal of LGBT Issues in Counseling, 1,* 77–98. doi:10.1300/J462v01n04_06

Doss, B. D., Cicila, L, N., Georgia, E. J., Roddy, M. K., Nowlan, K. M., Benson, L. A., & Christensen, A. (2016). A randomized controlled trial of the web-based OurRelationship program: Effects on relationship and individual functioning. *Journal of Consulting and Clinical Psychology, 84*(4), 285–296. doi:10.1037/ccp0000063

Doss, B. D., Rhoades, G., Stanley, S., & Markman, H. J. (2009). Marital therapy, retreats, and books: The who, what, when, and why of relationship help-seeking. *Journal of Marital and Family Therapy, 35,* 18–29. doi:10.1111/j.1752-0606.2008.00093.x

Fals-Stewart, W., O'Farrell, T. J., & Lam, W. K. K. (2009). Behavioral couple therapy for gay and lesbian couples with alcohol use disorders. *Journal of Substance Abuse Treatment, 37*(4), 379–387. doi:10.1016/j.jsat.2009.05.001

Frost, D. M. (2011). Similarities and differences in the pursuit of intimacy among sexual minority and heterosexual individuals: A personal projects analysis. *Journal of Social Issues, 67,* 282–301. doi:10.1111/j.1540-4560-2011.01698.x

Frost, D. M., & Meyer, I. H. (2009). Internalized homophobia and relationship quality among lesbians, gay men, and bisexuals. *Journal of Counseling Psychology, 56,* 97–109. doi:10.1037/a0012844

Garcia, J. R., Lloyd, E. A., Wallen, K., & Fisher, H. E. (2014). Variation in orgasm occurrence by sexual orientation in a sample of US singles. *Journal of Sexual Medicine, 11*(11), 2645–2652. doi:10.1111/jsm.12669

Gottman, J. M., Levenson, R. W., Gross, J., Fredrickson, B. L., McCoy, K., Rosenthal, L., . . . Yoshimoto, D. (2003). Correlates of gay and lesbian couples' relationship satisfaction and relationship dissolution. *Journal of Homosexuality, 45*(1), 23–43. doi:10.1300/J082v45n01_02

Halford, W. K., & Bodenmann, G. (2013). Effects of relationship education on maintenance of couple relationship satisfaction. *Clinical Psychology Review, 33,* 512–525. doi:10.1016/j.cpr.2013.02.001

Halford, W. K., Markman, H. J., & Stanley, S. (2008). Strengthening couples' relationships with education: Social policy and public health perspectives. *Journal of Family Psychology, 22*(4), 497–505. doi:10.1037/a0012789

Halford, W. K., Moore, E. M., Wilson, K., Dyer, C., Farrugia, C., & Judge, K. (2006). *Couple commitment and relationship enhancement.* Brisbane, Australia: Australian Academic Press.

Halford, W. K., & Pepping, C. A. (2015). *Rainbow Couple CARE: Program manual for relationship education for same-sex couples.*

Halford, W. K., Pepping, C. A., Hilpert, P., Bodenmann, G., Wilson, K. L., Busby, D., . . . Holman, T. (2015). Immediate effect of couple relationship education on low-satisfaction couples: A randomized clinical trial plus and uncontrolled trial replication. *Behavior Therapy*, 46, 409–421. doi:10.1016/j.beth.2015.02.001

Halford, W. K., & Simons, M. (2005). Couple relationship education in Australia. *Family Process*, 44, 147–159. doi:10.1111/j.1545-5300.2005.00050.x

Halford, W. K., Wilson, K., Watson, B., Verner, T., Larson, J., Busby, D., & Holman, T. (2010). Couple relationship education at home: Does skill training enhance relationship assessment and feedback? *Journal of Family Psychology*, 24(2), 188. doi:10.1037/a0018786

Hawkins, A. J., Blanchard, V. L., Baldwin, S. A., & Fawcett, E. B. (2008). Does marriage and relationship education work? A meta-analytic study. *Journal of Consulting and Clinical Psychology*, 76(5), 723–734. doi:10.1037/a0012584

Hawkins, A, J., & Erickson, S. E. (2015). Is couple and relationship education effective for lower income participants? A meta-analytic study. *Journal of Family Psychology*, 29 (1), 59–68. doi:10.1037/fam0000045

Hosking, W. (2013a). Agreements about extra-dyadic sex in gay men's relationships: Exploring differences in relationship quality by agreement type and rule-breaking behaviour. *Journal of Homosexuality*, 60, 711–733. doi:10.1080/00918369.2013.773819

Hosking, W. (2013b). Satisfaction with open sexual agreements in Australian gay men's relationships: The role of perceived discrepancies in benefit. *Archives of Sexual Behavior*, 42, 1309–1317. doi:10.1007/s10508-012-0005-9

Johnson, C. A., Stanley, S. M., Glenn, N. D., Amato, P. R., Nock, S. L., Markman, H. J., & Dion, R. (2002). *Marriage in Oklahoma: 2001 baseline statewide survey on marriage and divorce*. Oklahoma City, OK: Oklahoma Department of Human Services.

Kalmijn, M., Loeve, A., & Manting, D. (2007). Income dynamics in couples and the dissolution of marriage and cohabitation. *Demography*, 44(1), 159–179. doi:10.1353/dem.2007.0005

Khaddouma, A., Norona, J. C., & Whitton, S. W. (2015). Individual, couple, and contextual factors associated with same-sex relationship instability. *Couple and Family Psychology: Research and Practice*, 4, 106–125. doi:10.1037/cfp0000043

Kjeldstad, R., & Lappegard, T. (2014). How do gender values and household practices cohere? Value-practice configurations in a gender-egalitarian context. *Nordic Journal of Feminist and Gender Research*, 22, 219–237. doi:10.1080/08038740.2013.864703

Kurdek, L. A. (1993). The allocation of household labor in gay, lesbian, and heterosexual married couples. *Journal of Social Issues*, 49, 127–139.

Kurdek, L. A. (1994). Areas of conflict for gay, lesbian, and heterosexual couples: What couples argue about influences relationship satisfaction. *Journal of Marriage and Family*, 56(4), 923–934. doi:10.2307/353603

Kurdek, L. A. (1995). Developmental changes in relationship quality in gay and lesbian cohabiting couples. *Developmental Psychology*, 31, 86–94. doi:10.1037/0012-1649.31.1.86

Kurdek, L. A. (2004). Are gay and lesbian cohabiting couples really that different from heterosexual couples? *Journal of Marriage and Family*, 66(4), 880–890. doi:10.1111/j.0022-2445.2004.00060.x

Lebow, J. L., Chambers, A. L., Christensen, A., & Johnson, S. M. (2012). Research on the treatment of couple distress. *Journal of Marital and Family Therapy, 38*(1), 145–168. doi:10.1111/j.1752-0606.2011.00249.x

Lewis, R. J., Derlega, V. J., Berndt, A., Morris, L. M., & Rose, S. (2001). An empirical analysis of stressors for gay men and lesbians. *Journal of Homosexuality, 42*, 63–88.

Lingiardi, V., Baiocco, R., & Nardelli, N. (2012). Measure of internalized sexual stigma for lesbians and gay men: A new scale. *Journal of Homosexuality, 59*(8), 1191–1210. doi:10.1080/00918369.2012.712850

Lucier-Greer, M., & Adler-Baeder, F. (2012). Does couple and relationship education work for individuals in step-families? A meta-analytic study. *Family Relations, 61*, 756–769. doi:10.1111/j.1741-3729.2012.00728.x

Lyons, A., & Hosking, W. (2014). Prevalence and correlates of sexual partner concurrency among Australian gay men aged 18–39. *AIDS and Behavior, 18*, 801–809. doi:10.1007/s10461-013-0613-y

Lyons, A., Rozbroj, T., Pitts, M., Mitchell, A., & Christensen, H. (2015). *Improving E-therapy for mood disorders among lesbians and gay men: A practical toolkit for developing tailored web and mobile phone-based depression and anxiety interventions.* Retrieved from http://lgbtihealth.org.au/wp-content/uploads/2015/04/bw0293-toolkit-improving-e-therapy-for-lesbians-and-gay-men.pdf

Markman, H. J., Stanley, S. M., & Blumberg, S. L. (2010). *Fighting for your marriage* (3rd ed.). San Francisco, CA: Jossey-Bass.

Meyer, I. H. (2003). Prejudice, social stress and mental health in lesbian, gay and bisexual populations: Conceptual issues and research evidence. *Psychological Bulletin, 129*, 674–697. doi:10.1037/0033-2909.129.5.674

Meyer, I. H., & Dean, L. (1998). *Internalized homophobia, intimacy and sexual behavior among gay and bisexual men.* Thousand Oaks, CA: Sage.

Mohr, J. J., & Fassinger, R. E. (2006). Sexual orientation identity and romantic relationship quality in same-sex couples. *Personality and Social Psychology Bulletin, 32*(8), 1085–1099. doi:10.1177/0146167206288281

Moradi, B., Mohr, J. J., Worthington, R. L., & Fassinger, R. E. (2009). Counseling psychology research on sexual (orientation) minority issues: Conceptual and methodological challenges and opportunities. *Journal of Counseling Psychology, 56, 56*(1), 5–22. doi:10.1037/a0014572

Newcomb, M. E., & Mustanski, B. (2010). Internalized homophobia and internalizing mental health problems: A meta-analytic review. *Clinical Psychology Review, 30*(8), 1019–1029. doi:10.1016/j.cpr.2010.07.003

Otis, M., Rostosky, S., Riggle, E. & Hamrin, R. (2006). Stress and relationship quality in same-sex couples. *Journal of Social and Personal Relationships, 23*(1), 81–99. doi:10.1177/0265407506060179

Parsons, J. T., Starks, T. J., Gamarel, K. E., & Grov, C. (2012). Non-monogamy and sexual relationship quality among same-sex male couples. *Journal of Family Psychology, 26*, 669–677. doi:10.1037/a0029561

Patterson, C. J. (2000). Family relationships of lesbians and gay men. *Journal of Marriage and the Family, 62*, 1052–1069. doi:10.1111/j.1741-3737.2000.01052.x

Peplau, L. A., & Cochran, S. D. (1990). A relationship perspective on homosexuality. In D. P. McWhirter, S. A. Sanders, & J. M. Reinisch (Eds.), *Homosexuality/heterosexuality: Concepts of sexual orientation* (pp. 312–349). New York, NY: Oxford University Press.

Peplau, L. A., & Fingerhut, A. W. (2007). The close relationships of lesbians and gay men. *Annual Review of Psychology, 58,* 405–424. doi:10.1146/annurev.psych.58.110405.085701

Pepping, C. A., & Halford, W. K. (2014). Relationship education and therapy for same-sex couples. *Australian and New Zealand Journal of Family Therapy, 35,* 431–444. doi:10.1002/anzf.1075

Pepping, C. A., Lyons, A., Halford, W. K., Cronin, T. J., & Pachankis, J. (2017). Couple interventions for same-sex couples: A consumer survey. Manuscript under review.

Petch, J., Halford, W. K., Creedy, D. K., & Gamble, J. (2012). Couple relationship education at the transition to parenthood: A window of opportunity to reach high-risk couples. *Family Process, 51*(4), 498–511. doi:10.1111/j.1545-5300.2012.01420.x

Relationships Australia. (2011). *Issues and concerns for Australian relationships today: Relationship indicators survey 2011.* Retrieved from https://www.relationships.com.au

Rosenfeld, M. J. (2014). Couple longevity in the era of same-sex marriage in the United States. *Journal of Marriage and Family, 76,* 905–918. doi:10.1111/jomf.12141

Rostosky, S. S., Riggle, E. D., Gray, B. E., & Hatton, R. L. (2007). Minority stress experiences in committed same-sex couple relationships. *Professional Psychology: Research and Practice, 38*(4), 392–400. doi:10.1037/0735-7028.38.4.392

Rozbroj, T., Lyons, A., Pitts, M., Mitchell, A., & Christensen, H. (2014). Assessing the applicability of e-therapies for depression, anxiety, and other mood disorders among lesbians and gay men: Analysis of 24 web- and mobile phone-based self-help interventions. *Journal of Medical Internet Research, 16*(7), e166. doi:10.2196/jmir.3529

Sanders, M. R. (2008). Triple P positive parenting programs as a public health approach to strengthening parenting. *Journal of Family Psychology, 22*(3), 506–517. doi:10.1037/0893-3200.22.3.506

Shadish, W. R., & Baldwin, S. A. (2003). Meta-analysis of marriage and family therapy interventions. *Journal of Marital and Family Therapy, 29*(4), 547–570. doi:10.1111/j.1752-0606.2003.tb01694.x

Snyder, D. K., Castellani, A. M., & Whisman, M. A. (2006). Current status and future directions in couple therapy. *Annual Review of Psychology, 57*(1), 317–344. doi:10.1146/annurev.psych.56.091103.070154

Trail, T. E., Goff, P. A., Bradbury, T. N., & Karney, B. R. (2012). The costs of racism for marriage: How racial discrimination hurts, and ethnic identity protects, newlywed marriages among Latinos. *Personality and Social Psychology Bulletin, 38*(4), 454–465. doi:10.1177/0146167211429450

Todosijevic, J., Rothblum, E. D., & Solomon, S. E. (2005). Relationship satisfaction, affectivity, and gay-specific stressors in same-sex couples joined in civil unions. *Psychology of Women Quarterly, 29*(2), 158–166. doi:10.1111/j.1471-6402.2005.00178.x

Whitton, S. W., & Buzzella, B. A. (2012). Using relationship education programs with same-sex couples: A preliminary evaluation of program utility and needed modifications. *Marriage & Family Review, 48*(7), 667–688.

Whitton, S. W., Weitbrecht, E. M., Kuryluk, A. D., & Hutsell, D. W. (2016). A randomized waitlist-controlled trial of culturally sensitive relationship education for male same-sex couples. *Journal of Family Psychology, 30*(6), 763–768. doi:10.1037/fam0000199

6

Sexual Minority Parent Families

Research and Implications for Parenting Interventions

ABBIE E. GOLDBERG, REIHONNA L. FROST,
AND NÉSTOR NOYOLA ■

OVERVIEW

Parents' preparedness for parenthood, parenting skills, and adjustment have implications for child development and family functioning (Sandler, Ingram, Wolchik, Tein, & Winslow, 2015). Thus, there is value in addressing, via prevention and intervention, parenting practices, including preparedness for parenthood and parenting skills, as well as parents' mental health and intimate relationship quality, which have implications for parenting processes. Despite a modest literature on the use of empirically validated parenting interventions with heterosexual couples (Sandler et al., 2015), even less research has examined the utility or validity of empirically validated parenting interventions for lesbian, gay, bisexual, or queer (LGBQ) parents. This chapter addresses this gap. First, we provide an overview of select research on LGBQ family building, the transition to parenthood, parents' well-being and relationship quality, and parenting practices and parent child relationships. In discussing LGBQ parents' experiences creating families and raising children, we attend to key issues that may have implications for the implementation of preventive and intervention programs that address the transition to parenthood and parenting. Then, we discuss evidence-based parenting interventions in four areas: (1) the transition to parenthood, (2) parenting skills, (3) co-parenting and relationships, and (4) foster/adoptive parenting. In discussing these intervention targets, we highlight areas in which LGBQ parenting research should inform unique intervention approaches or the modification of existing approaches. We conclude with a case study that illustrates some of the challenges that a lesbian couple might face in building their family and navigating parenting issues, the frustrations that they encounter while interfacing with traditional therapeutic and support structures, and the potential for LGBQ-adapted parenting interventions to effectively address their needs and challenges.

LGBQ PARENTING

LGBQ parenting has grown more visible during the past several decades both within the United States and internationally (Goldberg & Gartrell, 2014). In addition to greater media coverage of topics related to LGBQ parents and their children (Herman, 2015), research on these families' experiences has also proliferated during the past few decades (Goldberg & Gartrell, 2014), although gaps in our understanding of these populations remain. This chapter emphasizes lesbian and gay (LG) parent families because these are the populations that have been most frequently studied. We present research on bisexual parent families when possible. Ross and Dobinson (2013) and Downing (2013) offer more complete reviews of bisexual and transgender parenting, respectively.

Family Building

Becoming a parent is often considered one of the major markers of adulthood, along with establishing a career, getting married, clarifying one's values, and exploring one's identity (Arnett & Tanner, 2006). In many ways, this transition may be different for LGBQ people in comparison to their heterosexual peers. Young adults who identify as LGBQ may delay or forgo parenthood due to societal stigma as well as different norms within LGBTQ communities that may not emphasize parenting; however, this tendency appears to be declining as LGBQ parenthood becomes more widely visible and accessible (Goldberg, 2010). The phenomenon of becoming a parent in the context of a same-sex relationship (e.g., via donor insemination, surrogacy, and adoption) has increased, due in part to increased societal acceptance of sexual minority parenting and advancements in reproductive technologies (Goldberg, 2010). Also, some sexual minorities become parents in the context of heterosexual relationships, as opposed to conceiving or adopting in the context of same-sex unions (Gates, 2013). They may enter same-sex relationships after their children are born/adopted, and their children may be raised in LGB stepfamilies (Tasker, 2013).[1]

---

1. Most LGB parents likely have their children within different-sex relationships (Gates, 2011). A 2013 Pew Research survey of LGBT Americans found that, consistent with other population-based surveys (Gates, 2013), more than one-third (35%) of LGBT individuals report having been a parent. But the findings suggest that parenting is higher among bisexual individuals than among gay men or lesbians. An estimated 59% of bisexual women and 32% of bisexual men report having had children, compared to 31% of lesbians and 16% of gay men. These figures, then, imply that nearly two-thirds of LGB parents (64%) are bisexual.

Of these family types, LGB stepfamily arrangements (formed post-heterosexual relationship dissolution) likely represent the most common arrangement (Gates, 2011, 2013). Such arrangements are particularly likely to occur among bisexual persons, who are more likely to be parents compared to gay men and lesbians (Gates, 2011, 2013) and for whom patterns of family formation are particularly diverse (i.e., bisexual people become parents in a variety of contexts, including same-sex relationships, different-sex relationships, and as single parents; Power et al., 2012).

Considering planned lesbian parent families, a common method of family building is donor insemination (DI). Female couples who use DI must first decide who will carry the child, a decision that may be made based on one partner's infertility (which can in turn lead to strain within the couple) and, relatedly, health and age considerations, in addition to a desire to be pregnant and breast-feed (Goldberg, 2006). Another key decision is what type of donor to use (known or anonymous). Women who select anonymous donors often do so out of a desire to avoid third-party involvement, unclear boundaries, or custody challenges (Chabot & Ames, 2004; Goldberg, 2006), whereas women who select known donors often feel strongly that their children deserve access to their biological heritage (Goldberg & Allen, 2013a; Touroni & Coyle, 2002).[2]

Female couples who build their families via DI are vulnerable to insensitive treatment by health professionals (e.g., failure to acknowledge the non-birthing partner in office visits) and medical forms that are inappropriate for lesbian/bisexual patients (e.g., they assume a heterosexual two-parent family; Goldberg, Downing, & Richardson, 2009; Ross, Steele, & Epstein, 2006; Yager, Brennan, Steele, Epstein, & Ross, 2010). In the event of infertility or miscarriage, sexual minority women may be vulnerable to additional forms of mistreatment (e.g., providers may minimize the grief of the non-carrying partner), which can exacerbate stress (Cacciatore & Raffo, 2011; Goldberg et al., 2009; Peel, 2010). Female

---

2. Historically, the decision of who will carry the child has also been significant in that the biological mother is automatically the legal parent, whereas the nonbiological mother in some states has been unable to complete a second-parent adoption to gain legal rights. With the US Supreme Court ruling that makes marriage by same-sex couples legal in all 50 states, many people have assumed that parental rights issues for same-sex couples will disappear. In fact, parentage is (generally) not conclusively established through marriage for same-sex or different-sex couples, although there is a marital presumption that applies: That is, the husband of a woman who gives birth is presumed to be the father of the child (although this presumption can be rebutted in certain circumstances through, for example, evidence of nonbiological connection). Hence, in some states, nonbiological married fathers who are the intended parents in different-sex marriages are also technically just as vulnerable to questions of parentage as nonbiological parents in same-sex marriages. In turn, the recommendation that nonbiological lesbian mothers complete second-parent (or step-parent) adoptions still stands (despite the reality that most husbands in different-sex marriage do not complete these). Advocacy is currently being focused on ensuring that marital presumptions of parentage apply equally regardless of whether marriage is same-sex or different-sex (D. NeJaime & G. J. Gates, personal communication, July 20, 2016).

couples who endure pregnancy loss may thus experience multiple forms of stress, including a lack of validation of their loss and lack of acknowledgment of and support for their same-sex relationship (Cacciatore & Raffo, 2011; Peel, 2010).

Female and male couples may also seek to adopt as a means of becoming parents. They are more likely to select adoption as their first choice than are heterosexual couples, who typically arrive at adoption after unsuccessful efforts to conceive. (Some female couples also arrive at adoption due to infertility but are less likely than heterosexual couples to identify infertility as the primary reason for pursuing adoption; Goldberg et al., 2009; Jennings, Mellish, Tasker, Lamb, & Golombok, 2014.) Same-sex couples are at least four times more likely to pursue adoption than are different-sex couples, and they are six times more likely to be foster parents (Gates, 2013). They are also more likely to adopt transracially (Farr & Patterson, 2009; Goldberg, 2009). In turn, many LGBQ adoptive families are also multiracial, which presents unique issues (e.g., families are highly visible and parents often navigate the challenge of engaging in socialization around a racial identity they do not share; Goldberg, 2009; Goldberg, Sweeney, Black, & Moyer, 2016). Same-sex couples may elect to pursue international adoption (although this is increasingly less of an option as sending countries tighten their criteria regarding who can adopt), public domestic adoption (via the child welfare system), or private domestic adoption (via a lawyer or agency). Although private domestic adoptions may be "open" or "closed," open adoptions[3] are increasingly becoming the norm in the United States (Child Welfare Information Gateway, 2013). LGBQ parents are often drawn to private domestic adoption because they desire openness (exchange of identifying information and/or ongoing contact with birth parents) or want to adopt an infant, whereas parents who pursue public adoption are often motivated by altruistic or financial reasons (Downing, Richardson, Kinkler, & Goldberg, 2009; Goldberg, 2012). Child welfare adoptions are technically "free," whereas private domestic and international adoptions cost between $15,000 and $50,000 (Child Welfare Information Gateway, 2016). LGBQ parents may pursue international adoption to avoid birth parent contact or because they have a special relationship with a country or culture (Downing et al., 2009).

Sexual minorities who decide to adopt often expend a great deal of energy researching adoption agencies for evidence that they are open to working with LGBQ people (Goldberg, Downing, & Sauck, 2007). Upon choosing an agency, sexual minorities may encounter professionals who hold discriminatory attitudes toward LGBQ people and who sabotage potential adoptive placements (Goldberg et al., 2007), as well as, on a more subtle level, heteronormative language in agency forms, materials, and support groups (Goldberg, 2012; Goldberg et al., 2007). For example, adoption professionals may assume that all parents are seeking to adopt

---

3. Open adoptions refer to arrangements that allow birth parents and adoptive parents to have information about and to communicate with each other before and/or after placement of the child. Closed adoptions refer to arrangements in which the birth parents and adoptive parents do not exchange identifying information and there is no contact between the birth parents and the adoptive parents.

because of infertility or may use terms such as "husbands and wives" (Goldberg et al., 2007). Affirming and supportive professionals, on the other hand, offer LGBQ parents resources relevant to their sexual minority status (e.g., legal resources about protecting their parental rights) and use terms such as "partner" and "parents" as opposed to husbands/wives and mothers/fathers (Goldberg, 2012). Gay men are vulnerable to the intersection of heterosexist and sexist stereotypes, such as the notion that gay men cannot be good parents because they are both male (i.e., not nurturing, not "mothers") and gay (Goldberg, 2012). Gay men may be turned down for certain placements because of the belief that children, especially girls, need a mother in the home (Goldberg, 2012). Bisexual people face stereotypes specific to bisexuality, such as the idea that bisexual people are overly sexual (Moss, 2012), which may lead agencies to assume that they are unfit to parent (Ross & Dobinson, 2013).

Due to its high cost (more than $100,000, on average) and the fact that it is not legal in all states, surrogacy is an option for only a small number of sexual minorities, mainly men (Bergman, Rubio, Green, & Padron, 2010; Berkowitz, 2013; Murphy, 2013). The limited work on sexual minorities' use of surrogacy suggests that a strong desire to have a biological child may be a powerful motivator in pursuing surrogacy over adoption (Berkowitz, 2013; Goldberg, 2012; Murphy, 2013).

Transitioning to Parenthood

Becoming a parent introduces unique forms of stress into couples' lives (Canario & Figueiredo, 2016; Cowan & Cowan, 1992), which can affect parents' mental health and relationship quality (Doss, Rhoades, Stanley, & Markman, 2009). Longitudinal studies that follow LG parents across the transition to parenthood have revealed that similar to parents in different-sex relationships, same-sex parents' well-being (Goldberg & Smith, 2011) and relationship quality (Goldberg, Smith, & Kashy, 2010) decline across the transition, although support from friends, family, co-workers, and supervisors tends to buffer all parents from experiencing these declines.

In female couples in which one partner has given birth, nonbiological mothers may experience unique mental health stressors related to the fact that they lack biogenetic ties to their children—inasmuch as biogenetic ties are deeply woven into notions of kinship in US society (Chateauneuf & Ouellette, 2017). Nonbiological mothers face less societal acknowledgment of their roles as mothers than do biological mothers, which can create feelings of frustration, sadness, and invisibility and may cause conflict within the couple (Abelsohn, Epstein, & Ross, 2013; Goldberg, Downing, & Sauck, 2008; Hunter, 2015). Nonbiological mothers may also perceive their children as "preferring" their biological mothers, which can create feelings of guilt and inadequacy and contribute to interparental tension (Goldberg et al., 2008). It is rare that mental health and support services explicitly focus on nonbiological LGBQ mothers—an invisibility that has consequences for their support networks and sense of community (Abelsohn, Epstein, & Ross, 2013).

Nonbiological mothers tend to be employed more hours in paid work, at least initially, whereas biological mothers do more child care, in part because of the demands of breast-feeding (Downing & Goldberg, 2010; Goldberg & Perry-Jenkins, 2007; Goldberg et al., 2008). Such divergences in partners' contribution to child care and paid work become less prominent over time (Goldberg et al., 2008), and same-sex couples generally share paid and unpaid work more equally than do different-sex couples (Chan, Brooks, Raboy, & Patterson, 1998; Goldberg, Smith, & Perry-Jenkins, 2012; Patterson, Sutfin, & Fulcher, 2004). When differences in paid and unpaid work contributions occur, these are often related to personal preferences, whereby one partner prefers to focus more energy in the work or home sphere, and also structural constraints, such as considerations related to work hours/flexibility, career commitment, and finances (Downing & Goldberg, 2010; Goldberg, 2012, 2013; Goldberg et al., 2012). Differing contributions to paid and unpaid labor may challenge couples in terms of ensuring that both partners feel similarly bonded to the child, requiring that both partners be cognizant of ways to facilitate closeness between the child and the parent who works more hours (Goldberg & Perry-Jenkins, 2007).

Changes in family support may also accompany the transition to parenthood (Goldberg, 2012). Compared to heterosexual parents, LGB parents may perceive less support from family (Goldberg & Smith, 2008a), but they tend to report greater support from family than do LGB individuals without children (DeMino, Appleby, & Fisk, 2007). Family members may become more supportive once a child enters the picture (Goldberg, 2006), such that they push aside negative views of homosexuality or seek to repair problematic relationships in the interest of developing a relationship with a grandchild or niece or nephew (Gartrell et al., 1999; Goldberg, 2012). In some cases, family ties may be strengthened by a child's arrival, such that LGB parents report greater closeness to their parents after becoming parents themselves (Gartrell et al., 1999; Goldberg, 2012).

Yet some sexual minorities who become parents encounter diminished support from their families, who may oppose this decision on moral or religious grounds or because they believe that life as a child of sexual minority parents will be too difficult (Gartrell et al., 1996; Goldberg, 2012). Notably, in female couples in which one partner gives birth, the nonbiological mother's family may be less excited about the child's arrival (Nordqvist, 2015) and ultimately less involved in the child's life (Patterson, Hurt, & Mason, 1998). Some family members may be explicitly resistant to the notion of adoption, particularly transracial adoption, and may in turn be unsupportive of a biologically unrelated, and possibly racially dissimilar, child (Goldberg, 2012; Sullivan, 2004).

In addition to potentially facing less support from family, same-sex couples who adopt encounter stressors unique to their adoptive status across the transition to parenthood. In particular, couples who seek to adopt via the child welfare system may encounter unique challenges, including greater stress, during this transition (Goldberg, Moyer, Kinkler, & Richardson, 2012). Such stress may stem from difficulties accessing needed supports and services, frustration with social service agencies, strained relationships with birth family members (who may be unhappy when children are placed with a same-sex couple), and anxieties about the potential removal of the child from their care (e.g., because of their sexual orientation; Goldberg et al., 2012).

For persons who had children in the context of heterosexual relationships prior to coming out as LGBQ, the transition at hand is coming out and merging their new LGBQ identity with that of being a parent (Lynch, 2004a, 2004b; Tasker, 2013). In some cases, coming out is accompanied by the formation of LGBQ stepparent families, and thus LGBQ parents may need to navigate the introduction of new same-sex partners into the family (Lynch, 2004a, 2004b). The formation of LGBQ stepfamilies is similar in many ways to that of heterosexual stepfamilies, in that children retain closer relationships to their biological parents (Goldberg & Allen, 2013b), but LGBQ stepfamilies face unique issues, such as coping with stigma (Robitaille & Saint-Jacques, 2009).

LGBQ Parents' Mental Health and Relationship Quality

Beyond the transition to parenthood, a body of research specifically addresses LGB parents' mental health, relationship quality, and the parenting process itself (including parenting style and co-parenting). Some studies have taken a comparative approach—that is, they compare LG and heterosexual parents in terms of mental health and parenting stress. Such studies have found few differences in such outcomes based on parent sexual orientation (Bos, van Balen, & van den Boom, 2004; Goldberg & Smith, 2009, 2011; Golombok et al., 2003; Shechner, Slone, Lobel, & Schecter, 2013). Another body of work has explored what factors within LGBQ parents are related to well-being and relationship outcomes and has found that LG parents who perceive less support from family and friends, and who live in less supportive legal contexts, report poorer mental health (Goldberg & Smith, 2008b, 2011, 2013; Shapiro, Peterson, & Stewart, 2009; Shechner et al., 2013). Other conditions that have been linked to poorer well-being in LG parent samples include internalized sexual stigma (Goldberg & Smith, 2011), child behavior problems (Goldberg & Smith, 2008b), and low parenting satisfaction (Lavner, Waterman, & Peplau, 2014). Within same-sex adoptive couples, parents who adopted older children report poorer mental health than those who adopted infants (Goldberg & Smith, 2013). Existing research on bisexual parents suggests that they experience bisexual erasure and invisibility in that their sexual identity is often inferred from the gender of their current partner (Ross & Dobinson, 2013). Such invisibility, as well as the exclusion that bisexual people often perceive within the LGBQ community, may contribute to distress in bisexual parents (Dodge & Sandfort, 2007; Ross, Siegel, Dobinson, Epstein, & Steele, 2012).

Regarding parents' intimate relationship quality, some studies have found similar levels of relationship quality (e.g., love and conflict) among LG and heterosexual parents (Farr, Forssell, & Patterson, 2010a; Goldberg et al., 2010), although at least one study (Baiocco et al., 2015) found higher levels of relationship quality in LG parents. Greater social support, a more positive sexual identity (e.g., lower levels of internalized sexual stigma), greater sexual satisfaction, and less work–family strain have been linked to greater self-reported intimate relationship quality among sexual minority parents (Farr et al., 2010a; Goldberg et al., 2010; Tornello, Johnson, & O'Connor, 2013).

Although there are few studies of relationship dissolution in LGBQ parent families, they suggest similar rates of dissolution across LG and heterosexual parent families (Goldberg & Garcia, 2015; Goldberg, Moyer, Black, & Henry, 2015). A study of 190 LG and heterosexual adoptive couples found that 15 couples (7.9%) dissolved their relationships during the first 5 years of parenthood. Seven of 57 lesbian couples (12.3%), 1 of 49 gay couples (2.0%), and 7 of 84 heterosexual couples (8.3%) dissolved their unions. Although the rate was highest among lesbian couples and lowest among gay couples, rates were not significantly different across family type. In the full sample, regardless of family type, dissolution was more likely among parents who had adopted an older child (vs. an infant) and among parents who felt less prepared for the adoption (Goldberg & Garcia, 2015), highlighting how stressors and their implications may vary among adoptive couples. Qualitative research on divorcing lesbian and heterosexual mothers showed that lesbian mothers were more likely than heterosexual mothers to cite problems with emotional and sexual intimacy, and inequities in the division of labor, as contributors to union dissolution (Goldberg et al., 2015).

Parenting Practices and Parent–Child Relationships

In addition to studying LGB parents' individual and relational well-being, some limited research has addressed their parenting practices and parent–child relationships. This work suggests some differences in parenting practices as a function of both sexual orientation and gender. One longitudinal study of LG and heterosexual parents found that all new parents perceived themselves as becoming more skilled at parenting across the transition to parenthood, but gay men's perceived skill increased the most and lesbians' perceived skill increased the least (Goldberg & Smith, 2014). The authors suggested that perhaps the experience of a man co-parenting with another man, coupled with their experience of performing the parental duties stereotypically associated with both mothers and fathers, leads gay men to develop greater confidence in their parenting skill over time. In contrast, the experience of a woman co-parenting with another woman may lessen parental confidence because sharing the mothering role can be challenging for lesbian partners, both of whom may feel pressure to embody intensive mothering ideologies and be somewhat more critical of their own parenting capacities over time as they measure them against those of their female partner (Goldberg et al., 2008).

Several other differences in parenting processes across family types have been documented. Observational research on co-parenting among LG and heterosexual couples found that lesbian couples exhibited the most supportive (e.g., warm and cooperative) and least undermining (e.g., cold and competitive) behavior, whereas gay couples exhibited the least supportive behavior and heterosexual couples the most undermining behavior (Farr & Patterson, 2013).

Overall, more supportive co-parenting was associated with better child adjustment (Farr & Patterson, 2013). Other recent work has explored the conditions that facilitate successful co-parenting among same-sex couples. For example, greater support from family of origin is related to a stronger parenting alliance among LG adoptive parents (Sumontha, Farr, & Patterson, 2016).

Studies comparing LG and heterosexual two-parent families suggest that parent–child relationships in these different family structures are more similar than different, such that few differences in parental warmth, parental emotional involvement, and parent–child relationship quality have been found across family type (Bos & van Balen, 2010; Bos, van Gelderen, & Gartrell, 2015; Golombok et al., 2003). However, one study found that gay fathers showed higher levels of warmth and responsiveness compared to heterosexual parents (but not lesbian mothers; Golombok et al., 2014). Furthermore, studies of lesbian mother families formed via DI indicate that children's relationships with their biological mothers and nonbiological mothers are similar in quality, which may be a reflection of the tendency for lesbian co-mothers to perform similar amounts of child care (Bos et al., 2004; Vanfraussen, Ponjaert-Kristoffersen, & Brewaeys, 2003). Yet nonbiological parent–child contact may be threatened if parents break up, inasmuch as societal and legal structures privilege the biological mother–child relationship. Nonbiological mothers who adopt their children are more likely to share custody, and to maintain contact and have a close relationship with their children, post-relationship dissolution (Gartrell, Bos, Peyser, Deck, & Rodas, 2011).

When parents adopt—which, as noted previously, sexual minority parents are more likely to do than are heterosexual parents—there may be greater challenges to the developing parent–child relationship. Parents who adopt older children are often confronted with a slower bonding process, as are parents who are placed with a child rather suddenly (Goldberg, Moyer, & Kinkler, 2013). Parenting a child with a history of abuse, neglect, or trauma may also pose challenges to bonding (Goldberg et al., 2013). Also, as mentioned previously, parents who build their families through private domestic adoption are likely to do so through open adoption, which means that in addition to developing a relationship with their child, they can also expect to have contact with their child's biological family (Goldberg, Kinkler, Richardson, & Downing, 2011). In fact, public domestic adoptions have recently been trending toward more openness as well, with adoptive families maintaining contact with their children's extended family members and biological siblings (Brodzinsky & Goldberg, 2016). Maintaining contact with birth family members can introduce complex issues. At the same time that adoptive parents are establishing their relationships with their children, they may also be managing the complex dynamics of maintaining contact and forming relationships with their children's birth families. Such relationships can sometimes be strained (e.g.,

LG parents may worry about potential homophobia by the birth family; Goldberg et al., 2012).

Children's Outcomes

Research has documented few differences in children's psychological adjustment as a function of family structure (Goldberg, 2010). That is, few differences have been observed between children raised by LG parents and children raised by heterosexual parents in terms of self-esteem, quality of life, internalizing problems (e.g., depression), externalizing problems (e.g., behavioral problems), or social functioning (Farr, Forssell, & Patterson, 2010b; Gartrell & Bos, 2010; Goldberg & Smith, 2013; Golombok et al., 2003; Shechner et al., 2013; van Gelderen, Bos, Gartrell, Hermanns, & Perrin, 2012). Exceptions include a study by Golombok et al. (2014) that found higher levels of externalizing problems among children in heterosexual-parent families than children in LG-parent families and a meta-analysis of 10 studies by Miller, Kors, and Macfie (2017) that determined that children of gay fathers demonstrate better psychological adjustment compared to children of heterosexual parents, which may in part be a function of gay fathers' relatively high socioeconomic status and tendency to share parenting roles.

Some studies point to strengths associated with growing up in a planned LG parent family. Studies of adolescents raised by lesbian mothers from birth found that adolescents were rated higher in social competence and self-esteem and lower in social problems, rule-breaking, aggressive behavior, and substance abuse compared to adolescents with heterosexual parents (Bos et al., 2015; Gartrell & Bos, 2010). In addition, young adults cite various strengths associated with growing up with LGB parents, including resilience and empathy toward marginalized groups (Goldberg, 2007; Titlestad & Pooley, 2014).

The social functioning and peer relationships of children and adolescents with LG parents appear to be similar to those of youth with heterosexual parents (Gartrell, Deck, Rodas, Peyser, & Banks, 2005; Goldberg & Smith, 2013; Wainright & Patterson, 2008). Indeed, family process variables (what happens within the family) are more important in predicting social competence than is family structure (parent sexual orientation; Goldberg, 2010). For example, adolescents with lesbian parents and adolescents with heterosexual parents do not differ in their self-reported quality of peer relationships (Goldberg, 2010; Wainright & Patterson, 2008). Regardless of family type, adolescents whose parents describe closer relationships with them tend to report having more friends and higher quality peer relationships (Wainright & Patterson, 2008).

Children with LGBQ parents may be socially skilled and have good relationships with friends but still be bullied due to their parents' sexual orientation. Studies that compare the teasing/bullying experiences of children with LG parents with those of children with heterosexual parents are conflicting: Some suggest higher rates of being bullied among the former group (Kosciw & Diaz, 2008) and others find no differences, according to self- and parent-report (Rivers, Poteat,

& Noret, 2008). Yet even if rates of teasing do not differ, the content of teasing might differ. Vanfraussen, Ponjaert-Kristoffersen, and Brewaeys (2002) compared school-age children from planned lesbian-mother households with children from heterosexual-parent families and found no differences in rates of teasing. Clothing, appearance, and intelligence were among the reasons for teasing in both groups, but family-related reasons for teasing were named only by children of lesbian mothers, one-fourth of whom had been teased about having two moms, having a lesbian mother, not having a father, or being gay. Notably, even when children are being teased about their families, they may not tell their parents (e.g., due to concerns about parents' response or worry that bullying invalidates their status as a "good" LG parent family; Goldberg, 2007).

Perceived stigmatization by peers has been linked to compromised mental health in children of LG parents (Bos & Gartrell, 2010). Notably, some work has found that although perceived stigmatization and homophobia by peers negatively impacts children's well-being overall, attending schools with LGBTQ curricula and having strong parent–child relationships can help buffer the negative impact of stigma on well-being (Bos & Gartrell, 2010).

EVIDENCE-BASED PARENTING INTERVENTIONS AND PROPOSED ADAPTATIONS FOR LGBQ PARENTS

Here, we review evidence-based parenting intervention programs focused on the transition to parenthood, parenthood in general, and adoptive/foster parenting. We then review suggested adaptations to these programs that can maximize their relevance to LGBQ parents and families.

Transition to Parenthood Programs

The transition to parenthood is a key life transition that may bring major disruptions in parents' lives and is linked to increased parental stress and strain between partners, which may or may not subside over time (Cowan & Cowan, 1992; Doss et al., 2009). Individual- and couple-level strains are linked to poorer parenting quality, which affects child outcomes (Karreman, van Tuijl, van Aken, & Dekovic, 2008; Krishnakumar & Buehler, 2000). In light of this, preventive programs have been developed to optimize mental and relational health after the transition and thus reduce the likelihood of problematic parenting, family violence, and relationship dissolution.

Schulz, Cowan, and Cowan (2006) developed a group intervention for couples making the transition to parenthood, and they found that couples who attended a couples group from mid-pregnancy to 3 months postpartum did not experience a decline in relationship satisfaction, whereas the no-treatment controls did experience a decline; effects were sustained for several years. Yet despite their innovative approach and its success in preventing marital decline, the program posed challenges for dissemination (e.g., 24 weekly meetings between mid-pregnancy and 3 months postpartum and limited manualization of content). Thus, building on Schultz et al.'s approach, Feinberg and colleagues (2010, 2014, 2016) developed Family Foundations (FF) as a universal prevention program for first-time expectant couples, which consists of nine classes, before and after birth, that aim to strengthen the co-parenting relationship. The program is based on evidence that parents' support of and coordination with each other is related to their well-being, parenting, and child outcomes (Feinberg, 2003; Feinberg, Kan, & Hetherington, 2007).

The FF program consists of five classes before birth (3 hours each) and four after birth (2 hours each) that focus on conflict resolution and problem-solving, communication, and mutual support. Feinberg et al. (2016) evaluated the effectiveness of the FF program in a randomized controlled trial (RCT), enrolling 399 couples who were expecting their first child, with assignment to either an intervention or a control condition after pretest. Classes consisting of 8–12 couples each involved presentation, discussion, couple and group skill-building exercises, and watching video vignettes. The FF prenatal classes also included general childbirth education. Control group families completed written materials on stages of child development and choosing quality child care. Trained coders examined parents' co-parenting, parenting, child behavior, and couple interaction. Feinberg et al. found that intervention couples demonstrated better post-test levels compared to control couples on more than two-thirds of measures of co-parenting, mental health, parenting, child adjustment, and family violence. Thus, the FF program has demonstrated efficacy in addressing processes that are often negatively impacted during the transition to parenthood.

Another intervention that focuses on the transition to parenthood is Towards Parenthood (TP) (Milgrom et al., 2005; Milgrom, Schembri, Ericksen, Ross, & Gemmill, 2011). The TP intervention is a book-based, guided self-help intervention targeted at the antenatal period with the goal of preventing postnatal depression and anxiety, strengthening the parent–child relationship, and promoting problem-solving skills. TP consists of a self-help, nine-unit workbook (Milgrom et al., 2009) that can be read at home by parents[4] or used in conjunction with therapy. The workbook covers a range of topics related to the transition to parenthood, including nurturing the mother–child relationship, developing realistic expectations, understanding role changes in couple relationships, and coping with depression/anxiety. Of the nine units, one explicitly focuses on fatherhood and covers topics such as fostering a healthy father–child relationship, managing stress, and how fathers can support their partners (e.g., helping to care for the

---

4. The intervention was originally aimed at couples, and there is content that couples (mothers and fathers) are supposed to read together. However, the implementation of this program ultimately involved the therapist talking only with mothers. This decision appears to have been made because fathers were not very engaged in the feasibility study.

baby). Although the fatherhood and motherhood units are separate, partners are encouraged to read both units together.

Milgrom et al. (2011) evaluated the effectiveness of the TP intervention in an RCT with pregnant women. In order for the study to be representative of women with and without symptoms of depression, anxiety, and stress, women between 20 and 32 weeks pregnant were screened for depressive symptoms and parenting difficulties. Women with scores above the cut-off for either scale were randomized into the high screening score intervention or routine care group; those scoring below it were randomized into the low screening score intervention or routine care group.

The intervention condition consisted of the TP self-help, nine-unit workbook, which was to be read at home by pregnant mothers and their partners and discussed in weekly half-hour sessions with a psychologist via phone.[5] Both parents received workbooks, but only the mother participated in phone sessions (eight prenatal sessions and one postnatal session). In the routine care condition, women continued to see their midwives or general practitioners for their care. Self-report measures of depression, anxiety, and stress were administered at baseline and post-treatment (12 weeks postpartum), and a self-report measure of parenting dysfunction was administered post-treatment. Milgrom et al. (2011) found that mothers who received the TP intervention reported lower post-treatment depression, stress, anxiety, and marginally lower parenting dysfunction compared to women in the routine care condition. Thus, the TP program shows efficacy in addressing adjustment difficulties in new mothers. Notably, despite regular attempts to encourage men to participate, the researchers documented poor engagement from men, as shown by their low rates of questionnaire completion.

Adaptation to LGBQ Parent Families

Given the promising efficacy of transition to parenthood programs such as FF and TP to improve the co-parenting relationship and prevent postpartum depressive and anxious symptoms and parenting difficulties, it is important to consider whether and how programs such as these need to be adapted to be appropriate for LGBQ parents and couples. Here, we offer some recommendations based on the literature:

- Transition to parenthood programs overwhelmingly focus on expectant biological mothers. Group leaders should be prepared to address the issues that arise with the coming of a new baby for nonbiological mothers (e.g., lack of societal recognition of their parental roles) and gay fathers (e.g., societal stereotypes of men as less nurturing and less skilled parents than mothers). Furthermore, some programs, such as TP,

---

5. Based on their research with TP, Milgrom et al. (2009) published *Towards Parenthood: Preparing for the Changes and Challenges of a New Baby*, a guidebook that expectant mothers and fathers can use as a self-help book or as a supplement to counseling with a professional.

consider the non-pregnant partner as playing a supporting role. This is likely to be problematic for many same-sex couples, who are more likely to share parenting than are heterosexual couples and will likely prefer an approach that centers on and seeks to support both partners' experiences as new parents.

- It is essential that program developers and group leaders be knowledgeable about LGBQ family building. For example, in female couples who use DI, one or both partners may have tried to become pregnant and/or experienced infertility or pregnancy loss. Sensitivity to such circumstances will enable group leaders to avoid assumptions about why couples "chose" one partner to carry the child. For instance, the partner who ultimately carries the child may have been chosen by default because one woman was unable to conceive.

- Program developers and group leaders should be trained to be mindful of heteronormative and gendered assumptions that are not supported by research. For example, group leaders should not assume that among female couples, one partner will be "more of" the mother than the other. Likewise, when presented with male couples, leaders should not assume that partners lack the necessary ingredients to "good parenting" because they are men.

- Group leaders should be sensitive to the makeup of groups in any group-based parenting intervention. A same-sex couple will likely be the minority in their group. In turn, group leaders should seek to cultivate a warm, respectful, and comfortable atmosphere and be vigilant about addressing heterosexist assumptions or remarks by group participants.

- Same-sex couples may present with unique challenges and strengths that could be the focus of an adapted protocol. Given their vulnerability to stigma within multiple spheres (e.g., legal, schools, and family), the FF could include a component aimed at enhancing resiliency and coping strategies (e.g., seeking a gay-friendly pediatrician and coping with homophobia from family). An adapted protocol could also address the fact that same-sex couples who became parents via DI and surrogacy face within-couple differences in their biolegal relationship to the child. Couples should also be guided to consider strategies for reducing feelings of invisibility on the part of the nonbiological parent (e.g., establishing legal parentage).

- Given the high rates of adoption among same-sex couples, group facilitators should be sensitive to the unique issues that may characterize their transition to parenthood, including birth family contact, racial dissimilarity between parents and child, and heightened visibility as a family. An adapted or enhanced protocol may be necessary to address such issues.

- Many protocols, including the TP self-help book, use heteronormative language and contain heteronormative and outdated assumptions (e.g., only dads go to work, not the birthing parent) and resources (e.g., separate lists of suggestions for moms and dads to "unwind"). Researchers and clinicians who use these protocols should adapt them to be more inclusive.

Parenting Programs

Many parenting programs are not implemented until after individuals or couples have become parents. A variety of behavioral parent training interventions are widely used because of strong evidence of their efficacy (Serketich & Dumas, 1996). Two of the most widely disseminated interventions are Parent–Child Interaction Therapy (PCIT) and the Triple P–Positive Parenting Program (Triple P), which have been shown to improve parenting behaviors and reduce child behavioral problems. The Couples Coping Enhancement Training (CCET), aimed at enhancing individual and dyadic coping (Bodenmann & Shantinath, 2004), is less widely disseminated but shows promise in impacting parent relationship quality and child well-being.

PCIT is an individualized intervention for parents of 4- to 7-year-old children with externalizing problems (Hembree-Kigin & McNeil, 1995). The outcome of interest in PCIT trials is observed changes in parent–child interactions, as opposed to parent-reported changes in the child's behavior only. Parents are guided toward behavior change via direct coaching; in turn, change in parental behavior is expected to change the child's behavior and improve parent–child interactions. In vivo coaching of parental behaviors differentiates PCIT from most other behavioral parent training interventions.

Treatment typically lasts 12–14 weeks. PCIT consists of two phases: child-directed interaction and parent-directed interaction. PCIT skills are taught via didactic instruction to parents and direct coaching of parents while they are interacting with their children. In the didactic sessions (usually two), the focus is on teaching the parent skills. Then, the remainder of PCIT involves direct coaching, whereby the parent and child interact in a play therapy room, with the therapist watching behind a one-way mirror and the therapist and parent communicating via a "bug in the ear" device that permits direct coaching of parents (Thomas & Zimmer-Gembeck, 2007).

Meta-analyses of PCIT RCTs show positive improvements in both parent and child behavior, according to observational and parent-report measures (Thomas & Zimmer-Gembeck, 2007). One RCT found that parents of preschool children with oppositional defiant disorder who received PCIT had more positive interactions with children and more success in achieving compliance compared to the control condition (Schuhmann, Foote, Eyberg, Boggs, & Algina, 1998). Bagner and Eyber (2007) found that among mothers of children with mental retardation, mothers in an immediate treatment condition reported fewer disruptive behaviors and more positive interactions with children than did mothers in a waitlist condition, which could be explained by an increase in positive parenting behaviors and a decrease in negative parenting behaviors in the context of mother–child interactions. Studies suggest that treatment outcomes are maintained 6 years later (Eyberg et al., 2001; Hood & Eyberg, 2003). Abbreviated forms of PCIT show promising results as well; long-term positive gains are comparable to those from the standard PCIT format for up to 2 years after treatment (Nixon, Sweeney, Erickson, & Touyz, 2003, 2004).

Triple P is a system of parenting support and intervention aimed at increasing parental confidence and skill in raising children, thus enhancing children's developmental and behavioral outcomes (Sanders & Pickering, 2014). It was designed to optimize positive parenting and relationship functioning between parents and children aged 2–16 years (Sanders, Cann, & Markie-Dadds, 2003). Families are offered information regarding parenting and behavior management strategies via a range of intervention structures (e.g., multimedia, professional consultations, and self-directed modules). Instruction, individual and group activities, and homework are incorporated to assist parents in using differential reinforcement, communication skills, and effective consequences for misbehavior. Lessons occur over approximately 10 sessions, although this depends on the version of Triple P that is being administered (Thomas & Zimmer-Gembeck, 2007). Pathways Triple P, for example, is a version that is designed for families at risk for child abuse or neglect, and it targets the attributional processes that parents have toward children's, and their own, behavior, as well as parental anger management deficits (Sanders & Pickering, 2014).

Meta-analyses of Triple P RCTs show positive improvements in parent and child behavior (Thomas & Zimmer-Gembeck, 2007), although some individual studies have documented only short-term maintenance of improvements in child behavior (e.g., Heinrichs, Kliem, & Hahlweg, 2014).

The CCET program, which is an example of a broader category of programs known as couple relationship education, consists of six modules aimed at improving knowledge of stress and coping processes, individual coping, dyadic coping, awareness of mutuality in relationships, communication, and problem-solving (Bodenmann & Shantinath, 2004; Ledermann, Bodenmann, & Cina, 2007). It is one of the first relationship education programs to go beyond teaching communication to address the enhancement of personal and dyadic skills to cope with stress (Zemp, Milek, Cummings, Cina, & Bodenmann, 2016).

CCET uses didactic elements (e.g., short lectures with video examples), quizzes for determining mastering of material, and feedback on the couple's behaviors (Bodenmann & Shantinath, 2004; Zemp et al., 2016). It can be offered as a weekend workshop in a group format of four to eight couples per workshop, with required homework after the workshop (Zemp et al., 2016). The program has been found to have positive effects on parents' relationship quality (Bodenmann, Bradbury, & Pihet, 2008; Halford & Bodenmann, 2013; see also Chapter 5, this volume) and child well-being (Bodenmann, Cina, Ledermann, & Sanders, 2008). One RCT examined parents' self-reports of relationship quality and parenting behavior and also child behavioral problems. It found that CCET enhanced couples' relationship functioning from pre- to post-test and reduced dysfunctional parenting. Children showed significantly fewer behavioral problems post-treatment (Bodenmann, Cina, et al., 2008).

ADAPTATION TO LGBQ PARENT FAMILIES

Interventions such as Triple P and PCIT hold promise for enhancing parental competence and improving parent and child behaviors; likewise, interventions such as CCETP have had success in the enhancement of individual and relational processes, thereby indirectly affecting family and child outcomes. In turn, it is important to consider how these types of programs could be applied to LGBQ parents. As with interventions aimed at LGBQ prospective and new parents, these could benefit from several adaptations:

- An adapted Triple P or PCIT protocol could address some of the unique determinants of stress for LGBQ parents and prospective parents. Given the role of internalized sexual stigma in parents' mental health and relationship quality, a psychoeducational component should promote awareness of ways that internalized sexual stigma may manifest (e.g., anxiety about whether a child's behavioral problems might be a result of one's sexual orientation). Helping parents recognize and challenge such beliefs can reduce their impact on personal, relational, and familial functioning.
- At the same time, particularly in a program such as Pathways Triple P, which focuses on parents' attributional processes, it is essential for coaches to assist parents in recognizing society's role in their own maladaptive self-schemas, as opposed to blaming themselves.
- Parenting interventions should address the unique sources of stress for children from LGBQ families, such as teasing related to their two-mom/ two-dad, adoptive, and/or multiracial family status. Interventions could be modified to include psychoeducation about the signs of bullying, reasons why children might hesitate to tell parents about bullying, and how to foster an environment that encourages children to talk about these issues. Interventions could also be adapted to empower parents with strategies for working with school personnel to create a safe environment for children (e.g., by sharing with schools the research showing linkages between school practices and the well-being of children of LGBQ parents).

Adoption and Foster Parenting Programs

Because same-sex couples are more likely to foster or adopt children than are their heterosexual counterparts (Gates, 2013), parenting intervention programs that focus on families built through adoption and foster care are of particular interest. The few intervention programs developed for adoptive families (e.g., Video-Feedback Intervention to Promote Positive Parenting; Juffer, Bakermans-Kranenburg, & van IJzendoorn, 2005) have not been tested in RCTs; therefore, we review those programs that have been tested in RCTs, which tend to focus on foster parents.

Families built through adoption may confront specific challenges that can be the focus of clinical treatment or intervention (Brodzinsky, 2013). One adoption-specific challenge that has been the focus of empirical study and intervention is parent–child attachment, particularly for adopted children who experienced early adversity. One attachment intervention that may be applicable for adoptive families is Attachment and Biobehavioral Catch-up (ABC), a short (10-session) manualized intervention focused on developing secure attachment in children exposed to early adversity (Bernard et al., 2012). Although this intervention was originally designed to be implemented with birth families involved in the child welfare system (e.g., parents at risk for having their children removed from their care), training caregivers to provide "therapeutic" parenting to children who have experienced abuse and neglect is relevant to, and can likely be adapted for, parents adopting from foster care.

Grounded in Ainsworth's attachment theory (Ainsworth, Blehar, Waters, & Wall, 1978), the ABC intervention recognizes that children exposed to early adversity may show insecure attachment patterns, including behaviors that discourage warm and caring responses from caregivers (e.g., turning away and fussiness). The manualized program consists of 10 videotaped home visits conducted by parent trainers—staff members trained in this model and supervised for fidelity to the program. The parent and child participate in home-based sessions together; other children and adults in the home are encouraged to join. Using a combination of observation, feedback, and psychoeducation, parent trainers guide families through sessions focusing on developing new skills in parents, including providing nurturance, "following the lead [of the child] with delight," decreasing parental behaviors that are frightening to the child, and recognizing influences from parents' own childhoods. During sessions, parent trainers observe as parents and children engage in an activity, during which the trainer provides in-the-moment feedback to parents about their behavior. Post-session, parents are given feedback using the videotaped interactions (Bernard et al., 2012).

The limited empirical evidence on the ABC approach is encouraging. In an RCT with 120 children (with 113 parents), Bernard et al. (2012) found that 1 month post-intervention, children in the intervention showed higher rates of secure attachment and lower rates of disorganized attachment compared to the control group. Three-month and 3-year follow-up results showed that the children had persisting biobehavioral changes (e.g., changes in cortisol level; Bernard, Hostinar, & Dozier, 2015).

Another intervention for foster families is Keeping Foster Parents Trained and Supported (KEEP). This program is intended to work preventatively with a universal foster care population. KEEP has been shown to be efficacious in improving foster parents' parenting skills and decreasing child behavior problems (Chamberlain et al., 2008).

The KEEP program focuses on improving foster parents' skills by providing 16 weeks of group-based behavior management training, including ongoing supervision. Behavior management practices are targeted in two ways. First, the frequency of discipline is reduced by teaching foster parents to provide more positive reinforcement than discipline (i.e., a ratio of four reinforcements to one discipline). Second, the program encourages non-harsh discipline techniques such as giving short time outs and removing privileges for reasonable periods of time (Chamberlain et al., 2008). Each of these group sessions lasts 90 minutes and includes a 15-minute didactic lesson by facilitators, followed by a guided group discussion of ways to implement the lessons at home. The sessions are led by trained paraprofessionals and supervised by clinicians (Chamberlain et al., 2008).

A randomized trial of KEEP, with 700 participating foster families (nearly entirely mothers), found that the intervention was successful in significantly increasing the proportion of positive reinforcement provided and significantly decreasing foster children's behavioral problems. The effects of the intervention were the strongest for families with foster children who started the program with more behavioral challenges (Chamberlain et al., 2008). Importantly, children whose foster parents were in the intervention were more likely to leave foster care to go back to their family of origin rather than being asked to leave the foster home because of problems (Price et al., 2008). In summary, the KEEP program showed efficacy in improving foster parents' parenting skills and, by extension, foster children's behavior and foster care outcomes.

Adaptation to LGBQ Parent Families

Interventions such as ABC and KEEP hold promise for addressing the needs of foster and adoptive parents and setting these families up for success by fostering secure attachment in children who have experienced early adversity, as well as by improving foster parents' parenting skills and by preventing child behavior problems. Therefore, it is important to consider how these types of programs might be applied to LGBQ parents and same-sex couples. As with interventions aimed at LGBQ parenting more generally, these interventions could benefit from the following adaptations and considerations:

- Both ABC and KEEP focus almost entirely on mothers and "mothering," without consideration or study of fathers. This leaves questions about the implementation and effectiveness for fathers, particularly gay fathers. For example, both programs require an interactive relational format (i.e., one-on-one coaching in ABC and group parenting programs in KEEP) that has mainly included female participants and coaches. Unknown is whether these programs would be successful if the ABC coaches were a different gender than that of parents or if the KEEP parenting groups were mixed-gender. A recent study found that gay men often felt uncomfortable or unwelcome at events such as Parent–Teacher Association meetings because of the female-dominated nature of schools and "primary" parenting (Goldberg, Black, Manley, & Frost, 2017). Thus, attention to the gender makeup of these groups in the context of addressing parenting issues is important.
- The focus of these groups is on "primary" parenting, which is less common in LGBQ parents, where responsibilities are more likely to

be split between parenting partners. Thus, the program will need to be reworked and adapted to effectively incorporate two parents.

- ABC's unique video feedback and in-the-moment feedback may present unique stressors for LGBQ parents, particularly fathers, who face societal skepticism of their parental fitness and stereotypes regarding gendered expectations of parenting. Specific training in stereotype threat might be essential for trainers to be able to anticipate and, it is hoped, alleviate concerns regarding feedback.

CASE STUDY

The following is a clinical vignette aimed at illuminating some of the issues that a same-sex couple might experience during the transition to parenthood and beyond and also the ways in which supports and interventions may need to be adapted to be sensitive and effective.

Jenny and Rebecca

Jenny (a social worker) and Rebecca (a tax attorney) are a lesbian couple living in a Northeast suburb. Both women tried to become pregnant for several years. First, Jenny tried—she had the greater desire to experience pregnancy, birth, and breast-feeding. After 2 years of undergoing in vitro fertilization (IVF), Jenny reluctantly terminated her efforts to conceive due to the lack of success and the high expense of IVF. After 6 months of "regrouping," the couple decided that Rebecca would try to become pregnant. Rebecca was initially less enthusiastic about the prospect of being the "carrying" partner; she worked long hours and was concerned about the effect that the pregnancy would have on her productivity at a crucial time in her career. But at Jenny's encouragement, she agreed to try to get pregnant—with the understanding that if Jenny found herself jealous or uncomfortable, she would stop her efforts and they would turn to adoption.

Rebecca became pregnant on her first insemination attempt. Both she and Jenny were elated—but also ambivalent, because Jenny realized that Rebecca would be experiencing a process (pregnancy) and event (birth) that she had always longed for. The two began to argue more frequently. Soon, Jenny became depressed and began calling into work sick. Eventually, she was fired, and she slipped into a deep depression.

In her second trimester, Rebecca miscarried after a car accident. Both women endured deep grief related to the lost pregnancy. Rebecca blamed herself for the accident and the loss of their child. Jenny blamed herself for not being "happier" for Rebecca and their future family, wondering whether God had caused this to happen because of her ambivalence about the pregnancy. Jenny and Rebecca entered couples therapy at this point to try to "find their way back" to each other and to decide what they would do next with respect to family building. However, their therapist did not seem to understand Jenny's grief about being unable to conceive. For instance, their therapist joked that he "thought that the great thing about being a lesbian couple was access to two wombs!" On another occasion, he expressed confusion as to how two females could both be the mothers to a child and inquired, "Who will fill the father role?" After that remark, feeling deeply alienated and misunderstood, Jenny and Rebecca terminated couples therapy and decided that it was better to "work it out" on their own.

After 6 months of what Rebecca wryly referred to as their "own brand of do-it-yourself therapy," whereby they took an hour walk on Mondays to talk about their feelings, scheduled a joint massage on Fridays, and spent time in their garden on weekends, the couple felt ready to pursue adoption. With their funds exhausted from IVF, they knew that adopting through the child welfare system "made the most sense." Rebecca was more hesitant about adopting through the foster care system than was Jenny; she worried about adopting a child with significant problems that they would not be able to handle. They agreed to only consider children younger than 1 year old, with no known prenatal drug exposure. This, they knew, would likely lengthen their wait time.

After enduring the paperwork, classes and trainings (in which they were the only same-sex couple), and a 6-month wait, they were placed with a 1-year-old biracial girl named Jade. This was a legally risky placement because the birth mother's rights had not yet been terminated, and she was still working with social workers to regain custody. Rebecca and Jenny fell in love with Jade. However, they were uneasily aware of the possibility that they would not be able to adopt her. Rebecca found herself protecting herself from this potential blow by not allowing herself to fully attach to Jade, and she downplayed the likelihood of them adopting her to friends and family. This upset Jenny, who found that she could not help but attach to Jade. The greatest stress in their life, however, was the visits that Jade continued to have with her birth mother—who, Jenny knew from a comment made by a social worker, "was not pleased" that Jade was placed with a two-mother family. During this time, Rebecca and Jenny sought out a support group for adoptive parents that was recommended by their social worker, but they found that it was a poor fit because all of the parents had actually adopted their children (they were not foster parents), and there were no other lesbian or gay adoptive parents. After attending a few sessions, Rebecca and Jenny decided that they had "gotten everything [they] were going to get" from the group, and they stopped going.

After a year of legal "hell," Jade's birth mother's rights were terminated, and Jade was legally free for adoption. Rebecca and Jenny joyfully had their day in court and became Jade's legal parents. Jenny and Rebecca both wept with relief. Although delighted that they were finally the legal parents of the child they had grown to love, Jenny and Rebecca found that the stress of infertility, miscarriage, and the adoption process had caught up with them. For instance, Jenny had gained 40 pounds during the past year, and Rebecca had become a heavier drinker than she had ever been in the past. Then, when Jade was 2½ years old, she began acting out at daycare and hitting other children. The daycare providers stated that Jade was "not like the other kids" and asked Jenny and Rebecca to stop bringing Jade until she could be safe around other children. This created a particularly high level of anxiety and hypervigilance in Jenny, who, in turn, constantly compared herself to Rebecca (whom both women agreed was the calmer, "type B" parent). The couple knew they needed support, but they were unsure where to find it. Thinking back to their isolating experiences with couple's therapy and the adoption support group, they decided to ask a local LGBTQ parenting group to recommend some LGBTQ-competent couples therapists.

Jenny and Rebecca began to work with one of the recommended therapists, Dr. Sun. After a few sessions, Dr. Sun recognized that Jenny and Rebecca were struggling to work together, manage stress, and solve problems as a unit. She suggested that the couple could benefit from a program that could help them improve the ways they interacted as a couple in order to better support each other and enhance family harmony. Jenny and Rebecca agreed that this could be useful; they recognized that they had "developed some bad habits" during their struggle to become parents. Dr. Sun invited them to participate in a couple's therapy group that used an evidence-based model, the Couples Coping Enhancement Training (CCET) program. Dr. Sun explained that the CCET group included same- and different-sex couples, and she provided some important background about the program. Specifically, she explained that CCET was developed for heterosexual couples and, although the facilitators had modified the handouts and other materials to reflect the experiences of diverse couples, the program included some instructional videos that featured only different-sex couples. Dr. Sun further explained that most of the same-sex couples who participated had reported that the program was helpful to them, despite the visual focus on different-sex couples. With this information—which reflected an awareness of heteronormativity on Dr. Sun's part—Jenny and Rebecca felt much more comfortable agreeing to try another group treatment setting.

During the CCET group program, Jenny and Rebecca learned to identify sources of stress in their family and developed new ways of coping with those stresses as a family. They particularly benefited from some of the material about stressors unique to same-sex couples (e.g., uncertainty about balancing housework and parenting responsibilities and fears that Jade's behavioral challenges would be viewed as being "caused" by having two moms), which Dr. Sun had added for her same-sex couple inclusive groups. They also benefited from hearing from another lesbian couple who had adopted two children via foster care and who described some similar struggles with IVF.

With their improved communication skills, Jenny and Rebecca were able to discuss some of their difficulties as parents. Jenny expressed that she worried that Rebecca still had not bonded fully with Jade and that she felt responsible for all of the emotional work of supporting their daughter. Rebecca was able to express her concerns that Jenny's "type A" parenting style seemed to "wind Jade up" and increase problem behaviors. Rebecca and Jenny agreed that they both needed to work on their parenting practices, and they hoped that Dr. Sun could provide them with family therapy. Dr. Sun agreed that the couple seemed to have identified important challenges that they needed to address, but she stated that she worked only with couples and did not have training to work with children. She recommended that the couple seek help from Jade's social worker to find adoption-related parenting interventions. Dr. Sun offered to talk with the provider of that program in order to provide them with resources and offer advice about working with LGBTQ parents. Jenny and Rebecca were disappointed that they would need to find a new practitioner, but they were more comfortable searching for a new program, knowing that Dr. Sun could assist them.

Jenny and Rebecca reached out to the social worker who had recommended the adoption support group. They explained the challenges that they had with the group and why they eventually left. The social worker was understanding and apologized for having not realized that the group would be a bad fit, noting that she would take their feedback and use it to try to help other families in the future. Jenny and Rebecca then asked the social worker for help finding a parenting program that might be appropriate for them. They explained Dr. Sun's offer to help a practitioner adapt their programs for two-mom families, and they asked if the social worker knew anyone who would be open to that sort of help. The social worker directed them to an adoption-focused organization that offered parenting interventions focused on parent–child relationships.

Jenny, Rebecca, and Jade were offered the Attachment and Biobehavioral Catch-up (ABC) program, which consisted of home visits, parent coaching, and psychoeducation. Jenny and Rebecca were hesitant to invite a provider into their home, but they tentatively agreed—explaining that Dr. Sun would soon be in touch to offer resources and guidance for working with diverse families. The provider enthusiastically agreed to talk to Dr. Sun and thanked them for the learning opportunity.

After that, the family began ABC sessions with the provider. The provider explained the program and acknowledged some ways that she had decided to adapt the program to make it suitable for a two-mom family. These adaptations included conducting sessions with both parents present and modifying some of the educational materials. She also encouraged Jenny and Rebecca to point out anything they thought could be improved for same-sex families.

During ABC sessions, the provider observed Jenny and Rebecca playing with Jade and provided real-time feedback about when they were "following her lead" or giving "warm and caring" responses. At some sessions, the provider videotaped interactions; in subsequent meetings, she played the videos and provided feedback to Jenny and Rebecca. She was able to point out problematic patterns, such as when Jenny would respond to Jade's behavior by becoming anxious and trying to control the situation, which would lead to Jade escalating her behavior. They talked about and practiced different ways of "responding with a plan." The provider also gave feedback to Rebecca about times that she missed opportunities to be warm and caring with Jade, and she was able to point out instances when Rebecca did not respond to Jade's cues or take opportunities to bond.

Both Jenny and Rebecca believed that their experiences of treatment with the CCETP and ABC programs were successful. Jade's behavior became more manageable, and she has had no incidents at her new preschool. Furthermore, Jenny and Rebecca believe that their relationship has improved. In fact, they are doing so much better that they are considering adopting another child. Rebecca joked that "Jade wouldn't be getting any brothers or sisters if we had stuck with our 'do-it-yourself' therapy!"

Considerations

- Jenny and Rebecca faced a lack of sensitivity to their unique experiences as a lesbian couple in the context of couples therapy and adoption support groups. Much could have been done to more sensitively and effectively treat this couple. For example, guidance could have been offered for addressing the complex feelings that arose due to not being the expectant mother in the couple. Also, had the therapist sought out education to correct his stereotypes and incorrect beliefs (e.g., the notion that children need a father to develop normally and the notion that in a female couple, one partner will play the "father role"), he might have been in a position to develop an authentic relationship with, and support, the couple. The willingness of both Dr. Sun and the ABC provider to learn and adapt programs for diverse families reflects some of the important work that therapists will need to do to effectively work with LGBQ clients. Indeed, in order to effectively implement parenting interventions with LGBQ parents, personnel will need to examine hidden biases about LGBQ parenting, receive appropriate psychoeducation about LGBQ parenting, and critically explore whether all aspects of the intervention are appropriate "as is" in the current context.
- Rebecca and Jenny experienced alienation as a result of being the only same-sex couple in their adoption trainings and support groups. Ultimately, this alienation factored into their decision to abandon their first support group. Parenting intervention programs, like the group-based CCET and KEEP programs, must anticipate and effectively plan for situations such as this. How can service providers provide a sensitive group learning/support environment for LGBTQ parents when they are—as they often will be—surrounded only by heterosexual parents? In such situations, providers may find it appropriate to connect LGBTQ parents with additional resources, such as LGBTQ-specific support groups or organizations.
- Jenny and Rebecca certainly benefited from the ABC parenting intervention. Their high level of personal and relational stress, and the likelihood that they may continue to face "bumps in the road" with respect to their daughter's externalizing behaviors, rendered them vulnerable to poor family functioning and negative parenting practices. As an effective parenting program, ABC provided them with important tools and resources to approach parenting challenges, and

the couples-focused CCET helped them learn to cope with the stress that they are facing in their lives. Importantly, the effectiveness of such programs hinges on their sensitivity to diverse families, the skillfulness of the group leaders, and the couple's own willingness to try such programs.

CONCLUSION

This chapter provided the state-of-the-science evidence for LGBQ parent interventions. We presented an overview of current research on LGBQ parents and their families, followed by a review of evidence-based parenting interventions and an illustration of some important adaptations and considerations that practitioners can apply to ensure the efficacy of such interventions for diverse families. By applying the evidence-based modifications discussed in this chapter, these interventions hold great promise for helping LGBTQ parents as they transition to parenthood and beyond. However, although our recommendations are based on the existing research on LGBQ parent families, it is important to note that such families have largely been absent from practice research. Future RCTs that test interventions specifically for LGBTQ parent families are needed to ensure that all families have access to treatments that are proven to work for families like theirs.

REFERENCES

Abelsohn, K. A., Epstein, R., & Ross, L. E. (2013). Celebrating the "other" parent: Mental health and wellness of expecting lesbian, bisexual, and queer non-birth parents. *Journal of Gay & Lesbian Mental Health, 17*(4), 387–405. doi:10.1080/19359705.2013.771808

Ainsworth, D. S., Blehar, M. C., Waters, E., & Wall, S. (1978). *Patterns of attachment: A psychological study of the Strange Situation.* Hillsdale, NJ: Erlbaum.

Arnett, J. J., & Tanner, J. L. (Eds.). (2006). *Emerging adults in America: Coming of age in the 21st century.* Washington, DC: American Psychological Association.

Bagner, D. M., & Eyberg, S. M. (2007). Parent–child interaction therapy for disruptive behavior in children with mental retardation: A randomized controlled trial. *Journal of Clinical Child and Adolescent Psychology, 36*(3), 418–429. doi:10.1080/15374410701448448

Baiocco, R., Santamaria, F., Ioverno, S., Fontanesi, L., Baumgartner, E., . . . Lingiardi, V. (2015). Lesbian mother families and gay father families in Italy: Family functioning, dyadic satisfaction, and child well-being. *Sexuality Research & Social Policy, 12*(3), 202–212. doi:10.1007/s13178-015-0185-x

Bergman, K., Rubio, R. J., Green, R.-J., & Padron, E. (2010). Gay men who become fathers via surrogacy: The transition to parenthood. *Journal of GLBT Family Studies, 6,* 111–141. doi:10.1080/15504281003704942

Berkowitz, D. (2013). Gay men and surrogacy. In A. E. Goldberg & K. R. Allen (Eds.), *LGBT-parent families: Innovations in research and implications for practice* (pp. 71–85). New York, NY: Springer.

Bernard, K., Dozier, M., Bick, J., Lewis-Morrarty, E., Lindhiem, O., & Carlson, E. (2012). Enhancing attachment organization among maltreated infants: Results of a randomized clinical trial. *Child Development, 83*, 623–636. doi:10.1111/j.1467-8624.2011.01712.x

Bernard, K., Hostinar, C., & Dozier, M. (2015). Intervention effects on diurnal cortisol rhythms of Child Protective Services-referred infants in early childhood: Preschool follow-up results of a randomized clinical trial. *JAMA Pediatrics, 169*(2), 112–119. doi:10.1001/jamapediatrics.2014.2369

Bodenmann, G., Bradbury, T. N., & Pihet, S. (2008). Relative contributions of treatment-related changes in communication skills and dyadic coping skills to the longitudinal course of marriage in the framework of marital distress prevention. *Journal of Divorce and Remarriage, 50*(1), 1–21. doi:10.1080/ 10502550802365391

Bodenmann, G., Cina, A., Ledermann, T., & Sanders, M. R. (2008b). The efficacy of the Triple P-Positive Parenting Program in improving parenting and child behavior: A comparison with two other treatment conditions. *Behaviour Research and Therapy, 46*(4), 411–427. doi:10.1016/j.brat.2008.01.001

Bodenmann, G., & Shantinath, S. D. (2004). The Couples Coping Enhancement Training (CCET): A new approach to prevention of marital distress based upon stress and coping. *Family Relations, 53*(5), 477–484. doi:10.1111/j.0197-6664.2004.00056.x

Bos, H., & Gartrell, N. (2010). Adolescents of the USA National Longitudinal Lesbian Family Study: Can family characteristics counteract the negative effects of stigmatization? *Family Process, 49*, 559–572. doi:10.1111/j.1545-5300.2010.01340.x

Bos, H., & van Balen, F. (2010). Children of the new reproductive technologies: Social and genetic parenthood. *Patient Education & Counseling, 81*, 429–435. doi:10.1016/j.pec.2010.09.012

Bos, H., van Gelderen, L., & Gartrell, N. (2015). Lesbian and heterosexual two-parent families: Adolescent–parent relationship quality and adolescent well-being. *Journal of Child and Family Studies, 24*(4), 1031–1046. doi:10.1007/s10826-014-9913-8

Bos, H. M., van Balen, F., & van den Boom, D. C. (2004). Experience of parenthood, couple relationship, social support, and child rearing goals in planned lesbian families. *Journal of Child Psychology and Psychiatry, 45*, 755–764. doi:10.1111/j.1469-7610.2004.00269.x

Brodzinsky, D. (2013). *A need to know: Enhancing adoption competence among mental health professionals: Policy perspective.* New York, NY: Donaldson Adoption Institute. Retrieved from https://www.adoptioninstitute.org

Brodzinsky, D. M., & Goldberg, A. E. (2016). Contact with birth family in adoptive families headed by lesbian, gay male, and heterosexual parents. *Children and Youth Services Review, 62*, 9–17. doi:10.1016/j.childyouth.2016.01.014

Cacciatore, J., & Raffo, Z. (2011). An exploration of lesbian maternal bereavement. *Social Work, 56*(2), 169–177. doi:10.1093/sw/56.2.159

Canario, C., & Figueiredo, B. (2016). Partner relationship from early pregnancy to 30 months postpartum: Gender and parity effects. *Couple and Family Psychology: Research & Practice, 5*, 226–239. doi:10.1037/cfp0000066

Chabot, J. M., & Ames, B. D. (2004). "It wasn't 'let's get pregnant and go do it'": Decision-making in lesbian couples planning motherhood via donor insemination. *Family Relations, 53*, 348–356. doi:10.1111/j.0197-6664.2004.00041.x

Chamberlain, P., Price, J., Leve, L. D., Laurent, H., Landsverk, J. A., & Reid, J. B. (2008). Prevention of behavior problems for children in foster care: Outcomes and mediation effects. *Prevention Science*, 9(1), 17–27. doi:10.1007/s11121-007-0080-7

Chan, R., Brooks, R., Raboy, B., & Patterson, C. (1998). Division of labor among lesbian and heterosexual parents: Associations with children's adjustment. *Journal of Family Psychology*, 12, 402–419. doi:10.1037//0893-3200.12.3.402

Chateauneuf, D., & Ouellette, F. R. (2017). Kinship within the context of new genetics: The experience of infertility from medical assistance to adoption. *Journal of Family Issues*, 38(2), 177–203. doi:10.1177/0192513X15596195

Child Welfare Information Gateway. (2013). Open adoption. Retrieved from https://www.childwelfare.gov/pubs/f_openadopt.pdf

Child Welfare Information Gateway. (2016). *Planning for adoption: Knowing the costs and resources*. Washington, DC: US Department of Health and Human Services, Children's Bureau.

Cowan, C. P., & Cowan, P. A. (1992). *When partners become parents: The big life change for couples*. New York, NY: Basic Books.

DeMino, K. A., Appleby, G., & Fisk, D. (2007). Lesbian mothers with planned families: A comparative study of internalized homophobia and social support. *American Journal of Orthopsychiatry*, 77, 165–173. doi:10.1037/0002-9432.77.1.165

Dodge, B., & Sandfort, T. G. M. (2007). A review of mental health research on bisexual individuals when compared to homosexual and heterosexual individuals. In B. A. Firestein (Ed.), *Becoming visible: Counseling bisexuals across the lifespan* (pp. 28–51). New York, NY: Columbia University Press.

Doss, B. D., Rhoades, G. K., Stanley, S. M., & Markman, H. J. (2009). The effect of the transition to parenthood on relationship quality: An 8-year prospective study. *Journal of Personality and Social Psychology*, 96, 601–619. doi:10.1037/a0013969

Downing, J. B. (2013). Transgender-parent families. In A. E. Goldberg & K. R. Allen (Eds.), *LGBT-parent families: Innovations in research and implications for practice* (pp. 105–115). New York, NY: Springer.

Downing, J. B., & Goldberg, A. E. (2010). Lesbian mothers' constructions of the division of paid and unpaid labor. *Feminism & Psychology*, 21(1), 100–120. doi:10.1177/0959353510375869

Downing, J. B., Richardson, H. B., Kinkler, L. A., & Goldberg, A. E. (2009). Making the decision: Factors influencing gay men's choice of an adoption path. *Adoption Quarterly*, 12, 247–271. doi:10.1080/10926750903313310

Eyberg, S. M., Funderburk, B. W., Hembree Kigin, T., McNeil, B., Querido, J. G., & Hood, K. K. (2001). Parent–child interaction therapy with behavior problem children: One and two year maintenance of treatment effects in the family. *Child & Family Behavior Therapy*, 23(4), 1–20. doi:10.1300/J019v23n04_01

Farr, R. H., Forssell, S. L., & Patterson, C. J. (2010a). Lesbian, gay, and heterosexual adoptive parents: Couple and relationship issues. *Journal of GLBT Family Studies*, 6(2), 199–213. doi:10.1080/15504281003705436

Farr, R. H., Forssell, S. L., & Patterson, C. J. (2010b). Parenting and child development in adoptive families: Does parental sexual orientation matter? *Applied Developmental Science*, 10, 164–178. doi:10.1080/10888691.2010.500958

Farr, R. H., & Patterson, C. J. (2009). Transracial adoption by lesbian, gay, and heterosexual couples: Who completes transracial adoptions and with what results? *Adoption Quarterly*, 12, 187–204. doi:10.1080/10926750903313328

Farr, R. H., & Patterson, C. J. (2013). Coparenting among lesbian, gay, and heterosexual couples: Associations with adopted children's outcomes. *Child Development, 84*(4), 1226–1240. doi:10.1111/cdev.12046

Feinberg, M. E. (2003). The internal structure and ecological context of coparenting: A framework for research and intervention. *Parenting: Science and Practice, 3*, 95–132. doi:10.1207/S15327922PAR0302_01

Feinberg, M. E., Jones, D. E., Hostetler, M. L., Roettger, M. E., Paul, I. M., & Ehrenthal, D.B. (2016). Couple-focused prevention at the transition to parenthood— A randomized trial: Effects on coparenting, parenting, family violence, and parent and child adjustment. *Prevention Science, 17*, 751–764. doi:10.1007/s11121-016-0674-z

Feinberg, M. E., Jones, D. E., Kan, M. L., & Goslin, M. C. (2010). Effects of family foundations on parents and children: 3.5 years after baseline. *Journal of Family Psychology, 24*, 532–542. doi:10.1037/a0020837

Feinberg, M. E., Jones, D. E., Roettger, M. E., Solmeyer, A., & Hostetler, M. L. (2014). Long-term follow-up of a randomized trial of family foundations: Effects on children's emotional, behavioral, and school adjustment. *Journal of Family Psychology, 28*, 821–831. doi:10.1037/fam0000037

Feinberg, M. E., Kan, M. L., & Hetherington, E. M. (2007). The longitudinal influence of coparenting conflict on parental negativity and adolescent maladjustment. *Journal of Marriage and Family, 69*, 687–702. doi:10.1111/j.1741-3737.2007.00400.x

Gartrell, N. K., Banks, A., Hamilton, J., Reed, N., Bishop, H., & Rodas, C. (1999). The National Lesbian Family Study: 2. Interviews with mothers of toddlers. *American Journal of Orthopsychiatry, 69*, 362–369. doi:10.1037/h0080410

Gartrell, N. K., Banks, A., Reed, N., Hamilton, J., Rodas, C., & Deck, A. (2000). The National Lesbian Family Study: 3. Interviews with mothers of five-year-olds. *American Journal of Orthopsychiatry, 70*, 542–548. doi:10.1037/h0087823

Gartrell, N. K., & Bos, H. M. W. (2010). US National Longitudinal Lesbian Family Study: Psychological adjustment of 17-year-old adolescents. *Pediatrics, 126*, 28–36. doi:10.1542/peds.2009-3153

Gartrell, N. K., Bos, H. M. W., Peyser, H., Deck, A., & Rodas, C. (2011). Family characteristics, custody arrangements, and adolescent psychological well-being after lesbian mothers break up. *Family Relations, 60*, 572–585. doi:10.1111/j.1741-3729.2011.00667.x

Gartrell, N. K., Deck, A., Rodas, C., Peyser, H., & Banks, A. (2005). The National Lesbian Family Study: 4. Interviews with the 10-year-old children. *American Journal of Orthopsychiatry, 75*, 518–524. doi:10.1037/0002-9432.75.4.518

Gartrell, N. K., Hamilton, J., Banks, A., Mosbacher, D., Reed, N., . . . Bishop, H. (1996). The National Lesbian Family Study: 1. Interviews with prospective mothers. *American Journal of Orthopsychiatry, 66*, 272–281. doi:10.1037/h0080178

Gates, G. (2011). *Family formation and raising children among same-sex couples* (NCFR Report, Issue FF51, pp. F1–F4). Retrieved from http://williamsinstitute.law.ucla.edu/wp-content/uploads/Gates-Badgett-NCFR-LGBT-Families-December-2011.pdf

Gates, G. (2013). LGBT parenting in the United States. Retrieved from http://williamsinstitute.law.ucla.edu/wp-content/uploads/LGBT-Parenting.pdf

Goldberg, A. E. (2006). The transition to parenthood for lesbian couples. *Journal of GLBT Family Studies, 2*, 13–42. doi:10.1300/j461v02n01_02

Goldberg, A. E. (2007). (How) does it make a difference? Perspectives of adults with lesbian, gay, and bisexual parents. *American Journal of Orthopsychiatry*, *77*, 550–562. doi:10.1037/0002-9432.77.4.550

Goldberg, A. E. (2009). Lesbian and heterosexual preadoptive couples' openness to transracial adoption. *American Journal of Orthopsychiatry*, 79(1), 103–117.

Goldberg, A. E. (2010). *Lesbian and gay parents and their children: Research on the family life cycle*. Washington, DC: American Psychological Association.

Goldberg, A. E. (2012). *Gay dads: Transitions to adoptive fatherhood*. New York, NY: New York University Press.

Goldberg, A. E. (2013). "Doing" and "undoing" gender: The meaning and division of housework in same-sex couples. *Journal of Family Theory and Review*, *5*, 85–104. doi:10.1111/jftr.12009

Goldberg, A. E., & Allen, K. A. (2013a). Donor, dad, or . . .? Young adults with lesbian parents' experiences with known donors. *Family Process*, *52*, 338–550. doi:10.1111/famp.12029

Goldberg, A. E., & Allen, K. R. (2013b). Same-sex relationship dissolution and LGB step-family formation: Perspectives of young adults with LGB parents. *Family Relations*, *62*, 529–544. doi:10.1111/fare.12024

Goldberg, A. E., Black, K. A., Manley, M. M., & Frost, R. (2017). "We told them that we are both really involved parents": Sexual minority and heterosexual adoptive parents' engagement in school communities. *Gender & Education*, *29*, 614–631. doi:10.1080/09540253.2017.1296114

Goldberg, A. E., Downing, J. B., & Richardson, H. B. (2009). The transition from infertility to adoption: Perceptions of lesbian and heterosexual preadoptive couples. *Journal of Social and Personal Relationships*, *26*, 938–963. doi:10.1177/0265407509345652

Goldberg, A. E., Downing, J. B., & Sauck, C. C. (2007). Choices, challenges, and tensions: Perspectives of lesbian prospective adoptive parents. *Adoption Quarterly*, *10*, 33–64. doi:10.1300/j145v10n02_02

Goldberg, A. E., Downing, J. B., & Sauck, C. C. (2008). Perceptions of children's parental preferences in lesbian two-mother households. *Journal of Marriage and Family*, *70*, 419–434. doi:10.1111/j.1741-3737.2008.00491.x

Goldberg, A. E., & Garcia, R. (2015). Predictors of relationship dissolution among lesbian, gay, and heterosexual adoptive couples. *Journal of Family Psychology*, *29*(3), 394–404. doi:10.1037/fam0000095

Goldberg, A. E., & Gartrell, N. (2014). Children with LGBT parents: Research trends, emerging issues, and future directions. In J. Benson (Ed.), *Advances in child development and behavior* (pp. 57–88). New York, NY: Elsevier.

Goldberg, A. E., Kinkler, L. A., Richardson, H. B., & Downing, J. B. (2011). Perceptions and experiences of open adoption among lesbian, gay, and heterosexual couples: A qualitative study. *Journal of Marriage and Family*, *73*, 502–518. doi:10.1111/j.1741-3737.2010.00821.x

Goldberg, A. E., Kinkler, L. A., Richardson, H. B., & Downing, J. B. (2012). On the border: Young adults with LGBQ parents navigate LGBTQ communities. *Journal of Counseling Psychology*, *59*, 71–85. doi:1 0.1037/a0024576

Goldberg, A. E., Moyer, A. M., Black, K., & Henry, A. (2015). Lesbian and heterosexual adoptive mothers' experiences of relationship dissolution. *Sex Roles*, *73*, 141–156.

Goldberg, A. E., Moyer, A. M., & Kinkler, L. A. (2013). Lesbian, gay, and heterosexual adoptive parents' perceptions of parental bonding during early parenthood. *Couple and Family Psychology: Research and Practice, 2*, 146–162. doi:10.1037/a0031834

Goldberg, A. E., Moyer, A. M., Kinkler, L. A., & Richardson, H. B. (2012). "When you're sitting on the fence, hope's the hardest part": Experiences and challenges of lesbian, gay, and heterosexual couples adopting through the child welfare system. *Adoption Quarterly, 15*, 1–28. doi:10.1080/10926755.2012.731032

Goldberg, A. E., & Perry-Jenkins, M. (2007). The division of labor and perceptions of parental roles: Lesbian couples across the transition to parenthood. *Journal of Social and Personal Relationships, 24*, 297–318. doi:10.1177/0265407507075415

Goldberg, A. E., & Smith, J. Z. (2008a). Social support and well-being in lesbian and heterosexual preadoptive parents. *Family Relations, 57*, 281–294. doi:10.1111/j.1741-3729.2008.00500.x

Goldberg, A. E., & Smith, J. Z. (2008b). The social context of lesbian mothers' anxiety during early parenthood. *Parenting: Science & Practice, 8*, 213–239. doi:10.1080/15295190802204801

Goldberg, A. E., & Smith, J. Z. (2009). Perceived parenting skill across the transition to adoptive parenthood among lesbian, gay, and heterosexual couples. *Journal of Family Psychology, 23*, 861–870. doi:10.1037/a0017009

Goldberg, A. E., & Smith, J. Z. (2011). Stigma, social context, and mental health: Lesbian and gay couples across the transition to adoptive parenthood. *Journal of Counseling Psychology, 58*, 139–150. doi:10.1037/a0021684

Goldberg, A. E., & Smith, J. Z. (2013). Predictors of psychological adjustment among early-placed adopted children with lesbian, gay, and heterosexual parents. *Journal of Family Psychology, 27*, 431–442. doi:10.1037/a0032911

Goldberg, A. E., & Smith, J. Z. (2014). Predictors of parenting stress during early parenthood in lesbian, gay, and heterosexual adoptive parents. *Journal of Family Psychology, 28*, 125–137. doi:10.1037/a0036007

Goldberg, A. E., Smith, J. Z., & Kashy, D. A. (2010). Pre-adoptive factors predicting lesbian, gay, and heterosexual couples' relationship quality across the transition to adoptive parenthood. *Journal of Family Psychology, 24*, 221–232. doi:10.1037/a0019615

Goldberg, A. E., Smith, J. Z., & Perry-Jenkins, M. (2012). The division of labor in lesbian, gay, and heterosexual new adoptive parents. *Journal of Marriage and Family, 74*, 812–828. doi:10.1111/j.1741-3737.2012.00992.x

Goldberg, A. E., Sweeney, K., Black, K., & Moyer, A. (2016). Lesbian, gay, and heterosexual parents' socialization approaches to children's minority statuses. *The Counseling Psychologist, 44*, 267–299.

Golombok, S., Mellish, L., Jennings, S., Casey, P., Tasker, F., & Lamb, M. E. (2014). Adoptive gay father families: Parent–child relationships and children's psychological adjustment. *Child Development, 85*(2), 456–468. doi:10.1111/cdev.12155

Golombok, S., Perry, B., Burston, A., Murray, C., Mooney-Somers, J., Stevens, M., & Golding, J. (2003). Children with lesbian parents: A community study. *Developmental Psychology, 39*, 20–33. doi:10.1037/0012-1649.39.1.20

Halford, W. K., & Bodenmann, G. (2013). Effects of relationship education on maintenance of couple relationship satisfaction. *Clinical Psychology Review, 33*(4), 512–525. doi:10.1016/j.cpr.2013.02.001

Heinrichs, N., Kliem, S., & Hahlweg, K. (2014). Four-year follow-up of a randomized controlled trial of Triple P Group for parent and child outcomes. *Prevention Science*, *15*(2), 233–245. doi:10.1007/s11121-012-0358-2

Hembree-Kigin, T. L., & McNeil, C. B. (1995). *Parent–child interaction therapy*. New York, NY: Plenum.

Herman, G. (2015, June 13). What could gay marriage mean for the kids? *New York Times*. Retrieved from https://www.nytimes.com/interactive/2015/06/12/sunday-review/same-sex-households-children.html

Hood, K. K., & Eyberg, S. M. (2003). Outcomes of parent–child interaction therapy: Mothers' reports of maintenance three to six years after treatment. *Journal of Clinical Child and Adolescent Psychology*, *32*(3), 419–429. doi:10.1207/S15374424JCCP3203_10

Hunter, A. (2015). Lesbian mommy blogging in Canada: Documenting subtle homophobia in Canadian society and building community online. *Journal of Lesbian Studies*, *19*, 212–229. doi:10.1080/10894160.2015.969077

Jennings, S., Mellish, L., Tasker, F., Lamb, M., & Golombok, S. (2014). Why adoption? Gay, lesbian, and heterosexual adoptive parents' reproductive experiences and reasons for adoption. *Adoption Quarterly*, *17*, 205–226. doi:10.1080/10926755.2014.891549

Juffer, F., Bakermans-Kranenburg, M. J., & IJzendoorn, M. H. (2005). The importance of parenting in the development of disorganized attachment: Evidence from a preventive intervention study in adoptive families. *Journal of Child Psychology and Psychiatry*, *46*(3), 263–274. doi:10.1111/j.1469-7610.2004.00353.x

Karreman, A., van Tuijl, C., van Aken, M. A. G., & Dekovic, M. (2008). Parenting, coparenting, and effortful control in preschoolers. *Journal of Family Psychology*, *22*, 30–40. doi:10.1037/0893-3200.22.1.30

Kosciw, J. G., & Diaz, E. M. (2008). *Involved, invisible, ignored: The experiences of lesbian, gay, bisexual, and transgender parents and their children in our nation's K–12 schools*. New York, NY: GLSEN.

Krishnakumar, A., & Buehler, C. (2000). Interparental conflict and parenting behaviors: A meta-analytic review. *Family Relations*, *49*, 25–44. doi:10.1111/j.1741-3729.2000.00025.x

Lavner, J. A., Waterman, J., & Peplau, L. A. (2014). Parent adjustment over time in gay, lesbian, and heterosexual parent families adopting from foster care. *American Journal of Orthopsychiatry*, *84*(1), 46–53. doi:10.1037/h0098853

Ledermann, T., Bodenmann, G., & Cina, A. (2007). The efficacy of the Couples Coping Enhancement Training (CCET) in improving relationship quality. *Journal of Social and Clinical Psychology*, *26*(8), 940–959. doi:10.1521/jscp.2007.26.8.940

Lynch, J. M. (2004a). Becoming a stepparent in gay/lesbian stepfamilies: Integrating identities. *Journal of Homosexuality*, *48*(2), 45–60. doi:10.1300/J082v48n02_03

Lynch, J. M. (2004b). The identity transformation of biological parents in lesbian/gay stepfamilies. *Journal of Homosexuality*, *47*(2), 91–107. doi:10.1300/J082v47n02_06

Milgrom, J., Ericksen, J., Leigh, B., Romeo, Y., Loughlin, E., McCarthy, R., & Saunders, B. (2009). *Towards parenthood: Preparing for the changes and challenges of a new baby*. Camberwell, Victoria, Australia: ACER Press.

Milgrom, J., Ericksen, J., McCarthy, R., Saunders, B., Loughlin, E., . . . Ross, J. (2005). Victorian intervention initiative: Antenatal support following depression—Enhancing the parent–infant relationship. In A. Buist & J. Bilszta (Eds.), *The beyondblue national postnatal depression program prevention and early intervention 2001–2005 final report—Volume II: State-based antenatal intervention initiatives* (pp. 8–25). Melbourne, Australia: beyondblue.

Milgrom, J., Schembri, C., Ericksen, J., Ross, J., & Gemmill, A. W. (2011). Towards parenthood: An antenatal intervention to reduce depression, anxiety and parenting difficulties. *Journal of Affective Disorders, 130*(3), 385–394.

Miller, B. G., Kors, S., & Macfie, J. (2017). No differences? Meta-analytic comparisons of psychological adjustment in children of gay fathers and heterosexual parents. *Psychology of Sexual Orientation and Gender Diversity, 4*(1), 14–22. doi:10.1037/sgd0000203

Moss, A. R. (2012). Alternative families, alternative lives: Married women doing bisexuality. *Journal of GLBT Family Studies, 8*(5), 405–427. doi:10.1080/1550428X.2012.729946

Murphy, D. A. (2013). The desire for parenthood: Gay men choosing to become parents through surrogacy. *Journal of Family Issues, 34*(8), 1104–1124. doi:10.1177/0192513X13484272

Nordqvist, P. (2015). "I've redeemed myself by being a 1950s 'housewife'": Parent-grandparent relationships in the context of lesbian childbirth. *Journal of Family Issues March, 36*(4), 480–500. doi:10.1177/0192513X14563798

Nixon, R. D., Sweeney, L., Erickson, D. B., & Touyz, S. W. (2003). Parent–child interaction therapy: A comparison of standard and abbreviated treatments for oppositional defiant preschoolers. *Journal of Consulting and Clinical Psychology, 71*(2), 251–260. doi:10.1037/0022-006X.71.2.251

Nixon, R. D., Sweeney, L., Erickson, D. B., & Touyz, S. W. (2004). Parent–child interaction therapy: One- and two-year follow-up of standard and abbreviated treatments for oppositional preschoolers. *Journal of Abnormal Child Psychology, 32*(3), 263–271. doi:10.1023/B:JACP.0000026140.60558.05

Patterson, C. J., Hurt, S., & Mason, C. D. (1998). Families of the lesbian baby boom: Children's contact with grandparents and other adults. *American Journal of Orthopsychiatry, 68*, 390–399. doi:10.1037/h0080348

Patterson, C. J., Sutfin, E. L., & Fulcher, M. (2004). Division of labor among lesbian and heterosexual parenting couples: Correlates of specialized versus shared patterns. *Journal of Adult Development, 11*, 179–189. doi:10.1023/B:JADE.0000035626.90331.47

Peel, E. (2010). Pregnancy loss in lesbian and bisexual women: An online survey of experiences. *Human Reproduction, 25*(3), 721–727. doi:10.1093/humrep/dep441

Power, J. J., Perlesz, A., Brown, R., Schofield, M. J., Pitts, M. K., McNair, R., & Bickerdike, A. (2012). Bisexual parents and family diversity: Findings from the Work, Love, Play Study. *Journal of Bisexuality, 12*, 519–538. doi:10.1080/15299716.2012.729432

Price, J. M., Chamberlain, P., Landsverk, J., Reid, J. B., Leve, L. D., & Laurent, H. (2008). Effects of a foster parent training intervention on placement changes of children in foster care. *Child Maltreatment, 13*(1), 64–75. doi:10.1177/1077559507310612

Rivers, I., Poteat, V. P., & Noret, N. (2008). Victimization, social support, and psychosocial functioning in same-sex and opposite-sex couples in the United States. *Developmental Psychology, 44*, 127–134. doi:10.1037/0012-1649.44.1.127

Robitaille, C., & Saint-Jacques, M. C. (2009). Social stigma and the situation of young people in lesbian and gay stepfamilies. *Journal of Homosexuality, 56*(4), 421–442. doi:10.1080/00918360902821429

Ross, L. E., & Dobinson, C. (2013). Where is the "B" in LGBT parenting? A call for research on bisexual parenting. In A. E. Goldberg & K. R. Allen (Eds.), *LGBT-parent families: Innovations in research and implications for practice* (pp. 87–103). New York, NY: Springer.

Ross, L. E., Siegel, A., Dobinson, C., Epstein, R., & Steele, L. S. (2012). "I don't want to turn totally invisible": Mental health stressors and supports among bisexual women during the perinatal period. *Journal of GLBT Family Studies, 8*(2), 137–154. doi:10.1080/1550428X.2012.660791

Ross, L. E., Steele, L. S., & Epstein, R. (2006). Service use and gaps in services for lesbian and bisexual women during donor insemination, pregnancy, and the postpartum period. *Journal of Obstetrics and Gynecology Canada, 28*, 505–511. doi:10.1016/S1701-2163(16)32181-8

Sanders, M. R., Cann, W., & Markie-Dadds, C. (2003). The Triple P-Positive Parenting Programme: A universal population-level approach to the prevention of child abuse. *Child Abuse Review, 12*(3), 155–171. doi:10.1002/car.798

Sanders, M. R., & Pickering, J. A. (2014). The importance of evidence-based parenting intervention to the prevention and treatment of child maltreatment. In S. Timmer & A. Urquiza (Eds.), *Evidence-based approaches for the treatment of maltreated children* (pp. 105–121). Houten, the Netherlands: Springer. doi:10.1007/978-94-007-7404-9_7

Sandler, I., Ingram, A., Wolchik, S., Tein, J. Y., & Winslow, E. (2015). Long-term effects of parenting-focused preventive interventions to promote resilience of children and adolescents. *Child Development Perspectives, 9*(3), 164–171. doi:10.1111/cdep.12126

Schuhmann, E. M., Foote, R. C., Eyberg, S. M., Boggs, S. R., & Algina, J. (1998). Efficacy of parent–child interaction therapy: Interim report of a randomized trial with short-term maintenance. *Journal of Clinical Child Psychology, 27*(1), 34–45. doi:10.1207/s15374424jccp2701_4

Schulz, M. S., Cowan, C. P., & Cowan, P. A. (2006). Promoting healthy beginnings: A randomized controlled trial of a preventive intervention to preserve marital quality during the transition to parenthood. *Journal of Consulting and Clinical Psychology, 74*(1), 20–31. doi:10.1037/0022-006X.74.1.20

Serketich, W. J., & Dumas, J. E. (1996). The effectiveness of behavioral parent training to modify antisocial behavior in children: A meta-analysis. *Behavior Therapy, 27*(2), 171–186. doi:10.1016/S0005-7894(96)80013-X

Shapiro, D. N., Peterson, C., & Stewart, A. J. (2009). Legal and social contexts and mental health among lesbian and heterosexual mothers. *Journal of Family Psychology, 23*, 255–262. doi:10.1037/a0014973

Shechner, T., Slone, M., Lobel, T., & Schecter, R. (2013). Children's adjustment in non-traditional families in Israel: The effect of parental sexual orientation and the number of parents on children's development. *Child: Care, Health, & Development, 29*, 178–184. doi:10.1111/j.1365-2214.2011.01337.x

Sullivan, M. (2004). *The family of woman: Lesbian mothers, their children, and the undoing of gender*. Berkeley, CA: University of California Press.

Sumontha, J., Farr, R. H., & Patterson, C. J. (2016). Social support and coparenting among lesbian, gay, and heterosexual adoptive parents. *Journal of Family Psychology, 30*(8), 987–996. doi:10.1037/fam0000253

Tasker, F. L. (2013). Lesbian and gay parenting post-heterosexual divorce and separation. In A. E. Goldberg & K. R. Allen (Eds.), *LGBT-parent families: Innovations in research and implications for practice* (pp. 3–20). New York, NY: Springer.

Thomas, R., & Zimmer-Gembeck, M. J. (2007). Behavioral outcomes of parent–child interaction therapy and Triple P—Positive Parenting Program: A review and meta-analysis. *Journal of Abnormal Child Psychology, 35*(3), 475–495. doi:10.1007/s10802-007-9104-9

Titlestad, A., & Pooley, J. A. (2014). Resilience in same-sex-parented families: The lived experience of adults with gay, lesbian, or bisexual parents. *Journal of GLBT Family Studies, 10*(4), 329–353. doi:10.1080/1550428X.2013.833065

Tornello, S. L., Johnson, S. M., & O'Connor, E. (2013). Relationship quality among lesbian mothers in planned families. *Journal of GLBT Family Studies, 9*(4), 346–363. doi:10.1080/1550428X.2013.801008

Touroni, E., & Coyle, A. (2002). Decision-making in planned lesbian parenting: An interpretative phenomenological analysis. *Journal of Community & Applied Social Psychology, 12*, 194–209. doi:10.1002/casp.672

van Gelderen, L., Bos, H. M.W., Gartrell, N. K., Hermanns, J., & Perrin, E. C. (2012). Quality of life of adolescents raised from birth by lesbian mothers: The US National Longitudinal Lesbian Family Study. *Journal of Developmental & Behavioral Pediatrics, 33*, 1–7. doi:10.1097/DBP.0b013e31823b62af

Vanfraussen, K., Ponjaert-Kristoffersen, I., & Brewaeys, A. (2002). What does it mean for youngsters to grow up in a lesbian family created by means of donor insemination? *Journal of Reproductive and Infant Psychology, 20*, 237–252. doi:10.1080/0264683021000033165

Vanfraussen, K., Ponjaert-Kristoffersen, I., & Brewaeys, A. (2003). Family functioning in lesbian families created by donor insemination. *American Journal of Orthopsychiatry, 73*, 78–90. doi:10.1037/0002-9432.73.1.78

Wainright, J. L., & Patterson, C. J. (2008). Peer relations among adolescents with female same-sex parents. *Developmental Psychology, 44*, 117–126. doi:10.1037/0012-1649.44.1.117

Yager, C., Brennan, D., Steele, L. S., Epstein, R., & Ross, L. E. (2010). Challenges and mental health experiences of lesbian and bisexual women who are trying to conceive. *Health & Social Work, 35*(3), 191–200. doi:10.1093/hsw/35.3.191

Zemp, M., Milek, A., Cummings, E. M., Cina, A., & Bodenmann, G. (2016). How couple- and parenting-focused programs affect child behavioral problems: A randomized controlled trial. *Journal of Child and Family Studies, 25*(3), 798–810. doi:10.1007/s10826-015-0260-1

7

Affirmative Mental Health Practice with Bisexual Clients

Evidence-Based Strategies

ANDREW YOUNG CHOI AND TANIA ISRAEL ■

Bisexuality is a sexual orientation characterized by "the potential to be attracted—romantically and/or sexually—to people of more than one sex and/or gender, not necessarily at the same time, not necessarily in the same way, and not necessarily to the same degree" (Ochs, 2005, p. 8). Population-based evidence suggests that in terms of attraction, behavior, and identity, there are more bisexual people than lesbians and gay men combined in the United States (Copen, Chandra, & Febo-Vazquez, 2016; Gates, 2011; Pew Research Center, 2013). Because bisexuals comprise the majority of sexual minorities, it is fitting to have a chapter devoted to evidence-based mental health practice with this largely invisible and underserved population.

Sexual minorities experience disproportionate mental health problems compared to heterosexuals; these problems are theorized to stem from minority stress (Meyer, 2003) and structural stigma (Hatzenbuehler, Phelan, & Link, 2013), and they have been empirically shown to be associated with both (Hatzenbuehler, 2016; Institute of Medicine, 2011; Mays & Cochran, 2001). Research also suggests that compared to heterosexuals and/or lesbians and gay men (e.g., monosexuals), bisexuals experience disparities in mental health (e.g., mood disorders), sexual health (e.g., sexually transmitted infections [STIs]), substance use, suicidality, and victimization such as child abuse and sexual violence (Feinstein & Dyar, 2017). Psychosocial problems also co-occur and are syndemic among bisexuals (Bauer, Flanders, MacLeod, & Ross, 2016; M. R. Friedman & Dodge, 2016). Finally, bisexuals report low social support (Jorm, Korten, Rodgers, Jacomb, & Christensen, 2002) and social well-being (Kertzner, Meyer, Frost, & Stirratt,

2009), in addition to access barriers to affordable health care tailored to bisexuality (MacKay, Robinson, Pinder, & Ross, 2017; Ross et al., 2016).

Research suggests that the vulnerabilities observed among bisexuals are linked to binegativity—a constellation of hostility, marginalization, stereotypes, and stigma that considers bisexuality as illegitimate and unstable and bisexuals as liars, untrustworthy, and flawed in character (Brewster & Moradi, 2010; Brewster, Moradi, DeBlaere, & Velez, 2013; Feinstein & Dyar, 2017; M. R. Friedman et al., 2014; Israel & Mohr, 2004; Ross, Dobinson, & Eady, 2010). Bisexuals experience binegativity in both heterosexual and lesbian and gay communities (Roberts, Horne, & Hoyt, 2015), in addition to unique complications related to coming out and identity disclosure (Dodge, Schnarrs, Reece, et al., 2012; McLean, 2007; Mohr, Jackson, & Sheets, 2017). Bisexuals are less open about their sexual orientation than are monosexuals (Balsam & Mohr, 2007), including to health care service providers (Durso & Meyer, 2013). Bisexuals also experience distinct negative disclosure consequences compared to monosexual minorities (Dobinson, MacDonnell, Hampson, Clipsham, & Chow, 2005), such as increased distress and mood disturbance after coming out (Pachankis, Cochran, & Mays, 2015). These patterns may be even more applicable to bisexual people of color who are behaviorally bisexual but do not identify publicly as bisexual due to cultural and/or safety reasons (Jeffries, 2014; Malebranche, Arriola, Jenkins, Dauria, & Patel, 2010).

Given the previously mentioned bisexual-specific disparities and stressors, practitioners are likely to encounter bisexuals in mental health practice. To support practitioners—in recognizing, understanding, and responding to bisexual clients in an affirmative, culturally responsive, and evidence-based manner—we present an applied and integrative review of bi-affirmative clinical practices emphasizing empirical evidence and its applications.

We first discuss how to effectively use the therapeutic alliance, including practitioner attitudes toward bisexuality and desirable practitioner characteristics. Here, we derived guidance primarily from qualitative and quantitative descriptive studies focused on bisexual people. Topics studied included bisexual people's experience and representation in mainstream heterosexual and lesbian, gay, bisexual, transgender, and queer (LGBTQ) communities, interpersonal relationships, and psychotherapy, as well as research examining practitioner experiences with bisexual clients. Next, we discuss efficacious therapy techniques for treating mental and behavioral health problems with bisexuals, supported by intervention research including randomized controlled trials (RCTs). The RCTs reviewed in this chapter were largely focused on cognitive–behavioral therapy (CBT) and included a small or unknown proportion of bisexuals in their samples. Nevertheless, findings suggest that CBT can be used for anxiety (Cruess et al., 2000), depression (Ironson et al., 2013; Pachankis, Hatzenbuehler, Rendina, Safren, & Parsons, 2015; Safren et al., 2009, 2012; Williams et al., 2013), psychological distress (Chesney, Chambers, Taylor, Johnson, & Folkman, 2003; Sikkema et al., 2006), post-traumatic stress symptoms (Ironson et al., 2013), sexual risk reduction (Fernandez et al., 2016; Harawa et al., 2013; Pachankis, Hatzenbuehler, et al., 2015; Parsons, Lelutiu-Weinberger, Botsko, & Golub, 2014; Roffman et al., 1997; Shoptaw et al., 2005; Velasquez et al., 2009; Williams et al., 2008, 2013), substance use (Parsons et al., 2014; Shoptaw et al., 2005; Velasquez et al., 2009), treatment adherence (de Bruin et al., 2010; Koenig et al., 2008; Safren et al., 2009, 2012), and promoting vocational behaviors such as job-seeking (Martin et al., 2012). We specifically discuss evidence bases for using psychoeducation, coping skills, behavioral interventions, and group work with bisexual clients. In a case example, we illustrate evidence-based practice with a client who is experiencing cultural conflicts related to bisexual attractions. This case describes therapist reflection and recognition of biases, acceptance, validation, collaboration, and application of CBT interventions. Finally, we present future research directions and evidence-based recommendations for mental health practice with bisexual clients.

THERAPEUTIC ALLIANCE WITH BISEXUAL CLIENTS

In this section, we discuss tailoring the therapeutic alliance when working with bisexuals. The therapeutic alliance refers to a helping relationship wherein a practitioner offers congruence, empathy, and unconditional positive regard to a client to facilitate an enduring and emotionally authentic bond, one in which mutually shared goals and tasks can be pursued to meet the client's needs. Consistent with general research on psychotherapy (Laska, Gurman, & Wampold, 2014), descriptive research shows that a robust therapeutic alliance with bisexual clients is fundamental across multiple therapeutic modalities (Burckell & Goldfried, 2006; Page, 2004; Victor & Nel, 2016). A deeply authentic relationship offering unconditional support and facilitation for bisexual exploration and identities can be a powerful intervention in and of itself.

Although relevant to working with all populations, an affirming therapeutic relationship may be especially important for bisexuals given some distinctive features of binegativity and bisexual health disparities. First, binegativity is distinct from general minority stress in terms of the wholesale erasure and invalidation of bisexuality's existence (Bostwick & Hequembourg, 2014), for which interpersonal affirmation may be a crucial intervention. Second, because involvement in mainstream LGBTQ communities—which have traditionally been viewed as a "safe haven" from minority stress for lesbians and gay men—can confer stress and negative health outcomes for bisexuals (Feinstein, Dyar, & London, 2017), practitioners may be called to serve as an exclusive source of acceptance and social support. Third, the elevated risk of childhood and adulthood physical and sexual victimization observed among bisexuals (Feinstein & Dyar, 2017) and evidence of binegativity within intimate relationships (Bostwick & Hequembourg, 2014) both indicate a therapeutic need for positive (and perhaps corrective) socioemotional experiences.

To establish a safe, secure, and supportive therapeutic environment, practitioners should offer acceptance, affirmation, and validation of the client's unique experience, identities, and strengths—bisexuality-related or otherwise (Brooks, Inman,

Klinger, Malouf, & Kaduvettoor, 2010; R. C. Friedman & Downey, 2010). Bisexual clients in mental health services report "validation of bisexuality" as their top suggestion to clinicians, followed by "viewing bisexuality as healthy per se" (Page, 2004, p. 148). Practitioners should be prepared to tolerate, normalize, and explore the ambiguity, complexity, and uncertainty that often typify bisexual lived experience (Dworkin, 2001; R. C. Friedman & Downey, 2010). It is important for clients to feel permitted to freely experience and process their bisexual attractions without the ridicule and persecution that they might otherwise incur in society. Survey research indeed indicates that bisexuals anticipate binegativity, a behavior linked with psychological distress and depressive symptoms (Brewster et al., 2013; Paul, Smith, Mohr, & Ross, 2014). Displaying nonjudgmental acceptance of bisexual feelings may be crucial for developing trust and quelling the suspicion that bisexuals often develop in response to binegativity, as suggested by qualitative research (Brooks et al., 2010; Eady, Dobinson, & Ross, 2011; Scherrer, 2013). Practitioners should also address concerns about confidentiality and privacy, which are salient aspects of accessing services for bisexually identified clients (Dobinson et al., 2005) and those who are behaviorally bisexual but without a bisexual identity (Dodge, Schnarrs, Goncalves, et al., 2012).

Practitioners can communicate bisexual validation verbally and nonverbally. Descriptive research suggests that practitioners should ask about and use client-preferred, inclusive language (e.g., gender-neutral terms) when referring to their client's partners or sexual identities (Victor & Nel, 2016). Appropriate language may be additionally relevant for bisexuals because they are more likely to use multiple sexual identity labels compared to monosexuals (Galupo, Mitchell, & Davis, 2015) and to use different labels across social contexts (Mohr et al., 2017). Because bisexuals are commonly assumed to be monosexual based on their partner's gender (Bostwick & Hequembourg, 2014; Dobinson et al., 2005), practitioner use of bi-affirming language can be an opportunity to counteract erasure and invisibility. However, practitioners should recognize that some behaviorally bisexual clients may be averse to mainstream labels (e.g., bisexual) and consider bisexual behaviors as a compartmentalized aspect of their experience rather than as a source of personal identity (Arnold et al., 2015; Dodge, Schnarrs, Goncalves, et al., 2012). These mixed findings thus reinforce the importance of using client-preferred labels.

Research indicates that tailoring structural aspects of service delivery to be inclusive and welcoming to the range of bisexual clients may be complex. Qualitative findings with openly bisexually identified clients suggest that visibility of bi-affirming symbols (e.g., bisexual flag) and signage in practice settings and marketing materials, as well as use of inclusive language on forms and by staff, may promote treatment access and outcome expectations (Dobinson et al., 2005; MacKay et al., 2017). Conversely, behaviorally bisexual clients report preferring indirect and non-explicit forms of marketing and outreach that do not include visible signals associated with mainstream LGBTQ communities of any kind (Arnold et al., 2015; Dodge, Schnarrs, Goncalves, et al., 2012). Practitioners should thus evaluate the cultural characteristics of their clientele and proximal community to adjust their structural practices accordingly.

Practitioner Attitudes Toward Bisexuality

Descriptive research and practitioners suggest that bi-specific awareness is needed for effective practice with this population (Brooks et al., 2010; Burckell & Goldfried, 2006; Dworkin, 2001; Eady et al., 2011; Israel, Gorcheva, Burnes, & Walther, 2008). Practitioners should examine reflexively their own sexual orientation and identity, assumptions about love and relationships, exposure to heterosexist and binegative messages, and how these may influence the helping encounter (Dobinson et al., 2005). Empirical findings and clinical expertise indicate that practitioners may hold unexplored assumptions about "healthy" relationships and sexuality, heteronormative attitudes, and bisexual stereotypes that impair judgment, lead them to intervene in inappropriate ways, and perpetuate the problems that bring bisexual clients into psychotherapy (Dworkin, 2001; Eady et al., 2011; MacKay et al., 2017; Mohr, Israel, & Sedlacek, 2001; Page, 2004; Victor & Nel, 2016). According to analog research, practitioners are more likely to stereotype bisexual clients (compared to monosexuals), especially when their presenting concerns approximate difficulties traditionally associated with stereotypes such as identity conflict and confusion or intimacy issues (Mohr, Chopp, & Wong, 2013; Mohr, Weiner, Chopp, & Wong, 2009). Given the prevalence of monosexism (Roberts et al., 2015), lesbian, gay, and heterosexual (including those identifying as LGBTQ-affirming) practitioners should examine their biases about bisexuality (Dobinson et al., 2005; Eady et al., 2011; MacKay et al., 2017).

Bisexual clients report unhelpful and harmful experiences in psychotherapy (Dobinson et al., 2005; Eady et al., 2011; MacKay et al., 2017; Page, 2004). To prevent relationship ruptures, practitioners should avoid committing microaggressions (MacKay et al., 2017; Shelton & Delgado-Romero, 2013), including pathologizing bisexuality as the root of the client's problems (Israel et al., 2008; Scherrer, 2013), conveying binegative and stereotypic attitudes (Dobinson et al., 2005), espousing a binary and inflexible view of human sexuality (Victor & Nel, 2016), or making assumptions about the client's sexual orientation (Burckell & Goldfried, 2006; Israel et al., 2008). Problematic psychotherapy encounters may foster discouragement and deter future help-seeking (Eady et al., 2011; MacKay et al., 2017).

Conversely, practitioners' bi-affirmative attitudes predict both perceived and actual counseling competence with bisexuals (Brooks & Inman, 2013). Practitioners who work toward developing LGB-affirmative attitudes and attaining security in their gender and sexual identities report higher counseling self-efficacy and affirmative behaviors in practice (Brooks & Inman, 2013; Dillon, Worthington, Soth-McNett, & Schwartz, 2008; Matthews, Selvidge, & Fisher, 2005). Practitioner affirmation of and curiosity about human diversity are likewise associated with increased therapeutic quality, as reported by practitioners and sexual minority clients (Matthews et al., 2005; Stracuzzi, Mohr, & Fuertes, 2011). According to descriptive research, practitioners can display affirmative attitudes by communicating that bisexuality is a natural variant of human sexual orientation (Israel et al., 2008; Victor & Nel, 2016) and discussing bisexual identity in the context of other meaningful aspects of the client's experience (Brooks et al., 2010; Burckell & Goldfried, 2006). To enhance the therapeutic alliance with bisexual clients, practitioners should develop fluency with the following topics within the therapeutic dialog: knowledge of and comfort with bisexuality (Eady et al., 2011; Page, 2004) and bisexual within-group differences (Dobinson et al., 2005; R. C. Friedman & Downey, 2010); bi-specific minority stress, including external and internalized binegativity (Page, 2004; Paul et al., 2014; Scherrer, 2013); intersectionality (Brooks et al., 2010; Brooks, Inman, Malouf, Klinger, & Kaduvettoor, 2008); and sexual fluidity (Diamond, 2016). Finally, the literature suggests that adopting a client-centered, continual learning perspective helps practitioners to affirm and privilege the client's bisexual experience (Dworkin, 2001; Page, 2004).

CULTURALLY ADAPTED THERAPY TECHNIQUES FOR BISEXUAL CLIENTS

In this section, we first discuss the relevance of cultural adaptation to mental health practice with bisexual clients. Next, we discuss enhancing case conceptualization with knowledge of bisexual identity development issues and a collaborative approach. Finally, we offer an applied discussion of evidence-based techniques for bisexuals, including psychoeducation, coping skills, behavioral interventions, and group work.

We encourage practitioners to culturally adapt manualized treatments to incorporate salient aspects of the bisexual experience and bi-specific mental health stressors. For example, Shoptaw et al. (2005) tested four variants of a CBT intervention to reduce substance use and risky sexual behaviors in bisexual and gay men. They found that men in the culturally adapted condition—which incorporated content on behavioral and cultural aspects of substance use and sexual activity in the bisexual and gay male community—exhibited the fastest and greatest reduction in risky sexual behaviors, substance use, and depression (Jaffe, Shoptaw, Stein, Reback, & Rotheram-Fuller, 2007). Readers are also referred to Pachankis, Hatzenbuehler, and colleagues (2015) for a more recent RCT reporting the efficacy of a manualized treatment that integrates sexual minority stress issues relevant to bisexual and gay men throughout the protocol.

Other client characteristics that may be helpful to incorporate into treatment include intersectionality (e.g., ethnic/racial diversity and identities), gender (e.g., culture-bound masculine norms), and clinical issues such as HIV status—as suggested by intervention (Arnold et al., 2015; Martínez-Donate et al., 2010; Operario, Smith, Arnold, & Kegeles, 2010) and descriptive (Brooks et al., 2010; Dyer, Regan, Pacek, Acheampong, & Khan, 2015; Malebranche et al., 2010) research. Several risk reduction RCTs with ethnic/racial minority bisexual clients show that treatments adapted to ethnic/racial diversity—including relationship building upon shared social identities (e.g., among group therapy members); conceptualization considering intersectional minority stress; and use of culture- and gender-bound concepts, motifs, symbols, terms, and values—are more efficacious than standard health promotion interventions (Fernandez et al., 2016; Harawa et al., 2013; Williams et al., 2008, 2013).

Bi-informed Case Conceptualization

Bi-affirmative practitioners strive to locate the client's distress in monosexist social structures rather than internally within the client. In doing so, practitioners prevent collusion with societal stereotypes of bisexuals as creating their own problems with confusion, lack of trustworthiness, and promiscuity (Israel & Mohr, 2004). Indeed, in an analog study exploring practitioner responses to a female bisexual client (Mohr et al., 2001), practitioners with higher anti-bisexual bias (compare to those with less bias) were more likely to rate the client as poorly functioning and as having more problems associated with bisexual stereotypes, even when sexual orientation was not a presenting problem; these practitioners were also more likely to anticipate that they might respond judgmentally toward the client. Conversely, many clinical issues in this population—emotion dysregulation, interpersonal ineffectiveness, mood disorders, and maladaptive coping with substances and/or sexual compulsivity—can be conceptualized as originating from minority stress (Hatzenbuehler, 2009; Pachankis, Rendina, et al., 2015).

Practitioners should recognize that for many bisexual clients, their feelings, thoughts, and interpersonal behaviors occur in a social context that is often ignorant or indifferent regarding bisexuality (Dworkin, 2001). Bisexuals perceive interpersonal and structural monosexism and binegativity as fundamental determinants of their mental health problems (Dodge, Schnarrs, Reece, et al., 2012; Ross et al., 2010). Moreover, bisexuals may experience internalized binegativity—which can include negative attitudes about one's bisexuality, endorsement of bisexual stereotypes, and devaluation of self-worth—adopted from exposure to binegative prejudice and discrimination (Balsam & Mohr, 2007; Dyar, Feinstein, Schick, & Davila, 2017; Paul et al., 2014; Ross et al., 2010; Sarno & Wright, 2013). Thus, practitioners working with bisexuals might normalize identity confusion and internalized binegativity as adaptive responses to the lack of affirmative narratives for bisexuality in mainstream society rather than a deficit inherent to one's sexual orientation (Lin & Israel, 2012).

In case conceptualization, practitioners should consider bisexual identity development; this includes facilitating clients to explore and reflect upon their bisexual behaviors, desires, fantasies, and the relationships in which they occur and also to articulate sexual identities that feel autonomously constructed and personally meaningful (Dobinson et al., 2005; Dworkin, 2001; R. C. Friedman & Downey, 2010; Scherrer, 2013). The Klein Sexual Orientation Grid (KSOG; Klein, 2014)—a multidimensional scale appreciated by sexual minorities, including bisexuals (Galupo, Mitchell, Grynkiewcz, & Davis, 2014)—may be used in this regard. Practitioners can use the KSOG to help clients identify aspects of their bisexuality that feel concerning, distressing, unclear, or relevant to identity development. Moreover, practitioners can empower clients by incorporating positive aspects of bisexuality, including resilience and strengths (Lin & Israel, 2012; Rostosky, Riggle, Pascale-Hague, & McCants, 2010).

With bisexuals, practitioners are also encouraged to use a collaborative approach to case conceptualization (MacKay et al., 2017). For example, a proactive conversation with bisexual clients may help practitioners to discern the extent to which the client's bisexuality is a salient aspect of the presenting concerns and prevent inappropriate emphasis on or excessive identification with bisexuality (Dworkin, 2001; Eady et al., 2011; Israel et al., 2008; Page, 2004; Shelton & Delgado-Romero, 2013; Victor & Nel, 2016). In cases of severe mental illness, practitioners should prioritize treating symptoms and helping clients with coping and self-care skills before considering deeper discussions about bisexuality (R. C. Friedman & Downey, 2010).

Psychoeducation with Bisexual Clients

It is important for bisexual clients to understand how early and current sexual minority stress can influence mental and behavioral health, including recognizing the typical ways they respond to stressful situations (Pachankis, Hatzenbuehler, et al., 2015). Practitioners should provide bi-specific education and support for bisexual clients to assimilate accurate information about their sexual orientation (Page, 2004), which can also help to reduce internalized stigma (Lin & Israel, 2012). Moreover, it may be important to discuss how minority stress influences problems that interfere with treatment adherence and foster maladaptive coping, relapse, and risk behaviors (Fernandez et al., 2016; Pachankis, Hatzenbuehler, et al., 2015). For example, in a group-based HIV risk-reduction intervention for Black bisexual men, Harawa et al. (2013) used a "holistic health" framework in which risky sexual behaviors were discussed in tandem with other health risks (e.g., substance use) relative to intersectional minority stress. Group discussions about cultural, developmental, and social determinants of sexual decision-making for each client facilitated individualized goal setting, change plans, values clarification, coping skills, and problem-solving strategies. The intervention was efficacious in reducing sexual risk behaviors with women. These and other similar findings suggest that psychoeducation should also address culture-bound messages or norms that may influence coping behaviors and health-related decision-making, especially for ethnic/racial minority bisexual clients (Arnold et al., 2015; Martínez-Donate et al., 2010; Operario et al., 2010; Williams et al., 2008, 2013).

Coping Skills to Encourage with Bisexual Clients

EMOTION REGULATION
Emotion regulation is a transdiagnostic process shown to mediate the associations among sexual minority stressors and health outcomes for bisexuals, such as

physical symptoms (Denton, Rostosky, & Danner, 2014) and sexual risk factors (Smith, Mohr, & Ross, 2018). Practitioners may need to help bisexual clients to recognize their typical response patterns to strong emotions, anticipate and manage triggers, and develop self-regulatory strategies (Pachankis, Hatzenbuehler, et al., 2015; Sikkema et al., 2006). Efficacious stress management techniques for reducing distress and managing negative mood in bisexual and gay men include diaphragmatic breathing exercises, guided imagery and meditation, and progressive muscle relaxation (Chesney et al., 2003; Cruess et al., 2000; Martin et al., 2012; Pachankis, Hatzenbuehler, et al., 2015; Safren et al., 2009, 2012). Evidence suggests that building emotion-related coping skills is more effective when they are practiced using real-life scenarios (Chesney et al., 2003), such as minority stress situations (Pachankis, Hatzenbuehler, et al., 2015), negotiating safer sex practices (Rotheram-Borus, Murphy, Fernandez, & Srinivasan, 1998), and treatment adherence (Safren et al., 2009, 2012). For example, Martin et al. performed an RCT of a career intervention involving training HIV-positive bisexual and gay clients to use distress tolerance techniques for handling workplace disclosure and discrimination issues. Clients receiving the intervention (compared to control) exhibited increased job-seeking and employment maintenance. Practitioners might similarly employ stress inoculation strategies wherein clients visualize binegative situations—such as being subtly invalidated or explicitly interrogated about their bisexuality—and experiment with a range of emotion regulation strategies to identify those that are best suited for each client in defusing difficult emotions. A role-play stress inoculation with the practitioner taking the role of an offending perpetrator may help clients to practice emotion regulation and interpersonal effectiveness when exposed to triggers in valued relationships.

Cognitive Restructuring

Randomized controlled trials have supported the use of several cognitive restructuring techniques with bisexuals, including self-monitoring, challenging, and reshaping thoughts that precede emotional distress and/or maladaptive behaviors, as well as identifying strengths related to one's sexual orientation and practicing self-affirmations (Cruess et al., 2000; de Bruin et al., 2010; Pachankis, Hatzenbuehler, et al., 2015; Safren et al., 2009, 2012; Shoptaw et al., 2005). For example, an online intervention successfully reduced internalized stigma with activities designed to guide bisexual and gay men to examine the external origins of heterosexist and binegative messages, deconstruct negative stereotypes with research-based psychoeducation, identify helpful strategies for rejecting the negative messages, and develop an affirmative attitude toward one's sexual identity (Lin & Israel, 2012). For stigma-related stress, practitioners might similarly use a thought record to help bisexual clients identify maladaptive thoughts that occur in response to binegative stereotypes—attending to those that elicit the strongest distress for each client, which can then be used for Socratic questioning and generating alternative interpretations that can be practiced through cognitive rehearsals and role-plays. Evidence also suggests promise for using expressive writing to help bisexual clients to privately examine and work through unprocessed emotional stressors and to identify their strengths, which may be especially beneficial for bisexuals given social support limitations (Feinstein, Dyar, & Pachankis, 2017). Finally, group interventions have been used to reduce depression among ethnic/racial minority bisexual men with childhood abuse histories, in part by addressing cognitive distortions and examining their trauma-related origins and behavioral consequences (Williams et al., 2013).

Behavioral Interventions with Bisexual Clients

Given that bisexuals are at risk for multiple behavioral health problems (Feinstein & Dyar, 2017), bisexual clients may benefit from skills related to health promotion and risk reduction. Motivational interviewing is one empirically supported approach to help bisexual clients to activate a sense of autonomy, control, intrinsic motivation, and responsibility that contribute to positive change (de Bruin et al., 2010; Fernandez et al., 2016; Koenig et al., 2008; Parsons et al., 2014; Safren et al., 2009; Williams et al., 2008, 2013; Wolfers, de Wit, Hospers, Richardus, & de Zwart, 2009). Establishing sufficient motivation may be crucial for bisexual clients, given evidence linking bisexual orientation with treatment dropout; lack of bisexual specificity among available interventions has been hypothesized as an explanation (Roffman et al., 1997).

Efficacious behavioral interventions for initiating and maintaining behavior change among bisexual clients include contingency management and skills training (de Bruin et al., 2010; Fernandez et al., 2016; Koenig et al., 2008; Ling Murtaugh, Krishnamurti, Davis, Reback, & Shoptaw, 2013; Pachankis, Hatzenbuehler, et al., 2015; Safren et al., 2009, 2012; Williams et al., 2008). For example, practitioners might use genograms to identify bi-supportive and stress-inducing relationships (Fernandez et al., 2016) in terms of minimizing triggers for maladaptive behaviors. For behavioral activation (Safren et al., 2009, 2012), practitioners might help clients to develop, schedule, and participate in pleasurable activities that integrate a bi-affirmative component (Pachankis, Hatzenbuehler, et al., 2015), such as expressing positive and meaningful aspects of one's bisexuality creatively (e.g., art, social media, or writing).

Other behavioral interventions, including problem-solving and assertiveness training, can be applied to address interpersonal issues relevant to bisexual health. For instance, problem-solving approaches can be used for helping bisexual clients to develop identity disclosure strategies matched with situational demands. Descriptive research suggests that bisexuals' coming out behaviors are diverse, including nondisclosure (e.g., "passing") or disclosing "as necessary," rejection of mainstream identity labels, successive approximation (e.g., initially gauging the reaction of the audience with "casual" or indirect disclosures), and/or using concurrent and multiple identity labels (Baldwin et al., 2015; McCormack, Wignall, & Anderson, 2015; McLean, 2007; Mohr et al., 2017). As such, guiding bisexual clients to systematically consider a wide range of disclosure strategies may foster perceived agency and interpersonal self-efficacy in managing social relationships

(Baldwin et al., 2015). Problem-solving may also be applied to community af-filiation issues, such as helping bisexual clients to weigh the advantages and disadvantages of involvement in mainstream LGBTQ networks via a decision-making process.

Assertive communication skills may help to address a range of issues associated with minority stress, such as risky sexual behaviors (Pachankis, 2015). For safer sex negotiation, preliminary intervention research suggests that practitioners should help bisexual clients to generate and practice separate scripts for female, male, casual, and/or long-term partners (Arnold et al., 2015; Operario et al., 2010). According to descriptive findings, practitioners should attend to nuances of cultural, gender, and sexual roles that may vary across relationships for bisexual clients, especially regarding interpersonal communication and sex-related issues (Hubach et al., 2014; Operario et al., 2010). Finally, self-advocacy skills seem to be an important facilitator of treatment access for bisexuals (MacKay, Robinson, Pinder, & Ross, 2017); thus, practitioners should assist clients to clarify their health care needs and learn how to convey them effectively to service providers.

Group Support for Bisexual Clients

Group-based services may be used as a powerful intervention for bisexual clients, given bi-specific barriers to belonging and inclusion (Balsam & Mohr, 2007; Dobinson et al., 2005). By facilitating a social context for bisexual clients to empower one another in a collective gesture of resisting binegativity and monosexism, practitioners can support aspects of positive bisexual identity devel-opment that are more difficult on an individual basis (Dobinson et al., 2005; Sarno & Wright, 2013). Bi-specific social support has been linked to reduced internalized binegativity (Sheets & Mohr, 2009), and bisexuals report that access to bisexual communities and healthy social support networks is salubrious for their mental health (Ross et al., 2010). Because bisexual clients report social networks as a common "first stop" for mental health support (MacKay et al., 2017), practitioners might facilitate bisexual community building by guiding group members to estab-lish health-promotive norms (e.g., mitigating sexual risk), increase mental health literacy (e.g., psychoeducation), and share health information targeted specifically to bisexuals (Dobinson et al., 2005). Many of the RCTs reviewed in this chapter were delivered in a group format or included a group component (Harawa et al., 2013; Koenig et al., 2008; Martin et al., 2012; Shoptaw et al., 2005; Sikkema et al., 2006; Velasquez et al., 2009; Williams et al., 2008, 2013). In mixed-orientation groups, practitioners may need to proactively prevent and address binegativity among monosexual group members (Page, 2004). In addition, groups may be less appropriate for bisexual clients who have extenuating privacy concerns or do not wish to have their bisexuality discussed with or known to others (Arnold et al., 2015; Dodge, Schnarrs, Goncalves, et al., 2012). Online social network re-sources may help clients who cannot or prefer not to access in-person bisexual communities (Ross et al., 2010).

CASE EXAMPLE

Idriss is a 20-year-old cisgender male student seen at the counseling center of a large university located on the West Coast of the United States. He is a bicultural Arab American born into an intact nuclear family of four siblings and immigrant parents from Algeria. Idriss lives with three roommates, has a monogamous and positive romantic relationship of 1 year with his girlfriend, and is undeclared in his major field of study. He is well groomed, attractive, and of average height and weight with no significant developmental conflicts, medical history, or safety risks. After noticing signs of anxiety and depression, one of his roommates suggested that Idriss seek counseling. Intake assessment reveals steep increases in anxiety and depression within the past month that have significantly impaired Idriss's ability to function academically and socially. Idriss is assigned to a lesbian psychologist named Alice who uses a person-centered theoretical orientation.

Alice explores the broader context of Idriss's life, including the quality of his social relationships and involvement in campus organizations. Idriss is cooperative and direct with responding but presents with significant internal preoccupation when discussing sexual and romantic history and satisfaction. When asked about his girlfriend, Idriss tentatively shares that he has been "distracted" and "not present" with her, although he cares for her very much, and he quickly redirects that "things are fine between them." Although Alice does not make assumptions about Idriss's sexual orientation, she is aware that bisexual clients are less likely to identify openly compared to other sexual minorities (Durso & Meyer, 2013), so she inquires further. In their third session, upon Alice's probing, Idriss discloses recently beginning to experience powerful attractions toward a male friend from the Muslim Student Association.

Guided by the KSOG, Alice asks about multiple aspects of his sexual orientation and changes over time (Galupo et al., 2014; Klein, 2014). Idriss reports first noticing attractions to women and men in high school but that he has not engaged in romantic or sexual relations with men, nor has he disclosed his attractions to men to anyone. He describes significant emotional distress and shame related to being confused and conflicted about his sexuality. He questions whether his attractions are stemming from the platonic, same-gender intimacy commonly expressed in North African culture or if they are romantic and sexual desires akin to what he experiences with his girlfriend. He shares that sexual minorities are viewed with hostility within his primary cultural, family, and religious networks and that he does not know anyone personally who identifies as bisexual or gay. Although he has a supportive social circle, he feels isolated and lonely and is very concerned about others "finding out." He does not wish to consult LGBTQ campus resources, never having viewed himself as "gay" and not wanting to inadvertently "out" himself. He reports spending lots of time searching for reliable bisexual information online.

Understanding the importance of building a strong therapeutic alliance with bisexual clients (Page, 2004) and recognizing unique barriers of invisibility and belongingness for this population (Bostwick & Hequembourg, 2014), Alice focuses on developing rapport and validating Idriss's experience. She attenuates shame by demonstrating acceptance of the full range of his bisexual feelings, and she affirms that Idriss's concerns are not inherently pathological and are shared by other bisexuals. She encourages Idriss to talk through his experience at his own pace, communicating empathy and encouraging Idriss to explore his sexuality (Scherrer, 2013). Also, she uses client-centered therapeutic assessments at each session—including the Outcome Rating Scale and the Session Rating Scale (Campbell & Hemsley, 2009)—to track Idriss's distress and gather feedback on his perception of the therapeutic alliance. These evidence-based practices foster and signal Alice's responsiveness and sensitivity to Idriss's clinical needs.

Following recommendations from the literature (Dobinson et al., 2005), Alice reflects privately on her own sexual identity development growing up in a Christian Belizean family and a community that predominantly espoused traditional gender expectations, including chastity, child-rearing, and heterosexual marriage for women. She reflects on prior experience with bisexual people in clinical settings, LGBTQ communities, mass media, and professional training. She consults with a colleague to explore internalized bisexual stereotypes with a free association exercise, which reveals assumptions connecting bisexuality with dishonesty, irresponsibility, and a belief that bisexual men are vectors for transmitting STIs to women (Israel & Mohr, 2004). She understands that bisexual stereotypes are often expressed in practice (Mohr et al., 2001, 2009), and she commits to using self-awareness to guide appropriate interventions (Dobinson et al., 2005). For example, instead of immediately presenting Idriss with HIV/STI information, she helps him to clarify the complexity and meaning of his same-sex desires and how they have influenced his relationships (R. C. Friedman & Downey, 2010). This allows her to more accurately assess his sexual health and prevent microaggressions related to assuming that he is sexually irresponsible or a health threat (MacKay et al., 2017) and also to demonstrate clinically appropriate emphasis on relevant aspects of his bisexuality (Dworkin, 2001).

She anticipates and finds that psychoeducation is helpful given Idriss's reported difficulty with locating credible information. Alice facilitates conversations about bisexuality, minority stress, and intersectionality, and she conveys that bisexuality is a normal variant of human sexuality and that bisexual people are subject to general and specific minority stressors (Feinstein & Dyar, 2017; Victor & Nel, 2016). She normalizes his identity conflict and confusion as problems that many bisexual people experience, especially in communities of color and religious networks. She validates his trouble locating information and finding communities given the relative invisibility of bisexuals compared to monosexuals (Dobinson et al., 2005), and she directs him to bi-affirming online resources (Ross et al., 2010) such as the Bisexual Resource Center (http://biresource.org) and the Movement Advancement Project (http://lgbtmap.org).

For symptom relief, Alice uses CBT approaches that have demonstrated efficacy with bisexuals (Harawa et al., 2013; Pachankis, Hatzenbuehler, et al., 2015; Safren et al., 2012; Williams et al., 2008), integrating cognitive restructuring, emotion regulation strategies, and problem-focused behavioral skills. She draws from intervention research (Lin & Israel, 2012) suggesting that cognitive restructuring exercises can help clients to revisit negative messages, challenge their veracity, recognize their external origin, generate strategies for overcoming internalized stigma, and practice cognitive rehearsals of alternative interpretations to replace maladaptive thoughts associated with bisexuality. She guides Idriss to practice emotion regulation (e.g., diaphragmatic breathing) in real and imagined situations, such as managing anticipatory anxiety when meeting his male friend at the mosque (Pachankis, Hatzenbuehler, et al., 2015). Alice and Idriss also identify aspects of his bisexuality that he appreciates and finds rewarding, and they explore the use of prayer for attaining insights, increasing self-awareness, and understanding meaningful intersections between his spirituality and sexuality. Finally, Alice uses problem-solving (Fernandez et al., 2016) with Idriss to explore self-disclosure considerations, including identity labels and coming out strategies. They weigh the advantages and disadvantages of multiple options for self-identification, ranging from an open bisexual identity to selection of another label (e.g., queer) or private self-acceptance. They discuss consequences of disclosure in his relationships with his family, girlfriend, friends, and other communities. Idriss believes that most people around him will respond negatively and with shock—given their lack of general knowledge of sexual diversity and bisexuality specifically—and Alice acknowledges that coming out can pose complex challenges for bisexuals (Dodge, Jeffries, & Sandfort, 2008). Because Alice understands the importance of, and barriers to, social support for bisexuals (Balsam & Mohr, 2007; Ross et al., 2010), she uses an adapted genogram (Fernandez et al., 2016) to help Idriss identify social relationships in which he can expect bi-specific acceptance and support.

Alice works with Idriss for a full academic year. At the end of the year, Idriss reports that although he has not decided whether to disclose his bisexual attractions nor defined a sexual identity label that fits him, he feels more accepting of his bisexuality, is better able to manage difficult emotions and maladaptive thoughts, feels equipped with coping skills to use when new concerns arise, and believes that he can continue maintaining positive relationships. Alice is familiar with the nonlinear identity development that bisexuals often experience (Diamond, 2016), so she has appropriate expectations and does not push Idriss in terms of disclosure, LGBTQ community affiliation, sexual identification, or engagement in same- or other-gender relationships. Although Alice recognizes her desire for cognitive closure in terms of Idriss's relationship choices, she understands that this need may be associated with negative attitudes toward bisexuality (Burke et al., 2017) and may not serve the client. Alice facilitates termination by reflecting on their work together to help Idriss consolidate his therapeutic gains and insights.

FUTURE RESEARCH DIRECTIONS

Research is needed to develop and test mental and behavioral health interventions for bisexuals to redress the scarcity of evidence-base practices and treatments specific to this population (Jeffries, 2014). Some of the guidance offered in this chapter draws on research using mixed-orientation samples (e.g., bisexual and gay men), limiting generalizability and specificity in whether interventions are differentially efficacious for bisexual versus monosexual clients. Advances in several specific areas are encouraged. Given the challenges of binegativity, psychotherapy process and outcome research with bisexual clients should identify aspects of treatment and psychotherapy relationships that are salient for this population. Couple treatments with bisexuals, including clinical practice with polyamory and nontraditional relationship structure issues, await empirical investigation. Finally, transdiagnostic treatments that address the processes driving the co-occurrence of mental and behavioral problems are encouraged over approaches that target problems in isolation, as discussed in Chapter 20 of this volume and elsewhere (Pachankis, 2015).

Areas of future descriptive research include individual differences in bisexual identity development trajectories, empirical examination of bi-specific structural stigma and minority stress models, bisexual resilience and well-being, and bisexual people's experience with intersecting identities and within-group differences. Although not focused on interventions per se, research in these areas may inform the development and/or adaptation of treatments to be responsive to a more diverse range of bisexual clients and support training efforts for practitioners building clinically appropriate attitudes and knowledge about this population.

Finally, more research on training and competence in mental health practice with bisexual clients is needed (Feinstein et al., 2017). Developing and evaluating interventions and programs targeted toward trainees' and practitioners' bisexual attitudes, knowledge, skills, and counseling self-efficacy are encouraged, including attention to applications across multiple practice settings. However, social contact with bisexuals has been shown to increase binegativity among lesbians and gay men, indicating that bisexual competence training may require bi-focused theoretical and empirical extensions (Cox, Bimbi, & Parsons, 2013).

CONCLUSION

Evidence-based practice with bisexual clients rests on a foundation of a strong therapeutic alliance. Although this is true of all psychotherapy, developing an alliance with bisexual clients has some distinct features. Given the pervasiveness of binegativity and stigmatizing stereotypes about bisexuals, practitioners will need to cultivate accurate knowledge of bisexuality, self-awareness of biases, and an affirmative therapeutic stance. Case conceptualization and collaboration should consider bisexual-specific concerns. Bisexual clients may need support and autonomy in their choices regarding self-identification, relationship structures, and affiliation with sexual minority communities. Treatments identified as efficacious with bisexual clients have typically been tested with mixed-orientation samples, generally with bisexual and gay men. Thus, practitioners may need to adapt such interventions when working with bisexual women and bisexual-specific presenting concerns. Overall, understanding the unique needs of bisexual clients can help practitioners to move toward providing affirming and effective mental health services for this vulnerable and underserved population.

ACKNOWLEDGMENTS

The authors thank the editors, Michael Barr, Jennifer J. Bordon, Kelly Edyburn, Daniel Meza, and Sruthi Swami for their helpful comments on earlier drafts of this chapter.

REFERENCES

Arnold, E., Operario, D., Cornwell, S., Benjamin, M., Dillard Smith, C., Lockett, G., & Kegeles, S. (2015). The development of a counseling based HIV prevention intervention for African American men who have sex with men and women: The Bruthas Project. *AIDS Education and Prevention, 27*(6), 505–521. https://doi.org/10.1521/aeap.2015.27.6.505

Baldwin, A., Dodge, B., Schick, V., Hubach, R. D., Bowling, J., Malebranche, D., . . . Fortenberry, J. D. (2015). Sexual self-identification among behaviorally bisexual men in the Midwestern United States. *Archives of Sexual Behavior, 44*(7), 2015–2026. https://doi.org/10.1007/s10508-014-0376-1

Balsam, K. F., & Mohr, J. J. (2007). Adaptation to sexual orientation stigma: A comparison of bisexual and lesbian/gay adults. *Journal of Counseling Psychology, 54*(3), 306–319. https://doi.org/10.1037/0022-0167.54.3.306

Bauer, G. R., Flanders, C., MacLeod, M. A., & Ross, L. E. (2016). Occurrence of multiple mental health or substance use outcomes among bisexuals: A respondent-driven sampling study. *BMC Public Health, 16,* 497. https://doi.org/10.1186/s12889-016-3173-z

Bostwick, W. B., & Hequembourg, A. (2014). "Just a little hint": Bisexual-specific microaggressions and their connection to epistemic injustices. *Culture, Health & Sexuality, 16*(5), 488–503. https://doi.org/10.1080/13691058.2014.889754

Brewster, M. E., & Moradi, B. (2010). Perceived experiences of anti-bisexual prejudice: Instrument development and evaluation. *Journal of Counseling Psychology, 57*(4), 451–468. https://doi.org/10.1037/a0021116

Brewster, M. E., Moradi, B., DeBlaere, C., & Velez, B. L. (2013). Navigating the borderlands: The roles of minority stressors, bicultural self-efficacy, and cognitive flexibility in the mental health of bisexual individuals. *Journal of Counseling Psychology, 60*(4), 543–556. https://doi.org/10.1037/a0033224

Brooks, L. M., & Inman, A. G. (2013). Bisexual counseling competence: Investigating the role of attitudes and empathy. *Journal of LGBT Issues in Counseling, 7*(1), 65–86. https://doi.org/10.1080/15538605.2013.756366

Brooks, L. M., Inman, A. G., Klinger, R. S., Malouf, M. A., & Kaduvettoor, A. (2010). In her own words: Ethnic-minority bisexual women's self-reported counseling needs. *Journal of Bisexuality, 10*(3), 253–267. https://doi.org/10.1080/15299716.2010.500959

Brooks, L. M., Inman, A. G., Malouf, M. A., Klinger, R. S., & Kaduvettoor, A. (2008). Ethnic minority bisexual women: Understanding the invisible population. *Journal of LGBT Issues in Counseling, 2*(4), 260–284. https://doi.org/10.1080/15538600802501953

Burckell, L. A., & Goldfried, M. R. (2006). Therapist qualities preferred by sexual-minority individuals. *Psychotherapy, 43*(1), 32–49. https://doi.org/10.1037/0033-3204.43.1.32

Burke, S. E., Dovidio, J. F., LaFrance, M., Przedworski, J. M., Perry, S. P., Phelan, S. M., . . . van Ryn, M. (2017). Beyond generalized sexual prejudice: Need for closure predicts negative attitudes toward bisexual people relative to gay/lesbian people. *Journal of Experimental Social Psychology, 71*(Suppl. C), 145–150. https://doi.org/10.1016/j.jesp.2017.02.003

Campbell, D. A., & Hemsley, S. (2009). Outcome Rating Scale and Session Rating Scale in psychological practice: Clinical utility of ultra-brief measures. *Clinical Psychologist, 13*(1), 1–9. https://doi.org/10.1080/13284200802676391

Chesney, M. A., Chambers, D. B., Taylor, J. M., Johnson, L. M., & Folkman, S. (2003). Coping effectiveness training for men living with HIV: Results from a randomized clinical trial testing a group-based intervention. *Psychosomatic Medicine, 65*(6), 1038–1046. https://doi.org/10.1097/01.PSY.0000097344.78697.ED

Copen, C. E., Chandra, A., & Febo-Vazquez, I. (2016, January 7). Sexual behavior, sexual attraction, and sexual orientation among adults aged 18–44 in the United States: Data from the 2011–2013 National Survey of Family Growth. *National Health Statistics Reports* (88), 1–14.

Cox, S., Bimbi, D. S., & Parsons, J. T. (2013). Examination of social contact on binegativity among lesbians and gay men. *Journal of Bisexuality, 13*(2), 215–228. https://doi.org/10.1080/15299716.2013.782596

Cruess, D. G., Antoni, M. H., Schneiderman, N., Ironson, G., McCabe, P., Fernandez, J. B., . . . Kumar, M. (2000). Cognitive–behavioral stress management increases free testosterone and decreases psychological distress in HIV-seropositive men. *Health Psychology, 19*(1), 12–20. https://doi.org/10.1037/0278-6133.19.1.12

de Bruin, M., Hospers, H. J., van Breukelen, G. J. P., Kok, G., Koevoets, W. M., & Prins, J. M. (2010). Electronic monitoring-based counseling to enhance adherence among HIV-infected patients: A randomized controlled trial. *Health Psychology, 29*(4), 421–428. https://doi.org/10.1037/a0020335

Denton, F. N., Rostosky, S. S., & Danner, F. (2014). Stigma-related stressors, coping self-efficacy, and physical health in lesbian, gay, and bisexual individuals. *Journal of Counseling Psychology, 61*(3), 383–391. https://doi.org/10.1037/a0036707

Diamond, L. M. (2016). Sexual fluidity in males and females. *Current Sexual Health Reports, 8*(4), 249–256. https://doi.org/10.1007/s11930-016-0092-z

Dillon, F. R., Worthington, R. L., Soth-McNett, A. M., & Schwartz, S. J. (2008). Gender and sexual identity-based predictors of lesbian, gay, and bisexual affirmative counseling self-efficacy. *Professional Psychology, 39*(3), 353–360. https://doi.org/10.1037/0735-7028.39.3.353

Dobinson, C., MacDonnell, J., Hampson, E., Clipsham, J., & Chow, K. (2005). Improving the access and quality of public health services for bisexuals. *Journal of Bisexuality, 5*(1), 39–78. https://doi.org/10.1300/J159v05n01_05

Dodge, B., Jeffries, W. L., & Sandfort, T. G. M. (2008). Beyond the down low: Sexual risk, protection, and disclosure among at-risk Black men who have sex with both men and women (MSMW). *Archives of Sexual Behavior, 37*(5), 683–696. https://doi.org/10.1007/s10508-008-9356-7

Dodge, B., Schnarrs, P. W., Goncalves, G., Malebranche, D., Martinez, O., Reece, M., . . . Fortenberry, J. D. (2012). The significance of privacy and trust in providing health-related services to behaviorally bisexual men in the United States. *AIDS Education and Prevention, 24*(3), 242–256. https://guilfordjournals.com/doi/10.1521/aeap.2012.24.3.242

Dodge, B., Schnarrs, P. W., Reece, M., Martinez, O., Goncalves, G., Malebranche, D., . . . Fortenberry, J. D. (2012). Individual and social factors related to mental health concerns among bisexual men in the Midwestern United States. *Journal of Bisexuality, 12*(2), 223–245. https://doi.org/10.1080/15299716.2012.674862

Durso, L. E., & Meyer, I. H. (2013). Patterns and predictors of disclosure of sexual orientation to healthcare providers among lesbians, gay men, and bisexuals. *Sexuality Research & Social Policy, 10*(1), 35–42. https://doi.org/10.1007/s13178-012-0105-2

Dworkin, S. H. (2001). Treating the bisexual client. *Journal of Clinical Psychology, 57*(5), 671–680.

Dyar, C., Feinstein, B. A., Schick, V., & Davila, J. (2017). Minority stress, sexual identity uncertainty, and partner gender decision making among nonmonosexual individuals. *Psychology of Sexual Orientation and Gender Diversity, 4*(1), 87–104. https://doi.org/10.1037/sgd0000213

Dyer, T. P., Regan, R., Pacek, L. R., Acheampong, A., & Khan, M. R. (2015). Psychosocial vulnerability and HIV-related sexual risk among men who have sex with men and women in the United States. *Archives of Sexual Behavior, 44*(2), 429–441. https://doi.org/10.1007/s10508-014-0346-7

Eady, A., Dobinson, C., & Ross, L. E. (2011). Bisexual people's experiences with mental health services: A qualitative investigation. *Community Mental Health Journal, 47*(4), 378–389. https://doi.org/10.1007/s10597-010-9329-x

Feinstein, B. A., & Dyar, C. (2017). Bisexuality, minority stress, and health. *Current Sexual Health Reports, 9*, 42–49.

Feinstein, B. A., Dyar, C., & London, B. (2017). Are outness and community involvement risk or protective factors for alcohol and drug abuse among sexual minority women? *Archives of Sexual Behavior, 46*(5), 1411–1423. https://doi.org/10.1007/s10508-016-0790-7

Feinstein, B. A., Dyar, C., & Pachankis, J. E. (2017). A multi-level approach for reducing mental health and substance use disparities affecting bisexual individuals. *Cognitive and Behavioral Practice*, advance online publication. https://doi.org/10.1016/j.cbpra.2017.10.003

Fernandez, M. I., Hosek, S. G., Hotton, A. L., Gaylord, S. E., Hernandez, N., Alfonso, S. V., & Joseph, H. (2016). A randomized controlled trial of POWER: An internet-based HIV prevention intervention for Black bisexual men. *AIDS and Behavior, 20*(9), 1951–1960. https://doi.org/10.1007/s10461-016-1403-0

Friedman, M. R., & Dodge, B. (2016). The role of syndemic in explaining health disparities among bisexual men: A blueprint for a theoretically informed perspective. In E. R. Wright & N. Carnes (Eds.), *Understanding the HIV/AIDS epidemic in the United States: The role of syndemics in the production of health disparities* (pp. 71–98). Cham, Switzerland: Springer.

Friedman, M. R., Dodge, B., Schick, V., Herbenick, D., Hubach, R. D., Bowling, J., . . . Reece, M. (2014). From bias to bisexual health disparities: Attitudes toward bisexual men and women in the United States. *LGBT Health*, *1*(4), 309–318. https://doi.org/ 10.1089/lgbt.2014.0005

Friedman, R. C., & Downey, J. I. (2010). Psychotherapy of bisexual men. *Journal of the American Academy of Psychoanalysis and Dynamic Psychiatry*, *38*(1), 181–197. https:// doi.org/10.1521/jaap.2010.38.1.181

Galupo, M. P., Mitchell, R. C., & Davis, K. S. (2015). Sexual minority self-identification: Multiple identities and complexity. *Psychology of Sexual Orientation and Gender Diversity*, *2*(4), 355–364. https://doi.org/10.1037/sgd0000131

Galupo, M. P., Mitchell, R. C., Grynkiewicz, A. L., & Davis, K. S. (2014). Sexual minority reflections on the Kinsey Scale and the Klein Sexual Orientation Grid: Conceptualization and measurement. *Journal of Bisexuality*, *14*(3-4), 404–432. https://doi.org/10.1080/15299716.2014.929553

Gates, G. J. (2011). *How many people are lesbian, gay, bisexual, and transgender?* Los Angeles, CA: Williams Institute.

Harawa, N. T., Williams, J. K., McCuller, W. J., Ramamurthi, H. C., Lee, M., Shapiro, M. F., . . . Cunningham, W. E. (2013). Efficacy of a culturally congruent HIV risk-reduction intervention for behaviorally bisexual Black men: Results of a randomized trial. *AIDS*, *27*(12), 1979–1988. https://doi.org/10.1097/QAD.0b013e3283617500

Hatzenbuehler, M. L. (2009). How does sexual minority stigma "get under the skin"? A psychological mediation framework. *Psychological Bulletin*, *135*(5), 707–730. https://doi.org/10.1037/a0016441

Hatzenbuehler, M. L. (2016). Structural stigma: Research evidence and implications for psychological science. *American Psychologist*, *71*(8), 742–751. https://doi.org/ 10.1037/amp0000068

Hatzenbuehler, M. L., Phelan, J. C., & Link, B. G. (2013). Stigma as a fundamental cause of population health inequalities. *American Journal of Public Health*, *103*(5), 813–821. https://doi.org/10.2105/AJPH.2012.301069

Hubach, R. D., Dodge, B., Goncalves, G., Malebranche, D., Reece, M., Van Der Pol, B., . . . Fortenberry, J. D. (2014). Gender matters: Condom use and nonuse among behaviorally bisexual men. *Archives of Sexual Behavior*, *43*(4), 707–717. https://doi.org/ 10.1007/s10508-013-0147-4

Institute of Medicine. (2011). *The health of lesbian, gay, bisexual, and transgender people: Building a foundation for better understanding*. Washington, DC: National Academies Press.

Ironson, G., O'Cleirigh, C., Leserman, J., Stuetzle, R., Fordiani, J., Fletcher, M., & Schneiderman, N. (2013). Gender-specific effects of an augmented written emotional disclosure intervention on posttraumatic, depressive, and HIV-disease-related outcomes: A randomized, controlled trial. *Journal of Consulting and Clinical Psychology*, *81*(2), 284–298. https://doi.org/10.1037/a0030814

Israel, T., Gorcheva, R., Burnes, T. R., & Walther, W. A. (2008). Helpful and unhelpful therapy experiences of LGBT clients. *Psychotherapy Research*, *18*(3), 294–305. https:// doi.org/10.1080/10503300701506920

Israel, T., & Mohr, J. J. (2004). Attitudes toward bisexual women and men. *Journal of Bisexuality*, *4*(1–2), 117–134. https://doi.org/10.1300/J159v04n01_09

Jaffe, A., Shoptaw, S., Stein, J. A., Reback, C. J., & Rotheram-Fuller, E. (2007). Depression ratings, reported sexual risk behaviors, and methamphetamine use: Latent growth curve models of positive change among gay and bisexual men in an outpatient treatment program. *Experimental and Clinical Psychopharmacology*, *15*(3), 301–307. https://doi.org/10.1037/1064-1297.15.3.301

Jeffries, W. L., IV. (2014). Beyond the bisexual bridge: Sexual health among U.S. men who have sex with men and women. *American Journal of Preventive Medicine*, *47*(3), 320–329. https://doi.org/10.1016/j.amepre.2014.05.002

Jorm, A. F., Korten, A. E., Rodgers, B., Jacomb, P. A., & Christensen, H. (2002). Sexual orientation and mental health: Results from a community survey of young and middle-aged adults. *British Journal of Psychiatry*, *180*(5), 423–427. https://doi.org/10.1192/bjp.180.5.423

Kertzner, R. M., Meyer, I. H., Frost, D. M., & Stirratt, M. J. (2009). Social and psychological well-being in lesbians, gay men, and bisexuals: The effects of race, gender, age, and sexual identity. *American Journal of Orthopsychiatry*, *79*(4), 500–510. https://doi.org/10.1037/a0016848

Klein, F. (2014). Are you sure you're heterosexual? Or homosexual? Or even bisexual? *Journal of Bisexuality*, *14*(3–4), 341–346. https://doi.org/10.1080/15299716.2014.953282

Koenig, L. J., Pals, S. L., Bush, T., Pratt Palmore, M., Stratford, D., & Ellerbrock, T. V. (2008). Randomized controlled trial of an intervention to prevent adherence failure among HIV-infected patients initiating antiretroviral therapy. *Health Psychology*, *27*(2), 159–169. https://doi.org/10.1037/0278-6133.27.2.159

Laska, K. M., Gurman, A. S., & Wampold, B. E. (2014). Expanding the lens of evidence-based practice in psychotherapy: A common factors perspective. *Psychotherapy*, *51*(4), 467–481. https://doi.org/10.1037/a0034332

Lin, Y.-J., & Israel, T. (2012). A computer-based intervention to reduce internalized heterosexism in men. *Journal of Counseling Psychology*, *59*(3), 458–464. https://doi.org/10.1037/a0028282

Ling Murtaugh, K., Krishnamurti, T., Davis, A. L., Reback, C. J., & Shoptaw, S. (2013). Spend today, clean tomorrow: Predicting methamphetamine abstinence in a randomized controlled trial. *Health Psychology*, *32*(9), 958–966. https://doi.org/10.1037/a0032922

MacKay, J., Robinson, M., Pinder, S., & Ross, L. E. (2017). A grounded theory of bisexual individuals' experiences of help seeking. *American Journal of Orthopsychiatry*, *87*(1), 52–61. https://doi.org/10.1037/ort0000184

Malebranche, D. J., Arriola, K. J., Jenkins, T. R., Dauria, E., & Patel, S. N. (2010). Exploring the "bisexual bridge": A qualitative study of risk behavior and disclosure of same-sex behavior among Black bisexual men. *American Journal of Public Health*, *100*(1), 159–164. https://doi.org/10.2105/AJPH.2008.158725

Martin, D. J., Chernoff, R. A., Buitron, M., Comulada, W. S., Liang, L.-J., & Wong, F. L. (2012). Helping people with HIV/AIDS return to work: A randomized clinical trial. *Rehabilitation Psychology*, *57*(4), 280–289. https://doi.org/10.1037/a0030207

Martínez-Donate, A. P., Zellner, J. A., Sañudo, F., Fernandez-Cerdeño, A., Hovell, M. F., Sipan, C. L., . . . Carrillo, H. (2010). Hombres Sanos: Evaluation of a social marketing campaign for heterosexually identified Latino men who have sex with men and women. *American Journal of Public Health*, *100*(12), 2532–2540. https://doi.org/10.2105/AJPH.2009.179648

Matthews, C. R., Selvidge, M. M. D., & Fisher, K. (2005). Addictions counselors' attitudes and behaviors toward gay, lesbian, and bisexual clients. *Journal of Counseling & Development*, *83*(1), 57–65.

Mays, V. M., & Cochran, S. D. (2001). Mental health correlates of perceived discrimination among lesbian, gay, and bisexual adults in the United States. *American Journal of Public Health*, *91*(11), 1869–1876. https://doi.org/10.2105/AJPH.91.11.1869

McCormack, M., Wignall, L., & Anderson, E. (2015). Identities and identifications: Changes in metropolitan bisexual men's attitudes and experiences. *Journal of Bisexuality*, *15*(1), 3–20. https://doi.org/10.1080/15299716.2014.984372

McLean, K. (2007). Hiding in the closet? Bisexuals, coming out and the disclosure imperative. *Journal of Sociology*, *43*(2), 151–166. https://doi.org/10.1177/1440783307076893

Meyer, I. H. (2003). Prejudice, social stress, and mental health in lesbian, gay, and bisexual populations: Conceptual issues and research evidence. *Psychological Bulletin*, *129*(5), 674–697. https://doi.org/10.1037/0033-2909.129.5.674

Mohr, J. J., Chopp, R. M., & Wong, S. J. (2013). Psychotherapists' stereotypes of heterosexual, gay, and bisexual men. *Journal of Gay & Lesbian Social Services*, *25*(1), 37–55. https://doi.org/10.1080/10538720.2013.751885

Mohr, J. J., Israel, T., & Sedlacek, W. E. (2001). Counselors' attitudes regarding bisexuality as predictors of counselors' clinical responses: An analogue study of a female bisexual client. *Journal of Counseling Psychology*, *48*(2), 212–222. https://doi.org/10.1037/0022-0167.48.2.212

Mohr, J. J., Jackson, S. D., & Sheets, R. L. (2017). Sexual orientation self-presentation among bisexual-identified women and men: Patterns and predictors. *Archives of Sexual Behavior*, *46*(5), 1465–1479. https://doi.org/10.1007/s10508-016-0808-1

Mohr, J. J., Weiner, J. L., Chopp, R. M., & Wong, S. J. (2009). Effects of client bisexuality on clinical judgment: When is bias most likely to occur? *Journal of Counseling Psychology*, *56*(1), 164–175. https://doi.org/10.1037/a0012816

Ochs, R. (2005). What is bisexuality? In R. Ochs & S. E. Rowley (Eds.), *Getting bi: Voices of bisexuals around the world* (pp. 7–15). Boston, MA: Bisexual Resource Center.

Operario, D., Smith, C. D., Arnold, E., & Kegeles, S. (2010). The Bruthas Project: Evaluation of a community-based HIV prevention intervention for African American men who have sex with men and women. *AIDS Education & Prevention*, *22*(1), 37–48.

Pachankis, J. E. (2015). A transdiagnostic minority stress treatment approach for gay and bisexual men's syndemic health conditions. *Archives of Sexual Behavior*, *44*(7), 1843–1860. https://doi.org/10.1007/s10508-015-0480-x

Pachankis, J. E., Cochran, S. D., & Mays, V. M. (2015). The mental health of sexual minority adults in and out of the closet: A population-based study. *Journal of Consulting and Clinical Psychology*, *83*(5), 890–901. https://doi.org/10.1037/ccp0000047

Pachankis, J. E., Hatzenbuehler, M. L., Rendina, H. J., Safren, S. A., & Parsons, J. T. (2015). LGB-affirmative cognitive–behavioral therapy for young adult gay and bisexual men: A randomized controlled trial of a transdiagnostic minority stress approach. *Journal of Consulting and Clinical Psychology*, *83*(5), 875–889. https://doi.org/10.1037/ccp0000037

Pachankis, J. E., Rendina, H. J., Restar, A., Ventuneac, A., Grov, C., & Parsons, J. T. (2015). A minority stress–emotion regulation model of sexual compulsivity among highly sexually active gay and bisexual men. *Health Psychology*, *34*(8), 829–840. https://doi.org/10.1037/hea0000180

Page, E. H. (2004). Mental health services experiences of bisexual women and bisexual men. *Journal of Bisexuality, 4*(1–2), 137–160. https://doi.org/10.1300/J159v04n01_11

Parsons, J. T., Lelutiu-Weinberger, C., Botsko, M., & Golub, S. A. (2014). A randomized controlled trial utilizing motivational interviewing to reduce HIV risk and drug use in young gay and bisexual men. *Journal of Consulting and Clinical Psychology, 82*(1), 9–18. https://doi.org/10.1037/a0035311

Paul, R., Smith, N. G., Mohr, J. J., & Ross, L. E. (2014). Measuring dimensions of bisexual identity: Initial development of the Bisexual Identity Inventory. *Psychology of Sexual Orientation and Gender Diversity, 1*(4), 452–460. https://doi.org/10.1037/sgd0000069

Pew Research Center. (2013). *A survey of LGBT Americans.* Washington, DC: Pew Research Center.

Roberts, T. S., Horne, S. G., & Hoyt, W. T. (2015). Between a gay and a straight place: Bisexual individuals' experiences with monosexism. *Journal of Bisexuality, 15*(4), 554–569. https://doi.org/10.1080/15299716.2015.1111183

Roffman, R. A., Downey, L., Beadnell, B., Gordon, J. R., Craver, J. N., & Stephens, R. S. (1997). Cognitive–behavioral group counseling to prevent HIV transmission in gay and bisexual men: Factors contributing to successful risk reduction. *Research on Social Work Practice, 7*(2), 165–186. https://doi.org/10.1177/104973159700700202

Ross, L. E., Dobinson, C., & Eady, A. (2010). Perceived determinants of mental health for bisexual people: A qualitative examination. *American Journal of Public Health, 100*(3), 496–502.

Ross, L. E., O'Gorman, L., MacLeod, M. A., Bauer, G. R., MacKay, J., & Robinson, M. (2016). Bisexuality, poverty and mental health: A mixed methods analysis. *Social Science & Medicine, 156,* 64–72. https://doi.org/10.1016/j.socscimed.2016.03.009

Rostosky, S. S., Riggle, E. D. B., Pascale-Hague, D., & McCants, L. E. (2010). The positive aspects of a bisexual self-identification. *Psychology & Sexuality, 1*(2), 131–144. https://doi.org/10.1080/19419899.2010.484595

Rotheram-Borus, M. J., Murphy, D. A., Fernandez, M. I., & Srinivasan, S. (1998). A brief HIV intervention for adolescents and young adults. *American Journal of Orthopsychiatry, 68*(4), 553–564. https://doi.org/10.1037/h0080364

Safren, S. A., O'Cleirigh, C. M., Bullis, J. R., Otto, M. W., Stein, M. D., & Pollack, M. H. (2012). Cognitive behavioral therapy for adherence and depression (CBT-AD) in HIV-infected injection drug users: A randomized controlled trial. *Journal of Consulting and Clinical Psychology, 80*(3), 404–415. https://doi.org/10.1037/a0028208

Safren, S. A., O'Cleirigh, C., Tan, J. Y., Raminani, S. R., Reilly, L. C., Otto, M. W., & Mayer, K. H. (2009). A randomized controlled trial of cognitive behavioral therapy for adherence and depression (CBT-AD) in HIV-infected individuals. *Health Psychology, 28*(1), 1–10. https://doi.org/10.1037/a0012715

Sarno, E., & Wright, A. J. (2013). Homonegative microaggressions and identity in bisexual men and women. *Journal of Bisexuality, 13*(1), 63–81. https://doi.org/10.1080/15299716.2013.756677

Scherrer, K. (2013). Culturally competent practice with bisexual individuals. *Clinical Social Work Journal, 41*(3), 238–248. https://doi.org/10.1007/s10615-013-0451-4

Sheets, R. L., & Mohr, J. J. (2009). Perceived social support from friends and family and psychosocial functioning in bisexual young adult college students. *Journal of Counseling Psychology, 56*(1), 152–163. https://doi.org/10.1037/0022-0167.56.1.152

Shelton, K., & Delgado-Romero, E. A. (2013). Sexual orientation microaggressions: The experience of lesbian, gay, bisexual, and queer clients in psychotherapy. *Psychology of Sexual Orientation and Gender Diversity, 1*(S), 59–70. https://doi.org/10.1037/2329-0382.1.S.59

Shoptaw, S., Reback, C. J., Peck, J. A., Yang, X., Rotheram-Fuller, E., Larkins, S., . . . Hucks-Ortiz, C. (2005). Behavioral treatment approaches for methamphetamine dependence and HIV-related sexual risk behaviors among urban gay and bisexual men. *Drug and Alcohol Dependence, 78*(2), 125–134. https://doi.org/10.1016/j.drugalcdep.2004.10.004

Sikkema, K. J., Hansen, N. B., Ghebremichael, M., Kochman, A., Tarakeshwar, N., Meade, C. S., & Zhang, H. (2006). A randomized controlled trial of a coping group intervention for adults with HIV who are AIDS bereaved: Longitudinal effects on grief. *Health Psychology, 25*(5), 563–570. https://doi.org/10.1037/0278-6133.25.5.563

Smith, N. G., Mohr, J. J., & Ross, L. E. (2018). The role of bisexual-specific minority stressors in sexual compulsivity among bisexual men. *Sexual and Relationship Therapy, 33*(1–2), 81–96. https://doi.org/10.1080/14681994.2017.1386301

Stracuzzi, T. I., Mohr, J. J., & Fuertes, J. N. (2011). Gay and bisexual male clients' perceptions of counseling: The role of perceived sexual orientation similarity and counselor universal-diverse orientation. *Journal of Counseling Psychology, 58*(3), 299–309. https://doi.org/10.1037/a0023603

Velasquez, M. M., von Sternberg, K., Johnson, D. H., Green, C., Carbonari, J. P., & Parsons, J. T. (2009). Reducing sexual risk behaviors and alcohol use among HIV-positive men who have sex with men: A randomized clinical trial. *Journal of Consulting and Clinical Psychology, 77*(4), 657–667. https://doi.org/10.1037/a0015519

Victor, C. J., & Nel, J. A. (2016). Lesbian, gay, and bisexual clients' experience with counselling and psychotherapy in South Africa: Implications for affirmative practice. *South African Journal of Psychology, 46*(3), 351–363. https://doi.org/10.1177/0081246315620774

Williams, J. K., Glover, D. A., Wyatt, G. E., Kisler, K., Liu, H., & Zhang, M. (2013). A sexual risk and stress reduction intervention designed for HIV-positive bisexual African American men with childhood sexual abuse histories. *American Journal of Public Health, 103*(8), 1476–1484. https://doi.org/10.2105/AJPH.2012.301121

Williams, J. K., Wyatt, G. E., Rivkin, I., Ramamurthi, H. C., Li, X., & Liu, H. (2008). Risk reduction for HIV-positive African American and Latino men with histories of childhood sexual abuse. *Archives of Sexual Behavior, 37*(5), 763–772. https://doi.org/10.1007/s10508-008-9366-5

Wolfers, M. E., de Wit, J. B., Hospers, H. J., Richardus, J. H., & de Zwart, O. (2009). Effects of a short individually tailored counselling session for HIV prevention in gay and bisexual men receiving hepatitis B vaccination. *BMC Public Health, 9*, 255–265. https://doi.org/10.1186/1471-2458-9-255

Evidence-Based Treatments for Specific Mental Health Problems Among Sexual and Gender Minority Clients

8

Anxiety Disorders and Obsessive–Compulsive Disorder

Evidence-Based Considerations for Affirmative Services for Sexual Minority Clients

NATALIE R. HOLT, ALLURA L. RALSTON,
AND DEBRA A. HOPE ■

Sexual minority adults face elevated rates of stress-related mental health problems, including anxiety disorders, compared to heterosexual adults (Meyer, 2003). The fifth edition of the *Diagnostic and Statistical Manual of Mental Disorders* (DSM-5; American Psychiatric Association, 2013) estimates 12-month prevalence rates of anxiety disorders in the general population between 1.2% (obsessive–compulsive disorder [OCD]) and 7% (social anxiety disorder). The lifetime prevalence of anxiety disorders among adults in the United States is nearly 30% (Kessler et al., 2005, 2009). This rate is substantially higher for lesbian, gay, and bisexual (LGB) adults,[1] who are at more than twice the risk of developing or being treated for an anxiety disorder compared to heterosexuals (Bränström, 2017; Cochran, Sullivan, & Mays, 2003; Meyer, 2003; Pakula, Shoveller, Ratner, & Carpiano, 2016). Within LGB adults, sexual minority men are at higher risk for a lifetime anxiety disorder compared to sexual minority women; however, bisexual men and women face the highest odds of any sexual identity group of developing an anxiety disorder (Bostwick, Boyd, Hughes, & McCabe, 2010).

1. Much of the literature cited in this chapter refers to LGB individuals who self-identify as a sexual minority. However, people may identify with a sexual orientation beyond lesbian, gay, and bisexual, and some individuals engage in same-sex sexual behavior but do not identify with a sexual minority label. Where possible, we include research from these broader sexual minority communities. In order to be consistent with previous literature and ease communication, this chapter uses sexual minority and LGB interchangeably.

Not surprisingly, elevated rates of mental health problems co-occur with elevated utilization of mental health services. A comparison of LGB individuals and their heterosexual siblings found 79.3% of LGB participants had a history of attending therapy compared to 52.5% of heterosexual siblings (Balsam, Beauchaine, Mickey, & Rothblum, 2005; Cochran, Björkenstam, & Mays, 2017). However, sexual minorities, like other marginalized groups, may face more barriers to obtaining care, such as poverty and lack of availability of appropriate services (Dahlhamer, Galinsky, Joestl, & Ward, 2016; Rosenkrantz, Black, Abreu, Aleshire, & Fallin-Bennett, 2017). Cultural competency for therapists working with LGB clients means awareness of LGB issues, positive attitudes toward LGB people, and any needed skills for LGB-affirmative therapy, according to the American Psychological Association (2012) guidelines. Therapists are more likely to have an awareness of LGB issues and have positive attitudes toward LGB people than they are to meet skill competencies for working with LGB clients, such as experience with counseling, assessment, and receiving supervision (Bidell, 2005). Unskilled treatment can be tempered by positive attitudes toward LGB people, but providing LGB-affirmative services requires more than good intentions.

This chapter addresses LGB-affirmative considerations in the evidence-based treatment and assessment of anxiety disorders and OCD[2] and the unique stressors that may sustain anxiety symptoms in LGB populations. In particular, this chapter explores how minority stress and sexual stigma may impact the presentation, assessment, and case conceptualization of anxiety disorders in LGB adults. Case examples illustrate how empirically supported treatments and techniques, such as cognitive restructuring and exposure, may be adapted for LGB-affirmative treatment. In addition, unique presentations of anxiety disorders related to sexual orientation, such as sexual orientation obsessions in OCD, and multicultural considerations sometimes related to sexual orientation, such as HIV status, are discussed. The chapter concludes with a consideration of future directions and emerging trends related to evidence-based treatment and dissemination strategies to improve the delivery of evidence-based anxiety treatment to LGB adults.

MINORITY STRESS AND SEXUAL STIGMA

LGB individuals are likely to experience marginalization, stress, and sexual stigma due to their sexual orientation. Meyer (1995, 2003) described a model of minority stress in which the unique societal stigma LGB individuals experience can cause and sustain mental health problems. Minority stress can arise from *distal stressors*, external events such as prejudice and victimization, and *proximal stressors*, wherein negative beliefs about a minority identity are internalized. Herek (2009) identified three types of sexual stigma that LGB individuals face. *Enacted stigma*, such as

---

2. Although DSM-5 no longer classifies OCD as an anxiety disorder, in this chapter, the term *anxiety disorders* is used to include OCD for ease of communication.

violence and hate crimes, operates similarly to distal stressors in Meyer's model to cause psychological stress and is associated with higher levels of anxiety (Herek, Gillis, & Cogan, 1999). *Felt stigma* refers to how an individual anticipates that stigma will arise in specific situations. LGB individuals' perceptions of felt stigma may lead to adaptive behavior or could increase avoidant behavior that restricts social, occupational, or academic functioning and maintains anxiety (Pachankis, Goldfried, & Ramrattan, 2008). For example, felt stigma may impact which occupational opportunities someone chooses to pursue. *Internalized stigma* operates as proximal stressors: An individual adopts negative attitudes about their identity and incorporates stigma into their self-concept. Similar to enacted stigma, higher levels of internalized stigma related to sexual orientation are associated with higher levels of anxiety (Newcomb & Mustanski, 2010).

HOW STIGMA INFLUENCES ANXIETY DISORDERS IN LGB ADULTS

Minority stress and sexual stigma not only can create and maintain anxiety symptoms in LGB adults but also may influence the presentation and treatment of anxiety disorders. Internalized homonegativity or internalized homophobia is the internalized stigma LGB individuals experience when they direct negative stereotypes about LGB people toward themselves, hold prejudicial attitudes about LGB communities, or feel shame about their own sexual orientation (Shidlo, 1994). Internalized homonegativity has been linked to treatment outcomes in LGB-affirmative cognitive–behavioral therapy (CBT; Millar, Wang, & Pachankis, 2016) and higher rates of internalizing disorders, especially among older LGB individuals (Newcomb & Mustanski, 2010). These findings suggest internalized homophobia may be an important domain to assess when developing a treatment plan and monitoring progress in therapy.

Additional constructs important to the development and maintenance of anxiety symptoms, particularly social anxiety symptoms, among LGB people are rejection sensitivity and fear of negative evaluation. Individuals high in rejection sensitivity and fear of negative evaluation are likely to anticipate, perceive, and overreact to being rejected in social situations. Compared to heterosexual men, gay men reported greater fear of negative evaluation, social interaction anxiety, and lower self-esteem (Pachankis & Goldfried, 2006), and being LGB is associated with a greater likelihood of social anxiety (Hatzenbuehler, Keyes, & Hasin, 2009). Keeping one's sexual orientation hidden and being less comfortable with being gay might also be associated with higher social anxiety. These findings fit within the minority stress model. LGB adults who anticipate and fear negative evaluation or rejection may have realistic assumptions of how they will be received in society due to their sexual orientation, suggesting that heightened social anxiety may not always be a maladaptive response. A thorough assessment is needed to distinguish between reasonable reactions to sexual stigma and overestimated fears of rejection that are characteristic of social anxiety. As discussed later, this distinction has important treatment implications.

Unlike individuals who possess a visible stigmatized identity, many, but not all, LGB adults must decide when and to whom to conceal and disclose their sexual orientation. Concealment and disclosure have been linked to mental health concerns and anxiety symptoms. Concealing sexual orientation predicts social anxiety symptoms among young adults (Cohen, Blasey, Taylor, Weiss, & Newman, 2016). More worry about one's sexual orientation, including worrying about coming out or being outed, is associated with higher negative affect and internalized homophobia and lower positive affect (Weiss & Hope, 2011). In fact, it may be that concealment, or actively hiding one's sexual orientation, is especially problematic for mental health. Pachankis (2007) argued that LGB individuals trying to conceal their sexual orientation may engage in avoidant behaviors that can create social dysfunction and/or sustain anxiety. For example, an LGB individual who fears being discovered as a sexual minority may change mannerisms they fear are associated with a LGB identity or avoid events or spaces connected to LGB communities, leading to a loss of social support. Only a few studies have disentangled concealment and disclosure. Meidlinger and Hope (2014) found concealment was more strongly associated with poor mental health outcomes than was nondisclosure, consistent with Pachankis' hypothesis. Another study found a similar pattern with behaviorally bisexual men (Schrimshaw, Siegel, Downing, & Parsons, 2013).

ASSESSMENT AND CASE CONCEPTUALIZATION FOR ANXIETY DISORDERS AMONG LGB ADULTS

In this section, we consider four key ideas to ensure the assessment process is LGB-affirmative and combats the heterocentrism often present in assessment tools for anxiety disorders. Heterocentrism, defined as the often implicit assumption that everyone is heterosexual, can disrupt the assessment process with LGB clients (Shulman & Hope, 2016). Four key approaches for avoiding heterocentrism and conducting an LGB-affirmative assessment are (1) assessing sexual orientation with all clients, not just those who are somehow perceived to be LGB; (2) assessing the role of sexual identity/orientation in case conceptualization; (3) using measures free of heterocentric language; and (4) distinguishing between maladaptive and adaptive safety behaviors. Failure to make these adaptations may isolate, confuse, or offend some LGB clients (Lindner, Martell, Bergstrom, Andersson, & Carlbring, 2013; Weiss, Hope, & Capozzoli, 2013) and lead to an unreliable and invalid assessment. Each of these key ideas is discussed next.

The first key idea is assessing sexual orientation with each client, not just those who are perceived somehow to be LGB, in order to open the door for discussion when needed. Each LGB client will have their own understanding of their identity. Their identity label, attraction pattern, and sexual behavior may appear inconsistent to the novice therapist. A man engaged in same-sex sexual behavior may or may not label himself as gay. A woman who is married and has children with a man may not label herself as heterosexual. Sexual orientation is complex and may be fluid over time (Klein, Sepekoff, & Wolf, 1985; Mock & Eibach, 2012). Therefore, inquiring about sexual orientation in an open manner allows clients to share their own understanding of themselves. The therapist's job is to listen carefully to what the client is and is not saying about their identity and then incorporate this information into the case conceptualization.

The second key idea is assessing the role of sexual identity/orientation in case conceptualization so the therapist can explore if and how minority stress may be relevant to the presenting problem. Both underemphasis and overemphasis of sexual orientation can strain the therapeutic relationship (Burckell & Goldfriend, 2006; Safren & Rogers, 2001). LGB clients vary in terms of how central their sexual orientation is to their identity, and the same client may place greater or lesser emphasis on their identity across time (Balsam, Martell, & Safren, 2006). Consider the following interaction between Gabriela, a married lesbian woman, and her therapist:

THERAPIST: I see you marked "lesbian" on our intake form. Tell me about how you see your sexual orientation?

GABRIELA: I have known I was gay since I was a little girl. I dated guys a few times in high school because of social pressure but then I met my wife and we have been together ever since.

THERAPIST: Do you see your identity and the stressors that can bring in our society playing a role in your anxiety?

GABRIELA: Not really. My wife and I are very happy and the kids are doing well. We have mostly set up our lives to be surrounded by supportive people. When I was first coming out, I was very anxious about what it meant, but not now.

THERAPIST: Now you are most anxious about what?

GABRIELA: Money. We just got bills paid off and are doing OK. However, I continue to worry a lot about our finances. I am anxious every time we spend money and lay awake at night worrying about whether we have overspent.

Although more information may be revealed later, it appears at this point that more discussion of sexual orientation is not warranted and further assessment of and then intervention on what appears to be excessive worry is more appropriate.

The third key idea is to use assessment measures free of heterocentric language and bias. Many self-report questionnaires exist for assessing anxiety and related concerns, including diagnostic measures (e.g., Connor, Kobak, Churchill, Katzelnick, & Davidson, 2001), symptom measures (e.g., Goodman et al., 1989), general anxiety scales (e.g., Beck, Epstein, Brown, & Steer, 1988), and scales of related cross-cutting constructs such as anxiety sensitivity (e.g. Taylor et al., 2007). Psychometric studies have not typically been conducted with LGB samples.

However, although most measures might not function differently according to sexual orientation, several measures of social anxiety include language about anxiety related to interacting with and/or attraction to the *opposite sex*. This language assumes that the respondent is heterosexual or is only attracted to members of another gender. Although the language was considered acceptable when the measures were developed, current scholarship has highlighted the problems of conflating sex and gender and the assumption that gender is binary (American Psychological Association, 2015). Some commonly used measures that include heterocentric language are the Social Interaction Anxiety Scale (SIAS; Mattick & Clarke, 1998), the Interaction Anxiousness Scale (IAS; Leary, 1983), the Social Phobia and Anxiety Inventory (SPAI; Turner, Beidel, Dancu, & Stanley, 1989), and the Social Avoidance and Distress Scale (SAD; Watson & Friend, 1969). Although a full review of how to modify these scales is outside the scope of this chapter, Weiss et al. (2013) have provided psychometrically sound alternatives for the SIAS, IAS, and SAD. In a follow-up study, Shulman and Hope (2016) identified wording changes for the SPAI that eliminated heterocentric language and expanded the scope of the assessment to be more inclusive. Furthermore, shortened forms of the SIAS (Fergus, Valentiner, McGrath, Gier-Lonsway, & Kim, 2012; Peters, Sunderland, Andrews, Rapee, & Mattick, 2012) are free of heterocentric bias and have been shown to be comparable to the longer form (Le Blanc et al., 2014).

The fourth key consideration in the assessment of LGB clients involves recognizing the difference between maladaptive thoughts and behaviors that unnecessarily impede functioning and thoughts and behaviors that are a realistic reaction to stigma and prejudice and keep clients safe. The following is an exchange between Leo, a 25-year-old gay man, and his therapist:

THERAPIST: Tell me about the promotion you turned down at work.

LEO: I have been working in the main store for a couple of years and it is going well. I feel comfortable there. I don't really have panic attacks there anymore. But even if it happens, I know I can just step outside for a few minutes and be OK. My manager wanted to me to join the distribution team that takes product out to a lot of stores in small towns. I was very anxious about that travel because I sometimes get panic attacks when driving and I didn't want to go deal with the people in the small towns.

THERAPIST: So part of it was about your fears about driving. Tell me about the part about dealing with people in the small towns.

LEO: I am out at work and everyone is OK with me being gay. That is part of what I like about this job. I grew up in a small town and was hassled my whole life. The idea of having to go to those rural areas and being unsure of their reactions is just too stressful. What if I had car trouble or got stuck in a snow storm and had to stay the night? I am not sure if it would be safe. I know everyone there is not prejudiced but the stores often have a lot of older conservative men I would have to deal with. The extra money just wasn't worth it.

In this exchange, it appears that Leo turned down the job in part because of panic and agoraphobic avoidance. However, his fears about experiencing harassment because of his sexual orientation were also important in his decision and warrant different consideration in the case conceptualization. A therapist might be tempted to conceptualize that his overestimation of danger seen in panic also extends to overestimating the danger of harassment. This approach could further marginalize Leo by suggesting that his experience might not be valid, especially if the therapist does not share his minority status. A more LGB-affirming approach would be to consider the possibility that he tends to avoid situations in which he has had a panic attack, which may correlate with situations in which he previously experienced harassment, such as in small towns. This developmental history of harassment may be important in understanding his reaction to stress, his self-schema, and his available coping skills. If the driving fears are independent of his concerns about being harassed in small towns, then treatment first can focus on the driving anxiety so that barrier is removed before the therapist helps Leo determine whether he wants to be able to take the new job that requires visiting small towns. If so, then the focus would be on empowering him to meet those challenges in a safe way. This approach is different than trying to convince him that his experiences and perceptions are inaccurate, which because of his history of homophobic stigma does not seem to be true. More details on how to address experiences of stigma and discrimination in treatment are described later in this chapter.

EVIDENCE FOR THE EFFICACY OF COGNITIVE–BEHAVIORAL THERAPY

Cognitive–behavioral therapy has been well established as an efficacious treatment for anxiety disorders in adults. Numerous meta-analyses provide support for the efficacy of CBT for panic disorder with or without agoraphobia (PD), social anxiety disorder (SAD), generalized anxiety disorder (GAD), and OCD. Many of these meta-analyses compared the effect sizes for CBT, wait-list, placebo, control, and pharmacological conditions. CBT and medications have been shown to be equally effective in treating PD (Bandelow, Seidler-Brandler, Becker, Wedekind, & Rüther, 2007; Cuijpers et al., 2014), with the combination of therapies more effective than either therapy alone (Bandelow et al., 2007). Some studies have shown CBT to be more effective than medication in treating PD (Bandelow et al., 2007; Mitte, 2005; Roshanaei-Moghaddam et al., 2011). CBT has also been shown to yield larger effect sizes for SAD compared to other treatments such as psychodynamic therapy and interpersonal therapy, no treatment, and placebo conditions (Mayo-Wilson et al., 2014). CBT and medication have been shown to be equally effective for GAD, with CBT producing greater post-treatment effects (Gould, Otto, Pollack, & Yap, 1997).

Randomized control trials for the treatment of GAD suggest that CBT maintains its effects at follow-up and is more effective than relaxation alone (Cuijpers et al.,

2014). Furthermore, CBT for GAD produces significantly higher effect sizes compared to wait-list controls (Cuijpers, et al., 2014). For OCD, CBT is similarly or significantly more effective than medication (Öst, Havnen, Hansen, & Kvale, 2015) and more effective than control conditions with therapist contact, such as relaxation training, and wait-list control conditions (Olatunji, Davis, Powers, & Smits, 2013). Norton and Price (2007) examined the efficacy of CBT using 108 studies spanning all anxiety disorder diagnoses. Consistent with results from studies of individual disorders, results from this study indicated that treatments using CBT techniques demonstrated significantly larger effect sizes compared to no-treatment or control conditions with therapist contact and other common factors only across all anxiety disorders. The efficacy of transdiagnostic CBT (TCBT) for anxiety disorders, in which a singular protocol is applied across multiple disorders, has been evaluated in a handful of studies. TCBT demonstrates better outcomes than wait-list and treatment-as-usual conditions (Reinholt & Krogh, 2014) and similar outcomes as diagnosis-specific treatment protocols (Barlow et al., 2017).

Although CBT represents the most investigated and established approach to treating anxiety disorders, other related psychosocial inventions have also shown efficacy. For instance, acceptance and commitment therapy (ACT; Hayes, Strosahl, & Wilson, 1999) is likely as effective as CBT (Arch et al., 2012).[3] Some studies also support the efficacy of brief psychodynamic psychotherapies for anxiety (Abbass et al., 2014), but the evidence does not support these approaches as a first choice for intervention.

Given that anxiety disorders and OCD occur at a higher rate in LGB individuals than heterosexual individuals, identifying the best evidence-based interventions for LGB individuals is especially important. Although strong evidence supports the efficacy of CBT for anxiety disorders and OCD in the general population, some culturally specific adaptations for LGB clients may be needed (Pachankis & Goldfried, 2013). These adaptations are described next and may apply to treatment approaches beyond CBT.

COMMON THERAPEUTIC FACTORS AND CLINICIAN CONSIDERATIONS

The treatments with the most empirical support for anxiety disorders tend to be CBT, but this does not preclude factors common across treatments in predicting positive outcomes. Common factors, such as an expectancy for change and a positive working alliance, are important mediators of treatment outcome (M. G. Newman & Fisher, 2010; Sauer-Zavala et al., 2018). A lack of multicultural competence may disrupt key common factors, such as therapeutic alliance, and

---

3. See Chapter 17 in this volume for a discussion of acceptance-based approaches with LGBT individuals.

thus impede intervention success (Owen et al., 2011). Unfortunately, most mental health providers have little formal training for working with LGB clients, and such training is not widely included in graduate training programs (Hope & Chappell, 2015). Sue (1991) identified three components of multicultural competence, including self-awareness of beliefs and attitudes, knowledge, and skills necessary for working with marginalized individuals. For all clinicians serving LGB clients, self-awareness includes an examination of one's own experience of sexual orientation and the influence of anti-LGB cultural messages on both the therapist and the client. For heterosexual clinicians, examination of the privilege that comes with heterosexuality, such as others' assumptions that one is heterosexual and safety when interacting with a partner in public settings, also represents necessary awareness. A clinician's limited comfort with and knowledge of sexual orientation and sexuality may impede therapy as well. Clinicians should be familiar with local LGB communities, including the cultural and legal climate for LGB individuals, diversity of the community, and available resources. The skills necessary for multicultural competent care are described later.

CASE CONCEPTUALIZATION

One important therapeutic skill that should be informed by multicultural considerations is case conceptualization, defined as the process or "crucible" in which psychological theory (e.g., relationships between events in a functional analysis) and research are combined with the client's experience to develop an understanding of the client's presenting problems that can be used to guide an individualized treatment plan (Kuyken, Padesky, & Dudley, 2008). Case conceptualizations include client demographics as a background against which to understand the client's experiences. However, due to heteronormativity, sexual orientation is often only explicitly stated in a case conceptualization when the client is LGB. We argue that sexual orientation should always be explicitly incorporated, if only to acknowledge that it is a contextual variable not necessarily central to the presenting problems. For example, consider the case of Paul, a gay man who is seeking treatment for frequent panic attacks occurring mostly at his job in the state government bureaucracy. In constructing a fear and avoidance hierarchy for Paul to help him address the increasing avoidance of situations in which he has had panic attacks, the therapist and Paul notice that the panic attacks occur most frequently around certain individuals who Paul perceives as holding anti-gay attitudes. Paul conceals his sexual orientation at work and fears a hostile work environment or even losing his job if his sexual orientation is discovered. The case conceptualization for Paul will consider the following: Paul is gay and not out at work, he has a hostile work environment that could get worse if he is outed, his mental and physical health are impacted by that hostile environment, and he has few legal protections in his city and state to help protect him from employment discrimination. It is tempting to question whether Paul's perception of the work climate is accurate, given the threat of hypervigilance common in anxiety disorders (Richards, Benson, Donnelly, & Hadwin, 2014). However, the clinician must tread carefully given the possible risks if Paul's assessment is accurate.

COGNITIVE RESTRUCTURING FOR ANXIETY DISORDERS AMONG LGB CLIENTS

Cognitive restructuring is one of the most commonly taught anxiety management strategies across evidence-based treatment for anxiety disorders (Antony & Norton, 2008; Craske & Barlow, 2006; Hope, Heimberg, & Turk, 2010). Based on the work of Beck and colleagues (e.g., Beck, Emery, & Greenberg, 2005), cognitive restructuring helps clients discover and change their maladaptive thoughts and core beliefs. Cognitive restructuring is based on the premise that anxiety results from the misinterpretation of internal or external events—for example, a pounding heart means a heart attack is imminent in panic disorder. As noted previously, LGB individuals, like other marginalized people, may be reacting to societal stigma and discrimination. In such situations, cognitive restructuring can still be useful but should not challenge perceptions of marginalizing experiences. Of course, LGB clients may also have catastrophic misinterpretations due to the cognitive biases in anxiety disorders, and these can be challenged as usual.

Several case studies of LGB clients with anxiety disorders include recommendations for using cognitive restructuring adapted to LGB-specific presenting concerns. Walsh and Hope (2010) described the use of CBT to treat social anxiety disorder in a European American gay man named Jason. Cognitive restructuring was used to examine Jason's fears about being harassed in public if he held hands with a partner and his concomitant concerns about his physical safety. Jason eventually created rational responses of "Even if I am verbally harassed by strangers, I know those words are coming from less open-minded individuals and I can cope" and "Although the risk of physical injury is probably low, I would rather risk my physical safety for a moment than risk my personal happiness for the rest of my life." Glassgold (2009) similarly reviewed the use of CBT for social anxiety disorder with Felix, a gay Latino man. Glassgold employed cognitive restructuring to examine automatic thoughts that stemmed from Felix's self-stigma about disclosure, such as "I am telling someone something bad." Through cognitive restructuring, Felix reappraised the negative biases he had about his own sexual orientation and more accurately assessed how his family members would respond to him coming out.

The cases of Jason and Felix show how cognitive restructuring can be applied to automatic thoughts that stem from fears of disclosure and victimization. Helping clients navigate and appropriately assess these types of automatic thoughts requires particular attention to the role of societal stigma and prejudice. Therapists must be aware of how social influences and clients' past experiences with stigma and discrimination contribute to the development and maintenance of anxious thoughts (Berg, Ross, Weatherburn, & Schmidt, 2013; Pachankis et al.,

2008). What appears to be an automatic thought may be an LGB client's accurate and rational assessment of a situation. As seen in Jason's case, cognitive restructuring does not have to be used to eliminate a client's fear that a situation is dangerous. Instead, rational responses can capture how to appropriately respond and cope in dangerous situations or weigh the costs and benefits of avoiding feared situations. Felix's case highlights the importance of clients understanding when their negative automatic thoughts come from internalized negative sentiments toward their sexual identity. Cognitive restructuring with LGB clients requires therapists and clients to discuss which thoughts and fears are maladaptive and which are prudent for ensuring clients' safety and security.

Consider the case of Jordan, a 20-year-old African American lesbian woman diagnosed with GAD. Jordan endorses worrying about her performance in school, finances, her health, and her sexual orientation, particularly being outed as a lesbian to her family and church members. Jordan describes herself as an activist and is a member of campus organizations dedicated to racial justice and social equality. However, her fears about disclosing her sexual orientation led her to stop participating in political activities. She worried that her family and friends from church would see her involved in protests and marches advocating for LGBTQ rights and would deduce her sexual orientation. Jordan says her church's pastor has spoken out against homosexuality, and she worries that her family will stop financially supporting her if they discover her sexual orientation. Cognitive therapy techniques, such as cognitive restructuring, can be used to examine if Jordan's fears are rational and determine how she should proceed. Jordan identifies thoughts such as "My family will never speak to me again if they find out I am gay" and "Advocating for LGBTQ rights will tell them I am gay." The following dialog shows Jordan and her therapist using Socratic questioning to negotiate which thoughts are maladaptive and could be fruitfully challenged:

THERAPIST: So it sounds like your worry that your family will find out you are gay is making you monitor how you act around them and keeping you from doing some things that are important to you.

JORDAN: Yes. It would be a disaster if they knew. After last weekend with them, I lay awake for hours replaying the conversations to see if I had slipped up.

THERAPIST: So let's use the cognitive restructuring skills to examine the thought "It would be a disaster if my family knew I am gay."

JORDAN: That sounds like catastrophizing but they would cut me off financially.

THERAPIST: Cutting you off financially means . . .

JORDAN: They would quit paying for college. Once I finish my degree, I would be OK.

THERAPIST: So you have two semesters left and you want to wait to come out to them. That seems like an option. But what would you do if suddenly tomorrow they stopped paying for school?

JORDAN: I would have to quit school and get a job to support myself.

THERAPIST: Would you ever be able to finish your degree?

JORDAN: Eventually, I guess. I could just take one class at a time while I worked.

THERAPIST: So it is much preferred to just finish now with your parents' support but you could get there eventually on your own.

JORDAN: Yes, I would make it somehow.

THERAPIST: So given you now have a plan if your parents find out you are gay and stop paying for college, let's think about what things you have been avoiding that you might be able to do.

JORDAN: I really feel badly that I am not more public about social justice and political causes I believe in. All my friends are very public and active.

THERAPIST: You said earlier that if your family saw you with a rainbow flag, they would know you are gay.

JORDAN: Yes.

THERAPIST: If they saw you at a vigil about hate crimes against Muslims, would they assume you are converting to Islam from Christianity?

JORDAN: No, I guess not.

THERAPIST: What if you spoke out about a lot of anti-discrimination issues, carried a lot of different flags and signs?

JORDAN: My parents might not be happy with some of the causes but they might see me as just an activist, a political person.

THERAPIST: So you could be more involved if you did show up for a lot of different causes.

JORDAN: Yes, and it would make me really happy to be more involved and making my voice heard.

As can be seen, the therapist did not challenge the client's experience of felt stigma from her family or whether hiding her identity was the best choice. The focus instead was on coping with possible consequences of enacted stigma. Coming out to her family is her choice to make. Concealing her identity likely has its own benefits and costs, but it is for the client, not the therapist, to decide whether to take that step. Contrast this with someone who has fears of an accident while driving. In this situation, cognitive restructuring would likely focus on the probability of an accident at some point. Although therapists might challenge the possibility that Jordan's parents could reject her, the ultimate responsibility of judging the risks and consequences of rejection lie much more with the client than it does in the case of a client who worries about having a driving accident. When treating the client with driving fears, the therapist has better information to challenge the client about how likely an accident is to occur. It is much more difficult for the therapist to accurately assess the probability that Jordan's family will reject her.

ADAPTING EXPOSURE THERAPY FOR ANXIETY DISORDERS AMONG LGB CLIENTS

Therapeutic exposure to feared situations and experiences is arguably the key ingredient in CBT for anxiety disorders (Foa et al., 2005; Hope, Heimberg, & Bruch, 1995). There are several types of exposure therapy, including in vivo, imaginal, virtual reality, and interoceptive exposure. For the most part, exposure can proceed as usual for individuals who identify as LGB. However, as discussed next, there are some situations in which additional safety considerations are needed.

Across anxiety disorders, exposure exercises usually proceed after the therapist and client create an individualized fear and avoidance hierarchy. As noted previously, in working with LGB clients, it is important to distinguish realistic fears of experiencing bias and discrimination from irrational fears characteristic of anxiety disorders when constructing the fear and avoidance hierarchy. Similarly, when planning exposures, especially in vivo exposures, therapists may need to attend to whether a given situation may present particular risks for an LGB client that may not be present for a heterosexual client. For example, when planning exposures for an LGB client who fears receiving medical care, the therapist and client first may need to identify an LGB-affirmative provider. This can ensure that concerns about discrimination or stigma in health care settings do not impact the exposure, allowing the focus to be on overcoming fears about medical experiences.

The case study of Felix (Glassgold, 2009), described previously, illustrates how exposure therapy can be helpful in reducing fears and self-evaluations specific to being a sexual minority. Felix first engaged in in vivo exposure to reduce his fear of disclosure and self-stigma. Exposure began with having Felix talk about LGB issues utilizing specific language, such as "gay" rather than "different lifestyle." Felix then constructed a hierarchy of exposure situations including people to whom to disclose his sexual orientation. Felix ranked individuals according to how difficult he perceived it would be to disclose to each person. He then began by disclosing to easier individuals (e.g., distant friends) and then to more difficult individuals (e.g., close family members). Felix role-played coming out to these individuals with his partner and other friends who already knew that he was gay. During role-playing exercises, Felix was encouraged to use cognitive restructuring skills, specifically rational responses, to challenge his negative thinking. This allowed Felix to reframe his automatic thoughts, such as "If they are upset, it is my fault," into affirming and rational statements, such as "If they are upset, it is due to their irrational fears or prejudices regarding homosexuality, which can be reduced." A few months after regular therapy sessions concluded, Felix came out to his family, most notably his father, to whom he anticipated having the most difficulty disclosing his sexual orientation.

Another case example is presented here. Patrick is working with his therapist to plan an exposure and response prevention homework assignment to address his fears about his alarm not going off. He has an elaborate bedtime ritual in which he checks multiple alarms. He worries about being late for work and losing his job if he oversleeps. These fears are exacerbated by his perception that his workplace is not LGB friendly and that his employer could use being late as a reason to dismiss him. The therapist modifies the exposure exercise by allowing a second alarm to account for the potential heightened consequence that, because he is gay, being late for work could be used as a cover for his dismissal. Over time, the therapist may encourage Patrick to give up the second alarm. Patrick and his therapist have the following conversation:

PATRICK: I understand that you want me to stop setting and checking all of my alarms before bed.

THERAPIST: You have had a lot of success with other exposures of just doing things once, instead of checking them over and over again.

PATRICK: Yes, I know it will be hard, but that the anxiety will come down and it won't bother me so much. This is different, though, because if my alarm does not go off, I will oversleep and be late work. They could use that as an excuse to fire me. They are very homophobic, but I really need this job.

THERAPIST: Because your workplace is not LGB friendly, it sounds like the potential consequences of your alarm not going off are pretty serious. Let's start with doing this exposure a bit differently than the ones in the past where the consequences of something bad happening were lower if what you feared actually happened.

PATRICK: That sounds good.

THERAPIST: What time does your alarm usually go off?

PATRICK: 6:15 a.m.

THERAPIST: What is the last possible time you could get up and still make it to work?

PATRICK: Well, if I didn't shower or eat breakfast, I could sleep until 7:15 and still make it by 8.

THERAPIST: So I want you to set just 2 alarms, one at 6:15 and one at 7:15. Just set them once and don't check them. When you get up with your 6:15 alarm, just shut the 7:15 one off. No checking.

PATRICK: I can set one on my phone and one on the alarm clock. I won't set all of the other back-up alarms. That will be hard. It will also be hard not to go back and double check.

Once some successful exposures have occurred, it can be especially important to discontinue all rituals in exposure-based treatment for OCD. However, it is possible that Patrick has realistic fears about losing his job if he is late, making the consequences of him not setting his alarm accurately much higher. It is also likely that he will never need the 7:15 a.m. alarm, which therefore could be discontinued eventually.

SEXUAL ORIENTATION OBSESSIONS IN OBSESSIVE–COMPULSIVE DISORDER

Individuals diagnosed with OCD who identify as heterosexual may experience an obsession that they are or may become gay or lesbian or engage in same-sex sexual behavior. Of particular relevance to this chapter, however, is the distinction between individuals who are heterosexual and have this particular obsession and individuals who may be coming to understand themselves as having same-sex attractions and are distressed about identifying as LGB. This variant of OCD, sometimes called *homosexual anxiety OCD* (Williams, 2008), occurs in approximately 1 in 10 cases of OCD and more commonly in men than women (Williams & Farris, 2011). Homosexual anxiety OCD may be missed in the clinical assessment, especially by clinicians who are less familiar with OCD or clinicians who misattribute the obsessions to so-called "latent homosexuality" (Gordon, 2002; Williams, Crozier, & Powers, 2011). In a case study, Williams and colleagues described the application of standard exposure and response prevention intervention for fears about being a sexual minority, and they noted that there is no evidence that treatment adaptations are needed. Williams (2008) argued that LGB individuals and heterosexual people with homosexual anxiety OCD can be distinguished by assessing whether there is any indication that same-sex behavior or attraction is experienced as pleasurable or desirable. Individuals with homosexual anxiety OCD are likely to demonstrate a pattern of heterosexual attraction and behavior, even if currently their sexual relationships are diminished by the OCD (Williams, 2008). In the majority of cases, homosexual anxiety obsessions and associated rituals occur in the context of other OCD obsessions, and an accurate conceptualization that the homosexual obsessions are another aspect of the OCD presentation may therefore be relatively easy to determine. However, in cases in which homosexual obsessions are the only presenting problem for a heterosexual individual, clinician find themselves at a crossroad. On the one hand, Williams et al. recommend against suggesting the person may be LGB as a form of exposure, because doing so might harm the therapeutic alliance and impede treatment if the client views an LGB identity as problematic. On the other hand, the clinician risks appearing to endorse anti-gay societal stigma by presenting LGB behavior or identity as a feared stimulus and suggesting that one might not want to be gay or that it might be possible to prevent "becoming gay." The latter, of course, falls within the admonition that therapeutic attempts to change sexual orientation are unethical and potentially harmful to the client (American Psychological Association, 2009). One possible resolution to this dilemma is to focus not on whether the client is LGB or heterosexual but, rather, on tolerating uncertainty about their sexual orientation (Tolin, Ambramowitz, Brigidi, & Foa, 2003).

MULTICULTURAL CONSIDERATIONS THAT CO-OCCUR WITH SEXUAL ORIENTATION

LGB individuals also share a variety of other identities, including racial or ethnic minority identities. Given that no studies have specifically examined anxiety treatment with LGB individuals who are also a racial or ethnic minority, we have to extrapolate from a combined review of evidence-based anxiety treatments for racial and ethnic minorities and the sexual minority literature. Previous studies of populations within the United States have consistently documented lower prevalence rates of anxiety disorders in ethnic and racial minorities (e.g., Latino, Black or African American, and Asian American) compared to their European American counterparts (Asnaani, Richey, Dimaite, Hinton, & Hofmann, 2010; Grant et al., 2005). A systematic review of global current prevalence rates indicated Ibero/Latin, African, Middle Eastern, and Indo/Asian cultures are at 20%–50% lower risk of anxiety disorders compared to Euro/Anglo cultures (Baxter, Scott, Vos, & Whiteford, 2013). It appears that people from non-Euro/Anglo cultures have a reduced risk of experiencing an anxiety disorder. Note that clarity is needed about whether these differences are related to measurement bias or lack of validity in diagnostic criteria (Baxter et al., 2013). For example, Asian populations are generally more likely than other populations to experience dizziness as a symptom of distress (Park & Hinton, 2002). This is one example of how current assessments might not accurately reflect cultural norms beyond Western norms. Although no treatment studies explicitly include racial and ethnicity minority LGB individuals, recent studies tend to have samples that are more reflective of the population in general. For example, Pachankis, Hatzenbuehler, Rendina, Safren, and Parsons (2015) included a sample that was nearly 50% non-White in their randomized control trial of CBT adapted for gay and bisexual men, and they demonstrated marginally significant reductions in anxiety symptoms between an immediate treatment group and a wait-list control group, suggesting LGB adaptations of empirically supported treatments for anxiety are likely beneficial for LGB racial and ethnic minority individuals. Whether race or ethnicity moderated the efficacy of this treatment is currently unknown.

Along with the many considerations already outlined for adapting treatment for LGB clients, it is important to recognize there are other multicultural considerations to make as well. Recognizing the intersectionality (Cole, 2009) of LGB individuals who are also part of other marginalized populations means that each identity creates its own context for understanding the individual's experience of anxiety. LGB clients from diverse backgrounds (e.g., racial, ethnic, cultural, religious, and spiritual) may find it difficult to incorporate their sexual identity with other cultural expectations or beliefs (American Psychological Association, 2012; Greene, 1994). For example, a Latino gay male may find his sexual identity and traditional family values (e.g., religion, marriage, and having children) at odds and struggle to feel like he fits in with either Latino or gay cultures (B. S. Newman & Muzzonigro, 1993). As with an individual's sexual orientation, clinicians should be mindful in determining how much emphasis to place on the role of culture in the presenting problems. Both overemphasis and underemphasis of the role of culture can challenge the therapeutic alliance. The diversity of cultures within racial and ethnic groups is also important to recognize because different subgroups may vary in their level of affirmation of LGB identities (Brown & Henriquez, 2008; Nelson & Golden, 2010; Ryan, Russell, Huebner, Diaz, & Sanchez, 2010).

HIV AND ANXIETY

Treating anxiety disorders among LGB individuals who are living with HIV and AIDS requires attention to the intersections of physical and mental health. Sewell and colleagues (2000) found no significant differences in the prevalence of lifetime anxiety disorders between gay men with and those without HIV. However, men who were HIV-positive and reported worse illness symptoms also reported more anxiety symptoms, which is a frequent reason HIV-positive men who have sex with men seek mental health services (Berg, Mimiaga, & Safren, 2004).

Although an HIV diagnosis may not make anxiety more likely, there appears to be a link between physical symptoms and anxiety symptoms. In particular, anxiety about one's HIV status can lead to avoiding situations relating to the disease, such as medical appointments, which in turn impedes disease management and medication adherence (O'Cleirigh, Hart, & James, 2008). HIV-positive patients with GAD and panic disorder have been found to be twice as likely to be non-adherent with medications compared to HIV-positive patients without anxiety disorders (Tucker, Burnam, Sherbourne, Kung, & Gifford, 2003). In addition, some panic symptoms are mimicked by certain antiretroviral drugs (Matthews & Trujillo, 2006). Despite these findings, O'Cleirigh and colleagues have noted a lack of research on psychosocial and psychopharmacological treatments for HIV-positive individuals with anxiety disorders. This gap is particularly pronounced for lesbian and bisexual women who are living with HIV and AIDS (O'Cleirigh et al., 2008).

FUTURE DIRECTIONS AND EMERGING TRENDS

Several emerging trends in the assessment and treatment of anxiety disorders are likely to benefit LGB clients. First, the development of transdiagnostic treatment packages in which multiple disorders are treated with the same intervention may make evidence-based treatments more accessible for everyone. Such treatments are also amenable to research on adaptations for smaller populations, such as members of the LGB community, because broader inclusion criteria facilitate recruitment (e.g., recruiting for all anxiety disorders, not just a specific disorder). A recent randomized controlled trial (Pachankis et al., 2015) utilizing an adaptation of Barlow's Unified Protocol (Barlow et al., 2010) for young gay and bisexual men is a good example of the utility of a transdiagnostic approach. The study by Pachankis et al. also suggests that transdiagnostic treatments may address the mechanisms underlying minority stress, reducing these risk factors for anxiety and other co-occurring mental health problems. A second emerging trend likely to benefit LGB clients is the use of teleconferencing to make treatment more accessible. Some LGB individuals live in areas where LGB-affirmative providers are not available, or they fear disclosure of their sexual orientation in rural communities. Telehealth can provide LGB clients with access to providers who live too far away for feasible in-person appointments. In our clinic, we have partnered with the Nebraska AIDS Project to provide telehealth psychological services for individuals living with HIV and AIDS, many of whom identify as LGB, across our very rural and underserved state. Finally, a third emerging trend is the change in social climate for individuals who identify as LGB. As anti-gay stigma decreases (Fetner, 2016), the research on health and mental health for LGB people may become dated, especially for younger cohorts of LGB people because their clinical needs may shift if they come of age in more affirming climates. Ongoing research on the impact of minority stress, resiliency, and cultural climate on the development and maintenance of anxiety disorders will be important to keep clinicians informed of the changing needs of their LGB clients.

CONCLUSION

Individuals who identify as lesbian, gay, or bisexual are at elevated risk for anxiety disorders and OCD, likely due to the mental health impact of stigma-related stress. There is a strong evidence base for the efficacy of CBT interventions for anxiety disorders and OCD, and there is no reason to think these CBT interventions are not equally helpful for sexual minorities. Provision of the best assessment and treatment services for LGB populations requires both cultural competency in LGB experiences and familiarity with LGB-focused research as well as modest adaptation of certain CBT procedures. These adaptations include integrating sexual orientation into case formulation; using self-report measures free of heterocentrism; and a careful consideration of the role of societal stigma and discrimination risk on the emotional, cognitive, and behavioral responses of anxiety disorders and OCD.

REFERENCES

Abbass, A. A., Kisely, S. R., Town, J. M., Leichsenring, F., Driessen, E., DeMaat S., . . . Croew, E. (2014). Short-term psychodynamic psychotherapies for common mental disorders. *Cochrane Database Systemic Reviews, 2014*(7). doi:10.1002/14651858. CD004687.pub4

American Psychiatric Association. (2013). *Diagnostic and statistical manual of mental disorders* (5th ed.). Arlington, VA: American Psychiatric Publishing.

American Psychological Association. (2009). *Report of the Task Force on Appropriate Therapeutic Responses to Sexual Orientation*. Retrieved from https://www.apa.org/pi/lgbt/resources/therapeutic-response.pdf

American Psychological Association. (2012). Guidelines for psychological practice with lesbian, gay, and bisexual clients. *American Psychologist, 67*, 10–42. doi:10.1037/a0024659

American Psychological Association. (2015). Guidelines for psychological practice with transgender and gender nonconforming people. *American Psychologist, 70*, 832–864. doi:10.1037/a0039906

Antony, M. M., & Norton, P. J. (2008). *The anti-anxiety workbook: Proven strategies to overcome worry, phobias, panic, and obsessions.* New York, NY: Guilford.

Arch, J., Eifert, G. H., Davies, C., Plumb Vilardaga, J. C., Rose, R. D., & Craske, M. G. (2012). Randomized clinical trial of cognitive behavior therapy (CBT) versus acceptance and commitment therapy (ACT) for mixed anxiety disorders. *Journal of Consulting and Clinical Psychology, 80*, 750–765. doi:10.1037/a0028310

Asnaani, A., Richey, J. A., Dimaite, R., Hinton, D. E., & Hofmann, S. G. (2010). A cross-ethnic comparison of lifetime prevalence rates of anxiety disorders. *Journal of Nervous and Mental Disease, 198*, 551–555. doi:10.1097/nmd.0b013e3181ea169f

Balsam, K. F., Beauchaine, T. P., Mickey, R. M., & Rothblum, E. D. (2005). Mental health of lesbian, gay, bisexual, and heterosexual siblings: Effects of gender, sexual orientation, and family. *Journal of Abnormal Psychology, 114*, 471–476. doi:10.1037/0021-843X.114.3.471

Balsam, K. F., Martell, C. R., & Safren, S. A. (2006). Affirmative cognitive–behavioral therapy with lesbian, gay, and bisexual people. In P. A. Hays & G. Y. Iwamasa (Eds.), *Culturally responsive cognitive–behavioral therapy: Assessment, practice, and supervision* (pp. 223–243). Washington, DC: American Psychological Association. doi:10.1037/11433-010

Bandelow, B., Seidler-Brandler, U., Becker, A., Wedekind, D., & Rüther, E. (2007). Meta-analysis of randomized controlled comparisons of psychopharmacological and psychological treatments for anxiety disorders. *World Journal of Biological Psychiatry, 8*, 175–187.

Barlow, D. H., Farchione, T. J., Bullis, J. R., Gallagher, M. W., Murray-Latin, H., Sauer-Zavala, S., . . . Ametaj, A. (2017). The unified protocol for transdiagnostic treatment of emotional disorders compared with diagnosis-specific protocols for anxiety disorders: A randomized clinical trial. *JAMA Psychiatry, 74*, 875–884. doi:10.1001/jamapsychiatry.2017.2164

Barlow, D. H., Farchione, T. J., Fairholme, C. P., Ellard, K. K., Boisseau, C. L., Allen, L. B., & Ehrenreich-May, J. T. (2010). *Unified protocol for transdiagnostic treatment of emotional disorders: Therapist guide.* New York, NY: Oxford University Press.

Baxter, A. J., Scott, K. M., Vos, T., & Whiteford, H. A. (2013). Global prevalence of anxiety disorders: A systematic review and meta-regression. *Psychological Medicine, 43*(5), 897–910. doi:10.1017/S003329171200147X

Beck, A., Emery, G., & Greenberg, R. L. (2005). *Anxiety disorders and phobias: A cognitive perspective.* New York, NY: Basic Books.

Beck, A. T., Epstein, N., Brown, G., & Steer, R. A. (1988). An inventory for measuring clinical anxiety: Psychometric properties. *Journal of Consulting and Clinical Psychology, 56*, 893–897. doi:10.1037/0022-006X.56.6.893

Berg, M. B., Mimiaga, M. J., & Safren, S. A. (2004). Mental health concerns of HIV-infected gay and bisexual men seeking mental health services: An observational study. *AIDS Patient Care and STDs, 18*, 635–643. doi:10.1089/apc.2004.18.635

Berg, R. C., Ross, M. W., Weatherburn, P., & Schmidt, A. J. (2013). Structural and environmental factors are associated with internalised homonegativity in men who have sex with men: Findings from the European MSM Internet Survey (EMIS) in 38 countries. *Social Science & Medicine, 78,* 61–69. doi:10.1016/j.socscimed.2012.11.033

Bidell, M. P. (2005). The Sexual Orientation Counselor Competency Scale: Assessing attitudes, skills, and knowledge of counselors working with lesbian, gay, and bisexual clients. *Counselor Education and Supervision, 44,* 267–279. doi:10.1002/j.1556-6978.2005.tb01755.x

Bostwick, W. B., Boyd, C. J., Hughes, T. L., & McCabe, S. E. (2010). Dimensions of sexual orientation and the prevalence of mood and anxiety disorders in the United States. *American Journal of Public Health, 100*(3), 468–475. doi:10.2105/AJPH.2008.152942

Bränström, R. (2017). Minority stress factors as mediators of sexual orientation disparities in mental health treatment: A longitudinal population-based study. *Journal of Epidemiology and Community Health, 71,* 446–452. doi:10.1136/jech-2016-207943

Brown, M. J., & Henriquez, E. (2008). Socio-demographic predictors of attitudes towards gays and lesbians. *Individual Differences Research, 6,* 193–202.

Burckell, L. A., & Goldfried, M. R. (2006). Therapist qualities preferred by sexual-minority individuals. *Psychotherapy, 43,* 32–49. http://dx.doi.org/10.1037/0033-3204.43.1.32

Cochran, S. D., Björkenstam, C., & Mays, V. M. (2017). Sexual orientation differences in functional limitations, disability, and mental health services use: Results from the 2013–2014 National Health Interview Survey. *Journal of Consulting and Clinical Psychology, 85*(4), 1111–1121. http://dx.doi.org/10.1037/ccp0000243

Cochran, S. D., Sullivan, J. G., & Mays, V. M. (2003). Prevalence of mental disorders, psychological distress, and mental health services use among lesbian, gay, and bisexual adults in the United States. *Journal of Consulting and Clinical Psychology, 71,* 53–61. http://dx.doi.org/10.1037/0022-006X.71.1.53

Cohen, J. M., Blasey, C., Taylor, C. B., Weiss, B. J., & Newman, M. G. (2016). Anxiety and related disorders and concealment in sexual minority young adults. *Behavior Therapy, 41,* 91–101. doi:10.1016/j.beth.2015.09.006

Cole, E. R. (2009). Intersectionality and research in psychology. *American Psychologist, 64,* 170–180. doi:10.1037/a0014564

Connor, K. M., Kobak, K. A., Churchill, L. E., Katzelnick, D., & Davidson, J. T. (2001). Mini-SPIN: A brief screening assessment for generalized social anxiety disorder. *Depression & Anxiety, 14*(2), 137–140.

Craske, M. G., & Barlow, D. H. (2006). *Mastery of your anxiety and panic: Therapist guide.* New York, NY: Oxford University Press.

Cuijpers, P., Sijbrandij, M., Koole, S., Huibers, M., Berking, M., & Andersson, G. (2014). Psychological treatment of generalized anxiety disorder: A meta-analysis. *Clinical Psychology Review, 34,* 130–140. doi:10.1016/j.cpr.2014.01.002

Dahlhamer, J. M., Galinsky, A. M., Joestl, S. S., & Ward, B. W. (2016). Barriers to health care among adults identifying as sexual minorities: A US national study. *American Journal of Public Health, 106,* 1116–1122. doi:10.2105/AJPH.2016.303049

Fergus, T. A., Valentiner, D. P., McGrath, P. B., Gier-Lonsway, S., & Kim, H. (2012). Short forms of the Social Interaction Anxiety Scale and the Social Phobia Scale. *Journal of Personality Assessment, 94,* 310–320. doi:10.1080/00223891.2012.660291

Fetner, T. (2016). U.S. attitudes towards lesbian and gay people are better than ever. *Contexts, 15,* 20–27. doi:10.1177/1536504216648147

Foa, E. B., Hembree, E. A., Cahill, S. P., Rauch, S. M., Riggs, D. S., Feeny, N. C., & Yadin, E. (2005). Randomized trial of prolonged exposure for posttraumatic stress disorder with and without cognitive restructuring: Outcome at academic and community clinics. *Journal of Consulting and Clinical Psychology, 73,* 953–964. doi:10.1037/0022-006X.73.5.953

Glassgold, J. M. (2009). The case of Felix: An example of gay-affirmative, cognitive-behavioral therapy. *Pragmatic Case Studies in Psychotherapy, 5*(4), 1–21. doi:10.14713/pcsp.v5i4.995

Goodman, W. K., Price, L. H., Rasmussen, S. A., Mazure, C., Fleischmann, R. L., Hill, C. L., . . . Charney, D. S. (1989). The Yale–Brown Obsessive Compulsive Scale: I. Development, use, and reliability. *Archives of General Psychiatry, 46*(11), 1006–1011. doi:10.1001/archpsyc.1989.01810110048007

Gordon, W. M. (2002). Sexual obsessions and OCD. *Sexual and Relationship Therapy, 17,* 343–354. doi:10.1080/1468199021000017191

Gould, R. A., Otto, M. W., Pollack, M. H., & Yap, L. (1997). Cognitive behavioral and pharmacological treatment of generalized anxiety disorder: A preliminary meta-analysis. *Behavior Therapist, 28,* 285–305. doi:10.1016/S0005-7894(97)80048-2

Grant, B. F., Hasin, D. S., Stinson, F. S., Dawson, D. A., Ruan, W. J., Goldstein, R. B., . . . Huang, B. (2005). Prevalence, correlates, co-morbidity, and comparative disability of DSM-IV generalized anxiety disorder in the USA: Results from the National Epidemiologic Survey on Alcohol and Related Conditions. *Psychological Medicine, 35*(12), 1747–1759.

Greene, B. (1994). Ethnic-minority lesbians and gay men: Mental health and treatment issues. *Journal of Consulting & Clinical Psychology, 62*(2), 243.

Hatzenbuehler, M. L., Keyes, K. M., & Hasin, D. S. (2009). State-level policies and psychiatric morbidity in lesbian, gay, and bisexual populations. *American Journal of Public Health, 99,* 2275–2281. doi:10.2105/AJPH.2008.153510

Hayes, S. C., Strosahl, K., & Wilson, K. G. (1999). *Acceptance and commitment therapy: An experiential approach to behavior change.* New York, NY: Guilford.

Herek, G. M. (2009). Sexual stigma and sexual prejudice in the United States: A conceptual framework. In D. A. Hope (Ed.), *Contemporary perspectives on lesbian, gay, and bisexual identities* (pp. 65–111). New York, NY: Springer. doi:10.1007/978-0-387-09556-1_4

Herek, G. M., Gillis, J. R., & Cogan, J. C. (1999). Psychological sequelae of hate-crime victimization among lesbian, gay, and bisexual adults. *Journal of Consulting and Clinical Psychology, 67*(6), 945–951.

Hope, D. A, & Chappell, C. L. (2015). Extending training in multicultural competencies to include individuals identifying as lesbian, gay and bisexual: Key choice points for clinical psychology training programs. *Clinical Psychology: Science and Practice, 22,* 105–118. doi:10.1111/cpsp.12099

Hope, D. A., Heimberg, R. G., & Bruch, M. A. (1995). Dismantling cognitive–behavioral group therapy for social phobia. *Behaviour Research and Therapy, 33,* 637–650. doi:10.1016/0005-7967(95)00013-N

Hope, D. A., Heimberg, R. G., & Turk, C. L. (2010). *Managing social anxiety: A cognitive-behavioral therapy approach.* New York, NY: Oxford University Press.

Kessler, R. C., Aguilar-Gaxiola, S., Alonso, J., Chatterji, S., Lee, S., Ormel, J., . . . Wang, P. S. (2009). The global burden of mental disorders: An update from the WHO World Mental Health (WMH) surveys. *Epidemiologia e Psichiatria Sociale, 18,* 23–33. doi:10.1017/S1121189X00001421

Kessler, R. C., Berglund, P., Demler, O., Jin, R., Merikangas, K. R., & Walters, E. E. (2005). Lifetime prevalence and age-of-onset distributions of DSM-IV disorders in the National Comorbidity Survey Replication. *Archives of General Psychiatry, 62*, 593–602. doi:10.1001/archpsyc.62.6.593

Klein, F., Sepekoff, B., & Wolf, T. J. (1985). Sexual orientation: A multi-variable dynamic process. *Journal of Homosexuality, 11*(1–2), 35–49.

Kuyken, W., Padesky, C. A., & Dudley, R. (2008). The science and practice of case conceptualization. *Behavioural and Cognitive Psychotherapy, 36*, 757–768. doi:10.1017/S1352465808004815

Le Blanc, A. L., Bruce, L. C., Heimberg, R. G., Hope, D. A., Blanco, C., Schneier, F. R., & Liebowitz, M. R. (2014). Evaluation of the psychometric properties of two short forms of the Social Interaction Anxiety Scale and the Social Phobia Scale. *Assessment, 21*(3), 312–323. doi:10.1177/1073191114521279

Leary, M. R. (1983). A brief version of the Fear of Negative Evaluation Scale. *Personality and Social Psychology Bulletin, 9*, 371–375. doi:10.1177/0146167283093007

Lindner, P., Martell, C., Bergstrom, J., Andersson, G., & Carlbring, P. (2013). Clinical validation of a non-heteronormative version of the Social Interaction Anxiety Scale (SIAS). *Health and Quality of Life Outcomes, 11*(1), 209–215. doi:10.1186/1477-7525-11-209

Matthews, A. M., & Trujillo, M. (2006). Anxiety disorders. In F. Fernandez & P. Ruiz (Eds.), *Psychiatric aspects of HIV/AIDS* (pp. 86–92). Philadelphia, PA: Lippincott Williams & Wilkins.

Mattick, R. P., & Clarke, J. C. (1998). Development and validation of measures of social phobia scrutiny fear and social interaction anxiety. *Behaviour Research and Therapy, 36*, 455–470. doi:10.1016/S0005-7967(97)10031-6

Mayo-Wilson, E., Dias, S., Mavranezouli, I., Kew, K., Clark, D. M., Ades, A. E., & Pilling, S. (2014). Psychological and pharmacological interventions for social anxiety disorder in adults: A systematic review and network meta-analysis. *The Lancet Psychiatry, 1*, 368–376.

Meidlinger, P. C., & Hope, D. A. (2014). Differentiating disclosure and concealment in measurement of outness for sexual minorities: The Nebraska Outness Scale. *Psychology of Sexual Orientation and Gender Diversity, 1*, 489–497. doi:10.1037/sgd0000080

Meyer, I. H. (1995). Minority stress and mental health in gay men. *Journal of Health and Social Behavior, 36*(1), 38–56. doi:10.2307/2137286

Meyer, I. H. (2003). Prejudice, social stress, and mental health in lesbian, gay, and bisexual populations: Conceptual issues and research evidence. *Psychological Bulletin, 129*, 674–697. doi:10.1037/0033-2909.129.5.674

Millar, B. M., Wang, K., & Pachankis, J. E. (2016). The moderating role of internalized homonegativity on the efficacy of LGB-affirmative psychotherapy: Results from a randomized controlled trial with young adult gay and bisexual men. *Journal of Consulting and Clinical Psychology, 84*, 565–570. doi:10.1037/ccp0000113

Mitte, K. (2005). A meta-analysis of the efficacy of psycho- and pharmacotherapy in panic disorder with and without agoraphobia. *Journal of Affective Disorders, 88*, 27–45.

Mock, S. E., & Eibach, R. P. (2012). Stability and change in sexual orientation identity over a 10-year period in adulthood. *Archives of Sexual Behavior, 41*, 641–648. doi:10.1007/s10508-011-9761-1

Nelson, S., & Golden, M. R. (2010). Persistence of racial differences in attitudes toward homosexuality in the United States. *Journal of Acquired Immune Deficiency Syndromes, 55*, 516–523.

Newcomb, M. E., & Mustanski, B. (2010). Internalized homophobia and internalizing mental health problems: A meta-analytic review. *Clinical Psychology Review, 30*, 1019–1029. http://dx.doi.org/10.1016/j.cpr .2010.07.003

Newman, B. S., & Muzzonigro, P. G. (1993). The effects of traditional family values on the coming out process of gay male adolescents. *Adolescence, 28*(109), 213–226.

Newman, M. G., & Fisher, A. J. (2010). Expectancy/credibility change as a mediator of cognitive behavioral therapy for generalized anxiety disorder: Mechanism of action or proxy for symptom change? *International Journal of Cognitive Therapy, 3*, 245–261. doi:10.1521/ijct.2010.3.3.245

Norton, P. J., & Price, E. C. (2007). A meta-analytic review of adult cognitive–behavioral treatment outcome across the anxiety disorders. *Journal of Nervous and Mental Disease, 195*(6), 521–531. doi:10.1097/01.nmd.0000253843.70149.9a

O'Cleirigh, C., Hart, T. A., & James, C. A. (2008). HIV and anxiety. In M. J. Zvolensky & J. J. Smits (Eds.), *Anxiety in health behaviors and physical illness* (pp. 317–340). New York, NY: Springer.

Olatunji, B. O., Davis, M. L., Powers, M. B., & Smits, J. J. (2013). Cognitive–behavioral therapy for obsessive–compulsive disorder: A meta-analysis of treatment outcome and moderators. *Journal of Psychiatric Research, 47*, 33–41. doi:10.1016/j.jpsychires.2012.08.020

Öst, L., Havnen, A., Hansen, B., & Kvale, G. (2015). Cognitive behavioral treatments of obsessive–compulsive disorder: A systematic review and meta-analysis of studies published 1993–2014. *Clinical Psychology Review, 40*, 156–169. doi:10.1016/j.cpr.2015.06.003

Owen, J., Imel, Z., Tao, K. W., Wampold, B., Smith, A., & Rodolfa, E. (2011). Cultural ruptures in short-term therapy: Working alliance as a mediator between clients' perceptions of microaggressions and therapy outcomes. *Counselling & Psychotherapy Research, 11*, 204–212. doi:10.1080/14733145.2010.49155

Pachankis, J. E. (2007). The psychological implications of concealing a stigma: A cognitive–affective–behavioral model. *Psychological Bulletin, 133*, 328–345.

Pachankis, J. E., & Goldfried, M. R. (2006). Social anxiety in young gay men. *Journal of Anxiety Disorders, 20*, 996–1015. doi:10.1016/j.janxdis.2006.01.001

Pachankis, J. E., & Goldfried, M. R. (2013). Clinical issues in working with lesbian, gay, and bisexual clients. *Psychology of Sexual Orientation and Gender Identity, 1*(S), 45–58. doi:10.1037/2329-0382.1.S.45

Pachankis, J. E., Goldfried, M. R., & Ramrattan, M. E. (2008). Extension of the rejection sensitivity construct to the interpersonal functioning of gay men. *Journal of Consulting and Clinical Psychology, 76*(2), 306–317. doi:10.1037/0022-006X.76.2.306

Pachankis, J. E., Hatzenbuehler, M. L., Rendina, H. J., Safren, S. A., & Parsons, J. T. (2015). LGB-affirmative cognitive–behavioral therapy for young adult gay and bisexual men: A randomized controlled trial of a transdiagnostic minority stress approach. *Journal of Consulting & Clinical Psychology, 83*(5), 875–889. doi:10.1037/ccp0000037

Pakula, B., Shoveller, J., Ratner, P. A., & Carpiano, R. (2016). Prevalence and co-occurrence of heavy drinking and anxiety and mood disorders among gay, lesbian, bisexual, and heterosexual Canadians. *American Journal of Public Health*, *106*, 1042–1048. doi:10.2105/AJPH.2016.303083

Park, L., & Hinton, D. (2002). Dizziness and panic in China: Associated sensations of Zang Fu organ disequilibrium. *Culture, Medicine and Psychiatry*, *26*, 225–257. doi:10.1023/A:1016341425842

Peters, L., Sunderland, M., Andrews, G., Rapee, R. M., & Mattick, R. P. (2012). Development of a short form Social Interaction Anxiety (SIAS) and Social Phobia Scale (SPS) using nonparametric item response theory: The SIAS-6 and the SPS-6. *Psychological Assessment*, *24*, 66–76. doi:10.1037/a0024544

Reinholt, N., & Krogh, J. (2014). Efficacy of transdiagnostic cognitive behaviour therapy for anxiety disorders: A systematic review and meta-analysis of published outcome studies. *Cognitive Behaviour Therapy*, *43*, 171–184. doi:10.1080/16506073.2014.897367

Richards, H. J., Benson, V., Donnelly, N., & Hadwin, J. A. (2014). Exploring the function of selective attention and hypervigilance for threat in anxiety. *Clinical Psychology Review*, *34*, 1–13. doi:10.1016/j.cpr.2013.10.006

Rosenkrantz, D. E., Black, W. W., Abreu, R. L., Aleshire, M. E., & Fallin-Bennett, K. (2017). Health and health care of rural sexual and gender minorities: A systematic review. *Stigma and Health*, *2*, 229–243. doi:10.1037/sah0000055

Roshanaei-Moghaddam, B., Pauly, M. C., Atkins, D. C., Baldwin, S. A., Stein, M. B., & Roy-Byrne, P. (2011). Relative effects of CBT and pharmacotherapy in depression versus anxiety: Is medication somewhat better for depression, and CBT somewhat better for anxiety? *Depression and Anxiety*, *28*, 560–567. doi:10.1002/da.20829

Ryan, C., Russell, S. T., Huebner, D., Diaz, R., & Sanchez, J. (2010). Family acceptance in adolescence and the health of LGBT young adults. *Journal of Child & Adolescent Psychiatric Nursing*, *23*, 205–213. doi:10.1111/j.1744-6171.2010.00246.x

Safren, S. A., & Rogers, T. (2001). Cognitive–behavioral therapy with gay, lesbian, and bisexual clients. *Journal of Clinical Psychology*, *57*(5), 629–643.

Sauer-Zavala, S., Boswell, J. F., Bentley, K. H., Thompson-Hollands, J., Farchione, T. J., & Barlow, D. H. (2018). Expectancies, working alliance, and outcome in transdiagnostic and single diagnosis treatment for anxiety disorders: An investigation of mediation. *Cognitive Therapy and Research*, *42*(2), 135–145. doi:10.1007/s10608-017-9855-8

Schrimshaw, E. W., Siegel, K., Downing, M. J., Jr., & Parsons, J. T. (2013). Disclosure and concealment of sexual orientation and the mental health of non-gay-identified, behaviorally bisexual men. *Journal of Consulting & Clinical Psychology*, *81*, 141–153. doi:10.1037/a0031272

Sewell, M. C., Goggin, K. J., Rabkin, J. G., Ferrando, S. J., McElhiney, M. C., & Evans, S. (2000). Anxiety syndromes and symptoms among men with AIDS: A longitudinal controlled study. *Psychosomatics*, *41*, 294–300. doi:10.1176/appi.psy.41.4.294

Shidlo, A. (1994). Internalized homophobia: Conceptual and empirical issues in measurement. In B. Greene & G. M. Herek (Eds.), *Lesbian and gay psychology: Theory, research, and clinical applications* (pp. 176–205). Thousand Oaks, CA: Sage. doi:10.4135/9781483326757.n10

Shulman, G. P., & Hope, D. A. (2016). Putting our multicultural training into practice: Assessing social anxiety disorder in sexual minorities. *The Behavior Therapist*, *39*, 315–319.

Sue, D. W. (1991). A model for cultural diversity training. *Journal of Counseling and Development*, *70*, 99–105. doi:10.1002/j.1556-6676.1991.tb01568.x

Taylor, S., Zvolensky, M. J., Cox, B. J., Deacon, B., Heimberg, R. G., Ledley, D. R., . . . Cardenas, S. J. (2007). Robust dimensions of anxiety sensitivity: Development and initial validation of the Anxiety Sensitivity Index-3. *Psychological Assessment, 19*, 176–188. doi:10.1037/1040-3590.19.2.176

Tolin, D. F., Abramowitz, J. S., Brigidi, B. D., & Foa, E. B. (2003). Intolerance of uncertainty in obsessive–compulsive disorder. *Journal of Anxiety Disorders, 17*(2), 233–242. doi:10.1016/S0887-6185(02)00182-2

Tucker, J. S., Burnam, M. A., Sherbourne, C. D., Kung, F. Y., & Gifford, A. L. (2003). Substance use and mental health correlates of nonadherence to antiretroviral medications in a sample of patients with human immunodeficiency virus infection. *American Journal of Medicine, 114*, 573–580.

Turner, S. M., Beidel, D. C., Dancu, C. V., & Stanley, M. A. (1989). An empirically derived inventory to measure social fears and anxiety: The Social Phobia and Anxiety Inventory. *Psychological Assessment, 1*, 35–40. doi:10.1037/1040-3590.1.1.35

Walsh, K., & Hope, D. A. (2010). LGB-affirmative cognitive behavioral treatment for social anxiety: A case study applying evidence-based practice principles. *Cognitive and Behavioral Practice, 17*, 56–65. doi:10.1016/j.cbpra.2009.04.007

Watson, D., & Friend, R. (1969). Measurement of social-evaluative anxiety. *Journal of Consulting and Clinical Psychology, 33*, 448–457. doi:10.1080/08917778908249324

Weiss, B. J., & Hope, D. A. (2011). A preliminary investigation of worry content in sexual minorities. *Journal of Anxiety Disorders, 25*, 244–250. doi:10.1016/j.janxdis.2010.09.009

Weiss, B. J., Hope, D. A., & Capozzoli, M. C. (2013). Heterocentric language in commonly used measures of social anxiety: Recommended alternate wording. *Behavior Therapy, 44*, 1–11. doi:10.1016/j.beth.2012.07.006

Williams, M. T. (2008). Homosexuality anxiety: A misunderstood form of OCD. In L. V. Sebeki (Ed.), *Leading-edge health education issues* (pp. 195–205). Hauppauge, NY: Nova Science.

Williams, M. T., Crozier, M., & Powers, M. (2011). Treatment of sexual-orientation obsessions in obsessive–compulsive disorder using exposure and ritual prevention. *Clinical Case Studies, 10*, 53–66. doi:10.1177/1534650110393732

Williams, M. T., & Farris, S. G. (2011). Sexual orientation obsessions in obsessive–compulsive disorder: Prevalence and correlates. *Psychiatry Research, 187*, 156–159. doi:10.1016/j.psychres.2010.10.019

9

Evidence-Based Approaches for Treating Depression Among Sexual and Gender Minority Clients

CHRISTOPHER R. MARTELL ■

Four weeks had gone by and Corey[1] continued to cry on a dime and felt completely overwhelmed with the latest round of work assignments. Corey was disappointed that the political tide had turned toward less tolerance of LGBTQ-supportive legislation and angry and a little scared when legislation supporting discrimination was proposed. Having always been involved in social justice issues, Corey was used to "fighting the good fight." Why so fatigued? Why the overwhelming sense of dread and hopelessness? It was like walking through life surrounded by mud rather than air. Frustrated with the inability to move forward, to move past the disappointments or to cope with so many horrible thoughts, Corey picked up the phone and called a psychologist who was known to do good work with sexual minority clients and set up an appointment 2 weeks out.

It has been clearly demonstrated that sexual minority individuals experience symptoms of depression at higher rates than their heterosexual counterparts (Cochran, Sullivan, & Mays, 2003). Although this chapter concerns the treatment of depression, and therefore focuses on rates of depression in lesbian, gay, bisexual, transgender, and queer (i.e., sexual minority or LGBTQ) communities, minority stress (I. H. Meyer, 1995) can not only result in poor outcomes and vulnerabilities but also sometimes promote resilience. Established treatments for depression do

---

1. Corey is a fictional character, although the presenting problem and course of treatment are based on actual therapy clients, disguised to preserve confidentiality.

not need to be modified extensively for sexual minority clients. However, particular vulnerabilities need to be taken into account and addressed when working with this population, and factors that enhance resilience in the face of minority stress must be considered as part of a treatment plan. This chapter discusses some of the literature on the discrepancies in the rates of depression for sexual minorities and relates the experiences of LGBTQ clients in terms of the minority stress model. After summarizing the various empirically supported treatments for depression, the chapter provides recommendations for best practices within these treatments when working with sexual minority clients. It then returns to the case of Corey and describes how LGBTQ-affirmative cognitive–behavioral therapy helped.

In what has become one of the most cited pieces of research on differential rates of depression and other disorders for sexual minority populations, Cochran et al. (2003) analyzed the 1995–1996 McArthur Foundation Study of Mid-Life (Brim et al., 1999). This database was impressive because it did not rely solely on sexual behavior to determine whether someone would be classified as a sexual minority but, rather, included self-identified sexual orientation. In addition, it was a truly random sample of non-institutionalized, English-speaking adults between the ages of 25 and 75 years rather than a convenience sample of people recruited from gay or lesbian bars, with such practices having been critiqued as adding bias to studies of sexual minority populations. Cochran et al. found that there was a greater incidence of depression and anxiety disorders in LGB-identified participants compared to the heterosexual majority. With increased vulnerability to these disorders in this population, adapting the best empirically supported treatments to LGBTQ clients is consistent with responsible, culturally responsive practice.

COGNITIVE–BEHAVIORAL THERAPY FOR DEPRESSION

Regardless of therapists' advertised specialties, nearly every therapist is likely to work with a client who identifies as a sexual minority from the outset or who begins to identity as part of that community while they are in therapy. Because depression and anxiety are relatively common problems experienced by sexual minority clients, it makes sense for therapists to be equipped to provide the best evidence-based treatments to their clients. Beck's cognitive therapy for depression (Beck, Rush, Shaw, & Emery, 1979) has the most robust empirical backing. Because there has always been a combination of strategies targeting behavior change as well as changing thoughts and beliefs, the treatment has also been called cognitive–behavior therapy (CBT). The terms can be used synonymously, but it is most commonly referred to as CBT. According to the model underlying this treatment (Beck, 1976), there are three psychological substrates for depression. The first is the cognitive triad or a negative view of the self, the world, and the future. Second are schema or deeply held, cross-situational, absolutistic core beliefs that have been learned from childhood on. Finally, there are cognitive errors or faulty information processing (Beck et al., 1979, p. 10). The treatment includes techniques to deal with cognition at all of these different levels as well as direct behavior change to improve mood. In Beck and colleagues' original development, behavioral techniques such as activity scheduling were used with more severely depressed clients at the beginning of treatment. Generally, regardless of severity, basic components of cognitive therapy include activity scheduling to get the client engaged and improve mood, thought records to address negative interpretations of events occurring in the client's life, behavioral experiments to examine beliefs, and other strategies for promoting change with unhelpful schema (Persons, Davidson, & Tompkins, 2001).

From the perspective of cognitive theory of depression, it is not surprising that sexual minority individuals are more vulnerable to depression. Although public opinion is demonstrably becoming more accepting of LGB individuals, the situation seems to be tenuous, even in the wake of the *Obergefell vs. Hodges* US Supreme Court decision that made marriage equality the law of the land in the United States. Whether public attitudes are favorable or not, it is clear that public attitudes toward and legal safeguards for sexual minorities are changeable, and this, in itself, is a stressor. In the United States, transgender and gender nonconforming individuals continue to face greater hostility and attempts to deny even the most basic of rights, such as access to public bathrooms and changing gender on official public documents to accurately reflect their identity. At various time points, different states, and even looming federal regulations, have turned to "religious freedom" to create laws that discriminate against sexual minority individuals. The strain of continuing to advocate for oneself and one's community can lead to the development of a negative view of the world and the future. In many instances, this is very rational and realistic. Individuals often must navigate the negative depictions of themselves in the popular media and work through their own internalized negativity about sexual minorities before they can benefit from social support or group identity that may promote resilience. Internalized negativity, referred to as "internalized homophobia "(Shidlo, 1994) or "internalized transphobia" (Hendricks & Testa, 2012), may also contribute to "relatively stable cognitive patterns" of interpretations of events (Beck et al., 1979, p. 12) and generally negative beliefs or schema about the self (Beck et al., 1979). This completes the "negative triad" of depression (Beck, 1976).

Understanding the negative triad and how minority stress may contribute is important in the treatment of depressed clients who are sexual minorities because therapists must be alert to deeply held beliefs that will become treatment goals for intervention in cognitive therapy. Even in the most progressive of families, the hegemony of cisgender, heterosexual social norms can be invalidating to children from birth. Infants are gendered based on their sexual characteristics at birth. The socialization process begins early on with, predominantly, expectations that children will be heterosexual and cisgender. With messages that may be well intended coupled with messages that are intentionally hostile, it is not surprising that some LGBTQ individuals develop a negative view of themselves. Not all do so, of course, and this is where factors that promote resilience may come into play; these are discussed later in this chapter.

Schema, or core beliefs, allow people to meaningfully interpret their experiences (Beck, 1976). Some schema are helpful and contribute to resilience (e.g., "I am a strong and competent person"), whereas others are unhelpful and contribute to vulnerability to emotional disorders (e.g., "I am sinful and unlovable"). According to Beck's theory, schema may be out of consciousness until triggered by a specific event or series of events. An individual can function very well in their life without being disturbed by a particularly unhelpful schema until that schema is triggered by something in the environment. Consider the following two scenarios:

William is a young man who, having been raised in a very conservative religious household, comes to terms with being gay but keeps his sexual orientation a secret from his family. He develops a small group of supportive friends in a large city in a state far from his family. Encouraged by his friends to become more active politically, he participates in a Pride march in his new city. During the parade, the small group of people with whom he is marching are stationed behind a float sponsored by a bar; on the float are a number of dancers in thongs tossing beads to the crowd. A local news channel, seeking a sensational angle on the story, films footage of the bar float, and William is prominently recognizable in the news footage. A conservative Christian televangelist picks up this footage and rebroadcasts it to show "the depravity" of the LGBTQ community. William's parents see the footage and are shocked. His mother calls him and tells him that she is deeply disappointed in him and that they would like him to change his plans to visit them on the Fourth of July holiday because they do not want him in their home but that they are praying for him. Most people would be distressed by such a message from their parents, but this also triggers William's schema that he is "sinful and unworthy." He stops calling his friends, withdraws from any social interactions, and falls into a deep depression that lasts for months.

Stuart has a core belief that he is "basically a good man who is ethical and intelligent." A very similar situation as occurred for William occurs for Stuart, and his parents tell him that they cannot accept his "lifestyle" and that they prefer that he not attend a family reunion. Stuart is understandably upset and feels sad about it. Stuart calls several of his best friends and asks if they will meet him for coffee so he can talk through this situation with them. His friends are able to offer support to him and to highlight many of Stuart's good qualities. In his angrier moments, Stuart's interpretation of this event is "My parents are ignorant and nasty," and in his less angry moments his interpretation is "My parents mean well but they just don't understand human behavior, and it is really disappointing that their love for me doesn't supersede their conservative beliefs." Stuart feels disappointed and sad, but he does not become depressed as he turns his attention to building a network of "chosen family" and hopes for a change in attitude from his biological family.

Persons et al. (2001) emphasize that good practice involves considering each individual case to be an experiment. Data such as those from Cochran et al. (2003) are starting points for developing hypotheses about sexual minority clients, which then need to be confirmed through a collaborative case formulation. Therapy begins with a thorough assessment of the problems experienced by the client as well as understanding their diagnosis. Results from the assessment are used in the development of a case conceptualization (Kuyken, Padesky, & Dudley, 2009; Nezu et al., 2004; Persons, 2008). Among other things, the case conceptualization takes into account the environmental context. With sexual minority clients, this should include current social and political attitudes toward this population. These macro-level factors will have more or less impact on any particular client. Even when a client does not state explicitly that they are distressed by attitudes or controversies affecting the LGBTQ community, the therapist should be aware of this context, which may have an impact on a client at some point during their treatment. Given that schema are tacit beliefs, overlearned to the point of "feeling" normal for the person, social/political/environmental events may activate a negative schema for a client without the client necessarily being able to articulate this connection. There could be innumerable moments when a client has had a negative emotional reaction to a posting on Facebook or a news story on television that presents an anti-LGBT message, but it has become so much a part of their life that they will not think to note it in therapy. However, over time, the impact of these messages perceived by someone who may already have unhelpful schema about themselves and the world can increase the veracity of the schema, which is known as "internalized homophobia." It might be useful in some cases to make this connection during therapy; recognizing these factors during the development of the case conceptualization can help set the therapist on the right path.

Therapy should proceed according to protocol for LGBTQ clients. Regardless of the type of therapy (cognitive, behavioral, or interpersonal), the therapist's demeanor, ability to validate the client's experience, and authentic expression of support are essential components of treatment. Many LGBTQ clients present for therapy with concerns that have little or nothing to do with their sexual orientation or gender identity. For these clients, their sexual minority status is important information for the therapist but would not impact a case conceptualization any more than would other demographic information. For others, because of internalized homophobia or transphobia, negative beliefs about self, or a tendency to interpret the actions of others as threatening or nonsupportive, may be a focus of treatment. An LGBTQ-affirmative cognitive therapist must take care to use his or her best Socratic skills and allow the client to test the accuracy of beliefs, many of which may, in fact, be realistic.

BEHAVIORAL TREATMENTS FOR DEPRESSION

Peter Lewinsohn and Lynn Rehm were, perhaps, the first researchers to develop treatments for depression that were rooted in the operant behavioral literature. Rehm's (1977) self-control therapy emphasized the need for depressed clients to experience proximal reinforcers because schedules of reinforcement that require high rates of behavior over longer periods of time demand that an individual maintain desired activity under such conditions of delayed reward. Rehm noted the difficulty for depressed individuals to remain engaged under such contingencies and developed strategies to help depressed clients reward themselves. In a study that exemplifies the use of an active psychotherapy control condition, Fuchs and Rehm (1977) compared self-control therapy to a nonspecific group therapy condition, and results showed that participants in the self-control conditions significantly improved on measures of depression compared to the control group and maintained gains at 6-week follow-up. Behavioral models that focused on interpersonal behaviors were also considered (McLean, Ogston, & Grauer, 1975). These behavioral treatments were the focus of much study in academic psychology from the late 1960s to the early 1980s, but they received less attention from the clinical community as the techniques developed by Beck, Ellis, and colleagues gained wider support. Due to the sociopolitical climate during the mid-20th century, the application of the therapies in a manner affirming sexual minority clients received no attention at all.

Nevertheless, the behavioral formulation of depression is relevant to sexual minority clients. Lewinsohn and colleagues noted that there are many possible reasons why there would be low rates of positive reinforcement or high rates of punishment. First, sources of reinforcement may not be present in the environment. Consider a child whose gender is more fluid. When the child desires to play with a doll and is forced to play with a truck, the positive attributes usually associated with a toy do not apply. Even when the child is showered with gifts, they miss the mark, and when caregivers heap loving comments on the child, they may do so in the context of holding certain expectations of behavior. "You are such a nice boy" is not necessarily a rewarding, loving statement to someone who wants to be a "nice human" who is not gendered by someone else. Contextual factors that differentially impact sexual minority youth and adults are myriad, and there are any number of scenarios that could illustrate the subtle ways in which behaviors that could be experienced by the individual as congruent are not reinforced or are punished, leading to destabilization of the individual with resulting dysphoria.

Behavioral activation (BA; Jacobson, Martell, & Dimidjian, 2001; Lejuez, Hopko, & Hopko, 2001) is a recent extension of the work of Lewinsohn and colleagues' pleasant events scheduling (MacPhillamy & Lewinsohn, 1982) and Skinners' operant behaviorism. Lewinsohn (1974) conceptualized depression as being associated with contingencies of low rates of positive reinforcement and high rates of punishment. As discussed previously, there are multiple reasons for decreases in or low rates of positive reinforcement. There may be a loss in life of either people or activities that were highly reinforcing. Consider, for example, Ali, a young transgender individual who's family raised as female and then could not except Ali's identification as gender queer, expressing traditionally male gender behaviors. Whereas family connections were once very reinforcing with hugs before bedtime, holiday celebrations, and enthusiasm over good grades, once they began expressing their gender as was appropriate for themselves, it was met with criticism, fear, and condemnation. The family environment no longer provided sources of positive reinforcement and, in fact, became punishing. When Ali would attempt to contact relatives, family members were critical over the phone and occasionally simply refused to speak to Ali. Over a very short period of time, Ali stopped calling family; their behavior had been sufficiently punished and extinguished. Without the support of family, Ali, who had not developed a social network in the LGBTQ community, felt lonely and rejected. Ali stopped calling friends from school and was unable to pursue university studies because of the loss of not only family social support but also their parents' commitment for financial support for university. The reinforcers that had been available to Ali were no longer present, and Ali lacked the emotional resources to seek alternative sources of reward.

Intrapersonal factors may also influence the availability of reinforcement. Research on the neural substrates of reward suggests that individuals who are depressed or who have a history of depression, even if not currently depressed, may not respond to reward in the same way as those who have never been depressed. Anhedonia, a decrease in the experience of pleasure, is one of the features of depression. It is not clear whether lower responsivity to reward is a characterological feature that may contribute to the onset of an initial depressive episode or whether it is a result of depression, but it contributes to the experience of low rates of reward, and repeatedly attempting to pursue activities in which one does not experience pleasure also serves to punish or extinguish the pursuit. Should research confirm that lower responsivity to reward is a characterological feature, punishing or invalidating experiences experienced from a very young age may contribute to dulling reward sensitivity for LGBTQ individuals, making them more vulnerable to depression.

The initial behavioral conceptualization of depression and the treatment thereof (Lewinsohn, 1974) sought to identify sources of reinforcement with which the depressed individual was no longer engaged. Because we can only know a behavior has been reinforced when we observe an increase in certain circumstances, and know the consequences that likely reinforced the behavior, it is difficult to identify reinforcers without this careful observation. Lewinsohn and colleagues, therefore, considered pleasant events as proxy for positively reinforced activities. Indeed, their research showed that lower rates of pleasant activities were associated with depression. The Pleasant Events Schedule (MacPhillamy & Lewinsohn, 1982) was used as a measure of baseline level of activity, and pleasant events scheduling was used to increase these activities, which resulted in improvements in depression symptoms. Lewinsohn, Antonuccio, Steinmetz-Breckenridge, and Teri (1984) developed the Coping with Depression Course, a group treatment for depression that has been adapted for treatment of adolescents as well as adults (Lewinsohn, Clarke, Hops, & Andrews, 1990). There have also been significant cultural adaptations of this treatment for depression (e.g., Muñoz, 1996). Contemporary BA uses the same principles of activity scheduling but does not rely on the identification of pleasant events; rather, the focus in on increasing activities that the individual identifies as meaningful or consistent with their values (Martell, Dimidjian, & Herman-Dunn, 2010). This idiographic approach avoids the potential for emphasizing potentially pleasant activities that are based on cisgender or heterocentric expectations, and it can more readily be used in an affirmative manner with sexual minority clients. A depressed transgender client may avoid eating at restaurants because of a fear of being confronted entering a gender-specific restroom. The idiographic approach considers both the absence of a potentially reinforcing experience (eating at a restaurant) and the avoidance of a fear-inducing situation. The LGBT-affirming BA therapist would collaborate with the client to develop small steps for testing the safety of certain places—perhaps by simply going to a restaurant and asking about reservations and determining if it has gender-neutral restrooms. Perhaps a step that would be more challenging for a depressed client who may also have some level of social anxiety would be to call a restaurant in advance and ask if it has gender-neutral restrooms. The consideration of restrooms is not typically considered a pleasant event-scheduling criterion, but it can be crucially relevant for certain sexual minority clients and is consistent with an idiographic approach to BA.

The LGBTQ-affirming BA therapist will also attempt to understand how a behavior serves an individual or a function of the behavior. Basically, the function of a behavior is determined by the short- and long-term consequences of the behavior in various situations. In the previous example of the concern regarding restrooms, the client not going to restaurants serves as avoidance behavior, reduces anxiety in the short term, but limits life experiences and may contribute to the maintenance of depression over the long term. Ferster (1973) examined depression from a behavioral perspective and suggested that many of the behaviors of depressed individuals function as avoidance behavior. In some cases, there is avoidance of activities or people who no longer provide the kinds of rewards they once did, because of either strains to relationships or the anhedonia experienced during a depressive episode. In other cases, a person may avoid aversive feelings such as sadness and anxiety. When one awakens feeling sad, having hopeless thoughts about how tides have turned against LGBT rights in recent months, and dreading the day, it is functional—momentarily—to roll over, pull up the covers, and turn off the alarm clock. However, this immediate escape from the aversive thoughts and feelings, which works in the short term, is likely to have negative long-term consequences, such as repeated tardiness or work absences and disruptions in family relations.

Behavioral activation is an idiographic treatment that begins with a conceptualization of the course of depression based on client interview to understand the life events that may have resulted in reductions in positive reinforcement or increases in punishment—referred to as a "less rewarding life" (Martell, Addis, &

Jacobson, 2001). Consistent with Lewinsohn and colleagues' theoretical model, a "less rewarding life" may contribute to low mood, anhedonia, lethargy, negative thinking, and an increased self-focus and rumination on one's aversive feelings. Behavioral responses are considered to be rational reactions to these feelings. For example, in the case of Ali, breaking contact with family after receiving criticism and not pursuing the development of new relationships make sense given the harsh treatment Ali received from those who were once a primary source of support. According to the BA model, depressed behavior becomes a repetitive "downward" cycle of feeling badly, with individuals responding in reaction to those feelings by becoming increasingly disengaged from former activities, having more difficulties as a result, and feeling worse. The goal of BA is to break this cycle and help the depressed client increasingly engage in "antidepressant behavior" (Martell et al., 2010).

Because the treatment is individualized, the protocol for adults does not include prescribed session-by-session strategies—although an adaptation for treating depressed adolescents involves modular treatment that follows a prescriptive structure (McCauley, Schloredt, Gudmundsen, Martell, & Dimidjian, 2016). In order to provide clarity for therapists, Martell et al. (2010) identified 10 principles that help in the conceptualization of the BA case and the structure of the individualized treatment. One of the principles is that change is easier when starting small. Given the understandable disengagement in response to the affective symptoms of depression, it is advised to collaborate with clients to plan and schedule activities that they are likely to have success completing. In Ali's case, it would be invalidating and insensitive, as well as unlikely to succeed, if a therapist asked Ali to schedule a meeting with family or to attend a local LGBTQ political gathering. Given that Ali has not identified with an LGBTQ community, such activity is too much, too soon. Rather, the therapist should discuss how Ali may be able to start the process of connecting with an alternative community that could provide support until such time (if ever) that Ali's family becomes more understanding and embracing. An initial plan may be for Ali to search on the internet for local resources for Queer or gender-nonconforming individuals and, if there are none in the local area, to identify resources online that Ali can utilize. Once Ali has identified a few resources, the assignment would be completed and the plan successful. The therapist and Ali would build from session to session on this activity in the hope that Ali would become increasingly motivated—that this behavior would serve an antidepressant purpose. Over time, the hope would be that Ali finds and begins to engage with a local or online community that can provide support.

INTERPERSONAL PSYCHOTHERAPY FOR DEPRESSION

Interpersonal psychotherapy therapy for depression (IPT; Klerman, Weissman, Rounsaville, & Chevron, 1984) was developed as the psychotherapeutic arm of a research study comparing psychotherapy with antidepressant medication. IPT focuses on helping clients ("patients" in IPT terms) solve interpersonal problems. Similar to BA, IPT conceptualizes current depression as being related to current life events. The focus of treatment is on identifying current interpersonal ruptures and helping solve these disputes or teaching skills to resolve interpersonal deficits. IPT has been adapted for use with depressed Puerto Rican adolescents (Roselló & Bernal, 1999) and as a group treatment for depression in Uganda (Bolton et al., 2003, 2007). It has also been adapted for other disorders, such as post-traumatic stress disorder (Bleiberg & Markowitz, 2005). When a client may have experienced a series of microaggressions from others, which is common among LGBTQ individuals, one can easily understand how IPT and the focus on repairing interpersonal ruptures may be of particular help. It is particularly challenging in IPT if the ruptures were caused by rejection from loved ones due to a client's sexual orientation or gender identity. The IPT therapist must help the client improve interpersonal functioning, perhaps apart from the people with whom there was a rupture, so that the client does not face further rejection despite their most skillful efforts at reconciliation.

Unlike the cognitive and behavioral therapies that de-emphasize the medical model, IPT takes the opposite view and uses the medical model as part of the formulation. The IPT conceptualization of depression stresses that it is a medical illness that results in impairment for the sufferer. The IPT therapist works with clients to assist them within the context of suffering from an illness. The focus, as is clear from the name of the treatment, is on impairment in their interpersonal relationships. Just as cognitive therapy was influenced by the earlier work of George Kelley, and behavioral activation was influenced by the work of B. F. Skinner and Charles Ferster and the early behaviorists, IPT was influenced by the work of Adolph Meyer (1957) and the interpersonal psychiatry approach of Harry Stack Sullivan (1953). Therapists practicing from an IPT model need to carefully distinguish between the client having an illness because of depression and any suggestion that the client is ill because they are gay, lesbian, bisexual, queer, or transgender.

PROBLEM-SOLVING THERAPY

Problem-solving therapy (PST; Nezu, Nezu, & D'Zurilla, 2013) also has the distinction of having strong evidence as an empirically supported treatment for depression according to the American Psychological Association, Society of Clinical Psychology (Division 12) listing (https://www.div12.org/psychological-treatments/treatments). In PST, therapists work with clients to orient toward problems in living as opportunities. The treatment helps teach clients to cope with daily or long-term problems. It is important to distinguish PST from simple problem-solving techniques for teaching problem-solving skills that are used in many cognitive and behavioral therapies. Nezu et al. distinguish the implementation of PST as a system of therapy from PST as skills training in that the latter does not emphasize skills that "foster a positive problem orientation and enhance emotion regulation skills" (p. 4). Like cognitive therapy and behavioral activation, PST is an active treatment, wherein therapists collaborate with clients to teach skills that will help them cope with stressful life events and manage emotional distress. PST provides a reasonable approach to helping LGBTQ clients identify challenges in their current life situations, deal with difficulty regulating emotions in the context of anti-LGBTQ sentiment or institutional biases, and identify possible strategies for resolving problems and managing affect.

USING EFFICACIOUS AND EFFECTIVE TREATMENTS WITH SEXUAL MINORITY CLIENTS

Due to the fact that there are higher rates of depression and greater use of behavioral health services among sexual minority individuals, therapists should be prepared to provide care that has been shown to have the greatest efficacy. That is the first step of affirmative therapy. We know, however, that there is a difference between efficacy and effectiveness. In efficacy research, certain well-screened research participants benefit from treatment and, in the best case, a smaller percentage do not benefit equally. Effectiveness research examines how well the therapy works in a less controlled clinical setting, with a population that experiences co-occurring disorders and life problems. Taking a case-conceptualization approach to treatment allows therapists to implement treatment that is likely to be more effective because in the formulation, situational factors (e.g., minority stress), individual differences (e.g., being a member of a sexual minority), co-occurring disorders, and the literature on the best treatments for those disorders are all taken into account. This is where the competent therapist should begin when treating depressed, sexual minority clients.

The treatments described in this chapter are relatively active—particularly in the case of BA and cognitive therapy—and all have demonstrated efficacy in the psychotherapy outcome literature. Because they were developed to be collaborative and to consider the individual situations of each client, they are ideally suited for work with sexual minority clients. The assumptions of these treatments have to do with the onset and maintenance of depression, but the theories of these treatments do not make assumptions about any particular intrapsychic structures (e.g., Oedipal urges) that may not account for the unique experiences of sexual minority clients.

Sexual minority clients have been participants in many of the treatment outcome trials for depression but not in sufficient numbers for statistical analysis of differences between sexual minority and majority participants. The treatments have also been studied for use with sexual minority clients with diagnoses other than depression or with co-occurring problems (e.g., crystal methamphetamine abuse; Mimiaga et al., 2012). Thus, a specific empirically based, LGBTQ-affirmative treatment for depression has not yet been developed and tested. Nevertheless, one can utilize the treatments summarized in this chapter in an affirmative way and not move away from practicing consistent with the empirical underpinnings of those treatments. Christine Nezu (personal communication, March, 28, 2017) states that contemporary PST is

> a comprehensive system of psychotherapy that increases patients' awareness of their inner experience, teaches specific skills regarding emotional understanding and regulation, and the intentional practice of newly learned problem-solving skills, in order to create an experiential learning process. The experiential component of PST is essential in that, suggestive of studies that document the plasticity of the brain, the intervention is designed to "train" patients' brains to react and attempt to manage challenging life stressors.

It is known from the literature that sexual minority individuals face a number of challenges and stressors that vary according to where they live, their occupation, their family structure, and many other factors. Even when sexual minority individuals live in highly accepting areas, individuals make mistakes that can be experienced as microaggressions. Such is true for the common occurrence, for example, of a gay man telling a colleague, "My partner and I are looking into buying a house" and the colleague responding, "Oh, tell me again what your wife does for a living." Microaggressions are often unintentional and committed without malice, but they add stressors. The gay man in this situation is faced momentarily with the decision to not embarrass his colleague and simply let the statement go, assert what his husband does for a living, or say "I don't have a wife." This momentary decision-making process is emotional, behavioral, and social—in essence, it is the perfect type of occurrence for which PCT is an excellent treatment choice. Nezu (personal communication, March 28, 2017) states that the nature of PCT

> translates to an approach with wide acceptability for individuals from traditionally under-represented populations in psychotherapy outcome studies, because it is practical, focused on individual goals, and informed by an individual's emotions (rather than in spite of negative feelings). For example, if a client was experiencing anger and fear associated with a discriminating cultural experience, the PST therapist would likely support accessing these negative feeling as essential sources of information to aid in personal goal setting and understanding of obstacles. In one case someone might conclude that brainstorming strategies to achieve a personal goal might need to take into account the very present obstacles of discrimination from others. In another instance one might discover in therapy how their awareness of their inner experience is informing relationship goals that they have been conditioned to avoid or, worse yet, become self-critical about. This value on one's internal experiences and emotional sensitivity as information about what makes life worth living and the practical way of seeking solutions free of self-judgment are aspects of PST that promote affirming experiences. The treatment, which is historically and theoretically rooted in a positive psychology

philosophy, is rooted in building strength and resilience to stressful problems in living, and increasing an individual's experience of empowerment.

A collaborative and individualized case conceptualization that takes into account the cultural context of the client's experiences enhances CBT, BA, and IPT and is consistent with the treatment processes. Therapists must ensure that the materials used are sensitive to LGBTQ clients; they can do so in the following ways:

1. Choose outcome measures that do not use heterosexist language, or modify those that do.
2. Modify forms to account for non-binary gender identities.
3. Use varied examples, metaphors, or analogies that are sensitive to the client. For example, in working with a depressed, pan-sexual woman, it would be better for the therapist to talk about "people for whom you have affection, or to whom you are attracted" than to say "when you meet a man or woman to whom you are attracted."

In BA and other contemporary behavioral or contextual therapies, such as acceptance and commitment therapy (ACT; Hayes, Strosahl, & Wilson, 1999), treatment includes a discussion of client values. Helping clients identify values guides action. In these treatments (particularly ACT), clients are encouraged to engage in activities that are consistent with their values rather than to wait for certain feelings to change before moving in a valued direction. Engaging in value-driven behavior, identified with each individual in treatment, can act as a powerful antidepressant for sexual minority clients. However, although the principle is to identify behavior that is meaningful to a particular individual, discussions of values can become a sticky issue for some clients, perhaps especially sexual minority clients. It is common to either confuse values with morals or only talk about values that are socially acceptable. For example, therapists will easily talk about interpersonal values that include being a good friend, spouse, or partner.

However, not all values fit neatly into categories that are socially acceptable to all therapists. For example, a client may begin to pursue goals to meet and enjoy sexual intimacy with a variety of partners. This individual may value personal freedom and may have a goal to have a sexually liberated life and physical connection with others. Sometimes, presentations of values seem to conflate morals and values. This is a particularly sensitive distinction for sexual minority clients, who are frequently confronted with allegations of being "immoral," "sinful," and "dangerous." Sexual minority clients rarely seek therapy to discuss morality. Values are not inherently good or bad. As defined by Hayes et al. (1999), "Values are verbally construed global desired life consequences" (p. 206); furthermore, "A value is a direction—a quality of action. By definition, values cannot be achieved and maintained in a static state, they must be lived out" (p. 231). Many therapists could get hung up in debates about whether the outcome of having multiple sexual partners is good or bad, implying that the value of personal freedom is somehow bad or that the stated goals of the client are not the right goals to pursue. However, if these activities are consistent with a person's values, it would be better to discuss topics such as healthier sexual practices and emotional reactions, and also to help the client negotiate goals that are consistent with the person's values, rather than considering positive or negative consequences with a hidden agenda of disapproving of the client's behavior. This could easily degenerate into the therapist attempting to impose their morals or values on the client. Sexual minority clients have historically had therapists' values, morals, and beliefs imposed on them, whether they sought this out or not.

SUMMARY

Depression is not easily treated, although several treatments have strong empirical support. It remains to be determined which therapies are best for which clients and when. Current best practices employ a case conceptualization that considers the client's diagnosis and treatments that have been developed for that diagnosis, transdiagnostic features of the client's presentation and corresponding treatment strategies that have been studied for these broader processes, and sets individualized treatment goals collaboratively with the client. Using these treatments in an LGBTQ-affirmative manner requires that therapists are aware of

- their own biases and attitudes about human sexuality and gender;
- their own privilege regarding sexual orientation or gender/gender identity; and
- limitations in their ability to respect sexual minority clients and affirm their realities.

Affirmative treatment is as much about attitude as it is about action. Data indicate that sexual minority individuals' lives may be complicated by the stressors of being a part of one or several oppressed or disenfranchised communities and therefore may be more vulnerable to depression and anxiety. However, data cannot tell us whether we should use cognitive reappraisal or brainstorming solutions with a particular individual. Rather, the empirically supported treatments all emphasize building a strong therapeutic relationship, being genuine and empathic, and, most important, working collaboratively in the process of treatment. These treatments can be empowering to people who face systematic disempowerment (consider the many decades when people of the same sex were not allowed to legally marry or the current legislative initiatives to prevent people from using bathrooms consistent with their gender identity). In summary, affirmative treatment for depression requires that clinicians learn the principles and protocols well, apply them according to the literature, and connect to each client they treat as a person of worth with diverse life experiences that add to the brilliant complexity of human behavior.

CASE EXAMPLE

Because the robust data support CBT in the treatment of depression, the case of Corey is presented from this perspective.

Demographic Information

Corey was a 37-year-old client who identified as gender-queer, and exclusively attracted to men, and therefore stated that their sexual orientation was "gay." Corey was of European American lineage and used the pronouns "they" and "their" because there is not a pronoun for the singular tense that would be for someone who is of a non-binary gender (e.g., he/him and she/her). Corey was the third of five children from a strict Catholic family but did not personally identify with any particular religion. Corey's relationship with family varied according to the individuals involved. Although their relationship with their Dad was "strained," their Mom was supportive of all her children, kind, but not emotionally demonstrative. Corey had an older brother from whom they were estranged. That brother was described as politically and socially conservative, extremely vocal about his views, and actively working against inclusive legislative agendas. Corey's older sister supported Corey but did not participate in politics apart from voting in "most" elections, although Corey remained on good terms with her, her husband, and their children. Corey's younger two siblings, both identified as female, were significantly younger and away at college. Corey thought they were both "great" and involved in "important work," but because of the age difference they did not interact much apart from communication on holidays and birthdays. Corey lived alone in a small apartment in a large western city close to the small suburban community where Corey was raised. Corey initially made statements such as "I am really proud of who I am and that I have been able to recognize complexities about myself that make me unique," but at the same time, Corey was easily influenced by the judgments of others and was prone to become highly self-critical.

Presenting Problems

At the urging of a close friend, Corey sought treatment following a break-up with a man whom Corey had dated for 6 months. Corey stated that they experienced low mood, extreme lethargy, and no longer found usual activities pleasurable. Corey had much anxiety about sharing their gender identity with others, particularly men in dating situations, although they did not attempt to act differently, wanting someone to "accept me for who I am." However, Corey feared that it would be very difficult to find someone who would be accepting. Corey had begun to refuse invitations to parties or weekend get-togethers with friends. This was a behavior that had concerned the friend because Corey had previously and typically been very social, enjoyed dancing at clubs on Friday nights, and was a regular at several annual parties, as well as very active in advocacy work. Corey also said that, although embarrassing to admit, they had not cleaned their apartment in more than 2 months and found it overwhelming to even begin with simple laundry. They would wash and dry a few clothes when "absolutely necessary" and had not cleaned bedding for more than 1 month.

Relevant History

Although Corey had always been a very social and outgoing person, it was rare that they were involved in a romantic relationship. Apart from the most recent relationship with a man named Henry, Corey had only dated one other man very briefly. There had also been several short-term sexual encounters in which the guy Corey began to date would end a continued relationship stating that Corey was "great, cute, but just not my type." Corey reported that the recent break-up that precipitated their symptoms was mutual and that Corey was surprised that it had such a negative emotional impact. In fact, Corey had reportedly found this 6-month relationship with Henry to be somewhat stressful. Throughout their relationship, Henry often made jokes referring to Corey as a "lady" or "girl," which Corey would laugh at but secretly felt lonely and sad, believing that they were being judged for not meeting stereotypical masculine gender norms. Corey described Henry as a "beefy jock type," and although Corey did not identify as "male," the jokes about behavior were embarrassing because Corey did not identify as female. Also, because Corey had never discussed gender identity with Henry, Corey feared that Henry had figured out that Corey "wasn't a real man" and was disapproving. Corey felt that Henry was a perfect example of the "type" of men that Corey typically ended up with—the type that would never reciprocate the admiration because Corey was not "masculine." After the break-up, Corey started to ruminate about the possibility of never meeting anyone and was plagued by the belief, "I will never find a partner, I'm just not attractive in that way to guys." Corey believed that a gay man would not accept anyone who did not identify as male and, therefore, disclose gender identity. Although Corey did not make attempts to act in ways that were inconsistent with their gender identity, would never put on an act for anyone, Corey still feared that disclosure to someone they initially could date may make Corey simply feel honest but would make the man less attracted.

As the public focus on gender and bathrooms began to increase in the media, Corey felt more self-conscious. The rhetoric used by those who believed people needed to use bathrooms according to their assigned sex at birth, rather than consistent with their identity, had a negative impact on Corey, who was feeling more vulnerable because of the recent break-up. Although Corey personally was comfortable using designated men's restrooms, they found the hostility in the conversations to be particularly disturbing. In all of Corey's former political activities—public protests against anti-LGBTQ legislation, marching in Pride parades, and so forth—Corey stood with Henry or with other friends as "gay men." Now, Corey started to shy away from fighting specifically anti-transgender legislation. Corey began to question whether it was worth the trouble to not just declare, "Alright, I'm male." Recognizing internalized transphobia, Corey began to feel guilty and think, "I am a fraud, and all of my work in support of sexual minorities was meaningless." This increased Corey's dysphoria and hopelessness.

Treatment

Corey's beliefs about masculinity and being attractive were a major focus of therapy. The internalized transphobia that was reinforced by Corey's father's criticism, as well as by Corey's own interpretation of why relationships did not work out, resulted in vulnerability to any form of perceived rejection by potential romantic partners and also vulnerability to become depressed. Although much of Corey's advocacy and activism revolved around broad issues of equality for LGBTQ people, Corey had greater difficulty being an activist for personal fulfillment and honesty. After the recent break-up, and the subsequent sadness and blue mood, Corey also began to avoid social encounters, which only served to exacerbate depression, lead to more avoidance, and provided limited opportunities to ameliorate the self-criticism. Corey's therapist proposed a cognitive–behavioral treatment plan that would emphasize behavioral activation elements of treatment to break the cycle of avoidance that Corey was in and also behavioral experiments to examine Corey's beliefs about masculinity and attractiveness. Corey's therapist also planned to examine Corey's beliefs about being a fraud through Socratic dialog, looking at the complexities of being influenced by a cisgender/heterocentric culture, internalizing negative beliefs while also believing that sexual minorities represented normal variations in human behavior.

Over 20 sessions of therapy, Corey experienced a marked reduction in depression symptoms as indicated by the Beck Depression Inventory–Second Edition (Beck, Steer, & Garbin, 1988; Beck, Ward, Mendelson, Mock, & Erbaugh, 1961), and Corey's scores on the Outcome Questionnaire-45 (Lambert et al., 2004) noted reliable change and suggested that the change was likely to be maintained following treatment. There were also notable improvements as the therapist and Corey moved through the varied stages of therapy. During the first 4 sessions, when treatment was focused on behavioral activation strategies, Corey noted that it was very important to be politically involved and felt particularly ashamed to have stopped engaging in local activities. Noting that contemporary behavioral activation emphasizes helping clients engage in activities that are meaningful and consistent with their values rather than just participating in activities that may be pleasurable, Corey's therapist asked Corey whether advocacy activities could be a reasonable place to begin. Therefore, as part of their behavioral activation plan, Corey identified a group that was working through a local church to help LGBTQ refugees and recent immigrants navigate appropriate social services.

Corey initially planned an activity to research the published information about this effort on the church's website, and Corey increased engagement with weekly therapy assignments. By session 4, Corey had visited the office and learned of a letter-writing effort to state officials to increase awareness of the plight of sexual minority refugees.

With Corey regularly engaging in activities, and stating that they were pleased with their renewed involvement with the refugee efforts as a way of helping others, cognitive reappraisal was added to the treatment. Namely, they began an examination of Corey's beliefs about not being attractive to other men due to not being "masculine enough." Corey had met several gay men through the aforementioned group, and Corey used a survey behavioral experiment to test the belief that "gay men only want to date distinctly male-identified, very masculine guys." Corey simply asked the two gay men with whom Corey was becoming acquainted, both of whom were single, "how they found the dating scene to be locally, and how compatible they felt with the men they dated." To Corey's surprise, both of the men said that they had rich dating lives because the area where they lived was culturally diverse, and they looked for potential partners who enjoyed the arts, good wine, and occasionally being "home-bodies." Corey was relieved to note that neither of these men noted that they wanted someone with a particular body type or demeanor. Although not a panacea, this behavioral experiment provided data disconfirming Corey's belief about what other gay men found attractive. Corey's therapist also followed up with questions about Corey's perceptions of these two men—for example, How masculine did they appear to Corey? Answer: "very." How attracted to or compatible might either of them be with Corey? Answer: "I could see myself interested in either of them." By the end of the 10th session of therapy, Corey had joined a "game night" group that one of the men from the Church group held every other Friday night. Not only did game night prove to be entertaining but also the participants shared hopes and frustrations with the current political climate locally, nationally, and internationally. The group consisted of a heterosexual couple, three gay men, and one gender-queer who identified as bisexual, in addition to Corey. Corey found the camaraderie of this group refreshing, and Corey increasingly shared personal details about their life and identity.

The success of Corey's involvement in "game night" led to a therapeutic focus on Corey's core belief that they were "a fraud." Corey was able to identify this belief and the factors that supported it: Corey seldom shared their gender identity and simply pretended to be male; Corey's ex-partner wanted someone more masculine. Corey also shared with their therapist that simply being gay and trying to pass through a heterocentric society led to the feeling of being a fraud. Corey's therapist used Socratic questioning and made some use of thought records to help Corey see that throughout daily life, we meet individuals about whom we know very little. We may make assumptions about people we see in a grocery store, for example, but just because our assumptions (that they are of a particular class, gender identity, or sexual orientation) may be incorrect simply makes us wrong, not them fraudulent. Corey began to practice accomplishing daily tasks making a mental note that "I am just me, this is me doing X, Y, or Z," and Corey focused less on worrying about what others believed.

Corey had a brief increase in depression scores between session 13 and session 14, when Corey asked one of the men from the Church group out on a date and was turned down. There was a resurgence of the belief about "not being loveable." Corey's therapist helped Corey examine these thoughts and view the broader context and circumstance about why this man had turned Corey down. Corey strongly believed the thought that "he doesn't think I'm his type even though he says he likes men that are into culture. It is because I need to be more butch." Using a white board to do an impromptu thought record, Corey and their therapist began to review evidence and clues to other possible interpretations. The man had actually stated that he had gone through a difficult break-up recently himself and was just not ready to start dating. Corey did not trust the veracity of this statement 100% but conceded that even if it was "mostly true" that gay men prefer masculine partners, it suggested that masculinity may have had little to do with being turned down in this particular situation. Furthermore, Corey was able to understand that predicting the future was not helpful and that it was not a foregone conclusion that nobody could ever find Corey sexy, attractive, and desirable as a partner.

A happy coincidence occurred, however, when that same man introduced Corey to an attractive friend of his, who asked Corey out, and they had begun casually dating during the period when therapy was coming to an end. Relapse prevention included Corey identifying potential situations that could result in rumination on the old beliefs or on disengaging from activities Corey found meaningful. Corey worked with their therapist to develop a plan for coping should these circumstances arise, and Corey was able to articulate how to activate and engage rather than avoid when feeling dysphoric and also how to question assumptions and beliefs that were occasioned by unpleasant events as a plan for "self-therapy" going forward.

Summary

As presented previously in this chapter, there are several empirically supported treatments that may have been used to help Corey, and evidence-based practice also suggests that therapists should begin with a good case conceptualization and modify treatment as indicated through ongoing assessment. In Corey's case, Beck's cognitive therapy for depression was used, informed by current literature on behavioral activation and with sensitivity to Corey's sexual orientation and gender identity insofar as these were associated with Corey's negative beliefs and current distress. The external pressures of being a member of a sexual minority when political climates and public sentiment are subject to variation, from supportive to oppressive, had a strong influence on Corey's depression. Culturally competent treatment of depression begins with the recognition that diversity in human identity and behavior is the norm. Implementation strategies for treatment evolve

around that fact and locate the individual being treated within the context of societal, political, and cultural pressures as well as individual beliefs and behavior.

REFERENCES

Beck, A. T. (1976). *Cognitive therapy and the emotional disorders*. New York,
NY: International Universities Press.

Beck, A. T., Rush, A. J., Shaw, B. F., & Emery, G. (1979). *Cognitive therapy of depression*.
New York, NY: Guilford.

Beck, A. T., Steer, R. A., & Garbin, M. G. (1988). Psychometric properties of the Beck
Depression Inventory: Twenty-five years of evaluation. *Clinical Psychology Review,
8*(1), 77–100.

Beck, A. T., Ward, C. H., Mendelson, M., Mock, J., & Erbaugh, J. (1961). An inventory
for measuring depression. *Archives of General Psychiatry, 4*, 561–571.

Bleiberg, K. L., & Markowitz, J. C. (2005). Interpersonal psychotherapy for posttraumatic
stress disorder. *American Journal of Psychiatry, 162*, 181–183.

Bolton, P., Bass, J., Neugebauer, R., Bentancourt, T., Speelman, L., Onyango, G., . . .
Verdeli, H. (2007). Interventions for depression symptoms among adolescent
survivors of war and displacement in northern Uganda: A randomized controlled
trial. *Journal of the American Medical Association, 298*(5), 519–527.

Bolton, P., Bass, J., Neugebauer, R., Verdeli, H., Clougherty, K.F., Wickramaratne, P., . . .
Weissman, M. (2003). Group interpersonal psychotherapy for depression in rural
Uganda: A randomized controlled trial. *Journal of the American Medical Association,
289*(23), 3117–3124. doi:10.1001/jama.289.23-3117

Brim, O. G., Baltes, P. B., Bumpass, L. L., Cleary, P. D., Featherman, D. L., Hazzard, W. R.,
. . . Shweder, R. A. (1999). *National Survey of Midlife Development in the United States
(MIDUS), 1995–1996*. Ann Arbor, MI: Inter-University Consortium for Political and
Social Research.

Cochran, S. D., Sullivan, J. G., & Mays, V. M. (2003).Prevalence of mental disorders, psychological distress, and mental health services use among lesbian, gay, and bisexual
adults in the United States. *Journal of Consulting and Clinical Psychology, 71*, 53–61.

Ferster, C. B. (1973). A functional analysis of depression. *American Psychologist, 28*,
857–870.

Fuchs, C. Z., & Rehm, L. P. (1977). A self-control behavior therapy program for depression. *Journal of Consulting and Clinical Psychology, 52*(2), 206–215. http://dx.doi.org/
10.1037/0022-006X.45.2.206

Hayes, S. C., Strosahl, K. D., & Wilson, K. G. (1999). *Acceptance and commitment
therapy: An experiential approach to behavior change*. New York, NY: Guilford.

Hendricks, M. L., & Testa, R. J. (2012). A conceptual framework for clinical work with
trans-gender and gender non-conforming clients: An adaptation of the minority
stress model. *Professional Psychology, 43*(5), 460–467.

Klerman, G. L., Weissman, M. M., Rounsaville, B. J., & Chevron, E. S. (1984). *Interpersonal
psychotherapy of depression*. New York: Basic.

Kuyken, W., Padesky, C. A., & Dudley, R. (2009). *Collaborative case conceptualization: Working effectively with clients in cognitive–behavioral therapy*. New York,
NY: Guilford.

Lejuez, C. W., Hopko, D. R., & Hopko, S. D. (2001). A brief behavioral activation treatment for depression: Treatment manual. *Behavior Modification, 25*(2), 255–286.

Lambert, M. J., Morton, J. J., Hatfield, D., Harmon, C., Hamilton, S., Reid, R. C., . . . Burlingame, G. (2004). *Administration and scoring manual for the Outcome Questionnaire (OQ-45.2)* (3rd ed.). Wilmington, DE: American Professional Credentialing Services.

Lewinsohn, P. M. (1974). A behavioral approach to depression. In R. M. Friedman & M. M. Katz (Eds.), *The psychology of depression: Contemporary theory and research* (pp. 157–185). New York, NY: Wiley.

Lewinsohn, P. M., Antonuccio, D. O., Steinmetz-Breckenridge, J., & Teri, L. (1984). *The coping with depression course*. Eugene, OR: Castalia.

Lewinsohn, P. M., Clarke, G. N., Hops, H., & Andrews, J. (1990). Cognitive–behavioral treatment for depressed adolescents. *Behavior Therapy, 21*, 251–264.

MacPhillamy, D. J., & Lewinsohn, P. M. (1982). The Pleasant Events Schedule: Studies in reliability, validity, and scale intercorrelation. *Journal of Consulting and Clinical Psychology, 50*, 363–380.

Martell, C. R., Addis, M. E., & Jacobson, N. S. (2001). *Depression in context: Strategies for guided action*. New York: Norton.

Martell, C. R., Dimidjian, S., & Herman-Dunn, R. (2010). *Behavioral activation for depression: A clinician's guide*. New York: Guilford.

McAuley, E., Schloredt, K. A., Gudmundsen, G. R., Martell, C. R., & Dimidjian, S. (2016). *Behavioral activation with adolescents: A clinician's guide*. New York: Guilford.

McLean, P. D., Ogston, K., & Grauer, L. (1975). Behavioral approach to the treatment of depression. In C. M. Franks & G. T. Wilson (Eds.), *Annual review of behavior therapy theory & practice* (Vol. 3, pp. 755–766). New York, NY: Bruner-Mazel.

Meyer, A. (1957). *Psychobiology: A science of man*. Springfield, IL: Thomas.

Meyer, I. H. (1995). Minority stress among gay men. *Journal of Health and Social Behavior, 36*, 38–56.

Mimiaga, M. J., Reisner, S. L., Pantalone, D. W., O'Cleirigh, C, Mayer, K., & Safren, S. A. (2012). A pilot trial of integrated behavioral activation and sexual risk reduction counseling for HIV-uninfected men who have sex with men abusing crystal methamphetamine. *AIDS Patient Care and STDs, 26*(11), 681–693. doi:10.1089/apc.2012.0216

Muñoz, R. G. (1996). *The healthy management of reality*. http://medschool2.ucsf.edu/latino/pdf/healthy_management.pdf

Nezu, A. M., Nezu, C. M., & D'Zurilla, T. J. (2013). *Problem-solving therapy: A treatment manual*. New York, NY: Springer.

Nezu, A. M., Nezu, C. M., & Lombardo, E. (2004). *Cognitive–behavioral case formulation and treatment: A problem-solving approach*. New York, NY: Springer.

Persons, J. B. (2008). *The case formulation approach to cognitive–behavior therapy*. New York, NY: Guilford.

Persons, J. B., Davidson, J., & Tompkins, M. A. (2001). *Essential components of cognitive–behavior therapy for depression*. Washington, DC: American Psychological Association.

Rehm, L. P. (1977). A self-control model of depression. *Behavior Therapy, 8*, 787–804.

Roselló, J., & Bernal, G. (1999). The efficacy of cognitive–behavioral and interpersonal treatments for depression in Puerto Rican adolescents. *Journal of Consulting and Clinical Psychology, 67*(5), 734–745.

Shidlo, A. (1994). Internalized homophobia: Conceptual and empirical issues in measurement. In B. Green & G. M. Herek (Eds.), *Lesbian and gay psychology: Theory, research, and clinical applications* (pp. 176–205). Thousand Oaks, CA: Sage.

Sullivan, H. S. (1953). *The interpersonal theory of psychiatry.* New York, NY: Norton.

10

Evidence-Based Alcohol and Substance Use Disorder Treatment with Sexual and Gender Minorities

ADAM W. CARRICO, WALTER GÓMEZ, AND CATHY J. REBACK ■

Sexual and gender minority (SGM) individuals who develop alcohol or substance use disorders face a debilitating, chronic condition. In order to more effectively address the pernicious problem of alcohol and substance use disparities that is facing SGM communities, the overarching goals of this chapter are threefold. First, we describe the existing literature documenting the nature and correlates of disparities in unhealthy drinking as well as substance use in specific SGM populations. Second, we review common barriers that SGM populations experience when attempting to access culturally tailored substance use disorder treatment as well as provide an overview of clinical research testing the efficacy of evidence-based interventions in various SGM populations. Third, we present clinical case studies highlighting how cognitive–behavioral techniques can be culturally tailored to assist sexual minority men in coping with multiple sources of social stigma that are potent triggers for unhealthy alcohol consumption and substance use.

DISPARITIES IN ALCOHOL AND SUBSTANCE USE DISORDERS IN SGM POPULATIONS

SGM populations are at elevated risk for developing alcohol and substance use disorders, which is likely attributable to the dynamic interplay of structural, social, and psychological factors. In the structural domain, it is well established that SGM populations experience substantial stigma and discrimination that have deleterious implications for health. For example, sexual minority individuals residing in environments characterized by higher levels of anti-gay prejudice die 12 years younger, on average, compared to SGM peers residing in settings with less prejudice (Hatzenbuehler et al., 2014). The experience of lifetime discrimination is also associated with fourfold greater odds of a substance use disorder in the past year among sexual minority men and women (McCabe, Bostwick, Hughes, West, & Boyd, 2010). These pervasive experiences of sexual minority stress have led to a sustained pattern of migration among SGM persons to urban communities that are affirming of their sexual and gender identities (Stall, Friedman, & Catania, 2008).

Although urban SGM communities can serve as an important source of support and resilience (Johns et al., 2013), these environments also possess unique risk factors for problematic patterns of alcohol and substance use (Egan et al., 2011). Because SGM-centric social spaces such as bars and nightclubs proliferate in major urban centers, they often become a focal point for socializing as well as meeting romantic and sexual partners. This may increase risk for unhealthy drinking, access to other substances, and contribute to permissive substance use norms in urban SGM communities, potentiating disparities in unhealthy drinking and substance use (Cochran, Grella, & Mays, 2012). The beneficial and deleterious effects of residing in SGM communities remain understudied, but it is important to consider the potent roles that structural and social factors play in developing culturally tailored interventions for alcohol and substance use disorders.

Many SGM individuals also struggle with the enduring effects of victimization beginning in childhood, including sexual abuse, parental abuse, and bullying (Friedman et al., 2011), that increase the risk of multiple, co-occurring psychosocial health problems (including polysubstance use). For example, these early traumatic life experiences contribute to the development of depressive disorders and sexual compulsivity that serve as key triggers for unhealthy drinking and substance use in sexual minority men (Carrico et al., 2012; Marshall et al., 2015; Parsons, Grov, & Golub, 2012; Stall et al., 2003). There is an urgent need for comprehensive prevention and treatment approaches that address the complex, multilevel drivers of disparities in unhealthy drinking and substance use in SGM communities.

The 2015 National Survey on Drug Use and Health observed that sexual minorities were almost twice as likely to screen positive for an alcohol use disorder and three times more likely to screen positive for a substance use disorder compared to their heterosexual counterparts (Medley et al., 2016). Sexual minority disparities were observed for every specific substance, and disparities persisted even among young adults, who tended to report higher prevalence of substance use overall. Results of a meta-analysis provide further support for the observation that sexual minority disparities in alcohol and substance use emerge during adolescence, such that sexual minority adolescents had 2.89 greater odds of reporting substance use compared to their heterosexual peers (Marshal et al., 2008).

Although broadly documenting these disparities in sexual minority populations is informative, gender has emerged as one important consideration in identifying specific disparities in alcohol and substance use disorders.

Sexual minority men appear to be at elevated risk for substance use disorders. In the National Epidemiologic Survey of Alcohol and Related Conditions, men who identified as sexual minorities had more than threefold greater odds of using drugs, other than marijuana, in the past year and screening positive for alcohol dependence in the past year (McCabe, Hughes, Bostwick, West, & Boyd, 2009). Most strikingly, sexual minority men had more than fourfold greater odds of screening positive for dependence on substances, other than marijuana, in the past year. An evidence-based review provides a more extensive summary of epidemiologic studies documenting disparities in substance use, but not alcohol use, in sexual minority men (Green & Feinstein, 2012).

There is also evidence that stimulants, such as methamphetamine, are a prevalent and particularly detrimental class of substances used by sexual minority men. Sexual minority men often report using stimulants while socializing and for sexual enhancement (Kurtz, 2005). Research in Washington state found that treatment-seeking sexual minority men were more likely to present with methamphetamine use as a primary focus for treatment but also less likely to present with problems related to alcohol or heroin relative to heterosexual men (Cochran & Cauce, 2006). In San Francisco, a similar study of treatment-seeking populations observed that sexual minority men displayed elevated prevalence of stimulant use (Flentje, Heck, & Sorensen, 2015). Gay and bisexual men were 6.43 and 2.94 times, respectively, more likely to endorse methamphetamine as their primary substance compared to heterosexual men. Also, gay (but not bisexual) men were more likely to start using cocaine and methamphetamine at a later age compared to heterosexual men. This underscores the unique context and patterns surrounding substance use among sexual minority men that require culturally tailored treatment approaches.

There is broad recognition regarding the primacy of sexual minority stress processes such as discrimination as key risk factors for substance use among sexual minority men. For example, one study of bereaved gay men observed that experiences of discrimination were associated with increased risk of substance use over 18 months (Hatzenbuehler, Nolen-Hoeksema, & Erickson, 2008). Other research with HIV-positive sexual minority men highlights that internalized heterosexism, arguably the most commonly examined indicator of sexual minority stress, is indirectly associated with increased stimulant use via higher negative affect (Johnson, Carrico, Chesney, & Morin, 2008). The crucial role of sexual minority stress processes is further supported by research conducted with young sexual minority men. Among these men, Feinstein and Newcomb (2016) observed that internalized heterosexism was associated with problems with alcohol and other substance use, and victimization was associated with problems with marijuana use. These direct associations were mediated by substance use coping motives. Clearly, sexual minority stress processes are an important trigger for unhealthy drinking and substance use in sexual minority men.

Among sexual minority men, co-occurring psychosocial health problems (Parsons et al., 2012; Stall et al., 2003) as well as social and psychological resilience (Carrico et al., 2013; Herrick et al., 2011) are important substance use disorder intervention targets. Findings from a meta-analysis highlight that young sexual minority men are almost five times more likely to experience childhood sexual abuse (Friedman et al., 2011), and greater prevalence of lifetime victimization (especially during childhood) may partially explain greater risk for alcohol and substance use disorders among both sexual minority men and women (Hughes, McCabe, Wilsnack, West, & Boyd, 2010). There is also evidence that co-occurring mental health problems such as sexual compulsivity and depressive symptoms are important triggers for substance use in sexual minority men (Carrico et al., 2012; Parsons et al., 2012). At the same time, positive affect appears to be a source of resilience for recovery among sexual minority men receiving outpatient substance use disorder treatment (Carrico et al., 2013). Positive affect is associated with higher cognitive–behavioral change processes (e.g., self-efficacy and abstinence-specific social support) that can assist with reducing stimulant use. There is emerging consensus that optimizing the effectiveness of substance use disorder interventions with sexual minority men will require greater attention to comorbid syndemic conditions and cultivating resilience (Carrico, Zepf, Meanley, Batchelder, & Stall, 2016).

On the other hand, disparities in unhealthy drinking are most pronounced among sexual minority women. In one large cohort study of participants aged 9–14 years (the Growing Up Today Study), sexual minority youth initiated alcohol use at younger ages than their heterosexual peers, and those who described themselves as "mostly heterosexual" had consistently elevated risk of unhealthy drinking (Corliss, Rosario, Wypij, Fisher, & Austin, 2008). In this study, sexual minority girls exhibited the highest risk of unhealthy drinking relative to their heterosexual peers. At the same time, there is other evidence that disparities in alcohol use disorders may persist well into adulthood. This is supported in part by another large study of adults older than age 50 years that reported greater prevalence of excessive drinking among sexual minority men and women, with the disparity being greatest when sexual minority women were compared to their heterosexual peers (Fredriksen-Goldsen, Kim, Barkan, Muraco, & Hoy-Ellis, 2013). In addition, a large national household survey in the United States found that only sexual minority women (but not sexual minority men) reported using alcohol more frequently, using alcohol in greater quantities, and experienced more alcohol-related problems relative to heterosexual women (Cochran, Keenan, Schober, & Mays, 2000). Taken together, there is strong evidence to support profound disparities in unhealthy drinking in sexual minority women.

Sexual minority stress processes such as victimization have also emerged as important risk factors for unhealthy drinking and substance use in sexual minority women. Lehavot and Simoni (2011) demonstrated that victimization, concealment of sexual orientation, and internalized heterosexism are indirectly associated with greater substance use (i.e., alcohol, tobacco, and other substances) via lower social–psychological resources. Interestingly, greater victimization was also directly associated with more substance use. Lending further support to the importance of victimization as a risk factor for unhealthy drinking, a recent longitudinal study with sexual minority women observed that severe sexual assault predicted a 71% greater number of weekly drinks and a 63% higher number of alcohol-related consequences over 2 years (Rhew, Stappenbeck, Bedard-Gilligan, Hughes, & Kaysen, 2017). Wilsnack and colleagues (2008) also reported that disparities in unhealthy drinking were paralleled by greater prevalence of childhood sexual abuse and depression in sexual minority women. Taken together, the role of sexual minority stress processes (including victimization) as drivers of alcohol and substance use among sexual minority women underscores the need for integrative, trauma-informed treatment approaches to mitigate alcohol-related disparities in this population.

Although there is evidence for substance use disparities among gender minorities (Edmiston et al., 2016), the literature is decidedly scarcer with regard to transgender women. Unhealthy drinking and stimulant use are prevalent drivers of the HIV epidemic in transgender women. A study performed in San Francisco by Flentje, Heck, and Sorensen (2014) found that transgender women entering substance use disorder treatment were six times more likely to endorse using methamphetamine as their primary substance of use compared to their cisgender counterparts. Much like sexual minority men, the high prevalence of stimulant use among transgender women is associated with greater HIV prevalence (Reback & Fletcher, 2014; Santos, Rapues, et al., 2014). These findings demonstrate the need for interventions targeting stimulant use in transgender women. At the same time, relatively little is known about what, if any, disparities in unhealthy drinking and substance use are experienced by gender minority men.

Gender minorities experience substantial social stigma and discrimination that often cause difficulties in meeting housing and subsistence needs. Discrimination experienced by gender minorities is also often nested within the institutions tasked with surveilling and managing their health needs. For example, Reisner and colleagues (2015) observed that both enacted and anticipated health care provider stigma toward transgender men served as possible risk factors for substance use. This is largely consistent with results from a large, national study reported by Klein and Golub (2016) suggesting that the common experience of familial rejection was associated with almost 3½ times the odds of attempting suicide and 2½times the odds of substance misuse. Substance use disorder interventions must be developed with a nuanced understanding of the structural and social barriers facing gender minority communities.

Consistent with the literature on sexual minorities, there is evidence that co-occurring psychosocial health problems among gender minorities are risk factors for substance use. For example, one cross-sectional study observed that the association of greater life stress with sexual risk was mediated by alcohol and substance use (Hotton, Garofalo, Kuhns, & Johnson, 2013). Other research has documented the high prevalence of mental health problems in gender minorities. For example, a study of transgender women in Boston reported that 61% met criteria for a psychiatric disorder and 65% reported regular alcohol use (Reisner, Bailey, & Sevelius, 2014). Further support for these findings is evident in another study of gender minorities, which observed that a high burden of syndemic conditions was associated with greater odds of a substance use disorder treatment history and current substance use (Keuroghlian, Reisner, White, & Weiss, 2015). The burden of co-occurring syndemic conditions among gender minorities underscores the potential benefits of testing integrative mental health approaches to reduce unhealthy drinking and substance use.

There is evidence that victimization can play an important role in the development of syndemic conditions and increases risk for substance use in transgender women (Nuttbrock et al., 2013, 2014). The experience of gender abuse is also associated with three or four times higher odds of alcohol, cannabis, or cocaine use as well as an eightfold increase in odds of use of any other substance. This association of gender abuse with substance use was mediated by depressive symptoms. In summary, these findings provide compelling evidence of the role of gender-based trauma as an important risk factor for depression and substance use in transgender women. This underscores the potential benefits of interventions that explicitly address needs for gender affirmation to assist gender minorities in coping with stigma and discrimination to decrease unhealthy drinking or substance use (Sevelius, 2013).

THE SEARCH FOR CULTURALLY TAILORED SUBSTANCE USE DISORDER TREATMENT APPROACHES

Culturally tailored treatment approaches are needed to address sexual minority stress processes, assist individuals in managing co-occurring syndemic conditions that serve as triggers for alcohol and substance use, support frank discussions of issues relevant to sexuality, and address unique spiritual dimensions of recovery (Hicks, 2000). Particularly outside of major urban centers, SGM patients often lack access to substance use disorder treatment programs that deliver culturally tailored services, and a substantial minority of substance use disorder treatment counselors may hold negative attitudes about SGM patients (Eliason, 2001). Approximately 7% of substance use disorder treatment programs in the United States provide culturally tailored substance use disorder treatment for SGM populations (Cochran, Peavy, & Robohm, 2007).

Although culturally tailored treatment is often inaccessible, sexual minorities with alcohol or substance use disorders may be more likely to access substance use disorder treatment (McCabe, West, Hughes, & Boyd, 2013). Interestingly, connection to the gay community is associated with greater odds of utilizing substance use disorder treatment, which highlights the potential role of gay community involvement with support for recovery (Flores, Santos, Makofane, Arreola, & Ayala, 2017). Innovative treatment models, potentially utilizing technology-based interventions, are desperately needed to expand the reach of culturally tailored substance use disorder treatment to SGM populations.

Although more SGM individuals appear to be initiating substance use disorder treatment, there appear to be disparities in degree of engagement and outcomes. This is supported in part by research conducted with individuals entering substance use disorder treatment programs in the state of Washington, where SGM patients reported significantly greater utilization of outpatient visits (Cochran & Cauce, 2006). This may reflect the search for a culturally competent substance use disorder treatment provider. SGM patients in Washington state also visited the emergency department significantly more often, highlighting the possibility of greater severity of alcohol and substance use without proper coverage of culturally tailored treatment services. Similarly, another study of treatment-seeking individuals observed that sexual minorities reported less satisfaction with substance use disorder treatment compared to their heterosexual peers (Senreich, 2009). Sexual minority men were also more likely to report leaving substance use disorder treatment early because their needs were not being met or they were not voluntarily discharged. Efforts to provide expanded access to culturally tailored substance use disorder treatment approaches could improve the efficient delivery of services and potentially optimize treatment outcomes with SGM populations. Next, we briefly review the literature testing the efficacy of culturally tailored, cognitive–behavioral and motivational interviewing interventions for sexual minority men. This is followed by a brief summary of limited clinical research conducted with other SGM populations.

We recently conducted a systematic literature review examining the efficacy of behavioral interventions to optimize HIV/AIDS prevention among substance-using sexual minority men (Carrico et al., 2016). There is evidence for the efficacy of brief cognitive–behavioral and motivational interviewing approaches, which may be more beneficial for populations with a lower severity of alcohol and substance use disorders. Compared to HIV counseling and testing alone, a single-session personalized cognitive counseling (PCC) intervention with HIV-negative, episodic substance-using sexual minority men significantly decreased alcohol, marijuana, and erectile dysfunction medication use (risk ratio [RR] = 0.51–0.93) during a 6-month follow-up (Santos, Coffin, et al., 2014). This brief intervention also decreased the frequency of drinking to intoxication (odds ratio [OR] = 0.58, 95% confidence interval [CI] = 0.36–0.90) and reduced the number of condomless anal intercourse partners while feeling the effects of methamphetamine (RR = 0.26, 95% CI = 0.08–0.84). One trial with young, HIV-negative sexual minority men who were using substances observed that those receiving a four-session motivational interviewing intervention were less likely to engage in condomless anal intercourse (OR = 0.76, 95% CI = 0.68–0.85) and also less likely to report any substance use (OR = 0.72, 95% CI = 0.75–0.89) during a 12-month follow-up compared to participants receiving education only (Parsons, Lelutiu-Weinberger, Botsko, & Golub, 2014). Taken together, there is evidence that brief cognitive and motivational interviewing approaches are effective for reducing alcohol and substance use.

The Matrix Model (Rawson et al., 2004) is an evidence-based, cognitive–behavioral outpatient substance use disorder treatment program that has been culturally tailored for substance-using sexual minority men (Reback & Shoptaw, 2014; Shoptaw et al., 2005, 2008). In a seminal randomized controlled trial, Shoptaw and colleagues (2005) tested the efficacy of the Matrix Model treatment with sexual minority men seeking treatment for methamphetamine abuse or dependence. In this trial, those receiving the culturally tailored Matrix Model achieved greater reductions in condomless anal intercourse at 1 month post-randomization relative to other active behavioral interventions. These intervention-related benefits of the culturally tailored Matrix Model for sexual risk reduction were not sustained during the 12-month follow-up. Interestingly, those receiving contingency management (CM) either alone (OR = 3.71, 95% CI = 1.77–7.80) or with cognitive–behavioral therapy (OR = 7.79, 95% CI = 3.53–17.17) achieved greater abstinence during treatment compared to those receiving cognitive–behavioral therapy alone. In a subsequent trial, substance-using sexual minority men were randomized to receive the culturally tailored Matrix Model or gay social support therapy. The culturally tailored Matrix Model achieved greater reductions in methamphetamine (OR = 0.44, 95% CI = 0.24–0.78) and marijuana (OR = 0.54, 95% CI = 0.30–0.96) use during a 12-month follow-up compared to gay social support therapy (Shoptaw et al., 2008). The culturally tailored Matrix Model substance use disorder treatment has emerged as one of the few evidence-based approaches to formal substance use disorder treatment for SGM populations. Given this success, it has been modified for implementation within community settings in major urban centers while maintaining most intervention effects (Reback & Shoptaw, 2014).

Other clinical research has documented the implementation of the culturally tailored Matrix Model from a harm reduction perspective with methamphetamine-using sexual minority men in San Francisco (Carrico et al., 2014). It is often the case that individuals with alcohol and substance use disorders are not ready, willing, or able to achieve complete abstinence at the outset of treatment. Harm reduction is a client-centered approach to cognitive–behavioral substance use disorder treatment in which individuals can pursue a spectrum of possible ways to change their substance use without requiring abstinence. For example, clients could focus on changing modes of methamphetamine administration (e.g., from injecting to snorting) to reduce its associated harms. Findings from two treatment outcome studies demonstrate that methamphetamine-using sexual minority men receiving outpatient, cognitive–behavioral substance use disorder treatment from a harm reduction perspective report reductions in stimulant use, decreases in addiction severity, and decreased sexual risk (Carrico et al., 2014). Findings indicate that it is feasible and acceptable to implement the culturally tailored Matrix Model with methamphetamine-using sexual minority men from a harm reduction perspective.

Other randomized controlled trials have tested moderately intensive, cognitive–behavioral approaches with substance-using sexual minority men who were not actively seeking formal substance use disorder treatment and have obtained mixed results. Mausbach, Semple, Strathdee, Zians, and Patterson (2007) reported that an individually delivered, eight-session intervention with HIV-positive, methamphetamine-using sexual minority men achieved sustained reductions in condomless anal intercourse during a 12-month follow-up, relative to a diet and exercise control condition (OR = 0.60, 95% CI = 0.42–0.85). However, concurrent intervention-related changes in alcohol and substance use were not examined. Another trial examined the efficacy of a 24-week CM intervention with HIV-positive and HIV-negative homeless sexual minority men (Reback et al., 2010). Those receiving CM reported sustained reductions in alcohol and methamphetamine use during the 12-month follow-up relative to a control condition that did not receive incentives for substance abstinence or engaging in health-promoting behaviors. Finally, Project MIX was a large, multisite randomized controlled trial that tested the efficacy of a 6-week cognitive–behavioral group intervention with HIV-positive and HIV-negative substance-using sexual minority men (Mansergh et al., 2010). There were no intent-to-treat effects on substance use during sex or condomless anal intercourse relative to an attention-control group during the 12-month follow-up.

To date, only one randomized controlled trial has examined an alcohol use disorder intervention with sexual minority women. Fals-Stewart, O'Farrell, and Lam (2009) tested the efficacy of behavioral couple therapy with gay and lesbian individuals with an alcohol use disorder and their same-sex partners who did not have alcohol or substance use disorders. Couples were randomized to receive behavioral couples therapy with individually delivered treatment for the partner with an alcohol use disorder or individually delivered treatment alone. During the 12-month follow-up, both gay and lesbian individuals with an alcohol use disorder reported decreases in days of heavy drinking and couples reported improved relationship adjustment compared to those receiving the individually delivered intervention alone. To our knowledge, this remains the only randomized controlled trial to test the efficacy of a couples-based approach to targeting alcohol use disorders in SGM populations.

No randomized controlled trial has tested the efficacy of interventions to reduce alcohol and substance use in gender minorities. One open-phase trial conducted by Empson and colleagues (2017) examined the feasibility and acceptability of Seeking Safety with seven transgender women. The intervention consisted of 12, 2-hour group sessions focusing on the tenets of the Seeking Safety modality. Participants reported a 23.9% decrease in alcohol use disorder screening scores and a 68.8% decrease in substance use disorder screening scores. More clinical research is needed to test the efficacy of culturally tailored approaches to substance use disorder treatment and prevention with gender minorities.

IMPLEMENTING EVIDENCE-BASED SUBSTANCE USE DISORDER INTERVENTIONS WITH SGM POPULATIONS

It is clear that the evidence-based techniques of cognitive–behavioral and motivational interviewing interventions can achieve meaningful reductions in alcohol or other substance use with SGM populations. For example, PCC focuses on identifying and reframing automatic thoughts (termed "self-justifications") that underlie engagement in substance use among sexual minority men (Santos, Coffin, et al., 2014). The directive, client-centered approach of motivational interviewing can also be helpful in enhancing intrinsic motivation and bolstering self-efficacy for reducing substance use in sexual minority men (Parsons et al., 2014). Similarly, strictly behavioral approaches, such as CM, that provide incentives as positive reinforcement for abstinence have been successfully implemented with sexual minority men (Gómez et al., 2018; Reback et al., 2010; Shoptaw et al., 2005). Although these relatively time-limited approaches may be effective, it is likely that those with moderate to severe alcohol or substance use disorders will require more intensive substance use disorder treatment. The Matrix Model is an evidence-based, cognitive–behavioral substance use disorder treatment that has been culturally tailored for sexual minority men (Carrico et al., 2014; Reback & Shoptaw, 2014). Although the vast majority of clinical research has focused on sexual minority men, it is likely that all SGM populations will derive meaningful benefits from these evidence-based techniques, which have been tested extensively in the broader substance use disorder treatment literature. Training in these evidence-based approaches is a necessary first step to delivering culturally tailored substance use disorder treatment.

At the same time, expanded efforts on the part of clinicians are often needed to adequately tailor these evidence-based approaches to the key social and contextual factors that contribute to unhealthy drinking as well as other substance use among SGM populations. This informs treatment in three key domains. First, clinicians can implement culturally tailored assessment approaches to identify unique triggers for substance use. These can include sexual and gender minority stress processes as well as contextual triggers such as the use of social networking applications to meet romantic and sexual partners. Conducting a culturally informed intake assessment is crucial to build rapport with SGM clients and develop a case conceptualization that identifies the most relevant triggers to address in treatment. Because SGM populations may use substances to escape, avoid, or cope with minority stress, culturally tailored case conceptualizations should include a functional analysis of these sorts of unique cognitive, affective, and behavioral antecedents of unhealthy drinking or substance use. Second, culturally informed interventions can assist clients with identifying the source of both risk and resilience within SGM communities that is relevant to their recovery. Many SGM clients face a struggle to forge a positive SGM identity that requires new efforts to build social relationships with other members of the community that are also consistent with their recovery. For example, gay community involvement can revolve around social and sexual contexts in which alcohol and other substances are used (e.g., bars, nightclubs, and sex clubs) that are triggers for relapse. However, engagement in other facets of the gay community may be an important social resource for recovery. One important goal of culturally informed treatment approaches is to support the sexual and gender identity development and community involvement of SGM clients in a way that minimizes risk of relapse. Finally, it is important to note that SGM populations are more likely to experience traumatic experiences such as childhood sexual abuse, victimization, and discrimination across the life course that can serve as potent triggers for unhealthy drinking and substance use. Culturally tailored treatment approaches must be trauma-informed by acknowledging the potent, often enduring impact of these events as key triggers. It is often the case that SGM clients require referrals to trauma treatment and other mental health treatment (see Chapters X and Y) to alleviate mental health symptoms that serve as triggers for unhealthy drinking and substance use.

GETTING OFF: IMPLEMENTATION OF CULTURALLY TAILORED COGNITIVE–BEHAVIORAL THERAPY

Here, we provide case studies from interviews with counselors to illustrate the ways in which culturally tailored cognitive–behavioral therapy is being implemented to assist methamphetamine-using sexual minority men to cope more effectively with sexual and ethnic minority stress processes as important triggers for alcohol and substance use. The Getting Off program was adapted and culturally tailored from the cognitive–behavioral Matrix Model approach to substance use disorder treatment for implementation among sexual minority men (Reback, Veniegas, & Shoptaw, 2014).

JULIO

Julio is a 25-year-old Hispanic/Latino gay man who is HIV-positive. Prior to enrolling in the Getting Off program, Julio had experienced multiple treatment episodes. At the time Julio started treatment, he was living with his parents. Julio's drugs of choice were methamphetamine and γ-hydroxybutyrate (GHB). In the program, Julio began to gain insights into the functions of his methamphetamine addiction, which helped him understand why he continued to use despite his many attempts to stop. Specifically, Julio grappled with self-acceptance and internalized heterosexism.

> COUNSELOR: Julio had a problem accepting himself as a gay man, who he was as a Latino gay man. Also, there was a lot of internalized heterosexism and methamphetamine helped him to escape all of that. Methamphetamine enabled Julio to have sex without shame or guilt. During the cognitive–behavioral group process, Julio identified how methamphetamine use allowed him to engage in a gay cultural and sexual life, and through the group process he continued to examine how his parents and his Latino culture did not accept his gay identity and did not accept him as a Hispanic/Latino male, which became his core beliefs. Julio was not comfortable being gay and, more specifically, he was not comfortable being Latino and gay; this led to negative self-talk and negative self-criticism.

To escape his internalized heterosexism, Julio enlisted in the armed forces so he could separate from his family pressures. However, as Julio explained, "That didn't work." In fact, nothing worked to counter his low self-esteem and lack of self-acceptance until he began using methamphetamine. Methamphetamine welcomed him into another world, and he felt comfortable with male sexual partners, including multiple male sexual partners. But that resulted in a vicious cycle in which he had internalized heterosexism, he used methamphetamine to escape the negative feelings and thoughts, then he engaged in high-risk sexual behaviors, which then reinforced the internalized heterosexism.

During the cognitive–behavioral group process, Julio began to realize that he was assigned the "hero" role in his family, partially due to the fact that he was born in the United States and had the highest level of acculturation. Familismo is common in many Hispanic/Latino cultures, leading Julio to prioritize the needs of his family over his sexual identity development. He was the family member who was responsible for assisting his family with effectively navigating in society. However, Julio was uncomfortable being assigned that role. In summary, Julio could never be himself, so methamphetamine filled a much needed role in allowing him to escape, both sexually and emotionally.

Although Julio had multiple previous attempts to stop using methamphetamine, all of his prior treatment experiences focused only on his substance use and did not connect that much of Julio's methamphetamine use was associated with his negative self-image related to being a Hispanic/Latino gay man. Julio communicated this directly during treatment, saying, "I'm not good enough. I'm never going to fit in. I need to use meth to feel comfortable."

According to Julio, the other treatment programs downplayed the fact that his sexual identity and internalized heterosexism influenced how he used methamphetamine. Then Julio enrolled in Getting Off, in which gay-specific culture and content are integrated into cognitive–behavioral therapy. This culturally tailored treatment setting helped Julio make important strides in his recovery.

> JULIO: I found a place where I can talk freely without judgment. That, you know, you guys are saying, "Yes, there may be a connection [between methamphetamine use and sexual behaviors] and why don't we talk about it?"

At the beginning of Julio's withdrawal period, he began to identify the role of triggers, thoughts, and cravings in his methamphetamine use and condomless sex. Through his experiences in the cognitive–behavioral skills group, Julio was able to learn skills for managing triggers more effectively, and this accelerated his process of recovery.

> COUNSELOR: He turned over all of his rigs. He had not just one or two needles, he had about 30 needles that he brought to the clinic and put in the sharps container. He turned over all of his other paraphernalia, too, his GHB bottle, the cotton swabs—everything that was associated with him

getting high and injecting and then having condomless sex. He identified all of the paraphernalia, which he came to understand were key triggers. In discarding his paraphernalia, Julio began to interrupt the "euphoric recall" by removing these key triggers for his methamphetamine use. Julio also began to identify that his methamphetamine use never changed as being attributable to the negative core beliefs that his parents instilled in him related to being deficient because of his sexual identity. Julio articulated this saying, "Meth is not going to change this truth for me." Julio's next step in his recovery process was when he identified how his feelings and thoughts influenced his behaviors. He began to look at his reaction to sexual minority stress processes as potent internal triggers.

Julio began to see that if he changed these internal triggers, then that's the quickest way to change the outcome. By identifying the thought, and reframing the thought, that's a sustainable way of moving forward and changing the outcome. Julio also began to catch himself internalizing negative thoughts and challenged these core beliefs, which would also result in positive outcomes. Next, Julio began scheduling positive events (an important form of behavioral activation) and goal setting to create time without methamphetamine. He started to re-engage in many of the activities he enjoyed doing without methamphetamine.

Scheduling. Structuring. He got a job while he was in treatment. He also started talking honestly about his feelings. Rather than just that "hero" approach of saying, "Oh no, everything is fine," when everything is not fine. He came to group and he'd say, "No, everything is not fine. Here's how I really feel and this is what's really going on." And he realized the world didn't end by saying that he was struggling. The support system around him in group was crucial to reinforce these treatment gains. So he didn't have to paint this perfect, pretty picture of things. He could just tell the truth and it was okay. And he also started creating boundaries with his mom, which was challenging for him because there's this dynamic that's been set in stone for so many years, but he would say, "No mom, this is the way it's gotta be, because I need to put myself first because I'm in recovery."

TOM

Tom is a 37-year-old African American/Black gay man who is HIV-negative. Tom had one prior treatment experience, several years ago. When Tom entered treatment, he was living alone in a rented apartment. Tom compartmentalized his life: He compartmentalized his co-workers, his parents, his non-work friends, his sexual hook-ups, the men with whom he used methamphetamine, and the men with whom he did not use methamphetamine; he compartmentalized himself. He compartmentalized his job; he would go out with his co-workers for drinks, and he never used methamphetamine with his co-workers. When he was at home,

Tom would go on social networking applications (e.g., Grindr and Scruff). When he met someone for a "hook-up," he would use methamphetamine with them. On the dating apps, he compartmentalized the methamphetamine-using sexual partners from the non-using sexual partners, and he never saw a sexual partner more than once. Sometimes he posted the profile of a non-using hook-up, and sometimes he posted a "party-and-play" (using drugs to party and have sex) hook-up profile. At times he would only hook-up for sex, and other times he would hook-up for sex and methamphetamine. His life was very much divided, which appeared to be partially due to the difficulties Tom experienced with accepting himself as a gay Black man; he did not quite know where he fit in with himself or with other people, including other gay men.

> COUNSELOR: He would do methamphetamine to break down the energy that it took to manage a compartmentalized existence. It took a lot of energy to keep all of those walls up, and being able to function within each metaphorical room. Tom could accept himself when he was high. The walls came down on the compartmentalization, he was uninhibited and he didn't have to deal with the internalized heterosexism when he was high. A major part of Tom's treatment plan was to identify why he compartmentalized all aspects of his life. In addition to sexual minority stress, Tom identified the experiences of acculturation stress within his family of origin at a very young age as an important area for exploration in treatment. Through the group process, Tom acknowledged the heterosexism within his family of origin. He began to see how both the acculturation stress and homophobia within his family interacted, and how that resulted in a lifelong coping mechanism of compartmentalizing his life to be both gay and Black.
>
> TOM: They would say things to me like, "You're not Black enough." That suddenly was like there was this distrust of me within my own family because what was implied, the message I got was, "I need to be Blacker in order to be accepted by my family, and I'm not Black enough."
>
> COUNSELOR: As a gay Black man, Tom didn't feel that he fit in and so he kept his sexual identity completely hidden. Tom identified that these developmental experiences were the source of him building that metaphorical condominium so that he could be different things to different people. So that he could be accepted, he didn't accept himself and had to compartmentalize so that he could be accepted in his family, by other sexual minority men, and in society.

As expected, Tom's negative feelings resulted in self-criticism. Given that he did not have a positive self-image of a Black gay man, Tom did not know how to be authentically sexual or where he fit within gay culture. Thus, he played upon the stereotype of what he believed was expected of him, which was the dominant African American insertive sexual partner. Tom described experiences in which his sexual partners used racism to sexualize him, and methamphetamine allowed him to participate in the sexual role play of the dominant Black top. Tom describes how using methamphetamine helped him manage experiences of ethnic minority stress in his sexual experiences with other sexual minority men:

> TOM: I'm gonna run with people objectifying me as a gay, Black man. I'm gonna make the decision that, maybe if I don't know how I fit authentically into this situation I'm just going to play up the fact that I'm gay and you can fetishize me, and let's do meth so I can tolerate this.

The Getting Off cognitive–behavioral therapy group was utilized as a safe place for Tom to begin to explore the potent effects of sexual and ethnic minority stress in his life. The counselor began by helping Tom identify his internal triggers and his thoughts and then see how these thoughts influenced his emotional responses and behaviors (thinking–feeling–doing). Once Tom began to identify the patterns, he realized that he could change the thoughts and then change the outcome. He began to see that his pattern of methamphetamine use and condomless sex always began at approximately 40 days into his recovery. Once he recognized that pattern, he was able to utilize relapse prevention strategies and prepare for the cravings; cognitive reframing and urge surfing became a fundamental component of Tom's relapse prevention plan.

In addition, Tom began to see the role that alcohol and marijuana use played in his relapse. Initially, Tom compartmentalized his substance use just like he compartmentalized his work life, his family life, and his sexual life. Alcohol was in one compartment, marijuana was in another compartment, and methamphetamine was in yet another compartment. However, following a relapse, he realized that once he took a drink and he smoked marijuana, he knew what was coming next, which was the social networking applications followed by methamphetamine use. Through behavioral analysis, Tom was able to understand that although it might not be true that methamphetamine use follows alcohol or marijuana use for others, it was true for him.

> COUNSELOR: Tom put the sequence together. He was like, well, "Maybe if I don't drink and I don't go out with my work friends and don't drink alcohol, maybe I won't get on the app and use meth afterwards." Tom began to redefine his place in the world. In the group setting, he explored what it meant to be a gay man and his sexuality. In Getting Off, an important part of recovery is finding how to bring healthy sexual behaviors into the life of a gay man without using methamphetamine. Tom realized that he used methamphetamine and objectified sex to escape the self-critical thoughts that stemmed from the heterosexism and racism experiences in early in life. Tom also started to identify what he wanted from sex, which had nothing to do with objectification as a Black man and had everything to do with intimacy.

Tom also began exploring the ways in which his social connections contributed to methamphetamine use. Tom clearly identified how he compartmentalized everyone and everything in his life. None of his networks were connected. He utilized goal setting and scheduling to plan coffee and dinner dates with those who would be supportive of his goal to not use methamphetamine.

> COUNSELOR: As part of his relapse prevention, Tom began to identify the self-justifications that led to his meth use. Through identifying justifications, he wouldn't get stuck in the "euphoric recall," he was able to bring logic back to the situation and remind himself how that sequence always played out. So, if he could identify the justification first, then that could change the outcome later on. And, he also began pre-exposure prophylaxis (PrEP) while he was in Getting Off, which helped him to begin to enjoy sex without the ever present fear of acquiring HIV.

SUMMARY AND RECOMMENDATIONS

SGM populations display distinct disparities in alcohol and substance use disorders that are driven in part by experiences of sexual and gender minority stress. To date, the vast majority of research has focused on documenting the prevalence and correlates of these disparities in sexual minority men and women, with some limited descriptive research on gender minorities. Efforts to develop and test novel substance use disorder intervention approaches to mitigate these profound disparities have focused extensively on optimizing HIV/AIDS prevention in sexual minority men. The dominant focus on culturally tailoring evidence-based substance use disorder interventions such as cognitive–behavioral therapy and motivational interviewing has yielded some important successes, but expanded efforts are needed in multiple domains to more effectively target alcohol and substance use disparities in SGM populations. Clearly, clinical research is desperately needed with sexual minority women and gender minorities.

Clinical research is needed to develop and test novel approaches that more effectively target sexual, ethnic, and gender minority stress processes. It is important to note that many SGM populations experience multiple, overlapping sources of social stigma and oppression. New behavioral approaches are needed to assist SGM individuals with navigating the often complex structural and social barriers they encounter that contribute to the onset as well as maintenance of alcohol and substance use disorders. It is also important to note that evidence-based interventions that have demonstrated efficacy with sexual minority men will need to be adapted for the other SGM populations, with input from the community, and evaluated for efficacy through randomized controlled trials.

In addition, more research is needed with ethnic minority populations to examine how best to modify the dominant focus on sexual and gender minority stress processes to include a recognition of the role of ethnic minority stress. Although substantial research has been conducted to document the nature and correlates of disparities in SGM populations, this has often not included sufficient numbers of ethnic minorities to examine their unique experiences. More research examining drivers of alcohol and substance use disorders in ethnic minority SGM populations is a necessary first step to inform better cultural tailoring of substance use disorder interventions.

It is also clear that even when evidence-based substance use disorder interventions for SGM populations are identified, there are profound structural barriers to implementing them. This is evidenced in part by the implementation of the culturally tailored Matrix Model, Getting Off, with methamphetamine-using sexual minority men. It is noteworthy, however, that limited funds for substance use disorder treatment will dictate that evidence-based substance use disorder interventions for SGM populations will operate predominantly in major urban centers, where a large number of individuals migrate. It is important to test the efficacy and effectiveness of technology-based approaches that can have a broader impact, particularly in rural areas, where SGM populations are likely to have difficulties accessing culturally tailored substance use disorder treatment at brick-and-mortar facilities. The potential promise of technology-based approaches is supported in part by a recent open-phase trial of a text messaging intervention to reduce methamphetamine use and condomless anal intercourse in sexual minority men (Reback et al., 2012). More clinical research like this is needed to develop and test mobile health interventions to reduce alcohol and substance use in SGM populations.

There are also important considerations with regard to the critical developmental periods for intervention and testing novel intervention modalities. At least among sexual minority men and women, there is evidence that disparities in alcohol and substance use emerge during adolescence (Marshal et al., 2008), and there is a need for such research among gender minority individuals. However, relatively few randomized controlled trials of substance use disorder interventions have focused on youth. Another important consideration is that interventions tested to date have not attempted to address the role of family processes such as rejection that serve as important risk factors for substance use. More clinical research is needed to develop and test family-based interventions, particularly with youth, to prevent the onset of alcohol or substance use disorders in SGM populations.

Despite the challenges we face in pursuing clinical research to address the heightened risk for alcohol and substance use disorders in SGM populations, there are multiple pathways forward. We have an important obligation to continue to pursue evidence-based treatments for alleviating the human suffering that SGM populations experience related to alcohol and substance use disorders. In the words of Oscar Wilde, "We are all in the gutter, but some of us are looking at the stars."

REFERENCES

Carrico, A. W., Flentje, A., Gruber, V. A., Woods, W. J., Discepola, M. V., Dilworth, S. E., . . . Siever, M. D. (2014). Community-based harm reduction substance abuse treatment with methamphetamine-using men who have sex with men. *Journal of Urban Health, 91*(3), 555–567.

Carrico, A. W., Pollack, L. M., Stall, R. D., Shade, S. B., Neilands, T. B., Rice, T. M., . . . Moskowitz, J. T. (2012). Psychological processes and stimulant use among men who have sex with men. *Drug and Alcohol Dependence, 123*(1), 79–83.

Carrico, A. W., Woods, W. J., Siever, M. D., Discepola, M. V., Dilworth, S. E., Neilands, T. B., . . . Moskowitz, J. T. (2013). Positive affect and processes of recovery among treatment-seeking methamphetamine users. *Drug and Alcohol Dependence, 132*(3), 624–629.

Carrico, A. W., Zepf, R., Meanley, S., Batchelder, A., & Stall, R. (2016). When the party is over: A systematic review of behavioral interventions for substance-using men who have sex with men. *Journal of Acquired Immune Deficiency Syndromes, 73*(3), 299–306.

Cochran, B. N., & Cauce, A. M. (2006). Characteristics of lesbian, gay, bisexual, and transgender individuals entering substance abuse treatment. *Journal of Substance Abuse Treatment, 30*(2), 135–146.

Cochran, B. N., Peavy, K. M., & Robohm, J. S. (2007). Do specialized services exist for LGBT individuals seeking treatment for substance misuse? A study of available treatment programs. *Substance Use & Misuse, 42*(1), 161–176.

Cochran, S. D., Grella, C. E., & Mays, V. M. (2012). Do substance use norms and perceived drug availability mediate sexual orientation differences in patterns of substance use? Results from the California Quality of Life Survey II. *Journal of Studies on Alcohol and Drugs, 73*(4), 675–685.

Cochran, S. D., Keenan, C., Schober, C., & Mays, V. M. (2000). Estimates of alcohol use and clinical treatment needs among homosexually active men and women in the US population. *Journal of Consulting and Clinical Psychology, 68*(6), 1062.

Corliss, H. L., Rosario, M., Wypij, D., Fisher, L. B., & Austin, S. B. (2008). Sexual orientation disparities in longitudinal alcohol use patterns among adolescents: Findings from the Growing Up Today Study. *Archives of Pediatrics & Adolescent Medicine, 162*(11), 1071–1078.

Edmiston, E. K., Donald, C. A., Sattler, A. R., Peebles, J. K., Ehrenfeld, J. M., & Eckstrand, K. L. (2016). Opportunities and gaps in primary care preventative health services for transgender patients: A systematic review. *Transgender Health, 1*(1), 216–230.

Egan, J. E., Frye, V., Kurtz, S. P., Latkin, C., Chen, M., Tobin, K., . . . Koblin, B. A. (2011). Migration, neighborhoods, and networks: Approaches to understanding how urban environmental conditions affect syndemic adverse health outcomes among gay, bisexual and other men who have sex with men. *AIDS and Behavior, 15*(1), 35–50.

Eliason, M. J. (2001). Substance abuse counselor's attitudes regarding lesbian, gay, bisexual, and transgendered clients. *Journal of Substance Abuse, 12*(4), 311–328.

Empson, S., Cuca, Y. P., Cocohoba, J., Dawson-Rose, C., Davis, K., & Machtinger, E. L. (2017). Seeking safety group therapy for co-occurring substance use disorder and PTSD among transgender women living with HIV: A pilot study. *Journal of Psychoactive Drugs*, *49*(4), 344–351.

Fals-Stewart, W., O'Farrell, T. J., & Lam, W. K. (2009). Behavioral couple therapy for gay and lesbian couples with alcohol use disorders. *Journal of Substance Abuse Treatment*, *37*(4), 379–387.

Feinstein, B. A., & Newcomb, M. E. (2016). The role of substance use motives in the associations between minority stressors and substance use problems among young men who have sex with men. *Psychology of Sexual Orientation and Gender Diversity*, *3*(3), 357.

Flentje, A., Heck, N. C., & Sorensen, J. L. (2014). Characteristics of transgender individuals entering substance abuse treatment. *Addictive Behaviors*, *39*(5), 969–975.

Flentje, A., Heck, N. C., & Sorensen, J. L. (2015). Substance use among lesbian, gay, and bisexual clients entering substance abuse treatment: Comparisons to heterosexual clients. *Journal of Consulting and Clinical Psychology*, *83*(2), 325–334. http://psycnet. apa.org/doiLanding?doi=10.1037%2Fa0038724

Flores, J. M., Santos, G. M., Makofane, K., Arreola, S., & Ayala, G. (2017). Availability and use of substance abuse treatment programs among substance-using men who have sex with men worldwide. *Substance Use & Misuse*, *52*(5), 666–673.

Fredriksen-Goldsen, K. I., Kim, H. J., Barkan, S. E., Muraco, A., & Hoy-Ellis, C. P. (2013). Health disparities among lesbian, gay, and bisexual older adults: Results from a population-based study. *American Journal of Public Health*, *103*(10), 1802–1809.

Friedman, M. S., Marshal, M. P., Guadamuz, T. E., Wei, C., Wong, C. F., Saewyc, E. M., & Stall, R. (2011). A meta-analysis of disparities in childhood sexual abuse, parental physical abuse, and peer victimization among sexual minority and sexual nonminority individuals. *American Journal of Public Health*, *101*(8), 1481–1494.

Gómez, W., Olem, D., Andrews, R., Discepola, M. V., Ambrose, P., Dilworth, S. E., & Carrico, A. W. (2018). Optimizing contingency management with methamphetamine-using men who have sex with men. *Cognitive and Behavioral Practice*, *25*(2), 286–295.

Green, K. E., & Feinstein, B. A. (2012). Substance use in lesbian, gay, and bisexual populations: An update on empirical research and implications for treatment. *Psychology of Addictive Behaviors*, *26*(2), 265.

Hatzenbuehler, M. L., Bellatorre, A., Lee, Y., Finch, B. K., Muennig, P., & Fiscella, K. (2014). Structural stigma and all-cause mortality in sexual minority populations. *Social Science & Medicine*, *103*, 33–41.

Hatzenbuehler, M. L., Nolen-Hoeksema, S., & Erickson, S. J. (2008). Minority stress predictors of HIV risk behavior, substance use, and depressive symptoms: Results from a prospective study of bereaved gay men. *Health Psychology*, *27*(4), 455.

Herrick, A. L., Lim, S. H., Wei, C., Smith, H., Guadamuz, T., Friedman, M. S., & Stall, R. (2011). Resilience as an untapped resource in behavioral intervention design for gay men. *AIDS and Behavior*, *15*(1), 25–29.

Hicks, D. (2000). The importance of specialized treatment programs for lesbian and gay patients. *Journal of Gay & Lesbian Psychotherapy*, *3*(3–4), 81–94.

Hotton, A. L., Garofalo, R., Kuhns, L. M., & Johnson, A. K. (2013). Substance use as a mediator of the relationship between life stress and sexual risk among young transgender women. *AIDS Education and Prevention*, *25*(1), 62–71.

Hughes, T., McCabe, S. E., Wilsnack, S. C., West, B. T., & Boyd, C. J. (2010). Victimization and substance use disorders in a national sample of heterosexual and sexual minority women and men. *Addiction*, *105*(12), 2130–2140.

Johns, M. M., Pingel, E. S., Youatt, E. J., Soler, J. H., McClelland, S. I., & Bauermeister, J. A. (2013). LGBT community, social network characteristics, and smoking behaviors in young sexual minority women. *American Journal of Community Psychology*, *52*(1–2), 141–154.

Johnson, M. O., Carrico, A. W., Chesney, M. A., & Morin, S. F. (2008). Internalized heterosexism among HIV-positive, gay-identified men: Implications for HIV prevention and care. *Journal of Consulting and Clinical Psychology*, *76*(5), 829.

Keuroghlian, A. S., Reisner, S. L., White, J. M., & Weiss, R. D. (2015). Substance use and treatment of substance use disorders in a community sample of transgender adults. *Drug and Alcohol Dependence*, *152*, 139–146.

Klein, A., & Golub, S. A. (2016). Family rejection as a predictor of suicide attempts and substance misuse among transgender and gender nonconforming adults. *LGBT Health*, *3*(3), 193–199.

Kurtz, S. P. (2005). Post-circuit blues: Motivations and consequences of crystal meth use among gay men in Miami. *AIDS and Behavior*, *9*(1), 63–72.

Lehavot, K., & Simoni, J. M. (2011). The impact of minority stress on mental health and substance use among sexual minority women. *Journal of Consulting and Clinical Psychology*, *79*(2), 159.

Mansergh, G., Koblin, B. A., McKirnan, D. J., Hudson, S. M., Flores, S. A., Wiegand, R. E., . . . Colfax, G. N.; Project MIX Study Team. (2010). An intervention to reduce HIV risk behavior of substance-using men who have sex with men: A two-group randomized trial with a nonrandomized third group. *PLoS Medicine*, *7*(8), e1000329.

Marshal, M. P., Friedman, M. S., Stall, R., King, K. M., Miles, J., Gold, M. A., . . . Morse, J. Q. (2008). Sexual orientation and adolescent substance use: A meta-analysis and methodological review. *Addiction*, *103*(4), 546–556.

Marshall, B. D., Shoveller, J. A., Kahler, C. W., Koblin, B. A., Mayer, K. H., Mimiaga, M. J., . . . Operario, D. (2015). Heavy drinking trajectories among men who have sex with men: A longitudinal, group-based analysis. *Alcoholism: Clinical and Experimental Research*, *39*(2), 380–389.

Mausbach, B. T., Semple, S. J., Strathdee, S. A., Zians, J., & Patterson, T. L. (2007). Efficacy of a behavioral intervention for increasing safer sex behaviors in HIV-positive MSM methamphetamine users: Results from the EDGE study. *Drug and Alcohol Dependence*, *87*(2), 249–257.

McCabe, S. E., Bostwick, W. B., Hughes, T. L., West, B. T., & Boyd, C. J. (2010). The relationship between discrimination and substance use disorders among lesbian, gay, and bisexual adults in the United States. *American Journal of Public Health*, *100*(10), 1946–1952.

McCabe, S. E., Hughes, T. L., Bostwick, W. B., West, B. T., & Boyd, C. J. (2009). Sexual orientation, substance use behaviors and substance dependence in the United States. *Addiction*, *104*(8), 1333–1345.

McCabe, S. E., West, B. T., Hughes, T. L., & Boyd, C. J. (2013). Sexual orientation and substance abuse treatment utilization in the United States: Results from a national survey. *Journal of Substance Abuse Treatment*, *44*(1), 4–12.

Medley, G., Lipari, R. N., Bose, J., Cribb, D. S., Kroutil, L. A., & McHenry, G. (2016). *Sexual orientation and estimates of adult substance use and mental health: Results from the 2015 National Survey on Drug Use and Health*. Retrieved from https://www.samhsa.gov/data/sites/default/files/NSDUH-SexualOrientation-2015/NSDUH-SexualOrientation-2015/NSDUH-SexualOrientation-2015.htm

Nuttbrock, L., Bockting, W., Rosenblum, A., Hwahng, S., Mason, M., Macri, M., & Becker, J. (2013). Gender abuse, depressive symptoms, and HIV and other sexually transmitted infections among male-to-female transgender persons: A three-year prospective study. *American Journal of Public Health, 103*(2), 300–307.

Nuttbrock, L., Bockting, W., Rosenblum, A., Hwahng, S., Mason, M., Macri, M., & Becker, J. (2014). Gender abuse, depressive symptoms, and substance use among transgender women: A 3-year prospective study. *American Journal of Public Health, 104*(11), 2199–2206.

Parsons, J. T., Grov, C., & Golub, S. A. (2012). Sexual compulsivity, co-occurring psychosocial health problems, and HIV risk among gay and bisexual men: Further evidence of a syndemic. *American Journal of Public Health, 102*(1), 156–162.

Parsons, J. T., Lelutiu-Weinberger, C., Botsko, M., & Golub, S. A. (2014). A randomized controlled trial utilizing motivational interviewing to reduce HIV risk and drug use in young gay and bisexual men. *Journal of Consulting and Clinical Psychology, 82*(1), 9.

Rawson, R. A., Marinelli-Casey, P., Anglin, M. D., Dickow, A., Frazier, Y., Gallagher, C., . . . Obert, J. (2004). A multi-site comparison of psychosocial approaches for the treatment of methamphetamine dependence. *Addiction, 99*(6), 708–717.

Reback, C. J., & Fletcher, J. B. (2014). HIV prevalence, substance use, and sexual risk behaviors among transgender women recruited through outreach. *AIDS and Behavior, 18*(7), 1359–1367.

Reback, C. J., Grant, D. L., Fletcher, J. B., Branson, C. M., Shoptaw, S., Bowers, J. R., . . . Mansergh, G. (2012). Text messaging reduces HIV risk behaviors among methamphetamine-using men who have sex with men. *AIDS and Behavior, 16*(7), 1993–2002.

Reback, C. J., Peck, J. A., Dierst-Davies, R., Nuno, M., Kamien, J. B., & Amass, L. (2010). Contingency management among homeless, out-of-treatment men who have sex with men. *Journal of Substance Abuse Treatment, 39*(3), 255–263.

Reback, C. J., & Shoptaw, S. (2014). Development of an evidence-based, gay-specific cognitive behavioral therapy intervention for methamphetamine-abusing gay and bisexual men. *Addictive Behaviors, 39*(8), 1286–1291.

Reback, C. J., Veniegas, R., & Shoptaw, S. (2014). Getting Off: Development of a model program for gay and bisexual male methamphetamine users. *Journal of Homosexuality, 61*(4), 540–553.

Reisner, S. L., Bailey, Z., & Sevelius, J. (2014). Racial/ethnic disparities in history of incarceration, experiences of victimization, and associated health indicators among transgender women in the U.S. *Women & Health, 54,* 750–767. doi:10.1080/03630242.2014.932891

Reisner, S. L., Pardo, S. T., Gamarel, K. E., Hughto, J. M. W., Pardee, D. J., & Keo-Meier, C. L. (2015). Substance use to cope with stigma in healthcare among US female-to-male trans masculine adults. *LGBT Health, 2*(4), 324–332.

Rhew, I. C., Stappenbeck, C. A., Bedard-Gilligan, M., Hughes, T., & Kaysen, D. (2017). Effects of sexual assault on alcohol use and consequences among young adult sexual minority women. *Journal of Consulting and Clinical Psychology, 85*(5), 424.

Santos, G. M., Coffin, P. O., Vittinghoff, E., DeMicco, E., Das, M., Matheson, T., . . . Dilley, J. W. (2014). Substance use and drinking outcomes in Personalized Cognitive Counseling randomized trial for episodic substance-using men who have sex with men. *Drug and Alcohol Dependence, 138,* 234–239.

Santos, G. M., Rapues, J., Wilson, E. C., Macias, O., Packer, T., Colfax, G., & Raymond, H. F. (2014). Alcohol and substance use among transgender women in San Francisco: Prevalence and association with human immunodeficiency virus infection. *Drug and Alcohol Review, 33*(3), 287–295.

Senreich, E. (2009). A comparison of perceptions, reported abstinence, and completion rates of gay, lesbian, bisexual, and heterosexual clients in substance abuse treatment. *Journal of Gay & Lesbian Mental Health, 13*(3), 145–169.

Sevelius, J. M. (2013). Gender affirmation: A framework for conceptualizing risk behavior among transgender women of color. *Sex Roles, 68*(11–12), 675–689.

Shoptaw, S., Reback, C. J., Larkins, S., Wang, P. C., Rotheram-Fuller, E., Dang, J., & Yang, X. (2008). Outcomes using two tailored behavioral treatments for substance abuse in urban gay and bisexual men. *Journal of Substance Abuse Treatment, 35*(3), 285–293.

Shoptaw, S., Reback, C. J., Peck, J. A., Yang, X., Rotheram-Fuller, E., Larkins, S., . . . Hucks-Ortiz, C. (2005). Behavioral treatment approaches for methamphetamine dependence and HIV-related sexual risk behaviors among urban gay and bisexual men. *Drug and Alcohol Dependence, 78*(2), 125–134.

Stall, R., Friedman, M., & Catania, J. A. (2008). Interacting epidemics and gay men's health: A theory of syndemic production among urban gay men. *Unequal Opportunity, 1*, 251–274.

Stall, R., Mills, T. C., Williamson, J., Hart, T., Greenwood, G., Paul, J., . . . Catania, J. A. (2003). Association of co-occurring psychosocial health problems and increased vulnerability to HIV/AIDS among urban men who have sex with men. *American Journal of Public Health, 93*(6), 939–942. doi:10.2105/AJPH.93.6.939

Wilsnack, S. C., Hughes, T. L., Johnson, T. P., Bostwick, W. B., Szalacha, L. A., Benson, P., . . . Kinnison, K. E. (2008). Drinking and drinking-related problems among heterosexual and sexual minority women. *Journal of Studies on Alcohol and Drugs, 69*(1), 129–139.

11

Application of Evidence-Based Practices for Trauma-Related Disorders Among Sexual Minority Women

DEBRA KAYSEN, KEREN LEHAVOT, AND EMILY R. DWORKIN ■

This chapter begins by defining, describing, and reporting the prevalence of trauma exposure and related mental health disorders among sexual minority women (SMW). We review theoretical models that explain the ways in which trauma exposure among SMW may lead to mental health concerns, including minority stress, insidious trauma, and psychological mediation theoretical frameworks, as well as how other theoretical frameworks such as emotional processing theory and social cognitive theory may be applied to SMW. Next, we review the literature on assessment and on leading treatment approaches for trauma-related disorders in the general population, and we discuss how these may be tailored for SMW. We then present illustrative case examples of how to apply these principles with SMW. Finally, we conclude with a discussion of future directions and emerging trends in the field.

TRAUMA EXPOSURE AMONG SEXUAL MINORITY WOMEN

Exposure to traumatic experiences is common among SMW (Roberts, Austin, Corliss, Vandermorris, & Koenen, 2010). In a review of the literature, sexual assault rates were high among SMW, with lifetime sexual assault prevalence across studies ranging from 16% to 85% (Rothman, Exner, & Baughman, 2011). The most common types of sexual victimization across studies were child sexual abuse (median = 35%) and adult sexual assault (median = 23%). In addition,

SMW report higher rates of both childhood and adult sexual and physical abuse compared to heterosexual women in representative and convenience samples (Austin et al., 2008; Balsam, Rothblum, & Beauchaine, 2005; Hughes, Johnson, & Wilsnack, 2001; Hughes, McCabe, Wilsnack, West, & Boyd, 2010; Roberts et al., 2010). SMW also may be more likely to experience injury or shocking events (e.g., life-threatening illness) as well as to learn of trauma to a close friend or relative compared to heterosexual women (Roberts et al., 2010).

Among SMW, experiences of bias-related stressors, such as discrimination and hate crimes, are also relatively common. In a national sample of sexual minority men and women, nearly two-thirds of the sample reported at least one experience of discrimination in the past year due to sexual orientation, race/ethnicity, or gender (Bostwick, Boyd, Hughes, West, & McCabe, 2014). A separate study found that 11% of sexual minority men and women were called offensive names because of race, sex, or sexual orientation and 4% were pushed, shoved, or threatened during the past 12 months (McLaughlin, Hatzenbuehler, & Keyes, 2010). Approximately 15% of SMW in a national sample reported actual or attempted violence or property crimes based on their sexual orientation (Herek, 2009). In a review of the literature, a median of 5% of SMW across studies reported hate crime-related sexual assault (Rothman et al., 2011).

TRAUMA-RELATED PSYCHIATRIC DISORDERS AMONG SEXUAL MINORITY WOMEN

Experiences of trauma and bias-related stressors have significant consequences for SMW. One such consequence is post-traumatic stress disorder (PTSD), which is a mental disorder that develops in response to a traumatic event. Traumatic events that meet criteria for diagnosis, termed criterion A events, involve exposure to actual or threatened death, serious injury, or sexual violence. According to the fifth edition of the *Diagnostic and Statistical Manual of Mental Disorders* (DSM-5; American Psychiatric Association, 2013), PTSD is characterized by intrusive thoughts and memories of the traumatic event, avoidance of external and/or internal reminders of the event, negative changes in cognition and mood, and changes in arousal and reactivity. Studies using nationally-representative samples have found that SMW are two to three times more likely to meet criteria for PTSD compared to heterosexual women (Gilman et al., 2001; Roberts et al., 2010; Roberts, Rosario, Corliss, Koenen, & Austin, 2012); lifetime prevalence estimates were 7%–13% for heterosexual women, 18% to 19% for lesbian women, and 26% to 27% for bisexual women.

Trauma exposure is also a risk factor for other conditions, such as depression and substance misuse. In studies of SMW, traumatic events such as child sexual abuse, adult sexual victimization, intimate partner violence, and hate crimes have been associated with elevated risk for depression and substance use disorders (Descamps, Rothblum, Bradford, & Ryan, 2000; Drabble, Trocki, Hughes, Korcha, & Lown, 2013; Lehavot & Simpson, 2014). Child sexual abuse and revictimization also appear to be risk factors for high-risk drinking among SMW (Gilmore et al., 2014; Hughes, Szalacha, et al., 2010). Sexual assault has been prospectively associated with increased risk of alcohol use and consequences among young SMW 1 year after the assault (Rhew, Stappenbeck, Bedard-Gilligan, Hughes, & Kaysen, 2017).

THEORETICAL MODELS FOR TRAUMA-RELATED PSYCHOPATHOLOGY AMONG SEXUAL MINORITY WOMEN

Multiple theoretical models can be applied to understand the impact of trauma on SMW's mental health. Next, we review models that explain elevated rates of mental disorders in minority populations. Then, we review models of the development of PTSD in the general population.

Models of Mental Disorder Risk in Sexual Minority Populations

Minority stress theory posits that sexual minorities face greater rates of violence, discrimination, and other stressors due to a negative social environment, which in turn contribute to mental health problems (Meyer, 2003). As reviewed previously, SMW do have a higher prevalence of PTSD as well as other mood, anxiety, and substance use disorders compared to their heterosexual counterparts (Cochran & Mays, 2000; Cochran, Sullivan, & Mays, 2003; Gilman et al., 2001; King et al., 2008; Sandfort, de Graaf, Bijl, & Schnabel, 2001). In a nationally representative sample, SMW's higher risk for PTSD was largely accounted for by their greater exposure to violence, exposure to more traumatic events, and earlier age of trauma exposure, in support of this theory (Roberts et al., 2010). Furthermore, among sexual minorities, those reporting traumatic events perceived to be related to sexual orientation-based prejudice have reported more symptoms of posttraumatic stress, depression, anger, and anxiety compared to sexual minorities reporting traumatic events not perceived to be prejudice related (Herek, Gillis, & Cogan, 1999).

Insidious trauma theory suggests that subtler forms of trauma, such as heterosexist discrimination and microaggressions, may heighten vulnerability to PTSD (Brown, 2003; Root, 1992). This theory proposes that even in the absence of a criterion A event, the ongoing negative experiences associated with being a member of a stigmatized group can result in PTSD symptoms. Although this theory diverges from current conceptualization of PTSD as necessarily stemming from criterion A traumatic events, as described in the DSM-5, several studies have found support for this theory. In an online convenience sample of lesbian women, heterosexist hate crime victimization (a criterion A event) as well as heterosexist discrimination (not a criterion A event) were both uniquely and significantly associated with PTSD symptoms (Szymanski & Balsam, 2011). This finding was replicated with a larger sample of sexual minorities (Bandermann & Szymanski, 2014). Another study found an association between greater experiences of heterosexist microaggressions (i.e., subtle or indirect discrimination) and PTSD symptoms in a sexual minority sample (Robinson & Rubin, 2016).

Minority stress and insidious trauma theories highlight the need for macrolevel societal intervention strategies (e.g., reducing discrimination) in order to reduce psychopathology and related disparities for SMW. Nonetheless, they do not identify specific mechanisms that explain the development or maintenance of psychopathology that could inform individual-level interventions (e.g., psychotherapy). The psychological mediation framework fills this gap by explaining how traumatic events and experiences of discrimination lead to psychopathology such as PTSD (Hatzenbuehler, 2009). This framework suggests that stressors in the environment result in elevations in emotion dysregulation, social and interpersonal problems, and cognitive processes, which in turn confer risk for mental health problems. These psychological processes may be non-minority specific (e.g., coping strategies and cognitive processes that are relevant across groups) as well as minority specific, including internal processes unique to SMW, such as internalized sexism and/or heterosexism, concealing sexual orientation, and expectations of rejection. Several studies provide support for the psychological mediation framework in relation to trauma-related disorders. For example, lesbian women who experienced more heterosexist discrimination had lower self-esteem, which in turn contributed to higher PTSD symptoms (Szymanski & Balsam, 2011). In a different study of sexual minorities, people who experienced more heterosexist discrimination were more likely to use coping strategies such as internalization and detachment. Individuals who used those strategies more, in turn, had higher PTSD symptoms (Bandermann & Szymanski, 2014). Among young SMW meeting criteria for PTSD (using traditional definitions of criterion A), experiences of daily heterosexism predicted more negative post-traumatic cognitions later in time, including thoughts about the self, world, and self-blame (Dworkin, Gilmore, Bedard-Gilligan, Lehavot, & Kaysen, 2018). Findings suggested that daily heterosexism contributed to negative views about the self that, in turn, promoted maintenance or exacerbation of PTSD symptoms.

Models of the Development of PTSD

In addition to the previously-mentioned minority-specific theories of health disparities, theories of the development and maintenance of PTSD that have been developed in the general population may have implications for SMW. Here, we review two such models: emotional processing theory and the social cognitive model.

Emotional processing theory builds from the premise that fear is represented in memory structures that drive fearful behavior (Lang, 1977, 1979). For people with PTSD, these fear structures are pathological in that they (1) are activated by an excessive, generalized set of stimuli;(2) drive fearful behaviors, such as avoidance, that are excessive in relation to the reality of the feared stimulus; (3) include pathological meaning elements (e.g., clients often believe that anxiety will persist indefinitely once activated); and (4) are resistant to modification (Foa & Rothbaum, 1998). As a result of avoidance of feared stimuli, people with PTSD do not have opportunities to encounter cognitive and affective information that is incompatible with the fear structures. In therapy, these fear structures are activated and disconfirming information is incorporated, which modifies the fear structures (Foa & Kozak, 1986). Although no studies have been conducted with SMW that directly address emotional processing theory, studies with SMW provide support for the role of avoidance in maintaining symptoms. Specifically, in a study with a community sample of lesbian women, those who had experienced childhood physical abuse reported higher experiential avoidance, which was in turn associated with higher PTSD symptoms (Gold, Feinstein, Skidmore, & Marx, 2011). In another study with lesbian sexual assault survivors, women who endorsed higher internalized heterosexism also reported higher experiential avoidance, which was in turn associated with higher PTSD symptom severity (Gold, Dickstein, Marx, & Lexington, 2009). These findings highlight the critical role that both trauma-specific (child physical abuse) and nonspecific (internalized heterosexism) factors may have for SMW in leading to avoidance and the role that avoidance plays in PTSD.

Social cognitive theory focuses on the impact of trauma exposure on beliefs and the emotions that arise from these altered beliefs (Cahill, Rothbaum, Resick, & Follette, 2008). This theory builds from the concept of "schemas," which are defined as individuals' mental frameworks that help organize and categorize information and make predictions about what one can expect in various circumstances. Traumatic experiences are thought to generate information that is incompatible with previously held schemas, leading to changes in these previously held schemas and in beliefs about the trauma. These new beliefs generate secondary, manufactured emotions (e.g., guilt and shame) and interfere with the expression of natural, primary emotions (e.g., fear and sadness). Avoidance of trauma-related emotions and memories helps maintain both the natural emotions and the maladaptive beliefs (Nishith, Resick, & Griffin, 2002). The goals of therapy are thus to stop avoidance; express natural emotions to allow them to run their course; and identify and correct distorted trauma-related beliefs, which in turn results in reductions in manufactured emotions. Comorbidities such as depression or substance use are viewed as by-products of avoidance (Resick, Monson, & Chard, 2006). This theory is consistent with the psychological mediation framework, although social cognitive theory emphasizes that the ways in which people create meaning out of events are much of what drives the development and maintenance of PTSD (LoSavio, Dillon, & Resick, 2017). Thus, experiences such as hate crimes or discrimination may be particularly devastating because of their impact on how SMW understand themselves, others, and the world. This is consistent with the studies reviewed previously that demonstrate the impact of trauma-related cognitions on PTSD among SMW (e.g., Dworkin et al., 2018). In addition, through this framework, internalized heterosexism can be conceptualized as negative self-related cognitions that could be reinforced by trauma exposure (Gold et al., 2009).

CLINICAL PRACTICE APPLICATIONS

Assessment of Trauma Exposure and PTSD

When working with populations that have high rates of potential trauma exposure, such as SMW, it is important to formally assess trauma exposure as part of a clinical assessment. There are several relatively brief measures of trauma exposure, either self-report or interviewer administered, many of which are available for free.[1] It is preferred to use measures that include specific, behaviorally based definitions of interpersonal traumatic events (Balsam, 2002). For example, women may be more likely to endorse that someone had forcible sex with them without their consent rather than endorsing that they had been raped. A thorough assessment of a client's history and experiences, the number and types of traumatic events she has experienced, her age when these events occurred, and her relationship with the perpetrator are important for treatment planning. To date, there have been no studies evaluating the extent to which these measures adequately capture important aspects of trauma exposure for SMW or the types of traumatic events to which SMW are exposed (e.g., childhood bullying) (D'Augelli, Grossman, & Starks, 2006). In addition, it may be important to understand whether SMW believe that the event occurred because of their gender, race/ethnicity, or sexual orientation, because trauma exposure may have a more severe impact for SMW who have experienced bias-based victimization (Herek et al., 1999). Last, these measures do not capture the effects of the chronic social stress (e.g., harassment and discrimination) and insidious trauma that may contribute additional risk for PTSD (Balsam et al., 2005; Katz-Wise & Hyde, 2012). Unfortunately, existing measures of minority stress (e.g., the Daily Heterosexist Experiences Questionnaire; Balsam, Beadnell, & Molina, 2013) do not capture the full range of trauma exposures covered by the trauma-specific measures. One option is to combine these two types of measures to conduct a fuller assessment of exposure to stressful and traumatic events relevant to SMW.

CASE EXAMPLE: JAINA

Jaina served in the Army. While stationed overseas, a member of her platoon with whom she had previously been friends, and who knew she identified as a lesbian, began to pressure her to have sex with him. She became fearful and tried to avoid

---

1. For a list of measures that assess trauma exposure and PTSD, see https://www.ptsd.va.gov/professional/assessment/all_measures.asp.

being alone with him. He threatened to disclose her sexual identity to others and told her it would ruin her military career. He informed her that if she did not have sex with him, everyone would know she was "a dyke." During an evening out while drinking together, he offered to take her home. On the way home, he pushed her up against a wall and raped her. Out of fear of the potential loss of her career, she did not disclose the rape. The effects of the sexual assault (criterion A) were worsened because of the underlying fear of losing her career and relationships and the concealment of her sexual orientation (non-criterion A stressors), and both were important to understand in addressing Jaina's concerns in treatment.

It is also important to systematically assess symptoms of PTSD because most individuals who experience traumatic events do not develop PTSD (Breslau, 2009). This can include a thorough structured or semistructured clinical interview and the use of brief screening measures such as the Primary Care PTSD Screen (Cameron & Gusman, 2003) or slightly longer self-report measures such as the Posttraumatic Checklist for DSM-5 (PCL-5) (Weathers et al., 2013). The PCL-5 and the Clinician-Administered PTSD Scale (CAPS; a structured clinical interview) are among the publicly available PTSD measures that have strong psychometrics and good sensitivity and specificity (Blevins, Weathers, Davis, Witte, & Domino, 2015; Weathers, Keane, & Davidson, 2001). However, it is important to note that these measures have not been validated with SMW, and several factors could lead SMW to respond differently to queries on these measures. It is unknown whether SMW's exposure to chronic social stress impacts endorsement of DSM-5 PTSD symptoms. For example, SMW may experience cognitive shifts, such as the internalization of heterosexist attitudes, which could manifest in the form of persistent and exaggerated negative beliefs related to a traumatic event (Alessi, Martin, Gyamerah, & Meyer, 2013; Szymanski & Balsam, 2011). It is possible that women in general may be less likely to endorse some PTSD symptoms, such as aggressive behavior (Archer & Haigh, 1999). One option may be to formally assess PTSD symptoms but to also include time in a diagnostic interview for women to describe their unique perspectives on how the traumatic events they have experienced have affected their lives and what reactions or symptoms they have noticed. These insights could then be incorporated into treatment planning.

CASE EXAMPLE: LORNA

Lorna presented to a therapist's office with complaints of nightmares, irritability, and constantly being on high alert. She described a series of sexual assaults. The worst one was perpetrated by a family friend who was angry that she was gay and had rejected his advances. During a formal CAPS interview, Lorna described that she has always believed that being gay is wrong; the assault made this belief stronger and led to the belief that being gay caused the trauma. She also endorsed negative feelings such as guilt and shame much of the time, but she said that she had had these negative feelings since she had known she was gay—they did not worsen after the assault. Lorna's therapist decided to treat these feelings as trauma-related given their connection to her beliefs about being gay, which was trauma-relevant.

Assessment of Other Comorbidities

As noted previously, the chronic social stressors experienced by SMW may also increase risk of other disorders among SMW, including depression and substance use disorders, which are also commonly comorbid with PTSD (King et al., 2008; Steele, Ross, Dobinson, Veldhuizen, & Tinmouth, 2009). SMW may also have an elevated risk of suicidality (King et al., 2008). Because these comorbidities have an impact on treatment course and planning, it is essential that clinical assessments include a good differential diagnostic evaluation and case conceptualization. In addition to assessment of symptoms, it can be helpful to conduct a functional analysis of the disorders, including examining the order of onset of disorders and how symptoms appear to interrelate. There may be a difference, for example, between a client who believes her alcohol use is a way of blocking out the traumatic event and one who views alcohol as a facilitator of socializing with her friends.

CASE EXAMPLE: MOIRA

Moira, a bisexual woman, presented for PTSD treatment following a history of childhood physical and sexual abuse. She had recently been hospitalized for suicidal ideation. She also met criteria for marijuana dependence and reported smoking three blunts of marijuana daily. The assessment included both a clinical interview and self-report measures of depression (Patient Health Questionnaire-9), PTSD (PCL), suicide risk (Suicide Behaviors Questionnaire–Revised), and substance use (Drug Use Disorders Identification Test). In discussing how her experiences fit together, Moira reported that she viewed her marijuana use as being closely linked with her PTSD symptoms, stating that she had tried to quit marijuana several times before but that she always relapsed because her PTSD was not treated. She reported, however, that since partnering with a man, she felt more isolated from her female friends and support network. Since that time, she noticed she had become more depressed and isolated, which had in turn led to the increase in suicidal ideation. She also reported that she was having trouble with sexual intimacy with her partner because some sex-related cues reminded her of the child sexual abuse. She would often cope by smoking prior to sexual intercourse to decrease her distress.

Cognitive–Behavioral Treatment Components for PTSD

To date, no clinical trials have evaluated evidence-based interventions for PTSD among SMW. In a systematic review of inclusion of sexual orientation in randomized controlled trials for anxiety and depression, only 1 article of 232 reported participants' sexual orientation (Heck, Mirabito, LaMaire, Linvingston, & Flentje, 2017). Thus, because it is currently unknown whether SMW have a differential treatment response to these treatments compared to their heterosexual counterparts, we next describe evidence-based interventions for PTSD that have established efficacy in general population samples. There are many psychological and pharmacological treatments for PTSD, but only cognitive–behavioral treatments received strong recommendations in the American Psychological Association's (2017) PTSD clinical practice guidelines based on a systematic review of the available research evidence. It is important to note that there are several different treatment guidelines with varying definitions of best practices with regard to PTSD (Forbes et al., 2010; National Institute for Health and Care Excellence, 2005; US Department of Veterans Affairs/US Department of Defense, 2010). Thus, our review is organized around common cognitive–behavioral strategies used in effective PTSD treatments for adult populations. When possible, we present evidence of the efficacy of treatments in sexual minority populations, which is mostly available in the form of case studies.

Cognitive–behavioral therapy (CBT) is a broad set of treatments that assist clients in practicing new patterns of thought and behavior. Evidence-based CBTs for PTSD typically address emotions and memories, and they use strategies including psychoeducation, teaching emotion regulation/coping skills, engaging in exposure, and/or assisting with cognitive restructuring (Schnyder et al., 2015). In several meta-analyses, CBT treatments were found to be efficacious in reducing PTSD symptoms (Bisson & Andrew, 2007; Bradley, Greene, Russ, Dutra, & Westen, 2005; Van Etten & Taylor, 1998). Since the publication of these meta-analyses, several randomized controlled studies have offered further support for the efficacy of CBT for PTSD (Hinton, Hofmann, Pollack, & Otto, 2009; Johnson, Zlotnick, & Perez, 2011; van Emmerik, Kamphuis, & Emmelkamp, 2008), including in internet-delivered form (Litz, Engel, Bryant, & Papa, 2007; Spence et al., 2011). A case study of the use of cognitive–behavioral conjoint therapy, a form of CBT, with a female active-duty service member with PTSD and her same-sex partner indicated that this treatment was associated with clinically meaningful reductions in PTSD symptoms that were maintained through a 2-month follow-up (Blount, Peterson, & Monson, 2017). A second case study that integrated exposure to trauma cues with cognitive restructuring in a gay man with PTSD and depression also reported reductions in symptoms of both disorders over the course of treatment (Chernoff, 2007).

Psychoeducation

Psychoeducation in CBT typically addresses information about the symptoms the person is experiencing, describes the treatment model and rationale, and describes what will be involved in treatment for both the client and the therapist. In PTSD treatments, psychoeducation often includes information that normalizes PTSD symptoms as common reactions to traumatic events. Although psychoeducation alone has not consistently been found to be effective for treatment of PTSD (Neuner,

Schauer, Klaschik, Karunakara, & Elbert, 2004; Oflaz, Hatipoğlu, & Aydin, 2008), it is a consistent element across trauma-focused CBTs. In working with SMW, additional elements may be useful to incorporate into psychoeducation, including discussion of the impact of societal bias on mental health, information on internal and external experiences of minority stress, and information on ways in which these experiences may increase vulnerability to trauma symptoms (Craig, Austin, & Alessi, 2013).

Skills Training

Emotion regulation and coping skills also may be taught as part of treatment and are part of some evidence-based treatments for PTSD (Cloitre, Koenen, Cohen, & Han, 2002). This may be accomplished overtly by addressing adaptive self-soothing skills, teaching mindfulness, introducing pleasant activity scheduling, or encouraging building social support. Skills training can also be conveyed indirectly through the process of tolerating affect through other parts of treatment. Given findings that experiential avoidance may play a role in maintaining PTSD among SMW (Gold et al., 2009, 2011), addressing emotional avoidance may be of particular importance in this population. Intervention strategies can include emotion identification and tolerating negative affect without avoiding, as well as strategies addressed next, such as exposure or cognitive restructuring. In adapting treatments for SMW, providers may also wish to work on identifying negative emotions related to minority stress (Pachankis, Hatzenbuehler, Rendina, Safren, & Parsons, 2015). Because clients may be unaware of the ways in which experiences of minority stress elicit various negative emotional states, increasing awareness of these effects may be helpful. For SMW, given the higher rates of substance misuse associated with trauma exposure (Pietrzak, Goldstein, Southwick, & Grant, 2011), it may be particularly helpful for providers to work with clients to identify means of coping with negative affect without the use of substances. Phase-based therapies that teach interpersonal and affect regulation skills have been found to be effective in treating PTSD and in increasing affect regulation (Cloitre et al., 2002, 2010). However, there is currently insufficient clinical literature about whether teaching emotional regulation or coping skills is necessary in PTSD treatment (Jongh et al., 2016) and particularly regarding when they are necessary when working with SMW.

Exposure

Several CBT treatments utilize exposure, with the rationale that repeated exposure to feared stimuli (e.g., thoughts, feelings, and situations associated with the trauma) extinguishes conditioned fear responses and creates new learning (Craske, Treanor, Conway, Zbozinek, & Vervliet, 2014; Foa, Rothbaum, Riggs, & Murdock, 1991). Examples of treatments utilizing exposure for PTSD include prolonged exposure (Foa et al., 1991), narrative exposure therapy (Schauer, Neuner, & Elbert, 2011), and virtual reality therapy (Rothbaum, Hodges, Ready, Graap, & Alarcon, 2001). In meta-analyses, therapies predominantly using exposure were highly effective in improving PTSD symptoms and secondary symptoms such as depression (Powers, Halpern, Ferenschak, Gillihan, & Foa, 2010). Although no studies to date have assessed the efficacy of exposure therapies for PTSD among sexual minorities per se, a study of men and women living with HIV that included many sexual minorities found that prolonged exposure was associated with significant reductions in PTSD symptoms, and these reductions were maintained at 6 months (Pacella et al., 2012). No studies to date have specifically examined exposure for PTSD among SMW.

Exposure can involve in vivo exposure, in which clients construct a list of feared stimuli that are then systematically confronted in real life either in session or between sessions. Clients typically remain in exposure situations until distress decreases by at least 50%; ending exposure exercises early can risk reinforcing avoidance. In vivo exposure can be a helpful way of addressing avoidance and has been found to have beneficial effects on depression as well as PTSD (Foa et al., 1999). When introducing in vivo exposures, it is important to identify a range of potential exposure targets. These are activities or situations the client has been avoiding because they are trauma-related reminders. The therapist should work collaboratively with the client to identify potential exposures that range from a low level of discomfort to a high level of discomfort and start the client at a level at which she can be successful. Starting too low is problematic because the client is likely to not experience enough distress to experience mastery, but if the exposure is too high in intensity, the client is more likely to avoid, especially when doing practice between sessions. Among SMW, incorporating exposure around minority stress may have additional benefits. For example, increasing social engagement through increasing community engagement and connectedness can be an in vivo exposure assignment and can also additionally reduce social withdrawal and isolation (Burton, Cooper, Feeny, & Zoellner, 2015). Examples of this include attending a community event even though there may be crowds or looking at books in the gay/lesbian section of a bookstore despite feelings of discomfort. As an additional consideration when conducting in vivo exposures, it is essential that exposures are, in fact, safe situations. This is standard clinical practice with in vivo exposures with any population; however, with sexual minorities, the clinician should be especially aware of any issues of concern regarding safety or hate crimes. Thus, being out as lesbian or bisexual in a situation with real risk would not be an appropriate in vivo exposure exercise.

Exposure can also take the form of imaginal exposure, in which the client verbally describes the trauma situation and revisits the memory until distress decreases. In some treatments, such as prolonged exposure, this may involve focusing on the worst memory, whereas in other treatments, such as narrative exposure therapy, this may involve working on each major traumatic memory. In general, when introducing the concept of imaginal exposure, it can be helpful to review the rationale, which can include the goal of organizing the memory, discriminating between a memory and the actual trauma, learning that one can tolerate the distress, and increasing a sense of mastery (Foa, Hembree, & Rothbaum, 2007; Hembree, Rauch, & Fa, 2004; Schauer et al., 2011). In implementing exposure-based techniques for SMW, there are several issues to consider. Given that SMW may have been exposed to multiple traumatic events (Morris & Balsam, 2003; Roberts et al., 2010), treatments that require the selection of a focal trauma, such as prolonged exposure, may be more clinically challenging (Mørkved et al., 2014), although it is important to note that prolonged exposure has been found to be effective for individuals who have experienced multiple traumatic events (McDonagh et al., 2005; Van Minnen, Arntz, & Keijsers, 2002). Similarly, events that are discriminatory or stressful, but which are not criterion A traumatic events, may increase PTSD symptoms among SMW (Robinson & Rubin, 2016), but these types of events are not typically included as focal events for imaginal exposure. It is unclear to what extent including non-criterion A traumatic events in imaginal exposure is beneficial. Evaluating potential ways to work with these types of events within an exposure-based treatment is one area in which more research is necessary.

CASE EXAMPLE: MOIRA

Moira and her therapist are working to identify the memory to focus on in imaginal exposure:

> THERAPIST: Moira, I know you've survived several traumatic events. Is there one memory that really haunts you? One that bothers you more than others?
>
> CLIENT: It's just all of it. It's hard to pick just one thing. The times that people have yelled horrible things at me, called me names, those were awful, especially when I was a teenager. My mom used to tell me I was disgusting, that I disgusted her.
>
> THERAPIST: What about in nightmares or thoughts you can't keep out of your head? Is there one that comes up more often than others?
>
> CLIENT: I really don't like to talk about it . . . but yeah. There are some really awful memories from when I was a kid.
>
> THERAPIST: Is there one you were hoping to never really have to talk about? Or if I had a magic wand and could make one go away right now, which would you choose? I know it's hard, but working on the worst memory is the best way to help you get better. And once you work on that memory, it tends to help with all of the other memories too.
>
> CLIENT: There was the first time my stepdad came into my bedroom and touched me. I was so scared. I was hoping to never tell anyone about that.
>
> THERAPIST: That may be our memory to start with then.

COGNITIVE RESTRUCTURING

The last element found in many of the evidence-based treatments for PTSD is cognitive restructuring, which involves identifying and replacing distorted thoughts stemming from trauma exposure. Beliefs targeted in trauma-focused CBTs may be beliefs about the meaning, causes, and consequences of the traumatic event; beliefs about the meaning of the PTSD symptoms themselves; or non-trauma specific negative cognitions (Schnyder et al., 2015). Cognitive restructuring also tends to address metacognition, or increasing one's own awareness of thoughts and feelings, and cognitive flexibility. Examples of treatments utilizing cognitive restructuring for PTSD include cognitive processing therapy (CPT; Resick & Schnicke, 1993) and Ehler and Clark's cognitive therapy for PTSD (Ehlers, Clark, Hackmann, McManus, & Fennell, 2005; Ehlers et al., 2003). In meta-analyses, therapies using cognitive restructuring were highly effective in improving PTSD symptoms and secondary symptoms such as depression (Watts et al., 2013), and trauma-focused CBTs decreased trauma-related cognitions more than did other treatments (Diehle, Schmitt, Daams, Boer, & Lindauer, 2014). In addition, changes in cognitions predict PTSD and depression changes during treatment (McLean, Yeh, Rosenfield, & Foa, 2015). Although no studies have evaluated the efficacy of CPT among SMW, a case study describing the use of CPT with a gay man who had experienced a bias-based physical assault reported lower acute stress disorder and symptoms of depression at post-treatment and 3-month follow-up (Kaysen, Lostutter, & Goines, 2005). In addition, PTSD-related cognitions and internalized heterosexism improved over the course of treatment.

When using cognitive restructuring to address PTSD and other trauma-related symptoms among SMW, clinicians should be prepared to address cognitions related to minority stress. This may include negative beliefs about the self related to one's sexual identity or negative beliefs about other sexual minority individuals based on internalized societal messages (Meyer, 2003). These beliefs contribute to depression and anxiety and can increase the risk of PTSD following trauma exposure (Cerezo, 2016; Szymanski, Kashubeck-West, & Meyer, 2008). In situations in which the traumatic event is viewed as being "caused" by one's sexual identity or in which individuals believe they were targeted due to their sexual identity, this could potentially reinforce these types of negative cognitions (Herek, Cogan, & Gillis, 2002; Herek, Gillis, & Cogan, 1999; Levin, 1999). Conversely, individuals who have experienced sexual trauma may believe the cultural myth that the sexual assault "caused" their sexual identity, which may be a further source of distress (Balsam, 2002). Bisexual women may find additional challenges due to biphobia within the lesbian, gay, bisexual, and transgender (LGBT) community, which can lead to further maladaptive beliefs about self or others that can maintain PTSD and depression. Examples of maladaptive cognitions that SMW may endorse following traumatic events are presented in the following list. This list is in no way meant to be comprehensive but, rather, is meant to highlight some of the complexities between sexual identity and trauma. Some of these cognitions are more trauma specific, and others are more general:

Because I was rejected by people I trusted, I cannot trust anyone.
I was targeted because I'm a lesbian; therefore I can never be safe.
If I hadn't been so "out," it wouldn't have happened.

(In the case of same-sex intimate partner violence) If I tell people my
    partner hurt me, it will be bad for the LGBT community.
When bad things happened to me, like the traumatic events, it's because
    I deserved them.
The child sexual abuse made me gay because it made me scared of men.
(In the case of a bisexual woman) If my lesbian friends knew I was raped on
    a date with a guy, they would tell me I should have known better and that
    it was my fault.
Wanting sex with a woman is immoral.
It was my fault because I was drunk.
If people know I'm lesbian/bisexual, they'll reject me.
Bad things always happen to gay people.
Any sign of discrimination means I'm going to be raped again.
The world hates me.
Other lesbian/bisexual women won't accept me.

It is important to note that the job of the therapist in conducting cognitive
restructuring is not to develop a new thought for the client, nor is it to try to
convince the client out of the old thought or to prove a point. Doing so may feel
especially invalidating to SMW whose therapists have different sexual identities
or worldviews than their own. Indeed, the therapist may not be correct in their assessment of the client's environment and experiences; it is important to remember
that the client understands her own world better than any therapist can. The job of
the cognitive therapist is to ask curious questions in a spirit of collaborative em-
piricism to help the client develop a new understanding of herself and her world
that is accurate and balanced. This will also include the reality of the discrimination and challenges that the client faces, without going too far.

CASE EXAMPLE: JAINA

Jaina and her therapist are working on beliefs about the sexual assault:

THERAPIST: One of the beliefs you've said is hard for you is that you should
    have fought back. Is that one that still feels true for you now?
CLIENT: Yeah . . . I was a soldier. I was trained to fight. But I just lay there
    and let him rape me.
THERAPIST: Is that one you want to work on together?
CLIENT: I think so. It's one where I just feel so ashamed that I let it happen.
THERAPIST: That feeling of shame is usually a tip off for us that it's a good
    belief for us to tackle together.
CLIENT: OK.
THERAPIST: Alright, so you are saying you let him rape you. Tell me a little
    about the context. What was going on that that time?

CLIENT: Well, he was a member of my platoon. We were buddies and hung out a lot. I thought I could trust him, that he had my back. I was so stupid!

THERAPIST: So, this was someone you thought you could rely on. Were there reasons you had at that time to think otherwise?

CLIENT: No. Until he started hitting on me, things were fine.

THERAPIST: And once he starting hitting on you?

CLIENT: Then he threatened he would tell the guys in my platoon I was a dyke. I was terrified! It could destroy my career. I was worried they would rape me. Anyway, I didn't really think he would hurt me. He was my friend.

THERAPIST: And during the rape?

CLIENT: During the rape, I just froze. I couldn't believe it was happening. And I was still so scared he would tell. That was what kept going through my head.

THERAPIST: What might have happened if you had fought back? How might it have ended differently?

CLIENT: Well I could have stopped it!

THERAPIST: Yes, that's one possibility. Do rapes always stop when people fight back?

CLIENT: I don't know, probably not. And he was stronger than me. He might have raped me anyway. He might have killed me. He was pretty jacked up. I guess maybe . . . there was nothing I could have done.

THERAPIST: Right. It sounds to me like you did the best you could to get through it. When you think about it that way, does it change how you feel about it?

CLIENT: I feel less ashamed. I feel more pissed at him and sad.

Implications of Common Comorbidities on Treatment

In most of the clinical trials on treatment of PTSD, common comorbidities such as depression, other anxiety disorders, and personality disorders have been included. In addition, the individuals included in the research trials have typically been exposed to multiple traumatic events rather than a single trauma. Thus, clinical trials tend to be representative of many clients seen in clinical practice, including those who are relatively complex. However, there are other comorbidities that are more likely to be excluded from clinical trials, such as psychotic disorders or serious self-harm or suicidal behavior. In addition, some comorbidities may alter the course of treatment. For example, women with depression and PTSD may be more likely to drop out of PTSD treatment (Bryant, Moulds, Guthrie, Dang, & Nixon, 2003; McDonagh et al., 2005). Women who are experiencing more dissociation and emotional numbing may respond better to treatments that include more exposure rather than purely cognitive interventions (Resick, Suvak, Johnides, Mitchell, & Iverson, 2012). For women with PTSD and substance use disorders, as may be somewhat more common among SMW, the research is still evolving. It appears that both substance use treatment alone and combined treatments that include coping skills and trauma-related content are effective in addressing comorbid PTSD and substance use (van Dam, Vedel, Ehring, & Emmelkamp, 2012). Some preliminary research suggests that with proper support, standard PTSD treatments may be well-tolerated by those with PTSD and substance use disorders (Coffey et al., 2016; Mills et al., 2012; Sannibale et al., 2013). In general, this is an area that broadly needs more research attention in order to best guide clinical decision-making.

FUTURE DIRECTIONS AND EMERGING TRENDS

There are highly effective treatments for PTSD and related symptoms that have been tested in large, well-conducted research trials among (presumably) predominantly heterosexual samples. Across these treatments, helping the client acquire a sense of mastery over the traumatic event, approach the memory of the trauma, and access emotions about the event appear to be important in addressing PTSD. However, there is minimal information about how these treatments may work for SMW. Existing studies often do not report the sexual orientation of their participants, and those that do so do not examine differences in treatment response in SMW compared to other groups. Thus, clinicians must rely on evidence-based principles rather than being able to truly assess the fit of these treatments for SMW.

One challenge in adapting treatment approaches for the needs of SMW is the need for theory to better address the issue of comorbidity in clinical presentations. Application of syndemic theory to SMW may be one way to address this challenge. Syndemic theory proposes that there are mutually reinforcing interactions between diseases and social conditions, which contribute to health disparities (Singer, 2010). For example, as noted in Moira's example presented previously, social conditions such as child abuse and other experiences of discrimination and biphobia interact with her experiences of PTSD, marijuana use, and suicidality, which also reinforce each other. Based on this theory, treating PTSD in isolation without addressing the contributions of societal stressors, ongoing insidious trauma, and other mental health concerns such as suicidality, substance use, or depression will be less likely to be successful. Given interrelationships between these disorders, as well as other health conditions that occur more frequently among SMW such as obesity and cardiovascular disease (Mayer et al., 2008), it may be particularly important to consider health disparities in a more holistic way. One option may be to move toward more transdiagnostic interventions that address mental health, health risk behaviors, and physical health in an integrative way. It is also important to target social conditions directly through anti-bias initiatives, policy changes, and other direct action.

Currently, we do not know the ways in which treatment adaptation may be useful and necessary in meeting the clinical needs of SMW. This ranges from whether additional content should be included in existing PTSD treatment manuals or whether it is better to use unadapted manuals enriched with clinical examples and suggestions for how to make the protocol culturally sensitive to the needs of SMW. Adaptation for SMW could include changes to treatment content (e.g., use of culturally relevant examples or homework assignments), clinician training, or delivery method of the treatment. For example, it may be that SMW prefer to receive therapy remotely due to concerns about stigma or difficulty finding supportive clinicians. The ability to access remote providers with appropriate cultural expertise could be of particular interest. Development of technology-based interventions, such as apps or web-based treatments, that are created particularly for SMW may also be helpful, especially for women in rural areas or who have difficulty finding providers. Treatments may also need to be adapted to better account for insidious trauma and to guide therapists in how best to address these types of events within a trauma-focused treatment. In summary, studies that examine SMW's response to existing evidence-based PTSD treatments and studies that empirically test the impact of adaptation are needed.

A final area in need of research relates to how best to guide clinical training programs, both in the adaptation of evidence-based practice and in application of those principles to SMW. This includes attention to both didactic training as well as to clinical training and supervision. Training programs also need to develop more nuanced curriculum that can attend to the intersectionality of multiple marginalized identities. There is a surprising dearth of research on what is effective about *how* we teach in general or what evidence-based teaching consists of, especially in the acquisition of complex clinical skills. Being able to apply those skills and adapt them to the unique needs of the client in the room, while also being aware of the therapist's (or supervisor's) own culturally based viewpoint, is essential. Training the next generation of clinicians to be sensitive to and aware of SMW's treatment needs is an essential component of providing them with equitable, effective care and ultimately reducing health disparities.

REFERENCES

Alessi, E. J., Martin, J. I., Gyamerah, A., & Meyer, I. H. (2013). Prejudice events and traumatic stress among heterosexuals and lesbians, gay men, and bisexuals. *Journal of Aggression, Maltreatment & Trauma, 22*(5), 510–526.

American Psychiatric Association. (2013). *Diagnostic and statistical manual of mental disorders* (5th ed.). Arlington, VA: American Psychiatric Publishing.

American Psychological Association. (2017). Clinical practice guideline for the treatment of posttraumatic stress disorder (PTSD) in adults. Retrieved from https://www. apa.org/about/offices/directorates/guidelines/ptsd.pdf

Archer, J., & Haigh, A. (1999). Sex differences in beliefs about aggression: Opponent's sex and the form of aggression. *British Journal of Social Psychology, 38*(1), 71–84.

Austin, S. B., Jun, H., Jackson, B., Spiegelman, D., Rick-Edwards, J., Corliss, H. L., & Wright, R. J. (2008). Disparities in child abuse victimization in lesbian, bisexual, and heterosexual women in the Nurses' Health Study II. *Journal of Women's Health, 17*, 597–606.

Balsam, K. F. (2002). Traumatic victimization in the lives of lesbian and bisexual women: A contextual approach. *Journal of Lesbian Studies, 7*(1), 1–14.

Balsam, K. F., Beadnell, B., & Molina, Y. (2013). The Daily Heterosexist Experiences Questionnaire: Measuring minority stress among lesbian, gay, bisexual, and transgender adults. *Measurement and Evaluation in Counseling and Development, 46*(1), 3–25.

Balsam, K. F., Rothblum, E. D., & Beauchaine, T. P. (2005). Victimization over the life span: A comparison of lesbian, gay, bisexual, and heterosexual siblings. *Journal of Consulting and Clinical Psychology, 73*, 477–487.

Bandermann, K. M., & Szymanski, D. M. (2014). Exploring coping mediators between heterosexist oppression and posttraumatic stress symptoms among lesbian, gay, and bisexual persons. *Psychology of Sexual Orientation and Gender Diversity, 1*, 213–224.

Bisson, J., & Andrew, M. (2007). Psychological treatment of post-traumatic stress disorder (PTSD). *Cochrane Database of Systematic Reviews, 18*(3), CD003388.

Blevins, C. A., Weathers, F. W., Davis, M. T., Witte, T. K., & Domino, J. L. (2015). The Posttraumatic Stress Disorder Checklist for DSM-5 (PCL-5): Development and initial psychometric evaluation. *Journal of Traumatic Stress, 28*(6), 489–498.

Blount, T. H., Peterson, A. L., & Monson, C. M. (2017). A case study of cognitive-behavioral conjoint therapy for combat-related PTSD in a same-sex military couple. *Cognitive and Behavioral Practice, 24*(3), 319–328.

Bostwick, W. B., Boyd, C. J., Hughes, T. L., West, B. T., & McCabe, S. E. (2014). Discrimination and mental health among lesbian, gay, and bisexual adults in the United States. *American Journal of Orthopsychiatry, 84*(1), 35–45.

Bradley, R., Greene, J., Russ, E., Dutra, L., & Westen, D. (2005). A multidimensional meta-analysis of psychotherapy for PTSD. *American Journal of Psychiatry, 162*, 214–227.

Breslau, N. (2009). The epidemiology of trauma, PTSD, and other posttrauma disorders. *Trauma, Violence, & Abuse, 10*(3), 198–210.

Brown, L. S. (2003). Sexuality, lies, and loss: Lesbian, gay, and bisexual perspectives on trauma. *Journal of Trauma Practice, 2*, 55–68.

Bryant, R. A., Moulds, M. L., Guthrie, R. M., Dang, S. T., & Nixon, R. D. V. (2003). Imaginal exposure alone and imaginal exposure with cognitive restructuring in treatment of posttraumatic stress disorder. *Journal of Consulting and Clinical Psychology, 71*, 706–712.

Burton, M. S., Cooper, A. A., Feeny, N. C., & Zoellner, L. A. (2015). The enhancement of natural resilience in trauma interventions. *Journal of Contemporary Psychotherapy, 45*, 193–204.

Cahill, S. P., Rothbaum, B. O., Resick, P. A., & Follette, V. M. (2008). Cognitive-behavioral therapy for adults. In E. B. Foa, T. M. Keane, M. J. Friedman, & J. A. Cohen (Eds.), *Effective treatments for PTSD: Practice guidelines from the International Society for Traumatic Stress Studies* (2nd ed., 139–222). New York, NY: Guilford.

Cameron, R. P., & Gusman, D. (2003). The Primary Care PTSD Screen (PC-PTSD): Development and operating characteristics. *Primary Care Psychiatry, 9*(1), 9–14.

Cerezo, A. (2016). The impact of discrimination on mental health symptomatology in sexual minority immigrant Latinas. *Psychology of Sexual Orientation and Gender Diversity, 3*(3), 283–292.

Chernoff, R. A. (2007). Treating an HIV/AIDS patient's PTSD and medication nonadherence with cognitive–behavioral therapy: A principle-based approach. *Cognitive and Behavioral Practice, 14*(1), 107–117.

Cloitre, M., Koenen, K. C., Cohen, L. R., & Han, H. (2002). Skills training in affective and interpersonal regulation followed by exposure: A phase-based treatment for PTSD related to childhood abuse. *Journal of Consulting and Clinical Psychology, 70*(5), 1067–1074.

Cloitre, M., Stovall-McClough, K. C., Nooner, K., Zorbas, P., Cherry, S., Jackson, C. L., ... Petkova, E. (2010). Treatment for PTSD related to childhood abuse: A randomized controlled trial. *American Journal of Psychiatry, 167*(8), 915–924.

Cochran, S. D., & Mays, V. M. (2000). Relation between psychiatric syndromes and behaviorally defined sexual orientation in a sample of the US population. *American Journal of Epidemiology, 151*, 516–523.

Cochran, S. D., Sullivan, J. G., & Mays, V. M. (2003). Prevalence of mental disorders, psychological distress, and mental health services use among lesbian, gay, and bisexual adults in the United States. *Journal of Consulting and Clinical Psychology, 71*, 53–61.

Coffey, S. F., Schumacher, J. A., Nosen, E., Henslee, A. M., Lappen, A., & Stasiewicz, P. (2016). Trauma-focused exposure therapy for chronic posttraumatic stress disorder in alcohol and drug dependent patients: A randomized clinical trial. *Psychology of Addictive Behaviors, 30*(7), 778–790. http://doi.org/10.1037/adb0000201

Craig, S. L., Austin, A., & Alessi, E. (2013). Gay affirmative cognitive behavioral therapy for sexual minority youth: A clinical adaptation. *Clinical Social Work Journal, 41*, 258–266.

Craske, M. G., Treanor, M., Conway, C. C., Zbozinek, T., & Vervliet, B. (2014). Maximizing exposure therapy: An inhibitory learning approach. *Behaviour Research and Therapy, 58*, 10–23.

D'Augelli, A. R., Grossman, A. H., & Starks, M. T. (2006). Childhood gender atypicality, victimization, and PTSD among lesbian, gay, and bisexual youth. *Journal of Interpersonal Violence, 21*, 1462–1482.

Descamps, M. J., Rothblum, E., Bradford, J., & Ryan, C. (2000). Mental health impact of child sexual abuse, rape, intimate partner violence, and hate crimes in the National Lesbian Health Care Survey. *Journal of Gay & Lesbian Social Services, 11*(1), 27–55.

Diehle, J., Schmitt, K., Daams, J. G., Boer, F., & Lindauer, R. J. (2014). Effects of psychotherapy on trauma-related cognitions in posttraumatic stress disorder: A meta-analysis. *Journal of Traumatic Stress, 27*(3), 257–264.

Drabble, L., Trocki, K. F., Hughes, T. L., Korcha, R. A., & Lown, A. E. (2013). Sexual orientation differences in the relationship between victimization and hazardous drinking among women in the National Alcohol Survey. *Psychology of Addictive Behaviors, 27*(3), 639–648.

Dworkin, E. R., Gilmore, A. K., Bedard-Gilligan, M., Lehavot, K., & Kaysen, D. (2018). Predicting PTSD severity from experiences of trauma and heterosexism in lesbian and bisexual women: A longitudinal study of cognitive mediators. *Journal of Counseling Psychology, 65*(3), 324–333.

Ehlers, A., Clark, D. M., Hackmann, A., McManus, F., & Fennell, M. (2005). Cognitive therapy for post-traumatic stress disorder: Development and evaluation. *Behaviour Research and Therapy, 43*(4), 413–431. http://doi.org/10.1016/j.brat.2004.03.006

Ehlers, A., Clark, D. M., Hackmann, A., McManus, F., Fennell, M., Herbert, C., & Mayou, R. (2003). A randomized controlled trial of cognitive therapy, a self-help booklet, and repeated assessments as early interventions for posttraumatic stress disorder. *Archives of General Psychiatry, 60*(10), 1024–1032. http://doi.org/10.1001/archpsyc.60.10.1024

Foa, E. B., Dancu, C. V., Hembree, E. A., Jaycox, L. H., Meadows, E. A., & Street, G. P. (1999). A comparison of exposure therapy, stress inoculation training, and their combination for reducing posttraumatic stress disorder in female assault victims. *Journal of Consulting and Clinical Psychology, 67*(2), 194–200.

Foa, E. B., Hembree, E. A., & Rothbaum, B. O. (2007). *Prolonged exposure therapy for PTSD*. New York, NY: Oxford University Press.

Foa, E. B., & Kozak, M. J. (1986). Emotional processing of fear: Exposure to corrective information. *Psychological Bulletin, 99*(1), 20–35.

Foa, E. B., & Rothbaum, B. O. (1998). *Treating the trauma of rape. Cognitive–behaviour therapy for PTSD*. New York, NY: Guilford.

Foa, E. B., Rothbaum, B. O., Riggs, D. S., & Murdock, T. B. (1991). Treatment of posttraumatic stress disorder in rape victims: A comparison between cognitive–behavioral procedures and counseling. *Journal of Consulting and Clinical Psychology, 59*(5), 715.

Forbes, D., Creamer, M., Bisson, J. I., Cohen, J. A., Crow, B. E., Foa, E. B., . . . Ursano, R. J. (2010). A guide to guidelines for the treatment of PTSD and related conditions. *Journal of Traumatic Stress, 23*(5), 537–552.

Gilman, S. E., Cochran, S. D., Mays, V. M., Hughes, M., Ostrow, D., & Kessler, R. C. (2001). Risk of psychiatric disorders among individuals reporting same-sex sexual partners in the National Comorbidity Survey. *American Journal of Public Health, 91*, 933–939.

Gilmore, A. K., Koo, K. H., Nguyen, H. V., Granato, H. F., Hughes, T. L., & Kaysen, D. (2014). Sexual assault, drinking norms, and drinking behavior among a national sample of lesbian and bisexual women. *Addictive Behaviors, 39*(3), 630–636.

Gold, S. D., Dickstein, B. D., Marx, B. P., & Lexington, J. M. (2009). Psychological outcomes among lesbian sexual assault survivors: An examination of the roles of internalized homophobia and experiential avoidance. *Psychology of Women Quarterly, 33*, 54–66.

Gold, S. D., Feinstein, B. A., Skidmore, W. C., & Marx, B. P. (2011). Childhood physical abuse, internalized homophobia, and experiential avoidance among lesbians and gay men. *Psychological Trauma, 3*, 50–60.

Hatzenbuehler, M. L. (2009). How does sexual minority stigma "get under the skin"? A psychological mediation framework. *Psychological Bulletin, 135*, 707–730.

Heck, N. C., Mirabito, L. A., LaMaire, K., Linvingston, N. A., & Flentje, A. (2017). Omitted data in randomized controlled trials for anxiety and depression: A systematic review of the inclusion of sexual orientation and gender identity. *Journal of Consulting and Clinical Psychology, 85*, 72–76.

Hembree, E. A., Rauch, S. A., & Foa, E. B. (2004). Beyond the manual: The insider's guide to prolonged exposure therapy for PTSD. *Cognitive and Behavioral Practice, 10*(1), 22–30.

Herek, G. M. (2009). Hate crimes and stigma-related experiences among sexual minority adults in the United States: Prevalence estimates from a national probability sample. *Journal of Interpersonal Violence, 24*(1), 54–74.

Herek, G. M., Cogan, J. C., & Gillis, J. R. (2002). Victim experiences in hate crimes based on sexual orientation. *Journal of Social Issues, 58*(2), 319–339.

Herek, G. M., Gillis, J. R., & Cogan, J. C. (1999). Psychological sequelae of hate-crime victimization among lesbian, gay, and bisexual adults. *Journal of Consulting and Clinical Psychology, 67,* 945–951.

Hinton, D. E., Hofmann, S. G., Pollack, M. H., & Otto, M. W. (2009). Mechanisms of efficacy of CBT for Cambodian refugees with PTSD: Improvement in emotion regulation and orthostatic blood pressure response. *CNS Neuroscience & Therapeutics, 15*(3), 255–263.

Hughes, T., McCabe, S. E., Wilsnack, S. C., West, B. T., & Boyd, C. J. (2010). Victimization and substance use disorders in a national sample of heterosexual and sexual minority women and men. *Addiction, 105,* 2130–2140.

Hughes T. L., Johnson T., & Wilsnack, S. C. (2001). Sexual assault and alcohol abuse: A comparison of lesbians and heterosexual women. *Journal of Substance Abuse, 13,* 515–532.

Hughes, T. L., Szalacha, L. A., Johnson, T. P., Kinnison, K. E., Wilsnack, S. C., & Cho, Y. (2010). Sexual victimization and hazardous drinking among heterosexual and sexual minority women. *Addictive Behaviors, 35*(12), 1152–1156.

Johnson, D. M., Zlotnick, C., & Perez, S. (2011). Cognitive behavioral treatment of PTSD in residents of battered women's shelters: Results of a randomized clinical trial. *Journal of Consulting and Clinical Psychology, 79*(4), 542–551.

Jongh, A., Resick, P. A., Zoellner, L. A., Minnen, A., Lee, C. W., Monson, C. M., . . . Rauch, S. A. (2016). Critical analysis of the current treatment guidelines for complex PTSD in adults. *Depression and Anxiety, 33*(5), 359–369.

Katz-Wise, S. L., & Hyde, J. S. (2012). Victimization experiences of lesbian, gay, and bisexual individuals: A meta-analysis. *Journal of Sex Research, 49*(2–3), 142–167.

Kaysen, D., Lostutter, T., & Goines, M. (2005). Cognitive processing therapy for acute stress disorder resulting from an anti-gay assault. *Cognitive & Behavioral Practice, 12*(3), 278–289.

King, M., Semlyen, J., Tai, S. S., Killaspy, H., Osborn, D., Popelyuk, D., & Nazareth, I. (2008). A systematic review of mental disorder, suicide, and deliberate self harm in lesbian, gay and bisexual people. *BMC Psychiatry, 8,* 70.

Lang, P. J. (1977). Imagery in therapy: An information processing analysis of fear. *Behavior Therapy, 8,* 862–886.

Lang, P. J. (1979). A bio-informational theory of emotional imagery. *Psychophysiology, 16,* 495–512.

Lehavot, K., & Simpson, T. L. (2014). Trauma, posttraumatic stress disorder, and depression among sexual minority and heterosexual women veterans. *Journal of Counseling Psychology, 61*(3), 392.

Levin, B. (1999). Hate crimes worse by definition. *Journal of Contemporary Criminal Justice, 15*(1), 6–21.

Litz, B. T., Engel, C. C., Bryant, R. A., & Papa, A. (2007). A randomized, controlled proof-of-concept trial of an internet-based, therapist-assisted self-management treatment for posttraumatic stress disorder. *American Journal of Psychiatry, 164*(11), 1676–1684.

LoSavio, S. T., Dillon, K. H., & Resick, P. A. (2017). Cognitive factors in the development, maintenance, and treatment of post-traumatic stress disorder. *Current Opinion in Psychology, 14,* 18–22.

Mayer, K. H., Bradford, J. B., Makadon, H. J., Stall, R., Goldhammer, H., & Landers, S. (2008). Sexual and gender minority health: What we know and what needs to be done. *American Journal of Public Health, 98*(6), 989–995. http://doi.org/10.2105/AJPH.2007.127811

McDonagh, A., Friedman, M., McHugo, G., Ford, J., Sengupta, A., Mueser, K., . . . Descamps, M. (2005). Randomized trial of cognitive–behavioral therapy for chronic posttraumatic stress disorder in adult female survivors of childhood sexual abuse. *Journal of Consulting and Clinical Psychology, 73*(3), 515–524.

McLaughlin, K. A., Hatzenbuehler, M. L., & Keyes, K. M. (2010). Responses to discrimination and psychiatric disorders among Black, Hispanic, female, and lesbian, gay, and bisexual individuals. *American Journal of Public Health, 100*(8), 1477–1484.

McLean, C. P., Yeh, R., Rosenfield, D., & Foa, E. B. (2015). Changes in negative cognitions mediate PTSD symptom reductions during client-centered therapy and prolonged exposure for adolescents. *Behaviour Research and Therapy, 68*, 64–69.

Meyer, I. H. (2003). Prejudice, social stress, and mental health in lesbian, gay, and bisexual populations: Conceptual issues and research evidence. *Psychological Bulletin, 129*, 674–697.

Mills, K. L., Teesson, M., Back, S. E., Brady, K. T., Baker, A. L., Hopwood, S., . . . Ewer, P. L. (2012). Integrated exposure-based therapy for co-occurring posttraumatic stress disorder and substance dependence: A randomized controlled trial. *Journal of the American Medical Association, 308*, 690–699. http://dx.doi.org/10.1001/jama.2012.9071

Mørkved, N., Hartmann, K., Aarsheim, L. M., Holen, D., Milde, A. M., Bomyea, J., & Thorp, S. R. (2014). A comparison of narrative exposure therapy and prolonged exposure therapy for PTSD. *Clinical Psychology Review, 34*(6), 453–467.

Morris, J. F., & Balsam, K. F. (2003). Lesbian and bisexual women's experiences of victimization: Mental health, revictimization, and sexual identity development. *Journal of Lesbian Studies, 7*(4), 67–85.

National Institute for Health and Care Excellence. (2005). Post-traumatic stress disorder: Management. Retrieved from https://www.nice.org.uk/guidance/cg26

Neuner, F., Schauer, M., Klaschik, C., Karunakara, U., & Elbert, T. (2004). A comparison of narrative exposure therapy, supportive counseling, and psychoeducation for treating posttraumatic stress disorder in an African refugee settlement. *Journal of Consulting and Clinical Psychology, 72*(4), 579–587.

Nishith, P., Resick, P. A., & Griffin, M. G. (2002). Pattern of change in prolonged exposure and cognitive-processing therapy for female rape victims with posttraumatic stress disorder. *Journal of Consulting and Clinical Psychology, 70*(4), 880–886.

Oflaz, F., Hatipoğlu, S., & Aydin, H. (2008). Effectiveness of psychoeducation intervention on post-traumatic stress disorder and coping styles of earthquake survivors. *Journal of Clinical Nursing, 17*(5), 677–687.

Pacella, M. L., Armelie, A., Boarts, J., Wagner, G., Jones, T., Feeny, N., & Delahanty, D. L. (2012). The impact of prolonged exposure on PTSD symptoms and associated psychopathology in people living with HIV: A randomized test of concept. *AIDS and Behavior, 16*(5), 1327–1340. http://doi.org/10.1007/s10461-011-0076-y

Pachankis, J., Hatzenbuehler, M., Rendina, J., Safren, S., & Parsons, J. (2015). LGB-affirmative cognitive–behavioral therapy for young adult gay and bisexual men: A randomized controlled trial of a transdiagnostic minority stress approach. *Journal of Consulting and Clinical Psychology, 33*(4), 395–401.

Pietrzak, R. H., Goldstein, R. B., Southwick, S. M., & Grant, B. F. (2011). Prevalence and Axis I comorbidity of full and partial posttraumatic stress disorder in the United States: Results from Wave 2 of the National Epidemiologic Survey on Alcohol and Related Conditions. *Journal of Anxiety Disorders, 25*, 456–465.

Powers, M. B., Halpern, J. M., Ferenschak, M. P., Gillihan, S. J., & Foa, E. B. (2010). A meta-analytic review of prolonged exposure for posttraumatic stress disorder. *Clinical Psychology Review, 30*(6), 635–641.

Resick, P. A., Monson, C. M., & Chard, K. M. (2006). Cognitive processing therapy: Veteran/military version. *Clinical Psychology, 74*, 898–907.

Resick, P. A., & Schnicke, M. (1993). *Cognitive processing therapy for rape victims: A treatment manual* (Vol. 4). Thousand Oaks, CA: Sage.

Resick, P. A., Suvak, M. K., Johnides, B. D., Mitchell, K. S., & Iverson, K. M. (2012). The impact of dissociation on PTSD treatment with cognitive processing therapy. *Depression and Anxiety, 29*, 718–730.

Rhew, I. C., Stappenbeck, C. A., Bedard-Gilligan, M., Hughes, T., & Kaysen, D. (2017). Effects of sexual assault on alcohol use and consequences among young adult sexual minority women. *Journal of Consulting and Clinical Psychology, 85*(5), 424–433.

Roberts, A. L., Austin, S. B., Corliss, H. L., Vandermorris, A. K., & Koenen, K. C. (2010). Pervasive trauma exposure among US sexual orientation minority adults and risk of posttraumatic stress disorder. *American Journal of Public Health, 100*(12), 2433–2441.

Roberts, A. L., Rosaria, M., Corliss, H. L., Koenen, K. C., & Austin, S. B. (2012). Elevated risk of posttraumatic stress in sexual minority youths: Mediation by childhood abuse and gender nonconformity. *American Journal of Public Health, 102*, 1587–1593.

Robinson, J. L., & Rubin, L. J. (2016). Homonegative microaggressions and posttraumatic stress symptoms. *Journal of Gay & Lesbian Mental Health, 20*, 57–69.

Root, M. P. (1992). Reconstructing the impact of trauma on personality development: A feminist perspective. In L. S. Brown & M. Ballou (Eds.), *Personality and psychopathology: Feminist reappraisals* (pp. 229–266). New York, NY: Guilford.

Rothbaum, B. O., Hodges, L. F., Ready, D., Graap, K., & Alarcon, R. D. (2001). Virtual reality exposure therapy for Vietnam veterans with posttraumatic stress disorder. *Journal of Clinical Psychiatry, 62*(8), 617–622.

Rothman, E. F., Exner, D., & Baughman, A. L. (2011). The prevalence of sexual assault against people who identify as gay, lesbian, or bisexual in the United States: A systematic review. *Trauma, Violence, & Abuse, 12*(2), 55–66.

Sandfort, T. G., de Graaf, R., Bijl, R. V., & Schnabel, P. (2001). Same-sex sexual behavior and psychiatric disorders: Findings from the Netherlands Mental Health Survey and Incidence Study (NEMESIS). *Archives of General Psychiatry, 58*, 85–91.

Sannibale, C., Teesson, M., Creamer, M., Sitharthan, T., Bryant, R. A., Sutherland, K., ... Peek-O'Leary, M. (2013). Randomized controlled trial of cognitive behaviour therapy for comorbid post-traumatic stress disorder and alcohol use disorders. *Addiction, 108*, 1397–1410. http:// dx.doi.org/10.1111/add.12167

Schauer, M., Neuner, F., & Elbert, T. (2011). *Narrative exposure therapy: A short-term treatment for traumatic stress disorders*. Cambridge, MA: Hogrefe.

Schnyder, U., Ehlers, A., Elbert, T., Foa, E. B., Gersons, B. P., Resick, P. A., ... Cloitre, M. (2015). Psychotherapies for PTSD: What do they have in common? *European Journal of Psychotraumatology, 6*.

Singer, M. (2010). Pathogen–pathogen interaction: A syndemic model of complex bio-social processes in disease. *Virulence*, *1*(1), 10–18.

Spence, J., Titov, N., Dear, B. F., Johnston, L., Solley, K., Lorian, C., . . . Schwenke, G. (2011). Randomized controlled trial of internet-delivered cognitive behavioral therapy for posttraumatic stress disorder. *Depression and Anxiety*, *28*(7), 541–550.

Steele, L. S., Ross, L. E., Dobinson, C., Veldhuizen, S., & Tinmouth, J. M. (2009). Women's sexual orientation and health: Results from a Canadian population-based survey. *Women & Health*, *49*(5), 353–367.

Szymanski, D. M., & Balsam, K. F. (2011). Insidious trauma: Examining the relationship between heterosexism and lesbians' PTSD symptoms. *Traumatology*, *17*, 4–13.

Szymanski, D. M., Kashubeck-West, S., & Meyer, J. (2008). Internalized heterosexism: A historical and theoretical overview. *The Counseling Psychologist*, *36*(4), 510–524.

US Department of Veterans Affairs/US Department of Defense. (2010). VA/DoD clinical practice guideline for management of post-traumatic stress. Retrieved from https://www.healthquality.va.gov/guidelines/MH/ptsd/cpg_PTSD-full-201011612.PDF

van Dam, D., Vedel, E., Ehring, T., & Emmelkamp, P. M. G. (2012). Psychological treatments for concurrent posttraumatic stress disorder and substance use disorder: A systematic review. *Clinical Psychology Review*, *32*, 202–214. http://doi.org/10.1016/j.cpr.2012.01.004

van Emmerik, A. A., Kamphuis, J. H., & Emmelkamp, P. M. (2008). Treating acute stress disorder and posttraumatic stress disorder with cognitive behavioral therapy or structured writing therapy: A randomized controlled trial. *Psychotherapy and Psychosomatics*, *77*(2), 93–100.

Van Etten, M. L., & Taylor, S. (1998). Comparative efficacy of treatments for post-traumatic stress disorder: A meta-analysis. *Clinical Psychology and Psychotherapy*, *5*, 126–144.

van Minnen, A., Arntz, A., & Keijsers, G. P. J. (2002). Prolonged exposure in patients with chronic PTSD: Predictors of treatment outcome and dropout. *Behaviour Research and Therapy*, *40*(4), 439–457.

Watts, B. V., Schnurr, P. P., Mayo, L., Young-Xu, Y., Weeks, W. B., & Friedman, M. J. (2013). Meta-analysis of the efficacy of treatments for posttraumatic stress disorder. *Journal of Clinical Psychiatry*, *74*(6), 541–550.

Weathers, F. W., Keane, T. M., & Davidson, J. R. (2001). Clinician-administered PTSD scale: A review of the first ten years of research. *Depression and Anxiety*, *13*(3), 132–156.

Weathers, F. W., Litz, B. T., Keane, T. M., Palmieri, P. A., Marx, B. P., & Schnurr, P. P. (2013). *The PTSD Checklist for DSM-5 (PCL-5)*. Available from the National Center for PTSD at https://www.ptsd.va.gov.

12

An Evidence-Based Approach to Conceptualizing Trauma Responses Among Transgender and Gender Nonconforming Adults

SARAH E. VALENTINE, JULIE WOULFE,
AND JILLIAN C. SHIPHERD ■

Transgender and gender nonconforming (TGNC) people face stigma, discrimination, and trauma at rates that are startlingly high—nearly universal. As such, providers who are interested in offering care to TGNC people need to be well-versed in the effects of these types of experiences as part of providing affirmative care. In this chapter, we offer an overview of the literature on these adverse experiences and their sequelae, present a framework for understanding the effects of these exposures, and provide guidance on treatment conceptualization.

First, we orient the reader to the various types of adverse events to which TGNC people may be exposed over the life course. Second, we review the literature on the prevalence of each type of exposure among TGNC people. Third, we discuss the common symptoms associated with exposure to various adverse experiences by describing the literature on mental health symptoms and substance use in TGNC people. Fourth, we describe a cumulative stress model to assist with case conceptualization with TGNC people that draws upon the minority stress and allostatic load theories. Finally, we summarize the limitations of the empirical literature and offer an illustrative case example that is trauma-informed and affirmative to transgender identities.

Before discussing appropriate treatments for trauma survivors, it is important to state at the outset that no randomized controlled trials have been conducted for TGNC people. The recommendations we propose are based on the existing literature and our clinical experience. In this chapter, we use specific language to describe and define traumatic events among TGNC clients because our experience tells us that definitions of what experiences may qualify as "traumatic" may differ among laypeople and professionals. We argue for precision in language because terminology informs assessment and, by extension, treatment. Of course, the majority of trauma survivors demonstrate resilience in the face of adversity, and TGNC people are no different. However, the cumulative burden of these experiences my lead to presentation for treatment even in cases in which symptoms do not meet diagnostic threshold. We suggest that if a TGNC client presents for treatment, affirmative care would be to offer treatment, even if symptoms are subthreshold at assessment.

DEFINING TRAUMA

Laypeople often use the words "traumatic" and "traumatizing" to describe emotional experiences (a divorce, losing a job, etc.), and TGNC people are no different. Well-intentioned providers often mirror this language as a way to validate the client's emotional experiences. However, we argue that there are better ways to validate a client's experience than to reify a description that may not be clinically accurate. Using the term "trauma" for an overly inclusive group of emotional experiences introduces problematic heterogeneity and implies that an appropriate treatment plan would target post-traumatic stress disorder (PTSD) symptoms, even when other treatments better fit the client's profile of symptoms.

Unfortunately, very little work has been done to understand the concepts being conveyed with the use of the term "trauma" by TGNC clients. In an ideal world, this chapter would summarize qualitative data about how to clarify concepts. However, given that this literature does not exist, we utilize our combined clinical experiences with TGNC people to further define the heterogeneous use of "trauma." We believe that these constructs can best be defined as (1) transgender-related discrimination (including both chronic minority stress experiences and extreme minority stressors), (2) events during which the body or its functions elicit distress and feel like a betrayal, and (3) potentially traumatic events.

The first type of event that TGNC people may sometimes describe as "traumatic" is *transgender-related discrimination*. The first subcategory is characterized by chronic and pervasive discrimination experiences, such as being the target of laughter, stares, or pointing in public spaces—termed here *chronic minority stress*. These types of experiences take a toll on a person's overall well-being and can certainly lead to mental health symptoms such as anxiety, hypervigilance toward threat, and even a desire to consume alcohol or use drugs before entering public spaces as a way to self-medicate. Some clients have referred to this experience as "death by a thousand cuts" and it is a positive sign when a transgender person seeks therapy to assist with the distress associated with these experiences.

Also within this category of minority stress are *extreme minority stressors*, such as being fired from a job or evicted from a home or apartment as a result of gender identity, which can clearly be a very difficult experience. Anyone might seek mental health treatment in the aftermath of being fired, especially when the perceived cause is related to an aspect of identity (as is the case for many TGNC people). This type of event is not unique to TGNC people, but due to structural (e.g., lack of legal protections) and social stigma, these experiences are common in TGNC lives (Grant et al., 2011; James et al., 2016).

Both types of transgender-related discrimination experiences provide important context for PTSD treatment, and sequelae of these events (anxiety, mood, and/or substance abuse symptoms) can also be a focus of treatment. Indeed, prevention of such experiences is ideal, and providers may want to get involved with local advocacy work to improve cultural awareness about TGNC people.

A second type of event that TGNC clients sometimes describe as "traumatic" involves secondary sex characteristics of their body (or their functions). For example, a transgender man may say that the experience of a menstrual cycle was "traumatic." Clearly, this is an event that would be upsetting for a male-identified person, but it is "traumatic" for a transgender man because his bodily functions are at odds with his self-conceptualization. Similarly, some transgender women report that getting an erection "feels traumatic." Specifically, the lack of control over bodily functions that are contrary with identity is stressful. Although no studies exist on this topic, our experience tells us that these types of concerns are sometimes raised over the course of treatment. As such, the probable best treatment to reduce distress associated with these types of experiences is a combination of hormone therapy to prevent additional menstruation or reduce erections coupled with transgender support groups and coping skills. In addition, mental health providers might find acceptance-based or third-wave cognitive–behavioral interventions useful in developing strategies for coping with distress triggered by reminders of the discrepancy between physiological responses associated with birth sex and gender self-concept. In one description of applying these techniques to the TGNC population, Sloan, Berke, and Shipherd (2017) detail the application of a dialectical behavior therapy framework to the treatment of TGNC clients. In this approach, they teach validation of unavoidable distress (e.g., bodily functions) through the application of mindfulness and acceptance strategies, balanced with change-based interventions associated with building coping skills and accessing medical interventions (e.g., hormones and surgeries).

The third type of trauma (and the primary focus of this chapter) is *potentially traumatic events* that would qualify for criterion A for a diagnosis of PTSD (American Psychiatric Association, 2013). Criterion A can be summarized as follows:

> The person was exposed to: death, threatened death, actual or threatened serious injury, or actual or threatened sexual violence, in the following

way(s): Direct exposure, witnessing the trauma, learning that a relative or close friend was exposed to a trauma, indirect exposure to aversive details of the trauma, usually in the course of professional duties (e.g., first responders, medics).

Importantly, these experiences are only one criterion for the diagnosis of PTSD; a set of intrusive, avoidance, negative thoughts, mood, and arousal symptoms must also be present and persist for at least 1 month. The vast majority of trauma survivors, including TGNC people, will not develop PTSD. Resilience in the aftermath of trauma exposure is the most common outcome (Foa, Rothbaum, Riggs, & Murdock, 1991). However, according to theories that support the cumulative burden of stress, TGNC people may be at increased risk for PTSD due to (1) elevated rates of exposure to potentially traumatic events, (2) elevated rates of additional minority stressors (e.g., transgender-related discrimination), and (3) less access to community and social supports (i.e., social marginalization/isolation). These conditions reduce one's capacity to cope with stressors, thereby increasing risk of developing PTSD, and as described later, these suspicions are borne out with empirical examinations.

Overlap between extreme minority stressors and potentially traumatic events is not uncommon. For example, there can be experiences of discrimination-based traumatic events (e.g., being beaten due to gender identity), which we call *bias-related events*. These types of trauma are not unique to TGNC people, although later we describe how TGNC people experience bias-related events at high rates. Although not previously examined in TGNC samples, gender nonconformity has been identified as a risk factor for discrimination and violence against lesbian, gay, and bisexual (LGB) people, with one study finding that 19% of potentially traumatic events were precipitated by gender nonconformity (Gordon & Meyer, 2007). In cases in which a person has experienced a bias-related event, some combination of treatments might be needed.

In summary, exposure to chronic minority stress, extreme minority stressors, secondary sex characteristics and their biological functions, and potentially traumatic events (including bias-related events) can all be associated with a range of mental health symptoms for TGNC individuals, which are described later.

EXPOSURE TO TRANSGENDER-RELATED DISCRIMINATION

The National Transgender Discrimination Survey (NTDS) is the largest study of transgender people in the United States, with a sample of 27,715 (James et al., 2016). The executive summary highlights the extent and reach of transgender-related discrimination in the United States, with 46% reporting verbal harassment in the prior year. The unemployment rate was three times higher than that of the general US population (15% vs. 5%, respectively), with 27% reporting being fired or denied a promotion because of their gender identity. An alarming 77% of respondents reported taking steps to avoid mistreatment at work, such as hiding or delaying their transition. Nearly 30% of the sample reported being homeless at some point, with 23% reporting being evicted or denied housing due to their identity, and for racial minority TGNC, the rates of homelessness and incarceration are even worse (Brown & Jones, 2014). A discouraging 33% of TGNC individuals in this survey reported that they had been refused care or harassed by a health care provider based on their gender identity, and 23% reported delaying needed health care due to anticipated stigma from providers. Unfortunately, these findings are consistent with those of other studies that have documented similar challenges (Reisner et al., 2015; Shipherd, Green, & Abramovitz, 2010). In summary, transgender-related discrimination limits opportunities and access to resources, including health care, housing, and employment. Indeed, these structural factors place TGNC people at higher risk for potentially traumatic events, including exposure to interpersonal violence.

EXPOSURE TO POTENTIALLY TRAUMATIC EVENTS

There is a growing body of evidence that suggests TGNC individuals are more likely to experience potentially traumatic events compared to their cisgender counterparts. A review of US data on rates and types of violence by group suggests that TGNC individuals are more likely to experience violence (especially sexual violence) compared to cisgender individuals—and this disparity starts early in life and continues across the lifespan (Beckman, Shipherd, Simpson, & Lehavot, 2018; Stotzer, 2009). Examining NTDS data (James et al., 2016), 47% endorsed being sexually assaulted in their lifetimes, and 10% were sexually assaulted in the past year. More than half (54%) had experienced some intimate partner violence, with 24% experiencing severe physical violence. Another study found that 98% of TGNC individuals who reported male sex at birth reported exposure to at least one potentially traumatic event, 91% had multiple lifetime potentially traumatic events, and 42% reported at least one potentially traumatic event as a transgender bias-related event (Shipherd, Maguen, Skidmore, & Abramovitz, 2011). An online study of 221 transgender veterans found that 100% of the sample had at least one potentially traumatic event exposure (Beckman et al., 2018).

Existing literature on exposure to violence among TGNC individuals has focused on experiences of childhood abuse, adult assault (including hate crimes), and partner violence. A recent study found that 55% of TGNC individuals (compared to 20% of cisgender individuals) reported a history of childhood abuse (Beckman et al., 2018; Reisner, White, Bradford, & Mimiaga, 2014). A growing body of research suggests that TGNC individuals are more likely to receive threats of violence relative to cisgender sexual minority and heterosexual individuals (35% vs. 14% and 12%, respectively; Landers & Gilsanz, 2009). TGNC individuals are also twice as likely to report having experienced sexual assault or rape compared to their LGB peers (Langender-Magruder, Walls, Kattari, Whitfield, & Ramos, 2016). In one study of partner violence among sexual and gender minority adults, TGNC individuals reported higher lifetime exposure to partner violence compared to their cisgender sexual minority peers (31% vs. 20%, respectively; Langenderfer-Magruder, Whitfield, Walls, Kattari, & Ramos, 2016). A recent study conducted through a primary care screener found that TGNC adults, especially transgender women, were more likely to experience past-year partner violence compared to cisgender women (Valentine et al., 2017). Dank, Lachman, Zweig, and Yahner (2010) similarly found that compared to heterosexual students, sexual and gender minority youth were at higher risk for all types of dating violence and that TGNC individuals and cisgender sexual minority women were at highest risk.

MENTAL HEALTH AND SUBSTANCE USE IN TGNC POPULATIONS

Given the previously discussed context, TGNC people are at increased risk for a variety of mental health concerns. Thus, it is important to consider the scope of problems that should be included in clinical assessment.

Suicidality and Symptoms of Depression

Given the pervasive nature of the challenges faced by the TGNC community, it is not surprising that the symptoms of depression and rates of suicide are elevated. For example, Budge, Adelson, and Howard (2013) found that nearly half of 351 TGNC survey participants reported clinically significant depressive symptoms. Another survey found that 64% of TGNC participants endorsed clinically significant depressive symptoms (Shipherd et al., 2011). In a 3-year prospective study of TGNC women, Nuttbrock and Colleagues (2010) found a four- to sevenfold increase in odds for clinical depression among those who had experienced transgender-related discrimination.

TGNC people are more likely to endorse lifetime suicide attempt or ideation compared to cisgender people (Reisner et al., 2014). The NTDS found that 40% of TGNC people reported past suicide attempt (James et al., 2016). A needs assessment of TGNC individuals living in Chicago found that nearly two-thirds of the sample had thought about attempting suicide (Kenagy & Bostwick, 2005). Risk for suicidal behavior among TGNC people is associated with family rejection (Klein & Golub, 2016), younger age, depressive symptoms, history of substance abuse treatment (Clements-Nolle, Marx, & Katz, 2006), transgender-related discrimination, exposure to potentially traumatic events such as interpersonal victimization and rape (Irwin, Coleman, Fischer, & Marasco, 2014), and internalized transphobia (Perez-Brumer, Hatzenbuehler, Oldenburg, & Bockting, 2015). Some points during social or medical transition (Grossman & D'Augelli, 2007; Rood, Puckett, Pantalone, & Bradford, 2015) may also convey elevated risk for suicide.

Recent reviews of the literature on TGNC individuals' mental health have highlighted several variables that contribute to higher rates of depressive symptoms among TGNC individuals compared to the general US population. Key variables may include a lack of social support (general), identity support, violence exposure, sex work, transgender-related discrimination, and socioeconomic factors (for review, see Hoffman, 2014). In a study on experiences of race- and transgender-related discrimination among TGNC of color, Jefferson, Neilands, and Sevelius (2013) found that exposure to both types of discriminatory events was associated with depressive symptoms. Jefferson and colleagues also found that increased TGNC identity (accompanied by increased coping self-efficacy) appeared to buffer associations between discrimination and depressive symptoms. This preliminary work suggests that access to identity support, increase in coping skills, and reduction of internalized transphobia may buffer people from some adverse mental health consequences of transgender-related discrimination.

Similar associations between TGNC status, transgender-related discrimination, and suicidality have been documented in veteran samples (Lehavot, Simpson, & Shipherd, 2016). Multiple studies have examined suicidality among TGNC veterans utilizing Veterans Health Administration (VHA) care. One study examining VHA medical record data found evidence of health disparities across mental health conditions, including PTSD, depression, suicidality, and serious mental illness, among transgender veterans compared to cisgender veterans (Brown & Jones, 2016). This study also found that TGNC veterans were more likely to have been homeless, to have experienced sexual trauma while on active duty, and to have been incarcerated compared to cisgender veterans (Brown & Jones, 2016). Another study of VHA data demonstrated a 20 times higher prevalence of suicide attempts among veterans with gender identity disorder (Blosnich et al., 2013). In addition, a survey study reported that 57% of TGNC veterans endorsed past-year suicidal ideation (SI), and 66% reported a history of suicide plan or attempt (Lehavot et al., 2016).

Substance Use

Although research in this area is limited, studies have found an elevated prevalence of alcohol and drug use among TGNC individuals compared to the general population (Benotsch, Snipes, Martin, & Bull, 2013; Keuroghlian, Reisner, White, & Weiss, 2015; Santos et al., 2014) and that racial disparities exist in alcohol abuse among TGNC veterans (Brown & Jones, 2014). Reportedly, 26%–28% of TGNC misuse substances to cope with transgender-related discrimination (Benotsch et al., 2013; Klein & Golub, 2016; Reisner et al., 2015). Substance use among transgender women has been associated with PTSD symptoms and transgender-related discrimination, and the presence of both was associated with drug use concurrent with sex and use of multiple drugs (Rowe, Santos, McFarland, & Wilson, 2015). In another survey study of TGNC adults, one-third of the sample reported medically unsupervised hormone use; however, transgender-related discrimination was not associated with non-medical use of hormones (Benotsch et al., 2013).

Posttraumatic Stress Disorder

Although we are advocating for more precision when describing trauma recovery in TGNC populations, most of the research has not utilized diagnostic clinical assessments of PTSD. Instead, the majority of studies use self-report symptom inventories (e.g., primary care screeners) that often fail to link symptoms to a criterion A event or rely on International Classification of Diseases, Ninth Revision (ICD-9), codes in medical record data. Thus, it is unclear if endorsed symptoms are indications of PTSD following exposure to a criterion A event or if the symptoms are indications of general distress. Three studies have utilized ICD-9 codes in Veterans Administration health records to report on rates of PTSD in transgender veteran samples. One study found that 23.7% of transgender veterans ($N = 1,640$) had a diagnosis of PTSD (Blosnich et al., 2016), whereas the other two studies found that 38.7% and 40.8% of transgender veterans had a diagnosis of PTSD ($N = 5,135$ and 6,308, respectively; Blosnich et al., 2017). In two studies that employed a primary care screen to identify PTSD (although not linked to a specific event) in a racially and ethnically diverse sample of transwomen youth, researchers found that 62% of the participants screened positive for PTSD (Wilson, Chen, Arayasirikul, Raymond, & McFarland, 2016). Although these studies consistently report high rates of PTSD among TGNC individuals, the available evidence on PTSD prevalence does not represent the overall TGNC population. For example, the current literature may not be representative of those without transgender-related diagnoses, those who do not disclose TGNC identity to providers, or those who do not experience distress or desire medical transition. As such, these rates may be overestimates of PTSD among TGNC people.

One study from our group was careful in its definition of trauma and assessment of exposure to potentially traumatic events, and it found that approximately 17.8% of the non-treatment-seeking sample of TGNC individuals endorsed significant PTSD symptoms related to the events (Shipherd et al., 2011). This finding is interesting because 98% of the sample had experienced a potentially traumatic event (42% bias-related events) and only 17.8% developed clinical significant levels of PTSD. Thus, despite nearly universal exposure to potentially traumatic events, the rates of significant levels of PTSD were only roughly double what is seen in the general population (7.8% prevalence; Kessler, Sonnega, Bromet, Hughes, & Nelson, 1995). These studies strongly suggest that high rates of exposure to potentially traumatic events, as well as additional experiences of transgender-related discrimination, may elevate risk for poor mental health sequelae.

DEVELOPING A THEORY: CUMULATIVE NATURE OF STRESS AMONG TGNC POPULATIONS

The Meyer minority stress model, as applied to TGNC individuals (Hendricks & Testa, 2012), posits that (1) TGNC individuals represent a disadvantaged social group that is frequently subjected to stigma and discrimination in the form of internal (identity concealment, internalized transphobia, and expectations of rejection) and external (discrimination and violence) minority stressors (Blosnich et al., 2016; Rood et al., 2015); (2) internal and external minority stressors related to gender identity predispose TGNC individuals to excess stress relative to cisgender individuals; and (3), in turn, excess stress may lead to mental or physical health problems (Meyer, 2003).

In applying the minority stress model, it is important to consider allostatic load or the "wear and tear" on the body that is the result of exposure to chronic stressors (i.e., transgender-related discrimination and marginalization). Allostatic load theory has also been used to explain how the cumulative burden of trauma has negative effects on both psychological and physical health (Borrell, Dallo, & Nguyen, 2010; Schnurr, 2015). Recently, allostatic load has also been used to conceptualize the detrimental effects of chronic minority stress, over and above discrete potentially traumatic events, including bias-related events such as hate crimes (Reisner et al., 2016). Thus, we advocate the use of a cumulative stress model when addressing sequelae of potentially traumatic events because it is important to recognize the added burden of everyday minority stress experiences when assessing, conceptualizing, and treating PTSD in TGNC individuals.

LIMITATIONS OF THE EXISTING LITERATURE

TGNC have been underrepresented in research, even among previous studies with LGBT samples, so the limitations are many. One reason may be that gender identity is poorly assessed in most clinical or population-based surveillance data sets. Where studies exist, transgender men, transgender women, and people with nonbinary identifications (i.e., any gender self-identification that is not exclusively man or woman; e.g., "gender fluid," "genderqueer," and "third gender") are often grouped together; important differences and nuances of experiences are certainly missed with this approach (Pantalone, Valentine, & Shipherd, 2016; Valentine & Shipherd, 2018). Most of the existing data derive from clinical samples (found in medical records based on diagnosis of "gender identity disorder" or "gender dysphoria") or online survey research. People meeting criteria for gender dysphoria are not representative of all TGNC people, and their willingness to be identified in a medical record suggests that they are unlikely representative of the general population of TGNC individuals. Because more services for TGNC people are available in urban areas, rural TGNC persons remain largely unrepresented.

However, in the past few years, there has been a major increase in the number of published studies focused on TGNC health. The majority of TGNC health studies have focused on the documentation of the alarming prevalence of exposure to potentially traumatic events, including bias-related events and other transgender-related discrimination. Moreover, although transgender-related discrimination experiences including both chronic minority stress and extreme minority stressors are often a focus in TGNC health studies, there is no consistent nomenclature to describe these experiences. For example, some studies report chronic "everyday" exposure to discrimination or "microaggressions" (Reisner et al., 2016; Robinson & Rubin, 2016); whereas others use terms such as "insidious trauma" to capture discrimination (Watson, DeBlaere, Langrehr, Zelaya, & Flores, 2016).

Furthermore, assessments of potentially traumatic event exposure among TGNC individuals have not been comprehensive, with few exceptions (Shipherd et al., 2011). Studies of potentially traumatic events among TGNC individuals are often limited to assessment of one type of violence exposure (i.e., child abuse, partner violence, and hate crimes), and most studies have not assessed whether the survivor perceives these events as bias-related (Holmes, Facemire, & DaFonseca, 2016). Existing data provide valuable information regarding the prevalence of violence and discrimination, but these studies do not elucidate mechanisms by which some TGNC people recover and some develop mental health symptoms.

Heterogeneity of experiences that are classified as traumatic, including transgender-related discrimination that does not represent potentially traumatic events, prevents the field from determining which treatments work best for recovery from each type of experience. For example, application of coping skills and cognitive–behavioral therapy among sexual minority men to address symptoms in the aftermath of minority stress experiences (Panchankis, Hatzenbuehler, Rendina, Safren, & Parsons, 2015) has yet to be generalized to TGNC people. Treatments designed to bolster coping with transgender-related discrimination could be useful when clients are seeking treatment, but symptoms are not specific to PTSD.

In summary, TGNC people suffer under the burden of transgender-related discrimination, although the relations between these experiences and their psychological sequelae are only beginning to be documented. Although there are no treatment studies of trauma recovery in TGNC people, our clinical practice has shown that transgender people respond to evidence-based PTSD treatment in similar ways as other clients (Maguen, Shipherd, & Harris, 2005). However, this care must be delivered following appropriate assessment of potentially traumatic event exposure in a setting that is sensitive to the TGNC experience. The case presented next offers an example of how TGNC identity can be explicitly incorporated into assessment and treatment of PTSD.

CASE EXAMPLE: COGNITIVE PROCESSING THERAPY FOR PTSD

Background and Treatment History

Annette was a 35-year-old White transgender woman who had been living with her partner of 5 years. She presented as anxious in her intake session—making infrequent eye contact, responding in short sentences, and nervously fidgeting in her chair. When asked what had brought her to therapy, she stated that she had been referred for trauma-focused therapy by her clinical social worker of 1 year. She described her previous therapeutic course as helpful, which mainly focused on reducing gender dysphoria, developing skills to cope with chronic minority stress, and providing psychoeducation on the effects of childhood physical and sexual abuse. With regard to reducing gender dysphoria, Annette worked with her therapist to come out as transgender and identify her goals for transition. This included pursuing a legal name change, accurate identity documents, beginning feminizing hormone therapy, and identifying her options for gender-affirming medical procedures. As Annette progressed in her transition, the focus of her therapeutic work expanded to include addressing negative self-judgments or prejudicial beliefs she had developed during the course of her life related to her identity as a transgender woman—termed "internalized transphobia"; managing distress associated with transphobia (discrimination or prejudice toward TGNC persons) in her daily interactions with others (e.g., others not using preferred pronouns, being misgendered, derogatory comments or staring, overhearing comments regarding TGNC people generally, and others asking intrusive questions about her anatomy); and cultivating resilience by developing more affirming social support. In particular, Annette found the skills-building component of therapy (dialectical behavior therapy [DBT] skills; Linehan, 2014) useful as she learned healthy distress tolerance skills (e.g., for coping with situations that she cannot change) and interpersonal effectiveness (e.g., for social situations in which change is possible). As Annette's symptoms of gender dysphoria began to subside and her skills in managing minority stress increased, she disclosed having experienced pervasive abuse in her family. Annette and her social worker agreed that Annette would benefit from a referral for PTSD-focused treatment.

PTSD-Focused Assessment and Treatment Planning

After the referral, Annette was seen for two assessment sessions that included self-report measures and diagnostic interviews. These visits were conducted by a therapist (psychologist) trained in evidence-based treatments for PTSD, who would later deliver the selected intervention.

Self-Report Measures

As part of her PTSD assessment, Annette's therapist screened for exposure to a range of potentially traumatic events using the Life Events Checklist (LEC; Weathers et al., 2013b), a 16-item self-report measure designed to screen for potentially traumatic events over the lifetime. For each endorsed potentially traumatic event, Annette was asked to report whether the event was bias-related. Annette's therapist assessed broadly for additional experiences of transgender-related discrimination using a modified self-report Heterosexist Harassment Rejection and Discrimination Scale (HHRDS; Szymanski, 2006). This 14-item scale assesses for harassment and rejection (e.g., "In the past year, how many times have you been treated unfairly by your family because you are TGNC person?"), workplace/school discrimination (e.g., "In the past year, how many times were you denied a raise, a promotion, tenure, a good assignment, a job, or other such thing at work that you deserved because you are a TGNC person?"), and other discrimination (e.g., "In the past year, how many times have you been treated unfairly by people in helping jobs because you are a TGNC person?"). The measure was amended to ask about TGNC identity and assess lifetime exposure.

Diagnostic Interviews

Annette screened positive on the LEC for multiple events of physical, psychological, and sexual abuse that qualified as potentially traumatic events, including bias-related events. A Clinician-Administered PTSD Scale for DSM-5 (CAPS-5; Weathers et al., 2013a) was administered. CAPS-5 is a 30-item structured clinical interview that is used to assess for past month and lifetime diagnoses of PTSD. The therapist asked Annette to consider (without going into great detail about any one event) whether there was one experience that she thought about more than others (e.g., had the most intrusive symptoms about) or avoided thinking about more than others. Annette initially seemed overwhelmed by the prospect of identifying a single experience, noting that "they are all kind of connected." Her therapist validated this difficulty, sharing the rationale for why it might be helpful to identify a single event (e.g., "Even though we are working with one event, treatment can generalize to other experiences—it can keep us from becoming overwhelmed"). Using these prompts as a guide, Annette described coming out as transgender at age 8 years and soon thereafter being molested by her father. Annette's father continued to sexually abuse her until he died when she was age 15 years. A specific childhood sexual abuse event was then identified as the index event for the CAPS assessment.

Case Conceptualization Summary

All survey and interview data were used in the case conceptualization. Annette met diagnostic criteria for PTSD because she reported severe symptomatology related to the event across all domains, including (1) re-experiencing, (2) avoidance, (3) negative cognition and mood, and (4) arousal and reactivity. Annette's therapist assessed for commonly co-occurring disorders using the Structured Clinical Interview for DSM 5 (SCID; First, Williams, Karg, & Spitzer, 2015). Annette also met criteria for major depressive disorder, recurrent episode, with moderate severity. Annette denied a history of substance use. She endorsed chronic passive SI; however, she denied having current or a history of suicidal gestures, plan, or intent to act on her SI.

Annette's responses also indicated family rejection, workplace discrimination, and anticipated rejection and enacted discrimination by health care providers. When prompted, Annette provided illustrative examples for each of these items: Her family members did not use her preferred name and pronouns, she had been "pushed out" of several jobs when she started to socially transition, and she had never disclosed her gender identity with her primary care doctor.

Treatment Planning

There are three evidence-based treatments for adults with PTSD: prolonged exposure (PE; Foa, Chrestman, & Gilboa-Schechtman, 2008). cognitive processing therapy (CPT; Resick, Monson, & Chard, 2016), and eye movement desensitization and reprocessing (EMDR; Shapiro, 2005). Annette's PTSD therapist was certified in two of these. The therapist presented Annette with two treatment options—PE and CPT—by briefly describing each approach. Annette chose to engage in CPT.

CPT is composed of four main components: (1) education about PTSD and CPT, (2) processing the trauma, (3) restructuring of post-traumatic cognitions, and (4) review of trauma themes. To track symptoms over time, each CPT session includes review of self-reported PTSD symptoms using the PTSD Checklist for DSM-5 (PCL-5; Weathers, Litz, et al., 2013) and self-reported depressive symptoms (including SI) using the Beck Depression Inventory–II (BDI-II; Beck, Steer, & Brown, 1996).

In CPT, clients are coached to write an "impact statement" that describes the ways their index trauma continues to affect their present functioning, including beliefs about self, others, and the world. The impact statement is used to identify extreme or inaccurate beliefs about the trauma (e.g., self-blame), as well as extreme or inaccurate beliefs about one's sense of safety, trust, power/control, intimacy, and esteem that interfere with natural recovery following trauma—the cognitions (beliefs) identified in CPT are referred to as "stuck points." The following excerpt is from Annette's impact statement (altered to preserve confidentiality):

> I was molested for coming out as a girl to my family. I was hurt because I was a girl, and because I'm transgender. The abuse damaged me, and I should have been stronger to stop it. I didn't know then that nobody can be trusted. On one hand, it wasn't my fault. My father was seriously messed up and children should never be treated like that. But it has affected my trust in people. I know now that I can't trust anyone. Too many people could harm me because of who I am. Especially now, being transgender makes me unsafe. It also affected my trust in myself. I didn't try hard enough to stop it, so it's my fault for allowing it to continue.

By reviewing Annette's impact statement in session, Annette and her therapist identified adaptive and balanced beliefs about her experiences of sexual trauma (e.g., "It wasn't my fault" and "children should never be treated like that") as well as stuck points. Stuck points included "nobody can be trusted," "I was hurt because I was a girl," and "I didn't try hard enough to stop it." In reviewing the impact statement, Annette also described how her stuck points—although adaptive at one point in her life—contribute to current problems with social isolation and distress. The remainder of CPT focused on learning and applying various cognitive restructuring exercises to stuck points.

Clinical Relevance of TGNC Identity

Several of Annette's identified stuck points (e.g., "being transgender makes me unsafe") were maintained by the experiences of transgender-related discrimination. Prior to challenging her stuck points through cognitive restructuring exercises (i.e., formal handouts practiced as homework and reviewed in session) and Socratic questioning (i.e., a clinician's open-ended questioning to guide the client toward more balanced thinking), the therapist spent time validating the realistic (and sometimes adaptive or protective) aspects of these thoughts. For example, when asked to elaborate on her statement "being transgender makes me unsafe," Annette described the ways in which disclosing her gender identity had indeed been dangerous to her physical well-being as well as to her livelihood.

Stuck points about safety are common in all clients with PTSD, but navigating both realistic and unrealistic aspects of stuck points is particularly important when working with TGNC and other minority status clients. Minority status clients may have realistic expectations regarding their own vulnerability to further rejection, discrimination, and abuse based on their identity. Thus, it is important to validate realistic aspects of beliefs and also spend time refining the stuck points or identifying related stuck points that have fewer realistic components. For example, follow-up questioning allowed Annette to refine the stuck point to "If I dress as a woman, I will always be assaulted." The process of refining stuck points allows clients to differentiate thoughts that are realistic or unrealistic from thoughts that have both realistic and unrealistic components. Starting with mainly unrealistic stuck points is particularly helpful when first teaching cognitive restructuring as clients are working toward gaining a sense of mastery.

Rather than challenging the *accuracy* of this belief, the therapist chose to explore the *utility* of it for Annette. The therapist reflected on how concealment can be a critical survival strategy in various situations and then gently inquired whether this thought represented only part of the truth (e.g., Were there other ways in which concealing her gender identity had been dangerous? Were there times when she was in a public space and she was not assaulted?). By re-evaluating the risk of openly identifying as her affirmed gender, Annette was able to balance her concern for being targeted for transgender-related discrimination with her need for social connection. This enabled her to discuss her strategies for developing physical and psychological safety in a more flexible and adaptive way (e.g., noting that she had been able to develop relationships with affirming people in her life, which has allowed her to be out and safe).

Additional Clinical Considerations

Evidence-based treatments for PTSD (PE, CPT, and EMDR) can at times be presented as a clear and linear path toward symptom reduction. However, in practice, many clients with PTSD find that it can be difficult to determine the best sequence of treatments to meet their needs. In this example, Annette came to treatment specifically seeking trauma-focused treatment. In other cases, clients with significant PTSD and transgender-related discrimination may benefit from integrated approaches that address PTSD symptoms while also bolstering coping skills.

The chronicity and scope of transgender-related discrimination that many TGNC clients face may create actual threats to their stability (e.g., financial, housing, and emotional) that may need to be addressed before they engage in trauma-focused interventions. Providers can help their TGNC clients consciously navigate treatment by providing several treatment options, outlining the costs and benefits, and providing a sense of what might inform their next steps. For example, Annette had a successful treatment episode focusing on her earlier treatment goal of developing her identity as a transgender woman and bolstering coping skills. This work allowed Annette to realize how her traumatic early childhood experiences continued to impact her life and to regain a sense of trust in mental health providers; thus, she was willing to consider PTSD treatment.

A second guiding principle for practitioners is that although trauma-informed practitioners make distinctions between potentially traumatic events and transgender-related discrimination, we have found that clients often do not. This can present a challenge for practitioners engaging in trauma-focused work because clients may be more focused on addressing the effect of chronic minority stress events rather than on a potentially traumatic event that would qualify for a PTSD diagnosis. This is another instance in which it is important to follow the client's lead. If a client reports both experiences and prefers to begin therapy by focusing on non-potentially traumatic experiences of transgender-related discrimination, the therapist might use that time to build skills to assist the client in coping with these experiences (e.g., DBT; Linehan, 2014) or to use an integrated approach that assists the client in building coping skills in preparation for trauma-focused treatment (e.g., Skills Training in Affect and Interpersonal Regulation [STAIR]; Cloitre et al., 2010; Levitt & Cloitre, 2006). In using either of these approaches, the therapist and client can attend to common themes of understanding and coping with transgender-related discrimination as well as potentially traumatic events.

Clinicians may encounter clients seeking trauma-focused treatment for transgender-related discrimination and may find that clients either have not experienced potentially traumatic events or do not meet criteria for a PTSD diagnosis.

In these cases, it is important to both offer hope about the absence of a PTSD diagnosis and simultaneously validate the difficult emotions associated with their history of discrimination. For example, a clinician may validate the effect of chronic discrimination and also state, for example,

> While discrimination like this is certainly distressing and can result in symptoms of anxiety and depression, the good news is that you do not also need to cope with the distressing symptoms that accompany a PTSD diagnosis. We are still learning best practices for addressing these symptoms that happen following the difficult stressors you have faced, but I have had success with other transgender people by building up their skills for coping with this experience.

The therapist can then offer more information about interventions that could be helpful, such as ESTEEM therapy (Pachankis & Goldfried, 2010; Pachankis, Hatzenbuehler, Rendina, Safren, & Parsons, 2015), Acceptance and Commitment Therapy (ACT; Hayes & Lillis, 2012), and DBT (Linehan, 2014).

COMMON THEMES EMERGING IN PTSD TREATMENT WITH TGNC PEOPLE

Many clients interpret their traumatic experience as having *caused* their gender identity—that is, they believe that they would have self-identified as cisgender had they not experienced sexual abuse. This interpretation is distinct from the association between gender identity and abuse that was described by Annette, in which she believes she was targeted for abuse because of her gender identity. Annette's belief is likely an accurate appraisal of her context for abuse; however, therapists should generally explore whether the appraisal is related to self-blaming or shame-based beliefs (e.g., "I deserved the abuse because I am transgender"). It is important that providers inform clients that although it is true that gender identity can create a vulnerability for interpersonal violence, there is no causal relation between abuse and "becoming" transgender. For example, a clinician working from a CPT perspective may use a cognitive restructuring technique by asking the client, "Are all people who experience abuse TGNC? Are all TGNC people abused?"

Annette's case also demonstrated how experiences of bias-related traumatic events led her to increase behaviors associated with identity concealment, even with health care providers. Identity concealment also led to further isolation as a self-protection strategy, as she withdrew socially. Other studies have found that concealment in and of itself is stressful and is related to greater symptoms of PTSD (Cochran, Balsam, Flentje, Malte, & Simpson, 2013). In the case of Annette, the social transition process was delayed by years, until she found the assistance of a gender-affirming therapist.

THE FUTURE OF HEALTH SERVICES FOR TGNC PEOPLE

Literature on adapting evidence-based treatments for PTSD and enhancing service delivery for TGNC clients does not exist. Therefore, we have provided a few avenues for researchers to consider in future treatment development and/or implementation of effectiveness trials that could aim to address PTSD disparities among TGNC people. To date, these approaches have only been tested with other minority groups (e.g., racial, ethnic, or sexual minorities) generally, where service delivery models aim to reduce stigma, enhance therapeutic relationships, and improve access and quality of care.

Addressing Stigma- and Discrimination-Related Barriers to Accessing Care

The extant literature on engagement and retention in mental health care has documented the role of stigma related to mental illness as well as related to aspects of identity (i.e., race, ethnicity, and immigration status) in under-engagement, poor retention, and poorer response to evidence-based treatments for PTSD (Lester, Artz, Resick, & Young-Xu, 2010). Preliminary research in this area for TGNC patients indicates that transgender-related discrimination may also create barriers to treatment (Sherman et al., 2014). Sherman and colleagues found that approximately one-third of TGNC individuals reported delaying needed medical treatment or avoiding routine preventive care visits due to anticipated discrimination. These data suggest that creating a safe environment may be critical to TGNC individuals' decisions to seek help. To date, no studies have examined engagement, retention, or response to PTSD treatment among TGNC people.

Increasing the Number of TGNC-Identified Providers

Peer and community identity support have been identified in the TGNC health literature as important resilience factors (Jefferson et al., 2013). A recent online survey study of TGNC people found that peer support from other TGNC individuals moderated the relationship between experiences of transgender-related discrimination and psychological distress (Bockting, Miner, Swinburne Romine, Hamilton, & Coleman, 2013). This suggests that helping TGNC clients access affirming social networks and peer-to-peer supports may be particularly helpful in buffering against experiences of discrimination. Indeed, group-based transgender treatment was found to be helpful in a study of six women who were working toward transition goals, with depression and anxiety symptoms decreasing and propensity to utilize social support networks increasing during the 12-week treatment (Maguen et al., 2005). Future studies may benefit from the inclusion of peers in care delivery models.

Research on racial and ethnic minority health has leveraged race and language-matched professional and paraprofessional (or peer) health workers to extend the reach of evidence-based treatments to groups that have historically been mistrustful of the health care system due to experiences of discrimination (Dinwiddie, Gaskin, Chan, Norrington, & McCleary, 2013). Lessons learned from this body of work suggest a need to increase the number of TGNC-identified formal and informal supports. Peers may be particularly helpful in engaging difficult-to-reach (or hidden) TGNC populations. First, TGNC peers can serve as "ambassadors" for health care and can create an initial safe and welcoming environment, thus facilitating engagement in treatment by reducing anticipated discrimination. Second, clinically supervised TGNC peers may be able to provide psychoeducation to help TGNC individuals understand PTSD symptoms as well as available evidence-based treatment options. There remains a need to empirically evaluate strategies for addressing stigma-related barriers to care among TGNC people. If efficacious, these strategies may help TGNC people engage and fully benefit from evidence-based PTSD treatments.

Creating a Safe and Welcome Environment

Given that NTDS data indicate that 33% of TGNC people report having had a negative interaction (harassment or being asked about TGNC health issues) with providers, and 25%–55% have been denied gender confirming services (James et al., 2016), there are clear implications for health care providers. Providers must actively work against a justifiable expectation of discrimination. This starts with seeking out education about the unique needs of TGNC people and committing to training all staff in the clinical environment about the importance of creating a welcoming environment. Providers should work hard to identify ways of demonstrating a safe space for TGNC, including the use of language in advertising for services; intake forms that ask about gender identity and preferred name and pronouns; creating safe spaces in waiting areas and treatment rooms with TGNC-inclusive posters, brochures, and fact sheets; the availability of preferred name over legal name in communications and documentation; dissemination of nondiscrimination policies that specifically include gender identity and expression; and the availability of gender-neutral restrooms. Therapists should also invite clients to name discriminatory experiences that occur during the course of the treatment process so that clinicians can apologize, change their behavior, and respond in an affirmative way. When working with TGNC clients, therapists are often placed in the role of advocating for the clients, especially with regard to experiences of discrimination that occur in the context of accessing and receiving care. Thus, therapists should also invite clients to report any issues that arise as a result of interaction with other staff in the clinic or hospital (e.g., front desk staff and security guards) and be aware of the hospital or local policies regarding nondiscrimination.

Currently, there are several legal battles taking place throughout the world related to TGNC rights. As a provider to this population, knowing your local protections (or lack thereof) is essential to offering informed treatment. Although this is a personal choice, as providers become more attuned to the chronic and pervasive discrimination experienced by TGNC people, social justice reform becomes one pathway for improved health in the TGNC community. Many providers feel pulled to finding solutions to these societal and cultural challenges as part of their commitment to reducing suffering and creating safety for this vulnerable population. We acknowledge that many providers have not had contact with TGNC clients in their practice. It is okay to not have background and expertise at the outset of receiving your first TGNC client. We have provided general guidance on the importance of directly assessing for experiences of discrimination and interpersonal violence (and their relations to current mental health and substance use symptoms) when working with TGNC clients. We encourage providers new to this population to keep in mind that, like all clients, TGNC clients deserve to receive care in a validating environment.

DISCLOSURE

This chapter represents the personal views of the authors and not those of the US Department of Veterans Affairs.

REFERENCES

American Psychiatric Association. (2013). *Diagnostic and statistical manual of mental disorders* (5th ed.). Arlington, VA: American Psychiatric Publishing.

Beck, A. T., Steer, R. A., & Brown, G. K. (1996). *Beck Depression Inventory–II*. San Antonio, TX: Pearson.

Beckman, K., Shipherd, J. C., Simpson. T. L., & Lehavot, K. (2018). Military sexual assault and mental health in transgender veterans: Results from a nationwide survey. *Journal of Traumatic Stress, 31*, 181–190. doi:10.1002/jts.22280

Benotsch, E. G., Snipes, D. J., Martin, A. M., & Bull, S. S. (2013). Sexting, substance use, and sexual risk behavior in young adults. *Journal of Adolescent Health, 52*(3), 307–313.

Blosnich, J. R., Brown, G. R., Shipherd, J. C., Kauth, M., Piegari, R., & Bossarte, R. (2013). Prevalence of gender identity disorder and suicide risk among transgender veterans utilizing Veterans Health Administration (VHA) care. *American Journal of Public Health, 103*(10), e27–e32. doi:10.2105/AJPH.2013.301507

Blosnich, J. R., Marsiglio, M. C., Dichter, M. E., Gao, S., Gordon, A. J., Shipherd, J. C., . . . Fine, M. J. (2017). Impact of social determinants of health on medical conditions among transgender veterans. *American Journal of Preventive Medicine, 52*(4), 491–498.

Blosnich, J. R., Marsiglio, M. C., Gao, S., Gordon, A. J., Shipherd, J. C., Kauth, M., . . . Fine, M. J. (2016). Mental health of transgender veterans in US states with and without discrimination and hate crime legal protection. *American Journal of Public Health, 106*(3), 534–540. https://doi.org/10.2105/AJPH.2015.302981

Bockting, W. O., Miner, M. H., Swinburne Romine, R. E., Hamilton, A., & Coleman, E. (2013). Stigma, mental health, and resilience in an online sample of the US transgender population. *American Journal of Public Health*, *103*(5), 943–951.

Borrell, L. N., Dallo, F. J., & Nguyen, N. (2010). Racial/ethnic disparities in all-cause mortality in US adults: The effect of allostatic load. *Public Health Reports*, *125*(6), 810–816.

Brown, G. R., & Jones, K. T. (2014). Racial health disparities in a cohort of 5,135 transgender veterans. *Journal of Racial and Ethnic Health Disparities*, *1*(4), 257–266.

Brown, G. R., & Jones, K. T. (2016). Mental health and medical health disparities in 5135 transgender veterans receiving healthcare in the Veterans Health Administration: A case–control study. *LGBT Health*, *3*, 122–131.

Budge, S. L., Adelson, J. L., & Howard, K. A. S. (2013). Anxiety and depression in transgender individuals: The roles of transition status, loss, social support, and coping. *Journal of Consulting and Clinical Psychology*, *81*(3), 545–557. https://doi.org/10.1037/a0031774

Clements-Nolle, K., Marx, R., & Katz, M. (2006). Attempted suicide among transgender persons: The influence of gender-based discrimination and victimization. *Journal of Homosexuality*, *51*, 53–69.

Cloitre, M., Stovall-McClough, K. C., Nooner, K., Zorbas, P., Cherry, S., Jackson, C. L., . . . Petkova, E. (2010). Treatment for PTSD related to childhood abuse: A randomized controlled trial. *American Journal of Psychiatry*, *167*(8), 915–924.

Cochran, B. N., Balsam, K., Flentje, A., Malte, C. A., & Simpson, T. (2013). Mental health characteristics of sexual minority veterans. *Journal of Homosexuality*, *60*(2–3), 419–435.

Dank, M., Lachman, P., Zweig, J. M., & Yahner, J. (2010). Dating violence experiences of lesbian, gay, bisexual, and transgender youth. *Journal of Youth and Adolescence*, *43*, 846–857. https://doi.org/10.1007/s10964-013-9975-8

Dinwiddie, G. Y., Gaskin, D. J., Chan, K. S., Norrington, J., & McCleary, R. (2013). Residential segregation, geographic proximity and type of services used: Evidence for racial/ethnic disparities in mental health. *Social Science & Medicine*, *80*, 67–75.

First, M. B., Williams, J. B. W., Karg, R. S., & Spitzer, R. L. (2015). *Structured Clinical Interview for DSM-5 Disorders, Clinician Version (SCID-5-CV)*. Arlington, VA: American Psychiatric Association.

Foa, E. B., Chrestman, K. R., & Gilboa-Schechtman, E. (2008). *Prolonged exposure therapy for adolescents with PTSD: Emotional processing of traumatic experiences—Therapist guide*. New York, NY: Oxford University Press.

Foa, E. B., Rothbaum, B. O., Riggs, D. S., & Murdock, T. B. (1991). Treatment of posttraumatic stress disorder in rape victims: A comparison between cognitive–behavioral procedures and counseling. *Journal of Consulting and Clinical Psychology*, *59*(5), 715–723.

Gordon, A. R., & Meyer, I. H. (2007). Gender nonconformity as a target of prejudice, discrimination, and violence against LGB individuals. *Journal of LGBT Health Research*, *3*(3), 55–71.

Grant, J. M., Mottet, L., Tanis, J. E., Harrison, J., Herman, J., & Keisling, M. (2011). *Injustice at every turn: A report of the National Transgender Discrimination Survey*. Washington, DC: National Center for Transgender Equality.

Grossman, A. H., & D'Augelli, A. R. (2007). Transgender youth and life-threatening behaviors. *Suicide Life Threat Behavior*, *37*(5), 527–537.

Hayes, S. C., & Lillis, J. (2012). *Acceptance and commitment therapy.* Washington, DC: American Psychological Association.

Hendricks, M. L., & Testa, R. J. (2012). A conceptual framework for clinical work with transgender and gender nonconforming clients: An adaptation of the minority stress model. *Professional Psychology-Research and Practice, 43*(5), 460.

Hoffman, B. R. (2014). The interaction of drug use, sex work, and HIV among transgender women. *Substance Use & Misuse, 49*(8), 1049–1053.

Holmes, S. C., Facemire, V. C., & DaFonseca, A. M. (2016). Expanding criterion A for posttraumatic stress disorder: Considering the deleterious impact of oppression. *Traumatology, 22*(4), 314–321.

Irwin, J. A., Coleman, J. D., Fisher, C. M., & Marasco, V. M. (2014). Correlates of Suicide Ideation Among LGBT Nebraskans. *Journal of Homosexuality, 61*(8), 1172–1191. doi:10.1080/00918369.2014.872521

James, S. E., Herman, J. L., Rankin, S., Keisling, M., Mottet, L., & Anafi, M. A. (2016). *The report of the 2015 US Transgender Survey.* Washington, DC: National Center for Transgender Equality.

Jefferson, K., Neilands, T., & Sevelius, J. (2013). Transgender women of color: Discrimination and depression symptoms. *Ethnicity and Inequalities in Health and Social Care, 6*(4), 121–136.

Kenagy, G. P., & Bostwick, W. B. (2005). Health and social service needs of transgender people in Chicago. *International Journal of Transgenderism, 8*(2–3), 57–66.

Kessler, R. C., Sonnega, A., Bromet, E., Hughes, M., & Nelson, C. B. (1995). Posttraumatic stress disorder in the National Comorbidity Survey. *Archives of General Psychiatry, 52*(12), 1048–1060.

Keuroghlian, A. S., Reisner, S. L., White, J. M., & Weiss, R. D. (2015). Substance use and treatment of substance use disorders in a community sample of transgender adults. *Drug and Alcohol Dependence, 152,* 139–146.

Klein, A., & Golub, S. A. (2016). Family rejection as a predictor of suicide attempts and substance misuse among transgender and gender nonconforming adults. *LGBT Health, 3*(3), 193–199.

Landers, S. J., & Gilsanz, P. (2009). *The health of lesbian, gay, bisexual and transgender (LGBT) persons in Massachusetts: A survey of health issues comparing LGBT persons with their heterosexual and non-transgender counterparts.* Boston, MA: Commonwealth of Massachusetts, Department of Public Health.

Langenderfer-Magruder, L., Whitfield, D. L., Walls, N. E., Kattari, S. K., & Ramos, D. (2016). Experiences of intimate partner violence and subsequent police reporting among lesbian, gay, bisexual, transgender, and queer adults in Colorado: Comparing rates of cisgender and transgender victimization. *Journal of Interpersonal Violence, 31*(5), 855–871.

Lehavot, K., Simpson, T. L., & Shipherd, J. C. (2016). Factors associated with suicidality among a national sample of transgender veterans. *Suicide and Life-Threatening Behavior, 46*(5), 507–524.

Lester, K., Artz, C., Resick, P. A., & Young-Xu, Y. (2010). Impact of race on early treatment termination and outcomes in posttraumatic stress disorder treatment. *Journal of Consulting and Clinical Psychology, 78*(4), 480–489.

Levitt, J. T., & Cloitre, M. (2006). A clinician's guide to STAIR/MPE: Treatment for PTSD related to childhood abuse. *Cognitive and Behavioral Practice, 12*(1), 40–52.

Linehan, M. M. (2014). *DBT skills training manual*. New York, NY: Guilford.

Maguen, S., Shipherd, J. C., & Harris, H. N. (2005). Providing culturally sensitive care for transgendered patients. *Cognitive and Behavioral Practice*, *12*(4), 479–490. doi:10.1016/S1077-7229(05)80075-6

Meyer, I. H. (2003). Prejudice as stress: Conceptual and measurement problems. *American Journal of Public Health*, *93*(2), 262–265. https://doi.org/10.2105/AJPH.93.2.262

Nuttbrock, L., Hwahng, S., Bockting, W., Rosenblum, A., Mason, M., Macri, M., & Becker, J. (2010). Psychiatric impact of gender-related abuse across the life course of male-to-female transgender persons. *Journal of Sex Research*, *47*(1), 12–23.

Pachankis, J. E., & Goldreid, M. R. (2010). Expressive writing for gay-related stress: Psychosocial benefits and mechanisms underlying improvement. *Journal of Consulting and Clinical Psychology*, *78*(1), 98–110.

Pachankis, J. E., Hatzenbuehler, M. L., Rendina, H. J., Safren, S. A., & Parsons, J. T. (2015). LGB-affirmative cognitive–behavioral therapy for young adult gay and bisexual men: A randomized controlled trial of a transdiagnostic minority stress approach. *Journal of Consulting and Clinical Psychology*, *83*(5), 875–889.

Pantalone, D. W., Valentine, S. E., & Shipherd, J. C. (2016). Working with survivors of trauma in the sexual minority and transgender/gender nonconforming populations. In K. DeBord, T. Perez, A. Fischer, & K. Bieschke (Eds.), *The Handbook of Sexual Orientation and Gender Diversity in Counseling and Psychotherapy* (pp. 61–68). Oxford University Press: New York, NY.

Perez-Brumer, A., Hatzenbuehler, M. L., Oldenburg, C. E., & Bockting, W. (2015). Individual- and structural-level risk factors for suicide attempts among transgender adults. *Behavioral Medicine*, *41*(3), 164–171.

Reisner, S. L., Hughto, J. M. W., Gamarel, K. E., Keuroghlian, A. S., Mizock, L., & Pachankis, J. E. (2016). Discriminatory experiences associated with posttraumatic stress disorder symptoms among transgender adults. *Journal of Counseling Psychology*, *63*(5), 509–519.

Reisner, S. L., Pardo, S. T., Gamarel, K. E., Hughto, J. M. W., Pardee, D. J., & Keo-Meier, C. L. (2015). Substance use to cope with stigma in healthcare among US female-to-male trans masculine adults. *LGBT Health*, *2*(4), 324–332.

Reisner, S. L., White, J. M., Bradford, J. B., & Mimiaga, M. J. (2014). Transgender health disparities: Comparing full cohort and nested matched-pair study designs in a community health center. *LGBT Health*, *1*(3), 177–184.

Resick, P. A., Monson, C. M., & Chard, K. M. (2016). *Cognitive processing therapy for PTSD. A comprehensive manual*. New York, NY: Guilford.

Robinson, J. L., & Rubin, L. J. (2016). Homonegative microaggressions and posttraumatic stress symptoms. *Journal of Gay & Lesbian Mental Health*, *20*(1), 57–69.

Rood, B. A., Puckett, J. A., Pantalone, D. W., & Bradford, J. B. (2015). Predictors of suicidal ideation in a statewide sample of transgender individuals. *LGBT Health*, *2*(3), 270–275.

Rowe, C., Santos, G.-M., McFarland, W., & Wilson, E. C. (2015). Prevalence and correlates of substance use among trans female youth ages 16–24 years in the San Francisco Bay Area. *Drug and Alcohol Dependence*, *147*, 160–166.

Santos, G. M., Rapues, J., Wilson, E. C., Macias, O., Packer, T., Colfax, G., & Raymond, H. F. (2014). Alcohol and substance use among transgender women in San Francisco: Prevalence and association with human immunodeficiency virus infection. *Drug and Alcohol Review*, *33*(3), 287–295.

Schnurr, P. P. (2015). Understanding pathways from traumatic exposure to physical health. In U. Schnyder & M. Cloitre (Eds.), *Evidence Based Treatments for Trauma-Related Psychological Disorders* (pp. 87–103). Cham, Switzerland: Springer. https://doi.org/10.1007/978-3-319-07109-1_5

Shapiro, F. (2005). *Eye movement desensitization and reprocessing (EMDR) training manual.* Watsonville, CA: EMDR Institute.

Sherman, M., Kauth, M., Ridener, L., Shipherd, J. C., Bratkovich, K., & Beaulieu, G. (2014). An empirical investigation of challenges and recommendations for welcoming sexual and gender minority veterans into VA care. *Professional Psychology: Research and Practice, 45*(6), 433–442. doi:10.1037/a0034826

Shipherd, J. C., Green, K. E., & Abramovitz, S. (2010). Transgender clients: Identifying and minimizing barriers to mental health treatment. *Journal of Gay and Lesbian Mental Health, 14*(2), 94–108. doi:10.1080/19359701003622875

Shipherd, J. C., Maguen, S., Skidmore, W. C., & Abramovitz, S. M. (2011). Potentially traumatic events in a transgender sample: Frequency and associated symptoms. *Traumatology, 17*(2), 56–67. https://doi.org/10.1177/1534765610395614

Sloan, C. A., Berke, D. S., & Shipherd, J. C. (2017). Utilizing a dialectical framework to inform conceptualization and treatment of gender dysphoria. *Professional Psychology: Research and Practice, 48*(5), 301–309.

Stotzer, R. L. (2009). Violence against transgender people: A review of United States data. *Aggression and Violent Behavior, 14*(3), 170–179.

Szymanski, D. M. (2006). Does internalized heterosexism moderate the link between heterosexist events and lesbians' psychological distress? *Sex Roles, 54*(3–4), 227–234.

Valentine, S. E., & Shipherd, J. C. (2018). A systematic review of social stress and mental health among transgender and gender non-conforming people in the United States. *Clinical Psychology Review.* doi:10.1016/j.cpr.2018.03.003.

Valentine, S. E., Peitzmeier S. M., King, D. S., O'Cleirigh, C., Marquez, S., Presley, C., & Potter, J. (2017). Disparities in exposure to intimate partner violence among transgender/gender nonconforming and sexual minority primary care patients. *LGBT Health, 4*(4), 260–267. doi:10.1089/lgbt.2016.0113

Watson, L. B., DeBlaere, C., Langrehr, K. J., Zelaya, D. G., & Flores, M. J. (2016). The influence of multiple oppressions on women of color's experiences with insidious trauma. *Journal of Counseling Psychology, 63*, 656–667. https://doi.org/10.1037/cou0000165

Weathers, F. W., Blake, D. D., Schnurr, P. P., Kaloupek, D. G., Marx, B. P., & Keane, T. M. (2013a). *The Clinician-Administered PTSD Scale for DSM-5 (CAPS-5).* Instrument available from the National Center for PTSD at https://www.ptsd.va.gov

Weathers, F. W., Blake, D. D., Schnurr, P. P., Kaloupek, D. G., Marx, B. P., & Keane, T. M. (2013b). *The Life Events Checklist for DSM-5 (LEC-5).* Instrument available from the National Center for PTSD at https://www.ptsd.va.gov

Weathers, F. W., Litz, B. T., Keane, T. M., Palmieri, P. A., Marx, B. P., & Schnurr, P. P. (2013). *The PTSD Checklist for DSM-5 (PCL-5).* Scale available from the National Center for PTSD at https://www.ptsd.va.gov

Wilson, E. C., Chen, Y. H., Arayasirikul, S., Raymond, H. F., & McFarland, W. (2016). The impact of discrimination on the mental health of trans* female youth and the protective effect of parental support. *AIDS and Behavior, 20*(10), 2203–2211.

13

Evidence-Based Practice for the Prevention and Treatment of Body Image Disturbance and Eating Pathology in Sexual Minority Men

AARON J. BLASHILL, TIFFANY A. BROWN, AND PATRYCJA KLIMEK ■

Eating disorders are serious mental health disorders that are associated with significant medical and psychiatric comorbidities, and they have one of the highest mortality rates of any psychiatric disorder (Arcelus, Mitchell, Wales, & Nielsen, 2011; Klump, Bulik, Kaye, Treasure, & Tyson, 2009; Mitchell & Crow, 2006). Although considerable research has demonstrated that sexual minority males represent a high-risk group for eating disorders and body image disturbance (BID), less research has been conducted on evidence-based practice for this population. In this chapter, we first define and discuss the prevalence of BID and eating disorders in sexual minority men. We then review theoretical models explaining increased risk for BID and eating disorders in sexual minority men. Next, we describe current empirically tested interventions targeting BID and eating disorder prevention and discuss eating disorder treatment approaches adapted for sexual minority men, including a case example. Finally, we discuss future and emerging directions within the field of evidence-based practice for eating disorders for sexual minority men.

DEFINITION OF EATING DISORDERS AND BODY IMAGE DISTURBANCE

The fifth edition of the *Diagnostic and Statistical Manual of Mental Disorders* (American Psychiatric Association, 2013) acknowledges several categories of eating disorders, including anorexia nervosa (AN), bulimia nervosa (BN), binge eating disorder, and avoidant restrictive food intake disorder. Individuals with a clinically significant disorder of eating who do not meet criteria for those mentioned previously are diagnosed with other specified feeding or eating disorder (OSFED).

Body image disturbance reflects the degree to which an individual has a distorted perception of his or her appearance, with associated distress and/or impairment (Thompson, Heinberg, Altabe, & Tantleff-Dunn, 1999). BID can occur within or outside the context of eating disorders (e.g., AN and BN). For males, BID can take the form of either underestimating one's level of muscularity or overestimating one's level of body fat or overall body size. Taken to the extreme, these disturbances can manifest as muscle dysmorphia disorder and AN, respectively (Murray et al., 2012). Importantly, BID is associated with body dissatisfaction, distress, functional impairment, depressive symptoms, and increased levels of eating pathology (Blashill & Wilhelm, 2014; McCreary, Hildebrandt, Heinberg, Boroughs, & Thompson, 2007; Thompson et al., 1999), highlighting the clinical significance of BID.

PREVALENCE OF BODY IMAGE DISTURBANCE AND EATING DISORDERS

Compared to their heterosexual counterparts, sexual minority males are more likely to be dissatisfied with their bodies, have a greater discrepancy between actual and ideal body shapes, engage in disordered eating behaviors, and be diagnosed with an eating disorder (Blashill, 2010; Brown & Keel, 2012; Calzo, Corliss, Blood, Field, & Austin, 2013; Carlat, Camargo, & Herzog, 1997; Morrison, Morrison, & Sager, 2004; Silberstein, Striegel-Moore, Timko, & Rodin, 1988). This disparity in BID and eating disorders appears to be more consistently and specifically found among sexual minority males, with research findings being more mixed for sexual minority females (Morrison et al., 2004).

Sexual minority men are typically overrepresented in eating disorder treatment-seeking samples, with up to 42% of male clinical samples identifying as gay or bisexual (Carlat et al., 1997). However, the overrepresentation of gay males is not limited to clinical samples; community-based studies support a greater prevalence of BID and eating disorders among this population. In one study, the lifetime prevalence for any eating disorder diagnosis among gay and bisexual men was 8.8% (15.6% subclinical) compared to a prevalence of 1.5% in heterosexual men (4.6% subclinical; Feldman & Meyer, 2007). Consistent with these results, another study found that the eating disorder prevalence rate was 10 times higher for gay men compared to heterosexual men (10% vs. 1%; Strong, Williamson, Netemeyer, & Geer, 2000). For comparison purposes, in female samples, the prevalence estimate for heterosexual women was 4.8% (8.0% subclinical) and that for sexual minority women was 7.2% (9.7% subclinical; Feldman & Meyer, 2007). Thus, there is considerable evidence that sexual minority men are at increased risk for eating disorders compared to heterosexual men and potentially compared to heterosexual women. Indeed, sexual minority men may represent the highest risk group for BID and eating disorders.

THEORETICAL MODELS

The development and maintenance of BID and eating disorders in gay men are best understood through three prevalent theoretical models: the tripartite model (Thompson, Heinberg, Altabe, & Tantleff-Dunn, 1999), sexual minority stress theory (Meyer, 1995), and objectification theory (Fredrickson & Roberts, 1997). All three models consider the unique pressures that are related to sexual minority status, such as appearance standards from the gay community and sexual minority stressors (e.g., harassment or stigma for not conforming to masculine ideals). A better understanding of these theoretical models and their role in gay men's BID and eating disorders may inform intervention and prevention efforts in this population.

Tripartite Model

The tripartite model (Thompson et al., 1999) implicates three direct influences on the development of BID: media, family, and peers. Individuals who compare their own bodies to idealistic images of and messages about others' bodies may develop BID (Thompson et al., 1999). Furthermore, by listening to these messages and viewing these media images, individuals might internalize what society views as the ideal body or, in other words, change their attitude toward what their body should look like. Internalization of the societal ideal might also lead to BID and, subsequently, body change behaviors, such as dieting or bulimic behavior (Thompson et al., 1999). In addition, family members and peers can provide pressure to conform to cultural expectations of beauty and negative evaluations about an individual's body. These social networks might also be a source of comparison, such as for modeling body change behaviors, which might influence individuals to change their own body. In addition, being surrounded by peers or family members who talk about their body image concerns may influence individuals to increasingly worry about their own body and compare their body to others. The influence of media, family, and peers may therefore manifest as pressure to fit perceptions of an ideal body, comparison to others' bodies, and internalization of the socially defined ideal body (e.g., mesomorphic ideal in men). Dissatisfaction and preoccupation over one's appearance, triggered by these sociocultural influences, may therefore lead individuals to develop clinically significant distress and/or maladaptive body change behaviors.

The tripartite model has been developed and supported primarily in adult and adolescent females, for whom the thin ideal is prominent (Shroff & Thompson, 2006; van den Berg, Thompson, Obremski-Brandon, & Coovert, 2002). Women experience links between perceived influence from peers, parents, and media; engagement in social comparison; internalization of the thin ideal; BID; and change behaviors (e.g., dieting and bulimic behaviors); however, the samples in these studies are mostly composed of White women, and sexual identity is not assessed.

Although the tripartite model was developed to explain body dissatisfaction in girls and women, recently it has guided studies of men. Specifically, men are exposed to the pressures of being more muscular yet lean (i.e., low body fat), which leads to internalization of the mesomorphic ideal (i.e., musculature combined with low body fat; Tylka, 2011). Research has suggested that pressure from peers, family, media, and, additionally, romantic partners leads men to internalize the mesomorphic ideal and subsequently develop body dissatisfaction (with muscularity or body fat) as well as muscle-building behaviors (e.g., steroid use) or disordered eating, in adult males (Karazsia & Crowther, 2009; Tylka, 2011). Furthermore, an application of the tripartite model among supplement users and steroid users indicated that relative to non-users, both supplement and steroid users endorsed greater importance of media, parent, and peer influences and were more likely to compare their bodies to others (Smolak, Murnan, & Thompson, 2005). These results indicate that in addition to explaining BID in men, the tripartite model may be applied to predict use of appearance and performance enhancing drugs (APEDs). However, existing research on the tripartite model has tested associations between these processes using cross-sectional designs; therefore, causality should be interpreted with caution.

Although the tripartite model is valid in describing the onset of BID and eating disorders in men, the majority of samples have included primarily heterosexual men, or else sexual identity was unmeasured. However, perceived social pressure to conform to appearance ideals and internalization of these ideals are more strongly related to drive for thinness and appearance anxiety among gay men than heterosexual men (Carper, Negy, & Tantleff-Dunn, 2010). In a sample of mostly White gay men, internalization of the mesomorphic ideal and appearance comparison were related to muscularity or body fat dissatisfaction and social pressures from media, romantic partners, friends, family, and the gay community (Tylka & Andorka, 2012). The perception that a lean and muscular body is the ideal form is common within the gay community and may lead to elevated pressure to conform to such ideals in order to be considered a viable sexual partner (Parent, 2013). Pressure to be lean and muscular may lead sexual minority men to compare themselves to other men in the community and to internalize the mesomorphic ideal, which then may lead them to alter their own bodies to fit the ideal. To our knowledge, few studies to date have investigated the tripartite model in gay men, indicating further need to validate this model in this population; however, the application of this model to bisexual and other sexual minority men, apart from self-identified gay men, is still unknown. Furthermore, reliance on cross-sectional research of the tripartite model limits our understanding of the mediating effects of social comparison and internalization in the relationship between social pressure and body image attitudes and behaviors. Support for the tripartite model for male BID, specifically among gay men, indicates the need to target internalization of the mesomorphic ideal in BID and eating disorder prevention and intervention efforts for this population.

Sexual Minority Stress Theory

Another theory that may help explain why sexual minority males are at increased risk for BID and eating disorders, compared to heterosexual males, is minority stress theory (Meyer, 1995). This theory posits that the stigma, prejudice, and discrimination that gay males face as being part of a minority group contribute to a disproportionately stressful environment, which in turn leads to elevated rates of mental health problems, including eating disorders, in sexual minorities compared to heterosexuals. Consistent with this, research has demonstrated that stress and negative affect contribute to eating disorder symptoms more broadly (Freeman & Gil, 2004; Jackson, Cooper, Mintz, & Albino, 2003). Specifically, research supports that social stress in sexual minority men, such as internalized homophobia, stigma, and victimization, is associated with body image dissatisfaction and masculine body ideal stress (Kimmel & Mahalik, 2005) and disordered eating (Watson, Adjei, Saewyc, Homma, & Goodenow, 2017).

Objectification Theory

Objectification theory (Fredrickson & Roberts, 1997) has been developed to explain women's experience of body image concern and cultural body-ideal internalization. This theory posits that the repeated experience of one's body or body parts being singled out, sexualized, and used to represent a woman as a whole, through catcalls and other forms of sexual harassment, leads women to direct this perspective toward themselves. In response to objectification, women may increase self-awareness and monitoring of their body, experience body shame, and attempt to engage in maladaptive behaviors, such as eating pathology, to meet these cultural standards. Women may also desire to be viewed as sexually appealing, if this is an important component of their self-esteem (Wiseman & Moradi, 2010), and could therefore also engage in body change behaviors and negative attitude about their bodies.

Similar to the objectification of the female body, male bodies are portrayed in the media with the ideal of low body fat and high muscularity (e.g., magazines and action toys; Leit, Pope, & Gray, 2001; Pope, Olivardia, Gruber, & Borowiecki, 1999). In samples of predominantly White men, internalizing the cultural standard of muscularity has been linked to body dissatisfaction and self-judgment based on body parts (i.e., self-objectification; Morry & Staska, 2001). Moreover, self-objectification is related to body shame and dissatisfaction to a greater extent for gay men than for heterosexual men because, similar to heterosexual women, gay men are seeking male partners, who are more concerned with physical attractiveness in sexual relationships compared to females (Martins, Tiggemann, & Kirkbride, 2007; Siever, 1994).

Objectification theory also overlaps with the tripartite model such that pressures from social networks might manifest as sexual objectifications (e.g., media images and sexual comments about body parts). For example, media (e.g., advertising) targeting the gay population often emphasizes sexual themes involving muscular bodies (Harvey & Robinson, 2003). In addition, objectification theory may interact with minority stress theory, such that minority stressors such as internalized homophobia have been linked to body shame for not conforming to the muscular body ideal (Wiseman & Moradi, 2010). Sexual minority men might be concerned about being targeted for their sexuality if they do not appear more "masculine" (i.e., muscular).

Summary

The tripartite model, sexual minority stress theory, and objectification theory indicate that sexual minority men may be subject to culturally specific risk factors for BID and eating disorders as well as other risky health behaviors, such as steroid use. North American gay male culture prioritizes physical appearance in pursuit of sexual partners, specifically the mesomorphic body ideal (Parent, 2013). Perceived pressure from social networks (including media, family, peers, sexual partners, and the gay community) to meet these standards of attractiveness may lead to social comparison, internalization of the mesomorphic ideal, and self-objectification. Moreover, sexual minority men are subject to unique stressors, such as prejudice and discrimination, that likely further increase pressures to fit the masculine body ideal. Sexual minority men may therefore develop preoccupation and dissatisfaction with one's appearance and subsequent behaviors to alter appearance, with varying etiology from heterosexual men and women. Thus, clinicians aiming to prevent or treat BID and eating disorders should consider the previously discussed theoretically informed risk factors when working with this population.

CLINICAL INTERVENTIONS

Prevention of Eating Disorders

The following section provides a discussion of empirically supported prevention programs tailored for sexual minority men. Although other eating disorder prevention efforts have been tested among women and men (e.g., psychoeducational, cognitive–behavioral, and dissonance-based; Stice, Shaw, & Marti, 2007), the PRIDE Body Project is the only prevention program developed and tested among sexual minority men. Therefore, this section outlines the components of the PRIDE Body Project and the efficacy of this prevention program in reducing BID and eating disorders among sexual minority men.

THE PRIDE BODY PROJECT

The PRIDE Body Project (Brown & Keel, 2015) is, to our knowledge, the only eating disorder prevention program that has been developed and empirically tested to reduce eating disorder risk among sexual minority men. The program is a two-session group eating disorder prevention program based on the Body Project, an eating disorder prevention program developed for female youth (Becker, Smith, & Ciao, 2006; Stice, Rohde, Gau, & Shaw, 2009; Stice, Shaw, Burton, & Wade, 2006). The program is peer co-facilitated and utilizes principles from cognitive dissonance theory to help elicit attitudinal and behavior change. Cognitive dissonance theory asserts that when people behave in a way that contradicts their beliefs, they will experience psychological discomfort, which will lead them to alter their beliefs to be more compatible with their actions to restore consistency (Festinger & Carlsmith, 1959). Thus, all activities within the PRIDE Body Project were designed to have participants actively argue against the lean, muscular body ideal for men in order to reduce eating disorder attitudes and behaviors.

In Session 1 of the PRIDE Body Project, participants (1) define the "ideal" body type within the gay male community; (2) discuss the origin and perpetuation of the "body ideal"; (3) brainstorm the costs of pursuing the "body ideal"; (4) participate in a verbal challenge during which they encounter the thin, muscular-ideal message; and (5) complete three homework assignments: a letter to an adolescent boy convincing him why pursuing the body ideal is problematic, a behavioral challenge to do something normally avoided due to body image concerns (e.g., going to the beach/pool/jogging without wearing a shirt), and a mirror exposure assignment (i.e., writing down characteristics that they appreciate about themselves, including physical, emotional, mental, and social, while standing in front of a mirror). In Session 2, participants (1) review homework; (2) engage in role plays to counter/discourage pursuit of the "ideal"; (3) discuss ways to challenge and avoid negative "body talk" statements; (4) list ways to resist the pressure to pursue this "ideal" both individually (e.g., posting an online article drawing attention to male body image issues on social media and stop buying magazines that promote the "ideal") and as a group within the gay male community (e.g., organizing a "love your body day" at the local PRIDE center)—these activities are termed "body activism" because they promote taking actions against the need to conform to the "ideal" body; (5) discuss barriers to body activism and how to overcome those barriers; and (6) individually select an exit exercise to continue actively challenging the body ideal.

Results from the preliminary randomized controlled trial of the PRIDE Body Project demonstrated significant and large reductions in body-ideal internalization, body dissatisfaction, drive for muscularity, dietary restraint, self and partner objectification, and bulimic symptoms compared to a wait-list control immediately post-intervention and 1 month after the intervention (Brown & Keel, 2015). In addition, body-ideal internalization mediated the relationship between intervention condition and bulimic symptoms, supporting that the program might work by reducing how much participants invest in trying to achieve a lean, muscular body.

Treatment of Eating Disorders

Although eating disorder and BID prevention efforts have been implemented for sexual minority men (i.e., the PRIDE Body Project), there are no treatments of full-threshold eating disorders tailored for this population. However, existing evidence-based treatments can be adapted to address specific client characteristics, including sexual orientation. As indicated by theoretical models applied to BID and eating disorders in sexual minority men—such as the tripartite model, objectification theory, and the minority stress model—sociocultural and interpersonal pressures unique to men, and specifically to sexual minority men, may be potential treatment targets. It is important to note, however, that little is known about the differential effects of evidence-based treatments by gender identity, sexual identity, race, or ethnicity (Shapiro et al., 2007). Evidence-based treatments of eating disorders (i.e., cognitive–behavioral therapy, interpersonal psychotherapy, family-based treatment, and dialectical behavior therapy) are described in the following sections as adapted for sexual minority men according to the theoretical models described previously. In addition, a case example is provided for cognitive–behavioral therapy in order to further illustrate the adaptation of eating disorder treatment in sexual minority men.

ENHANCED COGNITIVE–BEHAVIORAL THERAPY: A TRANSDIAGNOSTIC ADAPTATION

Enhanced cognitive–behavioral therapy (CBT-E) has been adapted for bulimia nervosa and applied to the full eating disorder spectrum, demonstrating stronger efficacy relative to the original CBT for bulimia nervosa (Fairburn, 2008; Fairburn et al., 2009). The transdiagnostic cognitive–behavioral theory of eating disorders is the purported mechanism of change in CBT-E. This theory indicates that the core psychopathology of eating disorders involves over-evaluation of shape and weight, which leads individuals to engage in various maladaptive behaviors to achieve body change (Fairburn, 2008). Specifically, the transdiagnostic theory indicates that perfectionism, core low self-esteem, and interpersonal difficulties maintain eating disorder symptoms.

A key feature of CBT-E is to develop a case formulation that identifies the factors maintaining each client's eating disorder symptoms and guides the treatment course. Fairburn (2008) provides a case formulation template in which therapists map out an individualized diagram of the disorder, such that over-evaluation of shape and weight is a starting point that leads to and maintains maladaptive eating behavior, all of which are exacerbated by interpersonal and affective difficulties. In cases of sexual minority men with eating disorders, it might be useful to consider the role of sociocultural pressures to maintain a muscular and lean physique in the case formulation.

The recommended format of CBT-E includes 20 sessions over 20 weeks, particularly for those who are not underweight (Fairburn, 2008). The first 4 weeks of treatment are devoted to understanding the client's history and eating disorder development—a pivotal time to understand the role that sexual identity status might play—and creating the case formulation. Clients are also introduced to self-monitoring, regular eating, and in-session weighing. At this time, therapists also address engagement in shape and weight control behaviors such as excessive exercise or purging. In relation to sexual minority men, another shape and weight control behavior that should be kept in mind is APED use. Furthermore, if sexual minority male clients also have a drive for the mesomorphic ideal, excessive muscle-building exercise may be important to address.

For the next 2 weeks, therapists help clients review progress and identify and incorporate treatment barriers into an edited case formulation. The next 8 weeks of treatment are devoted to addressing the factors that maintain the clients' eating disorders, including those potentially relevant to sexual minority men, such as shape and weight concerns, substance misuse, major life events (e.g., coming out), and interpersonal difficulties. When addressing dieting behavior, therapists should also be knowledgeable about common dieting behaviors related to achieving low body fat and high muscularity, such as increased lean protein and carbohydrate intake. The final stage of CBT-E addresses relapse prevention, which in sexual minority men might involve addressing ongoing environmental triggers, such as minority stress factors and sociocultural pressures to attain a gender-conforming ideal body.

INTERPERSONAL PSYCHOTHERAPY

Although CBT has been deemed the gold standard treatment for eating disorders, research indicated that at 1-year follow-up, interpersonal psychotherapy (IPT) displayed no differences from CBT in reduction of symptoms such as vomiting, dietary restraint, and binge eating (Fairburn, Jones, Peveler, Hope, & O'Connor, 1993), in addition to shape and weight concerns (Agras, Walsh, Fairburn, Wilson, & Kraemer, 2000), in clients with bulimia nervosa. However, there are mixed findings regarding IPT's efficacy (Agras et al., 2000). Understanding IPT in the context of eating disorder treatment and what types of clients may benefit the most from this treatment may therefore be important.

Interpersonal psychotherapy is characterized by addressing the relationship between social dysfunction and psychological symptoms (Rieger et al., 2010). The theoretical model of IPT for eating disorders stipulates that negative evaluation of one's body or eating habits from social networks (e.g., criticism of being "fat") leads to negative self-evaluation, such as BID, which triggers eating disorder behaviors aimed at achieving shape and weight changes (Rieger et al., 2010). IPT may be a viable option as a treatment for individuals for whom interpersonal factors are integral in the development and maintenance of eating disorder symptoms. In addition, given that IPT does not overtly address disordered eating behaviors, it may be a treatment option for patients who are resistant to explicitly discussing eating pathology but are open to discussing broader relationship issues. Clients also report high acceptability of IPT and perceived improvement and control of interpersonal functioning post-treatment (Fairburn, 2008). Fairburn further discussed combining an abbreviated IPT with CBT-E if interpersonal difficulty is a maintenance factor in an individual's case formulation; however, the efficacy of this form of IPT for eating disorders has not been tested.

Interpersonal psychotherapy for eating disorders consists of 12–16 weekly sessions (Weissman, Markowitz, & Klerman, 2000). Phase 1 includes a conceptualization of interpersonal difficulties as a maintenance factor for the individual's eating disorder and identification of specific difficulties (e.g., social comparison). In sexual minority men, this portion of treatment may include a discussion of any pressures from sexual partners or the gay male community about physical appearance. Sexual minority men may also endorse social comparison behaviors, also consistent with the tripartite model. Phase 2 is the longest portion of the treatment, with the goal of characterizing interpersonal difficulties into specific categories, such as grief, interpersonal role disputes (e.g., abuse), role transitions (e.g., coming out), and interpersonal deficits (e.g., low social support), and addressing them in everyday life. Sexual minority men, for example, may identify interpersonal role disputes, such as criticism or abuse from sexual or romantic partners, that may be linked to not meeting physical attractiveness standards. In addition, transitioning into a new sexual identity ("coming out") may be associated with desire to fit into the gay male community (e.g., meeting standards of attractiveness to be desired by sexual partners) and new stressors such as fear of discrimination, stigma, and victimization. Furthermore, preoccupation with appearance and comparing oneself to others may be paired with interpersonal deficits in sexual minority men, such as avoidance of bars, clubs, and other social events. Finally, Phase 3 sessions, during the last few weeks of IPT, involve relapse prevention. The therapist and client review progress and consolidate strategies to identify and target body image-related and eating disorder symptoms in an interpersonal context.

Interpersonal psychotherapy may therefore be an optimal choice if a client has body image and eating disorder concerns that are primarily maintained by pressures to have a socially defined ideal body from social networks (e.g., family, friends, and the media) or by social stress related to stigma or discrimination due to sexual orientation (e.g., not adhering to the traditional masculine body). However, the efficacy of IPT in sexual minority men has not been empirically tested.

FAMILY-BASED TREATMENT

Evidence supports the use of family-based treatment (FBT) for eating disorders in adolescents with anorexia nervosa and bulimia nervosa (Couturier, Kimber, & Szatmari, 2013). FBT consists of approximately 20 sessions during 6 months of treatment and is categorized by three phases (Loeb & le Grange, 2009). Phase 1 has the primary goal of weight restoration—for anorexia nervosa only, normalization of all eating behaviors and cessation of binge eating or purging behaviors. During this phase, parents are given control over the child's eating. In Phase 2 of treatment, control over eating is gradually returned to the adolescent. Finally, Phase 3 consists of focusing on interpersonal difficulties and other issues of development that might be relevant in the child's eating pathology. In sexual minority adolescent boys, Phase 3 may be a pivotal time to address the family's and other social networks' support of the child's sexual identity as well as the role of current and future sociocultural influences in maintaining or triggering eating disorder symptoms. Therapists may provide psychoeducation regarding how sexual minority status is a risk factor for body image concerns and eating disorders, highlighting relevant components of sexual minority stress theory, tripartite theory, and objectification theory. Therapists may help families and adolescent boys identify societal pressures regarding the ideal body for men and challenge that ideal in session and in their home environment (e.g., by asking the whole family to change the way they talk about magazines and media). Therapists may also ensure that adolescent boys can identify sexual minority discrimination or teasing and have social support systems in place (e.g., teachers, family, and peers).

DIALECTICAL BEHAVIOR THERAPY
Dialectical behavior therapy (DBT) is a cognitive–behavioral treatment originally developed for borderline personality disorder and incorporates both behavioral and acceptance-based interventions. The theoretical model underlying DBT for binge eating implicates emotion dysregulation as the primary cause of binge eating and purging (Wiser & Telch, 1999). DBT has been adapted for bulimia nervosa, in an individual format, and for binge eating disorder, in a group format, and consists of 20 weekly sessions (Safer, Telch, & Agras, 2001; Wiser & Telch, 1999). This adaptation focuses primarily on the mindfulness, emotion regulation, and distress tolerance skills-training modules (Safer et al., 2001; Telch, Agras, & Linehan, 2000). DBT for adolescents with anorexia and bulimia nervosa also includes a module for interpersonal effectiveness (Salbach, Klinkowski, Pfeiffer, Lehmkuhl, & Korte, 2007), which focuses on developing healthy relationships. There are three target behaviors in DBT: life-threatening behaviors (e.g., suicidality), therapy-interfering behaviors (e.g., non-adherence to homework and therapy non-attendance), and quality-of-life interfering behaviors (e.g., body checking and eating disorder behaviors). DBT may be more appropriate for clients with severe eating disorders or those who are highly impulsive and/or who have comorbid borderline personality disorder; however, moderators of DBT efficacy have not been thoroughly assessed when applied to eating disorders.

In sexual minority men, distress intolerance and emotion dysregulation may stem from sexual minority stressors, such as experiences of discrimination or stigma, and social comparison related to body shape and weight. Distress tolerance and mindfulness-based DBT techniques may be applied in this context in order to help clients accept these stressors as an unfortunate reality of their sexual minority status and to provide coping skills in response. These coping skills should replace maladaptive behaviors such as disordered eating. Case conceptualization may also indicate that the client has dysregulated emotional responses to social pressures from the gay male community or sexual partners, which leads to BID and eating disorder behaviors; therefore, emotion regulation skills can be implemented in response to these negative emotional responses. Furthermore, the interpersonal effectiveness module may be relevant for addressing eating disorder and body image symptoms among sexual minority men. Interpersonal effectiveness skills may help sexual minority men communicate more effectively with romantic partners and members of the gay community about physical appearance. For example, if romantic partners comment on their own body shape or about the client's body, the client can learn to respond effectively regarding their feelings about those comments. The four modules of DBT for eating disorders—mindfulness, distress tolerance, emotion regulation, and interpersonal effectiveness—are thus all applicable to address unique factors contributing to eating disorders in sexual minority men (e.g., gay-related discrimination and mesomorphic ideal pressures from the gay community).

Dialectical behavior therapy may be an appropriate treatment for sexual minority men with BID and eating disorders if pressures to conform to the mesomorphic ideal, social comparison, or minority stressors such as discrimination lead to emotion dysregulation that further maintains BID and eating disorder symptoms. Minority stress can be a source of significant distress for many sexual minority men, in which case distress tolerance skills and mindfulness can prove helpful. In addition, providing sexual minority men with emotion regulation skills may buffer them from maladaptive responses to shape- and weight-related social comparison. Interpersonal effectiveness skills may further help sexual minority men navigate pressures from social networks to adhere to the mesomorphic ideal.

CASE EXAMPLE: ENHANCED COGNITIVE–BEHAVIORAL THERAPY

Few existing treatments have been developed to address the specific needs of sexual minority males, including those experiencing body image or eating disturbance. However, given that CBT-E is a transdiagnostic form of CBT (Fairburn, 2008) that allows for a flexible framework and a personalized model of the patient's eating disorder, this approach could be effectively tailored to address how sexual identity may play a role in the patient's eating disorder maintenance. For example, clinicians could incorporate into treatment how specific pressures to conform to a mesomorphic body ideal among sexual minority clients, as outlined by objectification theory. This case example illustrates the application of CBT-E for a gay male client presenting with body image concerns and eating disorder symptoms.

Background

Kyle, a 22-year-old Caucasian, gay male undergraduate student, was referred to Dr. X, a psychologist specializing in eating disorder treatment. Kyle was born and raised in Jackson, Mississippi. At age 12 years, Kyle "came out" to his parents, who subsequently had difficulty accepting him being gay. Although he said he was aware that his parents loved him, they often avoided talking about his sexual orientation, which he believed indicated a lack of support. At the time of treatment, Kyle was not involved in a romantic relationship and was not connected with the lesbian, gay, bisexual, transgender, and queer (LGBTQ) organization at his school. Kyle self-referred for treatment due to his "obsessive food issues" and mood fluctuations.

Kyle reported that he had lost 75 pounds (highest weight, 233 pounds; lowest weight, 145 pounds; current weight, 150 pounds; current body mass index = 21.1) over 8 months during his sophomore year in college through "extreme dieting." Kyle attributed his motivation for this weight loss to pressures for gay men to look lean and "fit" and a belief that no one would find him attractive at his previous weight. Kyle also reported frequent negative thoughts related to eating and body image, including an intense fear of "becoming fat again" and needing to be thin in order to feel good about himself. Furthermore, he reported loss of control approximately once a week while eating normal amounts of food and endorsed several rituals around eating, including counting calories, fasting, and excessive exercise approximately 3 or 4 days per week.

Assessment

During the assessment phase, Kyle participated in a semi-structured clinical interview to determine eating disorder diagnosis and completed the Eating Disorders Examination Questionnaire (EDE-Q; Fairburn & Beglin, 1994) and the Clinical Impairment Assessment Questionnaire (CIA; Bohn & Fairburn, 2008). Kyle met all criteria for AN, excluding the weight criterion despite his substantial weight loss. Thus, Kyle was diagnosed with OSFED, atypical anorexia. Kyle's scores on the EDE-Q Restraint (score = 4.6), Eating Concern (score = 3.2), Weight Concern (score = 2.8), and Shape Concern (score = 2.8) subscales were all higher than the community norms for undergraduate males: Restraint mean (standard deviation) = 1.04 (1.19), Eating Concern = 0.43 (0.77), Weight Concern = 1.29 (1.27), and Shape Concern = 1.59 (1.38) (Lavender, De Young, & Anderson, 2010). His score on the CIA was higher than the suggested cut-off (score = 36; cut-off = 16).

Course of Treatment and Assessment of Progress

Stage I began with psychoeducation about eating disorder maintenance. Dr. X developed a comprehensive flow chart of the factors maintaining Kyle's eating disorder that guided the treatment focus. The primary maintenance factor for Kyle's eating disorder was his desire to look thin and muscular to attract a partner, which led him to engage in fasting, rigid rules about eating, and excessive exercise.

Although these behaviors led to weight loss, they also led to occasional loss-of-control eating (e.g., feeling that one cannot control what/how much they are eating and cannot stop eating once they start) and subsequent guilt about eating; this reinforced further restriction, which maintained the cycle of disordered eating. Additional triggers for Kyle's restrictive eating and loss-of-control eating included alcohol use and mood fluctuation. Furthermore, Kyle was highly perfectionistic and achievement focused, which also contributed to and maintained his restrictive eating pattern in order to look like the "perfect gay man." Kyle also reported limited engagement in the local LGBT community, partially due to concerns about his physical appearance.

During this stage, Kyle was asked to keep track of all food and beverage intake and thoughts regarding eating, weight, or shape in self-monitoring logs. Weekly weigh-ins were also introduced to monitor weight throughout treatment and to provide disconfirming evidence that regular eating would cause weight gain. Stage I goals first focused on regularizing his meal pattern by asking him to eat three meals and two snacks a day at regular times. Dr. X also determined that during this phase, Kyle should refrain from exercising because Kyle reported that he did not believe he could exercise moderately. Kyle was motivated to engage with treatment and quickly adapted to the eating plan. Triggers were discussed and problem-solved on days when Kyle engaged in dietary restriction. For example, Kyle had difficulty planning ahead and packing meals and snacks on busy school days, so Dr. X and Kyle decided that carrying granola bars in his backpack in the event that he forgot to pack a snack would help him keep on his eating schedule. During this period, Kyle also reduced his alcohol use on his own, after recognizing how his alcohol use increased his vulnerability to binge eating.

After six sessions, Kyle's scores on the dietary restraint subscale of the EDE-Q had decreased substantially to slightly above the community norm. Kyle's scores on the remaining cognitive subscales of the EDE-Q remained stable and within clinical ranges, which was expected given the behavioral focus of Stage I. Thus, Dr. X agreed that Kyle was ready to transition to Stage II. Given Kyle's motivation and progress thus far, Dr. X and Kyle spent one session in Stage II, which, as described previously, focuses on reviewing patient progress, identifying treatment barriers, and reviewing/updating the patient's case formulation. Dr. X and Kyle discussed Kyle's progress on the dietary restraint subscale of the EDE-Q, did not identify any immediate barriers to treatment, and agreed that his case formulation accurately reflected his eating disorder experience. As such, Dr. X decided to transition to Stage III.

Stage III included identifying and targeting the maintaining factors of Kyle's eating disorder, including dietary restraint, and dysfunctional cognitions and underlying beliefs. Although Kyle was eating regularly, he was still avoiding higher calorie foods and had considerable food rules. Thus, Dr. X formulated a feared food hierarchy to help expand Kyle's food choices, which eventually resulted in Kyle consuming his most feared food: a fried chicken sandwich with cheese.

During this stage, Dr. X and Kyle began identifying Kyle's negative automatic thoughts regarding his belief that he needed to be thin and muscular. These sessions also addressed the social factors maintaining Kyle's eating disorder, including distorted cognitions about dating and relationships ("I will never find a boyfriend at this weight") and his avoidance of eating in front of others. Dr. X worked with Kyle to challenge these thoughts (e.g., noting that Kyle knew normal and overweight gay men who were in relationships) and discussed ways to increase social support and expand Kyle's current network of friends, including attending campus LGBT activities to increase his sense of connectedness within the gay community. During these sessions, Dr. X and Kyle also discussed how to challenge potential pressures to conform to a lean, muscular ideal that might arise as Kyle became more involved in the gay male community (e.g., other men talking negatively about their bodies or specific foods, dieting, or the lean, muscular ideal).

Throughout the 10 sessions in Stage III, Kyle's scores on the EDE-Q dietary restraint subscale continued to decrease and ultimately stabilized below community norms, and his CIA scores declined below the clinical cut-off. Furthermore, his scores on the Eating, Shape, and Weight Concern subscales also showed substantial reductions from the beginning to the end of Stage III, when they reached the level of community norms. These scores, in conjunction with Kyle's self-reported improvement, led Dr. X to move to Stage IV, which consisted of 3 sessions focused on reviewing progress, building a relapse prevention plan, and clarifying the difference between a "lapse" and a "relapse."

FUTURE DIRECTIONS

There is a paucity of both theoretical and intervention/prevention research on BID and eating disorders in sexual minority men. The cross-sectional nature of the existing evidence base for BID and eating disorder theories indicates the need for experimental and longitudinal research to assess temporal and causal relationships between the sociocultural factors contributing to BID and body change behaviors. Without a deeper understanding of the development and maintenance of eating disorders and BID in sexual minority men, it is difficult to confidently apply existing evidence-based treatments, which were primarily validated in female samples, to this population.

The sexual minority male community also has considerable variability regarding the "ideal" body type (e.g., mesomorphic, thin, large, hairy, and hairless), which must be better understood, along with its implications for treatment. For example, the bear community, one of the gay male subcultures, has a larger body ideal, and members therefore may feel protected against eating disorders and pressures to adhere to the mesomorphic body ideal. Helping clients find more accepting subcultures within the gay community may be an important component of effective treatment. As a clinician, having cultural sensitivity to these differences might help guide treatment for a sexual minority male client. Further research on the heterogeneity within sexual minority cultures might strengthen clinician knowledge and self-efficacy in addressing these matters using an evidence-based practice approach.

In addition to the potential adaptations to existing evidence-based treatments for eating disorders and BID discussed previously, several other treatment adaptations may benefit sexual minority men. For example, investigators have begun to implement couples therapy in treating adults with eating disorders such as anorexia nervosa and binge eating disorder (Bulik, Baucom, Kirby, & Pisetsky, 2011; Kirby, Runfola, Fischer, Baucom, & Bulik, 2015). Gay and bisexual men have the unique experience of having a same-sex partner and, therefore, share the same societal body ideals, which might elicit competition, body comparison, and/or perceptions of pressure to adhere to the mesomorphic body ideal (Bailey, Markey, Markey, August, & Nave, 2015). Couples therapy for sexual minority men with BID or eating disorders could be helpful in addressing these unique experiences. Couples therapy for eating disorders attempts to facilitate a partner support system, provide psychoeducation, and increase understanding of each partner's body image experiences. Therapists should identify the client's and the partner's beliefs surrounding the mesomorphic body ideal and the role that physical appearance plays for each of them in their sexual and romantic relationships. Sexual minority male clients and their partners can be educated on the role that societal pressures and social comparison can play in internalizing the mesomorphic body ideal and subsequent maladaptive body change thoughts and behaviors. In addition, because sexual minority clients and their partners may both experience minority stressors, facilitating a support system will also be mutually beneficial, particularly if this stress plays a role in maintenance of eating disorders and BID. Furthermore, in couples therapy for binge eating disorder, an additional treatment goal is switching the focus in the relationship from discussions of weight to general health. The same shift in discussions of body image may be important among sexual minority men and their partners to reduce pressure to conform to the mesomorphic body ideal and curb body comparisons.

Online intervention and prevention efforts may also be an effective method of targeting BID and eating disorders in sexual minority men, among whom internet use is widespread in the form of social networking, such as dating websites (Brown, Maycock, & Burns, 2005). In addition, sexual minority men who exhibit sexual orientation concealment may explore their sexuality via the anonymity of the internet rather than going to gay bars or other public gay social events. Sexual minority men who are not openly out may not be willing to reveal their sexual identity in the therapeutic context; thus, the therapist may not be able to identify and target connections between sexual minority-specific factors contributing to BID and eating disorders. Online intervention options may therefore reach a wider sexual minority population. In addition, internet-based prevention efforts targeting internalization of the mesomorphic body ideal via exposure to gay-related media (e.g., advertisements and pornography) may be effective. HIV prevention efforts among sexual minority men, for example, have leveraged the prevalence of internet use among men who have sex with men by creating internet and cell phone-based HIV prevention and intervention programs (Ybarra & Bull, 2007). Furthermore, tests of internet-based interventions and prevention programs in body image-concerned women (Taylor et al., 2006) and college-age women at risk of developing an eating disorder (Zabinski, Wilfley, Calfas, Winzelberg, & Taylor, 2004) yielded high acceptability as well as improvements in shape and weight concern. Eating disorder internet-based prevention efforts specific to sexual minority men have the potential to reach both the openly gay community and men exhibiting greater concealment of their sexual orientation. However, more randomized controlled trials are needed to assess the benefits of online prevention and intervention efforts in sexual minority men with BID or eating disorders.

CONCLUSION

Sexual minority men experience BID and eating disorders at rates higher than those of heterosexual men and equal to or greater than those of women. Existing theoretical models of the development and maintenance of eating disorders have been primarily tested with women but more recently have been extended to sexual minority men. For example, the tripartite model and objectification theory apply to sexual minority men primarily via the pressures associated with being part of the gay community, such as the importance placed on the mesomorphic body ideal within the gay community. Moreover, minority stress theory further indicates a greater risk for overall mental health concerns, including eating disorders and BID. Understanding the role that sexual minority status may play in the development and maintenance of this pathology will help therapists tailor treatments to this population. The PRIDE Body Project is an example of a successfully tailored prevention program, and it can be a model for future intervention and prevention efforts in sexual minority men. In addition to modifying CBT-E, FBT, IPT, and DBT for sexual minority men, treatments such as couples therapy and internet-based intervention and prevention efforts should be explored and tested in this population. This chapter provides an informed yet introductory understanding of treating eating disorders in sexual minority men; future research is needed to validate evidence-based treatments specific to this population.

REFERENCES

Agras, W. S., Walsh, B. T., Fairburn, C. G., Wilson, G. T., & Kraemer, H. C. (2000). A multicenter comparison of cognitive–behavioral therapy and interpersonal psychotherapy for bulimia nervosa. *Archives of General Psychiatry, 57*, 459–466. doi:10.1001/archpsyc.57.5.459

American Psychiatric Association. (2013). *Diagnostic and statistical manual of mental disorders* (5th ed.). Arlington, VA: American Psychiatric Publishing.

Arcelus, J., Mitchell, A. J., Wales, J., & Nielsen, S. (2011). Mortality rates in patients with anorexia nervosa and other eating disorders: A meta-analysis of 36 studies. *Archives of General Psychiatry, 68*, 724–731. doi:10.1001/archgenpsychiatry.2011.74

Bailey, L., Markey, C. N., Markey, P. M., August, K. J., & Nave, C. S. (2015). Understanding same-sex male and female partners' restrained eating in the context of their relationships. *Journal of Health Psychology, 20*, 816–827. doi:10.1177/1359105315573431

Becker, C. B., Smith, L. M., & Ciao, A. C. (2006). Peer-facilitated eating disorder prevention: A randomized effectiveness trial of cognitive dissonance and media advocacy. *Journal of Counseling Psychology, 53*, 550. doi:10.1037/0022-0167.53.4.550

Blashill, A. J. (2010). Elements of male body image: Prediction of depression, eating pathology and social sensitivity among gay men. *Body Image, 7*, 310–316. doi:10.1016/j.bodyim.2010.07.006

Blashill, A. J., & Wilhelm, S. (2014). Body image distortions, weight, and depression in adolescent boys: Longitudinal trajectories into adulthood. *Psychology of Men & Masculinity, 15*, 445–451. doi:10.1037/a0034618

Bohn, K., & Fairburn, C. G. (2008). Clinical Impairment Assessment Questionnaire (CIA 3.0). In C. Fairburn (Ed.), *Cognitive behavior therapy for eating disorders* (pp. 315–317). New York, NY: Guilford.

Brown, G., Maycock, B., & Burns, S. (2005). Your picture is your bait: Use and meaning of cyberspace among gay men. *Journal of Sex Research, 42*, 63–73. doi:10.1080/00224490509552258

Brown, T. A., & Keel, P. K. (2012). The impact of relationships on the association between sexual orientation and disordered eating in men. *International Journal of Eating Disorders, 45*, 792–799. doi:10.1002/eat.22013

Brown, T. A., & Keel, P. K. (2015). A randomized controlled trial of a peer co-led dissonance-based eating disorder prevention program for gay men. *Behaviour Research and Therapy, 74*, 1–10. doi:10.1016/j.brat.2015.08.008

Bulik, C. M., Baucom, D. H., Kirby, J. S., & Pisetsky, E. (2011). Uniting Couples (in the treatment of) Anorexia Nervosa (UCAN). *International Journal of Eating Disorders, 44*, 19–28. doi:10.1002/eat.20790

Calzo, J. P., Corliss, H. L., Blood, E. A., Field, A. E., & Austin, S. B. (2013). Development of muscularity and weight concerns in heterosexual and sexual minority males. *Health Psychology, 32*, 42–51. doi:10.1037/a0028964

Carlat, D. J., Camargo, C. A., Jr., & Herzog, D. B. (1997). Eating disorders in males: A report on 135 patients. *American Journal of Psychiatry, 154*, 1127–1132. doi:10.1176/ajp.154.8.1127

Carper, T. L. M., Negy, C., & Tantleff-Dunn, S. (2010). Relations among media influence, body image, eating concerns, and sexual orientation in men: A preliminary investigation. *Body Image, 7*, 301–309. doi:10.1016/j.bodyim.2010.07.002

Couturier, J., Kimber, M., & Szatmari, P. (2013). Efficacy of family-based treatment for adolescents with eating disorders: A systematic review and meta-analysis. *International Journal of Eating Disorders, 46*, 3–11. doi:10.1002/eat.22042

Fairburn, C. G. (2008). *Cognitive behavior therapy and eating disorders*. New York, NY: Guilford.

Fairburn, C. G., & Beglin, S. J. (1994). Assessment of eating disorders: Interview or self-report questionnaire? *International Journal of Eating Disorders*, 16, 363–370.

Fairburn, C. G., Cooper, Z., Doll, H. A., O'Connor, M. E., Bohn, K., Hawker, D. M., . . . Palmer, R. L. (2009). Transdiagnostic cognitive–behavioral therapy for patients with eating disorders: A two-site trial with 60-week follow-up. *American Journal of Psychiatry*, 166, 311–319. doi:10.1176/appi.ajp.2008.08040608

Fairburn, C. G., Jones, R., Peveler, R. C., Hope, R. A., & O'Connor, M. (1993). Psychotherapy and bulimia nervosa: Longer-term effects of interpersonal psychotherapy, behavior therapy, and cognitive behavior therapy. *Archives of General Psychiatry*, 50, 419–428. doi:10.1001/archpsyc.1993.01820180009001

Feldman, M. B., & Meyer, I. H. (2007). Eating disorders in diverse lesbian, gay, and bisexual populations. *International Journal of Eating Disorders*, 40, 218–226. doi:10.1002/eat.20360

Festinger, L., & Carlsmith, J. M. (1959). Cognitive consequences of forced compliance. *Journal of Abnormal Psychology*, 58, 203–210.

Fredrickson, B. L., & Roberts, T. A. (1997). Objectification theory: Toward understanding women's lived experiences and mental health risks. *Psychology of Women Quarterly*, 21, 173–206. doi:10.1111/j.1471-6402.1997.tb00108.x

Freeman, L. M. Y., & Gil, K. M. (2004). Daily stress, coping, and dietary restraint in binge eating. *International Journal of Eating Disorders*, 36, 204–212. doi:10.1002/eat.20012

Harvey, J. A., & Robinson, J. D. (2003). Eating disorders in men: Current considerations. *Journal of Clinical Psychology in Medical Settings*, 10, 297–306. doi:10.1023/A:1026357505747

Jackson, B., Cooper, M. L., Mintz, L., & Albino, A. (2003). Motivations to eat: Scale development and validation. *Journal of Research in Personality*, 37, 297–318. doi:10.1016/S0092-6566(02)00574-3

Karazsia, B. T., & Crowther, J. H. (2009). Social body comparison and internalization: Mediators of social influences on men's muscularity-oriented body dissatisfaction. *Body Image*, 6, 105–112. doi:10.1016/j.bodyim.2008.12.003

Kimmel, S. B., & Mahalik, J. R. (2005). Body image concerns of gay men: The roles of minority stress and conformity to masculine norms. *Journal of Consulting and Clinical Psychology*, 73, 1185–1190. doi:10.1037/0022-006X.73.6.1185

Kirby, J. S., Runfola, C. D., Fischer, M. S., Baucom, D. H., & Bulik, C. M. (2015). Couple-based interventions for adults with eating disorders. *Eating Disorders*, 23, 356–365. doi:10.1080/10640266.2015.1044349

Klump, K. L., Bulik, C. M., Kaye, W. H., Treasure, J., & Tyson, E. (2009). Academy for eating disorders position paper: Eating disorders are serious mental illnesses. *International Journal of Eating Disorders*, 42, 97–103. doi:10.1002/eat.20589

Lavender, J. M., De Young, K. P., & Anderson, D. A. (2010). Eating Disorder Examination Questionnaire (EDE-Q): Norms for undergraduate men. *Eating Behaviors*, 11, 119–121. doi:10.1016/j.eatbeh.2009.09.005

Leit, R. A., Pope, H. G., & Gray, J. J. (2001). Cultural expectations of muscularity in men: The evolution of Playgirl centerfolds. *International Journal of Eating Disorders*, 29, 90–93. doi:10.1002/1098-108X(200101)29:1<90::AID-EAT15>3.0.CO;2-F

Loeb, K. L., & le Grange, D. (2009). Family-based treatment for adolescent eating disorders: Current status, new applications and future directions. *International Journal of Child and Adolescent Health*, 2, 243–254.

Martins, Y., Tiggemann, M., & Kirkbride, A. (2007). Those Speedos become them: The role of self-objectification in gay and heterosexual men's body image. *Personality and Social Psychology Bulletin, 33*, 634–647. doi:10.1177/0146167206297403

McCreary, D. R., Hildebrandt, T. B., Heinberg, L. J., Boroughs, M., & Thompson, J. K. (2007). A review of body image influences on men's fitness goals and supplement use. *American Journal of Men's Health, 1*, 307–316. doi:10.1177/1557988306309408

Meyer, I. H. (1995). Minority stress and mental health in gay men. *Journal of Health and Social Behavior, 36*, 38–56.

Mitchell, J. E., & Crow, S. (2006). Medical complications of anorexia nervosa and bulimia nervosa. *Current Opinion in Psychiatry, 19*, 438–443. doi:10.1097/01.yco.0000228768.79097.3e

Morrison, M. A., Morrison, T. G., & Sager, C. L. (2004). Does body satisfaction differ between gay men and lesbian women and heterosexual men and women? A meta-analytic review. *Body Image, 1*, 127–138. doi:10.1016/j.bodyim.2004.01.002

Morry, M. M., & Staska, S. L. (2001). Magazine exposure: Internalization, self-objectification, eating attitudes, and body satisfaction in male and female university students. *Canadian Journal of Behavioural Science, 33*, 269–279. doi:10.1037/h0087148

Murray, S. B., Rieger, E., Hildebrandt, T., Karlov, L., Russell, J., Boon, E., . . . Touyz, S. W. (2012). A comparison of eating, exercise, shape, and weight related symptomatology in males with muscle dysmorphia and anorexia nervosa. *Body Image, 9*, 193–200. doi:10.1016/j.bodyim.2012.01.008

Parent, M. C. (2013). Clinical considerations in etiology, assessment, and treatment of men's muscularity-focused body image disturbance. *Psychology of Men & Masculinity, 14*, 88–100. doi:10.1037/a0025644

Pope, H. G., Olivardia, R., Gruber, A., & Borowiecki, J. (1999). Evolving ideals of male body image as seen through action toys. *International Journal of Eating Disorders, 26*, 65–72. doi:10.1002/(SICI)1098-108X(199907)26:1<65::AID-EAT8>3.0.CO;2-D

Rieger, E., Van Buren, D. J., Bishop, M., Tanofsky-Kraff, M., Welch, R., & Wilfley, D. E. (2010). An eating disorder-specific model of interpersonal psychotherapy (IPT-ED): Causal pathways and treatment implications. *Clinical Psychology Review, 30*, 400–410. doi:10.1016/j.cpr.2010.02.001

Safer, D. L., Telch, C. F., & Agras, W. S. (2001). Dialectical behavior therapy for bulimia nervosa. *American Journal of Psychiatry, 158*, 632–634. doi:10.1176/appi.ajp.158.4.632

Salbach, H., Klinkowski, N., Pfeiffer, E., Lehmkuhl, U., & Korte, A. (2007). Dialectical behavior therapy for adolescents with anorexia and bulimia nervosa (DBT-AN/BN)—A pilot study. *Praxis der Kinderpsychologie und Kinderpsychiatrie, 56*, 91–108. doi:10.13109/prkk.2007.56.2.91

Shapiro, J. R., Berkman, N. D., Brownley, K. A., Sedway, J. A., Lohr, K. N., & Bulik, C. M. (2007). Bulimia nervosa treatment: A systematic review of randomized controlled trials. *International Journal of Eating Disorders, 40*, 321–336. doi:10.1002/eat.20372

Shroff, H., & Thompson, J. K. (2006). The tripartite influence model of body image and eating disturbance: A replication with adolescent girls. *Body Image, 3*, 17–23. doi:10.1016/j.bodyim.2005.10.004

Siever, M. D. (1994). Sexual orientation and gender as factors in socioculturally acquired vulnerability to body dissatisfaction and eating disorders. *Journal of Consulting and Clinical Psychology*, *62*, 252–260. doi:10.1037/0022-006X.62.2.252

Silberstein, L. R., Striegel-Moore, R. H., Timko, C., & Rodin, J. (1988). Behavioral and psychological implications of body dissatisfaction: Do men and women differ? *Sex Roles*, *19*, 219–232. doi:10.1007/BF00290156

Smolak, L., Murnen, S. K., & Thompson, J. K. (2005). Sociocultural influences and muscle building in adolescent boys. *Psychology of Men & Masculinity*, *6*, 227–239. doi:10.1037/1524-9220.6.4.227

Stice, E., Rohde, P., Gau, J., & Shaw, H. (2009). An effectiveness trial of a dissonance-based eating disorder prevention program for high-risk adolescent girls. *Journal of Consulting and Clinical Psychology*, *77*, 825–834. doi:10.1037/a0016132

Stice, E., Shaw, H., Burton, E., & Wade, E. (2006). Dissonance and healthy weight eating disorder prevention programs: A randomized efficacy trial. *Journal of Consulting and Clinical Psychology*, *74*, 263–275. doi:10.1037/0022-006X.74.2.263

Stice, E., Shaw, H., & Marti, C. N. (2007). A meta-analytic review of eating disorder prevention programs: Encouraging findings. *Annual Review of Clinical Psychology*, *3*, 207–231.

Strong, S. M., Williamson, D. A., Netemeyer, R. G., & Geer, J. H. (2000). Eating disorder symptoms and concerns about body differ as a function of gender and sexual orientation. *Journal of Social and Clinical Psychology*, *19*, 240–255. doi:10.1521/jscp.2000.19.2.240

Taylor, C. B., Bryson, S., Luce, K. H., Cunning, D., Doyle, A. C., Abascal, L. B., . . . Wilfley, D. E. (2006). Prevention of eating disorders in at-risk college-age women. *Archives of General Psychiatry*, *63*, 881–888. doi:10.1001/archpsyc.63.8.881

Telch, C. F., Agras, W. S., & Linehan, M. M. (2000). Group dialectical behavior therapy for binge-eating disorder: A preliminary, uncontrolled trial. *Behavior Therapy*, *31*, 569–582. doi:10.1016/S0005-7894(00)80031-3

Thompson, J. K., Heinberg, L. J., Altabe, M., & Tantleff-Dunn, S. (1999). *Exacting beauty: Theory, assessment, and treatment of body image disturbance*. Washington, DC: American Psychological Association.

Tylka, T. L. (2011). Refinement of the tripartite influence model for men: Dual body image pathways to body change behaviors. *Body Image*, *8*, 199–207. doi:10.1016/j.bodyim.2011.04.008

Tylka, T. L., & Andorka, M. J. (2012). Support for an expanded tripartite influence model with gay men. *Body Image*, *9*, 57–67. doi:10.1016/j.bodyim.2011.09.006

van den Berg, P., Thompson, J. K., Obremski-Brandon, K., & Coovert, M. (2002). The tripartite influence model of body image and eating disturbance: A covariance structure modeling investigation testing the mediational role of appearance comparison. *Journal of Psychosomatic Research*, *53*, 1007–1020. doi:10.1016/S0022-3999(02)00499-3

Watson, R. J., Adjei, J., Saewyc, E., Homma, Y., & Goodenow, C. (2017). Trends and disparities in disordered eating among heterosexual and sexual minority adolescents. *International Journal of Eating Disorders*, *50*, 22–31. doi:10.1002/eat.22576

Weissman, M. M., Markowitz, J. C., & Klerman, G. L. (2000). *Comprehensive guide to interpersonal psychotherapy*. New York, NY: Basic Books.

Wiseman, M. C., & Moradi, B. (2010). Body image and eating disorder symptoms in sexual minority men: A test and extension of objectification theory. *Journal of Counseling Psychology, 57,* 154–166. doi:10.1037/a0018937

Wiser, S., & Telch, C. F. (1999). Dialectical behavior therapy for binge-eating disorder. *Journal of Clinical Psychology, 55,* 755–768. doi:10.1002/(SICI)1097-4679(199906)55:6<755::AID-JCLP8>3.0.CO;2-R

Ybarra, M. L., & Bull, S. S. (2007). Current trends in internet- and cell phone-based HIV prevention and intervention programs. *Current HIV/AIDS Reports, 4,* 201–207. doi:10.1007/s11904-007-0029-2

Zabinski, M. F., Wilfley, D. E., Calfas, K. J., Winzelberg, A. J., & Taylor, C. B. (2004). An interactive psychoeducational intervention for women at risk of developing an eating disorder. *Journal of Consulting and Clinical Psychology, 72,* 914–919. doi:10.1037/0022-006X.72.5.914

14

Sexual Health Interventions for HIV-Negative Sexual Minority Men

TREVOR A. HART, JULIA R. G. VERNON,
AND NATHAN GRANT SMITH ■

Gay, bisexual, queer, and other men who have sex with men (MSM) continue to be a population at risk for significant negative sexual health outcomes. Sexual minority men comprise the majority of new HIV infections in most developed countries (Centers for Disease Control and Prevention, 2014; Public Health Agency of Canada, 2015). MSM are also disproportionately burdened by other sexually transmitted infections (STIs), especially syphilis and sexually transmitted hepatitis C virus (Centers for Disease Control and Prevention, 2016). The HIV and STI epidemics among MSM do not appear to be decreasing despite promising new biomedical treatments such as pre-exposure prophylaxis, which refers to the use of antiretroviral medications by HIV-negative individuals to reduce the chances of contracting HIV (Grant et al., 2010; McCormack et al., 2016).

HIV-negative MSM may also face other sexual health problems beyond contracting HIV. Sexual minority men report higher erectile dysfunction compared to heterosexual men (Hirshfield et al., 2010). This population may also experience concerns such as pain or discomfort in the anal sphincter or canal during anal sex (Rosser, Short, Thurmes, & Coleman, 1998), low sexual self-efficacy and sexual anxiety (Blashill et al., 2016), and problems with sexual assertiveness (Eisenberg, Bauermeister, Johns, Pingel, & Santana, 2011).

This chapter reviews the scientific literature on available interventions for HIV-negative MSM and provides information on how to integrate these approaches into clinicians' practice. The interventions reviewed are diverse in their theoretical background, format, and required counseling skills but may nevertheless be accessible to most mental health professionals. When available, the chapter presents clinically focused information regarding the content of each session, and it discusses how practitioners can integrate these interventions into their practice. The chapter first reviews empirically supported individual- and couples-based HIV prevention interventions and then discusses small group-based HIV prevention interventions. It then discusses the relatively more limited literature on sexual health interventions outside of HIV prevention. The chapter concludes by summarizing the available findings and suggesting future research to advance the science and practice of sexual health interventions for HIV-negative MSM.

INDIVIDUAL AND COUPLES HIV PREVENTION INTERVENTIONS

EXPLORE

EXPLORE is the first randomized controlled trial (RCT) of an HIV prevention intervention for MSM in the United States designed with a sample size large enough for HIV incidence to be the outcome (Koblin et al., 2003). EXPLORE is a 10-module cognitive–behavioral therapy (CBT) intervention that integrates the information motivation behavioral skills model and social learning theory (Chesney et al., 2003). Module 1 uses motivational interviewing techniques to discuss and strengthen reasons as to why the participant wants to remain HIV-negative. The counselor normalizes the client's ambivalence about engaging in behaviors that are consistent with this goal. In modules 2 and 3, the counselor asks about the client's current knowledge of HIV risk factors and helps him explore his own risk limits. Positive aspects of condomless anal sex (CAS; what is "good" about the current behavior) for the client are also discussed—for example, convenience and enhanced physical sensation.

Modules 4 and 5 focus on verbal and nonverbal sexual communication and the ways in which current attitudes and skills impede sexual communication of one's own risk limits. In module 6, the emphasis is on the role of substance use in perpetuating unwanted risk behavior. Modules 7–9 focus on the triggers that can facilitate the old behavior and on identifying and practicing skills to mitigate these triggers. Module 10 focuses on maintaining adherence to the client's sexual risk limits and strategies for relapse prevention.

In an RCT of 4,295 men residing in six cities in the United States, EXPLORE was compared to a two-session risk reduction intervention using the US Centers for Disease Control and Prevention's (CDC) Project RESPECT model, which was not originally designed for sexual minority men (Kamb et al., 1998). The rate of seroconversion was 15.7% (95% confidence interval [CI]: –8.4, 34.4) lower in EXPLORE participants than the comparison group at 48-month follow-up, controlling for baseline characteristics (EXPLORE Study Team, 2004). Although the target of a 35% difference in HIV incidence was observed at 12-month follow-up, differences waned over time and the HIV incidence target was not achieved at 48-month follow-up (EXPLORE Study Team, 2004). In terms of behavioral outcomes at 48-month follow-up, controlling for site and baseline characteristics, 13.2% (95% CI: 4.8, 20.9) fewer participants reported any CAS in the past 6 months in the EXPLORE group, 14.8% (95% CI: 6.5, 22.4) fewer participants reported serodiscordant CAS, and 22.5% (95% CI: 13.3, 30.7) fewer participants reported serodiscordant receptive CAS. Significant differences in biological outcomes were not observed four years later. An argument has been made, however, that the 35% incidence difference should not have been the sole indicator of the success or failure of the study and that, as a result, research interest in behavioral interventions to prevent HIV in HIV-negative MSM has been too harshly criticized in terms of affecting HIV prevention goals (Kalichman, Zohren, & Eaton, 2014). The intervention was successful, for example, in preventing HIV infections in the medium term and had lasting effects on sexual risk behavior.

Young Men's Health Project

The Young Men's Health Project is a four-session motivational interviewing intervention for MSM aged 18-29 years who use recreational drugs (Parsons, Lelutiu-Weinberger, Botsko, & Golub, 2014). Its use of motivational interviewing is an advantage because many mental health professionals are already trained in this modality. In Session 1, the therapist explains motivational interviewing, asks the participant to select the target behavior he would like to address first (CAS or substance use), and helps participant devise a plan for change, which includes goal setting and identifying barriers to change. Session 2 involves creating a plan for the other target behavior, discussing the links between CAS and substance use, and a decisional balance exercise examining the costs and benefits of change. Session 3 focuses on readiness to change, motivation, and resolving ambivalence about the goal behaviors, and the therapist affirms the participant's progress and commitment to change. In Session 4, plans for change are reviewed and revised as needed, and information about community resources is provided.

Parsons et al. (2014) compared the Young Men's Health Project to a four-session educational intervention with structured discussion questions in an RCT. Participants were men aged 18–29 years who reported use of cocaine, methamphetamine, γ-hydroxybutyrate, Ecstasy, ketamine, or poppers on at least 5 of the past 90 days and CAS with an HIV-positive or unknown status primary male partner or any casual male partner, or any sex with a casual partner, in the past 90 days. Participants also reported having anal sex with a casual male partner at least once within 30 days before the baseline assessment. From baseline to post-treatment and 3-, 6-, and 9-month follow-up assessments, the experimental condition resulted in a greater reduction of the number of days on which participants had CAS with a casual partner within the past 30 days even after controlling for drug use (adjusted odds ratio [OR] = 0.79; 95% CI: 0.70, 0.89). The Young Men's Health Project also demonstrated greater reductions in the number of days of drug use in the past 90 days compared to the control condition across the four follow-up assessments.

Personalized Cognitive Counseling

Personalized cognitive counseling (PCC) is a one-session intervention designed for MSM with a history of HIV testing on multiple occasions after engaging in high-risk sexual behavior (Dilley et al., 2002). The premise for the intervention is based on self-justifications (Gold & Rosenthal, 1998), stages of behavior change, and self-regulation theory, and it is designed for men who are already knowledgeable of the risks associated with their sexual practices but find themselves returning to the behavior (Coffin et al., 2014). Because of its focus on rational versus nonrational thinking and disputing maladaptive cognitions, PCC may be well suited to clinicians who are already trained in cognitive–behavioral therapies and other techniques focusing on increasing the adaptiveness of thoughts and behavior.

Clients complete a self-report questionnaire called the Self-Justification Elicitation Instrument (Gold & Rosenthal, 1998), in which they indicate the degree to which each of a list of statements of self-justifications for having CAS applies to them. The counselor introduces the objective of the intervention, which is to help the client pursue a fulfilling sex life while limiting risky sexual activities. The client relays a narrative of the most recent occasion during which he had CAS with an HIV-positive or unknown status partner. Next, the counselor asks the client to express his self-justifications for not using a condom during the encounter or his thoughts, feelings, and attitudes directly preceding the sexual activity. During the examination phase, the counselor leads the client in questioning or disputing his self-justifications by highlighting the distinction between *on-line thinking* and *off-line thinking*. The former takes place in the "heat of the moment" when the client is sexually aroused; this is when self-justifications are present and facilitate behavior contrary to one's preferred sexual risk limits. Off-line thinking refers to a state of more rational thinking, when the self-justifications seem less convincing and the client reports more accurate assessments of risk. The session concludes with plans for future behavior. In a first RCT, the PCC was delivered by mental health professionals and at 6-month follow-up was found to be successful compared to the standard of care plus a sexual behavior diary in terms of fewer CAS acts with an HIV-positive or unknown serostatus partner in the previous 90 days (Dilley et al., 2002). In another RCT, the researchers investigated whether PCC would be successful when delivered by paraprofessional HIV test counselors compared to the standard of care recommended by the CDC. Participants in the PCC condition still reported significantly fewer CAS events compared to the standard of care at 6-month follow-up (Dilley et al., 2007).

Adaptation of PCC: Project ECHO

Project ECHO is an adaptation of PCC for sexual minority men who engage in episodic substance use and have a pattern of repeated sexual risk behavior followed by HIV testing. Informed by qualitative interviews with episodic substance-using

MSM, Knight and colleagues (2014) created a modified version of the Self-Justification Elicitation Instrument that includes more items about substance use in sexual situations. Sample items are "Alcohol and/or drugs make it easier to have sex (or different kinds of sex)" and "Sex is better when I am drunk or high" (Coffin et al., 2014).

In Project ECHO, clients are asked to recall a recent sexual scenario in which they had CAS with a serodiscordant or unknown status partner and to complete the self-justification elicitation instrument based on their recollection of their thoughts, feelings, and attitudes that facilitated the non-use of a condom at that time. To prepare for future sexual situations, the participant and counselor weigh the evidence for and against each self-justification statement that was endorsed, discuss the function of these self-justifications, and brainstorm more positive self-statements as well as strategies for engaging in healthier sex moving forward.

In an RCT with men who had CAS while under the influence of methamphetamine, poppers, crack or powdered cocaine, or within 2 hours of binge drinking alcohol in the past 6 months, Coffin et al. (2014) did not find reductions in the number of insertive or receptive CAS events or the number of CAS partners in the past 3 months, or the number of CAS events with participants' three most recent non-primary partners. Project ECHO participants had a greater decrease in the number of receptive CAS occasions, although the reduction was not significantly different from controls. Among participants who did not meet criteria for substance dependence, Project ECHO participants had a greater reduction in the number of CAS occasions with their three most recent non-primary partners. Project ECHO may therefore be helpful for reducing sexual risk behavior in clients with mild substance use disorders or subclinical substance use concerns. In summary, although including substance use management is logical given that substance use is a risk factor for HIV among MSM (Koblin et al., 2006), more data are needed to support the use of this one-session intervention with episodic substance users.

Think Twice

Think Twice is a peer-delivered, 40-minute, one-session program for MSM engaging in high-risk sex and is designed to be implementable in public health settings (Eaton, Cherry, Cain, & Pope, 2011). It is focused on preparing men to make healthy decisions in high-risk scenarios by weighing the costs and benefits of possible choices. Think Twice also aims to dispel myths about serosorting through the use of a graphic novel. For example, the belief that it is safer to have CAS with a partner who reports being HIV-negative than with a partner who reports being HIV-positive may be incorrect if the former partner has an undiagnosed acute HIV infection and the latter partner has an undetectable viral load. Participants are guided through an exercise in which they identify possible HIV transmission routes using a visual sexual network diagram of the main character of the graphic novel. Participants then create their own sexual network diagram to extrapolate the new information into their own life and their own harm reduction plan.

Men who have sex with men reporting two or more CAS partners in the past 6 months were randomized to Think Twice or a time-matched, control condition following CDC guidelines for standard HIV risk reduction counseling. Compared to controls, Think Twice participants reported fewer male sexual partners at 1- and 3-month follow-up and fewer HIV-positive or unknown status partners. They also had greater condom use self-efficacy at 3-month follow-up. This intervention is not only efficacious but also could reach a wide variety of clients due to its short format and peer delivery. In addition, due to its use of a graphic novel and visual diagram, Think Twice may be particularly well suited to people who are visual learners.

Life-Steps for Pre-exposure Prophylaxis

One innovative HIV prevention intervention is focused not on reduction of sexual risk behaviors but, rather, on increasing adherence to antiretroviral medications used for pre-exposure prophylaxis (PrEP; Mayer et al., 2017). Life-Steps, a treatment originally designed to help HIV-positive participants with medication adherence (Safren, Otto, & Worth, 1999), was adapted with HIV-negative MSM focusing on improving PrEP adherence (for a case study and demonstration videos, see Taylor et al., 2017). This intervention is well suited for use by mental health professionals who are trained in both behavioral therapies and motivational interviewing.

Life-Steps uses a combination of education, motivational interviewing techniques, and problem-solving to address barriers to medication adherence. The educational component occurs mostly in Session 1 and includes both discussion about PrEP, how it works, and its side effects and a video that reinforces this information and introduces motivations for being adherent to PrEP. The motivational component occurs largely in Sessions 2 and 3. An example of motivational interviewing can be found in the decisional balance presented in Taylor et al. (2017). Advantages for being adherent to PrEP might include protection for HIV and increasing intimacy because the client feels safer, and disadvantages may include having to take daily pills. Advantages of not adhering to PrEP may include avoiding side effects, and disadvantages include remaining at risk for HIV. The problem-solving component occurs in Sessions 3 and 4 and includes discussion of barriers to HIV risk reduction, brainstorming of potential solutions, evaluation of potential solutions, and planning for implementation of a plan of the best rated solution.

In a pilot study of 50 MSM, four counseling sessions were conducted by a nurse, with follow-up visits at 1, 2, 3, and 6 months after enrollment. Plasma levels of tenofovir, the medication used for PrEP, were higher in the Life-Steps group than in the time-matched counseling intervention at 6-month follow-up using mean substitution analysis (i.e., computing missing variables), although not in the completer analyses. The lack of statistical significance is likely due to low statistical power in this pilot study. Although more data are needed on this program, this intervention is timely and innovative due to its focus on PrEP adherence.

2GETHER Couples Intervention

Mental health professionals now also have an option when counseling couples that want to focus on HIV prevention. The 2GETHER four-session intervention integrates HIV prevention and relationship education for young male couples (Newcomb et al., 2017). Sessions 1 and 2 are psychoeducational group sessions providing information on healthy relationships, communication skills, sexual health information including HIV and STI prevention, and strategies for coping with minority and relationship stressors. Sessions 3 and 4 involve couples coaching to apply skills to improve relationship functioning and sexual health promotion, including a relationship agreement to reduce the risk of transmitting HIV within a couple and with sexual partners outside of the couple. Among 57 couples, there was a minor reduction in the proportion of CAS partners and no effect for the total number of CAS acts. Although there were no differences in relationship functioning as assessed by the Dyadic Adjustment Scale (Spanier, 1976), there were increases in relationship investment and in relationship agreement among partners about sexual monogamy versus allowing outside sexual partners. This intervention is notable for its use of group and couples counseling, as well as its focus on couple dynamics. Its relative strengths are also a potential challenge for clinicians who are not trained in both group counseling and couples counseling. However, more research is merited to support its use. One future area for examination of 2GETHER may be with serodiscordant couples because clinicians may see more of these couples in their practices given that medical treatments have become increasingly effective in reducing HIV transmission.

INTERNET-BASED INTERVENTIONS

Internet-based counseling allows clinicians to reach clients in areas where relevant, culturally competent services may not be available. In rigorous evaluations, some internet-based HIV prevention interventions have been found to lead to reductions in sexual risk behavior. One of these, POWER (Fernandez et al., 2016), involves interacting with a live facilitator and is detailed next. The others are independent interactive self-learning tools and thus do not fall within the scope of a traditional counseling or psychotherapy session, but they are supported by evidence and may be useful adjuncts to therapy. These include Keep It Up! (Mustanski, Garofalo, Monahan, Gratzer, & Andrews, 2013), the Kinsey Institute Homework Intervention Strategy (KIHIS; Emetu et al., 2014), Hot and Safe M4M (Carpenter, Stoner, Nikko, Dhanak, & Parsons, 2010), and Project SMART (Schonnesson, Bowen, & Williams, 2016).

POWER

POWER consists of three 60- to 90-minute sessions and is designed for HIV-negative and HIV-positive Black men who have sex with men and women (MSMW; Fernandez et al., 2016). Like many of the individual interventions described previously, POWER is based on the information–motivation–behavioral skills model (Fisher & Fisher, 1992), but it is unique in that it involves live chat with a facilitator via the internet. Session 1 begins with viewing videos about media stereotypes of Black men and concludes with a motivational video about the client's agency in making change. Between video clips, using motivational interviewing, the facilitator helps the participant identify the important people in his life and reflect on whether or not they support the client's sexual health. In Session 2, the facilitator provides sexual health information and helps the client set sexual health goals and devise strategies to support these goals. Session 3 involves learning about verbal and nonverbal communication, practicing sexual communication skills, identifying social support, and finalizing and committing to a sexual health plan.

In an RCT in which POWER was compared to a one-session online intervention lasting 3 or 4 hours, Fernandez and colleagues (2016) found that after adjusting for HIV status and diagnosis of an STI in the past 12 months at baseline, participants in the POWER condition were less likely to report condomless anal or vaginal intercourse at the 3-month follow-up assessment (OR = 0.49; 95% CI: 0.25, 0.98). POWER also showed superior results for reductions in anal or vaginal sex with a serodiscordant partner irrespective of condom use (adjusted OR = 0.59; 95% CI: 0.36, 0.96). Examining male and female partners separately, there were significant differences only for male partners for both outcomes. POWER may be easily implementable for clinicians trained in motivational interviewing approaches.

Independent Internet-Based Interventions

Keep It Up! (Mustanski et al., 2013) is designed to reach ethnically diverse MSM aged 18–24 years who have received an HIV-negative test result. It consists of seven online modules completed during three sessions. The modules have informational video and interactive components, and the participant is prompted to develop a sexual health plan with specific goals pertaining to risk behavior and strategies for addressing barriers to implement the plan. Compared to a time-matched control condition consisting of an online information intervention, participants in the Keep It Up! condition reported fewer CAS events at 12-week follow-up.

KIHIS (Emetu et al., 2014) participants receive a selection of free condoms and view a demonstration on how to put on a condom correctly. As homework, participants are asked to practice applying at least six kinds of condoms and rate them in online surveys. In a one-armed trial, there was an increase in condom use self-efficacy and an increase in the percentage of occasions on which men used a condom for insertive anal sex (Emetu et al., 2014).

Hot and Safe M4M (Carpenter et al., 2010) is a 90- to 120-minute online tuto-rial inspired by the information motivation behavioral skills model and includes videos and interactive activities such as tests of HIV knowledge and a decisional balance exercise. Compared to participants assigned to an online stress-reduction training program, participants in Hot and Safe M4M had a greater decrease in the number of CAS events with HIV-positive or unknown status partners.

Project SMART is an adaptation of the Wyoming Rural AIDS Prevention Project (WRAPP; Bowen, Williams, Daniel, & Clayton, 2008) for the Swedish context. It is based on the information motivation behavioral skills model and consists of six online sessions. WRAPP consists of three modules: Module 1 provides information about HIV by depicting a conversation between a knowl-edgeable HIV-positive man educating an HIV-negative man who had recently engaged in risky sex, Module 2 targets motivation by highlighting the discrep-ancy between life goals and short-term goals in a risky sexual scenario, and Module 3 focuses on risk reduction strategies in a variety of contexts. There was no treatment control group in this study, but some subgroups of participants demonstrated increased condom use, decreased number of sex partners, and a reduced percentage of partners with whom they had anal sex. Compared to participants assigned to a 30-day wait-list period, participants in the Project SMART condition significantly reduced their frequency of anal sex with casual partners (Schonnesson et al., 2016).

The four interventions discussed in this section may be useful for clinicians who either cannot work with a client on a weekly basis (e.g., due to barriers such as finances or distance to the clinic) or are focusing clinically on presenting complaints outside of sexual health.

GROUP INTERVENTIONS

Group interventions have a number of benefits compared to individual interventions but also have some potential pitfalls. In general, group interventions can be provided to a greater number of individuals, making them potentially more cost- and time-efficient than individual interventions. In addition, group contexts may allow for the development of social support, sense of belonging, sense of universality, the ability to help others, social learning and modeling, and sharing of common experiences (Yalom & Leszcz, 2005). In the context of MSM, group interventions bring together men with similar sexual minority identities and may be useful in promoting community connectedness, which is positively related to social and psychological well-being (Frost & Meyer, 2012). A potential pitfall is the possibility of members developing sexual relationships with other members. For example, although it was not a group intervention, 31% of participants in the EXPLORE study reported having sex with other EXPLORE participants (Mimiaga et al., 2006). With these benefits and caveats in mind, this section reviews group interventions to promote MSM's sexual health.

Many Men, Many Voices

Many Men, Many Voices (3MV; Wilton et al., 2009) focuses on Black MSM and consists of six 2- or 3-hour sessions provided in a weekend retreat format. Session 1 links racism and homophobia to sexual risk behaviors and substance use. Session 2 focuses on the relative HIV and STI risk of various sexual acts, as well as sexual relationship dynamics. Session 3 helps participants identify options for safer sex. Session 4 focuses on increasing intentions to engage in safer sex. Session 5 deals with relationship dynamics. Session 6 includes role-playing partner communication skills, peer support for problem-solving, and identification of risk reduction strategies should relapse occur. Overall, 3MV focuses on the intersection of being Black and being a sexual minority. Familial, cultural, and religious norms are explored, as well as their impact on HIV and STI risk among participants. HIV risk behaviors are explored in the context of racism and homophobia. Finally, the intervention focuses on the nuances of relationship dynamics within Black MSM culture.

To test the efficacy of 3MV, 338 men were enrolled in an RCT and either received 3MV immediately or were placed on a wait list to receive 3MV after 6 months. The intervention was delivered by two trained Black MSM peers. At 3-month follow-up, those in the intervention condition reported significantly fewer male sex partners compared to controls. At 6-month follow-up, those in the intervention condition reported significantly fewer instances of CAS with casual partners (but not main partners) compared to controls. Finally, at 6-month follow-up, those in the intervention condition were more likely to report obtaining HIV testing than were controls.

40 & Forward

40 & Forward (Reisner et al., 2011) focuses on HIV-negative and HIV-positive MSM aged 40 years or older with self-reported mental health problems. The intervention consists of six 2-hour weekly sessions. The sessions cover the following topics: (1) identification of sources of social support, (2) prioritizing engaging in pleasant activities and identifying obstacles to doing so, (3) development of problem-solving skills, (4) HIV risk reduction psychoeducation and development of partner sexual communication skills, (5) development of general communication skills, and (6) active listening skills training. A primary focus is increasing social support and decreasing isolation. As such, it helps participants identify the underlying causes of social isolation (as well as depression and social anxiety), develop their interpersonal and communication skills, and expand their social support networks.

A total of 84 men completed the intervention and pre- and post-treatment assessments. There was no control group. Results revealed significant reductions from pre- to post-treatment in depression (a medium effect size), social anxiety, loneliness, and fear of negative evaluation (all small effect sizes). There was a large effect on increases in condom use self-efficacy. There were reductions in CAS, but these were not statistically significant.

LifeSkills for Men

LifeSkills for Men (LS4M; Reisner et al., 2016) targets transgender MSM aged 18–29 years. LS4M was adapted from the LifeSkills intervention (Garofalo et al., 2012), an intervention for young transgender women. It involves four weekly meetings, each lasting 2 hours. The first session focuses on identity affirmation, with exploration of the impact of positive and negative messages about gender identity on self, relationships, and coping. The second session focuses on partner communication, including strategies around disclosure of transgender identity. The third session focuses on safer sex practices. The fourth session includes a review of the topics covered and a focus on transgender community connection and support of cisgender allies. Throughout, it focuses on affirming participants' gender and sexual identities. The group explores the influence on their lives of masculinity norms and stereotypes of transgender and sexual minority people. These messages are unpacked and analyzed to identify how they impact participants' coping strategies, relationships, and general and sexual health. Next, LS4M provides participants with psychoeducation on partner communication and HIV and STI. This information is integrated with discussions of how to meet partners and navigate disclosure of their transgender and sexual orientation identities to sexual partners. The intervention concludes with a focus on transgender community connection and identification of social support.

A total of 18 participants enrolled in a one-armed pilot that included a pretreatment and 4-month post-treatment assessment. Self-report psychosocial (e.g., transgender-specific mental health adaptation) and sexual health outcomes (e.g., knowledge and self-efficacy) measures revealed changes in the expected direction from pre- to post-treatment; however, few effects were significant. There were significant increases in transgender community integration, gender identity adjustment, and condom use self-efficacy (for condom use self-efficacy, the result was marginally significant). In addition, no participant seroconverted during the study.

Males of African American Legacy Empowering Self

Males of African American Legacy Empowering Self (MAALES; Harawa et al., 2013; Williams, Ramamurthi, Manago, & Harawa, 2009) focuses on HIV-positive and HIV-negative African American MSMW. It consists of six 2-hour sessions over the course of 3 weeks, plus two 2-hour booster sessions at 6 and 18 weeks post-treatment. The first two sessions focus on past experiences and their impact on sexual behavior and sexual decision-making. Sessions 3 and 4 focus on current behaviors, including sexual behavior and substance use, as well as development of sexual risk reduction goals and communication skills. Sessions 5 and 6 focus on developing strategies for overcoming obstacles and maintaining commitment to sexual health goals. Historical events, such as the Tuskegee syphilis experiment, are used as discussion topics to explore cultural and historical issues facing African American MSMW. Current events are explored through media representations of African Americans and critical examination of stereotypes. Throughout these cultural–historical discussions, sexual decision-making and coping are evaluated to promote safer sex behaviors. Throughout, cultural and community values, such as collectivism, are emphasized.

Harawa et al. (2013) conducted an RCT of MAALES with 386 participants who were randomized to either MAALES or a single, individualized session of HIV risk reduction counseling. From baseline to 6-month post-treatment, the intervention group reported significant reductions in condomless sex with male and female partners. Corresponding changes for the control condition were all nonsignificant. In addition, compared to the control group, the intervention group had significantly fewer female sex partners.

Male Youth Pursuing Empowerment, Education and Prevention Around Sexuality

Male Youth Pursuing Empowerment, Education and Prevention Around Sexuality (MyPEEPS; Hidalgo et al., 2015) focuses on MSM aged 16–20 years. It consists of six 2-hour group sessions. The first session includes HIV and STI epidemiology as well as a focus on interpersonal communication. The second session focuses on safer sex skills, such as condom use, and specific STI information. The third session includes discussions of minority stress and how it impacts safer sex practices and also role-playing safer sex practices. The fourth session focuses on the role of emotion regulation in safer sex practices. The fifth session includes a focus on partner communication and substance use. The sixth session includes goal setting and review.

The efficacy of MyPEEPS was examined via an RCT of 101 participants who were randomized to MyPEEPS or a predominately lecture-based time-matched active control condition that included HIV and STI information. Compared to controls, MyPEEPS participants had lower rates of sex (with and without condoms) under the influence of alcohol or drugs at 12-weeks post-treatment, although neither was significant. There were no significant effects on other outcomes (e.g., number of partners and safer sex self-efficacy), although most results were in the expected direction.

No Excuses/Sin Buscar Excusas

No Excuses/Sin Buscar Excusas (O'Donnell, Stueve, Joseph, & Flores, 2014) is a one-session group intervention for Latino MSM. It was adapted from VOICES/

VOCES (Video Opportunities for Innovative Condom Education and Safer Sex; e.g., O'Donnell, San Doval, Duran, & O'Donnell, 1995), an intervention aimed at African American and Latino heterosexual adults. The adaptation focused on ensuring the content, especially the video component of the intervention, was relevant and appropriate for Latino MSM. This adapted intervention consists of information and discussion regarding safer sex and partner communication. It includes a video portraying condom negotiation, group discussion concerning condom negotiation and skill development, and provision of condoms and sexual health referral information.

O'Donnell and colleagues (2014) conducted an RCT of No Excuses/Sin Buscar Excusas with 370 participants who either received the intervention and were offered HIV testing or were offered HIV testing only (non-attention control). Participants completed baseline and 3-month follow-up assessments. At follow-up, there was a significantly greater reduction in condomless sex in the intervention group compared to the control group. The intervention group was also significantly more likely to report condom use at last intercourse compared to the control group.

Project PRIDE

Project PRIDE (Promoting Resilience in Discriminatory Environments; Smith et al., 2016, 2017) focuses on MSM aged 18–25 years to reduce HIV risk behaviors and substance use by helping participants develop adaptive coping strategies to deal with sexual minority stress. It involves eight 2½-hour sessions. Session 1 focuses on exploration of gay/bisexual/queer identity. Session 2 includes an overview of Meyer's (2003) minority stress model and discussion of how minority stress impacts participants' lives. Session 3 introduces Lazarus and Folkman's (1984) stress and coping model and adaptive and maladaptive coping strategies. Session 4 ties together the minority stress model with the stress and coping model and focuses on development of goals for overall and sexual health. Session 5 focuses on substance use in the context of minority stress. Sessions 6 and 7 focus on safer sex skill development, including partner communication skills. Session 8 reviews intervention content and application of adaptive coping strategies.

Smith and colleagues (2016, 2017) conducted a one-armed pilot of Project PRIDE that included pretreatment, post-treatment, and 3-month follow-up assessments. Smith et al. (2016) presented three case examples to describe the process and outcomes of select participants in the group. Smith et al. (2017) also provided estimates of effect size for the 33 participants enrolled in the pilot study. From pretreatment to follow-up, the number of sex partners decreased significantly, as did alcohol use, loneliness, and internalized homonegativity. In addition, self-esteem increased significantly. Finally, from pre- to post-treatment, condomless sex decreased with a small, but not significant, effect, although it returned to near baseline levels at follow-up.

CASE EXAMPLE FOR PROJECT PRIDE

Although many of the interventions discussed previously have more extensive empirical support, the first and last authors of this chapter co-developed Project PRIDE. Due to its focus on social cognitive theory, a focus shared with other HIV prevention interventions (e.g., 3MV, 40 & Forward, MyPEEPS, and No Excuses/ Sin Buscar Excusas), we present an amalgamated case example to illustrate how therapists and counselors can administer HIV prevention interventions in their practices. For more information on how to conduct Project PRIDE, and on this and other case examples, please see Smith et al. (2016).

Robert was a 20-year-old French-speaking man who was raised in downtown Montreal, Canada, a predominantly French-speaking but bilingual French–English speaking city. He presented for Project PRIDE in order to help ease his loneliness following the dissolution of a 1-year romantic relationship. Robert participated in six of the eight weekly group sessions. He participated well during the sessions he attended, sharing his own knowledge, thoughts, and experiences while also providing space for others to participate. Robert reported feeling down and lonely on most days due to his recently ended relationship.

In Session 1, when the group leaders were facilitating a discussion about challenges of homophobia among sexual minority youth, he reported being out as a gay man to most people in his life and not experiencing daily instances of homophobia, although he did report witnessing homophobic insults to others when he was a child and adolescent. In Session 2, which discusses the minority stress model, Robert reported he sometimes avoided holding hands in public with his ex-boyfriend during their previous relationship due to fears of people staring at him or making negative comments. During Session 3, which focuses on stress and adaptive and maladaptive coping strategies, Robert quickly grasped the stress and coping model and identified alternative adaptive coping strategies when working though the group stress and coping activity. For example, he reported that one stressor was that he was sometimes uncomfortable with his body, which Robert believed was too skinny. One of the facilitators asked Robert what his responses had been in the past when he felt insecure about his body, including when with other men. Robert responded that when with men he found attractive, it was more difficult to assert himself, including his desire to avoid CAS. The facilitator then asked about which coping strategies would work best, to which Robert noted he could cope by reminding himself that his body was great the way it was (emotion-focused coping) or by working out at the gym twice a week in order to build muscle strength (problem-focused coping). In Session 4, which links the stress and coping model to experiences of minority stress and helps participants identify SMART (specific, measureable, achievable, realistic, time-limited) goals to cope with minority stressors, Robert reported the stress and coping model to be useful in his everyday life. In Session 4 he also identified two SMART goals: communicating his desire to avoid CAS to two sexual partners in the next week and being assertive in asking two new partners about their HIV serostatus in the next week.

In Session 5 which focuses on how maladaptive coping strategies play out in terms of substance use and sexual behavior, Robert noted that sometimes he would drink more when he knew he was going to meet an attractive man for sex. One of the facilitators then asked to what extent drinking was adaptive or maladaptive for Robert. He responded that although the alcohol was helpful in that it "took off the edge" of his anxiety and self-consciousness, drinking also made it more difficult to assert himself sexually. One of the group members suggested that alcohol, per se, did not seem to be a problem, but the amount of it was more of a problem. The other facilitator then asked if he wanted to alter his SMART goals to incorporate these new insights about alcohol. Robert agreed and in Session 6, made an addition to his SMART goals, which was to limit his alcohol consumption to two drinks if he believed he might have sex that evening.

During Session 7, the participants role-played sexual risk situations that allowed them to practice their coping skills. The facilitators emphasized that although there were limits to what could be role-played during group counseling— for example, not being able to role-play safer sex behaviors such as putting a condom on a penis—there were other situations that could be role-played, including practicing verbal safer sex skills and refusing to engage in maladaptive substance use. Robert volunteered to participate in a role-play with two facilitators who were acting out a scene in which one man is pressuring another man to engage in CAS. The co-facilitators asked Robert and other participants to suggest ways the pressured character could reply. Robert suggested that the pressured character say, "I like you too. If you want to have sex with me, I always use condoms."

In Session 8, the facilitators asked about what each participant would take from Project PRIDE after the group ended. Robert responded that he realized that he wanted to be less judgmental toward himself and that "it was okay to ask for what I want," including sexually.

At baseline, Robert reported 25 acts of CAS in the past 3 months, which decreased to zero at both post-treatment and 3-month follow-up. He also reported decreases in alcohol use and drug use, as well as decreases in loneliness and increases in self-esteem. In addition, Robert reported becoming more comfortable asking about the HIV status of his partners early in the relationship or date and being more comfortable asserting his preference for using condoms with all partners.

SEXUAL HEALTH INTERVENTIONS BEYOND HIV/STI RISKS

There has been much less research on counseling interventions or psychotherapies that focus on areas outside of HIV/STI prevention. This is likely due to the relative difficulty in securing research funding that is not from the HIV/AIDS funding envelopes available in many developed countries. The lack of literature is problematic for clinicians who want to improve sexual health and well-being of clients but whose clients are not exclusively presenting with concerns related to HIV sexual risk behavior.

Most of the research that exists outside of HIV prevention is composed of case studies and clinical guidelines for working with MSM or other lesbian, gay, and bisexual (LGB) couples. Rutter (2012) provides an especially instructive approach to providing relationship or sex therapies for MSM couples. The approach outlined is gay affirmative, understands the discrimination and added stressors experienced by male couples, affirms the resiliency of MSM couples (e.g., use of humor to cope with problems), and takes an open approach to the nature of a relationship—whether a relationship is strictly monogamous or not. This section focuses on psychotherapies and counseling interventions with empirical support through clinical trials. However, due to the relative lack of RCTs for couples therapies, sex therapies, and other sexual health interventions that go beyond HIV/STI prevention, we also refer to studies that extend treatments found to be efficacious in the general population.

Relationship Education

One area in which researchers have added to the tool kit available to clinicians seeking to treat MSM clients is couples counseling. Two studies have tested Strengthening Same-Sex Relationships, a 10-hour group program that was designed to improve couples' long-term functioning (Whitton & Buzzella, 2012). This 10-hour program targets communication training and includes sessions to reduce the impact of minority stressors, such as coping with discrimination and getting support for one's same-sex relationship. In the pilot study, 12 married or engaged MSM couples were randomized to immediate or wait-list conditions. Large effects from pretreatment to post-treatment were found on the outcomes of relationship quality and satisfaction. There were also medium to large effects in three of the intervention's hypothesized mediators: communication, problem-solving, and support for the relationship. Although differences at post-treatment between groups were only in relationship quality, there were non-statistically significant trends for improvements on other relationship variables. Relationship improvements were mostly maintained at 3-month follow-up. Another wait-list controlled trial of 20 couples found significant improvements from pretreatment to 3-month follow-up in relationship satisfaction, relationship instability, couple communication, perceived stress, and social support, with small to medium effects for all variables (Whitton, Weitbrecht, Kuryluk, & Hutsell, 2016). Couples in the immediate treatment group had significantly improved couple communication, less perceived stress, and improved relationship satisfaction. Although the effects are not large, this program offers couples therapists a form of counseling that may help MSM clients presenting as a couple improve their relationship across a variety of domains. Clinicians may also wish to consider adapting this program when working with other LGB clients.

Other empirically supported treatment guidelines and case studies may be helpful for clinicians working with MSM couples, especially for clinicians who want guidance on how to use empirically supported treatments in ways that avoid heterosexist biases. Approaches based on existing empirically supported therapies include cognitive–behavioral couples therapy (Baucom & Epstein, 1990) when one partner is bisexual (Deacon, Reinke, & Viers, 1996) and emotion-focused therapy for couples (Johnson, Hunsley, Greenberg, & Schindler, 1999) extended for MSM couples (Allan & Johnson, 2017). One case study extended behavioral therapy for substance use disorders for an MSM couple in which one partner was a patient recruited from a drug and alcohol program (Hellmuth, Follansbee, Moore, & Stuart, 2008). At 12-month follow-up, the patient was 100% abstinent from substances.

Sexual Dysfunction

The literature for treating sexual dysfunction is quite limited, but it does offer some guidance to clinicians seeking to use empirically supported treatments, especially for those who are familiar with behavioral therapies. In an older study (Everaerd et al., 1982) consisting of rational emotive therapy, masturbation exercises, and social skills training in order to reduce sexual dysfunction, clients ($N = 21$) presented with a variety of complaints, including erectile dysfunction and premature or delayed ejaculation. The vast majority of clients were single, and one-third were MSM. At 2-month follow-up, 40% were determined to have made a "complete recovery" based on a sexual functioning scale that was not validated for use with MSM.

Only one case study has been conducted extending empirically supported treatment for sexual dysfunction to MSM. In this study, CBT was used successfully to treat erectile dysfunction among two nonpartnered MSM (Hart & Schwartz, 2010). This approach used a combination of psychoeducation on male sexual functioning, cognitive restructuring, exposure to sexual performance situations that induced anxiety, and behavioral experiments to test maladaptive beliefs. One other case study presents an example of how to extend an empirically supported treatment to MSM for HIV prevention purposes (Hart, Tulloch, & O'Cleirigh, 2014). This case study extended CBT for social anxiety disorder to include substance use management and assertiveness in sexual situations to reduce high-risk sexual behavior.

CONCLUSION

The literature on the sexual health of MSM offers several empirically supported options to reduce HIV risk behaviors, including individual, couples, and group and online counseling interventions. Many of these are based on models that may be familiar to many mental health clinicians and counselors, including social cognitive theory (Bandura, 1986) and motivational interviewing (Rollnick & Miller, 1995). Techniques used are also likely to be familiar to many mental health professionals, such as psychoeducation, identifying triggers for risky sexual or drug use behavior, completing decisional balance worksheets about the advantages and disadvantages of current behavior versus a desired changed behavior, and role-playing desired change behaviors. Interventions are also available for professionals working with youth aged 16 years or older (EXPLORE Study Team, 2004; Parsons et al., 2014).

One exciting development outlined in this chapter is the use of online tools for HIV prevention. These tools offer mental health professionals an adjunct to face-to-face counseling and psychotherapy. The advantage of these tools is obvious for mental health professionals who identify that their HIV-negative clients are at high risk for HIV contraction but who are not already well trained in HIV prevention counseling. These online interventions may also be of service to men living in areas without access to gay-affirmative counseling.

Limitations and Future Directions

Despite the existence of a number of effective, as well as promising, interventions, the rich HIV prevention literature has room for significant improvement. As noted previously, only PCC has been evaluated for efficacy by two independent research teams. The HIV prevention interventions are also limited in their generalizability in that they are almost exclusively tested in the United States. Furthermore, there is a dearth of interventions for older MSM, which is problematic due to cohort effects. For example, many men older 50 years of age lost a large number of friends to the HIV epidemic and some may avoid gettting close to people, including sexual partners, for fear of additional loss (Cherney & Verhey, 1996). Many older men may also have come out later in life and may have children from previous heterosexual relationships. There do not appear to be HIV prevention interventions specifically catering to these populations. Research is also needed on interventions for MSM from many ethnic minority communities, including East Asian, South Asian, and Native American and other indigenous communities. Given the frequent use of the internet by MSM to meet sexual partners (Ross et al., 2007), interventions focused on navigating communication, reducing sexual risks, and promoting sexual assertiveness in this context are needed.

Another limitation is that many HIV prevention interventions are not rooted in common empirically supported therapy modalities. This means that therapists who are trained in psychotherapies such as CBT, behavioral therapy, dialectical behavior therapy, and interpersonal therapy must take time to learn how to conduct the interventions reviewed here. There are also few case studies showing clinicians how to extend empirically supported therapies for MSM. This limitation is glaring given that many mental health problems are more common among MSM, such as social anxiety (Pachankis & Goldfried, 2006), post-traumatic stress disorder (Roberts, Austin, Corliss, Vandermorris, & Koenen, 2010), and mood disorders (Gilman et al., 2001; Sandfort, de Graaf, Bijl, & Schnabel, 2001), and are associated with sexual risk behaviors (Hart & Heimberg, 2005; Millar, Starks, Grov, & Parsons, 2017).

In addition, research disproportionately focuses on HIV prevention to the exclusion of most other aspects of sexual health. The state of the literature may be due to the relative lack of research funds for any LGBTQ population outside of HIV. There is an unfortunate absence of information for those counseling MSM in any other aspect of sexual health.

Sexual Health Beyond HIV Prevention

Some topics that have previously been identified in the literature as being problems for MSM, but for which there is still no empirically supported treatment, include sexual dysfunctions and pain (Hart & Schwartz, 2010; Hirshfield et al., 2010; Rosser, Short, Thurmes, & Coleman, 1998), low sexual self-efficacy and sexual anxiety (Blashill et al., 2016), and problems with sexual assertiveness (Eisenberg et al., 2011). Interventions focusing on sexual health can include other topics identified as problems among this population, such as finding a satisfying sexual relationship (Lawrance & Byers, 1995) and dating anxiety (Chorney & Morris, 2008). Sexual health for those in relationships might also include problems identified in the literature, such as conflicts regarding sexual roles during anal sex (i.e., insertive or receptive; Schwartz & Young, 2009) or differences in sexual drive between partners. The lack of MSM-specific data means that therapists must draw their own conclusions about how to generalize data from sexual dysfunction treatments and other sex therapies (Aubin, Heiman, Berger, Murallo, & Yung-Wen, 2009; Bach, Barlow, & Wincze, 2005; Masters & Johnson, 1986; for a review, see Berner & Günzler, 2012) that have empirical support with almost exclusively heterosexual samples.

The literature is even less advanced in testing interventions that promote sexual health from a nondeficit model. Likely due to the focus of the larger clinical psychology and psychiatric literature on sexual health problems, there is little emphasis on building on strengths already demonstrated by clients. Psychological theory offers some future directions for researchers and therapists seeking to build on resilience of MSM (for a review, see Smith, 2017). For example, the minority stress model (Meyer, 2003) posits that compensatory coping, which includes social support and support from one's community (e.g., LGBT community programs and social services provided by one's community), may mitigate the effects of anti-LGB stigma. Building on social support and community-level support may directly reduce HIV risk behaviors even when controlling for syndemic risk factors such as depression, multiple substance use, and childhood sexual abuse (Hart et al., 2017). Interventions that build on resilience in order to reduce HIV risks and to broadly promote sexual health and well-being are warranted.

Summary

Several interventions are available to reduce a client's risk of contracting HIV. These interventions, which typically involve eight sessions or less, are diverse in their modality, format (i.e., individual, group, or online), and target population. The literature is much less advanced on sexual health interventions beyond HIV prevention, although it is possible to extend empirically supported psychotherapies for use with HIV-negative MSM (for an extensive discussion, see Martell, Safren, & Prince, 2003). However, studies that test sexual health interventions are still sorely needed to increase the certainty of mental health professionals when working to promote the sexual health and well-being of HIV-negative MSM.

REFERENCES

Allan, R., & Johnson, S. M. (2017). Conceptual and application issues: Emotionally focused therapy with gay male couples. *Journal of Couple and Relationship Therapy, 16*, 286–305. doi:10.1080/15332691.2016.1238800

Aubin, S., Heiman, J. R., Berger, R. E., Murallo, A. V., & Yung-Wen, L. (2009). Comparing sildenafil alone vs. sildenafil plus brief couple sex therapy on erectile dysfunction and couples' sexual and marital quality of life: A pilot study. *Journal of Sex & Marital Therapy, 35*, 122–143. doi:10.1080/00926230802712319

Bach, A. K., Barlow, D. H., & Wincze, J. P. (2005). The enhancing effects of manualized treatment for erectile dysfunction among men using sildenafil: A preliminary investigation. *Behavior Therapy, 35*, 55–73. doi:10.1016/S0005-7894(04)80004-2

Bandura, A. (1986). *Social foundations of thought and action: A social cognitive perspective.* Englewood Cliffs, NJ: Princeton-Hall.

Baucom, D. H., & Epstein, N. (1990). *Cognitive–behavioral marital therapy.* New York, NY: Brunner/Mazel.

Berner, M., & Günzler, C. (2012). Efficacy of psychosocial interventions in men and women with sexual dysfunctions: A systematic review of controlled clinical trials. *Journal of Sexual Medicine, 9*, 3089–3107. doi:10.1111/j.1743-6109.2012.02970.x

Blashill, A. J., Tomassilli, J., Biello, K., O'Cleirigh, C., Safren, S. A., & Mayer, K. H. (2016). Body dissatisfaction among sexual minority men: Psychological and sexual health outcomes. *Archives of Sexual Behavior, 45*, 1241–1247. doi:10.1007/s10508-015-0683-1

Bowen, A. M., Williams, M. L., Daniel, C. M., & Clayton, S. (2008). Internet based HIV prevention research targeting rural MSM: Feasibility, acceptability, and preliminary efficacy. *Journal of Behavioral Medicine, 31*, 463–477. doi:10.1007/s10865-008-9171-6

Carpenter, K. M., Stoner, S. A., Mikko, A. N., Dhanak, L. P., & Parsons, J. T. (2010). Efficacy of a web-based intervention to reduce sexual risk in men who have sex with men. *AIDS and Behavior, 14*, 549–557. doi:10.1007/s10461-009-9578-2.

Centers for Disease Control and Prevention. (2014). *Diagnoses of HIV infection in the United States and dependent areas, 2014.* Retrieved from https://www.cdc.gov/hiv/pdf/library/reports/surveillance/cdc-hiv-surveillance-report-us.pdf

Centers for Disease Control and Prevention. (2016). *Sexually transmitted disease surveillance 2015.* Retrieved from https://www.cdc.gov/std/stats15/std-surveillance-2015-print.pdf

Cherney, P. M., & Verhey, M. P. (1996). Grief among gay men associated with multiple losses from AIDS. *Death Studies, 20*, 115–132. doi:10.1080/07481189608252745

Chesney, M. A., Koblin, B. A., Barresi, P. J., Husnik, M. J., Celum, C., Colfax, G., . . . the EXPLORE Study Team. (2003). An individually tailored intervention for HIV prevention: Baseline data from the EXPLORE study. *American Journal of Public Health, 96*, 933–938. doi:10.2105/AJPH.93.6.933

Chorney, D. B., & Morris, T. L. (2008). The changing face of dating anxiety: Issues in assessment with special populations. *Clinical Psychology: Science and Practice, 15*, 224–238. doi:10.1111/j.1468-2850.2008.00132.x

Coffin, P. O., Santos, G., Colfax, G., Das, M., Matheson, T., DeMicco, E., . . . Herbst, J. H. (2014). Adapted personalized cognitive counseling for episodic substance-using men who have sex with men: A randomized controlled trial. *AIDS and Behavior, 18*, 1390–1400. doi:10.1007/s10461-014-0712-4

Deacon, S., Reinke, L., & Viers, D. (1996). Cognitive–behavioural therapy for bisexual couples: Expanding the realms of therapy. *American Journal of Family Therapy, 24*, 242–257. doi:10.108/019 26189 608251037

Dilley, J. W., Woods, W. J., Loeb, L., Nelson, K., Sheon, N., Mullan, J., . . . McFarland, W. (2007). Brief cognitive counselling with HIV testing to reduce sexual risk among men who have sex with men. *Journal of Acquired Immune Deficiency Syndromes, 44*, 569–577. doi:10.1097/QAI.0b013e318033ffbd

Dilley, J. W., Woods, W. J., Sabatino, J., Lihatsh, T., Adler, B., Casey, S., . . . McFarland, W. (2002). Changing sexual behavior among gay male repeat testers of HIV: A randomized, controlled trial of a single-session intervention. *Journal of Acquired Immune Deficiency Syndromes, 30*, 177–186. doi:10.1097/01.QAI.0000016823.19906.41

Eaton, L. A., Cherry, C., Cain, D., & Pope, H. (2011). A novel approach to prevention for at-risk HIV-negative men who have sex with men: Creating a teachable moment to promote informed sexual decision-making. *American Journal of Public Health, 101*, 539–545. doi:10.2105/AJPH.2010.191791

Eisenberg, A., Bauermeister, J., Johns, M. M., Pingel, E., & Santana, M. L. (2011). Achieving safety: Safer sex, communication, and desire among young gay men. *Journal of Adolescent Research, 26*, 645–669. doi:10.1177/0743558411402342

Emetu, R. E., Marshall, A., Sanders, S. A., Yarber, W. L., Milhausen, R. R., Crosby, R. A., & Graham, C. A. (2014). A novel, self-guided, home-based intervention to improve condom use among young men who have sex with men. *Journal of American College Health, 62*, 118–124. doi:10.1080/07448481.2013.856914

Everaerd, W., Dekker, J., Dronkers, J., van der Rhee, K., Staffeleu, J., & Wiselius, G. (1982). Treatment of homosexual and heterosexual sexual dysfunction in male-only groups of mixed sexual orientation. *Archives of Sexual Behavior, 11*, 1–10. doi:10.1007/BF01541361

EXPLORE Study Team. (2004). Effects of a behavioural intervention to reduce acquisition of HIV infection among men who have sex with men: The EXPLORE randomized controlled study. *Lancet, 364*, 41–50. doi:10.1016/S0140-6736(04)16588-4

Fernandez, M. I., Hosek, S. G., Hotton, A. L., Gaylord, S. E., Hernandez, N., Alfonso, S. V., & Joseph, H. (2016). A randomized controlled trial of POWER: An internet-based HIV prevention intervention for Black bisexual men. *AIDS and Behavior, 20*, 1951–1960. doi:10.1007/s10461-016-1403-0

Fisher, W. A., & Fisher, J. D. (1992). Understanding and promoting AIDS preventive behaviour: A conceptual model and educational tools. *Canadian Journal of Human Sexuality, 1*(3), 99–106.

Frost, D. M., & Meyer, I. H. (2012). Measuring community connectedness among diverse sexual minority populations. *Journal of Sex Research, 49*(1), 36–49. doi:10.1080/00224499.2011.565427

Garofalo, R., Johnson, A. K., Kuhns, L. M., Cotton, C., Joseph, H., & Margolis, A. (2012). Life skills: Evaluation of a theory-driven behavioral HIV prevention intervention for young transgender women. *Journal of Urban Health, 89,* 419–431. doi:10.1007/s11524-011-9638-6

Gilman, S. E., Cochran, S. D., Mays, V. M., Hughes, M., Ostrow, D., & Kessler, R. C. (2001). Risk of psychiatric disorders among individuals reporting same-sex sexual partners in the National Comorbidity Survey. *American Journal of Public Health, 91,* 933–939. doi:10.2105/AJPH.91.6.933

Gold, R. S., & Rosenthal, D. A. (1998). Examining self-justifications for unsafe sex as a technique of AIDS education: The importance of personal relevance. *International Journal of STD and AIDS, 4,* 208–213.

Grant, R. M., Lama, J. R., Anderson, P. L., McMahan, V., Liu, A. Y., Vargas, L., . . . Montoya-Herrera, O. (2010). Preexposure chemoprophylaxis for HIV prevention in men who have sex with men. *New England Journal of Medicine, 363,* 2587–2599. doi:10.1056/NEJMoa1011205

Harawa, N. T., Williams, J. K., McCuller, W. J., Ramamurthi, H. C., Lee, M., Shapiro, M. F., . . . Cunningham, W. E. (2013). Efficacy of a culturally congruent HIV risk-reduction intervention for behaviorally bisexual Black men: Results of a randomized trial. *AIDS, 27,* 1979–1988. doi:10.1097/QAD.0b013e3283617500

Hart, T. A., & Heimberg, R. G. (2005). Social anxiety as a risk factor for unprotected intercourse among gay and bisexual male youth. *AIDS and Behavior, 9,* 505–512. doi:10.1007/s10461-005-9021-2

Hart, T. A., Noor, S. W., Adam, B. D., Vernon, J. R. G., Brennan, D. J., Gardner, S., . . . Myers, T. (2017). Number of psychosocial strengths predicts reduced HIV sexual risk behaviors above and beyond syndemic problems among gay and bisexual men. *AIDS and Behavior, 21,* 3035–3046. doi:10.1007/s10461-016-1669-2

Hart, T. A., & Schwartz, D. R. (2010). Cognitive–behavioral erectile dysfunction treatment for gay men. *Cognitive and Behavioral Practice, 17,* 66–76. doi:10.1016/j.cbpra.2009.04.009

Hart, T. A., Tulloch, T. G., & O'Cleirigh, C. (2014). Integrated cognitive behavioral therapy for social anxiety and HIV prevention for gay and bisexual men. *Cognitive and Behavioral Practice, 21,* 149–160. doi:10.1016/j.cbpra.2013.07.001

Hellmuth, J. C., Follansbee, K. W., Moore, T. M., & Stuart, G. L. (2008). Reduction of intimate partner violence in a gay couple following alcohol treatment. *Journal of Homosexuality, 54,* 439–448. doi:10.1080/00918360801991513

Hidalgo, M. A., Kuhns, L. M., Hotton, A. L., Johnson, A. K., Mustanski, B., & Garofalo, R. (2015). The MyPEEPS randomized controlled trial: A pilot of preliminary efficacy, feasibility, and acceptability of a group-level, HIV risk reduction intervention for young men who have sex with men. *Archives of Sexual Behavior, 44,* 475–485. doi:10.1007/s10508-014-0347-6

Hirshfield, S., Chiasson, M. A., Wagmiller, R. L, Jr., Remien, R. H., Humberstone, M., Scheinmann, R., & Grov, C. (2010). Sexual dysfunction in an internet sample of U.S. men who have sex with men. *Journal of Sexual Medicine, 7,* 3104–3114. doi:10.1111/j.1743-6109.2009.01636.x

Johnson, S. M., Hunsley, J., Greenberg, L., & Schindler, D. (1999). Emotionally focused couples therapy: Status and challenges. *Clinical Psychology: Science and Practice, 6*, 67–79. doi:10.1093/clipsy.6.1.67

Kalichman, S. C., Zohren, L., & Eaton, L. A. (2014). Setting the bar high or setting up to fail? Interpretations and implications of the EXPLORE study (HPTN 015). *AIDS and Behavior, 18*, 625–633. doi:10.1007/s10461-013-0603-0

Kamb, M. L., Fishbein, M., Douglas, J. M., Jr., Rhodes, F., Rogers, J., Bolan, G., . . . Kent, C. (1998). Efficacy of risk-reduction counseling to prevent human immunodeficiency virus and sexually transmitted diseases: A randomized controlled trial. *JAMA, 280*, 1161–1167. doi:10.1001/jama.280.13.1161

Knight, K. R., Das, M., DeMicco, E., Raiford, J. L., Matheson, T., Shook, A., . . . Herbst, J. H. (2014). A roadmap for adapting an evidence-based HIV prevention intervention: Personalized cognitive counseling (PCC) for episodic substance-using men who have sex with men. *Prevention Science, 15*, 364–375. doi:10.1007/s11121-013-0364-z

Koblin, B. A., Chesney, M. A., Husnik, M. J., Bozeman, S., Celum, C. L., Buchbinder, S., . . . Cotes, T. J. (2003). High-risk behaviors among men who have sex with men in 6 US cities: Baseline data from the EXPLORE study. *American Journal of Public Health, 93*, 926–932. doi:10.2105/AJPH.93.6.926

Koblin, B. A., Husnik, M. J., Colfax, G., Huang, Y., Maddison, M., Mayer, K., . . . Buchbinder, S. (2006). Risk factors for HIV infection among men who have sex with men. *AIDS Care, 20*, 731–739. doi:10.1097/01.aids.0000216374.61442.55

Lawrance, K. A., & Byers, E. S. (1995). Sexual satisfaction in long-term heterosexual relationships: The interpersonal exchange model of sexual satisfaction. *Personal Relationships, 2*, 267–285. doi:10.1111/j.1475-6811.1995.tb00092.x

Lazarus, R. S., & Folkman, S. (1984). *Stress, appraisal, and coping*. New York, NY: Springer.

Martell, C. R., Safren, S. A., & Prince, S. E. (2003).*Cognitive behavioral therapies with lesbian, gay, and bisexual clients*. New York, NY: Guildford.

Masters, W., & Johnson, V. (1986). *Sex and human loving*. Boston, MA: Little, Brown.

Mayer, K. H., Safren, S. A., Elsesser, S. A., Psaros, C., Tinsley, J. P., Marzinke, M., . . . Mimiaga, M. J. (2017). Optimizing pre-exposure antiretroviral prophylaxis adherence in men who have sex with men: Results of a pilot randomized controlled trial of "Life-Steps for PrEP." *AIDS and Behavior, 2*, 1350–1360. doi:10.1007/s10461-016-1606-4

McCormack, S., Dunn, D. T., Desai, M., Dolling, D. I., Gafos, M., Gilson, R., . . . Mackie, N. (2016). Pre-exposure prophylaxis to prevent the acquisition of HIV-1 infection (PROUD): Effectiveness results from the pilot phase of a pragmatic open-label randomised trial. *Lancet, 387*, 53–60. doi:10.1016/S0140-6736(15)00056-2

Meyer, I. H. (2003). Prejudice, social stress, and mental health in lesbian, gay, and bisexual populations: Conceptual issues and research evidence. *Psychological Bulletin, 129*, 674–697. doi:10.1037/0033-2909.129.5.674

Millar, B. M., Starks, T. J., Grov, C., & Parsons, J. T. (2017). Sexual risk-taking in HIV-negative gay and bisexual men increases with depression: Results from a US national study. *AIDS and Behavior, 21*, 1665–1675. doi:10.1007/s10461-016-1507-6

Mimiaga, M. J., Safren, S. A., Benet, D. J., Manseau, M. W., DeSousa, N., & Mayer, K. H. (2006). MSM in HIV-prevention trials are sexual partners with each other: An ancillary study to the EXPLORE intervention. *AIDS and Behavior, 10*, 27–34. doi:10.1007/s10461-005-9025-y

Mustanski, B., Garofalo, R., Monahan, C., Gratzer, B., & Andrews, R. (2013). Feasibility, acceptability, and preliminary efficacy of an online HIV prevention program for diverse young men who have sex with men: The Keep It Up! intervention. *AIDS and Behavior, 17*, 2999–3012. doi:10.1007/s10461-013-0507-z

Newcomb, M. E., Macapagal, K. R., Feinstein, B. A., Bettin, E., Swann, G., & Whitton, S. W. (2017). Integrating HIV prevention and relationship education for young same-sex male couples: A pilot trial of the 2GETHER intervention. *AIDS and Behavior, 21*, 2464–2478. doi:10.1007/s10461-017-1674-0

O'Donnell, L., San Doval, A., Duran, R., & O'Donnell, C. R. (1995). The effectiveness of video-based interventions in promoting condom acquisition among STD clinic patients. *Sexually Transmitted Diseases, 22*, 97–103.

O'Donnell, L., Stueve, A., Joseph, H. A., & Flores, S. (2014). Adapting the VOICES HIV behavioral intervention for Latino men who have sex with men. *AIDS and Behavior, 18*, 767–775. doi:10.1007/s10461-013-0653-3

Pachankis, J. E., & Goldfried, M. R. (2006). Social anxiety in young gay men. *Journal of Anxiety Disorders, 20*, 996–1015. doi:10.1016/j.janxdis.2006.01.001

Parsons, J. T., Lelutiu-Weinberger, C., Botsko, M., & Golub, S. A. (2014). A randomized controlled trial utilizing motivational interviewing to reduce HIV risk and drug use in young gay and bisexual men. *Journal of Consulting and Clinical Psychology, 82*, 9–18. doi:10.1037/a0035311

Public Health Agency of Canada. (2015). *HIV and AIDS in Canada: Surveillance report to December 31, 2014.* Retrieved from http://healthycanadians.gc.ca/publications/diseases-conditions-maladies-affections/hiv-aids-surveillance-2014-vih-sida/alt/hiv-aids-surveillance-2014-vih-sida-eng.pdf

Reisner, S. L., Hughto, J. M. W., Pardee, D. J., Kuhns, L., Garofalo, R., & Mimiaga, M. J. (2016). LifeSkills for Men (LS4M): Pilot evaluation of a gender-affirmative HIV and STI prevention intervention for young adult transgender men who have sex with men. *Journal of Urban Health, 93*, 189–205. doi:10.1007/s11524-015-0011-z

Reisner, S. L., O'Cleirigh, C., Hendriksen, E. S., McLain, J., Ebin, J., Lew, K., . . . Gonzalez, D. (2011). "40 & Forward": Preliminary evaluation of a group intervention to improve mental health outcomes and address HIV sexual risk behaviors among older gay and bisexual men. *Journal of Gay & Lesbian Social Services, 23*, 523–545. doi:10.1080/10538720.2011.611113

Roberts, A. L., Austin, S. B., Corliss, H. L., Vandermorris, A. K., & Koenen, K. C. (2010). Pervasive trauma exposure among US sexual orientation minority adults and risk of posttraumatic stress disorder. *American Journal of Public Health, 100*, 2433–2441. doi:10.2105/AJPH.2009.168971

Rollnick, S., & Miller, W. R. (1995). What is motivational interviewing? *Behavioural and Cognitive Psychotherapy, 23*, 325–334. doi:10.1017/S135246580001643X

Ross, M. W., Rosser, B. S., McCurdy, S., & Feldman, J. (2007). The advantages and limitations of seeking sex online: A comparison of reasons given for online and offline sexual liaisons by men who have sex with men. *Journal of Sex Research, 44*, 59–71. doi:10.1080/00224490709336793

Rosser, B. R., Short, B. J., Thurmes, P. J., & Coleman, E. (1998). Anodyspareunia, the unacknowledged sexual dysfunction: A validation study of painful receptive anal intercourse and its psychosexual concomitants in homosexual men. *Journal of Sex and Marital Therapy, 24*, 281–292. doi:10.1080/00926239808403963

Rutter, P. A. (2012). Sex therapy with gay male couples using affirmative therapy. *Sexual and Relationship Therapy, 27*, 35–45. doi:10.1080/14681994.2011.633078

Safren, S. A., Otto, M. W., & Worth, J. L. (1999). Life-steps: Applying cognitive behavioral therapy to HIV medication adherence. *Cognitive and Behavioral Practice, 6*, 332–341. doi:10.1016/S1077-7229(99)80052-2

Sandfort, T. G., de Graaf, R., Bijl, R. V., & Schnabel, P. (2001). Same-sex sexual behavior and psychiatric disorders: Findings from the Netherlands Mental Health Survey and Incidence Study (NEMESIS). *Archives of General Psychiatry, 58*, 85–91. doi:10.1001/archpsyc.58.1.85

Schonnesson, L. N., Bowen, A. N., & Williams, M. L. (2016). Project SMART: Preliminary results from a test of the efficacy of a Swedish internet-based HIV risk reduction intervention for men who have sex with men. *Archives of Sexual Behavior, 45*, 1501–1511. doi:10.1007/s10508-015-0608-z

Schwartz, P., & Young, L. (2009). Sexual satisfaction in committed relationships. *Sexuality Research and Social Policy, 6*, 1–17. doi:10.1525/srsp.2009.6.1.1

Smith, N. G. (2017). Resilience across the lifespan: Adulthood. In K. L. Eckstrand & J. Potter (Eds.), *Trauma, resilience, and health promotion in LGBT patients: What every healthcare provider should know* (pp. 75–88). New York, NY: Springer.

Smith, N. G., Hart, T. A., Kidwai, A., Vernon, J. R. G., Blais, M., & Adam, B. (2017). Results of a pilot study to ameliorate psychological and behavioral outcomes of minority stress among young gay and bisexual men. *Behavior Therapy, 48*, 664–677. doi:10.1016/j.beth.2017.03.005

Smith, N. G., Hart, T. A., Moody, C., Willis, A. C., Andersen, M. A., Blais, M., & Adam, B. (2016). Project PRIDE: A cognitive–behavioral group intervention to reduce HIV risk behaviors among HIV-negative young gay and bisexual men. *Cognitive and Behavioral Practice, 23*, 398–411. doi:10.1016/j.cbpra.2015.08.006

Spanier, G. B. (1976). Measuring dyadic adjustment: New scales for assessing the quality of marriage and similar dyads. *Journal of Marriage and the Family, 38*, 15–28. doi:10.2307/350547

Taylor, S. W., Psaros, C., Pantalone, D. W., Tinsley, J., Elsesser, S. A., Mayer, K. H., & Safren, S. A. (2017). "Life-Steps" for PrEP adherence: Demonstration of a CBT-based intervention to increase adherence to pre-exposure prophylaxis (PrEP) medication among sexual-minority men at high risk for HIV acquisition. *Cognitive and Behavioral Practice, 24*, 38–49. doi:10.1016/j.cbpra.2016.02.004

Whitton, S. W., & Buzzella, B. A. (2012). Using relationship education programs with same-sex couples: A preliminary evaluation of program utility and needed modifications. *Marriage and Family Review, 48*, 667–688. doi:10.1080/01494929.2012.700908

Whitton, S. W., Weitbrecht, E. M., Kuryluk, A. D., & Hutsell, D. W. (2016). A randomized waitlist-controlled trial of culturally sensitive relationship education for male same-sex couples. *Journal of Family Psychology, 30*, 763–768. doi:10.1037/fam0000199

Williams, J. K., Ramamurthi, H. C., Manago, C., & Harawa, N. T. (2009). Learning from successful interventions: A culturally congruent HIV risk-reduction intervention for African American men who have sex with men and women. *American Journal of Public Health, 99*, 1008–1012. doi:10.2105/AJPH.2008.140558

Wilton, L., Herbst, J. H., Coury-Doniger, P., Painter, T. M., English, G., Alvarez, M. E., ... Carey, J. W. (2009). Efficacy of an HIV/STI prevention intervention for Black men who have sex with men: Findings from the Many Men, Many Voices (3MV) project. *AIDS and Behavior, 13*, 532–544. doi:10.1007/s10461-009-9529-y

Yalom, I. D., & Leszcz, M. (2005). *The theory and practice of group psychotherapy* (5th ed.). New York, NY: Basic Books.

15

Evidence-Based Approaches to HIV-Positive Sexual Minority Men's Sexual Health

AUDREY HARKNESS AND STEVEN A. SAFREN ■

Sexual minority men, and other men who have sex with men (MSM), continue to be the demographic group most affected by HIV in the United States, making up more than half of those living with the virus (Centers for Disease Control and Prevention [CDC], 2016). Globally, sexual minority men and other MSM also continue to constitute a significant portion of those living with HIV (Beyrer et al., 2012), with MSM in low- and middle-income countries having approximately 19 times the risk of being HIV-positive compared to the general population of adults (Baral, Sifakis, Cleghorn, & Beyrer, 2007).

Evidence-based strategies for promoting sexual health among HIV-positive sexual minority men are needed (Wolitski & Fenton, 2011). Behavioral interventions can address several sexual health outcomes that can improve HIV-positive sexual minority men's personal health and reduce the onward transmission of HIV (secondary prevention). Increasing condom use can prevent acquisition and transmission of other sexually transmitted infections (STIs), re-infection or superinfection, and further transmission of HIV. Uptake and adherence to antiretroviral (ART) medication in pursuit of viral suppression is another strategy to reduce transmissibility—a strategy known as "treatment as prevention," which is also beneficial for personal HIV health (Gardner, McLees, Steiner, Del Rio, & Burman, 2011; Rodger et al., 2016). Practitioners working with HIV-positive sexual minority men can draw from evidence-based sexual health and psychosocial interventions in order to help clients achieve sexual health outcomes such as these.

Among sexual minority men, psychosocial problems such as substance use, depression, sexual abuse, and partner violence are prevalent, co-occurring, and cumulatively associated with behaviors such as condomless sex and non-adherence to ART (Friedman et al., 2015; Harkness et al., 2018; Stall et al., 2003). Essential to secondary prevention is addressing psychosocial issues that impede this population's health behaviors (Safren, Perry, Blashill, O'Cleirigh, & Mayer, 2015). Evidence-based approaches to prevention should address these psychosocial factors in order to curb the impact and transmission of HIV among sexual minority men.

This chapter begins with a review of the current state of research and theory regarding evidence-based sexual health interventions for HIV-positive sexual minority men. To facilitate practitioners' understanding and potential work with this population, we draw from experience with a specific intervention, Project Enhance, which involves using models informed by cognitive–behavioral therapy (CBT) and motivational interviewing (MI) to address sexual health and other related concerns in this population (Safren, O'Cleirigh, Skeer, Elsesser, & Mayer, 2013). We conclude with recommendations for practitioners working with HIV-positive sexual minority men and future directions for clinical research with this population.

CURRENT STATE OF RESEARCH AND THEORY

Evidence-based behavioral interventions for HIV-positive sexual minority men typically aim to increase condom use, reduce serodiscordant condomless anal sex (CAS), improve communication about HIV status, and/or lower viral load to reduce transmissibility. These interventions vary in their focus on contextual factors that contribute to each of these health behaviors, including mental health concerns, substance use, and stigma-related stress. Interventions also vary with regard to the evidence supporting their efficacy and effectiveness, ranging from pilot nonrandomized studies to large-scale randomized controlled trials (RCTs).

A systematic review of behavioral interventions for reducing HIV risk behaviors among people living with HIV found that evidence-based interventions addressed (1) HIV risk reduction behaviors (e.g., sexual risk reduction), (2) motivation for risk reduction behaviors, (3) knowledge about HIV, (4) mental health, and (5) medication adherence (Crepaz et al., 2014). Previously, a meta-analysis assessed common factors of efficacious interventions for reducing HIV risk behaviors among people living with HIV (Crepaz et al., 2006). Efficacious interventions utilized behavioral theory, focused on reducing transmission behaviors, addressed behavioral skills, were administered individually, used a health care provider or professional counselor, were delivered in HIV care settings, were intensive and longer in duration, and addressed contextual issues affecting HIV risk behaviors (e.g., mental health and ART adherence). Crepaz et al. (2006) concluded that successful secondary prevention interventions should be delivered in HIV care settings and address contextual factors that could contribute to sexual risk behaviors, including physical and mental health concerns. Some of the studies reviewed by Crepaz et al.

(2006, 2014) that focused on MSM and other studies that address sexual health for sexual minority men living with HIV are reviewed next.

Individual Interventions

Many evidence-based sexual health interventions for HIV-positive sexual minority men are delivered individually. These include the Healthy Living Project (Morin et al., 2008), the Treatment Advocacy Program (McKirnan, Tolou-Shams, & Courtenay-Quirk, 2010), Project Enhance (Safren et al., 2011, 2013), the Providers Advocating for Sexual Health Initiative (Bachmann et al., 2013), a disclosure intervention (Serovich, Reed, Grafsky, & Andrist, 2009), and Positive Choices (Sikkema et al., 2014). Advantages of individually administered interventions include individualized tailoring, intensity, and a sense of confidentiality, which may contribute to a greater sense of safety in disclosing highly personal information.

The Healthy Living Project (HLP) is an intensive secondary prevention intervention based on a prevention case management model that involves fifteen 90-minute individual sessions (Morin et al., 2008). HLP participants spent 5 sessions on each of three major content areas— (1) stress, coping, and adjustment; (2) safety (e.g., reducing sexual risk behaviors); and (3) optimizing health (e.g., medication adherence and accessing care)—with sessions being both structured and individually tailored. The intervention uses CBT techniques, including problem-solving and goal setting. A clinical trial ($N = 616$) found that HLP participants showed significant reductions in serodiscordant CAS over time (up to 20 months) compared to a wait-list control. Effects of HLP on sexual risk behaviors appeared to be associated with serosorting, or having a greater portion of condomless sex with partners who were also HIV-positive rather than unknown or negative partners, a strategy that prevents transmission to negative partners but risks transmission of other STIs and possible reinfection or super-infection (Poudel, Poudel-Tandukar, Yasuoka, & Jimba, 2007). Thus, serosorting involves additional sexual health implications that practitioners can address. Overall, results of this trial suggested that HLP is efficacious in reducing HIV-related sexual risk behavior among HIV-positive MSM.

Also delivered in a primary care setting, the Treatment Advocacy Program (TAP; McKirnan et al., 2010) aimed to reduce serodiscordant CAS through four 60- to 90-minute individual sessions, two booster sessions, and phone check-in sessions. TAP was developed based on basic coping and self-regulation frameworks and utilized CBT and MI. Session topics included HIV coping, medication adherence, intimacy and sexuality, and sexual safety skills. HIV-positive peer advocates (supervised by licensed therapists) facilitated each session using a computerized treatment manual, which allowed sessions to be structured yet tailored to individual goals, motivation, and experiences. Sessions began with a motivation and goal assessment, followed by structured MI and CBT prompts that led to the development of a concrete behavior change plan. Booster sessions focused on participants' challenges in implementing their initial behavior change plan. In an RCT ($N = 313$), TAP participants showed a significant reduction in serodiscordant CAS compared to participants in care as usual (McKirnan et al., 2010).

Project Enhance is a sex-positive and culturally appropriate secondary prevention intervention for HIV-positive MSM in HIV care (Knauz et al., 2007). This intervention aimed to reduce serodiscordant CAS, with an understanding of psychosocial factors that may contribute to sexual risk behaviors in this population. Enhance was developed using theoretical models such as the information, motivation, and behavior change (IMB) model (Fisher & Fisher, 1992) and the transtheoretical model of behavior change (Prochaska & DiClemente, 1982). The IMB model holds that individuals require accurate information about HIV transmission and prevention and the motivation and skills to make these changes (Fisher & Fisher, 1992). The transtheoretical model highlights that different psychosocial interventions are indicated depending on one's readiness for change (Prochaska & DiClemente, 1982). Stakeholders (e.g., focus groups, HIV providers, and a community advisory board) provided input to inform the development of Enhance. Interdisciplinary teams created a flexibly delivered workbook, used in 50-minute tailored individual sessions. Over 12 months, participants completed an intake, four core sessions, and four booster sessions. Participants selected session topics from the following modules: Having Sex; Party Drugs; Managing Stress; Triggers; Cultures, Communities, and You; Disclosure; and Getting the Relationships You Want.

The first evaluation of Project Enhance was a demonstration project with HIV-positive peer facilitators ($N = 176$; Safren et al., 2011). This study demonstrated the program's feasibility and acceptability using peer interventionists. Serodiscordant CAS decreased for those who reported it at the beginning of the study. Participants noted that nonjudgmental peer counselors who appropriately shared personal experiences and effectively used therapeutic skills were helpful. Most appreciated the option to choose session topics, and participants reflected on the positive overall impact of Enhance on their sexual health and behaviors.

The second study to evaluate this intervention was an RCT ($N = 201$) that compared Enhance, delivered by medical social workers, to usual HIV medical care (Safren et al., 2013). Both groups showed reduced serodiscordant CAS over time. However, among participants who were depressed at intake, those in the Enhance condition showed significant reductions in sexual risk behaviors compared to those in their usual medical care only. Among non-depressed participants, simply assessing one's own behavior following a recent sexual risk activity may have been enough to reduce future serodiscordant CAS, as has been shown elsewhere (Lightfoot, Rotheram-Borus, Comulada, Gundersen, & Reddy, 2007). However, among those with depression, intervention that is more intensive may be required. The proactive case management provided by medical social work interventionists and/or the Enhance topics may be particularly relevant for depressed individuals. Thus, tailoring secondary prevention to HIV-positive MSM's various psychosocial concerns, such as depression, may be a useful strategy.

The Providers Advocating for Sexual Health Initiative used primary care providers with computer assistance to engage patients in a secondary prevention intervention in medical care clinics in the Deep South, rather than adding another provider for behavioral health care. To evaluate this intervention, Bachmann et al. (2013) conducted a longitudinal demonstration project without a control group ($N = 234$). Participants completed computerized assessments of recent sexual risk behaviors and readiness for change at their regular primary care visits. Their providers received the results of these assessments with tailored risk reduction messages that they in turn provided to their patients. Messages were specific to patients' readiness for change and recent sexual behaviors. The demonstration project showed preliminary evidence of the effectiveness of this cost-effective option for integrating sexual health messaging into usual care, with participants showing significant decreases in CAS (insertive) over five sessions. This type of intervention may be particularly useful for those who would not be willing to receive additional psychosocial intervention beyond usual medical care.

Disclosure and communication about HIV status can be a difficult and complex concern for HIV-positive gay and bisexual men. Serovich et al. (2009) developed and pilot tested a four-session disclosure intervention guided by the theory that disclosure is more likely when anticipated rewards outweigh costs of disclosure. Participants identified goals and assessed current disclosure behaviors, evaluated the costs and benefits of disclosure, compared disclosure strategies, and rehearsed disclosure behaviors, with a special focus on disclosing to casual partners. A three-arm pilot RCT (facilitator-only, computer-assisted with facilitator, and wait-list control; $N = 77$) found that participants in the facilitator-only condition showed improved self-reported disclosure behaviors, attitudes, and intentions, consistent with the primary goal of the intervention. There were baseline differences between the three groups on frequency of CAS (the control group had a low frequency compared to the intervention groups); however, by 3-month follow-up, the frequency of CAS was similar across the facilitator-only group and control group. Serovich et al. postulated that a disclosure intervention might elicit serosorting and greater CAS in light of knowledge of partners' HIV statuses, again highlighting the importance of specifically addressing the advantages and disadvantages of serosorting in the context of sexual minority men's sexual health interventions.

Positive Choices (PC) is a behavioral intervention designed to meet the needs of newly diagnosed HIV-positive MSM (Sikkema et al., 2014). PC is informed by the transtheoretical model (Prochaska & DiClemente, 1982) and the IMB model (Fisher & Fisher, 1992), and it was delivered over the course of three 1-hour individually tailored sessions. In the first two sessions, participants received information about transmissibility, built motivation for behavior change, developed behavioral skills, and created a risk reduction plan. A booster session followed 1 month later to reinforce, practice, and rework the original risk reduction plan. Although the initial pilot trial ($N = 65$), which compared PC plus comprehensive standard care to comprehensive standard care alone (Sikkema et al., 2011), showed only nonsignificant effects of the treatment on sexual transmission risk behaviors and number of partners, a larger study did find significant effects (Sikkema et al., 2014). This larger study compared three sessions of PC to standard treatment ($N = 102$) and found that PC participants showed significant reductions in serodiscordant CAS up to 9 months after the intervention.

Group Interventions

Group interventions for HIV-positive sexual minority men's sexual health have also been developed and evaluated. Here, we review several evidence-based group interventions, including Prevention Options for Positives (Lapinski, Randall, Peterson, Peterson, & Klein, 2009), Gay Poz Sex (Hart, Willis, et al., 2016), the Seropositive Urban Men's Intervention Trial (Wolitski, Gómez, & Parsons, 2005), the Sexual Health Intervention for Men (Williams et al., 2008, 2013), and 40 & Forward (Reisner et al., 2011). Group interventions have several advantages, including opportunity for peer feedback, increased social support, exploration of peer experiences regarding mental and sexual health, and cost-effectiveness.

Prevention Options for Positives (POP) evaluated group plus individual counseling compared to individual counseling only as secondary prevention for HIV-positive MSM ($N = 74$; Lapinski et al., 2009). The structured POP group intervention addressed psychosocial issues, HIV status communication, safer sex, and substance use. Each group session was informed by the theory of reasoned action (Fishbein & Ajzen, 1975) and social cognitive theory (SCT; Bandura, 1977). Using this theoretical foundation, POP group participants explored subjective norms and their own sexual behaviors. SCT highlights the importance of modeling and vicarious learning in order to elicit behavior change (Bandura, 1977). Utilizing HIV-positive sexual minority men as peer facilitators is an example of one way that SCT informed the POP intervention. Group sessions also provided opportunities for interpersonal interaction and social support. Certified HIV prevention counselors provided client-centered individual counseling, assessing HIV risk behaviors and facilitating development of tailored risk reduction plans.

Participants who received the POP group counseling in addition to individual counseling were more likely to avoid sex while drunk or high, disclose HIV status, and engage in risk behavior communication with their main partner compared to those who only received individual counseling. This suggests the utility of theoretically grounded groups in enhancing HIV-positive sexual minority men's disclosure of status to main partners. Neither intervention showed significant effects on disclosure with other sex partners (e.g., casual partners). This remains a challenging area that may require additional assertiveness or interpersonal skill training (Serovich et al., 2009). Lapinski et al. 2009 highlight the importance of practitioners helping HIV-positive sexual minority men develop sexual risk reduction plans that address the range of situations in which different strategies may be more useful or accessible. For example, with a main partner, disclosing one's HIV status may be a viable option, whereas with casual partners, consistent condom use regardless of disclosure may be a more attainable goal.

Gay Poz Sex (GPS; Hart, Stratton, et al., 2016; Hart, Willis, et al., 2016) is another group intervention, which takes a sex-positive approach and is informed by the IMB model (Fisher & Fisher, 1992). Similar to the Enhance intervention (Safren et al., 2011), community organizations and HIV-positive community members collaborated to design GPS to maximize its clinical feasibility and implementation when used in community settings. HIV-positive peer counselors facilitated seven weekly 2-hour structured group sessions, during which they provided information about HIV transmission (e.g., transmission risk and viral load, seropositioning, and STI risk), built motivation for safer sex using MI (e.g., decisional balance exercise), and taught behavioral skills for safer sex (e.g., disclosure or safer sex negotiation role plays). A pilot study ($N = 59$) showed significant reductions in CAS while also positively impacting psychosocial concerns such as loneliness, sexual compulsivity, and fear of rejection for insisting on condom use (Hart, Stratton, et al., 2016). These findings suggest that a brief group intervention may reduce sexual risk and psychosocial concerns, although greater integration of mental health treatment may be needed to show effects on depressive symptoms, which were not significantly impacted.

The Seropositive Urban Men's Intervention Trial (SUMIT) compared a standard one-session safer sex psychoeducation intervention to an enhanced six-session group-based secondary prevention intervention ($N = 811$; Wolitski et al., 2005). The manualized enhanced intervention, based on behavioral theory, addressed sexual and romantic relationships, HIV and STI transmission, substance use, assumptions about others' HIV status, disclosure, and mental health. SUMIT goals were to increase knowledge about sexual behaviors associated with risk for HIV transmission, motivation and a sense of responsibility for safer sex, awareness of contextual factors' impact on sexual behaviors, and awareness of triggers for sexual risk. Techniques used included interactive learning activities, presentations, small group discussions, and exposure via videotape of peers navigating safer sex. Three months after the intervention, participants in the enhanced intervention had reduced serodiscordant CAS (receptive) compared to standard of care; however, other predicted outcomes were not observed at 3- or 6-month follow-up. Wolitski et al. suggested modifications to further increase the efficacy of the intervention, such as focusing participants on reducing one high-risk behavior instead of aiming for broad risk reduction, highlighting benefits of safer sex to participants' own sexual health, and structuring the group intervention to avoid negative role modeling from riskier participants.

Another group sexual health intervention, the Sexual Health Intervention for Men (S-HIM), addressed the unique needs of African American and Latino MSM and men who have sex with men and women with a history of childhood sexual abuse. Although African American and Latino MSM and men who have sex with men and women are disproportionately affected by HIV (CDC, 2016) and childhood sexual abuse history is associated with greater sexual risk behaviors (Stall et al., 2003), few interventions have been specifically developed for any of these populations and clinical issues. The Men's Health Project therefore compared S-HIM, a CBT and social learning theory group intervention, to a general six-session health promotion intervention that did not directly address sexual health (N = 137; Williams et al., 2008). Focus groups with African American and Latino men informed the development of S-HIM. Trained, ethnically matched facilitators delivered both interventions during six 2-hour group sessions. S-HIM addressed triple minority status (being HIV-positive, ethnic minority, and sexual minority) and the experience of CSA history as these related to sexual risk reduction and psychological distress. Across both conditions, participants' sexual risk behavior decreased over time; however, there were not significant effects of S-HIM compared to the control group. A follow-up RCT (N = 117) compared an enhanced version of S-HIM (ES-HIM) specifically for HIV-positive bisexual African American men with CSA histories to the standard health promotion intervention. ES-HIM was modified to include an ecological, culturally congruent framework focused on changing sexual behavior and improving mental health. ES-HIM participants showed significant reduction in CAS (insertive), with significant gains in mental health outcomes (e.g., reduced post-traumatic stress disorder and depression) not observed from the initial trial of S-HIM. Both trials highlight the value of addressing sexual health in the context of identity-based stressors (e.g., minority stress) and psychosocial concerns in a group setting.

Older HIV-positive sexual minority men are another group with unique sexual health needs. 40 & Forward is a manualized group intervention designed to reduce sexual risk for HIV-positive sexual minority men aged 40 years or older with depression, isolation or loneliness, or social anxiety (Reisner et al., 2011). Across six weekly group sessions, participants considered the causes of social isolation, depression, and anxiety; learned and implemented interpersonal skills to improve social and sexual interactions; and expanded their social networks. Techniques such as role plays, self-assessment of social support, activity scheduling, problem-solving, and psychoeducation addressed these content areas. A pre–post evaluation of the intervention (N = 84, no control) showed that participants in the peer-facilitated group intervention showed improved condom-use self-efficacy and improvements in mental health concerns such as depression, social anxiety, loneliness, and fear of negative evaluation. They also observed a nonsignificant decrease in CAS following the intervention. Although they did not measure overall sexual behavior, Reisner et al. proposed that reducing participants' depressive symptoms may have increased sexual interest and activity, thereby explaining the non-reduction in sexual risk. This possibility highlights the importance of addressing mental and sexual health simultaneously.

Behavioral Interventions for Physical Health

In addition to sexual risk reduction, another strategy for improving personal HIV health (Gardner et al., 2011) and preventing HIV transmission is uptake and adherence to ART, with the goal of viral suppression. Viral suppression has been shown definitively to prevent HIV transmission (Cohen et al., 2011; Rodger et al., 2016), meaning that ART treatment can be used as secondary prevention.

However, taking daily medication is a health behavior that can be challenging due to the burden of daily remembering, reminders of HIV stigma, medication side effects, and pragmatic concerns such as refilling prescriptions and accessing care. Complicating factors, such as substance use or other psychosocial problems, can also interfere with ART uptake and adherence (Blashill, Perry, & Safren, 2011; Harkness et al., 2018).

There are several evidence-based ART adherence interventions (Amico, Harman, & Johnson, 2006; Simoni, Pearson, Pantalone, Marks, & Crepaz, 2006), with general samples of those living with the virus versus MSM in particular. Here, we review two ART adherence interventions for sexual minority men and two interventions that were tested with a large portion of sexual minority participants.

An RCT compared a 10-week cognitive–behavioral stress management (CBSM) intervention plus medication adherence training ($n = 76$) to medication adherence training alone ($n = 54$) for HIV-positive gay men (Antoni et al., 2006). In the CBSM intervention, participants attended 135-minute group sessions that addressed stress management and relaxation. Facilitators encouraged participants to discuss, examine, and restructure their thoughts related to taking medication. Participants also learned problem-solving to increase adherence and relaxation skills to manage medication side effects. Advanced psychology trainees supervised by licensed mental health professionals facilitated the intervention using a treatment manual. Among those with detectable viral loads at baseline, CBSM participants showed reductions in viral load not observed in the control group. Furthermore, CBSM participants showed decreased depressive symptoms, which explained the intervention's positive effect on viral load. The findings highlight the importance of treating mental health concerns for HIV-positive sexual minority men who have difficulty adhering to ART.

Thrive with Me (TWM) was a preliminary efficacy study of another intervention designed to improve adherence specifically in MSM (Horvath et al., 2013). This 8-week online social support intervention ($n = 67$) was compared to usual care alone ($n = 57$) for HIV-positive sexual minority men. TWM participants could interact with other HIV-positive sexual minority men as well as track and receive feedback on their medication adherence online. Participants could opt in to receive text message or email medication reminders. TWM also offered interesting and engaging information about HIV (e.g., educational videos, articles about adherence, and links to online HIV-related resources). Horvath et al. found modest (nonsignificant) effects of TWM on adherence, whereas adherence worsened in the control group. However, among drug-using participants, TWM participants showed significantly improved ART adherence, suggesting the intervention was most useful for drug users.

Two recent studies evaluated the effects of CBT for adherence and depression (CBT-AD), an intervention designed for people living with HIV and co-occurring depression. A large percentage of participants in both trials of CBT-AD were sexual minorities. The first RCT ($N = 45$, 82.2% gay or bisexual men) aimed to improve ART adherence while simultaneously addressing co-occurring depression (Safren et al., 2009). CBT-AD began with an initial medical adherence session,

Life-Steps (Safren, Otto, & Worth, 1999), which used psychoeducation, problem-solving, and CBT skills to address adherence concerns. In Life-Steps, participants identified barriers and solutions to problems related to obtaining medication, communicating with their provider, scheduling and remembering medicine, managing side effects and cognitive barriers to adherence, and transportation. Following this, participants completed 11 sessions that incorporated five CBT modules to address both depressive symptoms and medication adherence, including MI (e.g., advantages and disadvantages of improving medication adherence and depressive symptoms), behavioral activation, cognitive restructuring (e.g., challenging thoughts that interfere with adherence), problem-solving, and relaxation training. In the enhanced treatment as usual condition, participants completed only the Life-Steps intervention. Those who received CBT-AD showed improved ART adherence and reduced depressive symptoms and viral load compared to those who received only Life-Steps, with gains generally maintained over 12 months.

To further test the efficacy of CBT-AD, a three-arm RCT ($N = 240$, 64.5% not exclusively heterosexual) compared the same intervention, CBT-AD, to (1) information and supportive psychotherapy or (2) enhanced treatment as usual, including 1 session of Life-Steps (Safren et al., 2016). CBT-AD and Life-Steps were delivered as described previously. Information and supportive psychotherapy began with 1 session of Life-Steps followed by 11 sessions of information about healthy living with HIV and client-centered supportive therapy for depression. The CBT-AD participants had improved adherence and reduced depressive symptoms compared to those who received only enhanced treatment as usual; however, CBT-AD was not superior to information and supportive therapy, suggesting the importance of addressing psychosocial concerns of people living with HIV, using evidence-based psychosocial and adherence interventions.

General Recommendations for Clinicians

Practitioners can choose from a variety of evidence-based interventions to promote HIV-positive sexual minority men's sexual health. Consistent with Crepaz et al.'s (2006) meta-analysis, many of the interventions were integrated into participants' existing medical care (Bachmann et al., 2013; McKirnan et al., 2010; Safren et al., 2013), which may facilitate access to care. Although some interventions utilized mental health professionals as interventionists (Safren et al., 2013), many successfully utilized HIV-positive peer interventionists (Hart, Willis, et al., 2016; McKirnan et al., 2010; Safren et al., 2011; Wolitski et al., 2005). However, it is important to have careful selection, training, and supervision from trained mental health professionals when utilizing peer interventionists (Safren et al., 2011). Training peer counselors may be an effective strategy for delivering sexual health interventions to HIV-positive sexual minority men with fewer co-occurring psychosocial problems, whereas mental health professionals may be more appropriate in clinically complex cases.

The interventions varied in their theoretical underpinnings and techniques. They often drew from or were consistent with a CBT framework (Antoni et al., 2006; Morin et al., 2008), the transtheoretical model of change (Safren et al., 2013; Sikkema et al., 2014), and the IMB model (Hart, Willis, et al., 2016; Safren et al., 2013). Although all were secondary prevention interventions, a majority addressed this goal in the context of HIV-positive sexual minority men's lives, addressing the unique challenges of various forms of minority stress (Williams et al., 2013) and psychosocial issues such as depression, substance use, and loneliness (Morin et al., 2008; Safren et al., 2013). This is consistent with findings that HIV-positive MSM prefer interventions that address coping challenges as well as sexual risk reduction (Vanable et al., 2012). Practitioners should consider this point when providing secondary prevention services to HIV-positive sexual minority men.

Interventions varied with regard to their intensity and duration, ranging from brief 3-session (Sikkema et al., 2011) to intensive 15-session interventions (Morin et al., 2008). Mental health professionals' choice of evidence-based intervention for HIV-positive sexual minority men may depend on a number of factors, including availability of resources, a client's co-occurring psychosocial problems, identity-based stress (e.g., minority stress and stigma), and readiness for change. Safren et al. (2015) highlight that people with more co-occurring, intertwined psychosocial problems have greater transmissibility due to ART non-adherence and greater sexual risk behavior, suggesting the cost-effectiveness (in terms of new HIV cases averted) of more intensive intervention for higher risk populations.

Finally, the evidence-based interventions described here all involved the development of a positive therapeutic relationship and are likely most effective coming from a gay/bisexual-affirming, sex-positive provider. HIV-positive MSM's positive experiences with peer counselors for HIV prevention counseling are associated with peer counselors maintaining a nonjudgmental stance and building rapport with participants (Driskell et al., 2010). Providers may be more culturally competent in their service delivery if they are willing to reflect upon and challenge any underlying beliefs or values they may have when using these interventions. Therapists responding to a hypothetical HIV-positive client demonstrated less empathy, assessed a client's functioning to be worse, and were less willing to work with the client if the hypothetical client was gay, if the provider reported more homophobic attitudes, and if the hypothetical client's source of HIV infection was not drugs (Hayes & Erkis, 2000). These findings highlight the importance of providers engaging in values exploration and building an affirming stance to build working alliances with their clients and provide effective care to this population.

Prior to delivering a sexual risk reduction intervention to an HIV-positive sexual minority client, practitioners may benefit from reflecting on the following:

Regarding client characteristics: What sexual risk behaviors is my client currently practicing? How motivated and prepared is my client to change their current behaviors? How might stigma, discrimination, or co-occurring psychosocial difficulties impact my client's current behaviors and psychosocial adjustment?

Regarding systemic issues: What resources are available? Am I able to provide intensive treatment, or am I restricted to short-term intervention? Can I train peer interventionists or medical providers to deliver these interventions? Would a group be an effective use of my resources?

Regarding the therapeutic relationship and cultural competence: Am I prepared to practice from a gay/bisexual-affirming, nonjudgmental, sex-positive perspective working with someone living with HIV? What biases might get in my way, and how can I address these?

APPLICATION OF FINDINGS TO PRACTICE

As described previously, Project Enhance is an evidence-based secondary prevention intervention for HIV-positive sexual minority men (Knauz et al., 2007). Enhance is flexibly delivered, with each module eliciting the client's knowledge of the topic, employing MI, and incorporating behavior change suggestions and practice assignments. Enhance is composed of an intake session followed by four core modules and four booster sessions over the course of 1 year. Clients select from the following modules: Having Sex (completed by all patients); Party Drugs; Managing Stress; Triggers; Cultures, Communities, and You; Disclosure; and Getting the Relationships You Want. Here, we present a case to illustrate the use of Enhance with "Andres." We de-identified and merged characteristics from several Enhance participants to formulate this case material.

CASE EXAMPLE

Prior to beginning the Enhance intervention, clients complete an intake session during which counselors review clients' HIV-related and psychosocial history and current needs. During Andres' intake, the counselor learned that Andres was a 35-year-old Latino gay man who was raised Catholic, an important aspect of his identity. Although out as gay to most people, religious stigma about being gay and HIV-positive led to anxiety and concealment in religious spaces, resulting in a compartmentalized sense of self. He was diagnosed with HIV approximately 2 years ago and only had casual sex partners since then. He described moderate symptoms of anxiety and depression, which permeated his sexual, social, family, and work life. The counselor listened nonjudgmentally and aimed to build rapport with Andres throughout the intake session.

Andres completed the Having Sex module as his first core session. In general, the goal of this module is to facilitate a nonjudgmental discussion about participants' current sexual risk behaviors and risk reduction activities. Andres reported inconsistent condom use, stating that he bottoms when not using a condom to reduce HIV transmission risk to a partner. The counselor, following the material provided as part of the intervention packet (hence diminishing the perception of judgment and too much didactic information), provided education about reinfection, superinfection, and STI transmission related to condomless anal sex.

The Having Sex module also contains a sexual risk limit exercise, which involves discussing sexual activities within and beyond the client's personal "risk limits." Andres reported that casual sex with a condom was within his limits, and condomless casual sex was past his limit. The counselor used MI to highlight the discrepancy that Andres sometimes had condomless casual sex, yet this is past his sexual limit. This elicited change talk from Andres, who acknowledged that he would prefer to use condoms with casual partners consistently, especially with the new information he learned about risks to his own sexual health. He explained that he has sex when he feels lonely and fears rejection if he were to disclose that the reason he wanted to use a condom was his HIV status. Andres developed a behavior change plan that did not require him to disclose his HIV status (e.g., requesting a condom to prevent STIs).

After the first core module, Enhance clients select modules that they believe are most relevant to them. Clients can focus on one module for all of their remaining sessions or on an assortment of modules. In this way, the Enhance intervention is individually tailored and patient-directed. Andres chose to cover the following three modules during his remaining core sessions: Disclosure; Getting the Relationships You Want; and Cultures, Communities, and You.

The goal of the Disclosure module is to reduce HIV transmission risk by addressing difficulties in telling partners one's HIV status. During Andres' session on disclosure, the counselor facilitated a discussion about his current disclosure practices (e.g., situations in which he would and would not disclose his HIV status). Andres explained that fear of rejection usually prevents him from disclosing. One past sexual partner rejected him after he disclosed, which exacerbated his anxiety and loneliness and led to greater reluctance about disclosure. He assumed that if someone were HIV-negative, they would ask to use condoms. Andres identified one exception to his non-disclosure tendency: He reported that he always discloses if a partner directly asks his status. Andres also discussed the double bind he experienced regarding disclosure. If he were to start a relationship with someone, the timing of disclosure would be a significant worry. Andres worried that if he disclosed too soon, the partner would not want to have sex or a relationship with him because he was HIV-positive. On the other hand, if he waited "too long," the partner would be upset that he did not tell him sooner.

The counselor facilitated a discussion whereby Andres examined his thoughts and feelings about disclosure. Andres acknowledged that he had disclosed his status several times in the past, and only one person explicitly rejected him for sex following this disclosure. For the most part, partners were comfortable as long as they used a condom. Andres felt some relief when he disclosed in the past because it was consistent with his values to be honest and protect others' sexual health. Using MI, the counselor highlighted Andres' change talk—that disclosing could be a way to honor two of his important values. Andres met most of his partners online and did not feel comfortable posting his HIV status. Because he was successful disclosing in the past when partners directly asked him his status, he posted "Ask me my status" in his profile to initiate the disclosure process without having to disclose his status in a public forum.

Next, Andres completed the Getting the Relationships You Want module. The goal of this module is to bolster clients' social support networks by either identifying strategies to build new relationships or improving existing relationships. Andres felt lonely much of the time. Although he valued his religious community, he minimized his gay identity in this setting, leading to increased loneliness. Reviewing a list of 12 relationship types, he identified wanting more meaningful and longer lasting connections with gay men, especially those who were religious, HIV-positive, and/or sexual minority men of color. Andres viewed sex as a way to connect with other gay men; however, he wanted to establish some nonsexual relationships with gay men. During this session, he explored strategies for locating these communities and practiced assertiveness and communication skills to express himself and set boundaries with new gay men in his life with whom he hoped to establish nonsexual friendships. He also practiced assertiveness and communication skills that he could use for condom negotiation and HIV status disclosure with casual versus repeat and/or main partners.

Andres completed his core modules with Cultures, Communities, and You. The general goal of this module is to explore intersections between an individual's identity statuses and their general and sexual decision-making. Andres mapped out his different identity statuses and explored how they contributed to his experiences and sexual decision-making. He discussed enjoying his social support community through church, but he also felt stressed by having to minimize his gay identity. He felt alienated from the local gay community, which he perceived to be predominantly White HIV-negative gay men. As a Latino HIV-positive gay man, he felt less entitled to be sexually assertive, whereas he viewed his partners as retaining more power and privilege than he did. Andres explored ways to advocate for his sexual safety and pleasure with others. He also continued his exploration from the prior session about ways to connect with groups within the gay community that shared some of his experiences and identity statuses, including religious and ethnic identity, as well as HIV status.

Following the core sessions, Andres completed four booster sessions (once every 3 months during the course of 1 year). Booster sessions track, reinforce, and build new skills from the core sessions. Clients can revisit core modules or review new modules, depending on their current needs. Andres located a social group for gay men of color and enjoyed participating in the group's activities, and he attributed his improved mood to this social connection. However, he continued to struggle with disclosure and asserting condom use during casual sex. Thus, he revisited the disclosure module for his booster sessions. The counselor facilitated an in-depth review of Andres' thoughts and feelings about disclosure, challenging unhelpful thoughts and restructuring these to be more balanced. For example,

Andres continued to feel anxious about partners rejecting him because of his HIV status, with great concern about the appropriate timing of disclosure. He reviewed the evidence for and against this belief. He had one experience of rejection in the past year, which he was able to tolerate especially because he felt less lonely now, and otherwise his sexual partners had been accepting. Andres also reviewed the benefits to his own sexual health of using condoms, which reinforced his motivation to use condoms, even in the absence of disclosure. At the final booster session, Andres reported increased HIV disclosure, which alleviated his anxiety about sex, as well as more consistent condom use.

FUTURE DIRECTIONS

As illustrated by this review of interventions and case illustration of secondary prevention interventions for HIV-positive sexual minority men, practitioners have several options regarding treatment. There are also issues that may be further explored in future clinical trials in order to improve services for HIV-positive sexual minority men. An ongoing concern is the development of interventions that meet the needs of different populations of HIV-positive sexual minority men. Some sexual minority men face a greater number of co-occurring psychosocial concerns and associated increases in transmissibility (Safren et al., 2015). Highlighting this issue, the effects of Enhance on reduced sexual risk were moderated by baseline depression (Safren et al., 2013), and the TAP intervention's effects were partially mediated by reductions in substance abuse (McKirnan et al., 2010). Among these individuals, mental health and substance use problems may be acting as barriers to change. Thus, intensive intervention addressing both psychosocial problems and sexual health may be required. To complement intensive intervention for individuals with higher sexual risk, Morin et al. (2008) suggest integrating short sexual risk assessments into routine medical care, a smaller scale intervention that could reduce sexual risk for those with greater motivation and fewer barriers to change.

Another current concern is the disproportionate impact of HIV on sexual minority men of color, specifically African American and Latino sexual minority men (CDC, 2016). Few secondary prevention trials address cultural context and racial or ethnic minority stress for HIV-positive sexual minority men. With continued health disparities across racial and ethnic groups, practitioners should consider the heterogeneity of facilitators and barriers to sexual health among different populations of HIV-positive sexual minority men.

There are also new mechanisms available for delivering evidence-based interventions to HIV-positive sexual minority men. Electronic and computer-assisted health interventions may be particularly useful and cost-effective for some populations of HIV-positive sexual minority men, increasing accessibility to underserved and over-affected populations, including racial and ethnic minority men and youth (CDC, 2016). Electronic and computer-assisted interventions may be especially useful in conservative or rural geographic areas with fewer gay/bisexual-affirming HIV behavioral health resources. For example, the Providers Advocating for Sexual Health Initiative was developed and tested at HIV clinics in the Deep South without the use of additional mental health services (Bachmann et al., 2013). Instead, through computer assistance, patients' usual medical providers provided sexual risk reduction messages. In this region, this type of intervention may be more accessible than adding a separate psychosocial intervention. Although some online interventions, such as Thrive with Me (Horvath et al., 2013), show high retention, some HIV-positive sexual minority men may prefer in-person rather than computer-assisted intervention (Serovich et al., 2009). Practitioners should consider the preferences of their clients when deciding whether to utilize in-person or electronic interventions.

From a risk reduction perspective, HIV-positive sexual minority men can engage in a range of behaviors to promote sexual health. Lapinski et al. (2009) suggest that psychosocial interventions should reflect these options in order to meet the needs of a heterogeneous population rather than focusing only on eliminating risk. The range of risk reduction options for HIV-positive sexual minority men continues to expand with emerging medical knowledge. There is now definitive evidence that viral suppression prevents HIV transmission in heterosexual (Cohen et al., 2011) and MSM (Rodger et al., 2016) sexual partners, knowledge of which HIV-positive sexual minority men can use to inform their sexual decision-making. Practitioners and clinical researchers need to incorporate messages about navigating sexual encounters with knowledge of one's own viral load. Similarly, the development of pre-exposure prophylaxis (PrEP), although designed for individuals who are HIV-negative, has implications for how HIV-positive sexual minority men navigate sex.

Both of these new developments also raise the issue of transmission of other STIs, which can be transmitted to or from HIV-positive sexual minority men when choosing not to use condoms due to suppressed viral load, a partner being adherent to PrEP, or because a partner is seroconcordant (Rodger et al., 2016). HIV-positive sexual minority men may be particularly impacted by acquisition of STIs due to having a compromised immune system, an issue that should be addressed in secondary prevention interventions (Serovich et al., 2009). To promote comprehensive sexual health for HIV-positive sexual minority men, practitioners should be aware of how their patients' behaviors not only impact transmission to others but also impact their patients' own health.

Overall, practitioners have a variety of options for evidence-based interventions that can be used and tailored to clinical practice with HIV-positive sexual minority men. Some of these interventions may be especially relevant to those with greater co-occurring psychosocial problems, whereas others might be implemented as a larger scale prevention program.

REFERENCES

Amico, K. R., Harman, J. J., & Johnson, B. T. (2006). Efficacy of antiretroviral therapy adherence interventions: A research synthesis of trials, 1996 to 2004. *Journal of*

Acquired Immune Deficiency Syndromes, *41*(3), 285–297. https://doi.org/10.1097/ 01.qai.0000197870.99196.ea

Antoni, M. H., Carrico, A. W., Durán, R. E., Spitzer, S., Penedo, F., Ironson, G., . . . Schneiderman, N. (2006). Randomized clinical trial of cognitive behavioral stress management on human immunodeficiency virus viral load in gay men treated with highly active antiretroviral therapy. *Psychosomatic Medicine*, *68*(1), 143–151. https:// doi.org/10.1097/01.psy.0000195749.60049.63

Bachmann, L. H., Grimley, D. M., Gao, H., Aban, I., Chen, H., Raper, J. L., . . . Hook, E. W. (2013). Impact of a computer-assisted, provider-delivered intervention on sexual risk behaviors in HIV-positive men who have sex with men (MSM) in a primary care setting. *AIDS Education and Prevention*, *25*(2), 87–101. https://doi.org/10.1521/ aeap.2013.25.2.87

Bandura, A. (1977). *Social learning theory*. Englewood Cliffs, NJ: Prentice Hall.

Baral, S., Sifakis, F., Cleghorn, F., & Beyrer, C. (2007). Elevated risk for HIV infection among men who have sex with men in low- and middle-income countries 2000– 2006: A systematic review. *PLoS Medicine*, *4*(12), e339. https://doi.org/10.1371/ journal.pmed.0040339

Beyrer, C., Baral, S. D., van Griensven, F., Goodreau, S. M., Chariyalertsak, S., Wirtz, A. L., & Brookmeyer, R. (2012). Global epidemiology of HIV infection in men who have sex with men. *Lancet*, *380*(9839), 367–377. https://doi.org/10.1016/ S0140-6736(12)60821-6

Blashill, A. J., Perry, N., & Safren, S. A. (2011). Mental health: A focus on stress, coping, and mental illness as it relates to treatment retention, adherence, and other health outcomes. *Current HIV/AIDS Reports*, *8*(4), 215–222. https://doi.org/10.1007/ s11904-011-0089-1

Centers for Disease Control and Prevention. (2016). *HIV surveillance report, 2015* (No. 27). Retrieved from http://www.cdc.gov/hiv/library/reports/hiv-surveillance.html

Cohen, M. S., Chen, Y. Q., McCauley, M., Gamble, T., Hosseinipour, M. C., Kumarasamy, N., . . . Fleming, T. R. (2011). Prevention of HIV-1 infection with early antiretroviral therapy. *New England Journal of Medicine*, *365*(6), 493–505. https://doi.org/10.1056/ NEJMoa1105243

Crepaz, N., Lyles, C. M., Wolitski, R. J., Passin, W. F., Rama, S. M., Herbst, J. H., . . . HIV/AIDS Prevention Research Synthesis (PRS) Team. (2006). Do prevention interventions reduce HIV risk behaviours among people living with HIV? A meta-analytic review of controlled trials. *AIDS*, *20*(2), 143–157. https://doi.org/10.1097/ 01.aids.0000196166.48518.a0

Crepaz, N., Tungol, M. L. V., Higa, D. H., Vosburgh, H. W., Mullins, M. M., Barham, T., . . . Lyles, C. M. (2014). A systematic review of interventions for reducing HIV risk behaviors among people living with HIV in the United States, 1988–2012. *AIDS*, *28*(5), 633–656. https://doi.org/10.1097/QAD.0000000000000108

Driskell, J. R., O'Cleirigh, C., Covahey, C., Ripton, J., Mayer, K., Perry, D., . . . Safren, S. (2010). Building program acceptability: Perceptions of gay and bisexual men on peer or prevention case manager relationships in secondary HIV prevention counseling. *Journal of Gay & Lesbian Social Services*, *22*(3), 269–286. https://doi.org/10.1080/ 10538720903426388

Fishbein, M., & Ajzen, I. (1975). *Belief, attitude, intention and behavior: An introduction to theory and research*. Reading, MA: Addison-Wesley.

Fisher, J. D., & Fisher, W. A. (1992). Changing AIDS-risk behavior. *Psychological Bulletin*, *111*(3), 455–474.

Friedman, M. R., Stall, R., Silvestre, A. J., Wei, C., Shoptaw, S., Herrick, A., . . . Plankey, M. W. (2015). Effects of syndemics on HIV viral load and medication adherence in the multicentre AIDS cohort study. *AIDS*, *29*(9), 1087–1096. https://doi.org/10.1097/QAD.0000000000000657

Gardner, E. M., McLees, M. P., Steiner, J. F., Del Rio, C., & Burman, W. J. (2011). The spectrum of engagement in HIV care and its relevance to test-and-treat strategies for prevention of HIV infection. *Clinical Infectious Diseases*, *52*(6), 793–800. https://doi.org/10.1093/cid/ciq243

Harkness, A., Bainter, S. A., O'Cleirigh, C., Mendez, N. A., Mayer, K. H., & Safren, S. A. (2018). Longitudinal effects of syndemics on ART non-adherence among sexual minority men. *AIDS and Behavior*, *22*(8), 2564–2574.

Hart, T. A., Stratton, N., Coleman, T. A., Wilson, H. A., Simpson, S. H., Julien, R. E., . . . Adam, B. D. (2016). A pilot trial of a sexual health counseling intervention for HIV-positive gay and bisexual men who report anal sex without condoms. *PLoS One*, *11*(4), e0152762. https://doi.org/10.1371/journal.pone.0152762

Hart, T. A., Willis, A. C., Simpson, S. H., Julien, R. E., Hoe, D., Leahy, B., . . . Adam, B. D. (2016). Gay Poz Sex: A sexual health promotion intervention for HIV-positive gay and bisexual men. *Cognitive and Behavioral Practice*, *23*(4), 517–529. https://doi.org/10.1016/j.cbpra.2015.11.002

Hayes, J. A., & Erkis, A. J. (2000). Therapist homophobia, client sexual orientation, and source of client HIV infection as predictors of therapist reactions to clients with HIV. *Journal of Counseling Psychology*, *47*(1), 71–78. https://doi.org/10.1037/0022-0167.47.1.71

Horvath, K. J., Oakes, J. M., Rosser, B. R., Danilenko, G., Vezina, H., Amico, K. R., . . . Simoni, J. (2013). Feasibility, acceptability and preliminary efficacy of an online peer-to-peer social support ART adherence intervention. *AIDS and Behavior*, *17*(6), 2031–2044. https://doi.org/10.1007/s10461-013-0469-1

Knauz, R. O., Safren, S. A., O'Cleirigh, C., Capistrant, B. D., Driskell, J. R., Aguilar, D., . . . Mayer, K. H. (2007). Developing an HIV-prevention intervention for HIV-infected men who have sex with men in HIV care: Project Enhance. *AIDS and Behavior*, *11*(5 Suppl.), S117–S126. https://doi.org/10.1007/s10461-007-9257-0

Lapinski, M. K., Randall, L. M., Peterson, M., Peterson, A., & Klein, K. A. (2009). Prevention Options for Positives: The effects of a health communication intervention for men who have sex with men living with HIV/AIDS. *Health Communication*, *24*(6), 562–571. https://doi.org/10.1080/10410230903104947

Lightfoot, M., Rotheram-Borus, M. J., Comulada, S., Gundersen, G., & Reddy, V. (2007). Self-monitoring of behaviour as a risk reduction strategy for persons living with HIV. *AIDS Care*, *19*(6), 757–763. https://doi.org/10.1080/09540120600971117

McKirnan, D. J., Tolou-Shams, M., & Courtenay-Quirk, C. (2010). The Treatment Advocacy Program: A randomized controlled trial of a peer-led safer sex intervention for HIV-infected men who have sex with men. *Journal of Consulting and Clinical Psychology*, *78*(6), 952–963. https://doi.org/10.1037/a0020759

Morin, S. F., Shade, S. B., Steward, W. T., Carrico, A. W., Remien, R. H., Rotheram-Borus, M. J., . . . Healthy Living Project Team. (2008). A behavioral intervention reduces HIV transmission risk by promoting sustained serosorting practices among HIV-infected men who have sex with men. *Journal of Acquired Immune Deficiency Syndromes*, *49*(5), 544–551. https://doi.org/10.1097/QAI.0b013e31818d5def

Poudel, K. C., Poudel-Tandukar, K., Yasuoka, J., & Jimba, M. (2007). HIV superinfection: Another reason to avoid serosorting practice. *Lancet, 370*(9581), 23. https://doi.org/10.1016/S0140-6736(07)61033-2

Prochaska, J. O., & DiClemente, C. C. (1982). Transtheoretical therapy: Toward a more integrative model of change. *Psychotherapy, 19*(3), 276–288. https://doi.org/10.1037/h0088437

Reisner, S. L., O'Cleirigh, C., Hendriksen, E. S., McLain, J., Ebin, J., Lew, K., . . . Mimiaga, M. J. (2011). "40 & Forward": Preliminary evaluation of a group intervention to improve mental health outcomes and address HIV sexual risk behaviors among older gay and bisexual men. *Journal of Gay & Lesbian Social Services, 23*(4), 523–545. https://doi.org/10.1080/10538720.2011.611113

Rodger, A. J., Cambiano, V., Bruun, T., Vernazza, P., Collins, S., van Lunzen, J., . . . Lundgren, J. (2016). Sexual activity without condoms and risk of HIV transmission in serodifferent couples when the HIV-positive partner is using suppressive antiretroviral therapy. *JAMA, 316*(2), 171–181. https://doi.org/10.1001/jama.2016.5148

Safren, S. A., Bedoya, C. A., O'Cleirigh, C., Biello, K. B., Pinkston, M. M., Stein, M. D., . . . Mayer, K. H. (2016). Cognitive behavioural therapy for adherence and depression in patients with HIV: A three-arm randomised controlled trial. *Lancet HIV, 3*(11), e529–e538. https://doi.org/10.1016/S2352-3018(16)30053-4

Safren, S. A., O'Cleirigh, C., Skeer, M. R., Driskell, J., Goshe, B. M., Covahey, C., & Mayer, K. H. (2011). Demonstration and evaluation of a peer-delivered, individually-tailored, HIV prevention intervention for HIV-infected MSM in their primary care setting. *AIDS and Behavior, 15*(5), 949–958. https://doi.org/10.1007/s10461-010-9807-8

Safren, S. A., O'Cleirigh, C., Tan, J. Y., Raminani, S. R., Reilly, L. C., Otto, M. W., & Mayer, K. H. (2009). A randomized controlled trial of cognitive behavioral therapy for adherence and depression (CBT-AD) in HIV-infected individuals. *Health Psychology, 28*(1), 1–10. https://doi.org/10.1037/a0012715

Safren, S. A., O'Cleirigh, C. M., Skeer, M., Elsesser, S. A., & Mayer, K. H. (2013). Project Enhance: A randomized controlled trial of an individualized HIV prevention intervention for HIV-infected men who have sex with men conducted in a primary care setting. *Health Psychology, 32*(2), 171–179. https://doi.org/10.1037/a0028581

Safren, S. A., Otto, M. W., & Worth, J. L. (1999). Life-steps: Applying cognitive behavioral therapy to HIV medication adherence. *Cognitive and Behavioral Practice, 6*(4), 332–341. https://doi.org/10.1016/S1077-7229(99)80052-2

Safren, S. A., Perry, N. S., Blashill, A. J., O'Cleirigh, C., & Mayer, K. H. (2015). The cost and intensity of behavioral interventions to promote HIV treatment for prevention among HIV-positive men who have sex with men. *Archives of Sexual Behavior, 44*(7), 1833–1841. https://doi.org/10.1007/s10508-014-0455-3

Serovich, J. M., Reed, S., Grafsky, E. L., & Andrist, D. (2009). An intervention to assist men who have sex with men disclose their serostatus to casual sex partners: Results from a pilot study. *AIDS Education and Prevention, 21*(3), 207–219. https://doi.org/10.1521/aeap.2009.21.3.207

Sikkema, K. J., Abler, L., Hansen, N. B., Wilson, P. A., Drabkin, A. S., Kochman, A., . . . Nazareth, W. (2014). Positive Choices: Outcomes of a brief risk reduction intervention for newly HIV-diagnosed men who have sex with men. *AIDS and Behavior, 18*(9), 1808–1819. https://doi.org/10.1007/s10461-014-0782-3

Sikkema, K. J., Hansen, N. B., Kochman, A., Santos, J., Watt, M. H., Wilson, P. A., . . . Mayer, G. (2011). The development and feasibility of a brief risk reduction intervention for newly HIV-diagnosed men who have sex with men. *Journal of Community Psychology, 39*(6), 717–732. https://doi.org/10.1002/jcop.20463

Simoni, J. M., Pearson, C. R., Pantalone, D. W., Marks, G., & Crepaz, N. (2006). Efficacy of interventions in improving highly active antiretroviral therapy adherence and HIV-1 RNA viral load: A meta-analytic review of randomized controlled trials. *Journal of Acquired Immune Deficiency Syndromes, 43*(*Suppl. 1*), S23–S35. https://doi.org/10.1097/01.qai.0000248342.05438.52

Stall, R., Mills, T. C., Williamson, J., Hart, T., Greenwood, G., Paul, J., . . . Catania, J. A. (2003). Association of co-occurring psychosocial health problems and increased vulnerability to HIV/AIDS among urban men who have sex with men. *American Journal of Public Health, 93*(6), 939–942. https://doi.org/10.2105/AJPH.93.6.939

Vanable, P. A., Carey, M. P., Brown, J. L., Littlewood, R. A., Bostwick, R., & Blair, D. (2012). What HIV-positive MSM want from sexual risk reduction interventions: Findings from a qualitative study. *AIDS and Behavior, 16*(3), 554–563. https://doi.org/10.1007/s10461-011-0047-3

Williams, J. K., Glover, D. A., Wyatt, G. E., Kisler, K., Liu, H., & Zhang, M. (2013). A sexual risk and stress reduction intervention designed for HIV-positive bisexual African American men with childhood sexual abuse histories. *American Journal of Public Health, 103*(8), 1476–1484. https://doi.org/10.2105/AJPH.2012.301121

Williams, J. K., Wyatt, G. E., Rivkin, I., Ramamurthi, H. C., Li, X., & Liu, H. (2008). Risk reduction for HIV-positive African American and Latino men with histories of childhood sexual abuse. *Archives of Sexual Behavior, 37*(5), 763–772. https://doi.org/10.1007/s10508-008-9366-5

Wolitski, R. J., & Fenton, K. A. (2011). Sexual health, HIV, and sexually transmitted infections among gay, bisexual, and other men who have sex with men in the United States. *AIDS and Behavior, 15*(1), 9–17. https://doi.org/10.1007/s10461-011-9901-6

Wolitski, R. J., Gómez, C. A., & Parsons, J. T. (2005). Effects of a peer-led behavioral intervention to reduce HIV transmission and promote serostatus disclosure among HIV-seropositive gay and bisexual men. *AIDS, 19*(*Suppl. 1*), S99–S109. https://doi.org/10.1097/01.aids.0000167356.94664.59

Evidence-Based Treatments for Sexual and Gender Minorities Using Novel Modalities

16

Group-Based Cognitive-
Behavioral Therapies with Sexual
Minority Clients

JEFFREY M. COHEN AND MICHELLE G. NEWMAN ■

As a socially stigmatized group, sexual minorities face threats to psychological well-being that are primarily social in nature. These unique and socially based stressors, conceptualized as minority stress, are transmitted at both the structural level through social institutions and the interpersonal level through social interactions (Meyer, 2003). Negative, discriminatory social exchanges can cause psychological distress (Hatzenbuehler, Nolen-Hoeksema, & Dovidio, 2009). Stigma, the experience of being devalued by others on the basis of a social group identity (Goffman, 1963), is also associated with negative perceptions of oneself, particularly when similar others are absent (Frable, Platt, & Hoey, 1998). However, being around similar others increases self-esteem and decreases anxiety and depression in sexual minorities and others with concealable stigmatized identities (Frable et al., 1998). Evidence that sexual minorities feel better around other sexual minorities positions group psychotherapy as a unique and worthwhile treatment for the mental health of sexual minorities. This chapter provides an overview of the existing research on evidence-based group psychotherapy for sexual minorities as well as recommendations for adapting group cognitive–behavioral therapies (CBTs) to meet the unique features of sexual minority mental health, including an illustrative example.

SEXUAL MINORITIES AS A SOCIALLY STIGMATIZED GROUP

Here, we provide an overview of stigma-related social stressors and related outcomes, such as loneliness, and consider increased contact with other sexual minorities as a potential antidote. To be socially stigmatized is to be shunned on the basis of a collective social identity that is considered undesirable (Goffman, 1963). Stigma can be transmitted at the interpersonal level, such as through rejection, and at the structural level through discriminatory public policy. Sexual minorities frequently encounter rejection due to their sexual minority status and are exposed to childhood maltreatment, bullying, and physical and sexual assault at rates much higher than those for heterosexuals, even their own siblings (Balsam, Beauchaine, Mickey, & Rothblum, 2005; Balsam & Hughes, 2013). In contrast to ethnic minorities, sexual minorities do not typically share their minority status with their family of origin and may be less likely to learn how to cope with minority stress (Rothblum & Factor, 2001). Moreover, this occurs within the context of unequal access to the same nondiscrimination opportunities provided to heterosexuals, such as school and employment. For example, less than half of US states prohibit discrimination in the workplace on the basis of sexual orientation, and the current presidential administration has denied that sexual orientation is protected under the Civil Rights Act of 1964 (Human Rights Campaign, 2017). Similarly, 19 states do not include sexual orientation in hate or bias crime laws, and only 15 states have laws that address discrimination on the basis of sexual orientation in schools (Human Rights Campaign, 2017).

It is now well documented that these minority stressors drive increased risk for psychiatric morbidity, including anxiety and depression (Cohen, Feinstein, Rodriguez-Seijas, Taylor, & Newman, 2016; Hatzenbuehler, McLaughlin, Keyes, & Hasin, 2010). Given the aforementioned social factors, it is understandable that having a minority sexual orientation is associated with more anxiety and lower mood and self-esteem (Frable et al., 1998). One mechanism proposed to underlie this relationship is isolation from similar others who also share this concealable identity because similar others are not readily apparent (Frable et al., 1998). Sexual minorities, in fact, do experience greater social isolation and loneliness relative to heterosexuals across the lifespan (Doyle & Molix, 2016; Fredriksen-Goldsen, Kim, Barkan, Muraco, & Hoy-Ellis, 2013).

Given sexual minorities' relative lack of social support compared to heterosexuals (Balsam et al., 2005) and studies showing that similar others can serve as models for stigmatized individuals (Purdie-Vaughns & Eibach, 2013), efforts to increase sexual minorities' psychological well-being through group interventions have become increasingly common. The presence of a sexual minority affirmative group, such as a Gay–Straight-Alliance, in a school setting has been associated with greater perceived safety and psychological well-being among sexual minority youth (Goodenow, Szalacha, & Wesheimer, 2006; Hatzenbuehler, 2011).

EVIDENCE-BASED GROUP TREATMENT FOR SEXUAL MINORITIES

American Psychological Association (2012) guidelines for practice with lesbian, gay, and bisexual clients recommend the adaptation of evidence-based treatments to meet the unique features of sexual minority mental health. However, evidence-based group treatments for sexual minorities are not widely available. In this section, we address this gap with a discussion on adapting evidence-based treatments for group work with sexual minorities.

Group-based CBTs are grounded in empirical support and enjoy a robust evidence base for treating many mental health diagnoses, including disorders that disproportionately impact sexual minorities, such as anxiety and depression (Bieling, McCabe, & Antony, 2006; Heimberg et al., 1998; Silverman et al., 1999; Wilfley et al., 2002). This framework readily lends itself to work with sexual minorities because it promotes positive coping strategies and explores the functional nature of social behaviors within the context of current environmental contingencies as well as social learning history, such as minority stress experiences throughout development (Balsam, Martell, & Safren, 2006).

Historically, group CBTs varied greatly between disorders; however, more recent iterations, such as dialectical behavior therapy (DBT; Linehan, 1993) and acceptance and commitment therapy (ACT; Hayes, Strosahl, & Wilson, 1999), as well as newer versions of CBT (Barlow, Ellard, Fairholme, Farchione, & Boisseau, 2010), favor transdiagnostic approaches to treatment. A transdiagnostic approach focuses on processes and symptoms that appear across multiple diagnostic categories. This approach lends itself to treating a heterogeneous client population with varying diagnoses and to addressing minority stress processes, such as rejection sensitivity, internalized stigma, and sexual orientation concealment, which do not necessarily fit into a diagnostic category. Targeting these transdiagnostic processes may also maximize treatment gains because this approach has been shown to reduce symptoms of multiple clinical conditions that share the same core underlying vulnerabilities (Sauer-Zavala et al., 2017). Pragmatically, transdiagnostic approaches appear amenable to work with a minority population, particularly in smaller and medium-sized settings, which may lack the patient flow required to support disorder-specific groups. Furthermore, sexual minorities' presenting concerns might be united, at least in part, by their roots in shared minority stress-related experiences. In addition, recent research shows that transdiagnostic CBT is an effective intervention for treating emotional disorders and components of minority stress in gay and bisexual young men individually (Pachankis, Hatzenbuehler, Rendina, Safren, & Parsons, 2015), which suggests that transdiagnostic CBT may be effective in a group format as well.

ACT and DBT, commonly referred to as third-wave CBTs, also focus on cognition and behavior while incorporating a focus on acceptance of internal experiences and external realities (Hayes, 2004). Acceptance-based approaches may be particularly well-suited for the experiences of sexual minority clients because experiences of stigmatization exist largely outside of one's control. These acceptance-based approaches also include core components developed for a group format, such as group skills training and group mindfulness practice. Emerging evidence does suggest that both ACT and DBT are promising interventions for targeting minority stress and emotional disorders in sexual minorities (Cohen & Yadavaia, 2017; Yadavaia & Hayes, 2012).

APPLYING COGNITIVE–BEHAVIORAL STRATEGIES IN A GROUP SETTING WITH SEXUAL MINORITIES

Cognitive–behavioral therapies focus on present concerns and problem-solving through the development of effective coping techniques (Newman, LaFreniere, & Shin, 2017). Traditional CBT focuses on changing maladaptive behaviors and modifying inaccurate thoughts in order to bring a client's thoughts in line with reality (Beck, 2005). Third-wave CBTsincorporate acceptance-based strategies. ACT integrates acceptance into cognitive work by asking the client to observe thoughts as cognitive events rather than evaluating thoughts as either accurate or erroneous (Hayes et al., 1999). DBT balances acceptance- and change-based approaches in addressing maladaptive cognitions and behaviors, and both ACT and DBT encourage clients to commit to behaviors in line with their values (Hayes et al., 1999; Linehan, 1993). In group CBTs, clients take on a significant role in the implementation of these aforementioned strategies (Bieling et al., 2006). The following sections offer suggestions for integrating cultural considerations into traditional and third wave cognitive and behavioral group based work with sexual minorities.

Cognitive Strategies

Group-based work offers unique opportunities for the application of both traditional and third-wave cognitive strategies to common problems experienced by sexual minorities. This section explains how to integrate cultural considerations into cognitive restructuring, dialectical thinking, and cognitive defusion with sexual minority clients in a group setting.

Traditional cognitive theories suggest that activating events, including external and internal prompts, in conjunction with distorted thinking about these experiences, drive negative moods. Maladaptive thought patterns, such as rumination, place a client at risk for multiple disorders (McLaughlin & Nolen-Hoeksema, 2011) and therefore are valuable transdiagnostic treatment targets applicable to most clients in a group setting. Sexual minorities exposed to societal stereotypes during development may internalize stigma-related beliefs, which may create maladaptive cognitions such as "I'm defective because I'm a lesbian" or "Others will reject me because I'm gay." Cognitive thinking errors such as catastrophizing and jumping to conclusions can be identified. As described next, group reality testing and cognitive restructuring can then be used to correct dysfunctional automatic thoughts, such as erroneous expectations of rejection (Bieling et al., 2006). This work can also modify negative core beliefs and reduce internalized stigma.

When conducting cognitive restructuring in a group, group members may begin to question the evidence for and against their own thoughts as well as the thoughts of other group members. In this way, group members take on an active role in the cognitive restructuring of other group members (Bieling et al., 2006). The presence of group members allows cognitions to be carefully considered from multiple perspectives. Worries related to discrimination, such as loss of employment due to sexual orientation, may at first appear to be distortions, although in fact it is possible to be legally fired for being a sexual minority in most US states (Human Rights Campaign, 2017). Group members may assess the probability of discrimination or victimization and distinguish whether or not there is legitimate evidence for worries. The multiple viewpoints of the group are particularly useful in conducting this type of reality testing.

In a recent psychotherapy group that the first author led with sexual minority veterans at a Veterans Affairs (VA) hospital, a group member reported waiting 30 minutes for a table at a local restaurant and attributed it to having a same-gender dining companion. Another group member, who frequently dines at that same restaurant with her wife, shared, "The restaurant is often short-staffed and there can be a wait for a table during busy times." In doing so, she offered evidence that the first group member had failed to consider. Given that clients tend to notice evidence that supports their cognitions and disregard evidence that does not (Newman et al., 2017), we have found that the multiple perspectives of group members provide excellent opportunities for clients to discover evidence that is contrary to existing thought patterns. This group process also affords the opportunity for members to recognize the potential mismatch between expectation and environment, and cognitive distortions can be corrected and maladaptive schemas can be revised (Bieling et al., 2006).

We have sometimes noticed an overlap in the thought patterns of different group members, such as the overestimation of the probability of rejection on the basis of sexual minority status. It is important to acknowledge that these expectations of rejection likely developed within the context of hostile environments and early minority stress, and therefore the goal is to re-evaluate the function of these beliefs within clients' current environment (Pachankis, Goldfried, & Ramrattan, 2008). Many clients who lack evidence to support or refute a negative thought may assume the negative thought to be true, despite the lack of evidence (Beck, 2005). In these instances, and in the clear absence of evidence that an environment is hostile, we encourage clients to engage in alternative thinking in order to expose themselves to previously feared situations.

Individuals who have been chronically socially invalidated, which is the case for many sexual minorities (Meyer, 2003), may not be able to tolerate traditional cognitive restructuring. Challenging thoughts can replicate the invalidating environment through communicating that the client's thoughts, and relatedly the client himself, are the source of the client's problems (Linehan, 1993). In these instances, as described next, alternative cognitive modification techniques that are not purely focused on change, such as dialectical thinking and cognitive defusion, may be uniquely effective.

Dialectics emphasize that every truth has an opposite truth and that these truths come together in synthesis (Linehan, 1993). A dialectical approach to cognition searches for the "kernel of truth" in a thought and also asks what is being left out, rather than labeling a thought as correct or incorrect (Linehan, 1993). The multiple perspectives of group members allow group leaders to illustrate dialectical thinking through identifying the kernel of truth in seemingly divergent perspectives and arriving at a synthesis in group. The balance of acceptance and change is the primary dialectic of DBT. This dialectic can be applied to the problem of discrimination—acceptance that we live in a world in which discrimination exists and also social advocacy to change this reality.

ACT (Hayes et al., 1999) employs cognitive defusion, which is the skill of noticing thoughts as ongoing cognitive events rather than treating thoughts as facts to be proven either accurate or erroneous. We have encouraged members in previous groups to defuse from stigmatizing thoughts by repeating a phrase over and over again until the phrase temporarily loses its meaning (Hayes et al., 1999). In practicing this technique, group members have chosen to work with self-stigmatizing thoughts such as "being gay is bad."

Behavioral Strategies

In this section, we discuss the function of avoidance in the lives of sexual minorities and provide suggestions for the application of exposure to problematic avoidance. Exposure is a hallmark of traditional and third-wave behavioral therapies (Newman et al., 2017), and the group format offers an excellent forum for exposure (Bieling et al., 2006).

From a behavioral perspective, stigma and social stressors associated with sexual minority status, such as harassment and bullying, often punish the expression of sexual minority identity and potentially lead to pervasive patterns of self-silencing (Pachankis, 2007). Avoidance, including avoidance of external situations as well as the experiential avoidance of internal thoughts and feelings, is a transdiagnostic mechanism of distress (Sauer-Zavala et al., 2017). In determining the role of avoidance, it is important to understand the function of the behavior and the context in which it exists. In a functional analysis of behavior, clinicians consider how a particular setting influences behaviors (Newman et al., 2017). Although public acceptance of sexual minorities has increased dramatically in recent years (Human Rights Campaign, 2017), avoidance of some external situations may still be adaptive if there is evidence that a specific situation is inherently dangerous. For instance, it may not be adaptive for a sexual minority adolescent to come out to her family if a parent has threatened, "If I found out you were gay, I would send you to conversion therapy."

We have found that current patterns of responding have often outlived their usefulness and no longer fit the facts of clients' lives. Exposure, a core behavioral technique based on principles of counterconditioning and extinction, is an effective strategy to weaken the association between a stimulus and an unwanted response, such as avoidance (Newman et al., 2017). In this approach, a man who was bullied by male peers as a youth and consequently fears and avoids male peers as an adult would expose himself to interactions with males. This allows fear extinction to occur and also facilitates new learning, which results in male peers no longer being perceived as fear-worthy or meriting avoidance.

The group itself can serve as an excellent opportunity for in vivo exposure, such as socially engaging other males or any feared stimuli that may be present in the group. In vivo exposure in group may also include self-disclosure, which can reduce anxiety, shame, and internalized stigma (Pachankis, 2007; Rizvi & Linehan, 2005). The first author recently led a DBT skills group for sexual minorities at a VA hospital. A 71-year-old group member, who had concealed his sexual orientation throughout his time in the military and subsequent decades during which he received care at the VA hospital, utilized the group as an opportunity to disclose his sexual orientation both to VA providers and to other veterans. This disclosure reduced his avoidance, shame, and internalized stigma, and it increased his self-esteem and willingness to receive support from other sexual minorities.

The group format also offers a valuable forum for conducting more formal in-session exposure, such as behavioral role-plays of coming out and role-plays designed to increase social skills and assertiveness (Bieling et al., 2006), which can be compromised among sexual minorities given histories of minority stress (Pachankis et al., 2008). DEARMAN is a DBT assertiveness skill that the first author utilized in a DBT skills group for sexual minorities to inform coming out conversations. DEARMAN enables clients to effectively obtain an interpersonal objective, such as asking for acceptance of sexual minority status, and involves writing out a script to guide a future conversation. In the group, DEARMAN helped clients solidify disclosure objectives and clarify what to say in a coming out conversation. The group format allowed members to practice using the DEARMAN to disclose a minority sexual orientation through role-plays in session, and homework encouraged members to utilize the skill outside of group. In a cohesive group, a sense of responsibility to the group may also motivate clients to follow through with behavioral work outside of session. Group members may encourage one another to try more challenging exposure tasks or, alternatively, catch the subtle avoidance behaviors of other members (Bieling et al., 2006).

When group members agree that avoidance of external situations may be adaptive, such as due to safety concerns, willingness to commit to internal exposure of one's inner experience, including feelings of anger or anxiety and related thoughts, may be a fitting approach (Yadavaia & Hayes, 2012). We discuss this approach further in the following section.

Acceptance-Based Strategies

This section discusses the application of acceptance-based strategies of third-wave CBTs, including radical acceptance, acceptance of internal experiences, mindfulness, and values clarification. Although there has been substantial progress toward equality in recent years, stigma and social stressors related to sexual minority status are unlikely to disappear; therefore, some degree of acceptance, or acknowledgment that sexual minority clients live in world in which stigma and prejudice exist, may be adaptive.

No one chooses to live in a world in which discrimination, victimization, and rejection occur simply because of one's identity. In this type of situation, Linehan (2015) suggests that acceptance is needed. Radical acceptance is "accepting all the way, with your mind, your heart, and your body" (Linehan, 2015, Distress Tolerance Handout 11) and "opening yourself to fully experiencing reality as it is in this one moment" (p. 453, Linehan, 2015). In working with sexual minority veterans, we have observed sadness, anger, and resentment surrounding the military's long-standing ban on gay and lesbian service members and its subsequent modification known as "don't ask, don't tell," which was repealed in 2010. Although understandable, this refusal to accept the reality of the military's history of discriminatory policy can keep sexual minority veterans stuck in suffering. In doing this work on radical acceptance, we are careful to clarify that acceptance does not mean approval; it simply means being open to the reality of facts as they are. For clients who confuse acceptance with approval or for those who struggle with the term "acceptance" more broadly, we initially use the word "acknowledgment" until the client is able to understand acceptance.

As conceptualized in ACT, acceptance involves willingly and intentionally experiencing one's private thoughts and emotions as an alternative to habitual patterns of experiential avoidance (Hayes et al., 1999). Acceptance of feelings of discomfort, shame, and anxiety surrounding sexual orientation may be useful both when a client wishes to disclose his or her sexual minority status and when a client chooses to conceal it, potentially due to a hostile environment. Acceptance of internal events also includes accepting one's own feelings of same-gender attraction as well as anxiety about others' reactions (Yadavaia & Hayes, 2012).

In groups, we encourage members to observe and accept their feelings that arise related to sexual orientation through mindfulness, a core intervention of acceptance-based approaches. Mindfulness involves paying attention to the present moment without judgment and with compassion (Hayes et al., 1999). We ask group members to consider what things upset them the most, and their answers typically reveal things that have either occurred in the past or have yet to happen. We then encourage connection with the present moment and offer formal mindfulness practice as a way to increase this ability. We have found that the group format lends itself well to formal mindfulness practice, and group members often describe an increase in feelings of connectedness to the present as well as an increased sense of connection to others when practicing in group.

Mindfulness scripts have been adapted or developed to address common presenting concerns of sexual minorities (Skinta & Curtin, 2016). One such mindfulness script describes a tiger that was released into an expansive environment after years of living in a small cage. After her release, the tiger spent her days pacing a small patch of her now expansive surroundings. In using this mindfulness script, we have asked group members to consider if there are any ways in which they might be placing themselves within a tiny box in relation to their sexual orientation and ask how they might be like that tiger. We have found that this mindfulness practice increases group members' awareness of the functionality of their current behaviors. Through this practice, past group members have become aware that they behave in ways that no longer match their current contexts and that hold them back from living their best lives.

Finally, valued living may be especially applicable for sexual minority clients whose values may differ from the values of the dominant culture. Values are chosen life directions and are person specific. ACT emphasizes a commitment to behaviors consistent with a client's values rather than attempting to promote positive thoughts related to sexual minority status while eliminating negative ones (Hayes et al., 1999). Similarly, DBT focuses on values as a means to build a fulfilling life (Linehan, 2015). Values clarification, the process of discovering what matters most, can be instrumental in guiding sexual orientation disclosure (Yadavia & Hayes, 2012). Disclosure considerations may look very different for a client who values authenticity versus a client who values interconnectedness, such that a client who values authenticity may place more importance on disclosure. Values may conflict, such as in the case of a client who values both authenticity and interconnectedness. In these instances, a group format lends itself to values clarification because discussing the values of multiple group members may help individual group members clarify their own values.

We have found that the third-wave CBTs' focus on acceptance, mindfulness, and valued living resonates with the sexual minority group members with whom we have worked. In fact, preliminary research suggests third-wave CBTs adapted for work with sexual minorities are promising interventions when delivered both individually (Yadavaia & Hayes, 2012) and in a group format (Cohen & Yadavaia, 2017).

VALIDATION AS A THERAPEUTIC STANCE

This section highlights the importance of validation as a key therapeutic stance for group work with sexual minority clients. Validation is a therapeutic strategy for communicating that behavior is understandable and makes sense within the context of a client's life (Linehan, 1997). It is important for group therapists to recognize assumptions and biases about sexual minority persons and ask direct, nonjudgmental questions that convey acceptance of minority sexual orientations and validation of relevant choices clients have made. In this way, group therapists model that the group is a safe place where members can talk openly about concerns related to sexual minority status (Skinta & Curtin, 2016).

Validation also means describing an individual's behavior as understandable given the client's learning history (Linehan, 1993). For instance, a bisexual patient with chronic shame who grew up in a rejecting fundamentalist Christian family can be validated with "It makes sense that you experience the thought, 'I'm unlovable,' given the messages that you have received about being unlovable from the environment." In a group context, leaders can model validation and encourage group members to validate other group members, which may result in a significantly more cohesive group.

LGBT-AFFIRMATIVE ADAPTATIONS OF GROUP-BASED COGNITIVE–BEHAVIORAL THERAPIES

Although there is not a robust evidence base to support group CBTs with sexual minority clients, some data have been collected from small samples of participants in studies of group CBTs without control conditions. In this section, we review this preliminary support for group-based CBTs adapted for sexual minority clients. First, we review an adaption of CBT for gay men with HIV/AIDS. Second, we discuss the use of CBT to promote authenticity among a group of gay men. Third, we discuss Project Pride, an eight-session manualized CBT targeting minority stress and related health outcomes in young sexual minority men. Finally, we review an adaptation of DBT skills training (DBT-ST) for transdiagnostic emotion dysregulation and minority stress in sexual minority veterans.

In 1999, CBT was adapted to treat depression in a group of gay men with AIDS or symptomatic HIV infection (Lee, Cohen, Hadley, & Goodwin, 1999). Adaptations of traditional CBT for this population included an extension of the treatment duration from 12 to 20 weeks in order to allow more intensive work on maladaptive core beliefs and to prevent relapse. The group focused on maladaptive cognitions, such as thoughts of being a failure due to HIV-positive status, and the impact of cognitions on depressed mood and self-defeating behaviors such as medication noncompliance. The first 10 weeks focused on distorted automatic thoughts, and the last 10 weeks focused on more deeply rooted core beliefs. Each session followed a structured agenda that included completion of a depression symptom checklist, homework review, and the week's content. The group was also flexible in order to meet specific concerns and crises raised by members of the group. Under these circumstances, group leaders focused on the issues raised by clients and drew on the group process for support. Thirteen of the 15 participants completed the group treatment, and results revealed substantial decreases on depression scores from pre- to post-treatment, with further decreases reported at 1-year follow-up. Participants identified cognitive restructuring as one of the most helpful components of the treatment.

Group-based CBT has also been used to promote authenticity and the coming out process in young gay men (Pachankis, 2009). In this lesbian, gay, bisexual, and transgender (LGBT)-affirmative adaptation of a traditional cognitive and behavioral assertiveness training group, early sessions focused on raising awareness of the threat posed to healthy development by heterocentric socialization and homophobic environments. Subsequent sessions focused on assertiveness training in order to equip participants with skills to express themselves effectively and authentically, such as through the disclosure of their sexual orientation. Members participated in role-plays in group in order to develop more assertive patterns of communication. The final sessions processed gains made by group members and instilled motivation to continue authentic living. No efficacy data were reported for this small pilot study.

Project PRIDE (Promoting Resilience in Discriminatory Environments) is a recently developed eight-session group-based CBT that targets minority stress and associated negative health outcomes in young sexual minority men (Smith et al., 2017). Early sessions introduce minority stress, and middle sessions teach coping skills and encourage group members to identify SMART (specific, measurable, attainable, realistic, and time-bound; Cothran, Wysocki, Farnsworth, & Clark, 2015) goals related to sexual health and substance use. Later sessions address the risk for sexually transmitted infections and HIV with psychoeducation on safer sex and by teaching assertive sexual communication skills. Throughout, group members complete homework assignments in order to increase skills acquisition and also practice relaxation exercises at the conclusion of each session. Results from a sample of 33 young gay and bisexual men suggest clinically significant increases in self-esteem as well as decreases in loneliness and minority stress from pre- to post-treatment. The intervention is manualized and designed to be delivered by paraprofessionals, who are not required to have extensive training in CBT, which may maximize this intervention's potential for dissemination or potentially limit its use by licensed social workers, psychologists, and psychiatrists.

Virtually no studies have investigated group-based treatment for sexual minorities with an intersectional identity—that is, an identity composed of multiple and overlapping social identities. In one exception, DBT-ST has been adapted for group-based work with sexual minority veterans (Cohen, & Yadavaia, 2017). Sexual minorities and veterans are both populations at elevated risk for suicide (Matarazzo et al., 2014), and research highlights the association of minority stressors with elevated levels of depression, post-traumatic stress disorder, and suicidality among sexual minority veterans (Cochran, Balsam, Flentje, Malte, & Simpson, 2013). DBT, a treatment initially designed to target suicidality, emphasizes an invalidating environment as a contributing factor to psychological distress. This framework readily lends itself to work with sexual minorities, a population exposed to chronic invalidation. Standard DBT includes group skills training as a core component, and research suggests skills utilization is a primary mechanism of change (Neacsiu, Rizvi, & Linehan, 2010).

DBT-ST for sexual minority veterans conceptualizes minority stress as part of the invalidating environment. Sexual minority veterans who served during the military's long-standing ban on gay and lesbian service members, and the subsequent modification known as don't ask, don't tell, experienced government-mandated sexual orientation concealment and associated harassment, fear of discharge, and/or discharge. This DBT-ST adaptation explicitly identifies this experience as an example of an invalidating environment and highlights the understandable reactions of concealment, rejection sensitivity, and internalized stigma in order to raise participants' awareness of minority stress and to normalize these responses as common reactions to social stigma. This adaptation of DBT-ST additionally targets minority stress with teaching points that have explicit relevance to the lives of sexual minority clients. For instance, the DBT model of emotions is taught utilizing an example of shame related to the prompt of hearing a homophobic comment in a locker room. Group members are also encouraged to use the DBT skills to address minority stress with weekly homework assignments. A client who anticipated and feared rejection from his medical providers due to his sexual minority status used "check the facts," a cognitive restructuring skill, to discover that his expectations and fears of rejection did not fit the facts, and he was able to modify his cognitions.

Preliminary data found that this adaptation of DBT-ST reduced symptoms of anxiety, depression, and minority stress and significantly increased emotion regulation in a small sample of five sexual minority veterans from pre- to post-treatment (Cohen & Yadavaia, 2017).

GROUP-BASED COGNITIVE–BEHAVIORAL THERAPY WITH SEXUAL MINORITY YOUTH

This section describes an adaptation of CBT for a group composed of sexual minority adolescents, thereby illustrating how to integrate cultural considerations into traditional and third-wave CBT techniques for the group treatment of anxiety, depression, and minority stress. The first author led this 12-week group for four sexual minority adolescents, who were in the early stages of coming out, in a high school setting.

The treatment development method included a review of the existing literature, consultation with mental health providers and teachers experienced in working with sexual minority adolescents, and an individual pre-group assessment of each group member. We considered recommendations for the use of CBT with sexual minority youth (Safren, Hollander, Hart, & Heimberg, 2001), which focuses on stressors including (1) abuse, harassment, and violence; (2) the impact of internalized stigma on identity development; (3) sexual orientation disclosure and lack of adult social support; and (4) friendships and romantic relationships with sexual minority peers. In our initial assessment of participants, we discovered concerns related to the aforementioned stressors, including sexual orientation disclosure, internalized stigma, and fears and expectations of rejection as well as symptoms of anxiety and depression. This pre-group assessment informed the focus of our treatment.

Initial sessions focused on identifying the unique stressors that adolescents were facing due to their sexual minority status and normalizing anxiety and depression as an understandable response to those stressors. We discussed group members' personal experiences of minority stress and responses, which included concealment, rejection sensitivity, and internalized stigma. We provided validation to convey that each member's individual response to minority stress made sense in their current life and school contexts. This helped participants accurately identify the sources of distress related to feelings such as shame. This process also allowed group members to shift attributions about sources of distress away from beliefs of personal shortcomings toward the unfair burden of minority stress.

We provided psychoeducation on the meaning of each of the identities covered by the LGBTQ acronym and distinguished sexual orientation from gender identity in line with prior guidelines, which suggest that affirmative CBT for sexual minority youth includes an awareness of the importance of terminology (Safren et al., 2001). The group was composed of sexual minorities, and no gender minorities, and therefore concerns related to sexual orientation were the primary focus. Group members shared that learning terminology related to sexual orientation and identity provided a feeling of empowerment and increased their confidence to talk about their own identities with friends, family, and teachers.

We then conducted a formal exercise to uncover automatic thoughts and core beliefs related to sexual orientation. We asked group members to write down all of their thoughts about sexual minorities in general and what it meant personally to be gay, lesbian, or bisexual (Safren & Rogers, 2001). Group members noticed how negatively they viewed sexual minorities. For instance, one group member shared that he frequently uses the phrase "that's so gay," and we collaboratively identified this as a manifestation of internalized stigma. Another group member shared her thought that lesbians are ugly, and several members described sexual minorities as defective. Next, we conducted reality testing with the help of group members in order to assess the evidence for and against the negative thoughts and beliefs related to sexual orientation. This group process helped correct dysfunctional automatic thoughts, such as expectations of rejection, and revise maladaptive core beliefs, such as those stemming from internalized stigma.

At the midway point, we introduced the concept of values in order to help participants clarify what makes life meaningful to them and subsequently identified goals in line with these values (Hayes et al., 1999). We utilized ACT's "tombstone" exercise, which involves writing two versions of the epitaph for one's own future tombstone: One version asks group members to write what might be engraved if the client continues to live life in the same way, and the other version asks clients to write what might be engraved if the client lives life in a way that is more consistent with the client's values. All of the group members identified the value of living authentically and being remembered for who they actually were, inclusive of sexual orientation. We then introduced the concept of taking committed action steps to achieve authentic and valued living.

Given participants identified barriers, primarily related to fear toward engaging in values-based action, each group member created a personal "fear hierarchy," a list of internal and external thoughts, emotions, and situations that members actively feared or avoided. We asked group members to rate on a scale from 1 to 100 how much they feared each situation and how much they avoided each item. Items that elicited less fear and avoidance were placed lower down on each member's fear hierarchy, whereas the most feared and avoided situations were placed higher. Although there was some variability in where group members placed particular items, lower items included attending the school's Gay–Straight Alliance meeting and conversing with other sexual minority adolescents. Items in the middle included initiating conversations with adults and saying no to unreasonable requests. Items that were the most intensely feared included conversing with other sexual minority youth whom clients found attractive and disclosing their sexual orientation to adults.

We then moved on to address each member's fear hierarchy, beginning with items that were low on the hierarchy. The group offered a unique opportunity to do this. We used in-session role-plays of anxiety-provoking situations, such as coming out to a family member, until participants were ready to move on to the in vivo exposures of coming out to actual family members.

One group member, Maria, identified the goal of coming out to her family and feared that her family would never accept her. Maria found it very uncomfortable to be living in a home where she perceived intense pressure to manage her impression and cover her sexual identity. From a compassionate stance, group members asked Maria to share the evidence that supported her thought, and she was able to identify homophobic remarks her mother had made. A group member who was a friend of Maria's pointed out that Maria's sisters were not likely to reject her and provided the evidence that Maria's oldest sister has a gay friend. This group process led Maria to modify her belief to a less black-and-white perspective, which was, "Some family members may accept me and some family members may reject me." Maria then committed to the action of disclosing her sexual orientation to her sister, who was affirming and suggested that she disclose to her grandmother. Maria's grandmother was also affirming and offered to talk to Maria's parents, who were initially non-affirming. Maria's parents were able to shift toward a more compassionate stance with the support of Maria's grandmother and sisters, although this shift took some time and did not happen until after the conclusion of group.

Through the group process of modifying Maria's thoughts, other group members recognized that some of their own family members might be affirming, whereas others may not be. Collectively, group members committed to disclosing to family members who were likely to be affirming as an important values-based action. Group members continually encouraged each other to commit to disclosing to loved ones who they thought would be affirming. This brought group members closer in line with their stated value of living authentically, despite their fears of rejection.

After initial exposure exercises, we noticed that group members evaluated effectiveness of the exposure based on their feelings, such as whether they felt anxious or sad. In line with an ACT perspective, we encouraged group members to additionally consider if a particular action was in line with their values, regardless of their emotional experience of the action (Hayes et al., 1999). By the end of treatment, group members were able to consider if an action was values-based and use values to guide behaviors, regardless of group members' current or anticipated emotional experience.

In the final sessions, we reviewed progress. Group members reported that the most helpful components of group were a reduction in feelings of isolation, feeling more connected with other sexual minority youth, and learning how to speak to family about sexual orientation. Group members also completed the PROMIS Emotional Distress–Depression questionnaire, a 14-item self-report inventory designed to measure *Diagnostic and Statistical Manual of Mental Disorders*, fifth edition (American Psychiatric Association, 2013), symptoms of depression in children aged 11–17 years, both before and after completion of the group. Results revealed a strong reduction in symptoms of depression (Cohen, Woicicki, Lui, & Wilson, 2015).

FUTURE DIRECTIONS

Given evidence suggesting that sexual minorities report less depression and higher self-esteem when in proximity to other sexual minorities, group psychotherapy may be a uniquely effective treatment for sexual minority clients. Although efficacy evidence is currently preliminary, the strengths of transdiagnostic CBTs for group work with sexual minorities include the conceptualization of thoughts, behaviors, and emotions using a developmental framework, which acknowledges the role of minority stress in a client's learning history, and the emphasis on a functional analysis of the maintaining determinants of clients' behaviors. CBTs utilize cognitive and behavioral modification strategies as well as acceptance-based techniques in order to help clients build their best lives. The group format offers the unique possibility for sexual minorities to feel better in the presence of similar others and improved opportunities to deliver treatment components including reality testing, behavioral exposure, mindfulness practice, and skills training in a social context. Preliminary evidence supports the efficacy of group-based CBTs, including CBT for depression in HIV-positive sexual minority men, CBT for minority stress and related health outcomes in young sexual minority men, CBT for minority stress and symptoms of emotional disorders in sexual minority adolescents, and DBT-ST for transdiagnostic emotion dysregulation and minority stress.

Although evidence is somewhat limited, a recent randomized controlled trial does support the preliminary efficacy of addressing minority stress in individually delivered psychotherapy with sexual minority young men (Pachankis et al., 2015). Future research is needed to test the efficacy of evidenced-based interventions adapted to treat minority stress in a group format. Clinicians might collect and report outcome data on their LGBT-affirmative adaptations of group-based treatments in order to determine the efficacy of these interventions. Randomized controlled trials utilizing control groups comparing group-based approaches to individual therapy approaches are needed to test the hypothesis that group treatment is a maximally effective approach to sexual minority mental health.

CONCLUSION

Group-based models have the distinct advantage of allowing more clients to access evidence-based treatments and may be amenable for the particularly social concerns of sexual minority clients, such as isolation and loneliness. A group-based approach may offer a uniquely effective intervention for stigmatized populations who may feel better in the presence of similar others. Gender minorities, including transgender and gender non-confirming people, are also a stigmatized group who may feel better in the presence of similar others. We encourage clinicians and researchers to adapt evidence-based psychotherapies for group work with sexual and gender minority clients by integrating culturally sensitive considerations into evidence-based treatments. We also encourage data collection of culturally adapted group-based treatment and recommend that interventions that appear promising, based on preliminary outcomes, be subsequently evaluated with more rigorous testing. Finally, we hope that group evidence-based treatments will be disseminated in order to provide more sexual and gender minority people access to evidence-based mental health treatment designed to meet the unique features of sexual and gender minority mental health.

REFERENCES

American Psychiatric Association. (2013). *Diagnostic and statistical manual of mental disorders* (5th ed.). Arlington, VA: American Psychiatric Publishing.

American Psychological Association. (2012). Guidelines for psychological practice with lesbian, gay, and bisexual clients. *American Psychologist, 67*, 10–42. doi:10.1037/a0024659

Balsam, K. F., Beauchaine, T. P., Mickey, R. M., & Rothblum, E. D. (2005). Mental health of lesbian, gay, bisexual, and heterosexual siblings: Effects of gender, sexual orientation, and family. *Journal of Abnormal Psychology, 114*, 471–476. doi:10.1037/0021-843x.114.3.471

Balsam, K. F., & Hughes, T. (2013). Sexual orientation, victimization, and hate crimes. In C. J. Patterson & A. R. D'Augelli (Eds.), *Handbook of psychology and sexual orientation* (pp. 267–280). New York, NY: Oxford University Press. doi:10.1093/acprof:oso/9780199765218.003.0019

Balsam, K. F., Martell, C. R., & Safren, S. A. (2006). Affirmative cognitive–behavioral therapy with lesbian, gay, and bisexual people. In P. A. Hays & G. Y. Iwamasa (Eds.), *Culturally responsive cognitive–behavioral therapy: Assessment, practice, and supervision* (pp. 223–243). Washington, DC: American Psychological Association. doi:10.1037/11433-010

Barlow, D. H., Ellard, K. K., Fairholme, C. P., Farchione, T. J., & Boisseau, C. L. (2010). *Unified protocol for transdiagnostic treatment of emotional disorders: Workbook.* New York, NY: Oxford University Press.

Beck, A. T. (2005). The current state of cognitive therapy: A 40-year retrospective. *Archives of General Psychiatry, 62*, 953–959. doi:10.1001/archpsyc.62.9.953

Bieling, P. J., McCabe, R. E., & Antony, M. M. (2006). *Cognitive–behavioral therapy in groups.* New York, NY: Guilford.

Cochran, B. N., Balsam, K., Flentje, A., Malte, C. A., & Simpson, T. (2013). Mental health characteristics of sexual minority veterans. *Journal of Homosexuality, 60*(2–3), 419–435. doi:10.1080/0091369.2013.744932

Cohen, J. M., Feinstein, B. A., Rodriguez-Seijas, C., Taylor, C. B., & Newman, M. G. (2016). Rejection sensitivity as a transdiagnostic risk factor for internalizing psychopathology among gay and bisexual men. *Psychology of Sexual Orientation and Gender Diversity, 3*, 259–264. doi:10.1037/sgd0000170

Cohen, J. M., Woicicki, K., Lui, M., & Wilson, H. (2015, November). *The development and implementation of a CBT informed group treatment for sexual minority adolescents.* Poster presented at the 49th annual convention of the Association for Behavioral and Cognitive Therapies, Chicago, IL.

Cohen, J. M., & Yadavaia, J. E. (2017, November). *Affirmative dialectical behavior therapy skills training as a transdiagnostic treatment for emotional disorders and minority stress.* In C. Beard (Chair), Cognitive behavioral therapy with lesbian, gay, bisexual, and transgender populations. Paper presented at the 51st annual convention of the Association for Behavioral and Cognitive Therapies, San Diego, CA.

Cothran, H. M., Wysocki, A. F., Farnsworth, D., & Clark, J. L. (2015). *Developing SMART goals for your organization.* Retrieved from http://edis.ifas.ufl.edu/pdffiles/FE/FE57700.pdf

Doyle, D. M., & Molix, L. (2016). Disparities in social health by sexual orientation and the etiologic role of self-reported discrimination. *Archives of Sexual Behavior, 45*, 1317–1327. doi:10.1007/s10508-015-0639-5

Frable, D. E. S., Platt, L., & Hoey, S. (1998). Concealable stigmas and positive self-perceptions: Feeling better around similar others. *Journal of Personality and Social Psychology, 74*, 909–922. doi:10.1037/0022-3514.74.4.909

Fredriksen-Goldsen, K. I., Kim, H. J., Barkan, S. E., Muraco, A., & Hoy-Ellis, C. P. (2013). Health disparities among lesbian, gay, and bisexual older adults: Results from a population-based study. *American Journal of Public Health, 103*(10), 1802–1809. doi:10.2105/AJPH.2012.301110

Goffman, E. (1963). *Stigma: Notes on the management of spoiled identity.* New York, NY: Simon & Schuster.

Goodenow, C., Szalacha, L., & Westheimer, K. (2006). School support groups, other school factors, and the safety of sexual minority adolescents. *Psychology in the Schools, 43*(5), 573–589.

Hatzenbuehler, M. L. (2011). The social environment and suicide attempts in lesbian, gay, and bisexual youth. *Pediatrics, 127*, 896–903. doi:10.1542/peds.2010-3020

Hatzenbuehler, M. L., Keyes, K. M., & Hasin, D. S. (2009). State-level policies and psychiatric morbidity in lesbian, gay, and bisexual populations. *American Journal of Public Health, 99*, 2275–2281. doi:10.2105/ajph.2008.153510

Hatzenbuehler, M. L., McLaughlin, K. A., Keyes, K. M., & Hasin, D. S. (2010). The impact of institutional discrimination on psychiatric disorders in lesbian, gay, and bisexual populations: A prospective study. *American Journal of Public Health, 100*(3), 452–459. doi:10.2105/AJPH.2009.168815

Hatzenbuehler, M. L., Nolen-Hoeksema, S., & Dovidio, J. (2009). How does stigma "get under the skin"? The mediating role of emotion regulation. *Psychological Science, 20*, 1282–1289. doi:10.1111/j.1467-9280.2009.02441.x

Hayes, S. C. (2004). Acceptance and commitment therapy, relational frame theory, and the third wave of behavioral and cognitive therapies. *Behavior Therapy, 35*(4), 639–665.

Hayes, S. C., Strosahl, K. D., & Wilson, K. G. (1999). *Acceptance and commitment therapy: An experiential approach to behavior change.* New York, NY: Guilford.

Heimberg, R. G., Liebowitz, M. R., Hope, D. A., Schneier, F. R., Holt, C. S., Welkowitz, L. A., . . . Fallon, B. (1998). Cognitive behavioral group therapy vs. phenelzine therapy for social phobia: 12-week outcome. *Archives of General Psychiatry, 55*(12), 1133–1141. doi:10.1001/archpsyc.55.12.1133

Human Rights Campaign. (2017). *State maps of laws & policies.* Retrieved March 2017 from https://www.hrc.org/state_maps

Lee, M. R., Cohen, L., Hadley, S. W., & Goodwin, F. K. (1999). Cognitive–behavioral group therapy with medication for depressed gay men with AIDS or symptomatic HIV infection. *Psychiatric Services, 50*, 948–952. doi:10.1176/ps.50.7.948

Linehan, M. M. (1993). *Cognitive–behavioral treatment of borderline personality disorder.* New York, NY: Guilford.

Linehan, M. M. (1997). Validation and psychotherapy. In A. C. Bohart & L. S. Greenberg (Eds.), *Empathy reconsidered: New directions in psychotherapy* (pp. 353–392). Washington, DC: American Psychological Association. doi:10.1037/10226-016

Linehan, M. M. (2015). *DBT skills training manual* (2nd ed.). New York, NY: Guilford.

Linehan, M. M. (2015). *DBT Skills Training Handouts and Worksheets.* Guilford Publications.

Matarazzo, B. B., Barnes, S. M., Pease, J. L., Russell, L. M., Hanson, J. E., Soberay, K. A., & Gutierrez, P. M. (2014). Suicide risk among lesbian, gay, bisexual, and transgender military personnel and veterans: What does the literature tell us?. *Suicide and Life-Threatening Behavior, 44*(2), 200–217.

McLaughlin, K. A., & Nolen-Hoeksema, S. (2011). Rumination as a transdiagnostic factor in depression and anxiety. *Behaviour Research and Therapy, 49*(3), 186–193. doi:10.1016/j.brat.2010.12.006

Meyer, I. H. (2003). Prejudice, social stress, and mental health in lesbian, gay, and bisexual populations: Conceptual issues and research evidence. *Psychological Bulletin, 129*, 674–697. doi:10.1037/0033-2909.129.5.674

Neacsiu, A. D., Rizvi, S. L., & Linehan, M. M. (2010). Dialectical behavior therapy skills use as a mediator and outcome of treatment for borderline personality disorder. *Behaviour Research and Therapy, 48*(9), 832–839. doi:10.1016/j.brat.2010.05.017

Newman, M. G., LaFreniere, L. L., & Shin, K. (2017). Cognitive–behavioral therapies in historical perspective. In A. J. Consoli, L. E. Beutler, & B. Bongar (Eds.), *Comprehensive textbook of psychotherapy: Theory and practice* (2nd ed., pp. 61–75). New York, NY: Oxford University Press.

Pachankis, J. E. (2007). The psychological implications of concealing a stigma: A cognitive–affective–behavioral model. *Psychological Bulletin, 133,* 328–345. doi:10.1037/0033-2909.133.2.328

Pachankis, J. E. (2009). The use of cognitive–behavioral therapy to promote authenticity. *Pragmatic Case Studies in Psychotherapy, 5,* 28–38. doi:10.14713/pcsp.v5i4.997

Pachankis, J. E., Clark, K., Burton, C., White Hughto, J. M., & Keene, D. E. Sex, status, competition, and exclusion: Stress from within the gay community and sexual minority men's mental health. Manuscript submitted for publication.

Pachankis, J. E., Goldfried, M. R., & Ramrattan, M. E. (2008). Extension of the rejection sensitivity construct to the interpersonal functioning of gay men. *Journal of Consulting and Clinical Psychology, 76,* 306–317. doi:10.1037/0022-006X.76.2.306

Pachankis, J. E., Hatzenbuehler, M. L., Rendina, H. J., Safren, S. A., & Parsons, J. T. (2015). LGB-affirmative cognitive–behavioral therapy for young adult gay and bisexual men: A randomized controlled trial of a transdiagnostic minority stress approach. *Journal of Consulting and Clinical Psychology, 83,* 875–889. doi:10.1037/ccp0000037

Purdie-Vaughns, V., & Eibach, R. R. (2013). The social psychology of symbolic firsts: Effects of Barack Obama's presidency on student achievement and perceptions of racial progress in America. In F. C. Harris & R. C. Lieberman (Eds.), *Beyond discrimination: Racial inequality in a postracist era* (pp. 186–211). New York, NY: Russell Sage Foundation.

Rizvi, S. L., & Linehan, M. M. (2005). The treatment of maladaptive shame in borderline personality disorder: A pilot study of "opposite action." *Cognitive and Behavioral Practice, 12,* 437–447. doi:10.1016/S1077-7229(05)80071-9

Rothblum, E. D., & Factor, R. (2001). Lesbians and their sisters as a control group: Demographic and mental health factors. *Psychological Science, 12*(1), 63–69. doi:10.1111/1467-9280.00311

Safren, S. A., Hollander, G., Hart, T. A., & Heimberg, R. G. (2001). Cognitive–behavioral therapy with lesbian, gay, and bisexual youth. *Cognitive and Behavioral Practice, 8,* 215–223. doi:10.1016/S1077-7229(01)80056-0

Safren, S. A., & Rogers, T. (2001). Cognitive–behavioral therapy with gay, lesbian, and bisexual clients. *Journal of Clinical Psychology, 57,* 629–643. doi:10.1002/jclp.1033

Sauer-Zavala, S., Gutner, C. A., Farchione, T. J., Boettcher, H. T., Bullis, J. R., & Barlow, D. H. (2017). Current definitions of "transdiagnostic" in treatment development: A search for consensus. *Behavior Therapy, 48,* 128–138. doi:10.1016/j.beth.2016.09.004

Silverman, W. K., Kurtines, W. M., Ginsburg, G. S., Weems, C. F., Lumpkin, P. W., & Carmichael, D. H. (1999). Treating anxiety disorders in children with group cognitive–behavioral therapy: A randomized clinical trial. *Journal of Consulting and Clinical Psychology, 67*(6), 995. doi:10.1037/0022-006X.67.6.995

Skinta, M. D., & Curtin, A. (Eds.). (2016). *Mindfulness and acceptance for gender and sexual minorities: A clinician's guide to fostering compassion, connection, and equality using contextual strategies.* New York, NY: New Harbinger.

Smith, N. G., Hart, T. A., Kidwai, A., Vernon, J. R. G., Blais, M., & Adam, B. (2017). Results of a pilot study to ameliorate psychological and behavioral outcomes of minority stress among young gay and bisexual men. *Behavior Therapy, 48,* 664–677. doi:10.1016/j.beth.2017.03.005

Wilfley, D. E., Welch, R. R., Stein, R. I., Spurrell, E. B., Cohen, L. R., Saelens, B. E., . . . Matt, G. E. (2002). A randomized comparison of group cognitive–behavioral therapy and group interpersonal psychotherapy for the treatment of overweight individuals with binge-eating disorder. *Archives of General Psychiatry, 59*(8), 713–721. doi:10.1001/archpsyc.59.8.713

Yadavaia, J. E., & Hayes, S. C. (2012). Acceptance and commitment therapy for self-stigma around sexual orientation: A multiple baseline evaluation. *Cognitive and Behavioral Practice, 19,* 545–559. doi:10.1016/j.cbpra.2011.09.002

17

Acceptance, Vulnerability, and Compassion

Contextual Behavioral Approaches for Sexual and Gender Minority Clients

**MATTHEW D. SKINTA, BRANDON HOEFLEIN,
AND DANIEL RYU ■**

Research on sexual and gender minority psychology has experienced a renaissance during recent decades, driven by theoretical and empirical advances. The selection and practice of effective mental health practice for sexual and gender minority individuals, however, has been minimally influenced by those findings. Even well-established empirically supported treatments that target known areas of vulnerability are neither systematically selected nor promoted for use among sexual and gender minority (SGM) clients. In addition, many empirically supported psychotherapies emphasize the manipulation of one's internal experiences or behavior, which privileges individual factors over environmental and contextual factors that may contain bias and discrimination. The alternative to this emphasis on individual factors includes therapies that emphasize mindfulness, a present-moment awareness of what contexts are occurring in the moment, alongside acceptance, or a willingness to be present with aversive internal experiences (e.g., thoughts and emotions) without requiring them to change and with an emphasis on engaging in new behaviors in the presence of those unwanted experiences (S. C. Hayes, Villate, Levin, & Hildebrandt, 2011). These approaches can allow for interventions that are sensitive to homophobia, transphobia, and additional forms of bias related to intersectional minority identities that impact SGM clients by encouraging new behaviors and relational responses without requiring exposure to stigmatizing climates to change as a condition of greater well-being. Although these techniques have primarily been developed within the context of cognitive–behavioral therapeutic approaches (Hofmann & Asmundson, 2008), these approaches emphasize the context and function of difficult thoughts and feelings rather than the validity or specific content of difficult thoughts or feelings (S. C. Hayes et al., 2011). In a world in which animus toward SGM individuals is slow to change, a therapy that shifts one's experience of intrapersonal or interpersonal encounters with animus seems to be an ideal route to incorporating SGM experiences of minority stress, rejection sensitivity, and shame into therapy.

MINORITY STRESS THEORY

Researchers and clinicians have long noted that stigma, particularly self-stigma (e.g., internalized transphobia), is a major negative contributor to the adverse mental health and distress of SGM clients (Malyon, 1982). However, mental health professionals have a checkered history of diagnostic attempts to capture this distress (e.g., ego-dystonic homosexuality; J. Smith, 1980). Although affirmative therapy models that promote acceptance of one's experiences and identities have been developed (Ritter & Terndrup, 2002; Singh & dickey, 2016), these protocols generally offer atheoretical suggestions unyoked from any specific theoretically or empirically derived intervention. These models stress the internalization of widely held cultural opprobrium for gender nonconformity and/or same-sex attraction as the primary source of this distress. Fortunately, recent research suggests that approaches that are more specific to the experiences of SGM clients and catered to incorporate themes associated with minority stress can improve psychological well-being (Pachankis, Hatzenbuehler, Rendina, Safren, & Parsons, 2015).

Currently, the dominant theoretical lens used to observe the impact of stigma on sexual and gender minorities' mental health is Meyer's (1995) minority stress theory, which emphasizes the mechanisms by which societal views can be conveyed and might impact the individual. Earlier research tended to emphasize either the impact of internalized anti-SGM thoughts or the burden of having experienced specific instances of discrimination or violence (D'Augelli, 1989; Malyon, 1982). This neglects the range of possible responses to homophobia and transphobia, such as interpersonal guardedness, fear of stigmatizing responses in the absence of direct past experience of discrimination, or the stress of active attempts to conceal one's identity (Meyer, 1995). Minority stress theory describes how chronic daily stressors related to minority status accumulate throughout the lifespan. The theory posits that one can only measure—and presumably mitigate— the impact of societal stigma when the full range of minority stress mechanisms is appreciated. This range generally includes internalized stigma (e.g., internalized homophobia, biphobia, or transphobia), the expectation of stigma from others, outness/concealment, and discrimination (e.g., overt acts of discrimination or violence). More recently, the case has been made to also include connection within the SGM community as a source of resilience (Frost & Meyer, 2012).

In subsequent research on minority stress, emotion dysregulation has been identified as a robust link between minority stress and psychological distress (Hatzenbuehler, 2009; Hatzenbuehler, McLaughlin, & Nolen-Hoeksema,

2008). Emotion dysregulation refers to the difficulty some individuals experience in controlling or coping with strong emotions. High levels of emotion dysregulation are associated with a broad array of psychopathological outcomes (Aldao, Nolen-Hoeksema, & Schweizer, 2010). Prospective studies of gay and lesbian adolescents reflect a linear sequence in which stigmatizing events lead to emotion dysregulation, which in turn leads to psychopathological symptoms (Hatzenbuehler, 2009). In addition, increased dysregulation has been observed in the days immediately following stigmatizing experiences (Hatzenbuehler et al., 2008). Although less robust, similar findings link minority stress to psychopathology among transgender and gender nonconforming people (Hendricks & Testa, 2012). These findings help explain the processes through which minority stress is related to marked elevations in psychological distress among SGM people compared to community baselines (Graham et al., 2011), while simultaneously offering an explanatory rationale for the range of externalizing and internalizing symptoms that are observed. To our knowledge, only one randomized controlled trial has occurred directly related to this work (Pachankis et al., 2015).

There is some suggestion that minority stress may differ for SGM people who are White compared to those who are persons of color (Moradi et al., 2010). This may be due to identity conflict of belonging to both a sexual or gender minority and racial minority group, although in the presence of qualitative findings supporting that LGB individuals experience a unified rather than a conflicted self, this additional distress may be due to the additive effects of racism, homophobia, biphobia, and transphobia (Balsam et al., 2015; Meyer & Ouellette, 2009; Nabors et al., 2001; Szymanski & Sung, 2010; P. A. Wilson & Yoshikawa, 2007). One example includes an increase in behavioral avoidance among African American sexual minority men who experienced distress at reminders of possessing a dual minority status, in contrast to lesser behavioral avoidance among African American sexual minority men more comfortable with both their racial and their sexual identities (Tucker-Seeley, Blow, Matsuo, & Taylor-Moore, 2010).

Rejection Sensitivity and Ruptured Relationships

Although minority stress theory has always included the expectation of stigma from others, rejection sensitivity merits specific attention as a major transdiagnostic psychological risk factor in the SGM community (Cohen, Feinstein, Rodriguez-Seijas, Taylor, & Newman, 2016; Dyar, Feinstein, Eaton, & London, 2018; Hendricks & Testa, 2012; Testa et al., 2015). Many SGM clients have histories of parental or familial rejection, with serious consequences ranging from psychopathology to suicidality (Pachankis, Goldfried, & Ramrattan, 2008; Puckett, Woodward, Mereish, & Pantalone, 2015; Ryan, Huebner, Diaz, & Sanchez, 2009; Ryan, Russell, Huebner, Diaz, & Sanchez, 2010;). The expectation of rejection among transgender and gender nonconforming individuals may be particularly associated with high rates of discriminatory, prejudicial, and violent acts (Hughto, Reisner, & Pachankis, 2015; Rood et al., 2016; Testa et al., 2012). These histories of rejection within close, previously loving interpersonal relationships can lead to a pattern of guardedness and interpersonal distance that damages future attempts to establish meaningful relationships and may increase loneliness and isolation (Mereish & Poteat, 2015). For these reasons, a neutral therapeutic stance may be less effective compared to approaches that intentionally amplify and intensify the therapeutic relationship.

The Role of Shame

Although an important part of the SGM experience, shame has not been as well described in minority stress models (Downs, 2005). Shame, although not a clinical diagnosis, has been linked to a number of different problems and psychopathologies, including depression (Orth, Berking, & Burkhardt, 2006; Thompson & Berenbaum, 2006), post-traumatic stress disorder (PTSD; Lee, Scragg, & Turner, 2001; Leskela, Dieperink, & Thuras, 2002; J. P. Wilson, Drozdek, & Turkovic, 2006; Wong & Cook, 1992), substance abuse (Dearing, Stuewig, & Tangney, 2005), and suicide (Hastings, Northman, & Tangney, 2000; Lester, 1998). Shame plays a significant role in addictive behaviors, including substance abuse and compulsive sexual behavior, among SGM clients (Matthews, Lorah, & Fenton, 2006; Skinta & D'Alton, 2016). Shame also contributes to HIV risk behaviors among transgender women (Hughto et al., 2015). Furthermore, the specific impact of shame on SGM people likely varies by identity because past research has suggested divergent patterns of internalizing or externalizing disorders across gay, bisexual, lesbian, and transgender individuals (Cochran & Mays, 2009). Although the minority stress concept of self-stigma focuses on the content of particular self-referential thoughts, shame is both an affective consequence of those thoughts and a stimulus for self-critical mental content (e.g., "My sexuality must mean something is wrong with me").

MINDFULNESS AND ACCEPTANCE IN SGM-AFFIRMATIVE PSYCHOTHERAPY

There are few interventions that specifically target minority stress, rejection sensitivity, and shame among SGM clients, and there are even fewer that are empirically based and assessed. Contextual behavioral therapies emphasizing mindfulness and acceptance, including acceptance and commitment therapy (ACT; S. C. Hayes, Strosahl, & Wilson, 1999), functional analytic psychotherapy (FAP; R. J. Kohlenberg & Tsai, 1991), compassion-focused therapy (CFT; Gilbert, 2010), dialectic behavioral therapy (Linehan, 1993), mindfulness-based cognitive therapy (MBCT; Segal, Williams, & Teasdale, 2001), and acceptance-based behavioral therapy (Roemer, Orsillo, & Salters-Pedneault, 2008), rely on mindfulness and acceptance strategies to support improved emotion regulation (Blackledge & Hayes, 2001; Chambers, Gullone, & Allen, 2009; Gratz & Tull,

2010; A. M. Hayes & Feldman, 2004). Rather than a comprehensive exploration of all therapies that incorporate mindfulness and acceptance, ACT, FAP, and CFT are reviewed in detail as therapies that target the SGM-relevant processes of emotion regulation, rejection sensitivity, and shame. Specifically, ACT emphasizes a greater willingness to experience and not avoid painful emotions and thoughts (S. C. Hayes et al., 1999), FAP was created to mitigate the impact of familial and interpersonal histories that have been found to contribute to rejection sensitivity (R. J. Kohlenberg & Tsai, 1991), and CFT was developed to reduce the experience of shame and its effect on well-being (Gilbert, 2010). These three therapies share an emphasis on mindfulness, both as a formal practice within therapy (Teasdale et al., 2000) and as a stance toward attending to the present moment within therapy sessions (K. G. Wilson, 2009). Each therapy also emphasizes the contextual behavioral stance that all behaviors are adaptive, that the contexts that gave rise to unworkable behaviors previously supported those behaviors, and that acceptance of this principle is a key stance from which to develop new behaviors (Chiesa, 1994). These approaches contrast with more traditional cognitive and behavioral methods that primarily seek to alter the form or frequency of private events (e.g., automatic thoughts; Gaudiano, 2008), and they take a stance that behavior change is not contingent on an a priori change in distressing thoughts or feelings. Next, the evidence base of three popular mindfulness and acceptance therapies (ACT, FAP, and CFT) that target the SGM-relevant processes of emotion regulation, rejection sensitivity, and shame is reviewed.

Acceptance and Commitment Therapy for SGM Clients

Acceptance and commitment therapy (S. C. Hayes et al., 1999) is a third-wave behavioral therapy that focuses on psychological flexibility and a commitment to living in accordance with values. ACT differs from traditional cognitive and behavioral approaches in that it does not attempt to remove or alter internal experiences and instead aims to change the way that people relate to their thoughts, emotions, and sensations. ACT focuses on the suffering that occurs as a result of cognitive fusion (i.e., an overreliance on the literalness of human language wherein painful verbal rules are overly attended to), experiential avoidance (i.e., behavioral attempts to avoid feeling or experiencing adverse emotional states), and psychological inflexibility (i.e., the restriction in behavioral and interpersonal repertoires that occur in part as a result of experiential avoidance and cognitive fusion). ACT works to foster psychological flexibility through six core processes: contact with the present moment, defusion, acceptance, perspective taking, values clarification, and committed action.

A variety of cross-sectional studies suggest that mindfulness and experiential avoidance, which refers to avoidant behaviors that occur in response to unwanted thoughts and feelings and serves as one of the primary targets of ACT, play an important role in psychological distress among SGM people. In a study of gay men aged 40 years or older from Australia, trait mindfulness mitigated the impact of discrimination on self-esteem and psychological distress (Lyons, 2016). Furthermore, experiential avoidance has been shown to completely mediate the relationship between internalized homophobia and PTSD symptoms in lesbian sexual assault victims (Gold, Dickstein, Marx, & Lexington, 2009) and partially mediate the impact of childhood abuse on PTSD symptomology among lesbians (Gold, Feinstein, Skidmore, & Marx, 2011). Experiential avoidance also impacts treatment outcomes among HIV-positive gay and bisexual men, including increased trauma symptomology and decreased self-efficacy related to HIV management (Chartier et al., 2010). In a sample of gay male sexual assault survivors, experiential avoidance partially mediated the relationship between internalized homophobia and depressive symptomology, as well as the relationship between internalized homophobia and PTSD symptomology (Gold, Marx, & Lexington, 2007). Finally, measures of experiential avoidance and inflexibility are associated with self-concealment in gay men, although not lesbians (Masuda et al., 2017), and the co-occurrence of experiential avoidance and self-concealment is associated with overall psychological distress (Leleux-Labarge, Hatton, Goodnight, & Masuda, 2015). These findings suggest that ACT, as a transdiagnostic approach, may offer broad benefit to SGM individuals given its focus on cultivating a meaningful life without requiring painful cognitions to be eliminated, altered, or considered untrue.

Conversations about the use of ACT with SGM clients have proliferated in recent years through book chapters, case studies, and theoretical articles that illustrate the ways in which ACT may be an ideal therapeutic approach for a community that faces a disproportionate amount of stigma, shame, and stressors beyond its control (Skinta, 2014; Skinta & Curtin, 2016; Walloch, Cerezo, & Heide, 2012). Despite the growing cross-sectional support for the applicability of an ACT framework for understanding SGM experiences, however, only a limited number of pilot studies explicitly consider the efficacy of ACT in clinical settings. First, a multiple-baseline across-participants study providing ACT for SGM individuals bothered by self-stigmatizing thoughts related to a minority sexual orientation found a decrease in intrusive thoughts and distress, as well as improvement on measures of depression, stress, social support, and quality of life (Yadavaia & Hayes, 2012). Yadavaia and Hayes emphasized defusion from those distressing thoughts specific to the participant's sexual orientation. In addition, a pilot group intervention focusing on the experiences of stigma among gay and bisexual-identified men living with HIV also reported marked reductions in psychological inflexibility and HIV-related stigma (Skinta, Lezama, Wells, & Dilley, 2015). However, neither pilot has been replicated with a randomized design. In a study of gay men aged 40 years or older from Australia, mindfulness trainings, a key part of ACT, were shown to reduce the adverse effects of discrimination on self-esteem and psychological distress (Lyons, 2016).

Functional Analytic Psychotherapy for SGM Clients

Functional analytic psychotherapy is a behaviorally based, interpersonal psycho-therapy for augmenting the therapeutic relationship through contingent, in-the-moment responses to client behaviors (R. J. Kohlenberg & Tsai, 1991). Recent training manuals have simplified this process through emphasizing the core ther-apist behaviors of awareness (mindful attention to the present moment), courage (taking behavioral risks in the presence of fear or worry), and love (affective warmth and responsiveness on the part of the therapist; Holman, Kanter, Tsai, & Kohlenberg, 2017). FAP is rooted in the values of vulnerability, awareness, authen-ticity, and courage (Tsai, Callaghan, & Kohlenberg, 2013). In short, FAP clinicians seek to establish an intense, genuine relationship with clients and then use this re-lationship as a roadmap for augmenting therapeutic interventions. FAP functions primarily through evoking behavior in session, contingently responding to this behavior in session, and facilitating out-of-session generalizations of intimacy-building behaviors such as authentic expression of emotion and vulnerability (Haworth et al., 2015; Landes, Kanter, Weeks, & Busch, 2013). FAP techniques have been shown to increase targeted behaviors outside of session, such as emo-tional expression (Lizarazo, Munoz-Martinez, Santos, & Kanter, 2015).

The therapeutic relationship in FAP is conceptualized as a "real" relationship between two people, which ideally permeates both the relationship in therapy and the patient's vulnerable and intimate behaviors in meaningful relationships out-side of therapy. As such, the FAP therapist seeks to propose activities or behave in an evocative manner in order to elicit responses that may represent out-of-session problem behaviors or more adaptive behaviors that the client's current social con-text may not be reinforcing. This allows the therapist to reinforce actions that promote closeness and to block or shape behaviors that would lead to emotional distance. Study designs that have assessed the systematic addition and withdrawal of FAP interventions support the relationship between FAP techniques and increases in interpersonally meaningful, clinically relevant behaviors (Oshiro, Kanter, & Meyer, 2012).

FAP focuses on clinically relevant behaviors (CRBs) as the unit of conceptu-alization and intervention (Tsai et al., 2013). CRBs have been defined as inter-personal behaviors, which move clients toward value-driven behaviors in their relationships (CRB2) or move clients away from value-driven behaviors in their personal relationships (CRB1). Throughout treatment, the clinician's goal is to naturally reinforce CRB2s (toward moves) and block or shape CRB1s (away moves). FAP functions with five basic rules: (1) Watch for CRB, (2) evoke CRB in session, (3) naturally reinforce CRB2s, (4) assess reinforcing versus extinguishing implications of therapist intervention, and, (5) interpret and generalize CRB2 be-havior to out-of-therapy relationships. Rule 3 (contingent, natural reinforcement) may provide a natural context for therapist self-disclosure. Relatedly, a therapist's disclosure of their SGM identity, although not the disclosure of a heterosexual orientation, has been found to increase therapeutic alliance with sexual minority clients (Halpert & Pfaller, 2001; Kronner, 2013), indicating that the therapist modeling of a comfortable, vulnerable openness about their sexual orientation with a client may have reinforcement value and serve as a meaningful response to a CRB2.

Past research has demonstrated FAP's efficacy both as a stand-alone treatment and as a supplement to other treatments. Empirical analyses indicate that it is an efficacious connection-building tool for clients suffering from anxiety disorders or avoidant personality disorder, specifically on measures of daily life interpersonal relations and therapist–client working alliance (Maitland et al., 2016). Case studies have shown that stand-alone FAP interventions increase CRB2s (behaviors likely to result in closeness and intimacy) and decrease CRB1s (interpersonal behavior that fosters distance) in personality disorders (Callaghan, Summers, & Weidman, 2003). In addition, case study evidence suggests that a stand-alone FAP intervention improves symptoms of major depressive disorder and anxiety disorders without agoraphobia (Ferro-Garcia, Lopez-Bermudez, & Valero-Aguyao, 2012; Lopez-Bermudez, Ferro-Garcia, & Calvillo, 2010). Randomized controlled trials indicate that FAP enhances psychopharmacological treatment for addictions, demonstrating that smoking cessation is more successful with the addition of FAP and ACT compared to bupropion alone (Gifford et al., 2011). FAP has also been found effective as an adjunctive intervention in the treatment of depression with both cognitive therapy (R. J. Kohlenberg, Kanter, Bolling, Parker, & Tsai, 2002) and cognitive–behavioral therapy (McClafferty, 2012).

FAP offers a unique treatment tool for use with SGM clients. Specifically, fear of intimacy has been shown to partially mediate the effect of internalized homophobia on relationship quality among gay and bisexual men (Szymanski & Hilton, 2013). In the therapy room, this pattern might present as a client who avoids relational trust risks or emotional vulnerability, which interferes with their ability to develop lasting romantic relationships. Data also suggest that self-concealment partially stems from social anxiety and results in lowered commitment to relationship values and goals (Potoczniak, Aldea, & DeBlaere, 2007).

Patterns of guardedness may also arise when the therapist is unable to respond to material related to sexual orientation or gender diversity in a warm, nonjudgmental manner. For instance, many SGM clients report failed therapeutic relationships due to the therapist expression of biased, negative attitudes regarding minority sexual orientation and gender identities (Israel, Gorcheva, Burnes, & Walther, 2008; Shelton & Delgado-Romero, 2011). SGM-sensitive cultural frameworks call for therapists to be sensitive to past harms experienced by SGM clients and to discuss issues of identity differences and power conflicts, although this is an aspirational model of professional practice that is not always met (American Psychological Association, 2011, 2015; Association for Lesbian, Gay, Bisexual, and Transgender Issues in Counseling Lesbian, Gay, Bisexual, Queer, Intersex, Questioning and Ally Competencies Taskforce, 2012; Association for Lesbian, Gay, Bisexual, and Transgender Issues in Counseling Transgender Committee, 2010; L. C. Smith, Shin, & Officer, 2012). Plummer (2010) articulated the application of FAP in the training of effective clinicians working with SGM clients. For instance, contingent responding to client CRB1s and CRB2s may not be possible depending on the degree to which the clinician avoids contact with or is uncomfortable with topics of sexuality and gender. Furthermore, FAP suggests that therapists are responding to CRBs regardless of case conceptualization or approach: A lack of clarity about the importance of interpersonal connection and the role of rejection sensitivity in SGM clients would likely lead to adverse therapeutic outcomes (Plummer, 2010). For a more thorough description of FAP with SGM clients, see Skinta, Balsam, and Singh (2016).

Compassion-Focused Therapy for SGM Clients

Compassion-focused therapy (Gilbert, 2010) arose out of the observation that self-critical and shameful experiences of one's self become a risk for both the experience of psychopathology and the reoccurrence of depressive symptoms (Pulcu et al., 2014). Shame is not just expressed as pathology, however; many SGM clients have historically managed the experience of shame through overachieving—constantly striving, through accomplishments, awards, and aplomb, to secure a sense of worthiness that their inner critic assures them is not real (Downs, 2005; Pachankis & Hatzenbuehler, 2013). CFT is grounded in a biopsychosocial model incorporating findings in evolutionary biology, neuropsychology, and attachment theory. CFT emphasizes the motivational drive systems of threat, or responses to perceived threats in the environment; achievement, or the intrinsic response to successful acquisition of resources and rank; and contentedness, deeply grounded in early experiences of attachment and safety in relation to others. The first two motivational systems, threat and achievement, are easily maintained and developed through the ubiquitous presence of threatening stimuli or rewards in the environment. The third system related to contentedness and connection, however, has the greatest likelihood of impairment if an individual's early life environment lacks warmth or safety. CFT processes are intended to buttress and build that specific capacity for experiencing connection and a sense of interpersonal safety (Gilbert, 2014). Many of the core practices of CFT—from imagining receiving care from an ideal, compassionate other to cultivating a voice of one's own inner "compassionate" self—build on the ability to view one's own life through a compassionate, caring lens (Shapira & Mongrain, 2010).

CFT has been supported in the treatment of a number of disorders, including psychotic disorders (Braehler et al., 2013; Mayhew & Gilbert, 2008), eating disorders (Gale, Gilbert, Read, & Goss, 2014), and personality disorders (Lucre & Corten, 2013). CFT has also been supported as a supplement to cognitive–behavioral therapy for depression (Beaumont, Galpin, & Jenkins, 2012). Additional explorations of shame have been studied under the self-compassion model proposed by Neff (2003). Self-compassion clarifies that experiencing compassion toward one's self requires mindfulness, or a focus on emotional experiences as they occur in the present moment; common humanity, or the awareness that one's suffering is neither isolated nor individual but, rather, a shared aspect of the human experience; and self-kindness, or the generation of warm feelings toward the self (Neff, Kirkpatrick, & Rude, 2007).

A variety of psychoeducation programs have been investigated regarding compassionate responding and self-compassion (Gilbert, 2010; Neff, 2003). Modeled off of the 8-week meditation course format used in mindfulness-based stress reduction (Kabat-Zinn, 2009) and MBCT (Teasdale et al., 2000), each program builds upon the initial practice of mindfulness meditation and expands to include an emphasis on compassion for the self or others. These approaches include compassionate mind training (Gilbert & Proctor, 2006), cognitive-based compassion therapy (Reddy et al., 2013), compassion cultivation training (Jazaieri et al., 2013), mindful self-compassion (Neff & Germer, 2013), and mindfulness-based compassionate living (van den Brink & Koster, 2015). None of these group training approaches have been explored with SGM individuals, although a protocol has been published in advance of the onset of a study of compassionate mind training for SGM people (Pepping et al., 2017). Unfortunately, no pilot studies appear to exist in the peer-reviewed literature of compassion interventions for SGM clients.

Despite the relative lack of empirical data regarding CFT, or the compassion training programs inspired by it, specifically for SGM clients, such approaches appear to hold promise for responding to the unique manifestations of shame that affect SGM communities. For instance, communal shaming messages are common both within the community, such as when a young trans client rejects a referral to a peer support group because of her perception that other trans women are likely to be sex workers, and outside the community, as seen in the history of HIV prevention campaigns with embedded shaming messages that gay men cannot trust one another to honestly discuss their sexual histories (Odets, 1995) or current debates regarding pre-exposure prophylaxis and the argument that mitigating the risk of HIV might only further disinhibit sex-focused gay men (Elsesser et al., 2015). Although primarily described in the psychoanalytic literature, these forms of intra-community shame may also affect the therapeutic relationship because there is a risk that SGM therapists might avoid topics that elicit their own experience of shame (Dearing & Tangney, 2011; Morrison, 2008). Self-compassion and trait mindfulness have been shown to moderate the relationship between gender nonconformity and psychological health among heterosexual and sexual minority individuals, which suggests some benefit from compassion-based therapy for SGM individuals whose gender expression is nonconforming (Keng & Liew, 2017). Differences in early life memories associated with shame have also been found between gay and heterosexual men, suggesting that whereas heterosexual men generally experience diverse sources of shame early in life, among gay men, shame memories are strongly linked to critical fathers (Matos, Carvalho, Cunha, Galhardo, & Sepodes, 2017).

CASE EXAMPLE: AN EVIDENCE-BASED ACCEPTANCE AND MINDFULNESS APPROACH TO SGM-AFFIRMATIVE PSYCHOTHERAPY

In the therapeutic process detailed here, the integration of ACT, FAP, and CFT is presented in a stepwise manner, with a consistent emphasis on mindful attention to the present and perspective-taking that threads through each intervention. The initial stage of therapy emphasizes ACT processes, and it explores and challenges the experiential avoidance that restricts behavioral and emotional responses and the cognitive fusion that allows stigmatizing messages to be experienced so painfully. The second stage, which hinges on deepening the therapeutic relationship with FAP, presents an opportunity to rehearse and generalize intimate and vulnerable behaviors. The final stage uses CFT to provide tools and practices to respond more kindly to oneself with regard to the experience of shame.

Mark is a 32-year-old gay man who has struggled with his experience being gay. He was raised in a close-knit family within the Church of Jesus Christ of Latter-Day Saints (Mormons) and deeply aligned with his religious beliefs as a child. Despite generally positive memories as a child, he recalls instances of shaming and criticism by his parents, who suspected he was too interested in other boys and men at a young age. When he came out as gay as a young adult, he was rejected by his parents and had minimal contact with them for the next 5 years. He is close to one sibling, but two others frequently voice their preference that he not visit them because they have young children and do not wish for a gay uncle to be around them.

Currently, he struggles with relationships. He often pursues men intensely or feels overwhelmed with thoughts of men he experiences as distant or aloof, although when his feelings of attraction are reciprocated, he finds himself losing interest. He came to therapy concerned that he was drinking alcohol more than he would like and often felt that he used sex to cope with feelings of self-criticism and depressed affect.

Introducing Elements of Acceptance and Commitment Therapy

Although it is tempting to implement ACT in the manner of other manualized forms of cognitive–behavioral therapy, it is important to bear in mind that ACT is a process-oriented, behavior analytic approach, meaning that no single process is required prior to others. Common techniques might include an emphasis on contact with the present moment through breathing and noticing, without reacting to, thoughts (e.g., "Imagine you were able to observe each thought as it appears and disappears without needing to do anything with it, like watching fireflies light up in a field at night"); defusion, or the use of verbal techniques intended to aid a client in attending to the distinction between thoughts and the consequences of believing those thoughts (e.g., extensive repetition of emotionally charged thoughts); acceptance exercises (e.g., openly accepting emotional and physical sensations when engaging with painful thoughts); perspective-taking (e.g., asking what his older, wiser self would say looking back from 40 years in the future); values clarification interventions (e.g., Personal Values Card Sort; Miller, C'de Baca, Matthews, & Wilbourne, 2001); and, finally, committed action, or the delineation of specific behaviors, guided by values, completed in the presence of aversive thoughts or emotions without acting to avoid contact with those internal experiences. A strong behavioral analysis should guide interventions as the therapist dances between defusion from painful cognitions and experiential avoidance and the identification of values and committed actions in the service of those values. In the following opening vignette, Mark is being introduced to the concept of acceptance of unwanted thoughts and feelings, as well as defusion from implicit rules that have had a restrictive impact on his interpersonal behaviors. In this instance, he is revisiting an experience involving familial rejection that mirrors interpersonal challenges in his romantic relationships:

MARK: I know we've talked about this, but I woke up and reached first for my phone to scroll through Facebook. My brother had been posting hateful homophobic comments and arguing with some of my friends through the night. Like those fake caring comments about how gays and lesbians my brother knows are so unhappy, and maybe we shouldn't rule out that we all need therapy.

THERAPIST: What does your mind tell you, when you read the comments posted by your brother?

MARK: Well, it's a mix. I mean, first there's that side that says if I really let people in or share when I'm down or anxious, it just feeds into all this. Then there's that dating part where I think about when I've told you I don't know if I can ever fall in love and have a happy life. (forced, loud laugh)

THERAPIST: That laugh seemed to be covering something painful . . .

MARK: Well, it's just hard to dip into this, no one wants to be around someone who is wallowing all the time.

THERAPIST: That sounds like your mind is handing you that same thought again: "If people see who I really am, they won't like it." How much do you believe that today? Just off the top of your head, from zero to 100%?

MARK: It feels pretty high right now. I don't know, 85%?

THERAPIST: It makes me think about that discussion last week, of the co-worker you were getting close to. How much do you think you'd have believed this thought last week?

MARK: Maybe 30%? I was feeling less guarded, I guess.

THERAPIST: So what happens to the sadness? I mean, I had the sense before that you were saying if you had to believe this thought, 100%, that no one wants to see you unhappy, then there was no point in showing your genuine emotions or being sad. What do you have to do with these emotions if you believed completely that others valued and would want to be near an authentic you?

MARK: Hmm. . . . If I really bought that, then I guess it would be to show that I'm sad. Wouldn't I just wind up sad all the time if I did that, though?

THERAPIST: Well, not necessarily. I mean, if I asked you, just for the next 30 seconds, not to picture or think of a white elephant, what would happen?

MARK (LAUGHS): I keep thinking of an elephant.

THERAPIST: Sometimes trying to push a thought away is a bit like putting our thumb over the end of a hose. We don't stop the water, we just feel more pressure and wind up soaked.

MARK: So if I'm sad or tired or put off on my date tonight, I just show it?

THERAPIST: Sure. . . . What's the worst that will happen? He might even see the real you.

In this session, the therapist has primarily focused on the process of defusion through orienting the client to the changing believability of his thoughts (e.g., "How much do you think you'd have believed this thought last week?"). The client has been encouraged to track the relative impact of a thought (i.e., "If people see who I really am, they won't like it") and the ways in which treating the thought as believable affects his behavior across contexts. The goal is to increase the client's awareness of how the focus on avoiding internal experiences has limited his contact with the consequences of his behaviors in the present moment. In the future, the client may be more aware of the moment when the problematic thought (i.e., "No one wants to be around someone who is wallowing all the time") arises and to choose to act in accordance with his values rather than behaving as though the thought were true.

Introducing Elements of Functional Analytic Psychotherapy

For a FAP-informed therapist working with an SGM client, the initial goal of therapy is to identify CRB2s (clinically relevant behavior that moves the client *toward* emotional intimacy and authenticity) and CRB1s (clinically relevant behavior that moves the client *away from* emotional intimacy and authenticity). Specific to work with SGM clients, however, the therapist will also attempt to consider and incorporate CRBs specific to a client's history of reinforcement or punishment specific to the client's gender identity and sexual orientation. Although some SGM clients have had meaningful verbal disclosures responded to with silence, a change of topic, or hurtful responses, other SGM clients might have been encouraged to monitor and restrict mannerisms or gestures associated with the other gender. In the spirit of reinforcing authenticity and blocking attempts at interpersonal distance, the FAP therapist might consider as CRB2s a looser control of body language or more detailed description of meaningful relationships. The FAP therapist's goal is to contingently respond to CRBs, with the most common CRB1s consisting of attempts to block closeness or vulnerability, and CRB2s including intimate disclosures and expressions of warmth (for further illustration and coded therapist dialog with SGM clients, see Skinta et al., 2016). One common evocative task, described next, is the use of an emotional risk log (Tsai et al., 2009). Clients are asked to choose a single interpersonal action each day that feels emotionally challenging in order to increase awareness of how pervasive the habit of avoiding emotional vulnerability has become, gain experience acting in the presence of feared outcomes, and increase tolerance to acting in the presence of a fear of rejection. Common examples include saying "no" in the face of a desire for approval, expressing a need, or directly addressing an avoided conflict. In this discussion, the FAP practice of contingent responding to CRBs is used to challenge Mark to engage in a more vulnerable, connected way with the therapist:

MARK: So it turned out to be another one of those dates—I had been so into the idea, and after sex I just couldn't get over wanting to be away from him. (laughs in a forced, loud way)

THERAPIST: There's that laugh we'd discussed before. Could we step back a second? What would you be feeling if that laugh wasn't there?

MARK: I guess some guilt. I mean . . . part of me remembers when I was younger and felt like men used me that way, I would feel valued and pursued and then ignored. Part of me feels like there's something wrong with me that I could feel that way about someone.

THERAPIST: What's it like to share this part of you with me? Both bringing back up how terrible you felt when this happened to you, and your fear something is wrong with you that you might be doing this to others?

MARK: It's scary. Part of me feels like you'd judge me.

THERAPIST: I'm feeling some care for you, and some sadness that life has made it so hard for you to feel and receive the love you deserve. What's it like for you to hear this, that even in this moment I'm thinking how much this speaks to your deserving love?

MARK: A part of me relaxes, though I also have this tension in my chest, like I don't want to let it in.

THERAPIST: Could you imagine opening your heart maybe 10% more? What would that be like?

MARK: I can. It's hard. How do I work on this?

THERAPIST: You already are with the risk logs. Would you be willing to emphasize risks where others can show you love this next week? Perhaps in sharing what your needs are?

MARK: What about with this date? I kind of planned to not respond to anymore texts.

THERAPIST: Could it be worth it to see him again? To see what it might be like to take a step back from the story and show up fully with him?

MARK: I almost asked what to do if that makes him more attached, though I know you'd only ask what's so bad about that! Okay, I'll text him.

In this case, initial CRB1s, such as laughter to avoid feeling negative affect, are blocked by the therapist, and evocative statements are used to prompt CRB2s, including the invitation to slow down, notice the function of that laughter, and attend to the physical responses of avoided emotions to aid in labeling them. Here, Mark is being oriented toward a practice outside of therapy that might promote generalization and reduce behaviors that restrict closeness with others.

Introducing Elements of Compassion-Focused Therapy

As Mark grew closer to his therapist and took risks by approaching painful or avoided emotions, he grew increasingly aware of how affected he was by self-criticism. First, the therapist presented the rationale of the three affect-regulation systems from CFT:

> MARK: What can I do with this? It's like no matter what I change, I still don't feel good.
>
> THERAPIST: I'd like to spend some time on this. There are three systems identified by psychological research as affecting how we are motivated by our emotions. Two are pretty easily learned. First is our system for achievement. From the moment you taste something sweet, or are given a reward, that dopamine system engages. Next is our threat system, that old fight-or-flight feeling. The cold air of birth, or a loud noise, quickly can engage a sense of fear. The trouble comes with the third system. We can call it "connectedness," or "self-soothing." Every time you see a photo of a parent gazing into the eyes of an infant, you get a sense of how we learn that sense of safety in the world. That's the trouble—when our relationships are not safe, or we experience betrayal or abandonment, that system gets underdeveloped. The other two grow on autopilot, but not that one. When we're restricted to achievement or threat systems, then the second we don't succeed, everything crashes down.
>
> MARK: That feels right. How do I change that, though? I can't have new parents.
>
> THERAPIST: Some of it we have already done. Your emotional risk logs build safety in your relationships. It's also worth practicing other ways to let love in.

At this point, the provider introduced the compassionate figure meditation (Gilbert, 2010). Mark first thought of his grandmother, who had passed away when he was a child. Over time, however, he occasionally began to replace this with the image of his therapist and of various male role models from childhood. This targets the fear surrounding accepting care from others, and it involves imagined exposure to accepting warmth and compassion from an ideal compassionate being.

Although these therapeutic responses have been developed separately, guidelines have been developed articulating both the integration of ACT and

FAP (B. S. Kohlenberg & Callaghan, 2010; Callaghan, Gregg, Marx, Kohlenberg, & Gifford, 2004) and this proposed integration of ACT, FAP, and CFT (Tirch, Schoendorff, & Silberstein, 2014). The evidence for this approach is primarily inductive rather than deductive. That is, lacking randomized controlled trials that would allow broad generalization, convergent findings in SGM and psychotherapy research support this approach. SGM individual are subject to minority stress (Hendricks & Testa, 2012; Meyer, 1995), which primarily affects psychological well-being through emotion dysregulation (Hatzenbuhler, 2009). Emotion regulation skills improve in treatments emphasizing mindfulness and acceptance (Blackledge & Hayes, 2001; A. M. Hayes & Feldman, 2004). The interpersonal betrayals and rejections so common in the lives of SGM people result in not only psychological distress but also patterns of guardedness and isolation due to rejection sensitivity (Klein & Golub, 2016; Pachankis et al., 2008). This guardedness can be reduced and shaped with FAP (R. J. Kohlenberg & Tsai, 1991; Oshiro et al., 2012). Finally, SGM people are subjected to critical thoughts and shame that also result from environments lacking interpersonal safety and containing societal bias (Matos et al., 2017), and the impact of those thoughts and shame may be lessened through the use of CFT (Gilbert, 2014).

FUTURE DIRECTIONS

Research on the use of mindfulness and acceptance therapies for SGM people is fragmented, unsystematic, and would benefit from the collection of future evidence to fill in existing gaps in the literature while taking advantage of a wider variety of methods. The evidence guiding these approaches is reliant on the inductive use of convergent areas of recent scholarship. This is an imperfect state for advancing treatment in this area, and it highlights the need for a more systematic program of research that would connect these disparate areas of research together with empirical data. Experiential avoidance, as the primary target of ACT, should be investigated further as a link between minority stress and psychopathology. Similarly, FAP appears well-suited for the treatment of rejection sensitivity, although data on the effectiveness of FAP specific to SGM-identified clients are lacking. Finally, despite a number of cross-sectional studies exploring the impact of shame on the lives of SGM individuals, none of the recent wave of compassion-based interventions have been assessed with SGM people. A number of steps might be taken to improve the quality of mindfulness and acceptance interventions. Next steps should focus on increasing the diversity of research participants, increasing overlap between SGM psychology and the broader trends within clinical psychology, and expanding the use of cost-effective designs that would increase our knowledge in this area.

Regarding broadening recruitment, many of the studies discussed in this chapter included primarily gay men, with fewer numbers of participants identifying as bisexual or lesbian. Of the studies inclusive of transgender participants, most did not include clients with non-binary gender identities who also experience minority stress and discrimination (Richards et al., 2016). This is a particularly important point given that across the pilot studies described in this chapter that have included SGM participants, only two cisgender women were included (Yadavaia & Hayes, 2012). Despite known disparities in rates of diagnosis, gender identity and sexual orientation data are rarely gathered or reported by investigators conducting randomized controlled trials for psychological interventions (Heck, Mirabito, LeMaire, Livingston, & Flentje, 2017). The collection and dissemination of these data would broaden our knowledge and confidence in treatment planning if they were to be systematically collected in future studies.

Furthermore, it is important that trends and development in clinical research are integrated and considered in advancing SGM psychology research. For example, it is perhaps unsurprising that the case example presented in this chapter maps closely to the recommendations of Courtois and Ford's (2015) sequenced, relationship-based approach to the treatment of complex trauma—those traumatic responses resulting primarily from interpersonal and relational betrayals and losses so frequently experienced by SGM individuals. FAP was discussed previously with regard to its promise as a targeted treatment for rejection sensitivity, which has a broad and transdiagnostic impact on internalizing disorders in gay and bisexual men (Cohen, Feinstein, Rodriguez-Seijas, Taylor, & Newman, 2016). FAP may also hold value, however, in future research on complex PTSD (CPTSD). Higher rates of trauma and repeated trauma related to one's gender (Mizock & Lewis, 2008) and sexuality (Roberts, Austin, Corliss, Vandermorris, & Koenen, 2010) place this population at greater risk for CPTSD. Hallmark interpersonal symptoms of CPTSD include patterns of inconsistent relationships, inability to connect with others, and emotional injuries (Pearlman & Courtois, 2005). The first stage of treatment recommended for CPTSD focuses on the therapeutic alliance as an opportunity to address patterns of relationship instability and disconnection (Courtois, 2004), for which FAP may play a helpful role. SGM individuals are referenced in only a fraction of articles on CPTSD, however, with most existing literature limited to explorations of CPTSD among asylum seekers and other populations exposed to extreme duress (Alessi, Kahn, & Chatterji, 2016). This is representative of an area in clinical psychology that is experiencing a great deal of growth and attention, albeit separate from the trends and discussions within SGM psychology.

Finally, although the standards established within our field recommend replicated, randomized controlled trials to most strongly establish the empirical support for a treatment (Chambless & Hollon, 1998), there are other ways to strengthen the evidence base for the proposed types of treatments described in this chapter. One is through well-designed, single-subject experiments (Kazdin, 2011). Much of the supportive literature for FAP and its impact on interpersonal functioning is already grounded in the careful evaluation of the use and withdrawal of FAP techniques in well-designed, single-case studies (Busch et al., 2009; Callaghan et al., 2003). One of the major strengths of such a design is that it allows for greater clarity with regard to the mechanisms occurring in therapy and resulting in change (Kazdin, 1981). Such data would strengthen the inductive inference from the existing literature described in this chapter that ACT might mitigate emotion dysregulation due to minority stress or that FAP might reduce the impact of rejection sensitivity on interpersonal difficulties. Although this would not replace the need for randomized, experimental evaluations of these therapies with SGM clients, this approach would allow the evidence base to advance in a resource-limited environment.

CONCLUSION

Therapies enhancing mindfulness, acceptance, compassion, and vulnerability among SGM clients offer the potential to reduce the impact of minority stress, rejection sensitivity, and shame. The therapies described in this chapter utilize mindfulness and acceptance processes to improve emotion regulation, increase genuineness and vulnerability in interpersonal relationships, and reduce the experience of shame. Although empirical evidence supports the effectiveness of these therapies on targets that SGM psychology suggests are areas of vulnerability for SGM clients, the bodies of empirical research describing these therapies and the well-being of SGM clients are still primarily separate and only beginning to be connected (Skinta & Curtin, 2016).

REFERENCES

Aldao, A., Nolen-Hoeksema, S., & Schweizer, S. (2010). Emotion-regulation strategies across psychopathology: A meta-analytic review. *Clinical Psychology Review, 30*(2), 217–237.

Alessi, E. J., Kahn, S., & Chatterji, S. (2016). "The darkest times of my life": Recollections of child abuse among forced migrants persecuted because of their sexual orientation and gender identity. *Child Abuse & Neglect, 51*, 93–105.

American Psychological Association. (2011). *Guidelines for psychological practice with lesbian, gay, and bisexual clients.* Washington, DC: Author.

American Psychological Association. (2015). *Guidelines for psychological practice with transgender and gender nonconforming people.* Washington, DC: Author.

Association for Lesbian, Gay, Bisexual, and Transgender Issues in Counseling Transgender Committee. (2010). American Counseling Association competencies for counseling with transgender clients. *Journal of LGBT Issues in Counseling, 4*, 135–159.

Association for Lesbian, Gay, Bisexual, and Transgender Issues in Counseling Lesbian, Gay, Bisexual, Queer, Intersex, Questioning and Ally Competencies Taskforce. (2012). *ALGBTIC competencies for counseling LGBQQIA individuals.* Retrieved from https://www.counseling.org/docs/ethics/algbtic-2012-07.pdf?sfvrsn=2

Balsam, K. F., Molina, Y., Blayney, J. A., Dillworth, T., Zimmerman, L., & Kaysen, D. (2015). Racial/ethnic differences in identity and mental health outcomes among young sexual minority women. *Cultural Diversity and Ethnic Minority Psychology, 21*(3), 380.

Beaumont, E. A., Galpin, A. J., & Jenkins, P. E. (2012). "Being kinder to myself": A prospective comparative study, exploring post-trauma therapy outcome measures, for two groups of clients, receiving either cognitive behaviour therapy or cognitive behaviour therapy and compassionate mind training. *Counselling Psychology Review, 27*(1), 31–43.

Blackledge, J. T., & Hayes, S. C. (2001). Emotion regulation in acceptance and commitment therapy. *Journal of Clinical Psychology, 57*(2), 243–255.

Braehler, C., Gumley, A., Harper, J., Wallace, S., Norrie, J., & Gilbert, P. (2013). Exploring change processes in compassion focused therapy in psychosis: Results of a feasibility randomized controlled trial. *British Journal of Clinical Psychology, 52*(2), 199–214.

Busch, A. M., Kanter, J. W., Callaghan, G. M., Baruch, D. E., Weeks, C. E., & Berlin, K. S. (2009). A micro-process analysis of functional analytic psychotherapy's mechanism of change. *Behavior Therapy, 40*(3), 280–290.

Callaghan, G. M., Gregg, J. A., Marx, B. P., Kohlenberg, B. S., & Gifford, E. (2004). FACT: The utility of an integration of functional analytic psychotherapy and acceptance and commitment therapy to alleviate human suffering. *Psychotherapy: Theory, Research, Practice, Training, 41*(3), 195–207.

Callaghan, G. M., Summers, C. J., & Weidman, M. (2003). The treatment of histrionic and narcissistic personality disorder behaviors: A single-subject demonstration of clinical improvement using functional analytic psychotherapy. *Journal of Contemporary Psychotherapy, 33*(4), 321–339.

Chambers, R., Gullone, E., & Allen, N. B. (2009). Mindful emotion regulation: An integrative review. *Clinical Psychology Review, 29*(6), 560–572.

Chambless, D. L., & Hollon, S. D. (1998). Defining empirically supported therapies. *Journal of Consulting and Clinical Psychology, 66*(1), 7.

Chartier, M., Vinatieri, T., DeLonga, K., McGlynn, L. M., Gore-Felton, C., & Koopman, C. (2010). A pilot study investigating the effects of trauma, experiential avoidance, and disease management in HIV-positive MSM using methamphetamine. *Journal of the International Association of Physicians in AIDS Care, 9*(2), 78–81.

Chiesa, M. (1994). *Radical behaviorism: The philosophy and the science.* Authors Cooperative.

Cochran, S. D., & Mays, V. M. (2009). Burden of psychiatric morbidity among lesbian, gay, and bisexual individuals in the California Quality of Life survey. *Journal of Abnormal Psychology, 118*(3), 647–658.

Cohen, J. M., Feinstein, B. A., Rodriguez-Seijas, C., Taylor, C. B., & Newman, M. G. (2016). Rejection sensitivity as a transdiagnostic risk factor for internalizing psychopathology among gay and bisexual men. *Psychology of Sexual Orientation and Gender Diversity, 3*(3), 259–264.

Courtois, C. A. (2004). Complex trauma, complex reactions: Assessment and treatment. *Psychotherapy: Therapy, Research, Practice, Training, 41*(4), 412–425.

Courtois, C. A., & Ford, J. D. (2012). *Treatment of complex trauma: A sequenced, relationship-based approach.* New York, NY: Guilford.

D'Augelli, A. R. (1989). Lesbians' and gay men's experiences of discrimination and harassment in a university community. *American Journal of Community Psychology, 17*(3), 317–321.

Dearing, R. L., Stuewig, J., & Tangney, J. P. (2005). On the importance of distinguishing shame from guilt: Relations to problematic alcohol and drug use. *Addictive Behaviors*, *30*(7), 1392–1404.

Dearing, R. L., & Tangney, J. P. E. (2011). *Shame in the therapy hour*. Washington, DC: American Psychological Association.

Downs, A. (2005). *The velvet rage*. Boston, MA: Da Capo Press.

Dyar, C., Feinstein, B. A., Eaton, N. R., & London, B. (2018). The mediating roles of rejection sensitivity and proximal stress in the association between discrimination and internalizing symptoms among sexual minority women. *Archives of Sexual Behavior*, *47*(1), 205–218.

Elsesser, S. A., Biello, K. B., Taylor, S. W., Tomassilli, J. C., Safren, S. A., & Mayer, K. H. (2015, July). *Absence of sexual behavioral disinhibition in a PrEP adherence trial: Considerations for medical providers who prescribe PrEP for men who have sex with men (MSM)*. Poster presented at the 8th International AIDS Society Conference on HIV Pathogenesis, Treatment & Prevention; Vancouver, Canada.

Ferro-Garcia, R., Lopez-Bermdez, M. A., & Valero-Aguayo, L. (2012). Treatment of a disorder of self through functional analytic psychotherapy. *International Journal of Behavioral Consultation and Therapy*, *7*(2–3), 45–51.

Frost, D. M., & Meyer, I. H. (2012). Measuring community connectedness among diverse sexual minority populations. *Journal of Sex Research*, *49*(1), 36–49.

Gale, C., Gilbert, P., Read, N., & Goss, K. (2014). An evaluation of the impact of introducing compassion focused therapy to a standard treatment programme for people with eating disorders. *Clinical Psychology & Psychotherapy*, *21*(1), 1–12.

Gaudiano, B. A. (2008). Cognitive–behavioral therapies: Achievements and challenges. *Evidence-Based Mental Health*, *11*(1), 5.

Gifford, E. V., Kohlenberg, B. S., Hayes, S. C., Pierson, H. M., Piasecki, M. P., Antonuccio, D. O., & Palm, K. M. (2011). Does acceptance and relationship focused behavior therapy contribute to bupropion outcomes? A randomized controlled trial of functional analytic psychotherapy and acceptance and commitment therapy for smoking cessation. *Behavior Therapy*, *42*, 700–715.

Gilbert, P. (2010). *Compassion focused therapy: Distinctive features*. New York, NY: Routledge.

Gilbert, P. (2014). The origins and nature of compassion focused therapy. *British Journal of Clinical Psychology*, *53*(1), 6–41.

Gilbert, P., & Procter, S. (2006). Compassionate mind training for people with high shame and self-criticism: Overview and pilot study of a group therapy approach. *Clinical Psychology & Psychotherapy*, *13*(6), 353–379.

Gold, S. D., Dickstein, B. D., Marx, B. P., & Lexington, J. M. (2009). Psychological outcomes among lesbian sexual assault survivors: An examination of the roles of internalized homophobia and experiential avoidance. *Psychology of Women Quarterly*, *33*(1), 54–66.

Gold, S. D., Feinstein, B. A., Skidmore, W. C., & Marx, B. P. (2011). Childhood physical abuse, internalized homophobia, and experiential avoidance among lesbians and gay men. *Psychological Trauma: Theory, Research, Practice, and Policy*, *3*(1), 50.

Gold, S. D., Marx, B. P., & Lexington, J. M. (2007). Gay male sexual assault survivors: The relations among internalized homophobia, experiential avoidance, and psychological symptom severity. *Behaviour Research and Therapy*, *45*(3), 549–562.

Graham, R., Berkowitz, B., Blum, R., Bockting, W., Bradford, J., de Vries, B., . . . Makadon, H. (2011). *The health of lesbian, gay, bisexual, and transgender people: Building a foundation for better understanding.* Washington, DC: Institute of Medicine.

Gratz, K. L., & Tull, M. T. (2010). Emotion regulation as a mechanism of change in acceptance- and mindfulness-based treatments. In R. A. Baer (Ed.), *Assessing mindfulness and acceptance processes in clients: Illuminating the theory and practice of change* (pp. 107–133). Oakland, CA: New Harbinger.

Halpert, S. C., & Pfaller, J. (2001). Sexual orientation and supervision: Theory and practice. *Journal of Gay & Lesbian Social Services, 13*(3), 23–40.

Hastings, M. E., Northman, L., & Tangney, J. P. (2000). Shame, guilt, and suicide. In T. Joiner & M. D. Rudd (Eds.), *Suicide science: Expanding the boundaries* (pp. 67–79). Norwell, MA: Kluwer.

Hatzenbuehler, M. L. (2009). How does sexual minority stigma "get under the skin"? A psychological mediation framework. *Psychological Bulletin, 135*(5), 707–730.

Hatzenbuehler, M. L., McLaughlin, K. A., & Nolen-Hoeksema, S. (2008). Emotion regulation and internalizing symptoms in a longitudinal study of sexual minority and heterosexual adolescents. *Journal of Child Psychology and Psychiatry, 49*(12), 1270–1278.

Haworth, K., Kanter, J. W., Tsai, M., Kuczynski, A. M., Rae, J. R., & Kohlenberg, R. J. (2015). Reinforcement matters: A preliminary, laboratory-based component-process analysis of functional analytic psychotherapy's model of social connection. *Journal of Contextual Behavioral Science, 4*, 281–291.

Hayes, A. M., & Feldman, G. (2004). Clarifying the construct of mindfulness in the context of emotion regulation and the process of change in therapy. *Clinical Psychology: Science and Practice, 11*(3), 255–262.

Hayes, S. C., Strosahl, K. D., & Wilson, K. G. (1999). *Acceptance and commitment therapy: An experiential approach to behavior change.* New York, NY: Guilford.

Hayes, S. C., Villatte, M., Levin, M., & Hildebrandt, M. (2011). Open, aware, and active: Contextual approaches as an emerging trend in the behavioral and cognitive therapies. *Annual Review of Clinical Psychology, 7*, 141–168.

Heck, N. C., Mirabito, L. A., LeMaire, K., Livingston, N. A., & Flentje, A. (2017). Omitted data in randomized controlled trials for anxiety and depression: A systematic review of the inclusion of sexual orientation and gender identity. *Journal of Consulting and Clinical Psychology, 85*(1), 72.

Hendricks, M. L., & Testa, R. J. (2012). A conceptual framework for clinical work with transgender and gender nonconforming clients: An adaptation of the minority stress model. *Professional Psychology: Research and Practice, 43*(5), 460.

Hofmann, S. G., & Asmundson, G. J. (2008). Acceptance and mindfulness-based therapy: New wave or old hat? *Clinical Psychology Review, 28*, 1–16.

Holman, G., Kanter, J., Tsai, M., & Kohlenberg, R. (2017). *Functional analytic psychotherapy made simple: A practical guide to therapeutic relationships.* Oakland, CA: New Harbinger.

Hughto, J. M. W., Reisner. S. L., & Pachankis, J. E. (2015). Transgender stigma and health: A critical review of stigma determinants, mechanisms, and interventions. *Social Science & Medicine, 147*, 222–231.

Israel, T., Gorcheva, R., Burnes, T. R., & Walther, W. A. (2008). Helpful and unhelpful therapy experiences of LGBT clients. *Psychotherapy Research, 18*(3), 294–305.

Jazaieri, H., Jinpa, G. T., McGonigal, K., Rosenberg, E. L., Finkelstein, J., Simon-Thomas, E., ... Goldin, P. R. (2013). Enhancing compassion: A randomized controlled trial of a compassion cultivation training program. *Journal of Happiness Studies, 14*(4), 1113–1126.

Kabat-Zinn, J. (2009). *Full catastrophe living: Using the wisdom of your body and mind to face stress, pain, and illness.* New York, NY: Delta.

Kazdin, A. E. (1981). Drawing valid inferences from case studies. *Journal of Consulting and Clinical Psychology, 49*(2), 183.

Kazdin, A. E. (2011). *Single-case research designs: Methods for clinical and applied settings.* New York, NY: Oxford University Press.

Keng, S. L., & Liew, K. W. L. (2017). Trait mindfulness and self-compassion as moderators of the association between gender nonconformity and psychological health. *Mindfulness, 8*(3), 615–626.

Klein, A., & Golub, S. A. (2016). Family rejection as a predictor of suicide attempts and substance misuse among transgender and gender nonconforming adults. *LGBT Health, 3*(3), 193–199.

Kohlenberg, B. S., & Callaghan, G. M. (2010). FAP and acceptance and commitment therapy (ACT): Similarities, divergence, and integration. In J. W. Kanter, M. Tsai, & R. J. Kolhenberg (Eds.), *The practice of functional analytic psychotherapy* (pp. 31–46). New York, NY: Springer.

Kohlenberg, R. J., Kanter, J. W., Bolling, M. Y., Parker, C. R., & Tsai, M. (2002). Enhancing cognitive therapy for depression with functional analytic psychotherapy: Treatment guidelines and empirical findings. *Cognitive and Behavioral Practice, 9*, 213–229.

Kohlenberg, R. J., & Tsai, M. (1991). *Functional analytic psychotherapy: Creating intense and curative therapeutic relationships.* New York, NY: Plenum.

Kronner, H. W. (2013). Use of self-disclosure for the gay male therapist: The impact on gay males in therapy. *Journal of Social Service Research, 39*(1), 78–94.

Landes, S. L., Kanter, J. W., Weeks, C. E., & Busch, A. M. (2013). The impact of the active components of functional analytic psychotherapy on idiographic target behaviors. *Journal of Contextual Behavioral Science, 2*, 49–57.

Lee, D. A., Scragg, P., & Turner, S. (2001). The role of shame and guilt in traumatic events: A clinical model of shame-based and guilt-based PTSD. *Psychology and Psychotherapy: Theory, Research, and Practice, 74*(4), 451–466.

Leleux-Labarge, K., Hatton, A. T., Goodnight, B. L., & Masuda, A. (2015). Psychological distress in sexual minorities: Examining the roles of self-concealment and psychological inflexibility. *Journal of Gay & Lesbian Mental Health, 19*(1), 40–54.

Leskela, J., Dieperink, M., & Thuras, P. (2002). Shame and posttraumatic stress disorder. *Journal of Traumatic Stress, 15*(3), 223–226.

Lester, D. (1998). The association of shame and guilt with suicidality. *Journal of Social Psychology, 138*(4), 535–536.

Linehan, M. (1993). *Cognitive–behavioral treatment of borderline personality disorder.* New York, NY: Guilford.

Lizarazo, N. E., Munoz-Martinez, A. M., Santos, M. M., & Kanter, J. W. (2015). A within-subjects evaluation of the effects of functional analytic psychotherapy on in-session and out-of-session client behavior. *Psychological Record, 65*, 463–474.

Lopez-Bermudez, M. A., Ferro-Garcia, R., & Calvillo, M. (2010). An application of functional analytic psychotherapy in a case of anxiety panic disorder without agoraphobia. *International Journal of Behavioral Consultation and Therapy, 6*(4), 356–372.

Lucre, K. M., & Corten, N. (2013). An exploration of group compassion-focused therapy for personality disorder. *Psychology and Psychotherapy: Theory, Research, and Practice, 86*(4), 387–400.

Lyons, A. (2016). Mindfulness attenuates the impact of discrimination on the mental health of middle-aged and older gay men. *Psychology of Sexual Orientation and Gender Diversity, 3*(2), 227.

Maitland, D. W., Petts, R. A., Knott, L. E., Briggs, C. A., Moore, J. A., & Gaynor, S. T. (2016). A randomized controlled trial of functional analytic psychotherapy versus watchful waiting: Enhancing social connectedness and reducing anxiety and avoidance. *Behavior Analysis: Research and Practice, 16*(3), 103.

Malyon, A. K. (1982). Psychotherapeutic implications of internalized homophobia in gay men. *Journal of Homosexuality, 7*(2–3), 59–69.

Masuda, A., Tully, E. C., Drake, C. E., Tarantino, N., Ames, A. M., & Larson, D. G. (2017). Examining self-concealment within the framework of psychological inflexibility and mindfulness: A preliminary cross-sectional investigation. *Current Psychology, 36*(1), 184–191.

Matos, M., Carvalho, S. A., Cunha, M., Galhardo, A., & Sepodes, C. (2017). Psychological flexibility and self-compassion in gay and heterosexual men: How they relate to childhood memories, shame, and depressive symptoms. *Journal of LGBT Issues in Counseling, 11*(2), 88–105.

Matthews, C. R., Lorah, P., & Fenton, J. (2006). Treatment experiences of gays and lesbians in recovery from addiction: A qualitative inquiry. *Journal of Mental Health Counseling, 28*(2), 111–132.

Mayhew, S. L., & Gilbert, P. (2008). Compassionate mind training with people who hear malevolent voices: A case series report. *Clinical Psychology & Psychotherapy, 15*(2), 113–138.

McClafferty, C. (2012). Expanding the cognitive behavioral therapy traditions: An application of functional analytic psychotherapy treatment in a case study of depression. *International Journal of Behavioral Consultation and Therapy, 7*(2–3), 90–95.

Mereish, E. H., & Poteat, V. P. (2015). A relational model of sexual minority mental health and physical health: The negative effects of shame on relationships, loneliness, and health. *Journal of Counseling Psychology, 62*(3), 425–437.

Meyer, I. H. (1995). Minority stress and mental health in gay men. *Journal of Health and Social Behavior, 36*, 38–56.

Meyer, I. H., & Ouellette, S. C. (2009). Unity and purpose at the intersections of racial/ethnic and sexual identities. In P. L. Hammack & B. J. Cohler (Eds.), *The story of sexual identity: Narrative perspectives on the gay and lesbian life course* (pp. 79–106). New York, NY: Oxford University Press.

Miller, W. R., C'de Baca, J., Matthews, D. B., & Wilbourne, P. L. (2001). *Personal values card sort.* Albuquerque, NM: University of New Mexico.

Mizock, L., & Lewis, T. K. (2008). Trauma in transgender populations: Risk, resilience, and clinical care. *Journal of Emotional Abuse, 8*(3), 335–354.

Moradi, B., Wiseman, M. C., DeBlaere, C., Goodman, M. B., Sarkees, A., Brewster, M. E., & Huang, Y. P. (2010). LGB of color and White individuals' perceptions of heterosexist stigma, internalized homophobia, and outness: Comparisons of levels and links. *The Counseling Psychologist, 38*(3), 397–424.

Morrison, A. P. (2008). The analyst's shame. *Contemporary Psychoanalysis, 44*(1), 65–82.

Nabors, N. A., Hall, R. L., Miville, M. L., Nettles, R., Pauling, M. L., & Ragsdale, B. L. (2001). Multiple minority group oppression: Divided we stand? *Journal of the Gay and Lesbian Medical Association, 5*(3), 101–105.

Neff, K. (2003). Self-compassion: An alternative conceptualization of a healthy attitude toward oneself. *Self and Identity, 2*(2), 85–101.

Neff, K. D., & Germer, C. K. (2013). A pilot study and randomized controlled trial of the mindful self-compassion program. *Journal of Clinical Psychology, 69*(1), 28–44.

Neff, K. D., Kirkpatrick, K. L., & Rude, S. S. (2007). Self-compassion and adaptive psychological functioning. *Journal of Research in Personality, 41*(1), 139–154.

Odets, W. (1995). *In the shadow of the epidemic: Being HIV-negative in the age of AIDS.* Durham, NC: Duke University Press.

Orth, U., Berking, M., & Burkhardt, S. (2006). Self-conscious emotions and depression: Rumination explains why shame but not guilt is maladaptive. *Personality and Social Psychology Bulletin, 32*(12), 1608–1619.

Oshiro, C. K. B., Kanter, J., & Meyer, S. B. (2012). A single-case experimental demonstration of functional analytic psychotherapy with two clients with severe interpersonal problems. *International Journal of Behavioral Consultation and Therapy, 7*(2–3), 111–116.

Pachankis, J. E., Goldfried, M. R., & Ramrattan, M. E. (2008). Extension of the rejection sensitivity construct to the interpersonal functioning of gay men. *Journal of Consulting and Clinical Psychology, 76*(2), 306.

Pachankis, J. E., & Hatzenbuehler, M. L. (2013). The social development of contingent self-worth in sexual minority young men: An empirical investigation of the "best little boy in the world" hypothesis. *Basic and Applied Social Psychology, 35*(2), 176–190.

Pachankis, J. E., Hatzenbuehler, M., L., Rendina, H. J., Safren, S. A., & Parsons, J. T. (2015). LGB-affirmative cognitive–behavioral therapy for young adult gay and bisexual men: A randomized controlled trial of a transdiagnostic minority stress approach. *Journal of Consulting and Clinical Psychology, 83*(5), 875–889.

Pearlman, L. A., & Courtois, C. A. (2005). Clinical applications of the attachment framework: Relational treatment of complex trauma. *Journal of Traumatic Stress, 18*(5), 449–459.

Pepping, C. A., Lyons, A., McNair, R., Kirby, J. N., Petrocchi, N., & Gilbert, P. (2017). A tailored compassion-focused therapy program for sexual minority young adults with depressive symptomatology: Study protocol for a randomized controlled trial. *BMC Psychology, 5*(1), 5.

Plummer, M. D. (2010). FAP with sexual minorities. In J. Kanter, M. Tsai, & R. J. Kohlenberg (Eds.), *The practice of functional analytic psychotherapy* (pp. 149–172). New York, NY: Springer.

Potoczniak, D. J., Aldea, M. A., & DeBlaere, C. (2007). Ego identity, social anxiety, social support, and self-concealment in lesbian, gay, and bisexual individuals. *Journal of Counseling Psychology, 54*(4), 447.

Puckett, J. A., Woodward, E. N., Mereish, E. H., & Pantalone, D. W. (2015). Parental rejection following sexual orientation disclosure: Impact on internalized homophobia, social support, and mental health. *LGBT Health, 2*(3), 265–269.

Pulcu, E., Lythe, K., Elliott, R., Green, S., Moll, J., Deakin, J. F., & Zahn, R. (2014). Increased amygdala response to shame in remitted major depressive disorder. *PLoS One, 9*(1), e86900.

Reddy, S. D., Negi, L. T., Dodson-Lavelle, B., Ozawa-de Silva, B., Pace, T. W., Cole, S. P., . . . Craighead, L. W. (2013). Cognitive-based compassion training: A promising prevention strategy for at-risk adolescents. *Journal of Child and Family Studies*, *22*(2), 219–230.

Richards, C., Bouman, W. P., Seal, L., Barker, M. J., Nieder, T. O., & T'Sjoen, G. (2016). Non-binary or genderqueer genders. *International Review of Psychiatry*, *28*(1), 95–102.

Ritter, K., & Terndrup, A. I. (2002). *Handbook of affirmative psychotherapy with lesbians and gay men*. New York, NY: Guilford.

Roberts, A. L., Austin, B., Corliss, H. L., Vandermorris, A. K., & Koenen, K. C. (2010). Pervasive trauma exposure among US sexual orientation minority adults and risk of posttraumatic stress disorder. *American Journal of Public Health*, *100*(12), 2433–2441.

Roemer, L., Orsillo, S. M., & Salters-Pedneault, K. (2008). Efficacy of an acceptance-based behavioral therapy for generalized anxiety disorder: Evaluation in a randomized controlled trial. *Journal of Consulting and Clinical Psychology*, *76*, 1083–1089.

Rood, B. A., Reisner, S. L., Surace, F. I., Puckett, J. A., Maroney, M. R., & Pantalone, D. W. (2016). Expecting rejection: Understanding the minority stress experiences of transgender and gender-nonconforming individuals. *Transgender Health*, *1*(1), 151–164.

Ryan, C., Huebner, D., Diaz, R. M., & Sanchez, J. (2009). Family rejection as a predictor of negative health outcomes in White and Latino lesbian, gay, and bisexual young adults. *Pediatrics*, *123*(1), 346–352.

Ryan, C., Russell, S. T., Huebner, D., Diaz, R., & Sanchez, J. (2010). Family acceptance in adolescence and the health of LGBT young adults. *Journal of Child and Adolescent Psychiatric Nursing*, *23*(4), 205–213.

Segal, Z. V., Williams, J. M. G., & Teasdale, J. D. (2001). *Mindfulness-based cognitive therapy for depression*. New York, NY: Guilford.

Shapira, L. B., & Mongrain, M. (2010). The benefits of self-compassion and optimism exercises for individuals vulnerable to depression. *Journal of Positive Psychology*, *5*(5), 377–389.

Shelton, K., & Delgado-Romero, E. A. (2011). Sexual orientation microaggression: The experience of lesbian, gay, bisexual, and queer clients in psychotherapy. *Journal of Counseling Psychology*, *58*(2), 210–221.

Singh, A. A., & dickey, L. M. (Eds.). (2017). *Handbook of trans-affirmative counseling and psychological practice*. Washington, DC: American Psychological Association.

Skinta, M. D. (2014). Acceptance-and compassion-based approaches for invisible minorities: Working with shame among sexual minorities. In A. Masuda (Ed.), *Mindfulness and acceptance in multicultural competency: A contextual approach to sociocultural diversity in theory and practice* (pp. 213–232). Oakland, CA: Context Press.

Skinta, M. D., Balsam, K., & Singh, R. S. (2016). Healing the wounds of rejection: Deepening vulnerability and intimacy with functional analytic psychotherapy. In M. D. Skinta & A. Curtin (Eds.), *Mindfulness and acceptance for gender and sexual minorities: A clinician's guide to fostering compassion, connection, and equality using contextual strategies*. Oakland, CA: Context Press.

Skinta, M. D., & Curtin, A. (Eds.). (2016). *Mindfulness and acceptance for gender and sexual minorities: A clinician's guide to fostering compassion, connection, and equality using contextual strategies*. Oakland, CA: Context Press.

Skinta, M. D., & D'Alton, P. (2016). Mindfulness and acceptance for malignant shame. In M. D. Skinta & A. Curtin (Eds.), *Mindfulness and acceptance for gender and sexual minorities: A clinician's guide to fostering compassion, connection, and equality using contextual strategies.* Oakland, CA: Context Press.

Skinta, M. D., Lezama, M., Wells, G., & Dilley, J. W. (2015). Acceptance and compassion-based group therapy to reduce HIV stigma. *Cognitive and Behavioral Practice, 22*(4), 481–490.

Smith, J. (1980). Ego-dystonic homosexuality. *Comprehensive Psychiatry, 21*(2), 119–127.

Smith, L. C., Shin, R. Q., & Officer, L. M. (2012). Moving counseling forward on LGB and transgender issues: Speaking queerly on discourses and microaggressions. *The Counseling Psychologist, 40*(3), 385–408.

Szymanski, D. M., & Hilton, A. N. (2013). Fear of intimacy as a mediator of the internalized heterosexism-relationship quality link among men in same-sex relationships. *Contemporary Family Therapy, 35*(4), 760–772.

Szymanski, D. M., & Sung, M. R. (2010). Minority stress and psychological distress among Asian American sexual minority persons. *The Counseling Psychologist, 38*(6), 848–872.

Teasdale, J. D., Segal, Z. V., Williams, J. M. G., Ridgeway, V. A., Soulsby, J. M., & Lau, M. A. (2000). Prevention of relapse/recurrence in major depression by mindfulness-based cognitive therapy. *Journal of Consulting and Clinical Psychology, 68*(4), 615.

Testa, R. J., Habarth, J., Peta, J., Balsam, K., & Bockting, W. (2015). Development of the Gender Minority Stress and Resilience Measure. *Psychology of Sexual Orientation and Gender Diversity, 2*(1), 65.

Testa, R. J., Sciacca, L. M., Wang, F., Hendricks, M. L., Goldblum, P., Bradford, J., & Bongar, B. (2012). Effects of violence on transgender people. *Professional Psychology: Research and Practice, 43*(5), 452–459.

Thompson, R. J., & Berenbaum, H. (2006). Shame reactions to everyday dilemmas are associated with depressive disorder. *Cognitive Research and Practice, 30*(4), 415–425.

Tirch, D., Schoendorff, B., & Silberstein, L. R. (2014). *The ACT practitioner's guide to the science of compassion: Tools for fostering psychological flexibility.* Oakland, CA: New Harbinger.

Tsai, M., Callaghan, G. M., & Kohlenberg, R. J. (2013). The use of awareness, courage, therapeutic love, and behavioral interpretations in functional analytic psychotherapy. *Psychotherapy, 50*(3), 366–370.

Tsai, M., Kohlenberg, R. J., Kanter, J. W., Kohlenberg, B., Follette, W. C., & Callaghan, G. M. (2009). *A guide to functional analytic psychotherapy: Awareness, courage, love and behaviorism.* New York, NY: Springer.

Tucker-Seeley, R. D., Blow, A. J., Matsuo, H., & Taylor-Moore, R. (2010). Behavioral escape avoidance coping in African-American men who have sex with men. *Journal of Gay & Lesbian Social Services, 3*, 250–268.

van den Brink, E., & Koster, F. (2015). *Mindfulness-based compassionate living: A new training programme to deepen mindfulness with heartfulness.* New York, NY: Routledge.

Walloch, J. C., Cerezo, A., & Heide, F. (2012). Acceptance and commitment therapy to address eating disorder symptomatology in gay men. *Journal of LGBT Issues in Counseling, 6*(4), 257–273. doi:10.1080/15538605.2012.725648

Wilson, K. G. (2009). *Mindfulness for two: An acceptance and commitment therapy approach to mindfulness in psychotherapy.* Oakland, CA: New Harbinger.

Wilson, J. P., Dorzdek, B., & Turkovic, S. (2006). Posttraumatic shame and guilt. *Trauma, Violence, & Abuse, 7*(2), 122–141.

Wilson, P. A., & Yoshikawa, H. (2007). Improving access to health care among African-American, Asian and Pacific Islander, and Latino lesbian, gay, and bisexual populations. In I. H. Meyer & M. E. Northridge (Eds.), *The health of sexual minorities* (pp. 607–637). New York, NY: Springer.

Wong, M. R., & Cook. D. (1992). Shame and its contributions to PTSD. *Journal of Traumatic Stress, 5*(4), 557–562.

Yadavaia, J. E., & Hayes, S. C. (2012). Acceptance and commitment therapy for self-stigma around sexual orientation: A multiple baseline evaluation. *Cognitive and Behavioral Practice, 19*(4), 545–559.

18

Dialectical Behavior Therapy for Borderline Personality Disorder and Suicidality Among Sexual and Gender Minority Individuals

DAVID W. PANTALONE, COLLEEN A. SLOAN, AND ADAM CARMEL ■

In this chapter, we review the scientific literature on the use of dialectical behavior therapy (DBT) to treat borderline personality disorder (BPD) and suicidality among lesbian, gay, bisexual, and transgender (LGBT) individuals. We use "suicidality" intentionally to include suicide attempts and suicidal ideation, as well as self-harm behaviors. We review the emerging literature on the use of DBT for LGBT individuals struggling with BPD or suicidality, discuss the theoretical framework, and make recommendations for ways that therapists can skillfully apply a DBT conceptualization and intervention techniques to work effectively with LGBT clients. We include several detailed case studies to exemplify the suggested approach and, finally, discuss potential future directions.

OVERVIEW OF DIALECTICAL BEHAVIOR THERAPY

Dialectical behavior therapy is an evidence-based cognitive–behavioral therapy with demonstrated efficacy for improving the lives of individuals struggling with chronic suicidal behavior (for a review, see Panos, Jackson, Hasan, & Panos, 2014), including those who meet criteria for BPD (for a meta-analysis, see Kliem, Kröger, & Kosfelder, 2010), as well as for individuals struggling with other significant clinical problems, such as substance use disorders (Dimeff, Rizvi, Brown, & Linehan, 2000), eating disorders (Bankoff, Forbes, Karpel, & Pantalone, 2012), and trauma-related problems (Steil, Dyer, Priebe, Kleindienst, & Bohus, 2011). DBT is a principle-based (vs. protocol-based) treatment that is delivered in its standard form as a more intensive outpatient treatment compared to other therapies with approximately only 1 hour of clinical contact each week. Clients in standard DBT receive, for a period of 1 year or more, weekly individual therapy (1 hour), weekly skills training (2½ hours), and as-needed telephone consultation. Furthermore, DBT therapists participate in consultation team, which is a team of DBT therapists providing support, case consultation, and training to each other. Applications of the treatment have also been shown to be helpful with adolescents (Groves, Backer, van den Bosch, & Miller, 2012) and in inpatient settings (Bloom, Woodward, Susmaras, & Pantalone, 2012). In addition, the skills training component alone has shown some benefit for clients presenting with less severe symptoms (Valentine, Bankoff, Poulin, Reidler, & Pantalone, 2015). Given the preponderance of evidence, DBT has earned a designation as a "well-established" empirically supported treatment for BPD by the American Psychological Association, according to the criteria outlined by Chambless and Hollon (1998), and is recommended as an efficacious treatment for BPD by the American Psychiatric Association (2001).

DBT was developed to fill an important gap in the field of mental health treatment: decreasing chronic suicidality and self-harm behavior and increasing functional, adaptive responses in the face of intense negative emotions. Overall, the treatment goal is to create "a life worth living," a focus on building and maintaining positive elements in one's life over and above symptom reduction alone. One core feature of how DBT facilitates these positive changes is by a sustained focus on helping clients understand, identify, and manage their emotions. The treatment encourages the therapist to take the perspective, in terms of conceptualization and treatment, that emotion dysregulation is at the heart of the client's problems, such that the client's problematic behaviors are the direct result of overwhelming emotions or that they are the client's best (yet dysfunctional) attempts to decrease their distress. Furthermore, the treatment has a built-in assumption about the major pathway toward decreasing behaviors associated with out-of-control emotions (e.g., impulsivity), namely through skills training. This assumption has been supported empirically, for example, via findings from a component analysis in which interventions with a group skills training component significantly outperformed those without in terms of rates of nonsuicidal self-injury, depression, and anxiety (Linehan et al., 2015).

DIALECTICAL BEHAVIOR THERAPY FOR LGBT CLIENTS

Currently, DBT is the most widely disseminated (Carmel, Fruzzetti, & Rose, 2014) and, therefore, the first-line treatment for clients presenting with BPD or chronic suicidality. How common is BPD among LGBT individuals? The literature on the prevalence of BPD among LGBT individuals remains scant. Part of the difficulty with understanding the rates of BPD among LGBT individuals is the result of sexual orientation not being measured directly in population-level epidemiologic surveys of mental health problems. The published studies have, instead, relied on clinical samples with high acuity (e.g., psychiatric inpatients) and substantial comorbidities (e.g., substance use disorders). The findings from this small body of research are equivocal, especially given the methodologic weaknesses. Early reports indicated that BPD and "homosexuality" were significantly associated, especially among men (Dulit, Fyer, Miller, Sacks, & Frances, 1993), although recent reports using personality disorder constructs from the fifth edition of the *Diagnostic and Statistical Manual of Mental Disorders* (DSM-5; American Psychiatric Association, 2013) found stronger associations for lesbian and bisexual women and bisexual men (Russell, Pocknell, & King, 2017). There are even fewer studies examining BPD among transgender individuals. Furthermore, there is one study that presents lab-based evidence of clinician diagnostic bias. The authors discovered a sexual orientation by gender interaction, such that clinicians were more likely to "see" BPD symptoms in gay men coming out compared to lesbian women coming out (Eubanks-Carter & Goldfried, 2006). Those same therapists reported feeling more confident and willing to treat the lesbian clients and proffered that they would have a more favorable prognosis.

On the other hand, there is ample evidence that, unfortunately, suicidality and self-harm are common among LGBT individuals. Research demonstrates that sexual minority individuals are at higher risk of considering suicide compared to their heterosexual peers (for a meta-analysis, see King et al., 2008). These findings have been replicated across multiple samples comprising a variety of intersectional identities, including Latino and Asian American adults (25.3% vs. 8.3%, respectively; Cochran, Mays, Alegria, Ortega, & Takeuchi, 2007) and youth (40% vs. 10%, respectively, Safren & Heimberg, 1999). This alarming disparity has generated significant national attention, especially after a spate of well-publicized suicides of young sexual minority individuals in recent years (Hibbard, 2012). One of the most notable cases was that of Tyler Clementi, a freshman at Rutgers University. Tyler was secretly recorded by his roommate, Dharun Ravi, and the recording, which featured Tyler engaged in a private sexual encounter, was posted on social media. The following day, Tyler jumped to his death from the George Washington Bridge into the Hudson River. That same month, there were at least four other teenagers who killed themselves in response to homophobic bullying, as reported by the Gay, Lesbian, & Straight Education Network (2010).

Several published studies have found nonsignificant differences in rates of death by suicide comparing sexual minority and heterosexual individuals, but unfortunately the data on higher rates of suicide attempts for LGB individuals from samples collected throughout the world are much more consistent (Haas et al., 2010). Transgender individuals may be at an even higher risk of suicide. Approximately one-third of transgender individuals across diverse samples reported a history of suicide attempts: veterans (Blosnich et al., 2013), Chicago adolescents (Mustanski & Liu, 2013), and a statewide sample from Virginia (Goldblum et al., 2012). The federal government also called attention to suicide in sexual minority individuals in *Healthy People 2020* (Koh, 2010). Some research indicates that bisexual individuals may be at an especially elevated risk (Bolton & Sareen, 2011).

Epidemiologic data indicate that, at the very least, suicidality and self-harm are highly prevalent among LGBT individuals—probably more so than among their heterosexual and cisgender peers—and, thus, these individuals could be effectively treated with DBT. There are few published data about LGBT individuals diagnosed with BPD. However, given that DBT is a treatment that focuses on an idiographic conceptualization of a given client, DBT certainly could be a great help for LGBT individuals struggling with the emotional dysregulation and other symptoms consistent with BPD—especially given that DBT aims to target emotion dysregulation and the associated out-of-control behaviors (Lynch, Chapman, Rosenthal, Kuo, & Linehan, 2006), which likely underlie suicidality and self-harm across demographic groups.

Thus, it is clear that DBT could theoretically be useful to LGBT individuals. What do the data indicate in practice? Unfortunately, data in this area are startlingly absent. We could locate no published, peer-reviewed studies testing any variant of DBT (standard DBT, DBT skills only, etc.) in an LGBT sample—not even uncontrolled pilot studies. A literature search yields a few relevant entries (e.g., unpublished dissertations such as Worhach, 2016), which leads us to believe that the literature in this nascent area will grow in the near future as those investigators publish their work and conduct follow-up studies.

In the meantime, there are LGBT-identified clients reporting for therapy each day, including those who might benefit from DBT to address their BPD or suicidality, or the emotional dysregulation that underlies those behaviors. Given the lack of empirical evidence and the importance of advancing mental health treatment in this area, the remainder of this chapter focuses on (1) a discussion of the theoretical framework for DBT and its application for LGBT individuals, (2) some suggestions for adaptations to standard DBT, and (3) case studies that aim to showcase our recommendations in action. All of the following text is based on the results of our synthesis of the literature—all of which should be rigorously evaluated empirically.

FROM THE LGBT LITERATURE: MEYER'S MINORITY STRESS MODEL

One potential mechanism that explains LGBT health disparities—including the potential for BPD disparities and the known disparities in suicidality—is the way sexual orientation and gender identity impact those individuals' life experiences. Meyer's (2003) minority stress model summarizes significant empirical data on increased vulnerability to mental and physical health disparities for sexual minority individuals. Its gender-specific extension, the gender minority stress model (Hendricks & Testa, 2012), provides a theoretical framework for understanding the additional, specific minority stressors faced by transgender and gender nonconforming individuals. Empirical data on the gender-specific extension are beginning to appear in the literature (Timmins, Rimes, & Rahman, 2017).

Although minority stress models provide an important framework for understanding the contribution of stigma and marginalization to population-level mental health disparities, these theories do not adequately describe the specific mechanisms that lead to clinically significant distress in LGBT people (Hatzenbuehler, 2009). Moreover, these models center on the individual identity in lieu of the clinical distress, which limits their utility for informing clinical interventions (Johnson, Shipherd, & Walton, 2016). The advancement of targeted, effective mental health interventions necessitates the development of theoretical frameworks that utilize etiological and mechanistic models of mental health problems and clinical distress that are targeted to the specific circumstances of unique populations. Hatzenbuehler presented a theoretical model identifying emotion dysregulation as a psychological mediator between identity-based stress and the development of psychopathology. Indeed, some recent empirical work has identified associations between various minority stress processes and emotion dysregulation that, in turn, predicted sexual compulsivity (distressing, out-of-control sexual behavior) in a sample of gay and bisexual men (Pachankis et al., 2015).

FROM THE DIALECTICAL BEHAVIOR THERAPY LITERATURE: LINEHAN'S BIOSOCIAL MODEL OF EMOTION DYSREGULATION

The biosocial model of emotion dysregulation proposed by Linehan (1993) as the basis for DBT presents a framework to account for the etiology and maintenance of emotion regulation difficulties and associated areas of dysfunction, which are well documented in LGBT populations (Balsam, Beauchaine, Mickey, & Rothblum, 2005; Clements-Nolle, Marx, & Katz, 2006). The biosocial model posits that emotion dysregulation is an expectable, reasonable outcome of a transactional process that occurs between an individual with an emotionally vulnerable temperament (bio-) and an invalidating environment (-social). An emotionally vulnerable temperament is marked by emotional sensitivity (i.e., low threshold for emotions), emotional intensity, and prolonged duration of emotional experiences with a slow return to baseline (Crowell, Beauchaine, & Linehan, 2009; Linehan, 1993, 2014). An invalidating environment is characterized by the failure of the environment to acknowledge, understand, or accept an individual's expression of internal experiences (Linehan, 1993). Invalidation is especially prominent when important people in an individual's life (e.g., family of origin and friends) openly reject and/or do not tolerate the individual's expression of private internal experiences (Rizvi, Steffel, & Carson-Wong, 2013), such as sexual and/or gender identities. Thus, the biosocial model informs both the conceptualization and the treatment of the clinical presentation and distress that may ensue as a consequence of chronic invalidation and marginalization of LGBT identities, experiences, and expressions—meeting an important goal that minority stress models alone do not.

A "transactional" process, as indicated in the biosocial model (Linehan, 1993), more effectively captures the relationship between a marginalized individual and their environment, in that a transactional process refers to one wherein both entities simultaneously and constantly influence one another over time. This process differs from that within an "interactional" model, as indicated in the minority stress models (Hendricks & Testa, 2012; Meyer, 2003), in which a variable at a given level (e.g., a mental health problem) is triggered by another variable at a different level (e.g., minority stress). Moreover, within an interactional model, each variable is considered to remain static over time. In contrast, variables within a transactional model are constantly changing via influence from other variables in the model. In the case of LGBT individuals, those who are living with LGBT identities and experiences are invalidated by the larger social environment by way of stigma and victimization (Ryan & Rivers, 2003), as well as discriminatory policies and legislation (e.g., bathroom bills and lack of workplace discrimination protections; Herman, 2013). This invalidation constantly affects the individual, who in turn may develop difficulties regulating emotions.

As difficulties increase and become more pervasive over time, a threshold-level clinical presentation of BPD may begin to develop that could, in turn, be misinterpreted by individuals in the social environment as being consistent with an LGBT identity—and not arising in response to the environment itself. This interpretation is, of course, further invalidating. Moreover, there is the potential for the environment to increasingly invalidate the expression of LGBT identities (e.g., public affection, pride parades, and self-disclosure). Overt displays of distress by LGBT individuals may elicit increasingly negative attention from the environment. As this transactional process continues, both dysregulation within the LGBT individual and the invalidating nature of environment could worsen.

The biosocial model of emotion dysregulation highlights the transaction between biological temperament and experiencing invalidation. Emotion dysregulation may result from the significant contribution of only one of the two factors, as with any diathesis–stress model; indeed, emotion dysregulation may occur even in the absence of strong biological vulnerability (Koerner, 2012). This point is an important consideration for the experiences of LGBT individuals, given the intensity, frequency, and chronicity of invalidation. Emotion dysregulation may be more common among LGBT individuals, which could be an important factor contributing to the identity-based health disparities they face.

BORDERLINE PERSONALITY DISORDER CRITERIA RECONCEPTUALIZED FOR TREATING LGBT CLIENTS

In developing DBT, Linehan (1993) reconceptualized the DSM diagnostic criteria for BPD to better fit the biosocial model of BPD and a behavioral model of case conceptualization. In DBT, problem behaviors are understood to arise from a transactional process occurring between emotional vulnerability (the bio-) and environments characterized by invalidation (the -social). This pattern informs how DBT therapists understand clients' problems and how to treat them. The reorganized categories include five areas of dysfunction: emotional, behavioral, interpersonal, cognitive, and self-dysfunction. Next, we consider each of the five categories in turn and discuss how DBT strategies can be used to treat them for LGBT clients.

Emotional dysregulation involves individuals experiencing difficulties regulating strong negative emotions such as sadness or shame. Heightened sensitivity to emotional cues might be common, as well as high reactivity and slow return to emotional baseline. Emotion regulation difficulties involve an inability to control physiological responses, to reorient attention away from emotion-related cues, and can account for mood-dependent behavior. Emotions are difficult to experience in the absence of escalation or blunting. Thus, individuals with emotional dysregulation can vacillate between emotional suppression and emotional outbursts.

LGBT individuals might be hesitant to disclose their sexual orientation or gender identity, and in the context of invalidating responses, they might disclose while in a state of high emotional arousal. For example, during a medical appointment, an individual might choose not to disclose that he is gay until after a provider engages in a heteronormative line of questioning about his physical health (e.g., presuming a client identifies as a heterosexual cisgender man and asking about his partners' choice of birth control methods). In this type of scenario, a client might reasonably experience frustration that one's sexual orientation or gender identity is assumed by the provider and might correct the provider while experiencing intense negative emotions of anger or shame. Thus, identity expression occurs in the context of high emotional intensity rather than from emotional baseline.

Behavioral dysregulation includes impulsive behaviors such as self-harm, binging and purging, fighting, or substance use. Individuals in a state of high emotional arousal might be more likely to experience behavioral dysregulation. In DBT, the maladaptive behaviors often serve to regulate negative emotions. Thus, problematic behavior might be conceptualized as negative reinforcement to distract from or decrease arousal. For example, when anger intensifies, self-injury (e.g., cutting) can have an effect of decreasing anger, thus increasing the likelihood that it will occur again in the future as a way to reduce strong negative affect.

LGBT individuals have been found to be at higher risk of substance use disorders, suicidality, and self-harm (McCabe, Hughes, Bostwick, West, & Boyd, 2009). Any problematic behaviors treated within therapy, which are collaboratively identified by both client and therapist, require in-depth discussion and analysis to determine the function(s) of that particular behavior for that client in various contexts. For example, suppose a client desires to reduce HIV exposure via decreasing the frequency of condomless sex. The therapist may hypothesize that this behavior functions as a way to increase intimacy and connection, despite the health risks. If the therapist and client determine, after engaging in a behavioral analysis of an episode of condomless sex, that the therapist is correct about the function and, thus, a desire for intimacy is motivating the behavior, it is essential for the therapist to validate the need for closeness while also working to meet the client's goal of reducing his HIV risk by changing the behavior through various other strategies, such as contingency clarification, to find more adaptive ways for the client to increase intimacy and connection.

Interpersonal dysregulation involves chaotic relationships, difficulties attending to relationships, ending relationships prematurely, and frantic efforts to avoid abandonment. Systemic oppression can result in many LGBT individuals having expectations of stigma and rejection in their relationships. As noted previously, LGBT individuals live with the invalidation of their identities and experiences by the larger social environment by way of stigma, victimization, and discriminatory policies and legislation. Core beliefs that one is unlovable or defective, and that others are likely to criticize or reject them, might be a possible outcome of this environment and must be considered within the context of the client's learning history because these views of self and others would be common and not dysfunctional thoughts.

One consequence of experiencing ongoing rejection is that an LGBT client might have difficulty making requests or saying no during interpersonal interactions, due to concerns that stating one's objectives might result in yet another rejection. The DBT interpersonal effectiveness skill of clarifying priorities of interpersonal effectiveness is relevant in these circumstances, in which an LGBT client might consider the styles of communication that might limit their self-respect, their ability to achieve their objectives, and alienate themselves within the relationships that are the most important. Interpersonal passivity is likely another consequence of experiencing ongoing rejection, where individuals might lack the ability to adequately express their objectives verbally or nonverbally. The options for intensity of making a request skill (which helps clients determine the optimal level of intensity they might use to make a request or say no) allows the therapist to coach the client to consider carefully the various factors influencing the intensity of communication to best fit the situation.

Cognitive dysregulation pertains to difficulties controlling attention, dissociation, paranoia, and transient stress-induced psychosis. One consequence of an invalidating environment is that individuals might struggle with balanced and objective thinking. Maintaining an objective position about one's environment is difficult when the environment is unsupportive, critical, or punishing of one's private experience—as is the case for many LGBT individuals. Mindfulness skills can allow the client to increase control of their mind, instead of letting their mind control them, and, more generally, to increase participation with awareness that often has the effect of improving cognitive regulation.

Cognitive dysregulation can also pertain to rigid and distorted thinking. Nonjudgmental awareness (mindfulness) is particularly useful for LGBT individuals who might have core beliefs of being defective and unlovable and who might have underlying assumptions that reflect this belief, as noted previously. For example, coaching a client to step back and notice the thought, "No one would ever date me" might have the effect of creating distance from the thought—and this decentering might have the effect of reducing the emotional intensity associated with these cognitions, such as shame. Cognitive dysregulation is also a component of high emotional arousal, such as in the treatment of dissociative symptoms or transient stress-induced psychosis. The therapist might consider coaching the client to use mindfulness or distress tolerance skills to reduce physiological arousal when encountering prompting events for dissociation or stress-related paranoid ideation. For example, while coaching a transgender client about having a difficult conversation with their medical provider (such that the dissociation would be likely to occur in their interaction because of the high emotional arousal), the therapist might encourage the client to practice the distress tolerance skills of paced breathing and paired muscle relaxation while in the waiting room prior to coming into contact with the challenging situation.

Self-dysregulation involves difficulties knowing who one is, what one's values are, and with an overall unstable sense of self. A product of the invalidating environment for many LGBT individuals is that their sense of identity, and expression of that identity, is actively punished by the larger sociocultural environment—such as public debates about sodomy laws, marriage rights, and bathroom bills—and, as a result, likely becomes associated with a deep shame or thoughts or beliefs about being defective. One characteristic of the invalidating environment is that it oversimplifies the ease of problem-solving. Transgender or gender non-binary individuals might take on the characteristics of this environmental pattern by, for example, setting unrealistic goals and expectations of themselves about their gender expression, such that they "need to pass 100% of the time" or else their gender affirmation process has been unsuccessful. Therapists use a variety of DBT mindfulness skills to increase self-regulation. The wise mind skill, which balances reason and rational thinking with emotional states of being, is a useful skill for working toward replacing the self-dysregulation deficits with self-regulation capabilities. Wise mind emphasizes the client accessing their own wisdom and making a decision on a given question while striking this balance (rather than making decisions in a state of mind driven purely by emotion). Therapists working with LGBT clients must remember that the clients' values may not always be aligned with the values of others in their environment. For example, the wise mind value of a gay adolescent might be that individuals should be encouraged to disclose their bisexual sexual orientation when meeting new people, which might be in sharp contrast to values emphasized in their larger family or community that might wish to minimize sexual orientation disclosure to manage the family's own sense of embarrassment.

APPLICATION/ADAPTATION OF STANDARD DIALECTICAL BEHAVIOR THERAPY FOR LGBT CLIENTS

The four modes of standard DBT are DBT skills training, individual therapy, telephone consultation, and consultation team for the therapist. We offer a conceptualization for applying these modes in the treatment of LGBT clients. The function of DBT skills group is to acquire and strengthen behavioral skills in regulating emotions, tolerating distress, increasing mindfulness, and interpersonal effectiveness. Several of these skills are particularly useful for working with problems experienced by LGBT individuals (Table 18.1). More generally, if the skills training occurs in a group (as in standard DBT), the therapist should consider whether the group dynamics provide an affirmative environment for LGBT clients. Based on their learning history, LGBT clients may expect others to be unwelcoming and dismissive of their social identities; indeed, this expectation of rejection is an important part of Meyer's (2003) minority stress model. Without the group leaders orienting the group to the use of pronouns in a sensitive manner, the use of same-sex relationships in hypothetical examples, and modeling nonjudgmental approaches to discussing sexual orientation or gender identity, the group runs the risk of becoming yet another invalidating environment for the LGBT client.

In individual therapy, the goal is for the therapist to help the client apply the behavioral skills learned within group toward addressing the relevant problem behaviors or problems in the client's life. Problems could include life-threatening (suicidal) behaviors and behaviors that interfere with therapy, as well as problems that interfere with overall quality of life. Problems unique to the LGBT community require individual therapists to think flexibility and compassionately while taking into account LGBT individuals' unique learning history. For example, a therapist working with a cisgender gay male client might target a behavior such as barebacking (intentional unprotected anal sex, which presents a high risk for HIV acquisition). However, it may be difficult for the therapist to balance acceptance and change, which might give the appearance that the therapist is failing to consider adequately the function of the behavior, or is responding to the behavior judgmentally. A client's barebacking behavior could be viewed as careless and risky; however, it would be important for the therapist to explore how this behavior might function instead to increase intimacy and connection. Validating the need for closeness would be warranted, if this were the case, while at the same time working toward understanding or reducing HIV sexual risk through whatever strategies the client was willing to try (e.g., behavioral analysis, contingency clarification, and problem-solving other ways to increase intimacy).

Telephone consultation involves supporting the client to phone the therapist for structured and skills-focused calls outside of session as a means of generalizing skills into the client's natural environment. LGBT individuals encounter numerous stressors within their everyday lives—because many basic aspects of their identity are often dismissed, overlooked, and invalidated, often in subtle ways, based on the invalidating environments in which they live—that a therapist could overlook easily. Thus, environments perceived as benign to a therapist may be filled with the high possibility of threat to a transgender client, for example. Effective skills generalization through telephone consultation with a transgender client involves mindfully identifying potential cues that might appear innocuous on their face (e.g., asking where the closest restroom is located) and applying skills to prepare

Table 18.1. APPLICATION OF DIALECTICAL PRINCIPLES AND DBT SKILLS TO WORK WITH LGBT CLIENTS

Acceptance Strategy		Change Strategy	
Mindfulness	• Encourage increased contact with a stable sense of self (e.g., attending to true sense of self despite societal context privileging the gender-binary and heteronormative identities). • Engage fully in identity-affirming activities. • Take a nonjudgmental stance toward oneself and others. • Practice loving kindness toward oneself in the face of discrimination. • Practice mindfulness of others to increase understanding of impact of gender transition and others' difficulties affirming identity (e.g., using wrong name or pronoun).	Emotion regulation	• Engage in value-congruent behavior to replace behaviors inconsistent with affirmed identity. • Problem-solve identity affirmation (e.g., seeking interventions to alter appearance/body) and barriers that emerge. • Problem-solve coping responses to discriminatory legislation, court cases, and news coverage of hate crimes or hate speakers. • Use opposite action to change emotions that interfere with self-affirmation or effective engagement in goal-directed behavior. • Increase social support and engagement in activities that elicit mastery or pleasure via engagement in identity-consistent activities.
Distress tolerance/ reality acceptance	• Acceptance of personal history (e.g., birth sex and given name, experiences as other gender, and previous identification as heterosexual). • Acceptance of discrimination history, binary gender, and heteronormative social systems and associated constructions. • Tolerate slow progress, unexpected outcomes of medical/physical interventions, lack of availability of services, and lack of widespread provider cultural competence. • Learn to self-sooth when experiencing psychological or physical pain. • Reduce suffering via acceptance of inevitable pain associated with societal marginalization.	Interpersonal effectiveness	• Cope ahead with anticipated identity disclosure difficulties. • Advocate for needs in health care settings specific to transition (e.g., request support letters from providers and change name or pronoun in medical record). • Effectively say "no" to experiences that are likely to increase identity-related distress (e.g., within relationships). • Request others to use preferred name and pronouns; request others to affirm relationship with same-sex partner. • Establish new relationships that affirm core identities, and renegotiate/end relationships that are non-affirming or destructive. • Learn to self-validate one's genuine identities despite invalidation.

and manage their response (e.g., the client is dismissed for wanting to use the restroom consistent with their gender identity and develops urges to self-harm). Individual therapy sessions can be spent identifying the cues and planning for relevant skills to improve the effectiveness of telephone consultation.

The DBT consultation team functions to address challenges to therapist motivation and manage therapist burnout through "therapy for the therapist," as well as to engage the group for assistance in conceptualization and treatment planning. DBT consultation teams should include time in their weekly meeting for the review of a recorded session or other ongoing didactic training. For teams to increase competence in working with LGBT clients, it can be helpful to plan for expert outside consultation to improve the clinicians' capacity to work effectively with LGBT clients. If there is expertise among a therapist on the team, part of the consultation team meeting can consist of reviewing their recorded sessions with LGBT clients and highlighting the interventions used and the culturally sensitive conceptualization followed. This modeling may aid other therapists on the team in working successfully with their own LGBT clients.

CASE STUDIES

Here, we present two case studies that aim to illustrate an LGBT-affirmative approach to DBT. Through these examples, we hope to demonstrate some ways that DBT can be culturally tailored for experiences of LGBT clients. The therapists in the examples consider the possibility that sexual orientation and gender identity are relevant to the client's developmental history and present challenges, without assuming that the identities themselves are pathological—and without assuming that the identities are related to the client's challenges per se. Our goal is to present a variety of clinical presentations, identities, and treatment settings across the examples.

CASE STUDY 1: LESBIAN CLIENT WITH SUICIDALITY HISTORY, TREATED WITH INDIVIDUAL DIALECTICAL BEHAVIOR THERAPY

In this case study, we present the conceptualization of a client in standard DBT's individual therapy. "Jen" is a 45-year-old, divorced, White, lesbian-identified cisgender women who met diagnostic criteria for bipolar I disorder and generalized anxiety disorder and had borderline personality features at intake. She has a history of poorly controlled bipolar I disorder due to medication non-adherence, and she reports that she is "taking meds more regularly" in the past year. She is the mother of a 17-year-old daughter from a previous marriage to a man that lasted for 20 years. They began divorce proceedings 3 years ago after Jen started the process of coming out to her family and friends as lesbian, and suicidal behaviors (e.g., suicide attempts of overdosing and suicide rehearsal behaviors of loading a gun) appear to have increased in the context of her coming out. During the 2-year period before coming out, she reported experiencing significant shame, self-doubt, social isolation, and behavioral withdrawal, leading to a significant decline in functioning. Jen was stable with a steady work history as an administrator in a small business; however, she stopped working during this time due to frequent hospitalizations following three suicide attempts. Jen is currently unemployed and is receiving psychiatric disability. She currently lives independently and is quite socially isolated compared to her situation several years ago. In the past year, Jen starting to become more involved in a sex-positive BDSM (bondage and discipline, sadism and masochism) "play community" and views this as her primary social group. She identifies that several members of this community have provided her with consistent social support, whereas others, including her family, have provided inconsistent support at best, and criticism and rejection at worst. Her experience of her family appears to fit the biosocial model in which she describes her opinions, views, and expressions of identity as being ignored and punished. Jen reports that she receives some financial support from her ex-husband and that she is estranged or distant from many other family members due to the turbulent nature of these relationships.

As a DBT clinician working with Jen, the primary target in the treatment hierarchy is her life-threatening behavior, specifically her suicidality. To target the behavior, the clinician conducted behavioral (chain) analyses of suicidal and any other life-threatening behaviors that occurred during the course of Jen's treatment, as well as previous behaviors with high lethality, to determine cues, triggers, and helpful strategies for moving through those dark periods. The clinician assesses both the topography and the function of Jen's suicidality (e.g., reducing painful affect), the prompting events that are likely to cue suicidal behavior (e.g., perceived criticism), and vulnerability factors related to Jen's physical health that increase her vulnerability to impulsivity or emotional reactivity (e.g., poor sleep and psychiatric medication non-adherence). Repeated behavioral analyses completed by Jen and her clinician over time enabled them to identify behavior patterns that facilitate better understanding of the factors that prompt, maintain, and reinforce suicidal behavior, thus resulting in an improved ability to cope by noticing these patterns earlier and working to modify the controlling variables to change the risky situation's trajectory.

One significant pattern for Jen is that her suicidal behavior appears to have increased in the context of her coming out. The clinician should consider research that supports the minority stress model, which posits that chronically high levels of stress are experienced by members of stigmatized minority groups, and that this might be relevant for Jen, particularly during various stages of the coming out process (Meyer, 2003). Jen's identity and social network shifted in this process from mother, wife, and employee within a heterosexual and middle-class community to homeless and indigent, with many of her former roles ending. The therapist infers and validates Jen's struggles as understandable, as anyone would be expected to struggle during the coming out process, especially in the context of losing important family and friend relationships, facing ostracism from one's heterosexual community, and a major shift in one's personal identity and values. The DBT therapist communicates the validity of Jen's position using high levels of validation. At the same time, using a primarily acceptance-based approach with Jen would overlook the important detail that she is becomes suicidal in response to these stressors and engages in a range of highly lethal suicidal behaviors. Jen will continue to be at high risk for suicide until her therapist can apply change-based interventions to expand her coping repertoire to more effectively manage problematic cognitions, emotions, and behaviors while she is in crisis. Finding the balance between the poles of acceptance and change is the task of the DBT therapist, guided by assistance from the larger consultation team. Although Jen's emotions of fear and sadness are justified given the significant losses and transitions she has experienced, the subsequent action of loading a gun and rehearsing her death is neither a justified nor a valid response. The therapist magnifies the dialectical tension between acceptance and change in certain moments, including by asking Jen for a commitment to "take suicide off the table" permanently, because a goal of DBT is to join collaboratively with the client to block pro-suicidal means of coping with pain and to actively work in therapy to address the problems that prompt suicidality. Jen's suicidality makes sense, given her significant distress (and lack of distress tolerance), and removing suicidality as a way of coping is the first priority in their work together.

Emotion regulation, distress tolerance, and mindfulness skills are helpful to integrate into situations when Jen encounters cues for suicidality. While having a difficult interaction with her daughter during their scheduled visitation, Jen observes judgmental thoughts ("I'm not worth being a mother") and related emotions (shame) and subsequent urges (to suicide). The DBT therapist works with Jen to generalize the DBT skills learned in her skills group to help reduce her emotional arousal and either change or accept the thoughts and emotions that arise.

The overarching goal in DBT is to help clients build and sustain a "life worth living." As such, DBT should not be considered a suicide prevention treatment. Thus, the DBT clinician must assess Jen's "life worth living" goals and allow these goals to be at the forefront of the treatment throughout. The DBT clinician understands that clients want to die for a good reason: Their lives are unbearable as they are currently being lived. Thus, it is imperative to identify the problems in life that drive the suicidality and actively work to resolve them. Jen's primary "life worth living" goals were to be more involved in an inclusive, sex-positive BDSM play community; to have close friendships with other lesbian mothers; to improve her relationship with her daughter; to have independent housing; and to start her own small business. If isolation, perceived abandonment, and thwarted belongingness are factors that drive suicidality, then increasing social contact, connectedness with a community, and creating a family of choice will likely result in a decrease in suicidality.

Emphasis on her goals, and the therapist communicating the belief to Jen that she could achieve them, was the typical meta-communication in each DBT session, regardless of whether the discussion explicitly focused on managing suicidal crises, accepting emotions that arose in response to grief/loss, or solving difficult problems relevant to her return to the workforce. Jen reduced all life-threatening behavior and stabilized after a year of standard DBT, and she noted that learning new coping skills and building more of a community related to her "life worth living" goals were key aspects to her recovery. Interpersonal effectiveness skills were particularly effective in helping Jen achieve her goals, including skills of connecting with people in her social circle, promoting self-respect, and enhancing relationship quality and depth. Jen's goal of increasing intimacy in her sex-positive BDSM play community can be achieved by generalizing these skills to communicate her preferences and limits with her community.

Case Study 2: Transgender Client with Borderline Personality Disorder, Treated in a Dialectical Behavior Therapy Skills Group

In this case study, we present the conceptualization of a client in DBT skills group, as part of standard DBT. "Sid" is a 25-year-old, partnered, Black, transgender man (female sex assigned at birth; male gender identity) with 12 years of formal education. At intake, Sid met diagnostic criteria for borderline personality disorder, major depressive disorder, post-traumatic stress disorder, and alcohol use disorder. Sid started a DBT skills training group 2 months ago, after being referred by an outpatient therapist. Six months ago, Sid changed her name (not legally) and identified as male, while also expressing a preference for the use of female pronouns (she/her). Sid recently switched her primary care to a clinic that specializes in LGBT health, and she has been exploring options for hormone treatment with her new primary care physician as a way to further her gender affirmation process. She currently binds her chest. She has been in a relationship with a women for the past 2 years and reports ongoing communication problems in their relationship that increased when Sid began sharing thoughts about transitioning. During group, Sid often discusses conflicts in her relationship. When the group seeks relevant examples to discuss skills use, she routinely shares examples of communication difficulties that she and her partner face. Sid lives independently with four roommates in what she describes as a "queer and trans friendly" home environment. She has worked in a number of retail positions since graduating high school. She denied a history of self-harm behavior; however, Sid endorsed periods of suicidal ideation during high school, including two instances when she communicated suicidal intent to friends. In response, she was escorted to the emergency department during one of these incidents but was not hospitalized. Since high school, Sid has struggled with problematic alcohol use and has maintained periods of sobriety for 2 or 3 months at a time. Relapsing on alcohol has resulted in Sid losing several jobs. She attends Alcoholics Anonymous meetings regularly. She is hopeful that DBT skills training group will help her "learn how to cope better with my drinking problem and my relationships."

The group leaders prepared themselves for Sid's arrival in group by considering that an incoming transgender client may have had a learning history such that, on the one hand, others are likely to be unwelcoming and dismissive of their gender identity or expression or, on the other hand, others may be overly attuned and invasive by asking intensely personal questions about their physicality (e.g., whether they have undergone surgery). A reaction consistent with either pole has the potential to alienate the transgender group members and activate emotions of anger, fear, or shame. Sid's group leaders discussed together in advance how to respond if such interactions were to occur. However, from the start, responsiveness, maintaining a nonjudgmental stance, expressing warm engagement, and explicitly communicating liking of the client are all components of reciprocal communication strategies that an LGBT-affirmative clinician will use. Sid identifies as male and prefers female pronouns, and the DBT group leaders use and model these strategies to be responsive and accommodating rather than impervious to the position of the client by overlooking their language preferences.

Reviewing group guidelines at the beginning of a new skills module provided an opportunity to create a culture of respect by discussing the use of gendered pronouns and the importance of observing limits about self-identification. The group leaders modeled fallibility and noted that anyone might make an error, while actively planning about how to respond when errors are made or if limits are crossed. Orienting the clients to group procedures and using didactic (psychoeducation) strategies are ways to provide more context for why the group would want to mindfully use gendered language or mindfully ask questions about one's gender identity. Contingency clarification, or highlighting the "if–then" association between behaviors and their consequences, might also prove useful if group members continue to struggle to understand why asking Sid personal questions about her physicality might have a negative impact. The group leaders hypothesized that clients who were insensitive to Sid in the group setting might communicate similarly in their relationships outside of group, thus indicating an interpersonal skills deficit that they targeted in the group itself. Group members' verbal and nonverbal communication styles were shaped by the group leaders over time to increase social awareness and overall interpersonal effectiveness, with benefits for Sid's comfort in the group and the other members' relationships within and outside of group.

Given DBT's emphasis on building a life worth living, group leaders worked with Sid to identify "life worth living" goals so that they could coach her in applying those skills to her relevant goals. The fact that Sid often referenced conflict with her partner was an indicator that improving relationship quality, increasing intimacy, and effective communication would likely be goals. Skills modules on mindfulness, interpersonal effectiveness, emotion regulation, and distress tolerance contain specific skills to increase behaviors consistent with these goals, and the group leaders helped Sid develop and generalize these skills across her contexts.

The group leaders taught the wise mind skill. The awareness of one's evolving gender identity is undoubtedly well-suited for the development of this skill. It becomes a wise mind decision for individuals such as Sid, who are faced with the dilemma of living as an outsider in one's body or living in a way that is consistent with one's gender identity despite the increased risk of loss and vulnerability to discrimination that comes with the process of gender affirmation.

Interpersonal effectiveness skills were, perhaps, most clearly linked with Sid's "life worth living" goal of improving her relationship with her partner. It appears that Sid's gender affirmation was an additional stressor in a relationship that already had significant conflict. When Sid expressed an interest in enhancing the relationship and increasing intimacy with her partner, the group leaders taught the GIVE skill, which emphasizes a *g*entle approach, *i*nterest in other person, *v*alidation of other perspective, and maintaining an *e*asy manner in one's interactions. With frequent miscommunication between Sid and her partner, especially about Sid's gender identity—that had the effect of Sid losing her self-respect—the group leaders suggested the FAST skill to increase self-respect in her communication by being fair and truthful, not apologizing excessively, and sticking to her values.

Distress tolerance skills were useful for Sid, given that her gender affirmation process resulted in turbulence within her closest relationships, which caused her significant anxiety. Sid dates women; therefore, the group leaders conceptualized that she had two phases of coming out—one for her sexual orientation and another for her gender identity—and both phases are likely to involve significant stressors, consistent with the minority stress model. The coming out process and the gender affirmation process both involved Sid's experiencing pain from losing aspects of her identity, experiencing conflict or rejection in her relationships, and increasing her vulnerability to further discrimination in addition to the discrimination she already experiences as a person of color. In the skill of radical acceptance, which is applicable to life-changing events that clients cannot change and therefore must adjust to, clients are taught the distinction between pain and suffering. Pain is the inevitable and understandable primary emotion response to environmental cues (e.g., Sid feels intense sadness when a close friend ends the friendship after Sid discloses her gender identity). Suffering is when one adds judgment, expectations, secondary emotions, and beliefs that increase overall distress and that are either not accurate or unnecessary to the situation (e.g., Sid blames herself for the relationship ending or contacts the friend, excessively asking if they can meet). If Sid has a tendency toward suffering (which is preventable) on top of pain (which is unpreventable), then a radical acceptance stance would involve coming into contact with the pain and reducing the suffering. A radically accepting stance does not condone discrimination or suggest the individual approves of or is passive in the face of discrimination; rather, it involves fully acknowledging the negative impact of the discrimination. Also included in the distress tolerance skills are the modified DBT skills for treating substance use disorders. Dialectical abstinence as applied to Sid's problematic drinking will involve maintaining sobriety (drawing from abstinence-based interventions) while simultaneously planning for a relapse by creating a crisis plan for her to follow if she starts drinking again in the future (drawing from harm reduction interventions).

Sid's response to 12 months of DBT skills group included increased skills and self-efficacy in managing difficult emotions and also tolerating distress in short-term crisis situations. This led to less problematic alcohol use and greater behavioral control even when strong emotions arose for her, including anger. The acceptance-based skills, such as radical acceptance, helped Sid tolerate long-term painful situations more skillfully, particularly in her relationship with her partner, while she simultaneously worked to utilize many change-based skills, such as the FAST skill in interpersonal effectiveness, to improve their communication.

FUTURE DIRECTIONS

Researchers interested in investigating DBT for treating BPD and suicidality have many potential future directions, given the dearth of published work in this area. Indeed, there are so few data in this area that each individual study that is published makes a contribution to the knowledge base. Future work should focus on four major areas.

First, studies with increased methodologic rigor (compared to that of existing studies) are sorely needed in the area of diagnosing BPD among LGBT individuals. Importantly, population-based studies that use random sampling strategies need to measure sexual orientation and gender identity alongside BPD, suicidality, and self-harm so that we can answer some of the basic epidemiologic questions about the co-occurrence of those experiences and identities. This could be accomplished by adding valid questions about sexual orientation and gender identity to future large-scale studies that examine the prevalence of mental disorders. Having this information would answer open questions about the true rates of BPD, suicidality, and self-harm in the general population, potentially providing information about the significance of the problem.

Another potentially fruitful area of research would be to replicate and extend the Eubanks-Carter and Goldfried (2006) study about provider bias in diagnosing BPD across genders—that is, gay versus lesbian identified clients. It is important to determine the extent to which clinician bias plays a role in what appear to be high rates of BPD diagnosis among LGBT individuals. Especially important would be to investigate the potential for the "identity disturbance" category of BPD symptoms, not to be conflated with the normative identity exploration that is typical for an individual coming to understand their non-cisgender or non-heterosexual identity in a strongly cisgenderist and heterosexist social context. It will be crucial to conduct research that helps clinicians understand and validate the identity development process of such individuals as anticipated and not pathological.

Pragmatically, it is essential to investigate what modifications should be made in terms of conceptualizing BPD, suicidality, and self-harm from a DBT framework and, consequently, the best ways to culturally tailor the components of standard DBT in order to provide the most effective treatment to LGBT clients. Relevant research questions would include the best, most efficacious changes to make to individual therapy, skills training, telephone consultation, and the consultation team. An excellent article on the rationale for cultural adaption of evidence-based treatments was written by Lau (2006). In it, she details the reasons why cultural adaption of an evidence-based treatment would be needed. For example, one principal reason would be if there are unique "contextual processes influencing vulnerability to and protection from target problems" (p. 297), which certainly appears to be the case for LGBT individuals. She also notes the types of adaptations that might be made: contextualizing content and enhancing engagement. Various adaptations are beginning to appear in the literature. For example, modifications to the teaching points in DBT skills, suggested by experts and sexual minority clients who had received DBT, have begun to be studied (as reported in a conference presentation by Cohen, Jackson, & Yadavaia, 2017). Significantly more of this type of research is needed to more fully understand the best ways to implement DBT for LGBT clients.

Finally, there are theoretical models that underlie LGBT health disparities (the minority stress model and the psychological mediation framework) and that facilitate the development and maintenance of BPD symptoms, including suicidality and self-harm (the biosocial model). In this chapter, we discussed some of the ways that the models might be integrated. However, empirical research is needed to investigate these constructs simultaneously in a diverse sample of LGBT individuals.

REFERENCES

American Psychiatric Association. (2001). Practice guideline for the treatment of patients with borderline personality disorder. *American Journal of Psychiatry, 158*(Suppl.), 1–5.

American Psychiatric Association. (2013). *Diagnostic and statistical manual of mental disorders* (5th ed.). Arlington, VA: American Psychiatric Publishing.

Balsam, K. F., Beauchaine, T. P., Mickey, R. M., & Rothblum, E. D. (2005). Mental health of lesbian, gay, bisexual, and heterosexual siblings: Effects of gender, sexual orientation, and family. *Journal of Abnormal Psychology, 114*(3), 471–476.

Bankoff, S. M., Forbes, H. E., Karpel, M. G., & Pantalone, D. W. (2012). A systematic review of dialectical behavior therapy for the treatment of eating disorders. *Eating Disorders, 20*(3), 196–215. doi:10.1080/10640266.2012.668478

Bloom, J. M., Woodward, E. N., Susmaras, T., & Pantalone, D. W. (2012). Use of dialectical behavior therapy in inpatient treatment of borderline personality disorder: A systematic review. *Psychiatric Services, 63*(9), 881–888. doi:10.1176/appi.ps.201100311

Blosnich, J. R., Brown, G. R., Shipherd, J. C., Kauth, M., Piegari, R. I., & Bossarte, R. M. (2013). Prevalence of gender identity disorder and suicide risk among transgender veterans utilizing Veterans Health Administration care. *American Journal of Public Health, 103*(10), e27–e32.

Bolton, S. L., & Sareen, J. (2011). Sexual orientation and its relation to mental disorders and suicide attempts: Findings from a nationally representative sample. *Canadian Journal of Psychiatry, 56*(1), 35–43.

Carmel, A., Fruzzetti, A. E., & Rose, M. L. (2014). Dialectical behavior therapy training to reduce clinical burnout in a public behavioral health system. *Community Mental Health Journal, 50*(1), 25–30.

Chambless, D. L., & Hollon, S. D. (1998). Defining empirically supported therapies. *Journal of Consulting and Clinical Psychology, 66*(1), 7–18.

Clements-Nolle, K., Marx, R., & Katz, M. (2006). Attempted suicide among transgender persons: The influence of gender-based discrimination and victimization. *Journal of Homosexuality, 51*, 53–69.

Cochran, S. D., Mays, V. M., Alegria, M., Ortega, A. N., & Takeuchi, D. (2007). Mental health and substance use disorders among Latino and Asian American lesbian, gay, and bisexual adults. *Journal of Consulting and Clinical Psychology, 75*(5), 785–794.

Cohen, J. M., Jackson, L., & Yadavaia, J. E. (2017, April). *LGB-affirmative DBT skills training for sexual minority veterans.* Poster presentation at the 37th Annual Conference of the Anxiety and Depression Association of America, San Francisco, CA.

Crowell, S. E., Beauchaine, T. P., & Linehan, M. M. (2009). A biosocial developmental model of borderline personality disorder: Elaborating and extending Linehan's theory. *Psychological Bulletin, 135*, 495–510.

Dimeff, L., Rizvi, S. L., Brown, M., & Linehan, M. M. (2000). Dialectical behavior therapy for substance abuse: A pilot application to methamphetamine-dependent women with borderline personality disorder. *Cognitive and Behavioral Practice, 7*(4), 457–468.

Dulit, R. A., Fyer, M. R., Miller, F. T., Sacks, M. H., & Frances, A. J. (1993). Gender differences in sexual preference and substance abuse of inpatients with borderline personality disorder. *Journal of Personality Disorders, 7*(2), 182–185.

Eubanks-Carter, C., & Goldfried, M. R. (2006). The impact of client sexual orientation and gender on clinical judgments and diagnosis of borderline personality disorder. *Journal of Clinical Psychology, 62*(6), 751–770.

Gay, Lesbian, and Straight Education Network. (2010). *GLSEN, PFLAG, the Trevor Project release statement on recent tragedies.* Retrieved from https://web.archive.org/web/20101004195050/http://www.glsen.org/cgi-bin/iowa/all/news/record/2634.html

Goldblum, P., Testa, R. J., Pflum, S., Hendricks, M. L., Bradford, J., & Bongar, B. (2012). The relationship between gender-based victimization and suicide attempts in transgender people. *Professional Psychology: Research and Practice, 43*(5), 468.

Groves, S., Backer, H. S., van den Bosch, W., & Miller, A. (2012). Dialectical behaviour therapy with adolescents. *Child and Adolescent Mental Health, 17*(2), 65–75.

Haas, A. P., Eliason, M., Mays, V. M., Mathy, R. M., Cochran, S. D., D'Augelli, A. R., . . . Russell, S. T. (2010). Suicide and suicide risk in lesbian, gay, bisexual, and transgender populations: Review and recommendations. *Journal of Homosexuality, 58*(1), 10–51.

Hatzenbuehler, M. L. (2009). How does sexual minority stigma "get under the skin"? A psychological mediation framework. *Psychological Bulletin, 135*(5), 707–730.

Hendricks, M. L., & Testa, R. J. (2012). A conceptual framework for clinical work with transgender and gender nonconforming clients: An adaptation of the minority stress model. *Professional Psychology: Research and Practice, 43*, 460–467.

Herman, J. L. (2013). Gendered restrooms and minority stress: The public regulation of gender and its impact on transgender people's lives. *Journal of Public Management & Social Policy, 19*(1), 65–80.

Hibbard, L. (2012). *Brandon Elizares, gay teen, commits suicide, writing "I couldn't make it. I love you guys."* Retrieved from https://www.huffingtonpost.com/2012/06/14/brandon-elizares-gay-teen-commits-suicide-leaves-note_n_1598272.html

Johnson, L., Shipherd, J., & Walton, H. M. (2016). The psychologist's role in transgender-specific care with US veterans. *Psychological Services, 13*(1), 69–76.

King, M., Semlyen, J., Tai, S. S., Killaspy, H., Osborn, D., Popelyuk, D., & Nazareth, I. (2008). A systematic review of mental disorder, suicide, and deliberate self harm in lesbian, gay and bisexual people. *BMC Psychiatry, 8*(1), 70.

Kliem, S., Kröger, C., & Kosfelder, J. (2010). Dialectical behavior therapy for borderline personality disorder: A meta-analysis using mixed-effects modeling. *Journal of Consulting and Clinical Psychology, 78*(6), 936–951.

Koerner, K. (2012). *Doing dialectical behavior therapy: A practical guide.* New York, NY: Guilford.

Koh, H. K. (2010). A 2020 vision for healthy people. *New England Journal of Medicine, 362*(18), 1653–1656.

Lau, A. S. (2006). Making the case for selective and directed cultural adaptations of evidence-based treatments: Examples from parent training. *Clinical Psychology: Science and Practice, 13*(4), 295–310.

Linehan, M. M. (1993). *Cognitive–behavioral treatment of borderline personality disorder.* New York, NY: Guilford.

Linehan, M. M. (2014). *DBT skills training manual.* New York, NY: Guilford.

Linehan, M. M., Korslund, K. E., Harned, M. S., Gallop, R. J., Lungu, A., Neacsiu, A. D., . . . Murray-Gregory, A. M. (2015). Dialectical behavior therapy for high suicide risk in individuals with borderline personality disorder: A randomized clinical trial and component analysis. *JAMA Psychiatry, 72*(5), 475–482.

Lynch, T. R., Chapman, A. L., Rosenthal, M. Z., Kuo, J. R., & Linehan, M. M. (2006). Mechanisms of change in dialectical behavior therapy: Theoretical and empirical observations. *Journal of Clinical Psychology, 62*(4), 459–480.

McCabe, S. E., Hughes, T. L., Bostwick, W. B., West, B. T., & Boyd, C. J. (2009). Sexual orientation, substance use behaviors and substance dependence in the United States. *Addiction, 104*(8), 1333–1345.

Meyer, I. H. (2003). Prejudice, social stress, and mental health in lesbian, gay, and bisexual populations: Conceptual issues and research evidence. *Psychological Bulletin, 129,* 674–697.

Mustanski, B., & Liu, R. T. (2013). A longitudinal study of predictors of suicide attempts among lesbian, gay, bisexual, and transgender youth. *Archives of Sexual Behavior, 42*(3), 437–448.

Pachankis, J. E., Rendina, H. J., Restar, A., Ventuneac, A., Grov, C., & Parsons, J. T. (2015). A minority stress–emotion regulation model of sexual compulsivity among highly sexually active gay and bisexual men. *Health Psychology, 34*(8), 829–840.

Panos, P. T., Jackson, J. W., Hasan, O., & Panos, A. (2014). Meta-analysis and systematic review assessing the efficacy of dialectical behavior therapy (DBT). *Research on Social Work Practice, 24*(2), 213–223.

Rizvi, S. L., Steffel, L. M., & Carson-Wong, A. (2013). An overview of dialectical behavior therapy for professional psychologists. *Professional Psychology: Research and Practice, 44,* 73–80.

Russell, T. D., Pocknell, V., & King, A. R. (2017). Lesbians and bisexual women and men have higher scores on the Personality Inventory for the DSM-5 (PID-5) than heterosexual counterparts. *Personality and Individual Differences, 110,* 119–124.

Ryan, C., & Rivers, I. (2003). Lesbian, gay, bisexual and transgender youth: Victimization and its correlates in the USA and UK. *Culture, Health & Sexuality, 5*(2), 103–119.

Safren, S. A., & Heimberg, R. G. (1999). Depression, hopelessness, suicidality, and related factors in sexual minority and heterosexual adolescents. *Journal of Consulting and Clinical Psychology, 67*(6), 859.

Steil, R., Dyer, A., Priebe, K., Kleindienst, N., & Bohus, M. (2011). Dialectical behavior therapy for posttraumatic stress disorder related to childhood sexual abuse: A pilot study of an intensive residential treatment program. *Journal of Traumatic Stress, 24*(1), 102–106.

Timmins, L., Rimes, K. A., & Rahman, Q. (2017). Minority stressors and psychological distress in transgender individuals. *Psychology of Sexual Orientation and Gender Diversity, 4*(3), 328–340.

Valentine, S. E., Bankoff, S. M., Poulin, R., Reidler, E. B., & Pantalone, D. W. (2015). The use of dialectical behavior therapy skills training as stand-alone treatment: A systematic review of the treatment outcome literature. *Journal of Clinical Psychology, 71*(1), 1–20.

Worhach, M. (2016). *Internalized homophobia, alcohol use, and risky sexual behaviors: The buffering role of DBT coping skills.* Unpublished doctoral dissertation, State University of New York at Albany, Albany, NY.

19

Relationship-Focused Therapy for Sexual and Gender Minority Individuals and Their Parents

GARY M. DIAMOND, ROTEM BORUCHOVITZ-ZAMIR,
INBAL GAT, AND OFIR NIR-GOTTLIEB ■

Finding out that one's child is gay, lesbian, bisexual, transgender, or in some way not heteronormative and/or cisgender is often a life-altering event.[1] Even among parents who are generally accepting of sexual and gender minority individuals, the realization that their own children are same-sex oriented and/or transgender can elicit a plethora of negative emotions, including shock, shame, anger, grief, and fear. Indeed, more than half of parents initially react to their children's disclosure of a same-sex orientation or transgender identity with some degree of negativity (D'Augelli, Grossman, Starks, & Sinclair, 2010; Grossman, D'Augelli, Howell, & Hubbard, 2005; Heatherington & Lavner, 2008; Robinson, Walters, & Skeen, 1989; Savin-Williams & Dube, 1998). As Stone Fish and Harvey (2005) note, "It is impossible to grow up in a hetero[trans]sexist, homo[trans]phobic culture like our own and not be influenced by some of the negative messages about queer people" (p. 27). Although many parents eventually become more accepting, or at least more tolerant, over time (Beals & Peplau, 2006; Cramer & Roach, 1988; Grossman et al., 2005; Samarova, Shilo, & Diamond, 2014; Savin-Williams & Ream, 2003), a substantial minority of parents remain non-accepting. For example, in a recent Israeli study, lesbian, gay, and bisexual (LGB) adolescents and young adults reported that 9% of their mothers and 12% of their fathers remained fully or almost

---

1. The term *same-sex oriented* is used to refer to individuals who identify in any way other than exclusively heterosexual. The term *transgender* is used to represent clients who self-identify as transgender, genderqueer, non-binary, or in any way non-cisgender.

fully rejecting 18 months post-disclosure (Samarova, Shilo, & Diamond, 2014). In a US-based study of transgender adolescents and young adults, 50% of the sample reported that their mothers still reacted negatively or very negatively to their gender identity 3 years (on average) after their identity was revealed, and 44% of the sample reported that their fathers did so (Grossman et al., 2005). Such rejection may be expressed in a myriad of forms, including emotional withdrawal, devaluation, criticism, invalidation, humiliation, coercion, anger, verbal abuse, and, in extreme cases, physical violence or banishment from the family.

Needless to say, ongoing parental criticism, invalidation, and rejection of one's sexual orientation or gender identity can take a psychological toll. Such messages from parents may not only be internalized and negatively affect one's sense of self (Carastathis, Cohen, Kaczmarek, & Chang, 2016) but also signal to the individual that it is not safe or helpful to turn to their parents for support when experiencing minority stress (e.g., discrimination, rejection, and victimization) outside of the family (e.g., at work and in the community). Indeed, research has shown that parental criticism, invalidation, and rejection are associated with internalized homophobia, expectations for future gay-related rejection by others (Pachankis, Goldfried, & Ramrattan, 2008), substantially increased risk for depression and suicidal ideation (D'Augelli, Grossman, & Starks, 2005; Hass, Rodgers, & Herman, 2014; Ryan, Huebner, Diaz, & Sanchez, 2009), and higher levels of drug and alcohol consumption (D'Amico & Julien, 2012; Padilla, Crisp, & Rew, 2010; Rothman, Sullivan, Keyes, & Boehmer, 2012). In contrast, parental support of LGB individuals has been associated with greater self-esteem and greater perceived social support and has been found to buffer against psychopathology (D'Augelli, 2002; Eisenberg & Resnick, 2006; Elizur & Ziv, 2001; Evans, Hawton, & Rodham, 2004; Feinstein, Wadsworth, Davila, & Goldfried, 2014; Floyd, Stein, Harter, Allison, & Nye, 1999; Haas et al., 2014; Hershberger & D'Augelli, 1995; Needham & Austin, 2010; Ryan, Russell, Huebner, Diaz, & Sanchez, 2010; Savin-Williams, 1989; Shilo, Antebi, & Mor, 2015). Given the negative impact of ongoing parental rejection, and the positive impact of parental acceptance, on sexual and gender minority individuals, the development and testing of family-based interventions designed to increase parental acceptance, decrease parental rejection, and promote more open, accepting relationships between sexual and gender minority individuals and their parents is warranted (Feinstein et al., 2014; Pachankis & Goldfried, 2004).

RELATIONSHIP-FOCUSED THERAPY

This chapter describes relationship-focused therapy for sexual and gender minority individuals and their parents (RFT-SGM). RFT-SGM is a time-limited (26-session), manualized, focused treatment designed for families in which the sexual or gender minority individual and/or their parents believe that tension, conflict, or distance related to the adult child's sexual or gender identity has negatively impacted upon their relationship and the well-being of family members.

In some cases, the adult child initiates treatment because they are distressed by their parents' rejecting behavior and/or are worried about their parents' welfare.[2] In other instances, parents initiate therapy because they themselves are in distress regarding their child's sexual orientation or gender identity and/or recognize that their struggle to accept their child is negatively affecting their child's welfare and undermining the relationship. The treatment is applicable when both the sexual and/or gender minority individual and their parents are committed to repairing or improving the relationship.

RFT-SGM is an experiential treatment that has its roots in structural family therapy (Minuchin, 1977), multidimensional family therapy (Liddle, 2002), and emotion-focused therapy and theory (Greenberg, 2011, 2012; Greenberg, Warwar, & Malcolm, 2010; Johnson & Greenberg, 1995). The treatment is also informed by developmental research on relationships between young adults and their parents. Such research demonstrates that young adults who develop autonomy in the context of close, affectionate relationships with parents fare better psychologically and emotionally, and evidence higher levels of functioning, than young adults who are in ongoing conflict with, or who are detached from, their parents (Allen & Hauser, 1996; O'Connor, Allen, Bell, & Hauser, 1996). Similar findings have been reported among a sample of exclusively sexual minority young adults (Floyd, Stein, Harter, Allison, & Nye, 1999).

The most immediate and significant influence on RFT-SGM, however, is attachment-based family therapy (ABFT; G. S. Diamond, Diamond, & Levy, 2014). ABFT is a focused, empirically informed family-based treatment originally developed for working with depressed and suicidal adolescents (G. S. Diamond, Reis, Diamond, Siqueland, & Isaacs, 2002; G. S. Diamond et al., 2010). ABFT was later adapted for working with depressed and suicidal LGB adolescents (G. M. Diamond et al., 2012) and with young adults reporting unresolved anger toward parents (G. M. Diamond, Shahar, Sabo, & Tsvieli, 2016). Similar to attachment-based family therapy, RFT-SGM targets the quality of adult children's relationships with their parents. RFT-SGM also utilizes a similar structure, moves through many of the same intermediary therapeutic steps (tasks), and employs many of the same change mechanisms as ABFT. The goal of RFT-SGM is to help sexual and gender minority individuals and their parents re-establish or develop loving, supportive, mutually respectful, meaningful relationships in which the adult child can authentically and openly express all aspects of their identity without fear of rejection or of being negatively judged, and with the expectation of being validated and prized. The model assumes that most people, regardless of their age, want to feel like their parents accept them, respect them, appreciate them, are proud of them, and will be there for them in times of need. This may be particularly true for sexual and gender minority individuals.

---

2. Throughout the chapter, the gender and number (singular vs. plural) of pronouns have intentionally been mixed.

In RFT-SGM, the purported primary change mechanism is corrective emotional experiences. Such experiences begin when the adult child, after being prepared during individual sessions with the therapist, directly expresses to their parents, in the context of conjoint sessions, their sense of loss, pain, fear, and assertive anger associated with their parents' rejection of their sexual or gender identity. For example, as one son was able to say to his mother,

> When I tell you that David and I are thinking about moving in together and all I see is sadness in your eyes, I feel like you are disappointed in me. That somehow I have failed you and that you would rather not hear about what is going on in my life. I want you to be excited for me.

When parents witness and register the depth of their adult child's distress, vulnerability, and need, often for the first time, their innate caregiving instincts are activated, motivating them to soothe, support, and protect their child (Bowlby, 1988). Indeed, findings from basic research show that perceiving the other to be vulnerable elicits feelings of tenderness, and perceiving them to be in need elicits sympathy (Dijker, 2014; Lishner, Batson, & Huss, 2011). Similarly, findings from studies of emotionally focused couple therapy suggest that expressions of vulnerability evoke compassion, validation, and support and facilitate relational repair (Greenberg, Ford, Alden, & Johnson, 1993; Johnson & Greenberg, 1985; McKinnon & Greenberg, 2013).

From this place of empathy and concern, parents are guided to invite their adult child to share more deeply about themselves, their feelings, and their needs. In most cases, the adult child will respond by elaborating on their experience of feeling rejected, of feeling like they are a burden, or of feeling like they are a source of disappointment and pain for their parent. They will also more explicitly share their attachment needs (e.g., the need to feel loved and protected) and identity needs (e.g., the need to be accepted for who they are). Theoretically, the more that parents reach out and listen with empathy and openness, the more the adult child feels understood, cared about, and safe to share in an open, authentic manner. Such enactments are called attachment/identity episodes. This positive interactive cycle is thought to not only increase intimacy, strengthen the connection between the adult child and their parents, and positively impact upon the adult child's sense of self but also help parents retrospectively construct a more coherent understanding of their child's identity, which in turn further increases parents' validating and affirming behaviors. Indeed, prior research on ABFT lends support for some of these proposed mechanisms.

In one study of ABFT for suicidal adolescents, maternal psychological control (e.g., invalidation, criticism, and guilt induction) decreased, and maternal psychological autonomy-granting (i.e., encouraging adolescents' independence of thoughts and feelings and tolerating differences in opinions and narratives) increased, over the course of treatment. Moreover, increases in maternal psychological autonomy-granting behaviors were associated with increases in adolescents' perceived maternal care and decreases in attachment-related anxiety and avoidance. Decreases in maternal psychological control behaviors were associated with reductions in adolescents' depressive symptoms (Shpigel, Diamond, & Diamond, 2012). In a study examining ABFT for young adults suffering from unresolved anger toward a parent, young adults' attachment anxiety, attachment avoidance, unresolved anger, state anger, and psychological symptoms decreased over the course of treatment, with greater amounts of emotional processing (i.e., young adult's expressions of primary, adaptive, and typically vulnerable emotions directly to parents during conjoint attachment/identity episodes) predicting greater decreases in psychological symptoms (G. M. Diamond et al., 2016). Follow-up interviews with these clients revealed that they attributed change to productive emotional processing, saying things directly to their parents that they had never said before, being vulnerable and seeing their parents' vulnerability during conjoint attachment/identity episodes (Steinmann, Gat, Nir-Gottlieb, Shahar, & Diamond, 2017).

Once some of the pain, anger, and unmet attachment and identity needs associated with feeling rejected have been processed, and trust has been restored, the adult child and their parents are ready to initiate conversations about other previously avoided, emotionally laden topics, such as the adult child's experience of coming out to self and others, past traumas (e.g., being bullied at school as a child), relationships with romantic partners, and plans for the future (e.g., marriage and having children). At this point, parents may also share some of their own fears regarding their child's sexual or gender identity, as long as such disclosures are not experienced by the child as excuses for not being more accepting and the parent is not emotionally overwhelmed. Such disclosures on the part of parents have the potential to facilitate adult children's empathy for their parents and lead to further intimacy and mutual acceptance in the relationship. In the following sections, the structure and intervention strategies of RFT-SGM are described, preliminary research findings supporting the model are summarized, a clinical vignette illustrating the treatment is presented, and some of the constraints and limitations of the model are noted.

CLINICAL MODEL

RFT-SGM is comprised of a series of five tasks. The successful completion of one task sets the stage for the next task, and the therapist helps the family move through the five tasks in sequence. The purpose of Task I, conducted in the first session with both the adult child and parents present, is to establish relationship building (e.g., increased openness, increased parental acceptance, and decreased parental rejection) as the primary goal of therapy. Task II, conducted over the course of individual sessions with the adult child, involves creating a therapeutic bond with the adult child, helping them fully connect with and articulate primary adaptive emotions and unmet attachment needs (e.g., the need to be safe and the need for affection) and identity needs (e.g., the need to be validated and the need to be viewed as competent) associated with the relational rupture, agreeing on the goal of sharing such feelings and needs with parents in subsequent conjoint attachment/identity episodes, and preparing the adult child for such episodes. Task III, conducted over the course of individual sessions with parents, involves creating a therapeutic bond with parents; exploring and working through their fear, shame, grief, and anger associated with having a sexual/gender minority offspring; highlighting the impact of their rejection and own distress on the welfare of their child and their relationship with them; exploring parents' own developmental histories in an effort to help them empathize further with their child's attachment and identity needs; and preparing parents to empathically reach out to their child in subsequent conjoint attachment/identity episodes. Task IV, conducted in the context of conjoint child–parent sessions, involves facilitating in-session corrective emotional experiences by helping the adult child share their emotions and unmet attachment and identity needs and helping parents respond in an empathic, accepting manner (i.e., attachment/identity episodes). After some or all of the relational ruptures have been worked through, tension in the relationship has subsided, and there is an increased sense of acceptance, trust, and connection, Task V is initiated. This task, also conducted over the course of conjoint sessions, involves helping family members collaboratively solve current problems, as well as anticipate and plan for future challenges. Next, each task is described in greater detail.

Task I

Task I begins with the therapist orienting the family to the therapy setting and structure. For example, the therapist will typically say,

> Today, I am going to spend some time getting to know each of you a little bit. Then, we will talk about why you came and what is going on in the relationship. After that, over the course of the next few weeks, I will meet alone with you [adult child], and alone with you two [parents] for a few sessions. Finally, we will all get back together again and try to help you work through some of the things that have been getting in the way of your feeling closer and more at ease as a family. All-in-all, we have 26 sessions to work together.

The therapist responds to any questions or concerns about the setting and structure of the therapy and then moves on to briefly join with each family member. She asks each family member to share a little about themselves, focusing on their strengths and competencies.

Once family members feel comfortable, and an initial bond has been formed, the therapist moves on to the next phase and asks each family member about their relationship and why they have come to therapy. For some sexual and/or gender minority individuals, their primary concern is attachment related and involves themes of closeness, intimacy, safety, and connection. For example, one young woman reported that she and her father had barely spoken over the past

3 years, since the day that she had come out. She described missing the times that they used to joke and laugh together. Another young adult reported being hurt and angry that his parents did not sufficiently protect him. He described how, during his visits home, his parents failed to intervene when his older sister abused him verbally. For other individuals, their primary concerns revolve around frustrated identity and autonomy needs. In one case, a transgender client reported that her father's attempt to control what clothes she wore when visiting home felt invalidating and even humiliating. Another client described the impact of her parents' repeated comments that, perhaps, she was not really a lesbian and that she should keep her mind open to finding a man who was compatible. Some adult children are struggling with trying to balance their concern for their parents' welfare, their desire to maintain constructive relationships with their parents, and their desire to live an authentic, open life out of the closet. For example, one client described the great personal sacrifices he had made, and was still making, in terms of not coming out to extended family, and not getting involved in a serious romantic relationship, all in an effort to protect his parents' feelings. He explained that he had now reached the point at which the cost of protecting his parents was too great, and that it was undermining his relationships with his cousins and thwarting his own personal development. These individuals come to treatment with the hope that therapy will help their parents work through their fears and shame so that they, the young adults, can move forward with their own lives without constantly worrying about their parents' welfare or feeling guilty. Finally, in some cases, parents initiate therapy. They do so because they feel stuck in their grief or shame, years after their child has come out, and recognize that their inability to accept their child's sexual or gender identity has negatively impacted upon their child, themselves, and the relationship. They are searching for a way to feel more at peace and a way to repair their relationship with their child.

As the adult child describes their experience, the therapist works to connect them to, and amplify, associated underlying and previously avoided adaptive emotions. The therapist uses interventions such as accurate empathy, focusing, and empathic conjecture (Greenberg & Paivio, 2003) to evoke feelings of loss, sadness, loneliness, fear, humiliation, worthlessness, assertive anger, and longing. In many cases, this is the first time that parents have witnessed and experienced the extent of their child's pain. Typically, such conversations about feelings and unmet needs either have never taken place or, when they have occurred, have ended up as arguments or with family members disengaging from one another. Optimally, when parents witness the full extent of their child's distress and longing, they become more empathic. In such moments, parents often recognize, for the first time, the dramatic and negative effect that their rejection and withdrawal has had on their child. The pain of seeing their child's pain typically, although not always, generates in parents a motivation to change. An urgency arises within them to find a way to support and comfort their child—to help them feel better about themselves, loved, competent, safe, and connected to the family. At this point, the therapist offers therapy as an opportunity for parents to be there for their children in a different manner: more accepting, supportive, loving, and affirming. In most cases, this resonates for parents, and they eagerly adopt this relational goal.

In other cases, however, parents initially respond to this goal with ambivalence or even fear. On the one hand, they want to alleviate their child's pain and establish a closer, more caring relationship. On the other hand, they are anxious about being asked to do things or to respond in ways that seem impossible to them. Their fear, shame, or aversion may seem insurmountable, and they feel trapped between their desire to protect and nurture their child and their need to protect themselves. As one father stated,

> I know that my daughter wants me to be proud of her, and be happy to see her and her girlfriend together, but I just can't do that. I am not there yet, and I don't think I am ever going to be. In my mind, it will always be unnatural. I will always be looking at her sitting at the table and thinking that she should be sitting beside a husband and her children, and that will never change.

Such responses are an opportunity for the therapist to acknowledge and empathize with the parent's sense of loss and fear and to assure them that the therapy process will not be coercive. The therapist respects the fact that for some parents, coming to terms with, let alone embracing, the fact that they have a sexual or gender minority offspring may be a complicated, difficult, and gradual process. At the same time, the therapist redirects the parent back to the pain, loneliness, and anger that their adult child is feeling as the result of their rejection or lack of acceptance. The therapist might say,

> I know that this is hard for you, and nobody expects you to change things you can't change. When we meet alone together, I want to hear more about what this has been like for you. Right now, however, I am curious about what it feels like to see your daughter's tears as she talks about how alone she feels, and how much she misses the close relationship you two once had.

Once the parent is refocused on their child's pain, the therapist again offers therapy as an opportunity for relational repair. For example, the therapist might say,

> If I could help you find a way to be there for your daughter, hear her pain and longing, help her to feel more connected and valued, without you having to do or say things that you don't believe in or that feel intolerable for you, would that be a reasonable goal of therapy?

To the adult child, the therapist might say,

> If I could help your parents hear what it has been like for you in a way that they have not heard you before, even if they can't necessarily do much differently at first, would that be a worthy goal of therapy?

The answers to these questions are inevitably "yes." At this point, the therapist intentionally refrains from talking about specific behavioral changes. The goal of Task I is not to solve problems. Instead, it is to bring to the surface the adult child's pain, loneliness, frustration, and longing associated with their parents' rejection of their sexual and/or gender identity; help parents see and connect with their child's pain and needs; and then harness parents' innate desire to support, validate, and care for their child in order to establish increased relational repair as the goal of treatment.

Task II

Task II sessions, conducted alone with the sexual/gender minority individual, begin with getting to know the adult child as a person. The therapist briefly explores the major domains in the individual's life, including work, friends, romantic relationships, nuclear family system, current stressors (unrelated to their relationships with parents), as well as interests, strengths, and support networks. Once the therapist has a sense of the broad strokes of the individual's life, they explore the adult child's coming out experience. In these sessions, the adult child will typically offer details about experiences that they previously could not speak about in front of their parents. Some describe a history of feeling ashamed, scared, defective, angry, and hopeless—typically dating back to before they came out to their parents. For example, one client who grew up in a family characterized by conservative, traditional values, and whose parents were overtly homophobic, reported praying each day that he would die instead of having to disclose his identity to his father. He reported being jealous of people who had died in car accidents or terror attacks, and he described the panic he regularly experienced at the thought of being "discovered." When he did actually come out to his parents, their response was to withdraw into their own sense of loss, grief, shame, and fear. As a result, not only did he lose what had remained of the connection he felt with his parents but also he felt guilty about causing them pain. As the adult child tells their story, the therapist works to connect them fully to their emotions. The therapist asks them to describe specific moments that were particularly painful—vivid, episodic memories. Typically, feelings such as hurt, sadness, grief, loneliness, helplessness, shame, disappointment, self-hate, terror, and anger arise. The therapist then asks them whether they have ever shared any of their feelings with the parents and whether their parents know the extent to which their rejection and withdrawal has impacted them.

In most instances, the adult child will report either that they have not shared their experiences and feelings with parents or that they have tried to do so and such attempts have resulted in conflict or avoidance. In some instances, they will say that they are afraid to start such conversations because they are embarrassed, feel vulnerable, are not sure their parents want to hear, or are not sure that their parents are strong enough to contain their pain, disappointment, and anger. In other instances, adult children describe past attempts to speak with their parents that ended up leaving them frustrated, angry, and in even greater despair. For example, one adult child reported that each time he has attempted to express his anger, sense of loneliness, and feeling of being abandoned when not being included in family events, his parents become defensive, denying that his sexual orientation is an issue for them and accusing him of being overly sensitive. Such conversations only serve to increase his distress and isolation, and deepen the rift in the relationship.

At this point in the task, the therapist again offers therapy as an opportunity for the adult child to be heard by their parents in a way that they have never been heard before. For example, the therapist might say,

> If I could help your parents really listen and hear how painful and lonely it has been for you throughout the years, and how much it hurts when you see that they are ashamed of you, would that be something you want?

The possibility of finally being heard and understood resonates for the adult child, and the answer to this question is typically "yes." In some instances, however, the adult child expresses ambivalence. Some are skeptical that their parents have the capacity to listen or fully understand. Some are unsure whether their parents really want to hear. Some are worried about causing their parents further pain. Some wonder if it will make a difference in the relationship. At this point, the therapist takes the position that the adult child deserves to be heard. The therapist states that she will work alone with their parents, in individual sessions, in order to prepare them to listen and respond in a more open manner. Finally, and importantly, the therapist assures the adult child that she will only convene conjoint session if she is convinced that her parents are willing and able to listen with greater openness. Although the therapist does not promise the moon, in most cases parents are able to listen to and understand their adult child's experience at least somewhat better. Sometimes even small changes mean a world of difference.

Once the adult child has agreed to the task of sharing their experiences and feelings with their parents, the therapist prepares them for upcoming attachment/identity episodes. Together, the therapist and adult child identify the most salient issues and feelings the adult child wants to talk about with their parents. Then, the therapist prepares the adult child to articulate their feelings and associated attachment and identity needs from a place of vulnerability and care, and convey them in a non-accusatory, regulated manner. Finally, the therapist works with the client to set realistic expectations. Parents are not always able to respond optimally during their first try at such conversations. People often fall back into old, habitual, maladaptive patterns of relating (e.g., defensiveness and reactivity). The therapist prepares the adult child for the fact that it will be a two-step forward, one-step backward process. Together, they try to anticipate different types of potential non-optimal parental reactions and discuss how the adult child can respond productively (e.g., assertively and non-defensively). Once the adult child is prepared for subsequent attachment/identity episodes, the therapist begins working individually with parents.

Task III

Task III begins with the therapist briefly joining with each parent and exploring the major domains of their lives. The therapist asks each parent about work, extended family, friends, support systems, and hobbies, paying special care to note parents' strengths and competencies. The therapist also briefly explores potential stressors in parents' lives, such as financial stress, marital stress, health issues, work-related stress, and caretaking of older parents. It is important that therapists explicitly recognize the personal challenges parents are facing, as well as acknowledge the commitment, effort, courage, and love for their child that are required for them to come to, and participate in, this type of therapy. Not all parents are willing to take part in such a process.

Once the therapist has a sense of the broad strokes of parents' lives, and an initial bond has been formed, she asks parents to share their experience of having a sexual/gender minority child. Many begin by describing their sense of shock, disbelief, loss, fear, and shame upon first learning of their child's minority identity. Others report that they suspected their child was different from a young age. Some share how painful it was to see their child bullied or excluded at school and in the neighborhood throughout the years. Often, parents describe the loss of their heteronormative dream, and they grieve the fact that they will never have what they imagined to be a "normal" family, with a daughter-in-law (or son-in-law) and two grandchildren sitting beside them at the dinner table. For parents of transgender children, the sense of loss and grief may be greater (Norwood, 2013; Wahlig, 2015), in part because gender is typically experienced as more core to a person's identity than sexual orientation, and gender transition often involves changes in physical appearance, name, and pronouns. Many parents focus on the shame they feel vis-à-vis friends, extended family, co-workers, and in public. They also describe their fear that if others find out, they will gossip about them behind their backs, pity them, judge them, and distance themselves (Robinson & Brewster, 2016). They are afraid to lose friends, their community, and their life as they know it. Some parents are concerned that if their own parents were to find out, it might place their health at risk or worse. Individual sessions are where parents can voice even their most unspeakable thoughts, such as "When I look at her, all I see is the son I lost" or "I sometimes wonder whether it would have been better if she wasn't born." During this part of the task, the therapist listens with compassion and empathizes with parents' pain, confusion, and fear. It is crucial that parents feel heard, accepted, and not judged. Many of them have themselves grown up in homophobic/transphobic environments—families and communities in which being gay, lesbian, or transgender is perceived of as a defect, sickness, or sin.

At this point in the task, therapists invite parents to more closely examine some of their fears, beliefs, and behaviors that have impeded their becoming more accepting of, or at least more comfortable with, their child's identity. Some parents report that they have not shared their secret with anybody. In such cases, the therapist might wonder aloud if there is a particular family member or friend who may be more accepting than others. In many instances, parents are able to identify at least one person who would be more likely to be accepting. Such questions by the therapist begin to tease apart the global fear that has paralyzed parents and lead to a more differentiated, reality-based perspective. The therapist might then ask, "What would it be like to tell that person? How do you think they would react? Would they embrace your daughter?" Such questions usually reveal possibilities, and they underscore the potential for change. Suddenly, parents feel that there may be a light at the end of the tunnel.

Some parents are preoccupied with the question of whether they are somehow responsible for their child's sexual/gender identity and/or whether their child was "born that way." In such cases, the therapist may explore the basis for parents' beliefs and then provide some short psychoeducation about what is, and is not, known regarding the causes of sexual orientation and gender identity (for one approach to this conversation, see Shpigel, Belsky, & Diamond, 2015). Some parents are skeptical about whether their child is "really" gay or transgender and/or wonder if their child made a choice to adopt or "give in to" such an identity. This skepticism is often fueled by what appears to parents to be disconfirming evidence, derived from their observations throughout the years. For example, as one father described it,

> To be honest, I have trouble accepting that my son is really gay. I was there throughout his high school years. Every six months he had a new girlfriend. He was the most sought-after boy in his school—and these weren't just "friends." I saw how he interacted with girls and it was clearly much more than that.

In such cases, the therapist must empathize with the parent's confusion and, at the same time, offer future conjoint sessions as an opportunity for them to ask their child, from a place of curiosity and openness, how it all goes together—how to make sense of it all.

Once parents have fully connected with their own disappointment, loss, grief, and shame, and they have a sense that the therapy will address some of their fears, questions, and concerns, the therapist invites them to reflect on how their feelings and responses to their child's sexual orientation/gender identity may have affected their child throughout the years. At this point, parents often become sad and remorseful. At some level, they know that their reactions have, at times, left their child feeling rejected, ashamed, frustrated, and alone. In order to help parents fully connect to their child's pain, therapists will ask for a specific example—an episodic memory. One mother, for example, tearfully described the look of humiliation in her transgender daughter's eyes when they told her that, at home, they would not call her by her chosen name, only her birth name. In another case, the father remembered how his gay son would come home from school after being bullied and ridiculed and go to his room. He regretted that, at those moments, he would angrily berate his son for not fighting back instead of comforting him and helping him process what he had been through. It is at this point in the treatment that the therapist offers therapy as an opportunity for parents to be emotionally present for their adult child in a manner in which they were not able to be in the past. The therapist might say,

> I can see how much you love your son. I can also see how bad you feel about what he must have gone through. I know that, back then, you may have been overwhelmed with your own fear, disappointment, and anger, and it may not have occurred to you to hear what he was going through or to comfort him, but now things are different. You are in a different spot. You have an opportunity to invite your son to open up and share what that time was like for him. Be there with him in those feelings now in a way that you couldn't back then.

Another part of the work with parents is exploring their own developmental history. The goal of this intergenerational work is to help parents connect with their own childhood experiences of needing their parents' support, care, and protection and wanting their parents to be proud of them. In some cases, parents describe having grown up in homes with parents who themselves may not have been available, did not necessarily recognize when they were in distress, or did not have the tools or capacity to reach out to them in a way that allowed them to share, feel comforted, and safe. In some cases, parents describe how their own parents made them feel bad about themselves. In these cases, the therapist works to help the parent connect to an episodic memory when they themselves experienced parental abandonment or rejection, in order to help them access associated feelings of loneliness, fear, and shame and identify what they needed in that moment. For example, one father described how, as a young child, his mother would react to his signs of distress by becoming emotionally overwhelmed, leaving him feeling as if he had to take care of her instead of her taking care of him. His father, on the other hand, would react with annoyance and disapproval. This father was able to connect to how alone and ashamed he felt in those moments and how he had needed his parents to comfort him without falling apart or shaming him.

Next, the therapist uses parents' own experiences in order to help them imagine how their adult child might feel and what they might need. In the previous example, the therapist remarked to the father,

> You know Tom, listening to you talk about your experiences with your own parents, I wonder if your daughter sometimes feels the same way. Like she doesn't want to go to her mom because she sees how hard it is for her, and that she doesn't open up to you about how alone she feels because she is afraid you are going to downplay or even ridicule her feelings or needs.

By connecting parents to their own history of unmet needs and associated emotions, parents often become more empathic to their adult child's pain and longing and become motivated to provide a different type of experience for their adult child. In some cases, parents describe growing up with parents who were attentive, supportive, validating, and accepting. In such instances, the therapist will help the parent connect with how meaningful that experience was for them and offer therapy as an opportunity for them to ensure that their adult child has a similar experience.

Once parents agree to the goal of reaching out to their child in a more empathic, accepting, validating manner, the therapist begins to prepare them for subsequent conjoint attachment/identity episodes. Again, the purpose of such episodes is to create corrective emotional experiences. Optimally, during such episodes, parents empathically reach out to their adult child and invite them to share their memories and feelings about past and present traumatic events and ruptures in the relationship. As a result, the adult child shares previously avoided vulnerable feelings and longings in an emotionally connected manner. Parents then respond in a nonjudgmental, accepting, validating, supportive manner.

In order to prepare parents for such episodes, the therapist helps them identify some of the past and current events or interactions they believe are fueling their child's sense of frustration and distress. Some parents already have a good idea about what might be bothering their child because, throughout the years, the child has voiced such complaints, often in the heat of arguments. As one father stated, "I know she is furious with me for suggesting that she try to go out with more men before deciding that she was a lesbian. She has told me so." Other parents may be less aware of their child's concerns. In either case, the therapist tells parents that there are some things their son or daughter will want to bring up during the conversations. The therapist emphasizes that their task, as parents, is to reach out and listen to their child's pain, frustration, and longing with openness and without defending themselves. Parents are coached to ask open-ended questions about feelings and to give their adult child permission to share potentially painful and hurtful experiences. The therapist points out to parents that during these upcoming episodes, they may have the impulse to "present their side of the story," clarify facts, or defend themselves. However, the therapist reminds them that the initial goal is for them to encourage their adult child to share in a way that they have never shared before and for them, as parents, to listen, empathize, validate, support, and comfort. The therapist assures parents that after their child has shared all that they want to share, and has felt heard and validated, there will then be time for them, as parents, to share some of what it has been like for them.

Task IV

By the end of the third task, both the adult child and their parents are prepared to productively participate in attachment/identity episodes. The adult child now has the clarity and language to describe the range and depth of feelings that their parents' rejection and lack of acceptance bring up in them and what they needed, and need now, from their parents. At the same time, parents have been prepared to listen attentively, non-defensively, and with empathy, and they have identified some core themes and interactions they believe may be fueling their adult child's distress. Consequently, the therapist plays a less central role during these episodes, instead allowing family members to speak directly to one another. When necessary, the therapist will refocus family members onto core attachment (e.g., safety and closeness) and identity (e.g., validation and psychological autonomy) themes, block any escalation of conflict or defensiveness, and remind parents to stay focused on their child's experience and emotions. However, once therapists get the conversation back on track, they then get out of the way to allow the conversation to progress.

Such episodes typically begin with the adult child bringing up a past incident or interaction that was particularly hurtful. In the following example, a young man begins by talking about the intense pain he had felt 4 years prior:

ADULT CHILD: I remember when you came to my room that evening to ask me why I looked so sad. I finally got up the courage to tell you that I thought that I was gay. All that you could say was that if I didn't find a way to overcome this nonsense, I was going to ruin my life and the lives of everybody else in the family.

MOTHER: How did that make you feel?

ADULT CHILD: I was devastated. I was so vulnerable and instead of making me feel better, you made me feel worse.

THERAPIST (TO MOTHER): Ask him what he needed from you in that moment.

MOM: What did you want me to say?

ADULT CHILD (CRYING): I just needed you to hug me and say that it was going to be OK.

THERAPIST (TO MOTHER, WHO HAD ALSO BEGUN TO CRY): What is going on for you right now, mom?

MOTHER: It hurts. It hurts to realize how much I hurt him, and that I wasn't there for him when he needed me the most.

THERAPIST (TO MOTHER): See if your son will tell more of what that was like for him.

Once past traumatic events have been processed, the focus typically turns to ongoing dynamics and current interactions that contribute to the adult child's sense of rejection. For example, in the following case, a lesbian client describes how she feels about her parents never inviting her partner over for dinner:

ADULT CHILD: It makes me angry that you have never reached out to Rose or made her feel comfortable enough to come over. Not only does it make her feel bad, it makes me feel like you don't care about me.

MOTHER: How does that make you feel like we don't care about you?

ADULT CHILD: She is a big part of my life. We have been together for two years. It's like you don't care about what is going on in my life, getting to know about a big part of me. What makes it so ironic is that I know you would love her if you meet her.

These episodes also provide the adult child the opportunity to teach their parents what they need from them at specific moments—how to respond in a way that they do not feel judged or rejected. For example, in one case, a son explained to his parents who were worried that he was in an unhealthy relationship,

> Instead of telling me that I am making a mistake, and bad mouthing him [romantic partner], I would rather you tell me that you are worried about me and ask how I am protecting myself. That would make me feel like it is coming from a place of care and concern rather than criticism.

When the adult child shares their frustration, pain, and longing, and parents are able to respond with openness, validation, and empathy, the child's experience of their parents, the parents' experience of their child, and the relationship itself are transformed. The adult child feels more heard, understood, and cared for. They feel like their identity and autonomy needs are recognized and respected. Parents better understand their child and are motivated to do more to help them feel good about themselves and connected. An atmosphere of closeness, intimacy, and care evolves.

Sometimes, family members also use this task to ask questions that they have never asked before because the relationship was too volatile, and every comment or question was interpreted as criticism or invalidation, or because there was too much distance and too little trust. Now, with a growing sense of understanding and trust, fewer topics are off limits. For example, in one of the cases mentioned previously, during the later phases of Task IV, the father was able to ask his son about things he had observed during his son's adolescence and that now confused him:

FATHER: Do you mind if I ask you a question about the girls I saw come over all of the time when you were in high school?
SON: Go ahead. What do you want to know?
FATHER: It seemed to me like you were definitely attracted to a number of them, especially Kim. I don't know. It seemed you guys couldn't keep your hands off of each other.
SON: To be honest, I think I was just trying to do whatever I could to not raise suspicions. I was so afraid of how you would react. With regards to Kim, she had a girlfriend at the time and I was seeing somebody as well. There was never anything romantic or sexual between the two of us.

Such conversations, which were not possible in the past, can be crucial. In this example, the son's revelations were both painful for his father, because his lingering hope that his son was not really gay was shattered, but at the same time calming, because he no longer was left struggling to put together seemingly contradictory pieces of information. He was now free to move on from being preoccupied with his doubts about the veracity of his son's sexual orientation and, instead, get on with the process of accepting his son for who he is.

Task V

Once the adult child feels heard, tension around previously unresolved conflicts has begun to dissipate, and past hurts start to resolve, there is a lighter, more relaxed and trusting atmosphere. A new sense of possibility and hopefulness arises. It is within this context that family members are able to keep each other's needs and feelings in mind as they collaboratively find ways to navigate current and future challenges. For example, one family used these sessions to plan together how to come out to various members of the extended family. They each discussed their fears related to telling specific family members, who should be told, when, and how to tell them. Another family planned together when their son would bring his partner home for a family dinner for the first time.

Summary

By the end of the five tasks, many of the adult children we have treated believe that they have finally been heard and understood, and many of the parents we have treated have made meaningful changes in terms of acceptance. Often, family members describe a new sense of togetherness, closeness, trust, collaboration, and possibility. Indeed, in some of the follow-up interviews conducted in the context of an ongoing open clinical trial, family members have reported that the treatment "changed their lives." Other families, however, have described more modest gains. For example, one male client reported that although his mother is still saddened by his being gay, she no longer makes homophobic remarks or encourages him to explore relationships with women. Parents come to the treatment at various points on the acceptance continuum, and what might seem like modest gains for some individuals can feel like a momentous change for others. However, not all families have benefited from the treatment. We have worked with parents who, even after hearing their child's pain and longing for recognition and connection, are not able to overcome their own sense of loss, embarrassment, fear, and anger, and they continue to reject their child's sexual orientation or gender identity. In such cases, the therapist continues working alone with the adult child in order to help them grieve and begin the process of accepting that their parents cannot fully accept them, at least not for the time being.

EMPIRICAL SUPPORT

Results from two small-scale clinical trials provide preliminary evidence for the efficacy of RFT-SGM. In one study, attachment-based family therapy, the predecessor of RFT-SGM, was adapted and delivered to suicidal and depressed LGB adolescents as part of a pilot open trial (G. M. Diamond et al., 2012). Results showed that by the end of treatment, these adolescents evidenced significant decreases in depressive symptoms and suicidal ideation, as well as attachment anxiety and avoidance. In another study, ABFT was adapted for, and tested with, young adults (as opposed to adolescents) suffering from unresolved anger toward a parent. Results indicated that both ABFT and a comparison treatment, individual emotion-focused therapy (Greenberg, 2011), led to significant decreases in unresolved anger (e.g., forgiveness and letting go), state anger (current feelings of anger toward parent), attachment anxiety, and psychological systems, and ABFT also led to reductions in attachment avoidance (G. M. Diamond et al., 2016). In 2014, the first clinical paper describing relationship-focused therapy for sexual minority adults and their persistently non-accepting parents was published (G. M. Diamond & Shpigel, 2014). Currently, a 5-year open clinical trial is in progress. The goal is to treat 60 LGBTQ families with adult children reporting moderate to high levels of parental rejection. Thus far, over 20 cases have completed the treatment. In approximately half of the cases treated, the parent(s) initiated therapy because they believed that their child had disengaged from them, they sensed that their child was in distress, or they themselves felt distress due to the tension or distance in the relationship. In the other half of the cases, the adult child initiated treatment. In some of the cases, their primary concern was that they sought greater closeness, more validation, or more autonomy. In other cases, they were primarily concerned for their parents' welfare and felt conflicted or guilty for causing them pain. Preliminary analyses found significant increases in both maternal and paternal acceptance, and significant decreases in both maternal and paternal rejection, from pre-treatment to 3 months post-treatment (Diamond, 2018). In a study of six pilot cases from this trial, researchers found that in cases in which the adult child reported increased parental acceptance and decreased parental rejection post treatment, independent observers rated parents as evidencing higher levels of empathy and lower levels of rejection during conjoint attachment/identity episodes (Boruchovitz-Zamir & Diamond, 2017).

CASE EXAMPLE

Ben, a 24-year-old gay man, called after seeing the project advertised online. At the time, he was studying economics at a local university. He is the youngest of three adult children. His father, Ron, who works as an accountant, and his mother, Hannah, a high school teacher, both joined him in the treatment. During the initial session, Ben described his family as generally warm and supportive, but he also expressed frustration that his parents had never once broached the subject of his being gay in the 3 years since he had come out. He described being worried about them and the pain they still felt regarding his sexual orientation. When the therapist invited his parents to share their thoughts, Ron (the father) said he was not quite sure why they needed therapy, because he believed that he had gotten past the initial crisis and had learned to cope. While Ron was speaking, however, Hannah (the mother) began to cry. She described feeling constantly overwhelmed with grief. She also described Ron as being very homophobic and suggested his homophobia made it difficult for Ben to feel accepted. Ron responded by saying,

> Yes, I am a homophobe. That is not going to change. When I see two men together, I feel disgusted. I am also not the type of person to run around and tell the whole world that my son is gay. But, I told Ben that I love him and that I will always be there for him.

At this point, the therapist acknowledged the parents' apparent love of their child and their willingness to come with him to treatment, while at the same time focusing the conversation on how their responses affected Ben and their relationship with him. The therapist said, "Ben, as you look at your parents now and hear what they are saying, how do you feel?" Ben responded by talking directly to his parents:

> I know it is hard for both of you. I know what types of families you grew up in. But when I see that you are disgusted by me and ashamed of me, it makes me feel like something is wrong with me. That is why I don't tell you anything about myself or what is going on in my life. That is why I rarely come home to visit.

Ron looked a bit shaken, and Hannah, again, began to cry. The therapist moved closer to both parents, asking, "What is going on for the two of you right now, as you hear Ben talk?" Hannah stated, "I feel horrible. He shouldn't have to feel this way. I feel like we have made things harder on him." The therapist then turned directly to Ron and asked, "What about you Ron?" Ron responded, "I didn't know he felt that way. We used to have a close relationship. Go to basketball games together, whatever. I want him to feel like he can come home whenever he wants to."

At this point, the therapist offers therapy as an opportunity to help parents work through their loss, shame, fear, and aversion and re-establish or develop trust, openness, and closeness in their relationships with their adult child:

> I know this is hard for you two [parents]. But if I could somehow help you both feel less overwhelmed, and more comfortable, in relation to Ben being gay—for your sake, for Ben's sake, and for the sake of the relationship— would that be something you are willing to work on in this therapy?

Turning to Ben, the therapist continued: "If somehow your mother was less overwhelmed with grief, and your dad was more open to, and comfortable with, your sexual orientation, is that something that would be important to you?" After all three family members endorsed these therapy goals, the therapist met with Ben and his parents separately for a number of sessions.

During the second task of therapy, the therapist asked Ben about his current life, unrelated to his parents and his relationships with them. Ben described enjoying his university studies and having a group of close friends whom he had known since his freshman year. He was not currently involved in a romantic relationship. The therapist then asked Ben about his childhood and his coming out process. Ben described a happy childhood, with lots of friends and family around. When he was approximately 12 years old, he realized he was different from other boys, and at age 15 years, he realized that he was gay. He described how that realization had left him feeling confused, ashamed, scared, and guilty. At approximately age 18 years, he started feeling more comfortable with his sexual orientation and came out to a close friend, who responded supportively. During the next 2 years, he came out to all his friends and his siblings, leaving his parents for last. Although most of the reactions he received were accepting, his parents' reactions were more complex. His mother began sobbing. His father, while saying "You are still our son," was clearly upset and immediately left the house to go outside for a long walk. From that moment on, he has felt tremendously distant from both of his parents. Over the course of the individual sessions with Ben, the therapist helped him connect to his profound sense of loneliness, grief, and anger at his parents for not being able to accept him. Although he was initially apprehensive about the idea of sharing such feelings with his parents in future conjoint sessions, he recognized that it was important to him that they know he felt this way. He and the therapist worked on planning what he wanted to say and how to say it.

During the third task, in sessions alone with the parents, the therapist first inquired about each parent's personal life, above and beyond their relationship with Ben. They talked about their jobs, friends, extended family, and interests. They seemed to have a loving and mutually supportive marriage. The therapist then spoke with them about their experience of Ben's coming out. Hannah spoke about her deep sense of loss. Ben was her only son, and she had felt especially close to him. She looked forward to his getting married and having children, and when he told her that he was gay, she felt like her whole life had crumbled. Ron spoke about how, after Ben had come out, he had withdrawn from his own circle of friends and work colleagues: "I am not as interested in spending time with other people as I was in the past. I don't feel like answering their questions about Ben and how he is doing, so I just keep my distance." The therapist empathically helped both parents connect to their deep sense of loss, pain, shame, and loneliness while at the same time gently exploring their fears about the future, how others might react, and the implications of their choice to withdraw. She then asked both parents how they thought that their difficulty accepting Ben has impacted him and his relationships with them. Both looked sad. "I know it hurts him. I would feel the same way. It isn't his fault. He is the same wonderful son he has always been. Smart, good hearted," Hannah said. Ron replied, "I am willing to do anything. I don't want him to feel like there is something wrong with him or that he can't go on with his life."

At this point, the therapist asked each parent about their own experiences growing up. Ron described coming from a small family whose parents were holocaust survivors. He described them as loving parents who took good care of him. He also reported, however, that because of all that his parents had been through during the war, he felt like he did not want to cause them any additional pain. In fact, he said that even today, he made sure to only tell them things that were positive or would make them feel proud. Hannah described growing up in a large, well-established family. She spoke with pride about how her mother and father were viewed as the "successful, strong ones" and were the envy of their brothers and sisters, even now. She reported that there was no room for failure, weakness, or imperfection as a child, and she remembers the emphasis her parents placed on how they appeared in the eyes of others.

At the end of these sessions, the therapist wondered aloud whether Ben might be experiencing some of the same things they had struggled with in their own families of origin. She wondered if Ben was concerned about burdening them and therefore kept his feelings of sadness, worthlessness, and helplessness to himself. Perhaps he was worried about how his coming out might reflect negatively on the family. Seeing that this resonated with both Ron and Hannah, the therapist offered treatment as an opportunity for them to invite Ben to share his feelings with them openly. Therapy was presented, among other things, as an opportunity for them to give him the message that they were strong enough to hear and contain his grief, fears, and anger and that he did not have to protect them or the family.

During the fourth task, attachment/identity episodes, Ron and Hannah dared to ask Ben, for the first time, about his own process of coming out to himself and friends. Ben described the confusion, shame, and fear that dominated his early high school years. He talked about all the effort he had invested in concealing his homosexuality and his fear that if they had found out, they would be disappointed. Both parents were clearly moved. Ron was the first to respond: "I want to make it clear that I don't care what anybody else thinks or says. You are my son and you have nothing to be ashamed of." The therapist checked with Ben regarding how he experienced his father's response. Ben turned directly to his father and said, "You say that, but at the same time you have kept it a secret from everybody. You haven't even told Uncle Joe or Uncle Richard! It makes me feel like you are ashamed." Hannah joined in, saying, "I don't want you to keep things inside. I want to know what is going on with you." When the therapist then asked Ben to tell his mother what makes it difficult to share with her, he responded, "Every time I do share with you, you break down in tears. I end up feeling worse than before I told you." Because of the work done in Task III, Hannah was able to say,

> It is true that it is hard for me. I know that in the past I have sometimes gotten sad. But it is more important to me than anything in the world for you to come to me, and for me to know what is going on in your life. I am strong enough to manage my feelings. You used to share everything with me, and I miss that.

The therapist then asked Ben, "How does that sound to you, hearing your mom say that? Do you believe your mom when she says that she wants to hear what is going on with you, and that she is strong enough?" "Yes," Ben replied. At this point, the therapist suggested that the family use the next few sessions to continue the process, with mom and dad inviting Ben to share more about how he has felt in the past and how he currently feels in the relationship.

Once Hannah, Ron, and Ben had productively processed past and current relational ruptures and associated feelings, the tension in their relationships decreased and there was a greater sense of closeness. The family used their Task V sessions to think and plan together how Ron and Ben could progressively come out to members of Ron's extended family. Hannah helped Ron think about which of his friends and co-workers might be more accepting and how to begin to tell them. Ben asked Hannah to accompany him to a Parents and Families of Lesbians and Gays (PFLAG) meeting, and she agreed. The therapy ended with the therapist and family reflecting on the good, hard work the family was able to do, despite their fears and other challenges. There was an emphasis on the gains the family made during treatment and the hope that the increased openness, acceptance, and trust in the relationship would continue to serve them in the future.

CONSTRAINTS AND LIMITATIONS OF RFT-SGM

Relationship-focused therapy for sexual and gender minority individuals and their parents is a time-limited, focused treatment specifically designed to improve the quality of the adult child–parent relationship with regard to the adult child's sexual orientation/gender identity. Sometimes during the course of the therapy, important issues arise that are not directly related to parental acceptance or the adult child–parent relationship (e.g., mental health challenges, sibling relationships, and career issues). In such instances, the therapist will mark these issues as important domains the adult child or parents might want to work on in individual or family therapy after RFT-SGM has ended. When appropriate, family members are referred to other professionals for concomitant treatment or for additional treatment once RFT-SGM has finished. In other instances, clients are already in individual or couple therapy when they present for RFT-SGM. In such cases, we conduct our work parallel to, and in synchrony with, the work they are doing in individual or couples therapy.

RFT-SGM requires that both the adult child and their parents be willing to work, in good faith, on finding ways to help the adult child feel less rejected and more accepted and to improve the quality of the relationship. That is not to say that all the family members need to be enthusiastic or optimistic when they present for treatment. Some families come after years of frustration, conflict, and/or disengagement, and they may be demoralized and skeptical about the possibility of change. However, all family members have to be willing to try. In some instances, we have been approached by adult children who want to bring their parents to treatment but are not sure whether their parents will agree. In such cases, we work with them to formulate their request to their parents. We help them reach out to their parents from a place of vulnerability and longing, not from a place of anger and blame. When adult children say to their parents,

> I know that my being gay it is hard for you, but you are my parents and my relationship with you is important to me. I love you and want you in my life. Let's try to find a way to work through this together rather than drift apart,

parents are usually willing to come in to at least meet us and hear more about the treatment. However, a minority of parents intransigently maintain that their child's sexual orientation or gender identity is unnatural, a bad choice, or immoral, even after their adult child reaches out. They remain focused on trying to change their child rather than accept them or improve the relationship. These parents are not (yet) candidates for this treatment.

It is also important to note that the model is designed for working with families in which the adult child has been out of the closet to their parents for at least a year. This model is not designed for working with parents who have just found out about their child's minority sexual orientation or gender identity. Parents who are experiencing severe distress immediately subsequent to their child's disclosure may first require more supportive interventions designed to normalize and contain their emotional reactions, including psychoeducation. For those willing, attending support groups in the community, such as PFLAG, can be important. We have found that once parents have regained their ground, and some time has passed, they are more available to reap the benefit from the type of relational work described in this chapter.

REFERENCES

Allen, J. P., & Hauser, S. T. (1996). Autonomy and relatedness in adolescent–family interactions as predictors of young adults' states of mind regarding attachment. *Development and Psychopathology, 8*(4), 793–809.

Beals, K. P., & Peplau, L. A. (2006). Disclosure patterns within social networks of gay men and lesbians. *Journal of Homosexuality, 51*, 101–120. doi:10.1300/J082v51n02_06

Boruchovitz-Zamir, R., & Diamond, G. M. (2017, June). *Changes in parental criticism and empathy over the course of attachment-based family therapy with LGBT young adults and their non-accepting parents.* Paper presented at the international conference of the Society for Psychotherapy Research, Jerusalem, Israel.

Bowlby, J. (1988). *A secure base: Parent–child attachment and healthy human development.* New York, NY: Basic Books.

Carastathis, G. S., Cohen, L., Kaczmarek, E., & Chang, P. (2016). Rejected by family for being gay or lesbian: Portrayals, perceptions, and resilience. *Journal of Homosexuality, 64*(3), 289–320.

Cramer, D. W., & Roach, A. J. (1988). Coming out to mom and dad: A study of gay males and their relationships with their parents. *Journal of Homosexuality, 15*, 79–92. doi:10.1300/J082v15n03_04

D'Amico, E., & Julien, D. (2012). Disclosure of sexual orientation and gay, lesbian, and bisexual youths' adjustment: Associations with past and current parental acceptance and rejection. *Journal of GLBT Family Studies, 8*(3), 215–242.

D'Augelli, A. R. (2002). Mental health problems among lesbian, gay, and bisexual youths ages 14 to 21. *Clinical Child Psychology and Psychiatry, 7,* 439–462. doi:10.1177/1359104502007003010

D'Augelli, A. R., Grossman, A. H., & Starks, M. T. (2005). Parents' awareness of lesbian, gay, and bisexual youths' sexual orientation. *Journal of Marriage and Family, 67,* 474–482. doi:10.1111/j.0022-445.2005.00129.x

D'Augelli, A. R., Grossman, A. H., Starks, M. T., & Sinclair, K. O. (2010). Factors associated with parents' knowledge of gay, lesbian, and bisexual youths' sexual orientation. *Journal of GLBT Family Studies, 6,* 178–198. doi:10.1080/15504281003705410

Diamond, G. M. (2018). *Relationship-focused therapy for sexual and gender minority young adults and their non-accepting parents.* Paper presented at the Association for Behavior and Cognitive Therapy conference. Washington, D.C.: November 15th.

Diamond, G. M., Diamond, G. S., Levy, S., Closs, C., Ladipo, T., & Siqueland, L. (2012). Attachment-based family therapy for suicidal lesbian, gay, and bisexual adolescents: A treatment development study and open trial with preliminary findings. *Psychotherapy, 49,* 62–71. doi:10.1037/a0026247

Diamond, G. M., Shahar, B., Sabo, D., & Tsvieli, N. (2016). Attachment-based family therapy and emotion-focused therapy for unresolved anger: The role of productive emotional processing. *Psychotherapy, 53*(1), 34–44.

Diamond, G. M., & Shpigel, M. S. (2014). Attachment-based family therapy for lesbian and gay young adults and their persistently nonaccepting parents. *Professional Psychology: Research and Practice, 45*(4), 258–268.

Diamond, G. S., Diamond, G. M., & Levy, S. L. (2014). *Attachment-based family therapy for depressed adolescents.* Washington, DC: American Psychological Association.

Diamond, G. S., Reis, B. F., Diamond, G. M., Siqueland, L., & Isaacs, L. (2002). Attachment-based family therapy for depressed adolescents: A treatment development study. *Journal of the American Academy of Child and Adolescent Psychiatry, 41,* 1190–1196. http://dx.doi.org/10.1097/00004583-200210000-00008

Diamond, G. S., Wintersteen, M. B., Brown, G. K., Diamond, G. M., Gallop, R., Shelef, K., & Levy, S. (2010). Attachment-based family therapy for adolescents with suicidal ideation: A randomized controlled trial. *Journal of the American Academy of Child and Adolescent Psychiatry, 49,* 122–131.

Dijker, A. J. M. (2014). A theory of vulnerability-based morality. *Emotion Review, 6,* 175–183.

Eisenberg, M. E., & Resnick, M. D. (2006). Suicidality among gay, lesbian and bisexual youth: The role of protective factors. *Journal of Adolescent Health, 39,* 662–668. doi:10.1016/j.jadohealth.2006.04.024

Elizur, Y., & Ziv, M. (2001). Family support and acceptance, gay male identity formation, and psychological adjustment: A path model. *Family Process, 40*(2), 125–144.

Evans, E., Hawton, K., & Rodham, K. (2004). Factors associated with suicidal phenomena in adolescents: A systematic review of population based studies. *Clinical Psychology Review, 24,* 957–979. doi:10.1016/j.cpr.2004.04.005

Feinstein, B. A., Wadsworth, L. P., Davila, J., & Goldfried, M. R. (2014). Do parental acceptance and family support moderate associations between dimensions of minority stress and depressive symptoms among lesbians and gay men? *Professional Psychology: Research and Practice, 45*(4), 239–246.

Floyd, F. J., Stein, T. S., Harter, K. S. M., Allison, A., & Nye, C. L. (1999). Gay, lesbian, and bisexual youths: Separation–individuation, parental attitudes, identity consolidation, and well-being. *Journal of Youth and Adolescence, 28*, 719–739. doi:10.1023/A:1021691601737

Greenberg, L., Warwar, S., & Malcolm, W. (2010). Emotion-focused couples therapy and the facilitation of forgiveness. *Journal of Marital and Family Therapy, 36*, 28–42.

Greenberg, L. S. (2011). *Emotion-focused therapy.* Washington, DC: American Psychological Association.

Greenberg, L. S. (2012). Emotions, the great captains of our lives: Their role in the process of change in psychotherapy. *American Psychologist, 67*, 697–707.

Greenberg, L. S., Ford, C. L., Alden, L. S., & Johnson, S. M. (1993). In-session change in emotionally focused therapy. *Journal of Consulting and Clinical Psychology, 61*, 78–84.

Greenberg, L. S., & Paivio, S. C. (2003). *Working with emotions in psychotherapy* (Vol. 13). New York, NY Guilford.

Grossman, A., D'Augelli, A. T., Howell, T. J., & Hubbard, S. (2005). Parent' reactions to transgender youth' gender nonconforming expression and identity. *Journal of Gay & Lesbian Social Services, 18*, 3–16.

Haas, A. P., Rodgers, P. L., & Herman, J. L. (2014). Suicide attempts among transgender and gender non-conforming adults: Findings of the national transgender discrimination survey. American Foundation for Suicide Prevention and Williams Institute.

Heatherington, L., & Lavner, J. A. (2008). Coming to terms with coming out: Review and recommendations for family systems-focused research. *Journal of Family Psychology, 22*, 329–343. doi:10.1037/0893-3200.22.3.329

Hershberger, S. L., & D'Augelli, A. R. (1995). The impact of victimization on the mental health and suicidality of lesbian, gay, and bisexual youths. *Developmental Psychology, 31*, 65–74. doi:10.1037/0012-1649.31.1.65

Johnson, S. M., & Greenberg, L. S. (1985). Emotionally focused couples therapy: An outcome study. *Journal of Marital and Family Therapy, 11*, 313–317.

Johnson, S. M., & Greenberg, L. S. (1995). The emotionally focused approach to problems in adult attachment. In N. S. Jacobson & A. S. Gurman (Eds.), *Clinical handbook of couple therapy* (pp. 121–141). New York, NY: Guilford.

Liddle, H. A. (2002). *Multidimensional family therapy for adolescent cannabis users: Cannabis Youth Treatment (CYT) series* (Vol. 5). Rockville, MD: Center for Substance Abuse Treatment, Substance Abuse and Mental Health Services Administration.

Lishner, D. A., Batson, C. D., & Huss, E. (2011). Tenderness and sympathy: Distinct empathic emotions elicited by different forms of need. *Personality and Social Psychology Bulletin, 37*, 614–625.

McKinnon, J. M., & Greenberg, L. S. (2013). Revealing underlying vulnerable emotion in couple therapy: Impact on session and final outcome. *Journal of Family Therapy, 35*, 303–319.

Minuchin, S. (1977). *Families and family therapy.* London, UK: Routledge.

Needham, B. L., & Austin, E. L. (2010). Sexual orientation, parental support, and health during the transition to young adulthood. *Journal of Youth and Adolescence, 39*, 1189–1198. doi:10.1007/s10964-010-9533-6

Norwood, K. (2013). Meaning matters: Framing trans identity in the context of family relationships. *Journal of GLBT Family Studies, 9*(2), 152–178. doi:10.1080/1550428X.2013.765262

O'Connor, T. G., Allen, J. P., Bell, K. L., & Hauser, S. T. (1996). Adolescent–parent relationships and leaving home in young adulthood. *New Directions for Child and Adolescent Development, 1996*(71), 39–52.

Pachankis, J. E., & Goldfried, M. R. (2004). Clinical Issues in Working With Lesbian, Gay, and Bisexual Clients. *Psychotherapy: Theory, Research, Practice, Training, 41*(3), 227–246. http://dx.doi.org/10.1037/0033-3204.41.3.227

Pachankis, J. E., Goldfried, M. R., & Ramrattan, M. E. (2008). Extension of the rejection sensitivity construct to the interpersonal functioning of gay men. *Journal of Consulting and Clinical Psychology, 76*, 306–317.

Padilla, Y. C., Crisp, C., & Rew, D. L. (2010). Parental acceptance and illegal drug use among gay, lesbian, and bisexual adolescents: Results from a national survey. *Social Work, 55*(3), 265–275.

Robinson, M. A., & Brewster, M. E. (2016). Understanding affiliate stigma faced by heterosexual family and friends of LGB people: A measurement development study. *Journal of Family Psychology, 30*(3), 353–363. http://dx.doi.org/10.1037/fam0000153

Robinson, B. E., Walters, L. H., & Skeen, P. (1989). Response of parents to learning that their child is homosexual and concern over AIDS: A national study. *Journal of Homosexuality, 18*, 59–80. doi:10.1300/J082v18n01_03

Rothman, E. F., Sullivan, M., Keyes, S., & Boehmer, U. (2012). Parents' supportive reactions to sexual orientation disclosure associated with better health: Results from a population-based survey of LGB adults in Massachusetts. *Journal of Homosexuality, 59*(2), 186–200.

Ryan, C., Huebner, D., Diaz, R. M., & Sanchez, J. (2009). Family rejection as a predictor of negative health outcomes in White and Latino lesbian, gay and bisexual young adults. *Pediatrics, 123*, 346–352. doi:10.1542/peds.2007-3524

Ryan, C., Russell, S. T., Huebner, D., Diaz, R. M., & Sanchez, J. (2010). Family acceptance in adolescence and the health of LGBT young adults. *Journal of Child and Adolescent Psychiatric Nursing, 23*, 205–213. doi:10.1111/j.1744-6171.2010.00246.x

Samarova, V., Shilo, G., & Diamond, G. M. (2014). Changes in youths' perceived parental acceptance of their sexual minority status over time. *Journal of Research on Adolescence, 24*(4), 681–688.

Savin-Williams, R. C. (1989). Coming out to parents and self-esteem among gay and lesbian youths. *Journal of Homosexuality, 18*, 1–35. doi:10.1300/J082v18n01_01

Savin-Williams, R. C., & Dube, E. M. (1998). Parental reactions to their child's disclosure of a gay/lesbian identity. *Family Relations, 47*, 7–13. doi:10.2307/584845

Savin-Williams, R. C., & Ream, G. L. (2003). Sex variations in the disclosure to parents of same-sex attractions. *Journal of Family Psychology, 17*, 429–438. doi:10.1037/0893-3200.17.3.429

Shilo, G., Antebi, N., & Mor, Z. (2015). Individual and community resilience factors among lesbian, gay, bisexual, queer and questioning youth and adults in Israel. *American Journal of Community Psychology, 55*(1–2), 215–227.

Shpigel, M. S., Belsky, Y., & Diamond, G. M. (2015). Clinical work with non-accepting parents of sexual minority children: Addressing causal and controllability attributions. *Professional Psychology: Research and Practice, 46*(1), 46–64.

Shpigel, M., Diamond, G. M., & Diamond, G. S. (2012). Changes in parenting behaviors in attachment-based family therapy. *Journal of Marital and Family Therapy, 38*, 271–283.

Steinmann, R., Gat, I., Nir-Gottlieb, O., Shahar, B., & Diamond, G. M. (2017). Attachment-based family therapy and individual emotion-focused therapy for unresolved anger: Qualitative analysis of treatment outcomes and change processes. *Psychotherapy, 54*(3), 281–291. http://dx.doi.org/10.1037/pst0000116

Stone Fish, L., & Harvey, R. G. (2005). *Nurturing queer youth: Family therapy transformed.* New York, NY: Norton.

Wahlig, J. L. (2015). Losing the child they thought they had: Therapeutic suggestions for an ambiguous loss perspective with parents of a transgender child. *Journal of GLBT Family Studies, 11*(4), 305–326. doi:10.1080/1550428X.2014.945676

20

Transdiagnostic Approaches to Improve Sexual Minority Individuals' Co-occurring Mental, Behavioral, and Sexual Health

CRAIG RODRIGUEZ-SEIJAS, CHARLES L. BURTON,
AND JOHN E. PACHANKIS ■

Sexual minority individuals (i.e., those who identity as lesbian, gay, or bisexual [LGB], engage in same-sex sexual behavior, or report persistent same-sex attractions) experience disproportionately higher rates of mood and anxiety disorders compared to heterosexual men and women (Cochran & Mays, 2000, 2006; Cochran, Sullivan, & Mays, 2003), as well as higher rates of behavioral co-morbidity, including substance use disorders (Cochran, Ackerman, Mays, & Ross, 2004; Drabble & Trocki, 2005), suicidality (de Graaf, Sandfort, & ten Have, 2006), sexual compulsivity (Parsons, Grov, & Golub, 2012), and HIV-transmission risk behavior (Brennan, Craig, & Thompson, 2012). These psychosocial health threats do not occur in isolation, and each exacerbates the impact of the others, thereby undermining sexual minority persons' health and presenting a unique challenge to clinicians (Stall et al., 2003). Still, evidence-based treatment approaches tailored to this population have been relatively lacking. The ESTEEM (Effective Skills to Empower Effective Men; Pachankis, 2014) protocol is the first transdiagnostic treatment approach designed to address the multiple co-occurring psychoso-cial health needs of sexual minority individuals and, in fact, is the first LGB-affirmative mental health treatment for sexual minority individuals ever tested in a randomized controlled trial. This chapter introduces this treatment paradigm, including the principles that underlie the therapeutic approach, evidence of its effectiveness across multiple domains of function, and illustrative examples taken from the administration of the protocol. It also presents future directions for both research and clinical work with sexual minority individuals.

Minority stress theory (Meyer, 2003) is useful for understanding how one's non-heterosexual sexual orientation can be associated with increased risk for detrimental psychosocial health conditions. Health threats faced by sexual minority individuals result from a social climate that stigmatizes non-heterosexual persons. Strong evidence suggests that minority stressors—structural, interpersonal, and intrapersonal stressors resulting from sexual minority persons' stigmatized social status (Meyer, 2003)—are an underlying cause of the mental, behavioral, and sexual health disparities observed in this population. Minority stressors not only compound the effect of general life stress to confer risk for psychopathology (Hatzenbuehler, 2009; Meyer, Schwartz, & Frost, 2008) but also are associated with multiple other negative health outcomes.

Minority stressors exert a transdiagnostic effect in their associations with deleterious outcomes. Stress reactions that result from exposure to minority stress can transcend diagnostic boundaries and are often associated with multiple domains of dysfunction, including mood and anxiety disorders, problematic substance use, and sexual-risk behavior. For example, depression and anxiety symptoms are associated with minority stressors such as victimization based on one's sexual orientation, discrimination, chronic expectations of rejection as a result of one's sexual orientation, internalized homophobia, and concealment of one's non-heterosexual orientation (Cohen, Feinstein, Rodriguez-Seijas, Taylor, & Newman, 2016; Feinstein, Goldfried, & Davila, 2012; Pachankis, Newcomb, Feinstein, & Sullivan, 2018); substance use problems are associated with gay-related rejection and internalized homophobia (Brubaker, Garrett, & Dew, 2009; Green & Feinstein, 2012; Pachankis, Hatzenbuehler, & Starks, 2014; Pachankis, Westmaas, & Dougherty, 2011); and sexual compulsivity—and associated HIV-risk behavior—is associated with childhood gender nonconformity, discrimination, internalized homophobia, and expectations of rejection (Pachankis, Rendina, et al., 2015). Furthermore, all of these outcomes are associated with each other (Parsons et al., 2012).

A number of studies have begun to chart the pathways through which minority stress influences health outcomes. Minority stress not only contributes to maladaptive behaviors in contexts in which an individual's sexual orientation may be salient (e.g., anxiously anticipating and perceiving rejection due to their sexual orientation; Feinstein et al., 2012), but also can increase broad, universal risks for myriad forms of mental, behavioral, and sexual ill-health (e.g., increasing rumination, hopelessness, and social isolation; Hatzenbuehler, 2009). For instance, sexual minority individuals experience higher rates of victimization, violence, and abuse across the lifespan that are associated with dysfunction both directly—such as substance use problems, as outlined previously—and indirectly through increases in emotional, cognitive, and behavioral forms of avoidance (Foa & Kozak, 1986; Marx & Sloan, 2002) and hypervigilance (Major & O'Brien, 2005; Pachankis, 2007). Avoidance is associated with substance use, sexual compulsivity, rumination and worry, and unassertive interpersonal behaviors (e.g., failing to assert condom usage during sexual encounters); hypervigilance as related to expectations of rejection based on one's sexual orientation has been associated with social anxiety, substance use, sexual compulsivity, and other negative outcomes (Feinstein et al., 2012; Pachankis, Goldfried, & Ramrattan, 2008; Pachankis, Hatzenbuehler, Rendina, Safren, & Parsons, 2015; Pachankis, Hatzenbuehler, Schmidt, et al., 2014; Pachankis, Newcomb, Feinstein, & Bernstein, 2014). Furthermore, communication of the social inferiority of sexual minority individuals—by virtue of the persistence of discriminatory laws, policies, and social attitudes—can lead to perceptions of low agency, poor social communication, and unassertiveness, with ramifications for sexual orientation concealment and enacting health-promoting behaviors such as asserting condom usage (Pachankis, 2007). Minority stress theory, therefore, offers a parsimonious and comprehensive explanation of the disparities observed among sexual minority men and women, and it provides one possible avenue through which intervention approaches can have maximum efficacy (Pachankis, 2015).

Despite existing guidelines for conducting therapeutic interventions with sexual minority individuals (American Psychological Association, 2012), there are relatively few evidence-based treatment paradigms tailored to this population. This lack of appropriate evidence-based interventions represents a particularly notable research priority given that sexual minority individuals are more likely to utilize treatment services compared to their heterosexual counterparts (Bränström, Pachankis, & Hatzenbuehler, 2017; Cochran et al., 2003). Furthermore, current treatment models require LGB persons to receive services from multiple specialists for their diverse health disparities, which is a cost-prohibitive approach that often fails to address the minority stress reactions underlying many of the patient's presenting problems. Effective intervention with sexual minority individuals must balance enacting change across the many health disparity clusters that affect this population against limited resources, such as provider training to address multiple presenting clinical complaints.

Aiming treatment at the multiple co-occurring psychosocial processes underlying health disparities among sexual minorities aligns with recent empirical and clinical advances toward a transdiagnostic approach within the general population, which similarly targets shared psychosocial mechanisms that underlie most mental health disorders (Barlow, Allen, & Choate, 2004; Barlow et al., 2010, 2017; Rodriguez-Seijas, Eaton, & Krueger, 2015). By systematically adapting an existing transdiagnostic treatment manual (Barlow et al., 2004, 2010), one new LGB-affirmative psychotherapy model applies a transdiagnostic approach to address the minority stress processes that underlie the numerous co-occurring psychosocial health problems disproportionately facing sexual minority individuals. The remainder of this chapter describes this treatment model; discusses the principles that underlie this form of transdiagnostic intervention, illustrated by case examples; discusses preliminary findings regarding its efficacy; and presents considerations for future research.

EFFECTIVE SKILLS TO EMPOWER EFFECTIVE MEN

Clinical Model

The Effective Skills to Empower Effective Men (ESTEEM; Pachankis, 2014) protocol is a 10-module, individually administered intervention based on the Unified Protocol for the Transdiagnostic Treatment of Emotional Disorders (Barlow et al., 2010)—adapted to reduce the co-occurring negative mental (e.g., depression), behavioral (e.g., substance abuse), and sexual (e.g., HIV risk) health outcomes of minority stress. ESTEEM utilizes transdiagnostic cognitive–behavioral techniques to specifically address gay and bisexual men's minority stress reactions that contribute to these negative health outcomes. In its current iteration, the ESTEEM intervention is tailored specifically to the needs of gay and bisexual men, given their relatively unique confluence of health threats—such as the significant prevalence of HIV (Centers for Disease Control and Prevention, 2013)—compared to sexual minority women. It is noteworthy, however, that a counterpart to the ESTEEM intervention is currently being developed to target the psychosocial health threats for sexual minority women.

The ESTEEM protocol was developed through systematic consultation with key stakeholders (Pachankis, 2014). Central themes for adaptation were distilled through dialog with stakeholder members of the target clinical population (i.e., gay and bisexual men with significant symptoms of one or more mental health disorders) as well as expert mental health professionals with significant experience providing services to LGBT populations. These interviews involved asking stakeholders about common stressors faced by gay and bisexual men and their impact on gay and bisexual men's mental, behavioral, and sexual health, as well as adaptive and maladaptive strategies that could be utilized for coping with minority stress. This consultation was followed by relevant modification of the Unified Protocol, as well as subsequent stakeholder review and a preliminary trial (Pachankis, 2014).

ESTEEM Protocol Modules

The following are the modules of the ESTEEM protocol:

1. Motivating engagement in ESTEEM treatment
2. Explaining the emotional impact of minority stress
3. Tracking minority stress-related emotional experiences
4. Increasing awareness of minority stress reactions
5. Reappraising minority stress cognitions
6. Addressing substance use, rumination, and other emotional avoidance strategies
7. Connecting minority stress to emotion-driven behaviors

8. Learning assertiveness and other behavioral skills
9. Experimenting with new reactions to minority stress
10. Preventing relapse through self-affirmation

The 10 modules of the ESTEEM protocol are predicated upon eight core underlying principles. In the next section, we describe these principles and explore how they can be enacted in practice. We also illustrate implementation of the principles through clinical examples drawn from actual administration of the ESTEEM protocol. Although these principles should permeate the entire protocol, some modules place greater attention on one or more of them. For instance, although an entire module is dedicated to assertiveness training, this principle can guide the content and goals of several other modules within the intervention.

Principles Underlying the ESTEEM Protocol

PRINCIPLE 1: MOOD AND ANXIETY DISORDERS ARE COMMON RESPONSES TO MINORITY STRESS

Stigma operates in insidious, subtle ways to compromise health (Hatzenbuehler, 2009). Consequently, sexual minorities may not attribute the source of their psychosocial difficulties to minority stress; they might instead misattribute their distress, and difficulty managing it, to other sources, including themselves. Thus, this first principle emphasizes the importance of highlighting the influence of minority stress on clients and outlining the scientific explanation of how stigma threatens the health of sexual minorities. In this way, clients are guided toward shifting their conceptualization of their mental, behavioral, and sexual health problems away from one of personal inferiority toward locating them as normative responses to minority stress.

Exposure to minority stress can influence the psychosocial development of sexual minorities in a variety of ways that later influence their health as adults. For example, many sexual minority individuals realize their non-heterosexual orientation in isolation, an experience that is associated with concerns of parental and peer rejection (D'Augelli, 2002). Furthermore, early experiences of gender nonconforming behavior in childhood and adolescence are common among gay and bisexual men (Lippa, 2008; Rahman & Wilson, 2003; Rieger, Linsenmeier, Gygax, & Bailey, 2008). As such, examining the responses of significant others to these behaviors can be a powerful tool that demonstrates the effects of minority stress in sexual minority persons' lives: Boys might be corrected for feminine hand and body movements, chastised for displaying interest in stereotypically feminine games and pursuits (e.g., interests in cooking), or even ridiculed for displaying inappropriate interest in members of the opposite sex. Collectively, these early experiences convey the message that acceptance and love are conditional on the social acceptability of one's behavior—a precursor for problems related to rejection sensitivity, which underlies multiple domains of dysfunction (Cohen et al., 2016).

Minority stress processes also drive stress within the gay community. For instance, internalized homophobia is related to perceived desirability of masculine presentations of self and partner among gay men (Sánchez & Vilain, 2012). Similarly, sexual minorities have fewer avenues for childhood development of self-esteem, which can lead to the development of a sense of self-worth contingent upon achievement-related factors, such as sexual desirability or financial status, as a means to cope with the stigma of possessing a sexual minority identity (Pachankis & Hatzenbuehler, 2013). Recent research suggests that intraminority stress among gay men, driven by these status-related concerns, may exert equal, or even greater, influence on mental health symptoms as do other forms of minority stress (Pachankis, Clark, Burton, White-Hughto, & Keene, 2017). Re-envisioning these difficulties as empirically established consequences of growing up in a stigmatizing environment can be a powerful tool that helps sexual minorities question how their unique experiences with minority stress impact their identity development, current functioning, and struggles interacting with other members of the gay community.

Not all sexual minority individuals, however, readily accept that their experiences of minority stress contribute to their current dysfunction. Identifying common shame-driven behaviors, such as partially or fully concealing one's sexual orientation, monitoring gender presentation, using gender-neutral pronouns to describe a romantic partner, or avoiding intimacy with heterosexual peers, can illuminate the unique ways in which minority stress influences day-to-day life. Presenting de-identified examples from other gay and bisexual men can also normalize the experience of minority stress and help clients engage in a discussion of the relevance of this stress in their own lives. Note that the centrality of minority stress in sexual minority clients' lives can vary from person to person, but it is unlikely that a client is not at least partially influenced by historical and current attitudes toward LGBT individuals. For clients who still believe minority stress is irrelevant for them, the therapist's role becomes one of setting a safe place for exploring this possibility in later sessions, continuing to formulate a functional analysis considering the possibility that minority stress may be operating more insidiously in the client's life, or drawing upon those aspects of ESTEEM that address maintaining factors of depression and anxiety outside of minority stress.

Principle 2: Challenge Maladaptive Negative Thoughts

The second principle of the ESTEEM protocol involves helping clients understand the ways in which minority stress can influence their cognitive patterns, thereby opening the possibility of challenging maladaptive cognitions. Gay and bisexual men report that early experiences with minority stress lead to self-conceptions of inferiority, deficiency, and impairment (Pachankis, Rendina, et al., 2015), which can contribute to their internalized homophobia and rejection sensitivity. Standard cognitive restructuring techniques, common to cognitive–behavioral therapy (CBT) intervention approaches, can be used to reduce minority stress-driven cognitive biases.

In the ESTEEM protocol, challenging maladaptive thoughts is accomplished through an affirmative lens that recognizes that current maladaptive perceptive biases had previously adaptive functions. For instance, disproportionate fears of rejection are rooted in the need to protect oneself from discrimination, and even violence, upon disclosure of one's sexual orientation (Pachankis & Goldfried, 2006). However, when individuals find themselves in more supportive environments, such fears can impair the formation of intimate relationships with both heterosexual and sexual minority others. Similarly, minority stress leads to low agency and poor self-efficacy for enacting health-promoting behaviors; concerns of rejection may lead individuals to avoid asserting condom usage during sexual encounters out of a belief that they might be rejected should they vocalize this health need (Hart & Heimberg, 2005).

The cognitive impact of minority stress manifests in subtle behaviors that detract from psychosocial health, but minority stress-driven cognitions are not set in stone and can be altered using traditional cognitive therapeutic techniques. Exploring how maladaptive cognitive biases have outlived their utility via Socratic questioning can help restructure these cognitions and thus facilitate the replacement of situationally maladaptive behaviors shaped by erroneous cognitions. It is important to note, however, that challenging maladaptive cognitions also considers the real-world implications and utility of these cognitions. For instance, reducing hypervigilance to rejection might not be appropriate for all sexual minorities, such as those living in pervasively discriminatory settings wherein danger and violence are unfortunate truths.

PRINCIPLE 3: ENCOURAGE ASSERTIVE AND OPEN COMMUNICATION ACROSS CONTEXTS

Sexual minority individuals are often led to believe that they do not have the right or ability to stand up for themselves in the face of minority stress or to assert their preferences and desires across situations. Minority stress reactions, such as hypersensitivity to rejection, predict unassertive communication (Pachankis et al., 2008). Having to conceal one's true identity and denying the emotional pain from early stigmatizing experiences might serve as precursors to unassertiveness in adulthood. The third principle of the ESTEEM protocol therefore focuses on helping sexual minority men learn to assertively communicate their wants and desires. This is particularly evident in the eighth module of the protocol, which involves explicitly discussing with clients ways in which they might deny their own wants and needs, the effects of such actions on their psychosocial well-being, and considering new ways of communicating with others.

Therapists assist clients with better understanding the ways in which they silence themselves and how to utilize skills built in previous modules, such as challenging maladaptive cognitive patterns, to engender assertive behaviors that are consistent with personal values. In keeping with Principle 1 of the ESTEEM protocol, unassertiveness is normalized as one consequence of minority stress experiences and stigmatizing social contexts. This facilitates a shift in the narrative from one of personal deficiency (e.g., "I'm a wimp") to one that normalizes and empowers the client (e.g., "I don't have to hide my true feelings anymore").

Unassertiveness manifests in multiple subtle ways in the lives of gay and bisexual men. For some, it might be difficult to vocalize simple preferences with close friends; asserting one's desire not to use drugs or alcohol in social contexts can be difficult. For others, however, unassertiveness might manifest in sexual risk-taking such as engaging in condomless anal sex (Hart & Heimberg, 2005). The repercussions of unassertive behavior might range from unsatisfactory social relationships to significant health risks, making it important to consider the unique ways in which a lack of assertive behavior and open communication might impact the lives of gay and bisexual men and also how these might be driven by maladaptive cognitions (Principle 2). For instance, fears of asserting one's preferences with friends and sexual partners might be resultant from concerns about rejection and social isolation. Therefore, it is important to account for the myriad forms and functions of unassertive behavior in gay and bisexual men's lives.

Earlier modules of the ESTEEM protocol set the stage for increasing assertiveness during the later modules of the intervention. In the first module, therapists assist clients in clearly elucidating their goals for treatment and the spheres in which they would like to witness improvement. Therapists and clients further engage in open communication about the discrepancies between their desires and the outcomes of current behaviors (Modules 4 and 5). These earlier activities serve the purpose of modeling assertive and open communication, thereby setting the stage for later modules that explicitly focus on reducing the distance between one's desires and current behaviors, such as engaging in exercises that explicitly aim at increasing assertiveness in everyday activities (Module 8). Furthermore, these principles become integrated in the final modules of the protocol, wherein clients design and begin implementing behavioral experiments aimed at reducing avoidance, altering maladaptive coping strategies in the face of minority stress, and increasing interpersonal assertiveness.

PRINCIPLE 4: VALIDATE SEXUAL MINORITIES' UNIQUE STRENGTHS

The fourth principle of the ESTEEM protocol involves highlighting the unique strengths of sexual minority communities. Unlike many other minority groups (e.g., racial/ethnic minorities, religious minorities, and persons from lower socioeconomic backgrounds), gay and bisexual men often do not share their sexual orientation with their parents and are thus rarely introduced to the rich culture and history of the LGBT community (Crocker & Major, 1989). As such, the ESTEEM protocol focuses on explicitly educating sexual minorities regarding the remarkable resilience of sexual minority men and women—as well as adapting an affirmative and strengths-based approach—to instill a sense of hope and optimism and to provide identity-related support. Explicit focus on these strengths can serve a motivational force, reminding clients that they too can overcome their struggles to live functional, fulfilling lives (Herrick et al., 2011; Kwon, 2013).

Because parents of sexual minorities do not typically share such a sexual orientation, sexual minorities typically do not inherit narratives of community resilience and personal stigma coping strategies from their parents. It can be helpful for sexual minority persons to be reminded of the unique forms of resilience demonstrated within their community: the LGBT community's history of—and continuing—activism toward understanding and eradicated HIV/AIDS (Trapence et al., 2012), continued advocacy against discrimination and inequality (Herrick et al., 2011), social creativity through the creation of families of choice in response to rejection from biological families (Weeks, Heaphy, & Donovan, 2001), and sexual creativity in exploring non-heteronormative romantic relationships (Parsons, Starks, DuBois, Grov, & Golub, 2013). Collectively, these characteristics of the LGBT community may increase pride in the unique experience of being a sexual minority and remind sexual minority individuals of their abilities to remain resourceful and connected despite societal constraints.

At the individual level, all sexual minorities navigate their own unique coming out process. Regardless of the extent to which an individual conceals their sexual orientation, they have had to make a conscious effort to choose with whom they share that identity and from whom it is concealed. Given that many sexual minorities spend considerable time concealing their sexual orientations—particularly during more formative years—to protect themselves from the effects of early invalidating environments, it is understandable that concerns with regard to self-presentation and judgment by others might remain long after "coming out" (Pachankis & Hatzenbuehler, 2013; Potoczniak, Aldea, & DeBlaere, 2007). Although persistent self-monitoring may lead to mental health symptoms (e.g., excessive social anxiety in less invalidating circumstances), it is important to note that many such behaviors result from navigating a stigmatizing society. The creativity, endurance, and pain inherent in concealing one's sexual minority status remind clients of their personal strength and resilience (Herrick et al., 2011; Herrick, Stall, Goldhammer, Egan, & Mayer, 2014). Reflecting a client's personal strengths can instill hope and increase their motivation for continued self-development and behavioral change.

PRINCIPLE 5: AFFIRM AND NORMALIZE SEXUAL MINORITIES' EXPRESSIONS OF SEXUALITY

Principle 5 of the ESTEEM protocol focuses on affirming healthy, rewarding expressions of sexuality. Awareness of a non-heterosexual sexual orientation often occurs in adolescence (Rosario, Schrimshaw, & Hunter, 2009) with an absence of relevant sexual health education (Kubicek, Beyer, Weiss, Iverson, & Kipke, 2010). In addition to facing confusion and lack of practical information regarding noncoital intercourse, sexual minorities may also internalize negative societal messages about same-sex sexual behavior (Herek, 2004), which can leave them feeling ashamed, undesirable, and incapable of forming loving relationships. Collectively, these developmental circumstances leave gay and bisexual men, in particular, disproportionately affected by several sexual health disparities, including sexual compulsivity (Missildine et al., 2005), erectile difficulties (Bancroft, Carnes, Janssen, Goodrich, & Long, 2005), and HIV infection risk (Centers for Disease Control and Prevention [CDC], 2013).

To address these issues, the ESTEEM protocol takes a sex-positive approach by embracing sex as an important component of health, and it examines the ways in which minority stress compromises individuals' sex lives. ESTEEM helps sexual minorities articulate their sexual health goals; identify their sexual needs and desires; and examine the ways in which minority stress might prevent them from sexual health, fulfillment, and satisfaction. Acceptance of sexual identity, attractions, fantasies, and behaviors is one way of affirming sexual minorities' sexualities. For instance, exploring the ways in which minority stress and masculine gender conceptualizations (Courtenay, 2005) interact to stigmatize sexual preferences (e.g., preference for anal receptive vs. anal insertive sex) can assist in reducing gay and bisexual men's shame and guilt associated with what might be considered a less masculine sexual behavior. Monitoring sexual patterns and sexual self-perceptions, as well as cognitive restructuring of rejection-related sexual beliefs—including those related to sexual safety—also exemplify this principle. For instance, clients might recognize their patterns of substance use during sex as being related to minority stress processes (e.g., attempting to reduce or escape negative emotions such as sexual shame). Furthermore, the acceptance of sexual needs, such as desires for non-monogamous sexual relationships, and assisting clients in discussing such desires with a current or potential partner comprise another way to validate and affirm sexual minorities' sexual identities.

Principle 6: Facilitate Supportive Relationships

The sixth principle of the ESTEEM protocol focuses on increasing social support. Social resources buffer against the deleterious effects of minority stress (Hershberger & D'Augelli, 1995; Rosario et al., 2009). However, sexual minorities experience greater social isolation and less social support compared to their heterosexual counterparts (Plöderl & Fartacek, 2005; Safren & Heimberg, 1999). Poor social support is closely linked with negative mental health (Hatzenbuehler, Nolen-Hoeksema, & Dovidio, 2009; Safren & Heimberg, 1999) and even LGB individuals' biological response to stress (Burton, Bonanno, & Hatzenbuehler, 2014). Therefore, the final principle of the ESTEEM protocol counters the deleterious effects of minority stress on sexual minorities' social functioning by helping clients identify supportive community connections and build healthy relationships.

The principles throughout the ESTEEM protocol are integrated to bolster pre-existing forms of social support. Increasing the ratio of healthy, compared to unhealthy, social interactions can have a positive influence on perceptions of social support (Marlatt & Donovan, 2005). This may take the form of utilizing assertiveness skills to further enhance current social relationships, such as assertively voicing one's preference for one social activity over another with friends. Improving relationships with parents and biological family members, when possible and appropriate, further increases feelings of support (LaSala, 2000). For instance, therapists can employ cognitive restructuring and role-playing exercise to help clients prepare for introducing a romantic partner to the family or for coming out to family members from whom one remained closeted. Therapists further assist sexual minorities in effectively navigating romantic relationships and primary partnerships; a client struggling with dissatisfaction in a long-term relationship would benefit from assertiveness and social skills training to help openly discuss the underlying issues with their romantic partner.

For some sexual minorities, increasing social support takes the form of forging new sources of social interaction and building previously nonexistent support networks. Therapists brainstorm and use problem-solving methods to assist clients in finding appropriate venues for developing new sources of social support. Interacting with local LGBT centers and engaging in LGBT-affirmative groups, such as sports leagues or choirs, supplement existing systems. Furthermore, attending venues in which sexual minorities can meet heterosexual peers who are likely to be LGBT-affirmative both increases social integration and serves as a strong experience of inclusion that counteracts minority stress.

Empirical Support

For several reasons, CBT is particularly well-suited to addressing sexual minority-related stress. First, it focuses on understanding the function of problematic behaviors in their historical and current contexts to determine how they developed and are maintained. Second, it promotes coping self-efficacy by empowering clients with skills to confront the underlying source of maladaptive behaviors in minority stress. Third, it explicitly encourages the replacement of problematic behaviors and cognitions with more functional alternatives. Finally, universal risk factors that underlie the disproportionate rates of mental, behavioral, and sexual health problems of sexual minority individuals are the explicit targets of CBT. For instance, in a CBT framework, chronic expectations of gay-related rejection can be an explicit target of treatment: Psychoeducation can reveal how a history of concealment from important others might have served in the development and maintenance of a chronic fear of rejection; mindfulness skills can help a client realize when they are experiencing rejection-laden thoughts; cognitive restructuring techniques can challenge the validity of these thoughts and enact alternative behaviors where appropriate; and confronting previously avoided circumstances and events where rejection due to one's sexual orientation is unlikely can reduce avoidance tendencies (Feinstein et al., 2012; Pachankis et al., 2017).

In the first wait-list-controlled trial to examine the efficacy of the ESTEEM intervention among young gay and bisexual men (Pachankis, Hatzenbuehler, Rendina, Safren, & Parsons, 2015), the ESTEEM intervention improved outcomes across several spheres of clinical significance. Compared to participants on the wait list, recipients of ESTEEM had greater reductions in depressive symptoms, alcohol use problems, sexual compulsivity, and condomless anal sex with casual partners. The initial findings of the utility of the ESTEEM protocol suggest that this brief psychological intervention is capable of enacting meaningful change across several dimensions of dysfunction. Furthermore, effect sizes of this treatment protocol were comparable to those of other standard single-treatment/single-problem intervention approaches—in some cases exceeding the typical effect size (e.g., for reductions in condomless anal sex). The transdiagnostic approach of ESTEEM circumvents the need to train clinicians across multiple distinct intervention protocols tailored to specific diagnoses and problematic behaviors—an important advantage of this treatment. More important, this can be achieved without sacrifice of treatment efficacy across numerous domains. That is, participation in the ESTEEM protocol results in reductions in not only outcomes (e.g., mood and anxiety symptoms, sexual compulsivity, and substance-related problems) but also minority stress processes (e.g., sexual orientation-related stress, rejection sensitivity, and concealment) and universal risk factors (e.g., rumination and social isolation) that underlie these outcomes.

CASE EXAMPLE

Luke, a 25-year-old gay man, presented for treatment of his social anxiety and depression. The last of three boys, Luke came from a religious, Roman Catholic family. Luke was out to both his parents as well as his brothers. He reported that although his mother had initial difficulty with his sexual orientation, his family was currently supportive and affirming of his gay identity. Luke reported a history of social difficulties: He was overweight in elementary through high school, had few friends, and was teased with regard to both his weight and for lacking interest in sports. Upon further discussion with his therapist, Luke revealed that he often drank alcohol to reduce discomfort in social situations, often resulting in his getting "blackout drunk" on a typical Friday night. He also reported symptoms of depression due to his lack of a close social network, further expressing frustration with his own inability to "get his life together."

When Luke's therapist initially presented the minority stress model, Luke was hesitant, stating that this was not an issue in his life; his family was now very accepting of his sexual orientation. The therapist used this statement as an opportunity to explore the nature of Luke's coming out process. Upon coming out at age 19 years, Luke recalled his mother suggesting that he seek pastoral counseling to overcome his "sinful temptations." He further recalled that during his childhood and adolescence, he attended church functions at which same-sex behavior and attraction were expressly condemned as immoral and sinful. Furthermore, he recalled his father often making homophobic jokes during family gatherings prior to his coming out. The therapist and Luke explored how growing up in such a climate might impact his current functioning. Luke revealed that despite his parents' current open support for his sexual orientation, he was still hesitant to behave in ways that might upset them; he had not invited past boyfriends to family gatherings, and he did not discuss romantic relationships with his family, such as his recent breakup with his last boyfriend. Following this discussion with his therapist, Luke agreed with the conceptualization that these early experiences conveyed the message that acceptance and love might be conditional on the social acceptability of his behavior. He further offered that these same sentiments could be related to his current problem behaviors.

Upon further exploration with his therapist, Luke was able to enunciate clearly how his current depressive and anxiety symptoms were maintained by concerns about rejection from others. In social interactions, Luke reported intense anxiety and concerns about the reactions of others to his behavior. He found it particularly difficult to interact with other gay men, often riddled with concerns about rejection due to his physical appearance and behavior. Following social interactions, he would often ruminate, replaying scenarios in his mind in attempts at reducing anxiety by examining whether or not he committed a social faux pas. In attempts at reducing his anxiety, Luke would drink whenever he went out, usually to the point of inebriation. Luke's anxiety and rejection sensitivity also extended into his sexual life; Luke would often be unable to assert his desire for utilizing condoms during sexual activity.

Together with his therapist, Luke first explored his own personal strengths related to standing up for his own rights and beliefs, in efforts at increasing motivation for change. For instance, Luke recounted that upon coming out, when his mother presented him with a book detailing how he could use his religious faith to overcome the "temptations" of same-sex attraction, Luke refused his mother's request that he read the book. Although difficult, Luke reported that his mother respected his decision. With this foothold, the therapist then implemented cognitive restructuring techniques to explore Luke's maintenance of the status quo with his family members. Luke and his therapist explored the possible outcomes if he were to discuss his romantic life with family members (e.g., his mother, father, or brothers). Luke expected a supportive response from each member, but he still believed that it would be uncomfortable to discuss something like this with them: "It still feels like I would be doing something wrong, you know, but I know that she'd [Luke's mother] be glad that I confided in her. She'd feel like a mother and I guess I'd be glad to talk to someone," responded Luke about the possibility of telling his mother that he had recently experienced a breakup. Motivated to have such a discussion with his family members, in an effort to increase his sense of social inclusion, Luke further located these sentiments in historical messages about the acceptability of his behavior. However, utilizing more proximal evidence of the (un)likelihood of a negative response from family members, Luke felt encouraged to address the topic with his mother.

With headway made in his social interactions with his family, Luke and his therapist next turned to the more ambiguous nature of social interactions outside the family context. Together they explored how these earlier messages, alongside Luke's personal history of being bullied, interacted to increase his anxiety in social situations. Luke identified his alcohol consumption as an avoidance mechanism; by drinking, he not only escaped anxiety-inducing thoughts about rejection but also avoided any corrective experiences. Luke's avoidant pattern of drinking led him to attribute social successes to his alcohol consumption instead of his own social capabilities or likeable qualities. Luke considered what it would be like to engage in alternative ways of being, such as not drinking alcohol on a night out.

Luke and his therapist also devised a hierarchy of potential exercises in which he could engage on his own to further expose himself to his social anxiety without any avoidance, ranging from simpler exercises such as inviting a colleague out to lunch to more difficult ones, such as striking up a conversation with a gay man while sober.

Luke and his therapist also examined how minority stress processes impacted his sexual life. Luke reported that he often felt regretful about his sexual choices. He would often refrain from vocalizing his sexual desires. Luke and his therapist utilized cognitive restructuring exercises aimed at further understanding his passivity during sexual encounters:

> LUKE: I feel anxious in the moment to just stop everything and ask the guy to put on a condom.
>
> THERAPIST: What would happen if you did that?
>
> LUKE: Well I guess it would kill the mood. I mean what if he isn't interested anymore? But then I feel terrible about myself after for not saying anything.
>
> THERAPIST: Let's take that concern at face value. What if he wasn't interested anymore after you said you wanted to use a condom?
>
> LUKE: Well, it wouldn't be that terrible. I mean it would feel uncomfortable, but I could handle it. I guess it's that initial concern of being rejected that we talked about. But in this case, if he rejected me, it wouldn't be a bad thing.

During the course of therapy, Luke found it helpful to view his social anxiety and unassertive behavior through a minority stress lens. He gradually began testing his concerns of rejection—with both family members and social others. By exposing himself gradually to various social situations, and resisting from engaging in avoidance behaviors such as consuming alcohol excessively and self-silencing, Luke's feeling of social belonging began to increase. As a result of feeling less socially isolated, Luke's symptoms of social anxiety and depression decreased. Similarly, he reported less problematic alcohol use. His increase in assertiveness also resulted in less risky sexual behavior and more satisfactory social relationships.

FUTURE DIRECTIONS

The ESTEEM protocol is the first transdiagnostic treatments designed to alleviate sexual minorities' overlapping health needs. Given its relative novelty, several key future directions for both research and practice exist for delivering transdiagnostic treatment to LGBT individuals.

First, the preliminary wait-list-controlled trial of ESTEEM necessitates replication in future randomly controlled trials to determine its treatment efficacy in comparison with other standard interventions. Such a trial is ongoing.

Second, investigating moderators of individual treatment outcomes can inform future implementation of ESTEEM as well as prioritize specific subpopulations of sexual minorities to receive the treatment. Some empirical evidence suggests that improvement following ESTEEM depends on individual levels of internalized homophobia; participants who report higher levels show the most improvement following the ESTEEM intervention (Millar, Wang, & Pachankis, 2016). Furthermore, sexual minority men's psychosocial health risks are most pronounced in areas with higher minority stress (e.g., in states without anti-discriminatory legislation; Hatzenbuehler, McLaughlin, Keyes, & Hasin, 2010). Consequently, dissemination of such an intervention might be particularly important in areas characterized by higher levels of public and/or institutional stigma of sexual minorities. Preliminary evidence suggests that delivering these principles by online or mobile platforms can successfully reach high-risk sexual minority men in stigmatizing locales, such as certain Eastern European countries, that lack brick-and-mortar LGBT-affirmative health services (Lelutiu-Weinberger & Pachankis, 2017).

Third, future studies should investigate the mechanisms by which ESTEEM improves health outcomes because these can inform modification of standard interventions that target individual psychosocial outcomes, buttressing these treatments with the other aspects of ESTEEM that would permit greater transdiagnostic efficacy across multiple domains of dysfunction. For instance, sexual minority men account for a large proportion of new HIV infections within the United Stated (CDC, 2013). Training service providers at HIV testing sites on the basic principles underlying the ESTEEM protocol can serve as an important first-line defense against HIV, other sexually transmitted infections, and potentially mental health problems. Although future empirical investigation is warranted to determine the exact components of the protocol that are related to reductions in health-risk behaviors, basic knowledge of the ESTEEM treatment principles and techniques permits provision of care related to minority stress, discrimination, avoidance, and how these impact sexual risk.

Fourth, ESTEEM is a single intervention that enacts change across multiple clinical spheres, making it a cost-effective form of intervention. Dissemination of such a protocol holds the potential to reduce the burden on clinicians to be versed in multiple distinct treatment paradigms for the separate problems afflicting sexual minorities.

Finally, in its current form, the ESTEEM protocol is specifically geared toward improving psychosocial health of sexual minority men. Because sexual minority women, and transgender individuals, face distinct stressors compared to sexual minority men, the use of all aspects of the ESTEEM protocol may not be appropriate in interventions for lesbian and bisexual women. It is therefore important that future research on transdiagnostic treatment perspectives fill this important gap in the literature. Indeed, such modifications to the ESTEEM protocol are currently underway.

CONCLUSION

Minority stressors faced by sexual minorities place this group at increased risk for a host of mental, behavioral, and sexual problems. Few interventions have been specifically designed to address the multiple concerns facing sexual minority individuals. The ESTEEM protocol—the first transdiagnostic intervention designed to address the multiple psychosocial concerns of sexual minority men— represents one treatment paradigm that addresses the broad and specific sequelae of minority stress. The principles of the ESTEEM protocol constitute an empirically supported foundation for alleviating the psychosocial health concerns of sexual minority individuals.

REFERENCES

American Psychological Association. (2012). Guidelines for psychological practice with lesbian, gay and bisexual clients. *American Psychologist, 67*, 10–42.

Bancroft, J., Carnes, L., Janssen, E., Goodrich, D., & Long, J. S. (2005). Erectile and ejaculatory problems in gay and heterosexual men. *Archives of Sexual Behavior, 34*(3), 285–297.

Barlow, D. H., Allen, L. B., & Choate, M. L. (2004). Toward a unified treatment for emotional disorders. *Behavior Therapy, 35*, 205–230.

Barlow, D. H., Farchione, T. J., Bullis, J. R., Gallagher, M. W., Murray-Latin. H., Sauer-Zavala, S., . . . Cassiello-Robbins, C. (2017). The Unified Protocol for Transdiagnostic Treatment of Emotional Disorders compared with diagnosis-specific protocols for anxiety disorders: A randomized clinical trial. *JAMA Psychiatry, 74*(9), 875–884. doi:10.1001/jamapsychiatry.2017.2164

Barlow, D. H., Farchione, T. J., Fairholme, C. P., Ellard, K. K., Boisseau, C. L., Allen, L. B., & May, J. T. E. (2010). *Unified Protocol for Transdiagnostic Treatment of Emotional Disorders: Therapist guide*: New York, NY: Oxford University Press.

Bränström, R., Hatzenbuehler, M. L., Tinghög, P., & Pachankis, J. E. (2018). Sexual orientation differences in outpatient psychiatric treatment and antidepressant usage: Evidence from a population-based study of siblings. *European Journal of Epidemiology, 33*, 591–599.

Brennan, D. J., Craig, S. L., & Thompson, D. E. (2012). Factors associated with a drive for muscularity among gay and bisexual men. *Culture, Health & Sexuality, 14*(1), 1–15.

Brubaker, M. D., Garrett, M. T., & Dew, B. J. (2009). Examining the relationship between internalized heterosexism and substance abuse among lesbian, gay, and bisexual individuals: A critical review. *Journal of LGBT Issues in Counseling, 3*(1), 62–89.

Burton, C. L., Bonanno, G. A., & Hatzenbuehler, M. L. (2014). Familial social support predicts a reduced cortisol response to stress in sexual minority young adults. *Psychoneuroendocrinology, 47*, 241–245.

Centers for Disease Control and Prevention. (2013). HIV testing and risk behaviors among gay, bisexual, and other men who have sex with men—United States. *Morbidity and Mortality Weekly Report, 62*(47), 958–962.

Cochran, S. D., Ackerman, D., Mays, V. M., & Ross, M. W. (2004). Prevalence of non-medical drug use and dependence among homosexually active men and women in the US population. *Addiction, 99*, 989–998.

Cochran, S. D., & Mays, V. M. (2000). Relation between psychiatric syndromes and behaviorally defined sexual orientation in a sample of the US population. *American Journal of Epidemiology, 151*(5), 516–523.

Cochran, S. D., & Mays, V. M. (2006). Estimating prevalence of mental and substance-using disorders among lesbians and gay men from existing national health data. *Sexual Orientation and Mental Health*, 143–166.

Cochran, S. D., Sullivan, J. G., & Mays, V. M. (2003). Prevalence of mental disorders, psychological distress, and mental health services use among lesbian, gay, and bisexual adults in the United States. *Journal of Consulting and Clinical Psychology, 71*(1), 53–61.

Cohen, J. M., Feinstein, B. A., Rodriguez-Seijas, C., Taylor, C. B., & Newman, M. G. (2016). Rejection sensitivity as a transdiagnostic risk factor for internalizing psychopathology among gay and bisexual men. *Psychology of Sexual Orientation and Gender Diversity, 3*(3), 259–264.

McCreary, D. R., Saucier, D. M., & Courtenay, W. H. (2005). The drive for muscularity and masculinity: Testing the associations among gender-role traits, behaviors, attitudes, and conflict. *Psychology of Men & Masculinity, 6*(2), 83–94.

Crocker, J., & Major, B. (1989). Social stigma and self-esteem: The self-protective properties of stigma. *Psychological Review, 96*(4), 608.

D'Augelli, A. R. (2002). Mental health problems among lesbian, gay, and bisexual youths ages 14 to 21. *Clinical Child Psychology and Psychiatry, 7*(3), 433–456.

de Graaf, R., Sandfort, T. G., & ten Have, M. (2006). Suicidality and sexual orientation: Differences between men and women in a general population-based sample from the Netherlands. *Archives of Sexual Behavior, 35*(3), 253–262.

Drabble, L., & Trocki, K. (2005). Alcohol consumption, alcohol-related problems, and other substance use among lesbian and bisexual women. *Journal of Lesbian Studies, 9*, 19–30.

Feinstein, B. A., Goldfried, M. R., & Davila, J. (2012). The relationship between experiences of discrimination and mental health among lesbians and gay men: An examination of internalized homonegativity and rejection sensitivity as potential mechanisms. *Journal of Consulting and Clinical Psychology, 80*(5), 917–927.

Foa, E. B., & Kozak, M. J. (1986). Emotional processing of fear: Exposure to corrective information. *Psychological Bulletin, 99*(1), 20–35.

Green, K. E., & Feinstein, B. A. (2012). Substance use in lesbian, gay, and bisexual populations: an update on empirical research and implications for treatment. *Psychology of Addictive Behaviors, 26*(2), 265–278.

Greene, M. L., Way, N., & Pahl, K. (2006). Trajectories of perceived adult and peer discrimination among Black, Latino, and Asian American adolescents: Patterns and psychological correlates. *Developmental Psychology, 42*(2), 218–236.

Hart, T. A., & Heimberg, R. G. (2005). Social anxiety as a risk factor for unprotected intercourse among gay and bisexual male youth. *AIDS and Behavior, 9*(4), 505–512.

Hatzenbuehler, M. L. (2009). How does sexual minority stigma "get under the skin"? A psychological mediation framework. *Psychological Bulletin, 135*(5), 707–730.

Hatzenbuehler, M. L., McLaughlin, K. A., Keyes, K. M., & Hasin, D. S. (2010). The impact of institutional discrimination on psychiatric disorders in lesbian, gay, and bisexual populations: A prospective study. *American Journal of Public Health, 100*(3), 452–459.

Hatzenbuehler, M. L., Nolen-Hoeksema, S., & Dovidio, J. (2009). How does stigma "get under the skin"? The mediating role of emotion regulation. *Psychological Science, 20*(10), 1282–1289.

Herek, G. M. (2004). Beyond "homophobia": Thinking about sexual prejudice and stigma in the twenty-first century. *Sexuality Research and Social Policy, 1*(2), 6–24.

Herrick, A. L., Lim, S. H., Wei, C., Smith, H., Guadamuz, T., Friedman, M. S., & Stall, R. (2011). Resilience as an untapped resource in behavioral intervention design for gay men. *AIDS and Behavior, 15*, 25–29.

Herrick, A. L., Stall, R., Goldhammer, H., Egan, J. E., & Mayer, K. H. (2014). Resilience as a research framework and as a cornerstone of prevention research for gay and bisexual men: Theory and evidence. *AIDS and Behavior, 18*(1), 1–9.

Hershberger, S. L., & D'Augelli, A. R. (1995). The impact of victimization on the mental health and suicidality of lesbian, gay, and bisexual youths. *Developmental Psychology, 31*(1), 65.

Kubicek, K., Beyer, W. J., Weiss, G., Iverson, E., & Kipke, M. D. (2010). In the dark: Young men's stories of sexual initiation in the absence of relevant sexual health information. *Health Education & Behavior, 37*(2), 243–263.

Kwon, P. (2013). Resilience in lesbian, gay, and bisexual individuals. *Personality and Social Psychology Review, 17*(4), 371–383.

LaSala, M. C. (2000). Lesbians, gay men, and their parents: Family therapy for the coming-out crisis. *Family Process, 39*(1), 67–81.

Lelutiu-Weinberger, C. T., & Pachankis, J. E. (2017). Acceptability and preliminary efficacy of an LGBT-affirmative mental health provider training in a highly stigmatizing national context. *LGBT Health, 4*(5), 360–370.

Lelutiu-Weinberger, C. T., Manu, M., Lascut, F., Dogaru, B., Kovacs, T., Dorobantescu, C., Predescu, M., Surace, A., & Pachankis, J. E. (in press). An mHealth intervention to improve young gay and bisexual men's sexual, behavioral, and mental health in a structurally stigmatizing national context. *Journal of Medical Internet Research.*

Lippa, R. A. (2008). The relation between childhood gender nonconformity and adult masculinity–femininity and anxiety in heterosexual and homosexual men and women. *Sex Roles, 59*, 684–693.

Major, B., & O'Brien, L. T. (2005). The social psychology of stigma. *Annual Review of Psychology, 56*, 393–421.

Marlatt, G. A., & Donovan, D. M. (Eds.). (2005). *Relapse prevention: Maintenance strategies in the treatment of addictive behaviors.* New York, NY: Guilford.

Marx, B. P., & Sloan, D. M. (2002). The role of emotion in the psychological functioning of adult survivors of childhood sexual abuse. *Behavior Therapy, 33*(4), 563–577.

Meyer, I. H. (2003). Prejudice, social stress, and mental health in lesbian, gay, and bisexual populations: Conceptual issues and research evidence. *Psychological Bulletin, 129*(5), 674–697.

Meyer, I. H., Schwartz, S., & Frost, D. M. (2008). Social patterning of stress and coping: Does disadvantaged social statuses confer more stress and fewer coping resources? *Social Science & Medicine, 67*(3), 368–379.

Millar, B. M., Wang, K., & Pachankis, J. E. (2016). The moderating role of internalized homonegativity on the efficacy of LGB-affirmative psychotherapy: Results from a randomized controlled trial with young adult gay and bisexual men. *Journal of Consulting and Clinical Psychology, 84*(7), 565–570.

Missildine, W., Feldstein, G., Punzalan, J. C., & Parsons, J. T. (2005). S/he loves me, s/he loves me not: Questioning heterosexist assumptions of gender differences for romantic and sexually motivated behaviors. *Sexual Addiction & Compulsivity, 12*(1), 65–74.

Pachankis, J. E. (2007). The psychological implications of concealing stigma: A cognitive–affective–behavioral model. *Psychological Bulletin, 133*(2), 328–345.

Pachankis, J. E. (2014). Uncovering clinical principles and techniques to address minority stress, mental health, and related health risks among gay and bisexual men. *Clinical Psychology, 21*(4), 313–330.

Pachankis, J. E. (2015). A transdiagnostic minority stress treatment approach for gay and bisexual men's syndemic health conditions. *Archives of Sexual Behavior, 44*(7), 1843–1860.

Pachankis, J. E., Clark, K., Burton, C., White Hughto, J. M., & Keene, D. E. (2017). Sex, status, competition, and exclusion: Intra-minority stress from within the gay community and sexual minority men's mental health. Unpublished manuscript. Yale University, New Haven, CT.

Pachankis, J. E., & Goldfried, M. R. (2006). Social anxiety in young gay men. *Journal of Anxiety Disorders, 20*(8), 996–1015.

Pachankis, J. E., Goldfried, M. R., & Ramrattan, M. E. (2008). Extension of the rejection sensitivity construct to the interpersonal functioning of gay men. *Journal of Consulting and Clinical Psychology, 76*(2), 306–317.

Pachankis, J. E., & Hatzenbuehler, M. L. (2013). The social development of contingent self-worth in sexual minority young men: An empirical investigation of the "best little boy in the world" hypothesis. *Basic and Applied Social Psychology, 35*(2), 176–190.

Pachankis, J. E., Hatzenbuehler, M. L., Rendina, H. J., Safren, S. A., & Parsons, J.T. (2015). *Cognitive behavior therapy for young adult gay and bisexual men's mental health and related health risks: A randomized controlled trial of a transdiagnostic minority stress approach.* Unpublished manuscript, Yale School of Public Health, Yale University, New Haven, CT.

Pachankis, J. E., Hatzenbuehler, M. L., Schmidt, A. J., Hickson, F., Weatherburn, P., Berg, R., & Marcus, U. (2014). *Hidden from health: Structural stigma, sexual orientation concealment, and HIV across 38 countries in the European MSM Internet Survey (EMIS).* Unpublished manuscript, Yale School of Public Health, Yale University, New Haven, CT.

Pachankis, J. E., Hatzenbuehler, M. L., & Starks, T. J. (2014). The influence of structural stigma and rejection sensitivity on young sexual minority men's daily tobacco and alcohol use. *Social Science and Medicine, 103*, 67–75.

Pachankis, J. E., Newcomb, M. E., Feinstein, B. A., & Bernstein, L. B. (2014). *Young gay and bisexual men's stigma experiences and mental health: A five-year longitudinal study.* Unpublished manuscript, Yale School of Public Health, Yale University, New Haven, CT.

Pachankis, J. E., Newcomb, M. E., Feinstein, B., & Sullivan, T. J. (2018). Young gay and bisexual men's stigma experiences and mental health: An 8-year longitudinal study. *Developmental Psychology, 54*(7), 1381–1393.

Pachankis, J. E., Rendina, H. J., Restar, A., Ventuneac, A., Grov, C., & Parsons, J. T. (2015). A minority stress–emotion regulation model of sexual compulsivity among highly sexually active gay and bisexual men. *Health Psychology, 34*(8), 829.

Pachankis, J. E., Westmaas, J. L., & Dougherty, L. R. (2011). The influence of sexual orientation and masculinity on young men's tobacco smoking. *Journal of Consulting and Clinical Psychology, 79*(2), 142–152.

Parsons, J. T., Grov, C., & Golub, S. A. (2012). Sexual compulsivity, co-occurring psychosocial health problems, and HIV risk among gay and bisexual men: Further evidence of a syndemic. *American Journal of Public Health, 102*(1), 156–162.

Parsons, J. T., Starks, T. J., DuBois, S., Grov, C., & Golub, S. A. (2013). Alternatives to monogamy among gay male couples in a community survey: Implications for mental health and sexual risk. *Archives of Sexual Behavior, 42*(2), 303–312.

Plöderl, M., & Fartacek, R. (2005). Suicidality and associated risk factors among lesbian, gay, and bisexual compared to heterosexual Austrian adults. *Suicide and Life-Threatening Behavior, 35*(6), 661–670.

Potoczniak, D. J., Aldea, M. A., & DeBlaere, C. (2007). Ego identity, social anxiety, social support, and self-concealment in lesbian, gay, and bisexual individuals. *Journal of Counseling Psychology, 54*(4), 447–457.

Rahman, Q., & Wilson, G. D. (2003). Born gay? The psychobiology of human sexual orientation. *Personality and Individual Differences, 34*(8), 1337–1382.

Rieger, G., Linsenmeier, J. A., Gygax, L., & Bailey, J. M. (2008). Sexual orientation and childhood gender nonconformity: Evidence from home videos. *Developmental Psychology, 44*(1), 46–58.

Rodriguez-Seijas, C., Eaton, N. R., & Krueger, R. F. (2015). How transdiagnostic factors of personality and psychopathology can inform clinical assessment and intervention. *Journal of Personality Assessment, 97*(5), 425–435.

Rosario, M., Schrimshaw, E. W., & Hunter, J. (2009). Disclosure of sexual orientation and subsequent substance use and abuse among lesbian, gay, and bisexual youths: Critical role of disclosure reactions. *Psychology of Addictive Behaviors, 23*(1), 175.

Safren, S. A., & Heimberg, R. G. (1999). Depression, hopelessness, suicidality, and related factors in sexual minority and heterosexual adolescents. *Journal of Consulting and Clinical Psychology, 67*(6), 859.

Sánchez, F. J., & Vilain, E. (2012). "Straight-acting gays": The relationship between masculine consciousness, anti-effeminacy, and negative gay identity. *Archives of Sexual Behavior, 41*(1), 111–119.

Stall, R., Mills, T. C., Williamson, J., Hart, T., Greenwood, G., Paul, J., . . . Catania, J. A. (2003). Association of co-occurring psychosocial health problems and increased vulnerability to HIV/AIDS among urban men who have sex with men. *American Journal of Public Health, 93*(6), 939–942.

Trapence, G., Collins, C., Avrett, S., Carr, R., Sanchez, H., Ayala, G., . . . Baral, S. D. (2012). From personal survival to public health: community leadership by men who have sex with men in the response to HIV. *The Lancet, 380*(9839), 400–410.

Weeks, J., Heaphy, B., & Donovan, C. (2001). *Same sex intimacies: Families of choice and other life experiments.* New York, NY: Routledge.

CPSIA information can be obtained
at www.ICGtesting.com
Printed in the USA
BVHW040007150520
579724BV00001B/1